T5-AGL-538

THE CLARENDON EDITION OF THE WORKS OF JOHN LOCKE

GENERAL EDITOR: JOHN W. YOLTON

A PARAPHRASE AND NOTES ON THE EPISTLES OF ST PAUL

A

PARAPHRASE

AND

NOTES

ON THE

Epiſtles of St. Paul

TO THE

	Galatians,		*Romans,*
I & II	*Corinthians,*		*Epheſians.*

To which is Prefix'd, An

ESSAY

FOR THE

Underſtanding of St. *Paul's* EPISTLES, by Conſulting St. *Paul* Himſelf.

LONDON,
Printed by *J. H.* for *Awnſham* and *John Churchill,* at the *Black Swan* in *Pater-noſter-Row.* 1707.

JOHN LOCKE

A PARAPHRASE AND NOTES ON THE EPISTLES OF ST PAUL TO THE GALATIANS, 1 AND 2 CORINTHIANS, ROMANS, EPHESIANS

EDITED BY

ARTHUR W. WAINWRIGHT

VOLUME I

OXFORD
AT THE CLARENDON PRESS
1987

Oxford University Press, Walton Street, Oxford OX2 6DP
Oxford New York Toronto Melbourne Auckland
Delhi Bombay Calcutta Madras Karachi
Petaling Jaya Singapore Hong Kong Tokyo
Nairobi Dar es Salaam Cape Town
Associated companies in Beirut Berlin Ibadan Nicosia

OXFORD *is a trade mark of Oxford University Press*

Published in the United States
by Oxford University Press, New York

British Library Cataloguing in Publication Data
Locke, John, 1632–1704
A paraphrase and notes on the Epistles of St. Paul: To the Galatians, 1 and 2 Corinthians, Romans, Ephesians.—(The Clarendon edition of the works of John Locke)
1. Bible. N.T. Epistles of Paul—Commentaries
I. Title II. Wainwright, Arthur
227'.07 BS2650.3
ISBN 0-19-824801-6

Library of Congress Cataloging-in-Publication Data
Locke, John, 1632–1704.
A paraphrase and notes on the Epistles of St. Paul to the Galations, 1 and 2 Corinthians, Romans, Ephesians.
(Clarendon edition of the works of John Locke)
Bibliography: p
Includes index.
1. Bible. N.T. Epistles of Paul—Paraphrases, English. 2. Bible. N.T. Epistles of Paul—Criticism, interpretation, etc.—Early works to 1800. I. Wainwright, Arthur William. II. Title. III. Series: Locke, John, 1632–1704. Works. 1975.
BS2658.L63 1985 227'.077 86-18008
ISBN 0-19-824801-6

Set by Joshua Associates Limited, Oxford
Printed in Great Britain
at the University Printing House, Oxford
by David Stanford
Printer to the University

To Martin and Philip

CONTENTS

VOLUME ONE

Contents

VOLUME TWO

ACKNOWLEDGEMENTS

To the Curators of the Bodleian Library I am grateful for permission to transcribe the following: MS Locke c. 27, fos. 131–4, 162–73, 213–14, 217–19, 221–3, 278; MS Locke c. 39, fo. 25; MS Locke e. 2, fos. 1–232; and excerpts from MS Locke f. 30, the interleaved Bible *Locke 16.25* (referred to below as LL no. 309), and the interleaved Testaments *Locke 9.40* and *Locke 9.103–107* (referred to below as LL nos. 2862 and 2864).

Many people have helped me in my work on this edition. Mr Peter Laslett encouraged me to develop my interest in Locke as a biblical interpreter. I benefited greatly from comments made by Dr Warren Thomas Smith and the late Philip Watson. Dr Esmond de Beer and Dr John Higgins-Biddle made their knowledge of various aspects of Locke studies available to me. The photographs of the title page of my copy of Locke's *Paraphrase* was taken by Elaine Ellerbee. June Caldwell did much of the typing. Help has been given to me by William Arnold, Deborah Corbin, Kathleen Crenshaw, Betty Durham, Janet Gary, Kathryn Kolb, Stacey Lanier, Serena McGuire, Stephen Pattison, Christian Rave, Jeannie Saylor, Donna Springer, and Stacy Weenick; and my wife has come to my aid on numerous occasions.

Sabbatical leave from the Candler School of Theology and awards from the Association of Theological Schools in the United States and Canada have enabled me to pursue this work with greater concentration. To Emory University I am indebted for a grant from its Research Fund and for the use of the resources of its Pitts and Woodruff Libraries. I am grateful to Mr Paul Mellon for permission to use his library at Oak Spring, Virginia, where I first examined Locke's interleaved volumes before their transfer to the Bodleian; and considerable assistance has been given me by the Bodleian Library, the British Library, and the University Library of Heidelberg.

Special mention needs to be made of the late Peter Nidditch, who was General Editor of the Clarendon Locke until his death in 1983, by which time this edition of the *Paraphrase* had almost reached its final form. I remember with gratitude the care and patience which he showed in discussing this work and in reading through my typescript. It was my good fortune to benefit from his expertise as I carried out this enterprise.

A.W.W.

Atlanta
January 1986

INTRODUCTION

I. THE CIRCUMSTANCES, PURPOSE, AND METHOD OF THE PARAPHRASE AND NOTES

The Unfinished Agenda

LOCKE'S *Paraphrase and Notes on the Epistles of St Paul* was published during the years 1705-7, the author himself having died on 28 October 1704. In writing the work he was carrying out an agenda which he had set himself several years earlier. He had argued in the *Reasonableness of Christianity* that the fundamental doctrines of the Christian faith were most easily to be discerned in the Gospels and the Acts of the Apostles. But he did not wish to overlook the Epistles, which he believed to contain important truths that clarified and confirmed Christian doctrine.[1] It is no surprise that he directed his attention to the study of Paul. In Paul's Epistles is to be found the terminology of justification, a doctrine which is central to Locke's own theology. Even though Locke did not regard the doctrine as exclusively Pauline, he could hardly neglect those writings in which it was given its most explicit and forceful expression.

Underlying the whole enterprise of writing the *Paraphrase* was Locke's conviction that it was the Christian's duty to study the Bible, 'receiving with stedfast belief, and ready obedience, all those things which the spirit of truth hath therein revealed'.[2] It was a person's willingness to seek and embrace truth in the Scriptures which would be taken into account on the Day of Judgement.[3] The condition for eternal salvation was faith combined with a sincere endeavour to obey the will of God; and the study of the Scriptures was part of the endeavour to be obedient.

If Locke had any hesitation about paying special attention to the Epistles, it would be removed by the controversies in which he was

[1] *The Reasonableness of Christianity, The Works of John Locke* (12th edn., 9 vols.: London, 1824), vi. 154-5: 'These holy writers, inspired from above, writ nothing but truth; and in most places, very weighty truths to us now; for the expounding, clearing, and confirming of the christian doctrine, and establishing those in it who had embraced it.'

[2] *Vindication of the Reasonableness of Christianity, Works*, vi. 176.

[3] *The Correspondence of John Locke*, ed. E. S. de Beer (8 vols.: Oxford, 1976-), vi. 629-30.

involved in the latter half of the 1690s. In his criticism of the *Reasonableness* John Edwards had accused Locke of commanding his readers not 'to stir a jot farther than the Acts'.[1] The appearance of a work by Locke on Paul's Epistles was a convincing answer to this criticism. Another controversy which involved the interpretation of Paul was Locke's dispute with Edward Stillingfleet, Bishop of Worcester. According to Stillingfleet, Locke's account of personal identity in the *Essay* implied that the dead might be raised with different bodies from those which they had had during their mortal lives. Locke did not deny the point, but argued that his teaching was consistent with the Scriptures.[2] The controversy continued after Stillingfleet's death in 1699. John Milner and Daniel Whitby supported Stillingfleet, while Samuel Bold and Catharine Trotter (later Cockburn) wrote in defence of Locke.[3] This debate, which laid special emphasis on the interpretation of passages in Paul's Epistles to the Corinthians and Romans, provided Locke with a strong incentive to study Paul's writings in greater detail.

There was also the challenge of the Epistles themselves, which contained many difficulties of interpretation. In his Preface to the *Paraphrase* Locke mentions some of these: the Semitic idiom of Paul's Greek, the presence of long parentheses, and the vehemence of his style. Added to these problems was the tendency of interpreters to read their own presuppositions into Paul's writings. The desire to give an objective account of the meaning of the Scriptures was a powerful factor in inducing Locke to embark on his attempt to understand Paul's Epistles 'by consulting St. Paul himself'.

Locke's interest in the Scriptures was no new development. There is evidence of it in his *Two Tracts on Government* (1660-1). His Journals contain numerous references to biblical commentaries and other theological works. His interleaved Bibles and Testaments and some of his notebooks contain allusions to a wide variety of writers on theology as well as his own comments on passages from the Bible. As the years went by he seems to have spent an increasing amount of time

[1] John Edwards (1637-1716), *Socinianism Unmask'd* (London, 1696), LL no. 1026, p. 42 (for LL see below, p. 88). Cf. Locke, *Second Vindication of the Reasonableness of Christianity, Works*, vi. 262.

[2] *Second Reply to the Bishop of Worcester, Works*, iii. 303-4.

[3] John Milner (1628-1702), a non-juring minister, and formerly Vicar of Leeds, *An Account of Mr. Lock's Religion* (London, 1700), LL no. 1802b. For Whitby, see below, p. 12. Samuel Bold (1649-1737), Rector of Steeple, Isle of Purbeck, *Some Considerations on the Principal Objections and Arguments which have been Publish'd against Mr. Locke's Essay* (London, 1699), LL no. 384; Catharine Cockburn, *A Defence of the Essay of Human Understanding* (London, 1702), LL no. 1801.

on biblical studies. During his exile in Holland, Damaris Cudworth (later Lady Masham) wrote to him: 'I cannot but Fancie by your Letter that you have learnt more Scripture there than ever you Knew in your whole life before, whom I little thought once would ever have writt me a letter not to be understood without turning to St Paul, and St Peters Epistles.'[1] The years in Holland, where he made the acquaintance of the theologians Limborch and Le Clerc,[2] gave him plenty of opportunity to study the Bible. His interest in the Scriptures is evident in works published after his return to England: the *Letters Concerning Toleration* (1689, 1690, 1692), the *Two Treatises of Government* (1690), and the *Essay Concerning Human Understanding* (1690). It came to fruition in the *Reasonableness of Christianity* (1695), its two *Vindications* (1695, 1697), the published correspondence with Stillingfleet (1697, 1699), and the *Discourse of Miracles*, written in 1702 but published posthumously. The final and most detailed manifestation of his zeal for biblical studies is the *Paraphrase and Notes on the Epistles of St. Paul*. His interest in the Epistles had been given additional impetus by the controversies in which he was involved. But above all he was spurred on by his belief that it was his Christian duty to study these writings, which would show him the way to salvation. His work on Paul was a remaining item on his agenda, an item for which his declining state of health convinced him that he had a limited amount of time.

Preliminary Drafts, Papers, and Notes Used in Writing the Paraphrase

Some papers in Locke's handwriting, dated 1703, provide evidence of his preparatory work on the *Paraphrase*. They include an incomplete draft of a preface to his work on the Corinthian Epistles.[3] At one stage he intended to publish his paraphrase and notes on these Epistles before the rest of the work. He later changed his mind and published the work on Galatians first; but some of this draft has been reproduced verbatim in the published preface to the *Paraphrase*. These 1703 papers also include some notes entitled 'Difficulties in St Pauls Epistles',[4] which have influenced the Preface; and there are notes on the chronology of the fourteen Epistles he regarded as Paul's.[5]

A paper, entitled 'Christianae Religionis Synopsis' ('Synopsis of the Christian Religion'), and dated 1702, contains observations which

[1] 8 Oct. 1684, *Corr*. ii. 640.
[2] See below, pp. 14-15.
[3] See Appendix I.
[4] See Appendix IV.
[5] See Appendix II.

may have influenced his work on Romans,[1] and another paper, 'Synopsis Epistolarum Pauli' ('Synopsis of Paul's Epistles'),[2] was written in 1703 or 1704, at a time when he seems to have been preparing his work on Ephesians. An extract from the paper, 'Resurrectio et quae sequuntur' ('The resurrection and what follows'),[3] written between 1690 and 1701, has been incorporated into a note in Locke's work on 1 Corinthians. Some undated notes on 'Spirit, Soul, and Body'[4] illuminate a few comments made by Locke in his preface and his work on the Corinthian Epistles. And other papers provide evidence of his study of Paul, even though they have not clearly influenced the composition of the *Paraphrase*.[5]

As well as the above-mentioned material there are an interleaved Bible, two interleaved Testaments, and a notebook, each of which contains a large number of entries by Locke on the New Testament. Most of the entries in these volumes are allusions to writers other than Locke himself. Sometimes he has recorded a verbatim or almost verbatim quotation from a book which he was reading. At other times he has summarized an author's statements. There is no guarantee that Locke always agreed with the opinions expressed; indeed, he sometimes takes a vastly different point of view in the *Paraphrase*. Many of the entries are not extracts from other writers but are followed by the letters 'JL', indicating that they represent Locke's own opinions. Other entries have neither 'JL' nor any other name appended to them; and many of these are likely to be presenting his own viewpoint.

The precise date of the entries cannot be determined. It is not even clear when he obtained the volumes in which he wrote them down. The Bible and Testaments were in his possession by 1693, and one of the Testaments belonged to him as early as 1678. Over four hundred of the entries, taken from as many as thirty-one different writers, comment on the five Epistles on which the *Paraphrase* is based. A few of them are repeated more or less verbatim in the work; and many others have influenced its contents. They are evidence of the intensity of Locke's application to the study of Paul and the extent and variety of his reading.[6]

[1] See Appendix VIII.
[2] See Appendix IX.
[3] See Appendix VI.
[4] See Appendix V.
[5] See Appendices III and VII.
[6] For a more detailed discussion of the interleaved Bible and Testaments and the notebook, see Appendix X.

The Completion of the Work

Since the part of the Bodleian manuscript of the *Paraphrase* dealing with the Corinthian Epistles is dated 1701, Locke is likely to have been working on it for one or more years previously. But he continued to revise it in subsequent years. In the autumn of 1702 Isaac Newton visited him at Oates and had a preliminary glance at the work. 'I shewd him my Essay upon the Corinthians', wrote Locke to Peter King, 'with which he seemd very well pleased, but had not time, staying but one night, to looke it all over. But promisd me if I would send it him he would carefully peruse it, and send me his observations and opinion.'[1] Locke duly sent the manuscript to Newton, who took a long time to reply. After Locke had urged King to persuade him to return it,[2] Newton sent it back on 15 May 1703, suggesting an alternative interpretation of 1 Cor. VII.14 and making other corrections:[3]

Upon my first receiving your papers I read over those concerning the first Epistle to the Corinthians, but by so many intermissions that I resolved to go over them again so soon as I could get leasure to do it with more attention. I have now read it over a second time and gone over also your papers on the second Epistle. Some faults which seemed to be faults of the Scribe I mended with my pen as I read the papers, Some others I have noted in the inclosed papers.

Newton's general verdict on the manuscript was highly favourable. 'I think your Paraphrase and Commentary on these two Epistles', he wrote, 'is done with very great care and judgement.'[4] Locke did not adopt the suggestion about 1 Cor. VII.14, and it is impossible to determine how he responded to the other points which Newton made.

Locke continued to work on the Corinthian Epistles and also on Romans, which in his manuscript is dated 1702. In his letter to Peter King, dated 30 April 1703, he mentions that he is busy on both these Epistles. He also received a letter from King dated 26 January 1704 outlining Thomas Goodwin's account of the 'princes of this world'[5] in 1 Cor. II. 6-8 as the Jewish leaders and Pilate. Locke gave his assent to this viewpoint in a letter dated 28 January 1704.[6] Later, on 19 June of the same year, he indicated to Anthony Collins that he wanted to discuss the Corinthian Epistles with him:[7]

In the mean time, give me leave to desire you, to bestow some of your spare hours on the *Epistles to the Corinthians*, and to try whether you can find them

[1] *Corr.* vii. 772 (30 Apr. 1703).
[2] *Corr.* vii. 772-3.
[3] *Corr.* viii. 1.
[4] *Corr.* viii. 2.
[5] *Corr.* viii. 179-80.
[6] *Corr.* viii. 181-2.
[7] *Corr.* viii. 330.

intelligible or no. You will easily guess the reason of this; and when I have you here, I hope to convince you it will not be lost labour: only permit me to tell you, you must read them with something more than an ordinary application.

Collins arrived at Oates in July;[1] presumably the manuscript of the Corinthian Epistles was still undergoing revision at that time. Galatians must have already been in the hands of the printer, since a proof of it was sent to Locke by his publisher, Awnsham Churchill, on 17 August 1704. The printing was not to Churchill's liking, as his accompanying letter makes plain:[2]

This afternoon just as mr Collins was taking Coach, the Printer brought me a foul proof ill wrought of the Galations. I made it up with the MMS. and sent it you by him. I had not time to consider it, but I perceived the Compositor had putt the figures of the verses ⟨on⟩ the wrong side of the page, which he shall mend–When you have considered the whole Composition, and whether the page and paper be not too large I begg youl give me your Directions–I thought the 1st page was begun to neer the Top.

Another letter from Churchill, dated 17 October, indicates that Locke had omitted to send him part of the manuscript:[3]

I Received yours per mr Collins with the MMS. Coppy which does not supply what the printer wants and is that part of the Coppy, which has the Paraphrase. I would begg you to send it by first post, and shall gett it soon despatched.

Since Locke died on 28 October, he was unable to check the final proofs of Galatians, which was published in 1705. His manuscript of his work on the Epistle is dated 1703, but he is likely to have given further attention to it between that time and his death.

The Manuscript and the Printed Editions

The only surviving manuscript of the *Paraphrase* is a partial one. It is housed in the Bodleian Library, Oxford, having previously been in the possession of the Earls of Lovelace, descendants of Peter King, Locke's second cousin, who inherited his papers. It contains Locke's work on Galatians, 1 and 2 Corinthians, and Romans, but does not include Ephesians or the Preface.[4] Although the manuscript differs continually from the first edition in spelling, capitalization, and

[1] *Corr.* viii. 365-6.
[2] *Corr.* viii. 380.
[3] *Corr.* viii. 410.
[4] MS Locke e. 2, fos. 1-233.

punctuation, it contains only a limited number of verbal differences from it.

Locke had at least two manuscripts of most of the *Paraphrase*. While Newton was in possession of a copy of the part on the Corinthian Epistles, Locke told Peter King that he was at work on the very same Epistles. Moreover, the copy sent to Newton was made by a scribe. Newton spoke of 'faults which seemed to be faults of the Scribe'.[1] The last letter of Locke to King, dated 4 October 1704, confirms that there was a second copy of most of the work. A deleted passage from the letter indicates that at first he intended to send one copy to his publisher, Churchill, and another to his friend Samuel Bold.[2]

I intend to leave a copy in Mr Churchils hands who I suppose will print it. If he does I desire the edition may be carefully inspected. Mr Bold I think a fit man to doe it. Who by the copy in Mr Churchils hands and the other which I leave in yours will be inabled to set it right every where though the writeing in some places may be wrong or perplexed. What Mr Churchil will value the copy at I desire Mr Bold may have for his pains in correcting

Locke changed his mind, however, and deleted these words from the letter, substituting an instruction to Peter King in which he referred to only one copy of the work.

[The sense] I have . . . endeavourd to follow impartialy every where and if it shall be judgd usefull to the Christian religion am not unwilling what I have donne on St Pauls Epistles should be published but in this method That after the Galatians the 1 to the Corinthians. The 2d to the Corinthians. To the Romans and to the Ephesians. Each of which Epistles in this order should not till after 3 months from the publication of the former and as much later as you shall see occasion be conveyd to Mr Churchil to be printed as that to the Galatians is. Accordingly you will find them sealed up seperately ready to be sent in their order when you find it seasonable. If Mr Churchill prints them tis well if not you may take your own measures

A postscript, written on 25 October 1704, three days before his death, gives King revised instructions, occasioned because the copy of Ephesians had not been completed by the scribe (probably William Shaw), and also because he wished King to have freedom to inspect the completed work before he sent it to Churchill:[3]

You will find what I have done upon St Pauls Epistles tied up in several bundles and directed to Mr Churchil in the order they should be conveyd to him. The distance of time I leave to your judgment. I have not sealed them because

[1] *Corr.* viii. 1. See above, p. 5.
[2] *Corr.* viii. 414.
[3] *Corr.* viii. 416-17.

my seales comeing to your hands you may doe that when it is time and may perhaps have occasion to open and look into them before they goe out of your hands, which when they doe conceale your self and let it not be known they come from you. If my Paraphrase and notes on the Ephesians are not wholy transcribed before I dye (as I fear they will not. For however earnestly I have pressed it again and again I have not been able to prevaile with *Will:* to dispatch the two first Chapters in three months) you must get it to be transcribed out of my filed papers after I am dead, that so it may be in a condition to be printed. *Will* after all will I think be the fitest to transcribe them because he can read my hand and knows my way of writeing with the use of the references

If by any backwardness you shall find (which I doe not suspect) in Mr Churchill, you should have any apprehension that the preface might be lost in his hands, pray consider whether you will think it worth while to take a copy of it in short hand before you let it goe out of your keeping, there being noe other copy of it but that first and foul draught which is directed to Mr Churchill

The surviving manuscript of the *Paraphrase*, in Locke's own handwriting, is probably that which he at first intended to be inspected by Samuel Bold and to be compared with the scribe's copy. It is not mentioned in the final form of the letter which he left for King to open after his death. But it may well have been left among the 'filed papers' to which he referred. Because it contained a large number of alterations, he would prefer the scribe's neat copy to be sent to the printer.

The absence of Ephesians and the Preface from the Bodleian manuscript can easily be explained. The manuscript of Ephesians had been sent to William Shaw for the purpose of transcribing. It was not left with the filed papers, either because Shaw retained it or because it was sent to someone else for transcription. The Preface, as the postscript to Locke's last letter indicates, had not been transcribed, and King was advised to make no more than a shorthand copy before dispatching it to Churchill. Locke's manuscript of the Preface was sent to the publisher. Only Galatians, 1 and 2 Corinthians, and Romans were left in the filed papers; and these constitute the present Bodleian manuscript.

When the work appeared in print, it was anonymous, like his *Two Treatises*, his *Letters on Toleration*, and his *Reasonableness of Christianity*. But there was never any secret about its authorship, which was openly acknowledged by its earliest reviewers and critics.[1] It was published in

[1] The reason for anonymity is not clear. It is possible that Locke was apprehensive about his safety in case his views should be judged heretical. Thomas Aikenhead had been hanged at Edinburgh in 1697 for blasphemy and denial of the doctrine of the Trinity. At the time of Locke's death Thomas Emlyn was imprisoned in Dublin because of his unorthodox theology. Although it is unlikely that Locke was in serious danger, he himself might have preferred the safety of being anonymous. But it is then

separate parts according to Locke's wish. The parts came out in the order which he had given. The first edition of Galatians, which appeared in 1705, was a faulty publication. Churchill himself had complained of the foul appearance of the proofs, and the published work had obvious defects: some of the footnotes were printed in the wrong order; frequently they were on different pages from the verses of the paraphrase on which they were commenting; and on numerous occasions the sign at the beginning of a footnote was different from the corresponding sign in the actual paraphrase. It was therefore a wise decision to print a second edition, which appeared in 1706, the year when 1 and 2 Corinthians were first published. This second edition of Galatians corrected many of the faults of the previous one, and the system of footnote-signs and scripture-references was brought into line with that of 1 and 2 Corinthians. The following year, 1707, Romans, Ephesians, and the Preface were published. The second edition of Galatians and the first editions of the rest of the work all had the same style of scripture-references and footnote-signs. A third edition of Galatians is dated 1708, and yet another 'third edition' of it is dated 1718. Another edition of 1 Corinthians appeared also in 1718, although it did not describe itself as a second edition.

These early printings were issued as separate publications, each with its own title-page. Some of them were bound together with a title-page dated 1707 and reading *A Paraphrase and Notes on the Epistles of St. Paul to the Galatians, 1 and 2 Corinthians, Romans, Ephesians, To which is Prefix'd, An Essay for the Understanding of St. Paul's Epistles, by Consulting St. Paul Himself*. For example, a collection, consisting entirely of the first edition of each part, has the order: Romans, title-page, Preface, Ephesians, 1 Corinthians, 2 Corinthians, and Galatians.[1] Another first edition has the order: title-page, Preface, Galatians, 1 Corinthians, 2 Corinthians, Romans, and Ephesians;[2] and various other combinations occur.[3] The *Paraphrase* was included in the collected works of

surprising that King and Churchill should have arranged for the anonymity to be preserved after Locke's death. Another possibility is that Locke's anonymity in his publications may have been motivated by a wish to appear *unegotistically* concerned with principles (cf. Nidditch, Foreword (p. xvi) to the paperback edition of the *Essay Concerning Human Understanding* (Oxford, 1979)).

[1] In the Bodleian Library.

[2] In the British Library.

[3] e.g. in the Bodleian Library there are the following combinations: (i) a 1707 title-page with the second edition of Galatians and the first edition of every other part; (ii) a 1709 title-page, described as the second edition, with the third edition (1708) of Galatians and the first edition of every other part; (iii) a 1707 title-page with the third edition

Locke, the first edition of which was published in 1714. It was not until 1733 that there was a separate printing of the *Paraphrase* as a whole rather than as a collection of individual parts; it was described as the third edition.[1] During the rest of the eighteenth century and in the first part of the nineteenth further editions of the work were published.[2]

Persons Who Advised Locke To Publish

In his Preface (p. 109) Locke says that he has been persuaded to publish the *Paraphrase* by 'some very sober judicious Christians, no Strangers to the Sacred Scriptures, nay learned Divines of the Church of England'. He never mentions the names of these divines, and there is no clear evidence of their identity from other sources. A likely possibility is Samuel Bold, a good friend of Locke, who had come to his defence against the attacks launched by Edwards on the *Reasonableness of Christianity*. At one stage Locke intended that Bold should be entrusted with the manuscript of the *Paraphrase* after his death for the purpose of checking and correcting. It is highly likely that Bold read some of the work and discussed it with Locke.

Another clergyman who may have encouraged Locke to publish was Edward Fowler, Bishop of Gloucester. Locke and Fowler exchanged correspondence during the years 1696-1704, and since Fowler visited Locke in May 1704,[3] he probably discussed the *Paraphrase* on that occasion. Of course, Locke must have made the decision to publish before that visit, since the proofs came from him to Churchill no later than August of that year. But at least Fowler is a person who may have encouraged Locke to go ahead with his plans for publication.

Yet another possibility is Pierre (or Peter) Allix, Chancellor of Salisbury, whose views are often quoted in the interleaved Bible LL no. 309. It is possible that Allix and Locke may have met each other

(1718) of Galatians, the 1718 edition of 1 Corinthians, and the first edition of every other part. All the above have the order: title-page, Preface, Galatians, 1 Corinthians, 2 Corinthians, Romans, Ephesians. Yet another collection in the Bodleian Library contains only the Preface, Romans, and Ephesians, all in the first edition.

[1] In the British Library.

[2] See also H. O. Christophersen, *A Bibliographical Introduction to the Study of John Locke* (Oslo, 1930), pp. 75-6, who mentions the separate publication of the Preface in various collections.

[3] *Corr.* viii. 293-4.

personally or corresponded with each other.[1] It is conceivable that Allix also might have encouraged Locke to publish the *Paraphrase*.

There are indications that it was not only clergymen who encouraged him to publish the work. In an unfinished draft of the Preface Locke mentions 'Some sober and learned friends of mine whom I shewd it to'.[2] And in his last letter to Peter King (4 and 25 October 1704) he writes that 'Those who have seen what I have done upon some of St Pauls Epistles are all very desirous it should be printed.'[3] Once the circle of friends who persuaded him to publish is enlarged beyond the boundaries of the clergy, it becomes easier to identify some of those who belonged to it. Newton was one of them. So were Anthony Collins and Peter King. All three of these men had read parts of the *Paraphrase*. And there can be no serious doubt that the contents of the work had been discussed with Damaris Masham. It is likely that she was the other person who he says watched the daily progress of the *Reasonableness* during the period of its composition.[4] He was residing at her home in Oates when he was writing the *Paraphrase*, and probably consulted her frequently about its contents.

Another person whom he may have consulted was Pierre Coste, who was tutor to the Mashams' son, Frank. 'Mr. Locke', wrote Coste, 'also thought it necessary always to communicate one's thoughts to some friend, especially if one proposed to offer them to the public; and this was what he constantly observed himself.'[5] Coste may have been speaking from experience. He too may have been the recipient of Locke's thoughts on theological matters, and may have been one of those who advised him to publish the *Paraphrase*.

The Writers Consulted by Locke

In writing the *Paraphrase* Locke endeavoured to free himself from theological and philosophical presuppositions and to examine the Epistles by consulting Paul himself rather than the works of biblical commentators. He admitted, however, that 'Labours of the Learned' could be useful (Preface, pp. 108-9); and in fact he was extremely well

[1] See below, p. 14.
[2] Appendix I, n.
[3] *Corr.* viii. 414.
[4] *Second Vindication, Works*, vi. 188; cf. H. R. Fox Bourne, *The Life of John Locke* (2 vols.: London, 1876), ii. 284.
[5] Locke, *Works*, ix. 171.

read in theology before he embarked on the composition of the *Paraphrase*. The interleaved Bible and Testaments and the New Testament notebook give an indication of the scope of his reading; but his studies were by no means confined to the works to which he alludes in those volumes.

One of the writers explicitly mentioned in the *Paraphrase* is Daniel Whitby, a well-known controversialist whose commentary on the New Testament was highly esteemed in English scholarship of the eighteenth century. His theology was Arminian, and he became especially famous for his post-millennial interpretation of the Book of Revelation. Towards the end of his life he accepted a Unitarian Christology, but in Locke's day he was a vigorous upholder of the doctrine of the Trinity. Locke had already been in correspondence with him about the resurrection of the body, an issue in which Whitby supported Stillingfleet.[1] While Whitby did not mention Locke by name in the first edition of his commentary, he did in fact attack both his view on the resurrection of the body and his claim that all articles necessary for salvation were clearly taught in the Gospels. In the *Paraphrase* Locke replied with a criticism of Whitby's account of the resurrection of the body. His attitude to Whitby was not entirely that of an adversary. Although he differed from him about Christology and the resurrection of the body, he was in general agreement with him about divine election and justification. The two writers also had much in common in their account of the time and circumstances of the composition of Paul's Epistles. Whether he was agreeing or disagreeing with Whitby, in some of his most important comments on the Epistles Locke was consciously reacting to him.[2]

Another writer who had an obvious influence on Locke was Henry Hammond, the scholar who came to be known as the father of English biblical criticism. Hammond, who was greatly indebted to Hugo Grotius, made a detailed study of the linguistic background to the New Testament, and attempted to understand the Epistles in the light of the circumstances in which they were written. Theologically he was an Arminian of the Laudian school. It was in linguistic matters that

[1] *Corr.* vi. 545, 548-9; vii. 676-7, 697-8.

[2] Daniel Whitby (1638-1726) was Rector of St Edmund's, Salisbury, and Precentor of Salisbury. He was the author of *A Paraphrase and Commentary on all the Epistles of the New Testament* (London 1700), LL no. 3149, which later formed part of *A Paraphrase and Commentary on the New Testament* (2 vols.: London, 1703), LL no. 3150. He is mentioned by name in Locke's *Paraphrase* at Rom. V.12*f.

Locke was chiefly influenced by him. But Locke gave no support to his theory that Paul had to contend with Gnostic opponents.[1]

Frequent use was made by Locke of the writings of John Lightfoot, who was a pioneer in the investigation of the relationship between the New Testament and rabbinic writings. In the interleaved Bible and Testaments there are more entries from Lightfoot than from any other individual; and Locke was heavily indebted to him in dealing with 1 Corinthians. It was not in specifically theological matters that Locke was influenced by him, but in the explanation of words and phrases and in information about the Jewish background. Locke did not always agree with Lightfoot, but there is no other scholar on whom he depended as much for the interpretation of points of detail.[2]

Locke also made considerable use of the discourses of the Cambridge scholar Joseph Mede.[3] He acknowledged his dependence in certain places on the philosopher and medical practitioner Richard Burthogge, with whom he exchanged correspondence on biblical matters.[4] Other writers to whom he alludes by name include the French Calvinist Theodore Beza,[5] the Dutch scholars Isaac Vossius and Campegius Vitringa, the Flemish scholar Ludovicus de Dieu, and the English jurist and orientalist John Selden.[6]

In addition to the authors mentioned by name in the *Paraphrase*,

[1] Henry Hammond (1605-60) was deprived of his canonry of Christ Church, Oxford, for his royalist sympathies. His main work, *A Paraphrase and Annotations upon all the Books of the New Testament* (London, 1653), was used by Locke in Le Clerc's Latin translation, *Novum Testamentum . . . cum Paraphrasi et Annotationibus* (2 vols.: Amsterdam, 1698-9), LL no. 1382. He is mentioned by name in the *Paraphrase* in Preface, p. 108; 1 Cor. I.2†; Eph. IV.19(*a*)b; V.3(*e*)a.

[2] John Lightfoot (1602-75), Master of St Catharine Hall, Cambridge, *Works* (2 vols.: London, 1684), LL no. 1748; *Opera Omnia* (2 vols.: Rotterdam, 1686), LL no. 1745. He is mentioned by name in the *Paraphrase* at 1 Cor. XII.28*; XIV.4*.

[3] Joseph Mede (1586-1638), Fellow of Christ's College, Cambridge, *Works* (2 vols.: London, 1664), LL no. 1952. He is mentioned by name in the *Paraphrase* at 1 Cor. VIII.5*c; XI.3*q. Although he is best known for his writings on apocalyptic, it was in other matters that Locke made use of him for the study of Paul.

[4] Richard Burthogge (born *c.* 1638), *Christianity a Revealed Mystery* (London, 1702), LL no. 542. He is mentioned by name in the *Paraphrase* at 1 Cor. II.7‡d; Rom. XVI.25‡c. He also dedicated his *An Essay upon Reason, and the Nature of Spirits* (London, 1694), LL no. 538, to Locke, and wrote *Of the Soul of the World; and of Particular Souls* (London, 1699), LL no. 541, in the form of a letter addressed to him. See also *Corr.* vii. 709-11, 777-80.

[5] Theodore Beza (de Bèze) (1519-1605). His *Annotationes Maiores in Novum Domini Nostri Jesu Christi Testamentum* (new and rev. edn., 1594), is not in LL, but contains interpretations of the Epistles of which Locke was undoubtedly aware. See Preface, p. 108.

[6] See explanatory notes on 1 Cor. IX.12* and XV.54, Para. (for Vossius); Rom. XII.8* (for Vitringa); 1 Cor. VI.4*b (for de Dieu); and Preface, p. 106 (for Selden).

there were numerous others to whom Locke paid attention. In his conclusions about chronology he relied mainly on John Pearson.[1] Several passages show a knowledge of the work of the Cambridge Platonist Ralph Cudworth.[2] Many others reveal the influence of Pierre Allix, the French Protestant theologian, who emigrated to England; in the interleaved Bible and Testaments there are more entries under Paul from Allix than from any other person except Lightfoot and Locke himself.[3] The interpretations of Paul given by the great Dutch jurist Hugo Grotius were used extensively by Hammond, and in that way had an indirect influence on Locke; but Locke is also likely to have read Grotius's commentary himself.[4] Among other commentators whose work was known to Locke were the Arminian Conradus Vorstius,[5] the Socinian Johannes Crellius,[6] the French Protestants Jacobus and Ludovicus Cappellus,[7] and the English scholar Sir Norton Knatchbull.[8]

While he was writing the *Paraphrase*, Locke acquired a copy of the commentary written by Obadiah Walker and others.[9] A work which

[1] John Pearson (1613-86), Bishop of Chester, *Opera Posthuma Chronologica* (London, 1688), LL no. 2243. See also Appendix II.

[2] Ralph Cudworth (1617-88), Master of Christ's College, Cambridge, *A Discourse Concerning the True Notion of the Lords Supper* (3rd edn. London, 1676), LL no. 897; *The True Intellectual System of the Universe* (London, 1678), LL no. 896. Cudworth was the father of Damaris Masham, at whose home Locke resided when he was writing the *Paraphrase*.

[3] Pierre (or Peter) Allix (1641-1717) became Chancellor of Salisbury. The entries for him under Paul's Epistles do not resemble any passages in his published works. It is likely that they are the product of discussion between him and Locke, although no documentary evidence has been discovered to support this conjecture.

[4] Hugo Grotius (Huig de Groot) (1583-1645), *Annotationes in Novum Testamentum*, ii (Paris, 1646), LL no. 1337. Other works by Grotius influenced Locke's political thought; see Richard Tuck, *Natural Rights Theories, their Origin and Development* (Cambridge, 1979), and James Tully, *A Discourse on Property* (Cambridge, 1980), pp. 98-100, 122-3.

[5] Conradus Vorstius (Konrad von der Vorst) (1569-1622), *Commentarius in Epistolas Apostolicas* (Amsterdam, 1631), LL no. 3106.

[6] Johannes Crellius (Johann Crell) (1590-1633), *Opera Omnia Exegetica* (2 vols. in 1: Eleutheropolis, sc. Amsterdam, 1656), LL no. 876.

[7] Jacobus Cappellus (Jacques Cappel) (1570-1624), *Observationes in Novum Testamentum* (Amsterdam, 1657), LL no. 581. His brother, Ludovicus Cappellus (Louis Cappel) (1585-1658), wrote *Spicilegium post Messem* (Amsterdam, 1657), LL no. 583; see also Appendix II.

[8] Sir Norton Knatchbull, MP (1602-85), *Animadversiones in Libros Novi Testamenti* (3rd edn. Oxford, 1677), LL no. 1645.

[9] *A Paraphrase and Annotations upon all St Pauls Epistles*, 'Done by several Eminent Men at Oxford. Corrected and Improved by the late Right Reverend and Learned Bishop Fell' (3rd edn. London, 1702), LL no. 1103. A 1708 edition ascribed it to Abraham Woodhead, Richard Allestree, and Obadiah Walker. Most of it is probably the work of Obadiah Walker (1616-99), Master of University College, Oxford. See W. Jacobson's edition (Oxford, 1852), pp. iii-ix. Locke lists it as by 'Fell, alias Walker' (MS Locke e. 3).

came into his hands during that period was Jean Le Clerc's French translation of the New Testament with commentative notes, some of which were taken from his supplement to Hammond.[1] Although he did not possess the *Paraphrases* of Erasmus, he had access to that scholar's *Annotationes*[2] in *Critici Sacri*, a collection of comments on the Bible by leading scholars from the time of the Renaissance onwards.[3] Many of the viewpoints stated by commentators of the sixteenth and seventeenth centuries were also available to him in *Synopsis Criticorum*, Matthew Poole's massive summary of the interpretations of the Bible by scholars during that period.[4]

He was fully aware of the main theological trends of his day. He had been reared in a Calvinistic environment at the very time when the Westminster Confession was being drawn up.[5] Although he did not possess the commentaries of Calvin and Beza, he was well acquainted with their doctrines.[6] As far as Arminian theology was concerned, he had studied Episcopius, Limborch,[7] and Whitby. The writings of the English Latitudinarians were well known to him; he had read works by Chillingworth, Tillotson, and Fowler.[8] Socinian

[1] Jean Le Clerc (1657-1736), the Swiss scholar who met Locke in Holland, and frequently exchanged correspondence with him, *A Supplement to Dr Hammond's Paraphrase and Annotations on the New Testament* (London, 1699), LL no. 722; *Le Nouveau Testament* (2 vols.: Amsterdam, 1703), LL no. 2879.

[2] Desiderius Erasmus (*c.* 1466-1536), *Opera Omnia*, ed. by Jean Le Clerc (10 vols. in 11: Leyden, 1703-6), vols. vi, vii.

[3] *Critici Sacri* (9 vols.: Amsterdam, 1698, LL no. 886; first edition, London, 1660). John Pearson's was the first of various names subscribed to the preface of this work.

[4] Matthew Poole (Matthaeus Polus) (1624-79), a Dissenting minister, *Synopsis Criticorum* (5 vols.: London, 1669-76), LL no. 2369.

[5] *The Confession of Faith together with the Larger and Lesser Catechisms Composed by the Reverend Assembly of Divines Sitting at Westminster*. Locke had made his own index to his copy of the third edition (London, 1688), LL no. 140. The confession was approved by Parliament in 1648, when Locke was at Westminster School.

[6] John Calvin (1509-64), *Institutio Christianae Religionis* (Geneva, 1585; Leyden, 1654), LL nos. 570-1. For his commentaries see *Corpus Reformatorum*, vols. lxxvii-lxxxiii (Brunswick, 1892-6). For his influence on Locke see Merwyn S. Johnson, *Locke on Freedom* (Austin, Texas, 1978), pp. 163-4. For Beza see above, p. 13.

[7] Simon Episcopius (Simon Bischop) (1583-1643), *Opera Theologica* (2nd edn., 2 vols.: London, 1678), LL no. 1060; Philip van Limborch (1633-1712), *Theologia Christiana* (Amsterdam, 1686; 2nd edn. Amsterdam, 1695), LL nos. 1754, 1757. He also possessed Stephanus Curcellaeus (Étienne de Courcelles) (1586-1659), *Opera Theologica* (Amsterdam, 1675), LL no. 902.

[8] William Chillingworth (1602-44), *The Religion of Protestants* (4th edn. London, 1674; 5th edn. London, 1684), LL nos. 685-6; see *Second Vindication, Works*, ii. 276-7; John Tillotson (1630-94), Archbishop of Canterbury, *Sermons* (4 vols.: London, 1688-94), LL no. 2910; *Works* (3 vols.: London, 1752); Edward Fowler (1632-1714), Bishop of Gloucester, *The Principles and Practices of Certain Moderate Divines of the Church of England* (2nd edn. London, 1671), LL no. 1163.

teaching was available to him through the Racovian Catechism,[1] and the writings of, among others, Volkelius, Crellius, Biddle, and Faustus Socinus himself.[2] Not many years earlier he denied having read even a page of Socinus or Crellius,[3] but, as far as Crellius was concerned, that denial was no longer valid when he was writing the *Paraphrase*. He also possessed copies of the Unitarian tracts published in England at the end of the seventeenth century, conspicuous among which were the writings of Stephen Nye.[4] He was acquainted with the work of the Deists Edward Herbert, Charles Blount, and John Toland.[5] He protested that his teaching on fundamental doctrines was not indebted to Hobbes,[6] and that protest may well have been true; but an interleaved Bible shows that he had been reading at least one of Hobbes's writings.[7] Among Roman Catholic authors Richard Simon, a pioneer of modern biblical criticism, had been closely studied by Locke.[8] Simon's provocative views were hardly typical of the Catholicism of that time, but Locke possessed the works of Catholics as diverse in their theology as Pascal and Bossuet,[9] and had access to official

[1] *Catechesis Ecclesiarum Polonarum* (Irenopolis, sc. Amsterdam, 1659; Stauropolis, sc. Amsterdam, 1680), LL nos. 878-9. References below are to *The Racovian Catechism* (London, 1818), Thomas Rees's translation of the 1680 edition.

[2] Johannes Volkelius (Johann Völkel) (d. 1618), *De Vera Religione* (Amsterdam? 1642?), LL no. 3103, also included Johannes Crellius, *Liber de Deo et eius Attributis* and *De Uno Deo Patre*. John Biddle (1615-62), *The Apostolical and True Opinion Concerning the Holy Trinity* (London, 1691), LL no. 336; *The Faith of One God . . . Asserted and Defended in Several Tracts* (London, 1691), LL no. 3007. Faustus Socinus (Fausto Sozzini) (1539-1604), *Opera Omnia* (2 vols.: Irenopolis, sc. Amsterdam, 1656), LL no. 2712.

[3] *Second Vindication, Works*, vi. 300.

[4] Stephen Nye (*c.* 1648-1719), Rector of Little Hormead, Hertfordshire. For his and other Unitarian writings see LL nos. 2107-9, 3007-22a. William Popple (d. 1708), author of *A Rational Catechism* (London, 1687), was a friend of Locke with Unitarian sympathies.

[5] Edward Herbert, First Baron Herbert of Cherbury (1583-1648), *De Veritate* (Paris, 1624). Charles Blount (1654-93), *Miscellaneous Works* (London, 1695), LL no. 353; see also LL nos. 354-7, 2391. John Toland (1670-1722), *Christianity Not Mysterious* (London, 1696), LL no. 2935; see also LL nos. 2936-40.

[6] *Second Vindication, Works*, vi. 420-1, referring to Thomas Hobbes (1588-1679), *Leviathan* (London, 1651), LL no. 1465.

[7] Hobbes, *The Questions Concerning Liberty, Necessity, Chance* (London, 1656), from which there are entries in LL no. 309 under Jer. XIX.5 and 1 Tim. II.4.

[8] Richard Simon (1638-1712), a French Jesuit, *Histoire critique du Vieux Testament* (Paris, 1680; new edn. Rotterdam, 1685), LL nos. 2673a, 2673, to which there are many references in MS Locke f. 32; *Histoire critique du texte du Nouveau Testament* (Rotterdam, 1689), LL no. 2675; see also explanatory note on Preface, p. 110 and LL nos. 2676-7.

[9] Blaise Pascal (1623-62), *Pensées* (Lyon, 1675; new edn. Paris, 1678), LL nos. 2222a, 2222; Jacques Bénigne Bossuet (1627-1704), Bishop of Meaux, *Doctrinae Catholicae . . . Expositio* (Antwerp, 1678), LL no. 398.

Catholic teaching in the Canons and Decrees of the Council of Trent.[1]

Discussions of the literary style of biblical writings and of methods of biblical criticism were of special interest to Locke. He had studied, in addition to the works of Simon, the books in these areas by Jean Le Clerc;[2] and he was acquainted with the writings on the subject by the physicist and chemist Robert Boyle and the philosopher Baruch Spinoza.[3]

Besides the varied collection of authors who have been mentioned, numerous other writers were regarded by Locke as relevant for the study of the Epistles.[4] His interleaved volumes and notebooks show that he had carefully attempted to gather from a large number of books such material as he believed to be relevant to the study of Paul; and it is clear that the material represents only part of his reading on the subject.

When Locke undertook to study Paul's Epistles by consulting Paul himself, he certainly did not blot out of his mind the knowledge which he had acquired from other sources. The *Paraphrase* shows the influence of many of the books which he had read. In addition to the limited number of passages in which he refers to other writers by name, there are many places in which he is following or opposing the viewpoints of various authors. He was not inconsistent in allowing himself to consult these sources. He contended that 'the Labours of the Learned' could only be of use when a rule had been established for knowing which of their expositions was true to Paul's meaning (Preface, pp. 108-9). He believed that he had discovered such a rule; it was to read each Epistle at one sitting, and afterwards to read it over

[1] *Sacrosancti et Oecumenici Concilii Tridentini* . . . *Canones et Decreta* . . . (Cologne, 1615), LL no. 2981.

[2] Jean Le Clerc, *Sentimens de quelques théologiens de Hollande sur l'histoire critique du Vieux Testament* (Amsterdam, 1685), LL no. 754; *Défense des sentimens*, etc. (Amsterdam, 1686), LL no. 755; *Ars Critica* (2 vols.: Amsterdam, 1697), LL no. 769.

[3] Robert Boyle (1627-91), *Some Considerations Touching the Style of the Holy Scriptures* (London, 1661), a work mentioned in Locke's Journal for 8 November 1685 (MS Locke f. 8, p. 300); Baruch (or Benedict) Spinoza (1632-77), *Tractatus Theologico-Politicus* (Amsterdam, 1674), LL no. 2743.

[4] See explanatory notes on Gal. III.19b (for John Spencer); 1 Cor. III.15 (for Thomas Burnet); V.1† (for Jeremy Taylor); VIII.2 (for René Descartes); XV.54 (for Simon Patrick); Rom. IV.15 (for Thomas Godwin). The *Paraphrase* does not appear to have been influenced by the writings of Locke's relative, Peter King (1669-1734), first Lord King, Baron of Ockham, *An Enquiry into the Constitution, Discipline, Unity and Worship* . . . *of the Primitive Church* (London, 1691), LL no. 1636, and *The History of the Apostles Creed with Critical Observations on its Several Articles* (London, 1702), LL no. 1637.

and over again; in this way it was possible to observe 'the Drift and Design of his writing it' (Preface, p. 110). By applying this method he endeavoured to be free from a slavish reliance on any interpreter.

Locke's Approach to the Study of Paul's Epistles

The Preface to the *Paraphrase* contains some important statements about the difficulties encountered in the study of Paul's Epistles and about Locke's method of overcoming them. First of all he recognizes the difficulty of understanding the situation in which an Epistle was written. This is a problem which arises from 'the Nature of Epistolary Writings' (p. 103), which often omit matters known to the persons addressed but unknown to later generations of readers. There is no narrative like that of the Acts of the Apostles to provide precise information about the circumstances which led Paul to write the Epistles (p. 111). Reliance has to be placed on the Epistles themselves to provide clues about these issues.

Other difficulties arise from Paul's language and style. Although the language is Greek, the idiom is Semitic. Because of the nature of the subject, he often employs words in senses different from their normal usage. Moreover, his 'Stile and Temper' (p. 104) create problems. Thoughts follow one another in his mind in rapid succession, with the result that he inserts long parentheses into his Epistles, which have a tendency to confuse his readers, making them forget his train of thought. Because he frequently oscillates between first person singular and first person plural, it is not always clear whether he refers to himself alone or to other people as well. He alludes to objections to his arguments in ways that can mislead his readers into assuming that he is expressing his own thoughts. The very warmth and vehemence of his style hinders the process of interpretation.

Another problem is the chapter- and verse-divisions in the Authorized Version, divisions which have been perpetuated in subsequent translations of the Bible. As far as the New Testament is concerned, the present chapter divisions go back to the thirteenth-century archbishop, Stephen Langton, and the verse divisions to the sixteenth-century French scholar, Robert Stephanus.[1] Locke regarded them as a great obstacle to the understanding of Paul. They made unnatural breaks in his line of thought. If he was to be properly understood, they

[1] E. Kutsch, 'Kapitel- und Verseinteilung in der Bibel', *Die Religion in Geschichte und Gegenwart* (3rd edn., 6 vols. and index: Tübingen, 1956-65), iii. 1141-2.

had to be neglected and the Epistles had to be read like ordinary letters, which had no artificial intrusions (pp. 105-7).

Locke also recognizes that there are difficulties arising from the presuppositions of interpreters. Much of Paul's phraseology, he points out, is so familiar that readers have already formed an opinion of its meaning before they give serious study to the Epistles. Commentators, in particular, approach their task with a whole array of doctrinal and philosophical presuppositions (pp. 107-9). And students of the Scriptures gravitate towards the commentator with whose theological opinions they are in agreement. It is preferable that they should consult a variety of commentators, in order to safeguard themselves from being exposed to only one point of view. But when they consult several commentaries, they become confused by the multiplicity of interpretations.

Having recognized the difficulties confronted by the interpreter of the Epistles, Locke outlines the procedure which he has adopted in order to overcome them. His aim is to interpret Paul by consulting Paul himself; to this end he set about reading each Epistle at one sitting. Previously he had read them chapter by chapter. Now he decided to look at each Epistle as a whole and 'to observe as well as I could the Drift and Design of his writing it' (p. 110). One reading was not enough. He insisted on reading it over and over again with a complete disregard for chapter- and verse-divisions, and 'with a close Attention to the Tenour of the Discourse'. In this way he could more easily detect the meaning of obscure passages.[1]

He admitted that he presupposed Paul to be a coherent thinker. Even when the train of thought was obscure, Locke would wrestle with a passage until he could see how it might fit intelligibly into Paul's argument. The attentive reader, he claimed, is one who can 'see how the scatter'd Parts of the Discourse hang together in a coherent well-agreeing Sense, that makes it all of a Piece' (p. 104). His assumption about Paul's coherence was based on the conviction that when God chose Paul as Apostle to the Gentiles, he chose a man who was capable of using convincing argument (p. 110). Yet although Locke approached his task with this dogmatic conviction, his enterprise was

[1] In a paper on 'Infallibility', written in 1661, Locke spoke of the need to interpret Scripture in the light of Scripture–a need which had been recognized even in the early Church. In the *Paraphrase*, however, his concern is to interpret each Epistle in the light of Paul's thought as a whole rather than in the light of the entire Bible. For the text of Locke's paper see John C. Biddle, 'John Locke's Essay on Infallibility: Introduction, Text and Translation', *Journal of Church and State*, xix (1977), 301-27.

not uncritical. He operated on the assumption that Paul was a coherent thinker, and believed that after close examination he had found the assumption to be sound.

A great merit of Locke's Preface is the memorable clarity and vigour with which it states the difficulties which he encountered and the principles by which he operated in the study of Paul. His confidence in the consistency of Paul's thought may sometimes be questioned. The extent to which he read the Epistles without paying attention to commentators may be debated. Nevertheless the Preface is an important statement of a method for dealing with the problems presented by the Epistles and for discovering Paul's meaning.

Locke's main concerns in the Preface had been recognized by others before him. Boyle and Simon had both drawn attention to the problems of style in the Scriptures. They had, for example, pointed out the difficulty caused by the Semitic idiom which was frequently present in New Testament Greek.[1] Locke's claim to demonstrate the coherence of Paul's thought is reminiscent of Boyle's insistence that Paul reasoned 'as Solidly and Acutely' as Aristotle.[2] As for Locke's emphasis on reading each Epistle over and over again in its entirety, Jenkin contended with good reason that this had always been the practice of the best commentators.[3] Nor was Locke alone in showing discontent with chapter- and verse-divisions. Calvin, Vorstius, and Boyle were among those who had shown this kind of dissatisfaction before him.[4] The strength of the Preface is not in the originality of its ideas but in its success in confronting a variety of important issues in a persuasive and powerful manner.

The principles stated in the Preface are applied in the body of the *Paraphrase*. Throughout the work Locke is concerned to demonstrate the coherence of Paul's thought and the cogency of his arguments.[5] He makes frequent reference to the 'tenor' and 'thread' of Paul's discourse and reasoning. He seeks to display the 'force'[6] of the arguments and the way in which they are developed by 'illation' and 'inference'.[7] He

[1] Boyle, *Style of the Holy Scriptures*, p. 157; Simon, *Histoire critique du texte du Nouveau Testament*, p. 315. See also explanatory note on Preface, p. 110.

[2] Boyle, *Style*, p. 63.

[3] Robert Jenkin, *Remarks on Some Books Lately Publish'd* (London, 1709), pp. 126-7.

[4] Boyle, *Style*, p. 60. See explanatory note on 1 Cor. XI.1*.

[5] e.g. Preface, pp. 103, 104, 106, 110, 111; 1 Cor. VIII.1*; Rom. I.7†; VI.8*a; VII.1†; Eph. I.13(*y*); I.14(*b*)e; II.1(*n*)a.

[6] e.g. Preface, pp. 103-4, 111; Rom. VI.14†a; XIV.20*.

[7] e.g. Rom. II.1*a; III.28*; V.1*a; V.18*a. See *Essay Concerning Human Understanding*, ed. Peter H. Nidditch (Oxford, 1975) IV. xvii. 2 (pp. 668-9).

claims that even when there are parentheses the digression reinforces the argument.[1] He also stresses the importance of particles for clarifying the thread of Paul's thought.[2]

He is sensitive to the meaning of particular words and phrases and notes how Paul sometimes departs from the common Greek usage or 'propriety' of a word;[3] in some instances the meaning is to be determined by the Hebrew equivalent;[4] in others attention must be paid to the context or 'the sense of the place'.[5]

Above all, Locke is concerned to bear in mind Paul's aim or design in writing these Epistles and to show how the argument serves that aim.[6] He emphasizes the skilfulness and adroitness with which Paul adapts the arguments to his needs. He praises his ability to achieve that end without recourse to the ornaments and rules of Greek rhetoric, although he also praises his use of figurative speech, a rhetorical practice condemned in the *Essay*.[7]

Locke's concern to show how the argument serves Paul's aim is reflected in his treatment of chapter- and verse-divisions. Although Calvin and Vorstius had recognized the inadequacy of these divisions, their commentaries were still organized according to the traditional chapters. Locke broke away from that restraint. In a variety of places his arrangement of the material into sections and sub-sections disregards the beginning and ending of chapters. Such a procedure is often adopted by modern commentators, but in Locke's day it was an innovation; and it is vivid evidence of his determination to uncover the thread of the argument in each Epistle.

The aim of the Epistles cannot be adequately discussed without a consideration of the situations for which they were written. Locke attempted to reconstruct those situations by examining the contents of the Epistles. He claimed that all five of them were written at a time when Paul's main opponents were Judaizing Christians, a viewpoint which is for the most part similar to that of Whitby but differs from that of Hammond, who held that the main opposition came from

[1] e.g. Rom. V.6*, 8*, 10*cc; V.18*b-c.

[2] e.g. Rom. V.6*, 8*, 10*cc; V.18*b; Eph. II.1(*n*)a; II.4(*u*); III.2(*w*)a. Cf. *Essay*, III. vii (pp. 471-3), where a whole chapter is devoted to particles.

[3] In *Essay*, III. ix. 8 (p. 479) he describes 'common Use' as 'the Rule of Propriety'.

[4] e.g. 1 Cor. VIII.3*; 2 Cor. IV.17*.

[5] e.g. 1 Cor. III.18†; Rom. III.7†.

[6] e.g. Preface, p. 110; Gal. I.1-5, Contents, a; 1 Cor. Synopsis, g; 2 Cor. I.3-14, Contents, c; Rom. Synopsis, g; III.5*b; Eph. IV.9,10(*w*)a.

[7] Gal. V.2-13, Contents, g; Rom. I.16-II.29, Contents, b, e; II.1†; V.12*; Eph. II.15(*r*)a; Preface, p. 111; *Essay*, III. x. 34 (p. 508).

Gnostics.[1] It would be a mistake to say that these background issues had not been previously considered by scholars. Early writers such as Chrysostom and Theodoret were aware of these issues as were Colet and Calvin in the sixteenth century. But Locke, like Grotius, Hammond, and Whitby, gives extended consideration to the question of the opposition with which Paul had to contend. His examination of this question helped him to understand Paul's arguments and to reach conclusions about the purposes for which the Epistles were written.[2]

Paraphrase as a Means of Interpretation

Paraphrases of Scripture had a long history before Locke decided to use the form as a means of interpreting Paul's Epistles. The Aramaic Targums of the Hebrew Scriptures were paraphrases, at first oral, of which the earliest written versions date back to the second century. Cædmon's seventh-century poetic versions of excerpts from the Bible can be classified as paraphrases, as can also the tenth-century rendering of the Gospels into Anglo-Saxon by Aldred. The fashion of explaining the New Testament by this means was given fresh impetus in the sixteenth century by Erasmus, whose Latin paraphrases covered every book of the New Testament except Revelation. Thereafter the fashion spread. In Venice Antonio Scaino published a paraphrase of Paul's Epistles, and in Scotland John Napier published one of Revelation.[3] In the seventeenth century William Day produced a paraphrase of Romans, and Antoine Godeau used the form to interpret all the New Testament Epistles.[4] Conradus Vorstius and Obadiah Walker paraphrased all Paul's Epistles, and Johannes Crellius used this method for dealing with some of them.[5] Other paraphrases were written by William Clagett on parts of John's Gospel, by Sebastian Schmid on a section of the Epistle to the Romans, and by Samuel

[1] See the introductory explanatory notes for each Epistle.

[2] For a discussion of Locke's method of biblical interpretation and its relation to his *Essay*, see P. A. Schouls, *The Imposition of Method, A Study of Descartes and Locke* (Oxford, 1980), pp. 216-51. For an examination of Locke's practice of literary criticism in the *Paraphrase*, see Gretchen Graf Pahl, 'John Locke as Literary Critic and Biblical Interpreter', in *Essays Critical and Historical Dedicated to Lily B. Campbell* (Berkeley and Los Angeles, 1950), pp. 137-57, 270-2.

[3] Antonio Scaino, *Paraphrasis in Omnes S. Pauli Epistolas, cum Adnotationibus* (Venice, 1589); John Napier, *A Plaine Discoverie of the Whole Revelation of Saint John* (Edinburgh, 1593).

[4] William Day, *A Paraphrase and Commentary upon the Epistle of Saint Paul to the Romans* (London, 1666); Antoine Godeau, *Paraphrase sur les Épistres de Saint Paul et sur les Épistres Canoniques* (new edn. Paris, 1650).

[5] See above, p. 14.

Cradock and Edward Waple on the Book of Revelation.[1] Paraphrases of the whole New Testament were written by Henry Hammond and Richard Baxter.[2] At the turn of the century Samuel Clarke and Jean Le Clerc used the form to interpret the Gospels,[3] and Daniel Whitby[4] employed it for all the books of the New Testament except Revelation. When Locke selected the form as an appropriate means for conveying his interpretation of the Epistles, paraphrases were already in vogue.

To translate, according to the Oxford English Dictionary, is 'to turn from one language into another'; to paraphrase is 'to express the meaning in other words, usually with the object of fuller and clearer exposition', or 'to translate with latitude'. The line between a translation and a paraphrase is often hard to draw. Whenever a translation makes an imaginative attempt to catch the author's meaning instead of being satisfied with a word-for-word equivalency, it contains an element of paraphrase. Generally speaking, a translation keeps close to the original and hesitates to expand it; a paraphrase is much freer, often expanding the original and introducing explanations in order to be more intelligible to the reader. Paraphrases vary in freedom and length. Erasmus and Crellius do not stick at all closely to the text, but are expansive in their treatment of it. Walker and Whitby, on the other hand, for the most part reproduce the Authorized Version, adding amplifications to the text whenever they regard them as necessary. Hammond sometimes does no more than reproduce the rendering of the Authorized Version; at other times he is greatly independent of it.

Locke varies in his treatment of the material. Sometimes, as in Rom. XVI.1-16 and Eph. VI.10-20, he keeps close to the Authorized Version. At other times he is more expansive, as in 1 Cor. II.14-16, III.1-11, XIII.10-13. In some places the paraphrase shows the influence of his philosophy; his treatment of 1 Cor. XIII.12 reflects his

[1] William Clagett, *Eleven Sermons . . . And a Paraphrase with Notes upon the First, Second, Third, Fourth, Fifth, Seventh, and Eighth Chapters of St. John* (London, 1693); *A Paraphrase, with Notes, and a Preface, upon the Sixth Chapter of St. John* (London, 1686); Sebastian Schmid, *In Divi Pauli ad Colossenses Epistolae* [sic] *Commentatio . . . Paraphrases in Capita VII–XI Epistolae ad Romanos*, etc. (Hamburg, 1696); Samuel Cradock, *A Brief and Plain Exposition and Paraphrase of the Whole of the Book of the Revelation* (London, 1696); Edward Waple, *The Book of the Revelation Paraphrased* (London, 1693).

[2] On Hammond, see above, pp. 12-13. Richard Baxter, *A Paraphrase on the New Testament, with Notes Doctrinal and Practical* (London, 1685).

[3] Samuel Clarke, *A Paraphrase on the Gospel of St Matthew* (London, 1701), . . . *St Mark and St Luke* (London, 1702), . . . *St John* (London, 1703), LL nos. 732-4; Jean Le Clerc, *The Harmony of the Evangelists* (London, 1701), LL no. 775.

[4] On Whitby, see above, p. 12.

views on epistemology, and his explanation of Rom. II.14 is based on the distinction between natural and positive law.[1] Much more numerous are the passages where the paraphrase reveals his own theological standpoint. Indeed, the work provides information about his opinions on a greater variety of theological topics than does any of his other writings.

Since his aim was to elucidate the argument of the Epistles and to show the coherence of Paul's thought, the paraphrase was an excellent means for him to achieve his end. It enabled him to supply connecting links which were absent from the text of the Epistles and to display the train of Paul's arguments. In addition to the actual paraphrase, he provided a synopsis at the beginning of each Epistle. Statements of contents, varying in length, were placed at the beginning of most of the sections. By these different means he endeavoured to show the development of Paul's arguments in each Epistle.

Commentative notes accompany the paraphrase, as they do in various other works of this kind, including those of Vorstius, Hammond, Walker, and Whitby. Some of these notes deal with details of translation; others give information about Jewish or Gentile background; others give further assistance in understanding Paul's argument; others comment on textual criticism. While Locke's work on 1 Corinthians has a greater number of expanded paraphrases than his work on the other Epistles, it is on Romans and Ephesians that he has included the greatest number of lengthy notes. Some of these are of great importance for the understanding of his theology. His discussions of redemption (Rom. III.24*), resurrection (Rom. VIII.11†), the headship of Christ (Eph. I.10(*t*)), salvation by grace (Eph. II.8(*c*)), and the abolition of the law (Eph. II.15(*p*)), to mention only a few instances, are rich sources of evidence about his thought on these matters.

At first, according to a remark in the Preface (p. 109), he intended the *Paraphrase* for his private use. When, however, he decided to send it for publication, it was obviously his intention to assist others in understanding the Epistles. In the *Reasonableness* he had argued that the fundamental teaching of Christianity, found in the Gospels and the Acts, was easily intelligible to people with little education or of limited intellectual ability.[2] In a paper written apparently in preparation for the Preface to his *Paraphrase*, he takes the position that it is possible also to make the Epistles intelligible to the general public.

[1] See explanatory notes ad loc.

[2] *Works*, vi. 157.

His work, he explains, is meant for the 'illiterate', i.e., the uneducated.[1] It may be questioned how far his lengthy notes, many of which quote the Greek text, would clarify matters for such readers; but there is no doubt that he had a sincere concern to help a wide variety of readers to understand the Epistles. The work, which was at first written to enable him to grasp the meaning of Paul's writings, and to prepare himself for eternal salvation, was published in order to assist others to achieve these ends. In the concluding sentence of the Preface (p. 115) he invites his readers to join him in betaking themselves 'in earnest to the Study of the way to Salvation'. The years which he had devoted to careful investigation into the meaning of the Epistles were not spent in an enterprise of merely intellectual interest. He believed at first his own eternal destiny to be at stake. Later his concern extended to the eternal destiny of others.

Textual Criticism of the Epistles

Modern developments in textual criticism of the New Testament began about two centuries before Locke wrote his *Paraphrase*. Among its pioneers were the sixteenth-century scholars Desiderius Erasmus, Robertus Stephanus, and Theodore Beza, copies of whose editions of the New Testament were in Locke's possession.[2] The text prepared by Stephanus, and Beza's text, which was largely derived from his, provided the foundation for what is known as the Textus Receptus or Received Text, on which the Authorized (King James) Version of the New Testament was based. The science of textual criticism was still in a rudimentary state at the end of the sixteenth century. Editions were based on relatively late manuscripts, most of them belonging to the tenth century or later, and only a limited amount of work had been done on the collation of variant readings.[3] Nevertheless, at the beginning of the seventeenth century a rich storehouse of material was available to scholars. Early Greek manuscripts, versions of the New Testament in other ancient languages, and the writings of the early Church fathers provided a vast assortment of evidence for textual scholars to sift.

As Locke studied Paul's Epistles, he was able to consult much of this varied material. The Codex Claromontanus, a sixth-century uncial manuscript, which had been in the possession of Beza, is cited

[1] Appendix I, a.
[2] LL nos. 2861, 2866, 2868, 2870.
[3] Bruce M. Metzger, *The Text of the New Testament* (2nd edn. Oxford, 1968), pp. 95-106.

by Locke[1] in support of some passages where he disagrees with the Authorized Version. Another important uncial manuscript, Codex Alexandrinus, which was probably written in the fifth century, was the subject of much discussion in Locke's day. In 1627 it was given to Charles I of England by the Patriarch of Constantinople, and was used extensively by both Grotius and Hammond.[2] It is also mentioned by Locke in some of his notes, and was probably used by him on other occasions as well.[3] The fourth-century uncial, Codex Vaticanus, which was kept in the Vatican Library, was known to scholars, and seems to have been followed in at least two places by Locke.[4] A large number of other manuscripts were available, and while Locke is unlikely to have studied the originals, he was acquainted with some of their readings through various collations that had been published. There were also numerous versions of the New Testament in ancient languages. Locke makes reference to several of them, including the Old Latin, the Vulgate (which was the Latin version officially recognized by the Roman Catholic Church), the Syriac, and the Arabic.[5] In addition to all these sources of information he was aware of some of the evidence provided by Church fathers.[6]

It was not necessary for Locke to search the original documents for the manuscript evidence. He had access to collations of readings by Erasmus, Stephanus, and Beza. He possessed a copy of Brian Walton's Polyglot Bible, which contained numerous collations, including a large number of variants from Codex Alexandrinus, and reproduced several versions, among which were the Latin, Syriac, and Arabic.[7] The edition of the Greek New Testament prepared by John Fell, of which Locke owned a copy, included many variants, although it did not indicate their sources.[8] And the various commentaries which Locke consulted provided considerable information about textual matters.

The monumental edition of the New Testament by John Mill was not published until 1707, three years after Locke's death. This work,

[1] See explanatory notes on Gal. III.29*; 1 Cor. X.28*; Rom. I.32†a.

[2] Grotius refers to it as 'the Manuscript' and Hammond calls it 'the King's Manuscript'.

[3] See 1 Cor. II.1*; X.28*; Rom. III.25†; V.16*; Eph. III.19, Para.; V.27(*t*).

[4] See explanatory notes on 1 Cor. X.28*; Rom. IX.23*a.

[5] See explanatory notes on 2 Cor. XII.1, Para.; Rom. I.32†a.

[6] See explanatory note on Rom. I.32†a.

[7] *Biblia Sacra Polyglotta* (6 vols.: London, 1655-7), LL no. 324. It also included Ethiopic and, in the Gospels, Persian versions, but Locke did not refer to these.

[8] *Novi Testamenti Libri Omnes* (Oxford, 1675), LL no. 2865.

which collected all the evidence which was available to Mill, had taken thirty years to prepare. Locke may have seen part of it before publication, probably material on the first chapter of Paul's Epistle to the Romans. Letters written to Locke by Peter King in January and February of 1704 indicate that King hoped to borrow the material on Locke's behalf from William Lloyd, Bishop of Worcester.[1] But there is no evidence that the excerpt from Mill's work ever reached Locke. It is most unlikely that Locke had any personal conversation or correspondence with Mill on textual matters. Mill was one of the leaders of the unsuccessful attempt to have Locke's books banned from the University of Oxford.[2]

Besides the various editions of the New Testament which were appearing there were books about the history and method of textual criticism. Locke possessed a copy of *Histoire critique du texte du Nouveau Testament* by the French Jesuit, Richard Simon. He also had a copy, given by the author, of Jean Le Clerc's *Ars Critica*, a treatise on the textual criticism of ancient books. The page lists which Locke had written in pencil in this copy are evidence that he had studied the book with care. And he had been in correspondence with Isaac Newton about the possibility of publishing the latter's comments on two textual problems in the New Testament.[3] Locke's interest in textual

[1] In his letter of 6 Jan. 1704, Peter King told Locke, 'I have made your Compliment to the Bishop of Worcester by his son–You may see Dr Mills, if you please, Assoon as I have the book I will send you the variae lectiones on the. 1. Rom.' (*Corr.* viii. 155). The book to which King refers is probably an excerpt from Mill's work. Although it was not published until 1707, part of it may have already been printed and sent to the bishop. In a letter dated 15 Feb. 1704, King wrote to Locke informing him that the excerpt from Mill had not yet arrived: 'The Bishop of Worcester is very well pleased with your letter, He will, I believe, write you in a little time, He speaks of you with a great deale of respect . . . I have not yet found him at home so as to take what you desire out of Dr. Mills, but I will do it' (*Corr.* viii. 195-6).

[2] John Mill (1645-1707), who was Principal of St Edmund Hall, Oxford, from 1685 until his death, proposed in Nov. 1703 that there should be a ban on the use of Locke's and Le Clerc's books by tutors for reading with their pupils. The evidence is provided by a letter from James Tyrrell to Locke, dated *c.* 17 Apr. 1704 by de Beer (*Corr.* viii. 269).

[3] On 14 Nov. 1690 Newton sent Locke some papers (the covering letter is in *Corr.* iv. 164-5) and apparently on Locke's suggestion had them sent to Le Clerc for publication. They were concerned with the text for 1 John V.7 and 1 Tim. III.16. Newton eventually decided not to publish them (see Le Clerc's letter to Locke, dated Feb. 1692, *Corr.* iv. 387). The work was not published until 1754 when it appeared under the title *Two Letters of Sir Isaac Newton to Mr. Le Clerc*. Its original title was *An Historical Account of Two Notable Corruptions of Scripture*. See Maurice Cranston, *John Locke: a Biography* (London, 1957), pp. 338-9, 354-5; Frank E. Manuel, *A Portrait of Isaac Newton* (rev. edn. Cambridge, Mass., 1979), pp. 184-5, 371-2. The manuscript of the work has been transcribed

criticism was already evident in the 1680s, when he studied both Simon's work on the Old Testament and responses to it.[1]

The method which Locke employed in dealing with textual problems in the Epistles was thoroughly consistent with his desire to show the coherence of Paul's arguments. Although he paid attention to the kind of support given to a reading by the manuscripts and versions, his final decision was determined by the smoothness with which a reading would fit into the context. While textual critics of later generations tended to prefer the more difficult to the easier variant reading, on the grounds that a copyist would smooth out difficulties,[2] Locke was inclined to choose the easier reading. He acted on the assumption that Paul's arguments were coherent and that difficult readings were more likely to be the product of a copyist than of Paul himself. In Rom. IX.23 the omission of the word καί ('and') means that Paul's argument 'runs plainly and smoothly' (Rom. IX.23*c). The reading selected in 2 Cor. XII.1 is defended because 'suiting better with the context' it 'renders the sense clearer' (2 Cor. XII.1*). An extreme example of this tendency is his treatment of Rom. I.32, where he chooses what is generally regarded as an unreliable variant on the grounds that it is more consistent with Paul's thought as a whole (Rom. I.32†). The underlying principle on which he acted was that the reading is to be preferred which fits most easily into Paul's argument.

II. LOCKE'S THOUGHT AS EXPRESSED IN THE PARAPHRASE AND NOTES

The *Paraphrase* provides evidence for Locke's thought during the last five years of his life. He devoted his time to the writing of the work with seriousness and dedication. He knew that it was likely to be his final literary production. Since he believed Paul to be a vehicle of divine revelation, most statements in the *Paraphrase* which give expression to Paul's theology may also be regarded as statements of Locke's theology. The lines of Locke's thinking can be most clearly

in *The Correspondence of Isaac Newton*, ed. H. W. Turnbull, J. F. Scott, A. Rupert Hall, and Laura Tilling (7 vols.: Cambridge, 1959-77), iii. 83-129.

[1] See Limborch's letter to Locke, 8/18 Oct. 1685, *Corr.* ii. 755, and Le Clerc's letter to Locke, 27 Nov./7 Dec. 1694, *Corr.* v. 197-8.

[2] The principle that the more difficult reading is the more likely gained publicity soon after Locke's time. It was stated by Bengel in the first half of the eighteenth century (Metzger, *Text*, p. 112) and was already recognized by Mill in his edition of 1707 (Adam Fox, *John Mill and Richard Bentley* (Oxford, 1954), pp. 147-8).

discerned in his footnote annotations and in those parts of the paraphrase which handle the original text with the greatest freedom. When he is least dependent on the words of the Authorized Version, he provides the surest evidence of his own reflections.

A writer's theology is not to be as easily discovered in a biblical commentary as in a treatise of systematic theology. The outlines of Locke's thought do not lie on the surface in the *Paraphrase*. But when his work is examined closely, it becomes apparent that he has taken a firm stand on some of the most controversial theological issues of his day. In many of his notes he is defining his interpretation by contrast with viewpoints which he rejects. Much of his thought has parallels in his earlier writings. But in some places new ideas emerge. The *Paraphrase* represents a distinctive stage in the history of Locke's thought.

To clarify the theology of the *Paraphrase* it is necessary to compare it with the thought of Locke's earlier writings and also with alternative theological positions. It was not his aim to write a systematic theology. But in the *Paraphrase* he provides evidence of his views on many issues of Christian doctrine as well as on some important questions of philosophy. In the following pages an attempt will be made to draw attention to these aspects of his thought.

The Bible and Revelation

Although Locke believed a limited number of chosen individuals like Moses and Paul to have been the recipients of 'immediate' (i.e. unmediated) divine revelation,[1] he thought that revelation was given to the majority of people only as mediated through the Bible.[2] He claimed to read the Bible 'with a full assurance, that all it delivers is true'.[3] 'The holy scripture', he said, 'is to me, and always will be, the constant guide of my assent; and I shall always hearken to it, as containing infallible truth, relating to things of the highest concernment.'[4]

He did not elaborate on his statement that 'all it delivers is true'. He appears to have regarded the Bible as a historically accurate record of events. But in one respect he admits that Paul was capable of error. In his *Paraphrase* he claims that Paul expected the return of Christ to earth in the near future (2 Cor. V.3*; Rom. XIII.11, 12*). Although Locke believed in the eventual return of Christ, he recognized that Paul was

[1] *A Discourse of Miracles, Works*, viii. 262-3; Preface, see below, p. 110.
[2] Cf. explanatory note on Eph. I.17(*h*).
[3] *Second Reply to the Bishop of Worcester, Works*, iii. 341.
[4] *Letter to the Bishop of Worcester, Works*, iii. 96.

mistaken in expecting it to be imminent. Apart from this exception, Locke showed no sign of doubting the accuracy of the scriptural writers.

He never gave a satisfactory explanation why the Scriptures could be relied on in this way. He argued that their truth was authenticated by miracles, which were either performed by the recipients of revelation in order to convince others[1] or directly enacted by God in order to persuade the recipients.[2] Yet there is a circularity in this argument. The miracles, which are supposed to attest the scriptural revelation, are themselves attested only by the Scriptures. Locke does not appear to be aware of this weakness in the argument, and assumes throughout his writings, early and late, that the Bible is an accurate record of divine revelation, because its message is miraculously confirmed. This assumption underlies his thought in the *Paraphrase*, where, in addition to his repeated emphasis on the coherence of Paul's reasoning, he attaches great importance to the authentication of revelation by miracles (1 Cor. II.4-5, Para.).

Not every part of the Bible was treated alike by Locke. While he did not dispute the historical accuracy of the Old Testament, he did not regard its ceremonial and civil laws as binding on Christians, although he believed its moral laws to be still authoritative.[3] The Old Testament, however, was highly relevant for his understanding of Christianity. It was not a record of merely historical interest. Besides its literal meaning, it had a spiritual meaning, which had been shrouded in mystery until the coming of Christ, but now could be understood through the guidance of the Spirit (2 Cor. III.6*). The very events of Israelite history foreshadowed the Christian dispensation. The crossing of the Red Sea was a type of baptism, and the miraculous food and drink received by the children of Israel in the wilderness prefigured the bread and wine of the Lord's Supper (1 Cor. X.1-5, Para.). Even the sacrificial laws of the Old Testament pointed forward to the sacrificial death of Christ (Rom. III.25†).

This typological method of interpreting the Old Testament had been generally accepted since the days of the early Church. But there was dispute about the extent to which the method should be used. Locke belongs to the more cautious practitioners who are not disposed to employ the method any more extensively than do the

[1] *Reasonableness, Works*, vi. 85; *A Discourse of Miracles, Works*, viii. 262-4.
[2] *Essay*, IV. xix. 15 (p. 705).
[3] *Reasonableness, Works*, vi. 13; *Paraphrase*, Rom. II.26*f-j.

New Testament writers themselves. Whenever he sees an aspect of the Christian Gospel in the Hebrew Scriptures, it is one which is seen there by a New Testament writer. This method of interpretation continues to regard the Old Testament as an inspired and historically reliable collection of Scriptures. But in practice it relies on the New Testament as the source of authority, because it is the medium through which the spiritual meaning of the Old is discovered.

Within the New Testament Locke gave pride of place to the Gospels and the Acts. It was in these books that he believed the fundamental articles of the Christian religion to be most clearly discerned. The Epistles were inspired writings, and their teaching was to be believed in so far as it could be understood. But the Gospels and the Acts had to be studied first in order to discover what was fundamental. Because the Epistles were for the most part written for particular occasions, they contain many statements which were relevant for those circumstances rather than for later ages.[1] It was only when people had studied the Gospels and the Acts that they were equipped to study the Epistles. It was for people who had progressed to this stage that the *Paraphrase* was intended.

Revelation and Reason

More than any of Locke's other writings the *Paraphrase* stresses the superiority of revelation to reason, and marks the climax of a process which can already be discerned in the *Essay*. Some of the comments in the *Paraphrase* are surprising in a writer who has a reputation for stressing the importance of reason. In his work on 1 Corinthians Locke repeatedly depicts Paul as a man who relied on divine revelation rather than on human reason or human learning. He explains that for Paul 'the gospel was not to be propagated nor men to be established in the faith by humane learning and eloquence but by the Evidence it had from the Revelation conteined in the old Testament and from the power of god accompanying and confirming it with miracles' (1 Cor. II.1-5, Contents). In 1 Cor. II.1*a-b he writes that the apostle 'made noe use of any humane science improvement or skil; no insinuations of Eloquence; no philosophical speculations, or ornaments of humane learning appeard in any thing he said, to perswade them'. He explains that 'the knowledg of the gospel was not attainable by our natural parts however they were improved by arts and philosophie, but was wholy

[1] *Reasonableness, Works*, vi. 152-5.

oweing to Revelation' (1 Cor. II.6-16, Contents). As for the principles of the Christian religion, Paul 'sees and acknowledges it to be all a pure revelation from god, and not in the least the product of humane discovery parts or learning' (1 Cor. II.6*a). The contrast between the 'animal man' and the 'spiritual man' is between the man 'that has noe higher principles to build on than those of natural reason' and the man 'that founds his faith and religion on divine revelation' (1 Cor. II.15*).

These assertions of the superiority of revelation to reason represent Locke's own opinion, and are not just his attempts to explain Paul's thought. Their relevance extends to Locke's own time, when Deists claimed to rely on reason to such an extent as to dispense with the need for revelation. Although he was describing Paul's world in Corinth, he had his eye on the intellectual world of his own day. Here the empirical aspect of his theology is clearly to be discerned. There are truths which are above reason, he contends, and are to be discovered by the study of the Scriptures.

In spite of his strong emphasis on the function of revelation, he gives recognition in the *Paraphrase* to the importance of reason. It can discover 'the invisible things of god' and make known 'the natural and eternal rule of *rectitude*'.[1] And throughout the *Paraphrase* Locke is concerned to show the coherence and consistency of Paul's thought. But revelation has the primacy.

There is a marked change of emphasis in this respect from his earlier writings. In his *Treatises of Government* Locke rejects the elaborate attempts of Filmer to ground the divine right of kings on revelation. In constructing his own theory of government Locke uses revelation merely to support the findings of reason.[2] He is concerned in the *Essay* to maintain a balance between the two; truths of revelation may be above reason, but they are subject to the scrutiny of reason.[3] The *Reasonableness* acknowledges the limitations of reason more than does the *Essay*. While the *Essay* entertains the possibility of a logical demonstration of the laws of morality,[4] the *Reasonableness* points out that not even the greatest philosophers have been able to

[1] Rom. I.20*; I.32, Para.; II.26*a. In Gal. V.16, 17†d Locke describes 'spirit' as the 'principle which dictates what is right and inclines to good'. In this sense 'spirit' is equivalent to 'reason'.

[2] John Locke, *Two Treatises of Government*, ed. by Peter Laslett (2nd edn. Cambridge, 1967), *First Treatise*, passim; *Second Treatise*, v. 25; vi. 52 (pp. 303-4, 321).

[3] *Essay*, iv. xvii. 23-4; iv. xix. 14 (pp. 687-8, 704).

[4] *Essay*, iii. xi. 16; iv. iii. 18; iv. xii. 8 (pp. 516-17, 548-50, 643-4).

deduce a system of morality comparable to that given by Jesus through revelation.[1] The *Paraphrase* goes even further. Its strong assertions about the limitations of reason, philosophy, and human discovery mark the culmination of an important shift in Locke's attitude.[2]

A partial explanation of the change is to be found in the nature of the subject-matter. That would certainly help to explain the difference from the *Treatises of Government*. Even the difference from the *Reasonableness* may be partly accounted for by the influence of Paul. It was Paul who stressed the inferiority of the wisdom of this world to the divine wisdom; and while Locke had long been a student of his thought, he was more deeply immersed in it than ever when he was writing the *Paraphrase*. But another factor is likely to have helped to produce the change in Locke's attitude to reason. He was becoming increasingly concerned with the question of his ultimate destiny;[3] and it was on revelation rather than reason that he relied when he adjusted himself to the prospect of a future life.

Fundamental Articles

Before Locke wrote the *Paraphrase*, he had already written extensively about his views on the fundamental articles of the Christian religion. His position is stated in the *Reasonableness* and its *Vindications*. Belief in the fundamental articles is 'absolutely required of all those to whom the gospel of Jesus Christ is preached'.[4] The other articles, which are not fundamental, are to be believed in so far as people understand them.[5]

Sometimes he gives the impression that the only fundamental article is the belief that Jesus is the Messiah.[6] At other times he speaks of 'concomitant articles' which are necessary for justification. They include 'his miracles, death, resurrection, dominion, and coming to judge the quick and the dead'.[7] He also mentions the belief 'that God

[1] *Works*, vi. 140-3.

[2] In his Introduction to his edition of *Two Treatises of Government*, pp. 87-8, Peter Laslett argues that in his later writings Locke recognized the insufficiency of reason and attempted to supplement it with revelation. This viewpoint is challenged by Peter A. Schouls, *The Imposition of Method*, pp. 219-29.

[3] In a letter to Anthony Collins, dated 23 Aug. 1704, Locke wrote that 'this life is a scene of vanity that soon passes away and affords no solid satisfaction but in the consciousness of doeing well and in the hopes of an other life' (*Corr.* viii. 419).

[4] *Reasonableness, Works*, vi. 155.

[5] Ibid., vi. 156.

[6] Ibid., vi. 57.

[7] *Second Vindication, Works*, vi. 341; in *Reasonableness, Works*, vi. 151, he lists 'his resurrection, rule, and coming again to judge the world' as concomitant articles.

is true' as fundamental,[1] and recognizes the Apostles' Creed as a summary of necessary beliefs.[2]

The distinction between fundamental and non-fundamental articles is presupposed in the *Paraphrase*. The doctrine of Jesus as the Christ, Locke writes, is the foundation (1 Cor. III.1-IV.20, Contents, c), and the resurrection of Jesus is 'one of the most fundamental articles of the Christian religion' (Rom. X.9†a). Beyond the foundation are 'more advanced truths' (1 Cor. III.1-IV.20, Contents, b). Locke does not explicitly say what those advanced truths are. But he probably believed them to include much of the teaching in Paul's Epistles.[3]

This concern to establish the content of the fundamental articles of Christianity was a reaction to the tendency of ecclesiastical authorities to impose detailed doctrinal requirements as essential to salvation. It was a concern which had been expressed by various writers, among whom were Chillingworth, Hammond, Hobbes, Jeremy Taylor, and Limborch.[4]

Locke had already become embroiled in controversy about fundamental articles when he wrote the *Paraphrase*. His *Vindications* contained answers to criticisms of his views on the matter by John Edwards. Further attacks were made by John Milner and Daniel Whitby.[5] Milner argued that, contrary to statements in the *Reasonableness*, the Epistles as well as the Gospels made a distinction between fundamentals and non-fundamentals. Although Locke never explicitly answers Milner's criticism, he seems to be conceding the point by recognizing that Paul makes a distinction between a foundational

[1] *Reasonableness, Works*, vi. 156.

[2] *Second Vindication, Works*, vi. 272-81. He refers, however, to a creed which does not include the clause about Christ's descent into hell.

[3] *Reasonableness, Works*, vi. 155. A large amount of the teaching in the Epistles corresponds to what Locke describes as 'superstructures' built on the foundation. These superstructures are listed by him as: 'explaining the occasion, necessity, use, and end of his coming'; 'proving him to be the person promised, by a correspondence of his birth, life, sufferings, death, and resurrection, to all those prophecies and types of him, which had given the expectation of such a Deliverer; and to those descriptions of him, whereby he might be known, when he did come'; 'the discovery of the sort, constitution, extent, and management of his kingdom'; and 'showing from what we are delivered by him, and how that deliverance is wrought out, and what are the consequences of it' (*Second Vindication, Works*, vi. 353).

[4] William Chillingworth, *The Religion of Protestants*; Henry Hammond, *Of Fundamentals in a Notion referring to Practise* (London, 1654); Thomas Hobbes, *Leviathan*, xliii; Jeremy Taylor, *Works* (15 vols.: London, 1839), vii. 445-8; Philip van Limborch, *Theologia Christiana*, VII. xxi. 4, 13.

[5] John Milner, *An Account of Mr. Lock's Religion*, pp. 42-53, 184-5; Daniel Whitby, *Epistles*, preface to 1 John.

doctrine and more advanced truths. On the other hand, he makes no actual concession to Whitby's claim that belief in Jesus's Messiahship was not the only fundamental article for the early Church. Even Locke's description of Jesus's resurrection as a fundamental article (Rom. X.9†a) is no real surrender to Whitby, because in his *Second Vindication* he had already described this doctrine as concomitant to the fundamental article of Messiahship. Although he no longer insisted on the impossibility of distinguishing fundamental articles in Paul's Epistles, he had not altered his views about the content of those articles.

Sin and Redemption

Locke's account of the condition of humanity after Adam's sin in the Garden of Eden is essentially the same in the *Paraphrase* as in the *Reasonableness*. As a punishment for his act of disobedience Adam was deprived of his original state of immortality. His posterity are not punished for his transgression but they have inherited his mortality.[1] Although they do not share his guilt for that first sin, they are in fact all sinners, because they themselves fail to keep God's law.[2]

Locke's position differs sharply from the Calvinism of his day, according to which the guilt of Adam and Eve was imputed to their descendants.[3] It differs too from the teaching of Calvin himself, who argued that all human beings inherited a condition of sinfulness from Adam, and that they were liable to punishment for their condition of sin.[4] Locke does not even go as far as Limborch, who claims that human beings inherit an inclination to do what pleases the flesh.[5] On the other hand he dissociates himself from the Deistic view that the human race is not in need of redemption at all.[6]

He admits that there is a sinful tendency in all men and women. The flesh functions in them as 'that principle which inclines and carrys men to ill'; it is the source of their 'deviations from the strait rule of rectitude'. It fights against the opposing principle of the spirit which 'dictates what is right and inclines to good' (Gal. V.16, 17†c-d).

1 *Reasonableness, Works*, vi. 4-6; *Paraphrase*, Rom. V.12-19, Contents; V.12, Para.

2 *Reasonableness, Works*, vi. 13; *Paraphrase*, Rom. III.1-31, Contents, a-b.

3 *Reasonableness, Works*, vi. 4; cf. Westminster Confession, vi. 3. Beza, *Annotationes*, on Rom. V.12, argued that the whole human race was guilty of Adam's sin because its seed was in his loins.

4 *Institutes*, II. i. 8.

5 *Theologia*, III. iii. 19.

6 *Reasonableness, Works*, vi. 4-5.

He never says that this tendency is inherited, but he recognizes that it is present in everybody: the Jews are under its power (Rom. VII.7†); the Gentiles are its vassals (Rom. VI.8*) and subjects of Satan's kingdom (Eph. I.10(*t*)b). Although he rejects any doctrine of original sin or original guilt, he has no hesitation in saying that all human beings are sinners.[1]

He was sharply criticized by John Edwards for his failure in the *Reasonableness* to develop a doctrine of the satisfaction made for sins by the death of Christ.[2] In reply he pointed out that, although he never used the word 'satisfaction', he spoke of redemption in reference to the same doctrine.[3] But his understanding of redemption would not have pleased Edwards, who accepted the position, upheld by Calvin, that the guilt of human beings was imputed to Christ, and that Christ died to pay the penalty required by God for their sin.[4] In the *Paraphrase* Locke clearly rejected that doctrine. God, he claimed, could not require an equivalent payment, since he justified sinners 'of his free bounty'. In any case, redemption implied the payment of a ransom, and it was difficult to imagine how in strict justice God could receive both the ransom payment and the person redeemed (Rom. III.24*f).

Paul's statements about the death of Christ were interpreted by Locke in such a way as to remove any suggestion that the guilt of sin was imputed to Christ or that he died as a substitute for others. Christ, according to Locke, was a sin-offering, not in the sense that he was sacrificed as a substitute for others, but in the sense that by his sinless life he 'extinguished or suppressed sin in the flesh' (Rom. VIII.3b, Para.). Locke refused to entertain the idea that Christ 'was condemned for sin, or in the place of sin' (Rom. VIII.3a). Christ is not to be regarded as a propitiation for sin but as the antitype of the mercy-seat. Under the old covenant the mercy-seat was the place where God declared his will; under the new covenant Christ is the place where

[1] He agrees with the Socinians in their rejection of the doctrine of original sin and original guilt, but he does not adopt the position of the Racovian Catechism, v. 10 (p. 326) that through habitual sinning human nature 'is infected with a certain stain, and a very strong disposition to wickedness'. He merely asserts the presence of the sinful tendency.

For Locke's dispute with Whitby about the extent to which death was a penalty inflicted on the victims of the Flood and the disaster at Sodom and Gomorrah, see explanatory note on Rom. V.13, Para. For the problem created by Rom. I.32 see explanatory note ad loc.

[2] John Edwards, *Some Thoughts Concerning the Several Causes and Occasions of Atheism* (London, 1695), LL no. 1024, p. 112; *Socinianism Unmask'd*, p. 45.

[3] *Second Vindication*, *Works*, vi. 375.

[4] Calvin, *Institutes*, II. xvi. 5.

God declares his righteousness (Rom. III.25*; III.25†). And when Paul said that Christ was 'made to be sin' (2 Cor. V.21, AV), Locke did not explain it as the imputation of people's guilt to Christ, but claimed that God had made Christ 'subject to sufferings and death the punishment and consequence of sin as if he had been a sinner' (2 Cor. V.21, Para.).

This paraphrase might suggest that, although Locke rejected the Calvinistic account of the death of Christ, he assented to Grotius's theory that God inflicted a punishment on Christ in order to preserve good order and government.[1] But Locke did not proceed to develop a theory of atonement along those lines. It might then be thought that his viewpoint was Socinian since he rejected any idea of substitution. Yet his position did not coincide with that of the Socinians. He did not attack the doctrine of satisfaction, as they did, nor did he, like them, develop the theme of Christ's continuing heavenly expiation of sins.[2] And, unlike them, he emphasized the death and resurrection of Christ as a victory over Satan.[3] This latter doctrine, which had a long ancestry in the Church's thought, influenced Locke in his comments on Ephesians. By his death and resurrection, Locke explained, Christ conquered the devil and was restored to his headship over all things. It was as a result of this victory that Christ's kingdom was established and the old covenant of works was superseded by the new covenant of grace (Eph. I.10(*t*)c; II.15(*p*)e). In his understanding of the meaning of Christ's death, as in other aspects of his theology, Locke did not fit into the mould of any particular school.

Christ

It has been customary to assume that Locke was heterodox in his beliefs about the person of Christ; and such a view is not unfounded. He shows some of the characteristics of Socinian teaching, not so much in the positive statements which he makes but in his failure to assert the traditional Christian doctrines about Christ and the Trinity. It was to these omissions that his critics drew attention.[4] They were

[1] Hugo Grotius, *Defensio Fidei Catholicae de Satisfactione Christi* (Leyden, 1617).

[2] Racovian Catechism, v. 8; vi. 6 (pp. 301-20, 350-9).

[3] While Crellius mentions the theme in his comments on Hebrews (*Opera*, ii. 97), he does not refer to it in his treatise on Christ's death (*De Causis Mortis Christi, Opera*, i. 611-21); nor does it appear in the section on the death of Christ in the Racovian Catechism, v. 8.

[4] John Edwards, *Socinianism Unmask'd*, p. 82; John Milner, *An Account of Mr. Lock's Religion*, pp. 33-8. Locke, *Letter to the Bishop of Worcester, Works*, iii. 4; *Second Reply to the Bishop of Worcester, Works*, iii. 195-208.

criticisms that had some weight; and while Locke protested that he never denied the doctrine of the Trinity, he never took the trouble to affirm it.

On the other hand, the extent to which he deviated from the traditional doctrine of Christ can be exaggerated. His failure to discern that doctrine in passages where Paul does not clearly state it does not provide overwhelming evidence about his own theology.[1] And the presence of references to Socinian interpretations in his unpublished papers[2] does not prove that he gave wholehearted assent to them. Moreover, he manifests a clear disagreement with the Socinians in his unqualified assertion of Christ's pre-existence, a doctrine to which he gives expression in one of his extended theological notes on Ephesians. Before the revolt of Satan, he explains, 'Christ at first had the Rule and Supremacy over all, and was Head over all' (Eph. I.10(*t*)a). There is no trace of this doctrine in the *Reasonableness*. But he clearly accepts it in the *Paraphrase*; and such a theology is inconsistent with Socinian teaching.[3]

Locke was no more in agreement with the Unitarians of his day than with the Socinians. The Unitarianism represented in the writings of Stephen Nye was prepared to affirm the doctrine of the Trinity with the proviso that the three persons were merely three properties of the Godhead.[4] Locke differed from this interpretation in two ways: he maintained a studied silence about the Trinity; but he also believed in the pre-existence of Christ as a distinct person.

While Locke's Christology differed from that of Socinians and Unitarians, it also differed from that of the mainstream Protestant theologians of his day. He did not assert the divinity of Christ in terms which would satisfy them; and his silence about the doctrine of the Trinity put his theology at a considerable distance from theirs. Just as he moved away from the traditional philosophical language in the *Essay*, so he moved away from the traditional theological language in the *Reasonableness* and the *Paraphrase*. But although he avoided much of the terminology that had been accumulated during sixteen hundred years of theological discussion, he did not avoid the terminology of the New Testament. His aim was to explain the Christian message as

[1] See explanatory notes on 1 Cor. VIII.5*c and Rom. IX.5, Para.

[2] See explanatory note on Rom. IX. 5, Para. for his allusion to Biddle's interpretation of the verse.

[3] See explanatory note on Eph. I.10(*t*)a.

[4] Stephen Nye, *The Agreement of the Unitarians with the Catholic Church* (London, 1697), LL no. 3021, pp. 19-54.

it had been communicated by Jesus and the apostles, among whom Paul was numbered. The resulting Christology did not fit the pattern of any existing school.[1]

The Way to Salvation

Locke's chief concern in examining the scriptures was to study 'the way to Salvation' (Preface, p. 116). In both the *Reasonableness* and the *Paraphrase* he develops his thoughts about this theme. There are four main stages by which he believes God to offer deliverance to the human race from the condition of mortality into which it has fallen as a result of Adam's transgression. The first of these stages is the giving of the law to the Children of Israel through the mediation of Moses. By the law a reward of life was offered to everyone who lived in perfect obedience to it.[2] The second stage was initiated by the death and resurrection of Christ when all humanity was restored to life. This restoration does not save them from physical death but is the promise of a resurrection in the future. As a result of Christ's death they are released from the inevitability of eternal death.[3] But they do not automatically receive immortality, a privilege which is reserved only for the righteous.[4] The third stage is that which Paul frequently calls justification. Those who have faith that Jesus is the Messiah, are accepted by God into the Kingdom of Christ, have their sins forgiven, and are made righteous and capable of eternal life.[5] The fourth and final stage includes the resurrection of the righteous and the unrighteous–two separate events according to Locke–and their respective judgements. At this stage all who have believed in Christ and have

[1] A paper entitled 'Some General Reflections upon the Beginning of St John's Gospel' (MS Locke e. 17, fos. 175-223), written in Sylvester Brownover's hand, criticizes the Gnostic separation between the Son of God or Word and the human Jesus; but it does not affirm the pre-existence of Christ. In any case, it is not clear to what extent Locke was responsible for its contents; but see also Merwyn S. Johnson, *Locke on Freedom*, p. 165.

[2] *Reasonableness, Works*, vi. 14; *Paraphrase*, Rom. V.20†f.

[3] *Reasonableness, Works*, vi. 9: 'From this estate of death, Jesus Christ restores all mankind to life . . . the life, which Jesus Christ restores to all men, is that life, which they receive again at the resurrection.' Cf. *Paraphrase*, Rom. V.12-VII.25, Contents, d: 'by Christs death all men are restored to life'.

[4] *Reasonableness, Works*, vi. 14: 'and so the believers are admitted to life and immortality, as if they were righteous'. Cf. *Paraphrase*, Rom. V.12-VII.25, Contents, d: 'By Christ also as many of them as beleive are instated in eternal life.'

[5] *Reasonableness, Works*, vi. 110-11; *Paraphrase*, Rom. III.1-31, Contents, c; Eph. II.8(*c*). Like Paul, Locke recognizes that Abraham was justified by faith before the time of Christ (Rom. IV.9-10, Para.). But he does not integrate it into his own doctrine of justification.

sincerely endeavoured to be obedient to God will have their faith counted for righteousness even though their obedience has been imperfect, and will therefore receive eternal life; the unrighteous, however, will receive the condemnation of punishment and death.[1]

Although Locke does not explicitly list these four stages in any given passage in his writings, this scheme of things underlies both the *Reasonableness* and the *Paraphrase*. The word 'justify' is used by him to refer to three of the four stages which have been mentioned. The first stage, the covenant of the law with its command, 'Do this and live', is said to offer the option of justification by works, although nobody in fact proved to be capable of fulfilling the conditions of this option.[2] The death and resurrection of Christ, the second stage, is said to effect justification there and then for everyone. 'But the justification of life here spoken of is what all men partake in by the benefit of Christs death, by which they are justified from all that was brought upon them by Adams sin, i.e. they are discharged from death the consequence of Adams transgression; and restored to life to stand or fall by that plea of righteousness, which they can make, either of their own by works, or of the righteousness of god by faith' (Rom. V.18§b-c). At the third stage justification is the act whereby God 'now admits all, who profess faith in Jesus Christ, to be equaly his people' (Rom. III.1-31, Contents, c). It is in this act that believers receive forgiveness of sins (Rom. IV.6, 8*a) and are admitted into God's favour (Rom. V.1-2, Para.). Locke uses the terminology of justification in the *Reasonableness* to refer also to the fourth stage, that of ultimate salvation; and it is significant that he supports his usage of the word from the Epistle of James.[3] In the *Paraphrase*, where Paul, not James, is being expounded, it is not clear that justification has this meaning. Yet it is certainly connected with this final stage, since, Locke affirms, eternal life is the consequence of justification (Rom. IV.25*b, e).[4]

The word normally used in the *Paraphrase* to describe ultimate deliverance is 'salvation'. Paul used the Greek equivalent and its cognates to refer to the past and the present as well as the future. While

[1] *Reasonableness, Works*, vi. 9, 113-14, 125-6; *Paraphrase*, 1 Cor. XV.42*; 2 Cor. V.10-11, Para.; V.9†; Rom. V.12-VII.25, Contents; VI.22, 23, Para.; Eph. II.8(*c*).

[2] *Reasonableness, Works*, vi. 11-12; *Paraphrase*, Rom. III.27*. There is no evidence that Locke was influenced by the 'covenant theology' of the seventeenth-century Reformed theologian, Cocceius, who argued that the covenant of works was in operation before the fall of Adam, and the covenant of grace thereafter.

[3] *Works*, vi. 111.

[4] In his paraphrase of 1 Cor. VI.11 he explains the word 'justify' in yet another sense, that of making 'advances in the reformation of your lives'.

Locke can speak of salvation as a present deliverance from sin (Rom. X.8, Para.; X.9*f), the future reference is normative for him. He paraphrases 'we are saved by hope' (Rom. VIII.24, AV) as 'we have hitherto been saved but in hope and expectation'. When Eph. II.8 speaks of salvation as a past event, Locke comments that 'they were in the way of Salvation, and if they persevered, could not miss attaining of it, though they were not yet in actual Possession' (Eph. II.8(*c*)b). In these last two passages Locke shifts the moment of salvation from the past to the future.

Locke gives great emphasis to Paul's teaching that the faith of believers is reckoned to them for righteousness.[1] But he avoids the doctrine, characteristic of Calvinism, that Christ's righteousness is imputed to believers.[2] He understands the righteousness of faith as the righteousness of God, but describes it as given in and by Christ rather than as being of Christ (2 Cor. V.21, Para.; cf. Eph. II.8(*c*)k). And in no sense does he regard faith as a work. It is a gift of God (Eph. II.8(*c*)i), and justification is God's gift, not a reward earned by faith.

In a way characteristic of both Arminians and Socinians,[3] Locke stresses the importance of the sincere endeavour to be obedient to God. He asserts that 'both Jews and Gentiles shall be saved from death, if they beleive in Jesus Christ and sincerely endeavour after righteousness though they doe not attain unto it their faith being counted to them for righteousness' (Rom. II.26*t).[4] But the sincere endeavour does not earn salvation, which is always the gift of God (Eph. II.8(*c*)k). Locke rejects the idea that at any stage of their lives men and women are accepted by God as the due reward for their works of obedience.

The account of faith given in the *Paraphrase* is different from that in Locke's earlier writings. In the *Essay*, faith is regarded as assent to truths of revelation.[5] In the *Reasonableness*, it is understood as belief that Jesus is the Messiah.[6] Locke defended himself in the latter work against the possible criticism that he was regarding only a historical and not a saving faith as necessary for salvation. He claimed that

[1] e.g. Rom. IV.24, Para.; Eph. II.8(*c*)k; cf. *Reasonableness, Works*, vi. 111.

[2] Calvin, *Institutes*, III. xiv. 12-13; Westminster Confession, xi. 1.

[3] Limborch, *Theologia*, VI. iv. 4, 37; Whitby, *Additional Annotations to the New Testament* (London, 1710), p. 73; Racovian Catechism, v. 9 (pp. 321, 324). See also John Milton, *Paradise Lost*, iii. 191-7.

[4] Cf. *Reasonableness, Works*, vi. 111.

[5] *Essay*, IV. xvi. 14; IV. xviii. 2 (pp. 667-8, 689).

[6] *Works*, vi. 101, 112.

salvation only took place when faith and repentance were combined. Repentance, he explained, was not just an initial act of sorrow, but included 'doing works meet for repentance' and 'a sincere obedience to the law of Christ, the remainder of our lives'.[1] This account of faith is not as consistently maintained in the *Paraphrase* as in the earlier writings. Even when it is interpreted as assent, it includes an element of personal allegiance to Christ. To 'confess with thy mouth the Lord Jesus' (Rom. X.9) is paraphrased as to 'openly own Jesus the Lord, i e Jesus to be the Messiah thy Lord'. This allegiance is indicated by his choice of the words 'thy Lord' rather than 'the Lord'. Faith is understood as reliance on God. Those who are 'of faith' are described as those 'who relye upon god and his promises of grace and not upon their own performances' (Gal. III.7, Para.).

By introducing the notion of faith as trust and allegiance Locke was moving from the meaning of the word in the Epistle of James to that which is characteristic of Paul. He was also drawing nearer to the interpretations given by Calvinists, Arminians, and Socinians, all of whom understood saving faith to include an element of trust.[2] But it is Paul himself who is most likely to have been responsible for Locke's change of emphasis. The infrequency of references to repentance in Paul's Epistles would incline Locke to move away from the position which he adopted in the *Reasonableness*, where repentance included the notion of turning to God. In the *Paraphrase* the word 'faith' includes the notion of trust and commitment. The *Paraphrase* presents a Pauline understanding of faith.

An important point made in the *Reasonableness* is noticeably absent from the *Paraphrase*. It concerns the salvation of people who have never heard the Gospel or the promises which preceded it. Both these writings affirm that men and women like Abraham, who received the promises of the Messiah and relied on the goodness and faithfulness of God, were justified.[3] But the *Reasonableness* goes even further. It holds out the hope of forgiveness and reconciliation to those who have received neither the Gospel nor the promises. They too would be forgiven by God, 'if they acknowledged their faults, disapproved the iniquity of their transgressions, begged his pardon, and resolved in earnest, for the future, to conform their actions to this rule, which they

[1] *Works*, vi. 105.

[2] Calvin, *Institutes*, III. ii. 16; Westminster Confession, xiv. 2; Limborch, *Theologia*, v. ix. 24; Whitby, *Epistles*, pp. 254-6; Racovian Catechism, v. 9 (pp. 321-3).

[3] *Reasonableness, Works*, vi. 127-33; *Paraphrase*, Rom. IV.11-13, Para.

owned to be just and right'.[1] No such concession is made in the *Paraphrase*. No hope apart from Christ is extended to the heathen world (Eph. II.8(*c*)m-n).[2]

The Church

The best-known statement by Locke about the Church is his description of it as 'a voluntary society of men, joining themselves together of their own accord in order to the public worshipping of God, in such a manner as they judge acceptable to him, and effectual to the salvation of their souls'.[3] This description applied to any religious organization, Christian or otherwise. It was not made from the standpoint of faith but from the standpoint of civil government, which Locke believed should tolerate different religious organizations. In the *Paraphrase*, however, the Church is understood from the viewpoint of faith. Locke, in agreement with Paul, draws attention to God's initiative in calling it into existence and empowering it to continue. He still speaks of it as a society, but as one activated by the Spirit (1 Cor. XII.19, Para., cf. 1 Cor. V.7, Para.).

Of the ideas used by Paul to express his doctrine of the Church, the one which appears most frequently in the *Paraphrase* is that of the people of God. By rejecting Christ, Locke argues, the Jewish nation ceased to be God's people. Under the covenant of grace all who believed in Christ succeeded to that privilege. 'And particularly as to the Nation of the Jews', he writes (Rom. IX.1-X.21, Contents, g), 'all but a small remnant were rejected and the Gentiles taken in in their room to be the people and Church of god'. From that time onwards the Church was God's people, the 'visible subjects of his kingdom here on earth' (Rom. XI.32*i). At first it was among the nation of the Jews that God set up his earthly Kingdom. But now his only Kingdom on earth is the Kingdom of his Son, which is called the Church and was inaugurated through Christ's death and resurrection (Eph. I.10(*t*)e).

Locke makes no attempt to discern the traditional orders of ministry in statements made by Paul in these Epistles. Indeed, while many interpreters explained 'helps, governments' (1 Cor. XII.28) as 'deacons and

[1] *Works*, vi. 133.

[2] In his treatment of Rom. II.13-15 Locke recognizes that unbelieving Gentiles may keep to the moral standard of the positive law through their obedience to the light of nature; but he says nothing about the possibility of their forgiveness and reconciliation. See explanatory note on Rom. II.14*.

[3] *A Letter Concerning Toleration*, *Works*, v. 13.

presbyters (or bishops)', Locke followed Lightfoot in identifying 'helps' with assistants to the apostles and 'governments' with those who discern spirits (1 Cor. XII.28* and XII.28†). As for Paul's own apostolate, Locke emphasized that his commission and instructions came by direct revelation from God (Gal. I.1-5, Contents, d).

In dealing with the place of women in the Church, Locke claimed that two apparently contradictory statements made by Paul were in fact consistent with each other. According to 1 Cor. XI.5, every woman praying or prophesying dishonours her head if she is unveiled. According to 1 Cor. XIV.34, women were to keep silent in churches. Locke tried to reconcile these two statements by arguing that Paul intended women in normal circumstances to be silent in religious assemblies, but allowed them to pray or prophesy if they had 'an extraordinary call and commission from god' and were acting 'by the motion and impulse of the holy-ghost' (1 Cor. XI.3*cc, z; cf. 1 Cor. XIV.34, 35*). At the same time he emphasized that a woman should not take upon herself the office of teacher or instructor in the Church. 'This would have had too great an air', he wrote, 'of standing upon even ground with the men, and would not have well comported with the subordination of the sex' (1 Cor. XI.3*y).

Although Locke could not be considered a champion of equal rights for women, his views gave more liberty in worship to women than did some other commentators, who by one means or another contrived to deny that Paul ever allowed women to speak in church, apart from their participation in corporate prayers and singing.[1] While Locke did not advocate the ordination of women, he at least admitted a woman's right to speak in church when she was specially inspired to do so.[2]

Sacraments

Although Locke says little about Baptism and the Lord's Supper in his other writings, the subject-matter of Paul's Epistles made it inevitable that he should give some account of them in the *Paraphrase*. Baptism, he claims, is a symbolical rite. Its 'typical signification' is 'to be dead to sin and alive to god' (Rom. VI.2*a). It teaches those who receive it that they ought to die to sin and rise to a life of obedience (Rom. VI.1-23, Contents, d). It is also an 'initiateing ceremony' (Rom.

[1] See explanatory note on 1 Cor. XI.3*d-e.

[2] He understands Phoebe to be an assistant at a church hostel rather than a member of an order of deaconesses (Rom. XVI.2*).

VI.1-23, Contents, c). Everyone who has faith is admitted to the Kingdom of God by means of it (Eph. II.15(*p*)e).[1] At the same time it is not just mere admittance to the Kingdom. In Baptism people receive forgiveness of sins; they are 'purged from sin by Baptisme' (1 Cor. X.1-22, Contents, b). And they also receive new life, brought by the Spirit of God (Eph. II.8(*c*)i).

Locke is far removed from the traditional Catholic position, which claims that, provided no obstacle is put in the way, grace is conveyed by the performance of the sacramental act. Nor is he content with the view that Baptism is merely an initiation and pledge. He gives the impression that God works an inner change in those who receive their Baptism in faith. He makes no attempt to face the issue of Infant Baptism, but always speaks in terms of a ceremony of initiation for those who have faith in Jesus Christ.

His treatment of the Lord's Supper, the name which he prefers to Communion or Eucharist, indicates that it, like Baptism, is a symbolical act. The bread and wine are 'typical representations' of Christ (1 Cor. X.4, Para.). The purpose of the Supper's institution was 'to represent Christs body and blood, and to be eaten and drunk in remembrance of him'. Like Baptism, the rite proclaims a truth. Its aim is to 'shew forth his death' (1 Cor. XI.28*c).

Locke also regards the Supper as a means through which God acts on those who share in it. They 'partake of the benefits purchased by Christs bloud shed for them upon the cross' (1 Cor. X.16, Para.). The meal is a means of receiving spiritual life and participating in unity. 'And the bloud of Christ which we all partake of in the Lords Supper makes us all have one life, one spirit, as the same blood diffused through the whole body communicates the same life and spirit to all the members' (1 Cor. XII.13, Para.; cf. X.17, Para.).

In his *Second Vindication* Locke outlines four possible interpretations of the function of the bread and wine in the Lord's Supper. The first interpretation is literal, claiming that the bread and wine are 'changed really' into the body and blood of Christ. According to the second interpretation, it is 'really the body and blood of Christ, without ceasing to be the true bread and wine'. The third view is that 'the body and blood of Christ are verily and indeed given and received, in the sacrament, in a spiritual manner'. And the fourth view is that the bread and wine are no more than 'a representation of his body and

[1] Cf. *Reasonableness, Works*, vi. 111: 'by baptism being made denizens, and solemnly incorporated into that kingdom'.

blood'.[1] The first of these interpretations, the Roman Catholic doctrine of transubstantiation, and the second, the Lutheran doctrine of consubstantiation, were rejected by Locke in his assertion in the *Essay* that 'we can never assent to a Proposition, that affirms the same Body to be in two distant Places at once, however it should pretend to the Authority of a divine *Revelation*'.[2] The language used by Locke about the Lord's Supper in his *Paraphrase* goes beyond the fourth interpretation, which is characteristic of Zwingli and also of the Socinians.[3] He is in agreement with the third viewpoint, which is characteristic of Calvinism. The blood of Christ, he says, received in the Supper, 'makes us all have one life, one spirit'. This viewpoint implies the spiritual presence of Christ in the sacrament. Locke asserts that those who drink the cup 'thereby partake of the benefits purchased by Christ's bloud' (1 Cor. X.16, Para.). The word 'thereby', which is not present in the actual text of the Epistle, is the key to his thought. He believes the Lord's Supper to be the means by which divine benefits are given to the participants. The unity of the Church is one of these benefits, and new life in the Spirit is another.

Morality

In the *Paraphrase* Locke gives a clear enough account of his beliefs about the relationship between the law of nature, and positive laws, moral, civil, and ceremonial. He claims that there is a 'natural and eternal rule of *rectitude* which is made known to men by the light of reason' (Rom. II.26*a). The rule 'came from god and was made by him the moral rule to all man kind, being laid within the discovery of their reason' (Rom. II.26*b). In the *Paraphrase* he more frequently calls it 'the rule of right' or 'the rule of rectitude' than the 'law of nature', although he does not altogether abandon this last term.[4] Besides this rule of rectitude there is the law of Moses, which does not await discovery by reason, but is clearly stated in terms that everyone can understand. This law has several parts to it: 'precepts' or moral laws, which are branches of the eternal rule of rectitude; 'ordinances of divine service', which are rules prescribed to the Jews for the worship of God; and 'carnal ordinances', which are rules for preserving or

[1] *Works*, vi. 390-1.

[2] *Essay*, IV. xviii. 5 (p. 692).

[3] Racovian Catechism, v. 4 (pp. 263-76).

[4] For 'rule of right' and 'rule of rectitude' see Rom. I.32, Para.; I.32*; II.26* *passim*; Eph. II.15(*p*)q. Reference to the law of nature is found in Eph. II.15(*p*)q.

obtaining 'a legal outward holyness or righteousness' (Rom. II.26*a-j). Under the Gospel, while the ordinances of divine service and the carnal ordinances were abrogated, the moral precepts were not. Indeed, the moral law or law of nature, of which these precepts are a part, has been promulgated anew by Jesus, 'fuller and clearer than it was in the Mosaical constitution, or any where else'. Jesus 'by adding to its Precepts the Sanction of his own Divine Authority, has made the Knowledge of the Law more easy and certain than it was before' (Eph. II.15(*p*)q).

This account of the relationship between the natural rule of rectitude, the law of Moses, and the law of Christ is consistent with Locke's position in the *Reasonableness*. In that work he explains that the parts of the Jewish law connected with 'outward worship or political constitution' have 'a limited and only temporary obligation', while the moral part of it is 'of eternal obligation'.[1] Moreover, his insistence that Jesus made the law of nature easier to understand reflects his claim in the *Reasonableness* that Jesus's teaching contained that law in its entirety.[2]

Locke's treatment of law in the *Paraphrase* contains statements which appear to be in harmony with the voluntarism that regards law as constituted by the will of a law-maker. It is not only the law of Moses and the law of the Gospel that have been given by God. The 'natural and eternal rule of *rectitude*' itself 'came from god and was made by him the moral rule to all man kind' (Rom. II.26*a-b). It is 'the rule of right prescribed them by god and discovered by the light of nature' (Rom. I.32, Para.). These statements give the impression that natural law as well as the positive law of Moses and Jesus is dependent on the will of God.

On the other hand, there is terminology in the *Paraphrase* which is consistent with the rationalistic or intellectualistic view, according to which right and wrong do not depend on the will of the law-maker but are in harmony with the nature of things. The very phrases 'natural and eternal rule of *rectitude*' (Rom. II.26*a), 'eternal immutable rule of right' (Rom. VIII.7†b), and 'unmoveable Rule of Right' (Eph. II.15(*p*)q) imply a law which cannot be altered even by God.

These two motifs, the voluntaristic and the rationalistic, had long

[1] *Reasonableness, Works*, vi. 13.

[2] Ibid., vi. 138-43. In his early *Two Tracts on Government*, trans. and ed. by Philip Abrams (Cambridge, 1967), pp. 203-4, 234, he gives recognition to the New Testament as the basis for moral law.

been present in Locke's thought about ethical issues.[1] But one aspect of his rationalistic approach is absent from the *Paraphrase*. It is the claim, made in the *Essay* and other writings, that morality is '*capable of Demonstration*, as well as Mathematicks'.[2] In the *Reasonableness* the emphasis is on the failure of philosophers and moral teachers to deduce any such system.[3] And the matter is not even mentioned in the *Paraphrase*. Nevertheless, in spite of the absence of this theme, there is ample evidence of Locke's continuing interest in the rationalistic approach.

It has been argued that Locke never satisfactorily resolved the tension between the voluntaristic and rationalistic elements in his ethics.[4] But the *Paraphrase* supports the view that he saw no inconsistency between the two.[5] He describes the natural law as 'that eternall law of right, the observance whereof god always requires and is pleased with' (Gal. V.16, 17†b). It is 'that rule of rectitude which god has given to man kind in giveing them reason' (Rom. I.32*). The eternal validity of the law is as important as its being decreed by God. Of lives lived in accordance with 'the flesh' Locke says: 'Such a setled contravention to his precepts cannot be sufferd by the supreme Lord and governor of the world in any of his creatures without foregoeing his soverainty and giveing up the eternal immutable rule of right to the overturning the very foundations of all order and moral rectitude in the intellectual world' (Rom. VIII.7†b).[6]

[1] *Two Tracts*, pp. 193-4, 221-3; *Essays on the Law of Nature*, trans. and ed. by Wolfgang von Leyden (Oxford, 1954), pp. 132-3, 148-9, 199; *Treatises of Government*, ii. 58-63, 134 (pp. 324-7, 373-5), *Reasonableness, Works*, vi. 13-14, 142-3; MS Locke c. 28, fos. 146-52; see Peter King, seventh Lord King, Baron of Ockham, *The Life and Letters of John Locke* (new edn. London, 1858), pp. 306-13.

[2] *Essay*, III. xi. 16; cf. IV. iii. 18; IV. xii. 8 (p. 516; cf. pp. 548-50, 643-4). See also *Essays on the Law of Nature*, pp. 198-210, and Locke's correspondence with William Molyneux (*Corr.* iv. 508, 524, 602, 649; v. 570). In a letter to Molyneux dated 30 Mar. 1696, though not completed until early Apr. (*Corr.* v. 595), he confirmed the position adopted in the *Reasonableness*. For varying interpretations of what Locke meant by this kind of demonstration see W. von Leyden's Introduction to *Essays on the Law of Nature*, p. 55; J. Kemp, *Reason, Action and Morality* (London, 1964), p. 21; John W. Yolton, *Locke and the Compass of the Human Understanding* (Cambridge, 1970), pp. 166-74.

[3] *Reasonableness, Works*, vi. 140-2.

[4] W. von Leyden in *Essays on the Law of Nature*, pp. 73-8. Sterling P. Lamprecht, *The Moral and Political Philosophy of John Locke* (New York, 1918), pp. 103-9, makes a similar point, but subsumes the voluntaristic under the hedonistic element.

[5] That he saw no inconsistency is argued by Yolton, op. cit., p. 172, and John C. Biddle, *John Locke on Christianity: His Context and Text* (Ann Arbor, 1972), p. 86.

[6] Cf. *Reasonableness, Works*, vi. 11, where he argues that to fail to require men and women to live by the law of reason would be to authorize 'disorder, confusion, and wickedness'.

A third motif, the hedonistic, is present in most of Locke's writings on ethical questions.[1] It is stated very forcibly in the *Essay*,[2] which gives the impression that moral good and evil can be understood in terms of pleasure and pain. It is implied in those passages of the *Reasonableness* where death is said to be the punishment of sin and eternal life the reward for complete obedience to God under the Jewish law. It is also present in those passages where eternal life is offered as God's gracious gift to those who combine faith in Christ with the sincere endeavour to be obedient to God's will.[3] The *Paraphrase* adopts a different attitude. Locke asserts that 'there is no certain determined punishment affixed to sin without a positive law declareing it' (Rom. V.13, Para.). Under natural law, he argues, there is a knowledge of right and wrong, but no knowledge of rewards for virtue or punishment for sin (Rom. V.13*).[4]

This claim that no punishment is affixed to natural law is a new development in Locke's thought and weakens its hedonistic element. In his *Essays on the Law of Nature* he had indicated that the threat of punishment in a future life was essential even to natural law. God and the soul's immortality, he wrote, 'must be necessarily presupposed if natural law is to exist. For there is no law without a law-maker, and law is to no purpose without punishment.'[5] In the *Essay*, referring both to natural and to revealed law, he says that God has power to enforce his law by rewards and punishments in another life and that the only 'true touchstone of *moral Rectitude*' is to judge whether actions will procure happiness or misery from God.[6] A similar position is stated in the *Reasonableness*. It is 'conformable to the eternal and established law of right and wrong' that the wages of sin should be exclusion from immortality.[7] The teaching of the *Paraphrase* marks a clear departure from Locke's previous position.

The hedonistic element is not totally absent from the *Paraphrase*. Locke still holds out the alternative prospects of life and death for those who have received a positive law such as the law of Moses, or indeed the law given by Christ. But good and evil are primarily understood in

[1] The motif occurs in his journal as early as 1676 and is found in *Of Ethick in General*, which was probably written in the eighties; see von Leyden in *Essays on the Law of Nature*, p. 69.

[2] *Essay*, II. xxviii. 5; II. xx. 2; II. xxi. 42 (pp. 351, 229, 258-9).

[3] *Reasonableness, Works*, vi. 122-3.

[4] See also explanatory note on Rom. I.32.

[5] *Essays on the Law of Nature*, p. 173.

[6] *Essay*, II. xxviii. 8 (p. 352).

[7] *Reasonableness, Works*, vi. 10.

voluntaristic and rationalistic terms. Locke may well have taken notice of the criticism levelled against him by Thomas Burnet, who accused him of basing his ethic on the arbitrary will of God and on rewards and punishments rather than on the divine nature and on human nature.[1] In the *Paraphrase* Locke's statements emphasize that the will of God is not arbitrary but in accordance with the natural and eternal rule of rectitude. The incentive of rewards and punishments is strictly limited in scope and recedes into the background. Burnet could not have sustained his criticism as far as the *Paraphrase* was concerned. Locke's understanding of moral law had undergone an important change in the last years of his life.

Civil Law

In the *Essay* Locke claimed that people generally judge their actions by three laws, the divine law, the civil law, and the law of opinion or reputation.[2] By the time he was writing the *Paraphrase*, he was giving great emphasis to the divine law[3] but offering no more than a slight hint about the law of opinion.[4] His neglect of this theme is partly to be explained by its absence from the Epistles on which he was commenting.[5] It may also be a reaction to the critics who accused him of setting up the law of opinion as a basic standard of morality.[6] The civil law, on the other hand, is given considerable prominence in the *Paraphrase*.

Christians, Locke affirms, have a duty to be obedient to the laws of the state. They must not use their liberty in the Gospel as an excuse for neglecting their civil duties. They share the rights of other citizens but have no special privilege as Christians:[7] converts must be loyal to

[1] Thomas Burnet, *Second Remarks upon an Essay Concerning Humane Understanding* (London, 1697), LL no. 1795, p. 2.

[2] *Essay*, II. xxviii. 7 (p. 352); cf. II. xxviii. 13 (p. 357).

[3] According to *Essay*, II. xxviii. 8 (p. 352), the divine law is that 'which God has set to the actions of Men, whether promulgated to them by the light of Nature, or the voice of Revelation'.

[4] In Gal. III.15, Para., he speaks of 'a known and allowed rule in humane affairs' that promises and compacts must be kept. This may be an allusion to the law of opinion, but he does not develop the point.

[5] According to *Essay*, II. xxviii. 11 (p. 356), 'whatsoever things are of good report' (Phil. IV.8) refers to the law of opinion. But it is unlikely that Paul attached much importance to that law. His characteristic theme is that he is not concerned to 'please men' (Gal. I.10; 1 Thess. II.4).

[6] His preface to the fourth edition of the *Essay* (1700) answers some of these criticisms (see Nidditch's edition of the *Essay*, pp. 354-5).

[7] Rom. XIII.1†c; cf. Rom. XIII.1-7, Contents, b-c.

their unconverted spouses, slaves should be obedient to their owners.[1] Underlying this teaching is the conviction that God has allotted to each person a position in life.[2] Yet, in agreement with Paul, Locke recognizes that men and women have a right to prefer freedom to slavery, if they can obtain it (1 Cor. VII.21, Para.).

In his discussion of Paul's teaching about the 'higher powers' (Rom. XIII.1-7), he enters into extremely controversial territory. This passage had been used by Filmer to support the divine right of kings,[3] and was a favourite proof-text of the opponents of political revolutions. Since Locke had already supported such a revolution, the passage was bound to cause him difficulty. According to Paul, anyone who resisted the higher power would receive condemnation (Rom. XIII.2). Locke went out of his way to draw attention to Paul's silence about the right qualifications for the office of magistrate. 'To have medled with that would have been to decide of civil rights, contrary to the designe and business of the gospel, and the example of our Saviour. . . .'[4] Paul, he explained, was speaking only of magistrates who exercised a lawful power (Rom. XIII.1†b). Locke's comments are so worded that the door is left open for civil disobedience.

The Future

Like many of his contemporaries, Locke was often preoccupied with the question of the ultimate destiny of the human race. Although he believed Paul to have mistakenly expected the return of Christ in the near future,[5] he regarded Paul as a reliable guide to Christian expectations in other respects. The controversy in which he became engaged with Stillingfleet about the nature of bodies at the resurrection was not a mere academic question for him, but a matter of supreme concern. While there is no systematic treatment of Christian doctrine about the future in the *Paraphrase*, there are several parts of the work in which Locke devotes considerable attention to it.

He probably began to write the *Paraphrase* about the time of the

[1] 1 Cor. VII.12-13, Para.; VII. 23; Eph. VI.5, Para.

[2] 1 Cor. VII.17, Para. John Dunn, *The Political Thought of John Locke* (Cambridge, 1969), pp. 245-54, argues that Locke was strongly influenced by the Calvinistic doctrine of calling, according to which God has appointed people to particular functions in society. As Dunn recognizes, Locke's version of the doctrine is influenced by Arminianism (p. 223). The doctrine is not developed in detail in the *Paraphrase*.

[3] Sir Robert Filmer, *Patriarcha and Other Political Works*, ed. by Peter Laslett (Oxford, 1949), pp. 100-1.

[4] Rom. XIII.1-7, Contents, i-j; see explanatory notes ad loc.

[5] See above, pp. 29-30.

conclusion of his controversy with Stillingfleet. He was also in correspondence with Whitby about the same question of the resurrection.[1] The controversy arose because Locke's accounts in the *Essay* of substance and personal identity posed a threat to the traditional doctrine that the dead would be raised with the bodies in which they had lived in their mortal lives. In answer to Stillingfleet's criticisms, Locke strenuously maintained that the Scriptures did not teach the resurrection of the same bodies in which people had previously lived. He contended that they spoke only of the resurrection of the dead, which would leave open the possibility that they would be raised up with different bodies from their previous ones.[2] Because his debate with Stillingfleet had concentrated mainly on passages from the Epistles to the Corinthians and the Romans, Locke could scarcely avoid the issue in his *Paraphrase*. His comments on the fifteenth chapter of the First Epistle to the Corinthians show that he still adopted the position which he had maintained against Stillingfleet. God 'can give to men at the resurrection bodys of very different constitutions and qualitys from those they had before' (1 Cor. XV.39*). His paraphrase of 1 Cor. XV.50 reads: 'This I say to you Brethren to satisfie those that ask with what bodys the dead shall come, that we shall not at the resurrection have such bodys as we have now˙ for flesh and blood cannot enter into the kingdom which the saints shall inherit in heaven: Nor are such fleeting corruptible things as our present bodys are fitted to that state of immutable incorruptibility.'[3]

He also made a distinction between the resurrection of the righteous and that of the wicked, which he believed to be separate events. The First Epistle to the Corinthians, he claimed, spoke only of the resurrection of the righteous and did not go on to deal with the fate of the wicked (1 Cor. XV.42*m). 'Christ the first-fruits is already risen: Next after him shall rise those who are his people his church and this shall be at his second comeing. After that shall be the Day of Judgement. which shall bring to a conclusion and finish the whole dispensation to the race and posterity of Adam in this world.' (1 Cor. XV.23–4, Para.)

In the *Paraphrase* Locke does not mention the possibility of eternal punishment for the wicked. He makes a contrast between life, the gift of God to believers, and death, the lot of the unrighteous. In this

[1] See above, p. 12.

[2] *Second Reply to the Bishop of Worcester, Works*, iii. 303–4. Peter King, *History of the Apostles Creed*, p. 404, agrees with Stillingfleet in affirming the resurrection of the same body.

[3] See also explanatory note on Rom. VIII.11, Para.

respect his emphasis is like that of Paul, who says that 'the wages of sin is death: but the gift of God is eternal life, through Jesus Christ our Lord' (Rom. VI.23, AV). The same point had already been made by Locke in the *Reasonableness*, where he wrote: 'Here then we have the standing and fixed measures of life and death. Immortality and bliss belong to the righteous; those who have lived in an exact conformity to the law of God, are out of the reach of death; but an exclusion from paradise and loss of immortality is the portion of sinners.'[1] Other passages in the *Reasonableness*, however, indicate that pain and torment await the wicked after the Last Judgement. Locke points out that Jesus forbids immorality and immoral desires 'upon pain of hell-fire'.[2] He says that Jesus's commands are delivered 'with the inforcement of unspeakable rewards and punishments in another world, according to their obedience or disobedience'.[3] Milner criticized Locke for inconsistency in this matter.[4] Although neither the *Reasonableness* nor the *Paraphrase* answers this criticism, his paper 'Resurrectio et quae sequuntur' shows his attitude to be consistent. He believes that the wicked will endure torments for a limited period of time, after which they will be completely annihilated.[5] This viewpoint is in conflict not only with Catholicism and mainstream Protestantism but also with some forms of Socinianism,[6] though other Socinians expected the final punishment to be annihilation. Locke's position is in agreement with that of Hobbes, according to whom the sufferings of the reprobate may be of limited duration even if the fire in which they burn is everlasting.[7] This interpretation is an attempt to reconcile the biblical references to eternal punishment with those which imply that death is the fate of the wicked.

Locke's beliefs about the fate of human beings during the interval

[1] *Reasonableness, Works*, vi. 10.

[2] Ibid., vi. 115.

[3] Ibid., vi. 122. See also *Essay*, II. xxi. 60 (pp. 273–4): 'let him look into the future State of Bliss or Misery, and see there God the righteous Judge, ready to *render to every Man according to his Deeds; To them who by patient continuance in well-doing, seek for Glory, and Honour, and Immortality, Eternal Life; but unto every Soul that doth Evil, Indignation and Wrath, Tribulation and Anguish*'. Cf. explanatory note on Rom. II.8–9, Para.

[4] Milner, *An Account of Mr. Lock's Religion*, pp. 151–2.

[5] See Appendix VI, dd–gg. Although another part of this paper was incorporated into 1 Cor. XV.42*, this passage about hell torments was left unpublished.

[6] Racovian Catechism, vii (p. 367).

[7] Hobbes, *Leviathan*, xxxviii. In Appendix VI, dd, Locke claims support from Tillotson. In fact, while Tillotson mentions this kind of interpretation, he does not accept it himself. But he argues that God has the power to set limits to hell torments. See John Tillotson, 'Of the eternity of Hell Torments', *Works*, i. 321–9.

between their physical deaths and the resurrection are not easy to determine. The traditional Catholic view held that there was an intermediate state of conscious existence between physical death and the return of Christ. This belief was also held by Calvin and many other Protestant theologians including, among Locke's contemporaries, Limborch, Whitby, and the Cambridge Platonists.[1] The alternative view, known as Mortalism, claimed that the human soul either ceased to exist or remained in an unconscious state of 'sleep' during this interim period.[2] Although Luther himself appears to have been a mortalist, the doctrine was suspect in Locke's day and was associated with heresy, in particular that of Socinianism.[3] Among other writers Milton and Hobbes were mortalists.[4] The language which Locke uses to describe the death and resurrection of human beings is usually consistent with mortalism. In his controversy with Stillingfleet and in *Reasonableness* he never mentions any intermediate state. Moreover, his repeated insistence that all human beings are mortal and that immortality is not bestowed on anyone until the resurrection confirms the impression that he is a mortalist. At one point in the *Paraphrase*, however, he makes statements which might imply a belief in a conscious existence during that interim period. In his paraphrase of 2 Cor. V.8 he speaks of 'quiting this habitation to get home to the Lord', and in his note on 2 Cor. V.9†c, he alludes to 'death which brings me home to Christ'. It is possible that he understands being home with Christ to be a conscious state. His critical remarks about the doctrine of aerial vehicles (Preface, p. 114), which was sometimes associated with a belief in a continuing existence during that interim period, do not necessarily imply a rejection of such a belief.[5] But his views on the matter are far from clear.

His expectations about the nature of the life enjoyed by the righteous after their resurrection are essentially the same in both the *Essay* and the *Paraphrase*. It will be a condition like that of the angels in which it will be possible to have an intuitive knowledge of things

[1] Ralph Cudworth, *True Intellectual System of the Universe*, p. 818.

[2] The first of these forms of mortalism is sometimes known as thnetopsychism, and the second as psychosomnolence: Maurice Kelley, *The Complete Prose Works of John Milton* (New Haven, Conn., 1953–), vi. 91. For a detailed discussion, see Norman T. Burns, *Christian Mortalism from Tyndale to Milton* (Cambridge, Mass., 1972).

[3] Crellius, *Opera*, ii. 315. George H. Williams, *The Radical Reformation* (Philadelphia, 1962), p. 107, gives the information about Luther.

[4] Milton, *Paradise Lost*, iii. 245–9; x. 789–92; xi. 61–5; xii. 434. See Christopher Hill, *Milton and the English Revolution* (London, 1977), pp. 317–23; Hobbes, *Leviathan*, xxxviii.

[5] See explanatory notes on Preface, p. 114 and on 2 Cor. V.1–10, Para.

without any need for demonstrative reasoning. 'Now,' he writes in his paraphrase of 1 Cor. XIII.12, 'we see but by reflection the dimn and as it were enigmatical representation of things: but then we shall see, things directly and as they are in themselves as a man sees another when they are face to face. Now I have but a superficial partial knowledg of things, but then I shall have an intuitive comprehensive knowledg of them, as I my self am known and lie open to the view of superior seraphick beings, not by the obscure and imperfect way of deductions and reasoning.'[1] The same ideas are expressed in his discussion of intuitive knowledge in the *Essay*,[2] where he suggests that this knowledge may be what 'Angels have now, and the Spirits of just Men made perfect, shall have, in a future State, of Thousands of Things, which now, either wholly escape our Apprehensions, or which, our short-sighted Reason having got some faint Glimpse of, we, in the Dark, grope after'.

The resurrection of the just, he believes, will take place at the time of Christ's second coming (1 Cor. XV.23, Para.), which will itself be preceded by two other important events, the coming in of 'the fullness of the Gentiles' and the conversion of the Jews. These events had been the subject of a great deal of speculation during the seventeenth century, and were still giving rise to sharp controversy.[3] Locke disagrees with the view that Paul was referring to the conversion of Gentiles and Jews in the time of the early Church.[4] He believes him to be speaking of future events. He does not explain very clearly what is meant by the coming in of the fullness of the Gentiles, but describes it as a time when 'the whole Gentile world shall enter in to the church and make profession of Christianity' (Rom. XI.25, Para.). He does not say whether this statement referred to the conversion of the majority of people in each nation or to the official recognition of Christianity by the governments of Gentile nations. He is more explicit about the destiny of the Jews. He claims that Paul anticipated the time when 'the Jews shall be a flourishing people again professeing Christianity in the land of promise' (Rom. XI.23*). But the conversion of Jews and Gentiles will not ensure the eternal salvation of all individual members of those nations. Paul, according to Locke, was only concerned at this

[1] Cf. 1 Cor. XV.44*c: 'they are equall to the angels. i e are of an Angelical nature and constitution'.

[2] *Essay*, IV. xvii. 14 (p. 683).

[3] Christopher Hill, *Antichrist in Seventeenth-Century England* (London, 1971), pp. 114–15.

[4] Grotius, *Annotationes*, on Rom. XI.25, 26; Hammond, *Paraphrase*, on Rom. XI.25, 26.

point to assert that these nations would profess Christianity on earth (Rom. XI.26*). In speaking of a restoration of the Jewish nation to the land of Israel, Locke is in agreement with an expectation widely entertained in the seventeenth century.[1] His interest in the matter shows that he took the issue of apocalyptic expectation seriously; and an unpublished paper of his provides evidence that he may have indulged in speculation about the dates of these events.[2] But in the *Paraphrase* no such conjectures appear; he is concerned with the nature rather than the chronology of the future.

Election, Grace, and Free Will

Locke categorically rejected the doctrine of absolute predestination, which he had encountered in the Calvinism of England and Holland. His theology had no place for the idea that God had from all eternity ordained that certain people should be saved and others should be damned.[3] In his interpretation of Romans IX, which was used to support the Calvinistic doctrine, he argued that Paul was not speaking of the eternal destiny of individuals but only of God's choice or election first of Jews and then of Gentiles to be his people. Paul's teaching, Locke claims, 'extends not to their eternal state in an other world considerd as particular persons' (Rom. IX.1–X.21, Contents, h–i).[4]

Although he was opposed to the Calvinistic teaching, there was no doubt in Locke's mind about the reality of God's grace. It is God who has endowed the spirit of men and women with light to recognize what is good (Gal. V.16, 17†c–d). Faith itself is a gift of God; to attain it 'Men do or can do nothing, Grace hitherto does all' (Eph. II.8(*c*)i). When God finally gives eternal life to those who have continued in faith and endeavoured to be obedient, that life is 'the Gift of God, the Gift of Free Grace' (Eph. II.8(*c*)k).

Alongside this emphasis on the divine initiative is Locke's insistence

[1] Hill, *Antichrist*, pp. 114–15.

[2] MS Locke c. 27, fos. 258–60 contains calculations based on F. M. van Helmont, *Seder Olam, sive Ordo Seculorum* (Leyden?, 1693), LL no. 1416a. According to these calculations, the fullness of the Gentiles would come in 1702, the conversion of the Jews would occur in 1732, and the Millennium, which would follow Christ's second coming, would begin in 1777. The date of this manuscript is not known; nor is it clear that Locke agreed with van Helmont's conjectures. At any rate he regarded the theory as worthy of consideration. A deletion from his paper 'Resurrectio et quae sequuntur' suggests that he expected the Millennium to begin after the second coming. See manuscript note on Appendix VI, hh.

[3] Calvin, *Institutes*, III. xxi. 1–7; Westminster Confession, iii. 1–8.

[4] See also Rom. VIII.28–30, Para.; Eph. I.3–6, Para.; and explanatory notes on Rom. VIII.28–30, Para., and Eph. I.4, Para.

on the freedom of human beings to accept or resist God's grace. Those who have been called are not inevitably justified, but only if they obey the truth (Rom. VIII.30, Para.). Those who belong to the Kingdom of the Son of God are sure to attain eternal life if they persevere in faith and sincere obedience (Eph. II.8(*c*)p). Such interpretations are characteristic of Arminian and Socinian theology.

There is a limit, however, to human freedom. The *Paraphrase* explains that Paul was 'forced against my will to doe the drudgery of Sin' and was not 'a willing agent of my own free purpose' (Rom. VII.14, 17, Para.). These statements conflict with the *Essay*. According to that work, individuals always do what they have willed, unless they are prevented by physical disability;[1] they may will to perform actions which are to their disadvantage,[2] but in normal circumstances they perform whatever actions they have willed. Under the influence of Paul, Locke presented a different account of the freedom of the will in the *Paraphrase*. It was an account which understood men and women to be under the power of sin, and unable to escape from it except in response to God's call.

Locke's Theology in Relation to the Thought of his Day

During Locke's lifetime he was described by his opponents as a Socinian.[3] More recently he has been called a Deist,[4] a Unitarian,[5] and a Latitudinarian.[6] He himself did not wish to be placed in any school of thought. He protested that he was 'of no sect', and denied that he was a Socinian. As for Deism, he explicitly claimed to be attacking it.[7] An examination of the *Paraphrase* shows that his refusal to be identified with any theological school was justifiable. He was certainly not a Calvinist,[8] although some of his observations about the meaning of

[1] *Essay*, II. xxi. 71 (p. 284).

[2] *Essay*, III. xxi. 33–5 (pp. 252–4).

[3] John Edwards, *Socinianism Unmask'd*, p. 82; John Milner, *An Account of Mr. Lock's Religion*, pp. 179 ff.

[4] Ernst Crous, *Die religionsphilosophischen Lehren Lockes und ihre Stellung zu dem Deismus seiner Zeit* (Halle, 1910). For a criticism of Crous see S. G. Hefelblower, *The Relation of John Locke to English Deism* (Chicago, 1918).

[5] H. McLachlan, *The Religious Opinions of Milton, Locke, and Newton* (Manchester, 1941), p. 107. H. John McLachlan, *Socinianism in Seventeenth Century England*, pp. 327–8.

[6] G. V. Lechler, *Geschichte des englischen Deismus* (Stuttgart and Tübingen, 1841), p. 172.

[7] *Second Vindication, Works*, vi. 359; *Vindication, Works*, vi. 162–3; *Second Vindication, Works*, vi. 264–5. Cf. refs cited by R. I. Aaron, *John Locke* (3rd edn. Oxford, 1971), p. 299.

[8] Herbert D. Foster, *Collected Papers* (New York, 1929), pp. 147–78, contends that Locke was a liberal Calvinist. But Foster also claims that Arminians belong to that category, and they were certainly not Calvinists in the sense of the word as it was

the Lord's Supper are not far removed from the position of Calvin. But on the issues of Christology, predestination, original sin, atonement, justification, and the resurrection of the body he was at variance with the Calvinistic theology of his day. His links with Arminianism were closer than with Calvinism. His views on predestination and justification were within the orbit of Arminian theology, but in his Christology and his attitude to the resurrection of the body and atonement he parted company with it. As for Socinianism, his Christology, though completely lacking any trinitarian emphasis, stressed the pre-existence of Christ, a view unacceptable to that school of thought; and while he is close to it in his doctrine of atonement, his emphasis on Christ's victory over Satan is not characteristic of Socinians. Whatever may have been his influence on later Deists, his belief in the inadequacy of reason for salvation separated him from them. He had much in common with Latitudinarians. In his love of toleration and his insistence that revealed truth was not contrary to reason he was at one with them; but they were so varied in their theologies as hardly to constitute a school, and he differed from most of them in his refusal to affirm the doctrine of the Trinity. He has been called a 'supernatural rationalist',[1] but even such a title is too general to place him within a particular school. On the theological map of his day he was somewhere between Socinianism and Arminianism. But he himself rejected all such descriptions. He owned no spiritual master but Christ.[2] His interpretation of Paul is independent of any particular school of thought; although at many points he shows the influence of one school or another, he is not bound to any of them. The *Paraphrase* is the work of a man with a mind of his own.

When Locke wrote the *Paraphrase*, he was not content to repeat the ideas which he had formulated in earlier writings. Many of his thoughts have parallels in his previous works. But he also introduces new themes, such as the pre-existence of Christ and the account of Christ's death as a victory over Satan. There are also changes of emphasis, the increased importance attached to revelation by contrast

understood in England at the time when Locke was writing. The theology of Arminians, and even more that of Locke, differed sharply in important respects from that of the Westminster Confession and the editions of Calvin's *Institutes* in general circulation in Locke's day.

[1] A. C. McGiffert, *Protestant Thought Before Kant* (New York, 1911), pp. 189 ff.; Conrad Wright, *The Liberal Christians: Essays on American Unitarian History* (Boston, Mass., 1970), pp. 5-18.

[2] *Second Vindication, Works*, vi. 359.

with reason, the understanding of faith as trust as well as assent, the decrease in the weight given to the hedonistic element in morality, and the account of the Church as a people called by God rather than as a voluntary society. Some of his ideas conflict with his previous positions. Among these features of the *Paraphrase* are his recognition that fundamental articles of faith are distinguishable from non-fundamental in Paul as well as in the Gospels and Acts, his claim that no punishment is affixed to natural law, and his assertion that human beings are unable to act in accordance with their wills. The total picture which emerges is not that of a thinker who had undergone a complete change of outlook; there is too much continuity with his previous writings for such a conclusion to be reached. But his mind was not in a state of rigidity. He was open to new ideas, and did not always endeavour to remain consistent with his previous thoughts. As his mind interacted with that of Paul, ideas emerged which were recognizably the product of the same Locke who was responsible for his earlier writings. But it was the same Locke at a different stage of his intellectual and spiritual pilgrimage.

III. RECEPTION OF THE PARAPHRASE AND NOTES

The First Reactions

The earliest review of any part of the *Paraphrase* appeared in *Nouvelles de la République des Lettres*, a journal founded by Pierre Bayle and published in Amsterdam. Its issue of April 1705 contained a review, on the whole favourable, of Locke's work on Galatians.[1] In January 1706 the journal gave a brief notice of his work on the First Epistle to the Corinthians, in which the reviewer observed: 'Il y a des explications bien singulieres, et la Paraphrase est souvent forcée.'[2] The editor of the journal, Jacques Bernard, seems to have lost any enthusiasm which he possessed for Locke's work, since in May 1706 he mentioned without comment the appearance of the paraphrase of the Second Epistle to the Corinthians,[3] and thereafter ceased to report the publication of the remaining parts of the work.

Meanwhile there was speculation about the nature of the *Paraphrase*

[1] *Nouvelles de la République des Lettres*, Apr. 1705, pp. 448-56.

[2] Ibid., Jan. 1706, p. 101.

[3] Ibid., May 1706, p. 590.

even among those who had not read any of its contents. Catharine Trotter, later Cockburn (1679-1749), who had written a defence of Locke's *Essay* in reply to Thomas Burnet,[1] looked forward with eager anticipation to reading the *Paraphrase*. 'To gratify some of these hours,' she wrote in a letter to George Burnet, 7 July 1705, 'I am very desirous to meet with a book, which yet I have only heard of, A Commentary upon some of the Epistles, I think, St. Paul's, written by Mr. *Locke*, which I am the more curious to see, because I imagine he would not write on such a subject, if he did not treat of it in some peculiar way, or with a different view from other commentators: but this is only my conjecture.'[2]

Very different was the attitude of *Mémoires pour l'histoire des sciences et des beaux-arts* (also known as *Journal de Trévoux*). Its issue of June 1705, announcing the death of Locke, had already formed a verdict on the *Paraphrase* before its contents had been examined. '*M. Looke* [*sic*]', it reported, 'est mort à la Campagne, on dit qu'on imprimera ses Ouvrages sur l'Ecriture Sainte. *Le livre de l'entendement humain* vous l'a fait connoître pour un impie Sadducéen qui nie toute substance immaterielle, un tel homme n'étoit guéres propre à commenter l'Ecriture.'[3] A year later, in June 1706, the same journal announced the publication of Locke's paraphrase on the First Epistle to the Corinthians. 'Le nouvel Interprete', it commented, 'cherche des sens écartez dans cette Epître, et ses explications ne sont rien moins que naturelles. Il étoit difficile qu'un Socinien outré tel que Mr. LOCKE, pût expliquer l'Apôtre sans lui faire violence.'[4]

The longest review of the *Paraphrase* came from the pen of Jean Le Clerc, who had waited till the whole work had been published before he issued his evaluation of it. In 1707 Le Clerc's journal, *Bibliothèque choisie*, contained a lengthy discussion of the *Paraphrase*, which included an extensive summary of the Preface and detailed comments on Locke's treatment of each of the Epistles.[5] Le Clerc's attitude to the work was not as favourable as might have been expected after his *Éloge* of Locke in a previous issue of *Bibliothèque choisie*.[6] He claimed

[1] Catharine Cockburn, *A Defence of the Essay of Human Understanding* (London, 1702), LL no. 1801. The works of Burnet which she attacked were *Remarks upon an Essay Concerning Humane Understanding* (London, 1694), *Second Remarks*, etc. (London, 1697), *Third Remarks*, etc. (London, 1699), LL nos. 1794-5, 1799. Locke wrote to her in appreciation of her support (*Corr.* vii. 730-1). See below, pp. 64-5.

[2] Cockburn, *Works*, ed. by Thomas Birch (2 vols.: London, 1751), ii. 189.

[3] *Mémoires pour l'histoire des sciences et des beaux-arts*, June 1705, p. 1090.

[4] Ibid., June 1706, p. 1077.

[5] *Bibliothèque choisie*, xiii. 37-178.

[6] Ibid., vi. 342-411.

that Locke would have been a more successful interpreter of Paul if he had acquired a better knowledge of biblical languages. He also pointed out that Locke was in fact indebted to other scholars with similar opinions.[1] He was especially sensitive because he himself had not been mentioned by name in the *Paraphrase*, although he believed that Locke was indebted to him in several places.[2] But Le Clerc's review is by no means wholly negative. He recognized Locke's achievement in tracing the thread of Paul's thought in the Epistles. 'Au reste,' he wrote, 'il faut rendre cette justice à Mr. *Locke*, que de reconnoître qu'il n'y avoit eu aucun Interprete de S. Paul, avant lui; qui eût plus pris de peine pour développer la liaison des discours et des raisonnemens de cet Apôtre, et pour découvrir le but géneral, qu'il s'est proposé en châque Epître; et qu'il a employé pour cela la meilleure méthode, que l'on pouvoit prendre.'[3]

The next year, 1708, saw the appearance of further comments on the *Paraphrase*. In its September issue the periodical *History of the Works of the Learned* gave an objective summary of the Preface.[4] In December of the same year *Mémoires pour l'histoire des sciences et des beaux-arts* printed an article which defended Locke against Le Clerc's complaint that no acknowledgement had been given to him in the comments on 1 Cor. XIV.15.[5] The editors pointed out that their own views were very much opposed to those of Locke's advocate but that it was their policy to allow their journal to be '*un champ de bataille libre*'.[6] Le Clerc himself showed no evidence that he had changed his mind. In a letter to Pierre Desmaizeaux, 19 March 1709, he claimed that his criticisms of Locke were completely true and not the product of envy.[7]

The Further Reception in Britain

In 1709 there was published a book by Robert Jenkin (1656-1727), Fellow and later Master of St John's College, Cambridge, which contained an attack on the *Paraphrase*. Jenkin had read with obvious delight the adverse criticisms which Le Clerc had made of Locke's work. His discussion of the *Paraphrase* consists mainly of detailed

[1] Ibid., xiii. 65-7.

[2] Ibid., xiii. 97.

[3] Ibid., xiii. 176.

[4] *History of the Works of the Learned*, Sept. 1708, pp. 556-60.

[5] *Mémoires*, Dec. 1708, pp. 2051-64.

[6] Ibid., p. 2064.

[7] British Library, Add. MS 4282, fo. 107. See Annie Barnes, *Jean Le Clerc (1657–1736) et la République des Lettres* (Paris, 1938), p. 159.

criticisms but also includes some comments of a general nature. 'Few men', he claims, 'perhaps ever wrote upon St. *Paul*'s Epistles, who took less pains to understand them, than Mr. Lock seems to have done. He read them over divers times, made a *Paraphrase*, wrote a few *Notes*, good or bad, partly his own, and partly taken from former Commentators, and then makes a Mock of *Orthodoxy, establish'd Orthodoxy*, in an invective Preface against all that had written before him upon these Epistles, or any other part of Scripture. Is there much Learning or study required in all this?'[1] Jenkin takes Locke to task for his opinions on Christology, the resurrection, and the death of Christ, and challenges many details of his interpretation. He criticizes Locke's claim to be independent of other commentators. 'It is something suspicious,' he observes, 'that a Commentator should endeavour to make Men diffident of all Commentators, that have wrote before him; and very strange, that he could hope by this means to recommend his own performance.'[2] As for Locke's insistence that the whole of an Epistle should be read over and over again, Jenkin points out with justice that the best commentators have done this very thing.[3] But his opinion of the *Paraphrase* is not entirely negative. After nearly sixty pages of adverse criticism he ends with some remarks of guarded generosity: 'And tho' I have detected divers Errors, of a very pernicious Nature and Consequence, which Mr. *Le Clerc* approves and commends as true and sound Doctrine; yet I so far agree with him, as to acknowledge that there is such a Sense of Religion express'd in this Work of Mr. *Lock*'s, as seldom is to be found in those who most admire him, and make use of his Name and Authority to patronize their Errors.'[4]

A favourable assessment of the *Paraphrase* was given by William Whiston (1667-1752), Newton's successor in his chair of mathematics at Cambridge. In a work published in 1709 Whiston affirmed that Locke had set an example to the clergy by his studious application to Paul's Epistles. Of Locke's achievement in the *Paraphrase* he claimed that 'some Allowance being made a Disputant, He, in the main, has proceeded with an uncommon degree of Impartiality, Judgment and Sagacity'.[5]

[1] Robert Jenkin, *Remarks on Some Books Lately Publish'd. viz. Mr. Basnage's History of the Jews. Mr. Whiston's Eight Sermons. Mr. Lock's Paraphrase and Notes on St. Paul's Epistles. Mr. Le Clerc's Bibliothèque Choisie* (London, 1709), p. 123.

[2] Ibid., p. 124. [3] Ibid., pp. 126-7. [4] Ibid., p. 173.

[5] William Whiston, *Sermons and Essays upon Several Subjects* (London, 1709), pp. 254-5. In 1710 Whiston was deprived of his Cambridge chair for heresy.

A vastly different reaction to Locke's work came from the Dissenting preacher and hymn-writer, Isaac Watts (1674-1748), who had previously given high praise to Locke as a philosopher. When he read the *Paraphrase*, Watts was sorely disappointed. He objected to Locke's failure to give adequate treatment of the doctrines of the Incarnation, the Trinity, and the Atonement.

> Reason could scarce sustain to see
> Th' Almighty One, th' Eternal Three,
> Or bear the Infant Deity;
> Scarce could her Pride descend to own
> Her Maker stooping from his Throne,
> And dress'd in Glories so unknown.
> A ransom'd World, a Bleeding God,
> And Heav'n appeas'd with flowing Blood,
> Were Themes too painful to be understood.[1]

Watts expressed the hope that Locke, now that he was in the heavenly realm, would wish his *Paraphrase* to be consigned to oblivion.

> 'Forgive,' he cries, 'ye Saints below
> The wavering and the cold Assent
> I gave to Themes divinely true;
> Can you admit the Blessed to repent?
> Eternal Darkness veil the Lines
> Of that unhappy Book,
> Where glimmering Reason with false Lustre shines,
> Where the mere mortal Pen mistook
> What the celestial meant.'[2]

Far from being consigned to eternal darkness, the *Paraphrase* remained very much in the conspicuousness of broad daylight. Whitby's *Additional Annotations*, published in 1710 as a supplement to his *Paraphrase and Commentary*, contained criticisms of Locke's work and rebuttals of adverse remarks which Locke had made about Whitby's interpretations. One of the main points of dispute between the two men was the resurrection of the body, a theme which continued to provoke debate for many years. Discussions of the matter ranged widely over Locke's works, dealing with statements in the *Essay*, the *Reasonableness*, the published correspondence with Stillingfleet, and

[1] Isaac Watts, *Horae Lyricae* (3rd edn. London, 1715), p. 189.

[2] Ibid., p. 190. For other observations on Locke by Watts see *Horae Lyricae*, p. 153, and Kenneth MacLean, *John Locke and English Literature of the Eighteenth Century* (New Haven, Conn., 1936), pp. 152-3.

the *Paraphrase* itself. As early as 1711 William Lupton and Benjamin Hampton had published works attacking Locke's views on the matter.[1] In 1719 Winch Holdsworth, Fellow of St John's College, Oxford, preached a sermon against Locke's teaching on the resurrection.[2] The sermon was read some years later by Catharine Cockburn, who had made a reputation in her teens as a writer of verse and drama, and had published a defence of Locke's *Essay* in 1702.[3] In 1727 she came out again in Locke's support with her *Letter to Dr. Holdsworth*. Later in the same year Holdsworth replied with *A Defence of the Doctrine of the Resurrection of the same Body, in two parts. In the first of which the character, writings, and religious principles of Mr. Locke, are distinctly considered; and in the second, the Doctrine of the Resurrection of the same Body is at large explained and defended, against the notions and principles of that gentleman*.[4] Holdsworth used the occasion to make an onslaught on Locke's theology as a whole, accusing him of Socinianism and quoting from the *Paraphrase* as well as from Locke's other writings. Catharine Cockburn wrote in reply *A Vindication of Mr. Locke's Christian Principles, from the injurious imputations of Dr. Holdsworth*. She was unable to find a publisher for the work, and it did not appear in print until it was included in her collected works, published in 1751, two years after her death.[5] It is an extensive treatise, in two parts like Holdsworth's. The first part deals with Locke's Christian principles in general, and the second with the resurrection of the same body. Her concern in the first part of the work was to refute the charge that Locke was a Socinian, and in the second to answer the accusation that Locke's teaching about the resurrection was heretical. She devoted a considerable amount of space to passages from the *Paraphrase*. Indeed the controversy itself is evidence that the *Paraphrase* was being carefully read in the second and third decades of the eighteenth century. Catharine Cockburn could say with conviction that 'many persons both of piety and

[1] William Lupton, *The Resurrection of the Same Body* (Oxford, 1711). Benjamin Hampton, *The Existence of the Human Soul after Death* (London, 1711).

[2] Winch Holdsworth, *A Sermon Preached . . . on Easter-Monday, 1719* (Oxford, 1720).

[3] See above, p. 60.

[4] The lateness of Catharine Cockburn's reply to Winch Holdsworth was occasioned by the fact that she did not read Holdsworth's sermon until several years after its publication, and she then engaged in private correspondence with him before her work was published (Birch in Cockburn, *Works*, i, pp. xxxv-xxxvi).

[5] Cockburn, *Works*, i. 157-378. See also Birch's introduction in Cockburn, *Works*, i, pp. xxxvi-xxxvii.

learning highly esteem his *Comments* on St. Paul's Epistles, and think his other writings greatly tend to promote true religion'.[1]

While Locke's writings provoked sharp antagonism,[2] the comments of Whiston and Cockburn show that he did not lack supporters. Indeed a school of biblical commentators emerged to continue his work. His influence can be seen in the writings of John Shute Barrington (1678-1734), who used Locke's style of paraphrase and notes, with sections independent of chapter-divisions, to comment on passages from Genesis and 1 Peter.[3] The most important development, however, was the publication of commentaries after Locke's manner on the remaining Epistles of the New Testament. These works were written by James Peirce, Joseph Hallett, and George Benson. Peirce (1674?-1726), a Presbyterian minister with Arian leanings, published a paraphrase and notes on Colossians, which expressly claimed to be in Locke's manner.[4] Later in the same year he published a similar work on Philippians.[5] He did not live to finish his commentary on Hebrews, but it was completed by his colleague, Joseph Hallett (1691?-1744), and the commentary on Colossians, Philippians, and Hebrews appeared in 1733.[6] Peirce's work followed the same arrangement as Locke's, with Authorized Version, paraphrase, and notes running concurrently. He divided the Epistles into sections independent of the chapter divisions, and endeavoured, as Locke had done, to demonstrate the coherence of Paul's thought in each Epistle. In dedicating his work on Colossians to Peter King, he paid tribute to 'the Great Mr. *Locke* to whom I am more indebted, than to any man, for what understanding I have in St. *Paul*'s Epistles and whose admirable rules and example, I have, the best I could, indeavoured to follow. . . . I am not the only person who have often lamented his not

[1] Cockburn, *Works*, i. 247. Her own estimate of Locke was that he was 'an eminent and worthy man, one, who on all occasions seems to have his *heart filled* with sacred awe and sincere veneration for the holy Scriptures' (*Works*, i. 153).

[2] Jenkin's *Remarks* were reprinted in 1715, and a revised edition came out in 1721. Cf. Henry Felton, *The Resurrection of the Same Numerical Body, and its Reunion to the Same Soul* (Oxford, 1725).

[3] John Shute Barrington, first Viscount Barrington, *Miscellanea Sacra* (2 vols.: London, 1725).

[4] James Peirce, *A Paraphrase and Notes on the Epistle of St. Paul to the Colossians. With an Appendix upon Ephesians iv. 8* (London, 1725).

[5] James Peirce, *A Paraphrase and Notes on the Epistle of St. Paul to the Philippians. To which are added two Dissertations: one on Gal. iv. 21–v. 1; the other on Matt. ii. 13–15* (London, 1725).

[6] James Peirce, *A Paraphrase and Notes on the Epistles of St. Paul to the Colossians, Philippians, Hebrews: after the Manner of Mr. Locke . . . with a Paraphrase and Notes on the Three Last Chapters of the Hebrews . . . by Joseph Hallett, Jr.* (London, 1733).

applying himself sooner to this study, and that we should have his *Paraphrase* and *Notes* only upon five of the Epistles; but we have reason to be thankful for them, not only for the light they give to those Epistles, but the use they may be of to imitate this Great Man.'[1]

Another Dissenting minister, George Benson (1699-1762), produced a series of volumes, conforming to the same pattern, which dealt with the rest of the New Testament Epistles. In 1731 he published *A Paraphrase and Notes on St. Paul's Epistle to Philemon. Attempted in Imitation of Mr. Locke's Manner*. The same year a similar work appeared on the First Epistle to the Thessalonians, and in 1732 another volume on the Second Epistle to the Thessalonians. During the next seventeen years he published works on all the remaining Epistles.[2] Like Peirce, he was inclined towards Arianism, and like Peirce, he wrote of Locke in adulatory, although not completely uncritical, terms. 'The World in general', he affirmed, 'ought to be grateful to the Great and Good Mr. Locke, for putting them into such a Way of studying St. Paul's Epistles.' Like Peirce, he regretted that Locke had not written about more of the Epistles. He also recognized faults in the work. 'He has certainly put us into the right Way of Studying them [the Epistles], tho' I don't reckon him infallible; for I have by me some Remarks upon Places which I apprehend him to have mistaken.'[3]

Peirce, Benson, and Hallett were all involved in the controversies which arose within English nonconformity about the doctrine of the Trinity. In 1719 both Peirce and Hallett's father had been expelled from the Exeter congregation because of their unorthodox beliefs. After his father's death, Hallett became Peirce's colleague, and they ministered to a newly-formed congregation in the same city. Benson belonged to the group of Dissenters who were known as Non-subscribers because of their refusal to subscribe to the doctrine of the Trinity as defined in the Thirty-Nine Articles and the Westminster Confession. All these three men who perpetuated a Lockean school of commentary were known to be unwilling to accept the traditional statements of the doctrine of the Trinity.[4]

[1] Peirce, *Colossians*, pp. iii, v.

[2] 1 Timothy and Titus (1733), 2 Timothy (1734), James (1738), 1 Peter (1742), 2 Peter and Jude (1745). A collected edition of his works on Paul's Epistles was published in 1734, and on the seven Catholic Epistles in 1749.

[3] George Benson, *Paraphrase and Notes on St. Paul's Epistle to Philemon. Attempted in Imitation of Mr. Locke's Manner* (London, 1731), p. iii.

[4] Earl Morse Wilbur, *A History of Unitarianism in Transylvania, England, and America* (Boston, Mass., 1964), pp. 252-66.

Another scholar with similar theological views was Nathanael Lardner (1684-1768), who makes several references to the *Paraphrase* in his works.[1] But a much greater debt to Locke was acknowledged by John Taylor (1694-1761), a Dissenting minister in Norwich. Although Taylor did not become involved in Trinitarian controversy, his views on the subject were unorthodox. He became well known for his work on *The Scripture Doctrine of Original Sin* (London, 1740), which attacked Calvinistic teaching, and was the subject of controversy on both sides of the Atlantic. In his work, *A Paraphrase with Notes on the Epistle to the Romans*, Taylor gave high praise to Locke. 'But to Mr. *Locke* I am so much indebted, for the Sense of the Epistle, that I question whether I could have wrote my Paraphrase and Notes, had he not first written his.'[2] He was not uncritical of Locke. He explained that he had noted his mistakes 'on purpose that I might freely leave, and encourage the Reader to peruse the rest'. But his method of dealing with the Epistle places him in the Lockean school of commentators.

The *Paraphrase* was also known to the Unitarian, Joseph Priestley (1733-1804), who alludes to it in writing about Paul.[3] It was indeed amongst the theologians who rejected or were ambivalent about the doctrine of the Trinity that Locke's commentary was the most admired. There were various features of his work that attracted them: in addition to his silence about the doctrine of the Trinity, there was his liberal attitude to the atonement and original sin, and his hesitation to speak of eternal punishment. Especially attractive was his combination of reverence for the Scripture with a serious attempt to make use of reason in the study of it.

Locke's *Paraphrase* was read by other theologians. Philip Doddridge (1702-51), the Nonconformist commentator and hymn-writer, took note of his views in his *Family Expositor*.[4] The Scots Presbyterian James Macknight (1721-1800) made reference to Locke's work, and accused him of 'strained criticisms, for the purpose of establishing particular doctrines'.[5] Macknight expressed the same misgivings about Calvin, Beza, Grotius, Hammond, Limborch, and Taylor. So

[1] Nathanael Lardner, *Works* (10 vols.: London, 1838), x. 110, 146, 152, 154.

[2] John Taylor, *A Paraphrase with Notes on the Epistle to the Romans* (London, 1745), p. clxix.

[3] Joseph Priestley, *The Theological and Miscellaneous Works* (25 vols. in 26: London, 1817-32), vii. 377, 411.

[4] Philip Doddridge, *The Family Expositor* (6 vols.: London, 1739-56).

[5] James Macknight, *A New Literal Translation from the Original Greek of all the Apostolical Epistles, with a Commentary, and Notes, Philological, Critical, Explanatory, and Practical* (2nd edn., 3 vols.: Edinburgh, 1795), i. 39.

his remarks do not convey information about any distinctive features of Locke's work. More positive was the attitude of the Methodist Thomas Coke (1747-1814), whose *Commentary on the New Testament* (London, 1812) contains numerous allusions to the *Paraphrase*. Coke obviously regarded the work as one of the leading and most reliable commentaries on Paul's Epistles. But this reaction was not shared by his fellow Methodist, Richard Watson (1781-1833), who observed that in the interpretation of Rom. III.24 Locke 'greatly trifles with this passage'.[1] Biblical scholars of those days were reading Locke's *Paraphrase*, although their reactions to him greatly varied. The famous Anglican theologian William Paley (1743-1805) mentions the *Paraphrase* in his *Horae Paulinae*.[2] Although he does not always agree with Locke's views, he alludes to it in such a fashion as to give the impression that it was a standard commentary. Far different was the reaction of the Anglican scholar Thomas Scott (1747-1821), who was a thorough-going Calvinist. He singled out Locke and Taylor for condemnation. Both of these commentators, he lamented, 'darken counsel by words without knowledge'. Only in some incidental matters could he 'deduce instruction from them'.[3]

On one issue a debate arose about the *Paraphrase* within the ranks of the Quakers. The question at issue was whether Locke supported the Quaker practice of allowing women to speak at religious meetings. Benjamin Coole had argued that Locke's interpretation of 1 Cor. XI.3 did not support the legitimacy of allowing women to preach. But his fellow Quaker Josiah Martin claimed that Locke's account of the matter was agreeable to Quaker doctrine and practice. This debate was conducted in an amicable manner and was cut short by Coole's death in 1717. Martin and Coole each published two contributions to the debate.[4] And almost a century later the matter was brought up

[1] Richard Watson, *Works* (13 vols.: London, 1846), xiii. 703.

[2] William Paley, *A View of the Evidences of Christianity in Three Parts; and the Horae Paulinae* (Cambridge, 1849), pp. 353, 384-5, 395.

[3] Thomas Scott, *The Holy Bible* (6 vols.: New York, 1810-12), vi, pref. to Rom. (no page no.)

[4] Benjamin Coole, *Some Brief Observations on the Paraphrase and Notes of the Judicious John Locke relating to the Women's Exercising their Spiritual Gifts in the Church* (London, n.d.); Josiah Martin, *A Letter to the Author of Some Brief Observations* (London, 1716); Benjamin Coole, *Reflections on a Letter to the Author of Some Brief Observations* (London, 1717); Josiah Martin, *A Vindication of Women's Preaching, as well from Holy Scripture on Antient Writings as from the Paraphrase and Notes of the Judicious John Locke, on 1 Cor xi, wherein the Brief Observations of the said B.C. on the Said Paraphrase and Notes, and the Arguments in his Book, intitled Reflections, etc, are Fully Consider'd* (London, 1717).

again in a pamphlet by William Rawes.[1] These writers regarded Locke as an authority. As far as they were concerned, his support for an opinion was in itself a powerful argument in its favour.

The *Paraphrase* hardly coincided with the views of eighteenth-century Deists, who tended to rely exclusively on reasón and relegated revelation to a subordinate function or even disregarded it completely. One of their number, Henry St. John, Viscount Bolingbroke (1678-1751), was unashamedly hostile to Paul,[2] and took issue with the *Paraphrase*. He regarded Locke's whole theological enterprise as at variance with the *Essay*. 'I confess, farther,' he wrote, 'that I have been and am still, at a loss to find any appearance of consistency in an author who published a commentary on the epistles of St. PAUL and a treatise of the reasonableness of Christianity, which he endeavours to prove by fact and by argument, after having stated as clearly, as he had done, the conditions and the measures of historical probability, and after having written as strongly, as he had done, against the abuse of words.'[3] Bolingbroke regarded Paul as a thoroughly inconsistent writer. Locke, he admitted, had 'succeeded better, perhaps, than any other expositor, by happier conjectures, and no greater licence of paraphrase, in giving an air of coherence, consistency, and rationality to these epistles'.[4] But Locke, he argued, had failed to make his case.

As a biblical commentator Locke had provoked the opposition of the Deist, Bolingbroke, as well as that of more orthodox thinkers. But he had also acquired some fervent supporters. Prominent among them were theologians whose views on the Trinity were regarded as heretical. But the ranks of his admirers were by no means confined to such thinkers. Although the influence of the *Paraphrase* began to wane in subsequent generations, it was one of the main commentaries on Paul's Epistles in eighteenth-century Britain.

[1] William Rawes, *The Gospel Ministry of Women, under the Christian Dispensation, Defended from the Scripture and from the Writings of John Locke, Josiah Martin*, etc. (London, 1801).

[2] Henry St. John, first Viscount Bolingbroke, *The Philosophical Works* (5 vols.: London, 1754-77), ii. 281, where he accuses Isaac Barrow of 'talking in a theological cant more worthy of PAUL than of a man like him'.

[3] Bolingbroke, *Works*, ii. 132.

[4] *Works*, ii. 349. In *Works*, v. 80 Bolingbroke argues that Locke misrepresents Paul's teaching about predestination. See also *Works*, ii. 159-65 (page numbers are confused in the cited edition), for Bolingbroke's criticism of Locke's discussion of Rom. I and II in the *Reasonableness*.

The Reception in America

In America, as in Britain, reactions to the *Paraphrase* were mixed. Ezra Stiles (1727-95), a Calvinist, who was President of Yale College, was critical of the mode of commentary which Locke had undertaken. The English Bible, he claimed, is 'too intelligible to need the Paraphrase of even a Locke'. Paraphrase, Stiles pronounced, was absurd. Notes or expositions were 'the only true Way of Commentary'.

In spite of his adverse remarks about the work, Stiles provides evidence of its popularity during the eighteenth century. It was, he mistakenly argued, 'a new *Mode* of Scripture Commentary' which Locke had invented. This mode had 'received great Applause' even from theologians who disagreed with Locke's views. But it was especially the Dissenting divines who were 'captivated with Mr. Locke's Manner'. Because 'his Arian and Arminian principles' had been widely accepted, his reputation as a commentator had been 'exceeding high with the public'.[1]

Although Stiles was satisfied with neither the mode nor the theology of the *Paraphrase*, it was highly esteemed by the Unitarian William Ellery Channing (1780-1842). 'His works', Channing wrote, 'on the "Epistles of Paul" and on the "Reasonableness of Christianity", formed an era in sacred literature; and he has the honor of having shed a new and bright light on the darkest parts of the New Testament, and in general on the Christian system.'[2] Channing compared the *Paraphrase* to the *Essay*, claiming that Locke 'carried into the interpretation of the Scriptures the same force of thought as into the philosophy of the mind'.[3] The *Paraphrase*, which had been a standard work in eighteenth-century America, was continuing to hold its own in the early part of the nineteenth century.[4]

The work was also read by Alexander Campbell (1788-1866), the important American religious leader. Campbell, who had been greatly influenced by Locke's *Essay*, did not come across the *Paraphrase* until 1825. It was then too late for him to consult it in preparing his translation of the New Testament, which was just about to be published. But

[1] *The Literary Diary of Ezra Stiles* (3 vols.: New York, 1901), i. 356-8. These excerpts are taken from his entry for 18 May 1775.

[2] William Ellery Channing, *Works* (Boston, Mass., 1896), p. 406.

[3] Channing, *Works*, p. 560.

[4] The Unitarian Joseph Stevens Buckminster (1784-1812) is on record as having studied the *Paraphrase*. See Jerry Wayne Brown, *The Rise of Biblical Criticism in America, 1800–1870* (Middletown, Conn., 1965), p. 15.

he went on record as saying that in his work as a translator and interpreter of the scriptures he was using the same principles as Locke.[1]

An edition of the *Paraphrase* appeared in Cambridge, Mass., in 1832, and the Preface appeared as part of two different collections of theological works published in America in 1826 and 1836.[2] The *Paraphrase* is mentioned in the commentary on Romans by Moses Stuart (1780–1852).[3] But with the decline in fashion of Locke's philosophy and with the rise of new methods of biblical criticism the *Paraphrase* ceased to be as influential as in the previous century.

The Reception on the Continent of Europe

It was not only in Britain and America that the *Paraphrase* was being read. Reaction to it appeared early with the comments in France of *Mémoires pour l'histoire des sciences et des beaux-arts*. From Holland came Le Clerc's review in *Bibliothèque choisie* and the briefer comments in *Nouvelles de la République des Lettres*. The Swiss scholar, Johann Jakob Wettstein (1693–1754), although he disagreed with Locke's interpretation of Rom. IX.5, regarded him as a man who desired to serve God seriously and whose outlook was Arminian. Wettstein also observed that in textual criticism Locke sometimes departed from the Textus Receptus and preferred the authority of Codex Alexandrinus or Codex Claromontanus or other manuscripts.[4] Another Swiss scholar, Jean Alphonse Turretin (1671–1737), made some remarks about the difficulties of Paul's Greek style which are very reminiscent of Locke's statements in his Preface to the *Paraphrase*. Although he made no direct acknowledgement to Locke, Turretin had visited England, and was probably acquainted with Locke's work on the Epistles.[5]

Translations of parts of the *Paraphrase* appeared. The Preface was translated into French,[6] and Romans into Dutch.[7] Considerable

[1] Cecil K. Thomas, *Alexander Campbell and his New Version* (St. Louis, Mo., 1958), p. 15.

[2] Christophersen, *Bibliographical Introduction*, p. 76.

[3] Moses Stuart, *A Commentary on the Epistle to the Romans* (Andover, Mass., 1832), pp. 167, 378. Locke is not included, however, in his list of leading commentators, pp. 575–6.

[4] Johann Jakob Wettstein, *Novum Testamentum Graecum* (2 vols.: Amsterdam, 1751), i. 185, 189.

[5] Jean Alphonse Turretin, *Opera Omnia* (3 vols.: Leeuwarden and Franeker, 1774–6), ii. 443–5.

[6] 'Essai sur la nécessité d'expliquer les Epîtres de S. Paul par S. Paul même', *Œuvres diverses de M. Locke* (new edn., 2 vols.: Amsterdam, 1732), vol. ii.

[7] J. Locke, *Over den brief van Paulus aan de Romeinen* (Amsterdam, 1768).

attention was paid to the work in Germany. It was mentioned by Christoph Wolle, who criticized Locke's discussion of Paul's parentheses.[1] There are numerous references to it in the commentary by Johann Christoph Wolf (1683-1739), who alluded to Locke's account of the causes of Paul's obscurity and criticized several of the opinions expressed in the *Paraphrase*.[2] Siegmund Jakob Baumgarten (1706-57) referred to the work in his commentaries and reviewed it in his journal, *Nachrichten von merkwürdigen Büchern*, where he noted Locke's lack of expertise in biblical languages but approved the arrangement of his material. He also reviewed the commentaries written in Locke's style by Peirce and Benson.[3] The influence of the *Paraphrase* was strong in the case of Johann David Michaelis (1717-91). In his Preface to the German translation Michaelis indicated that he had made regular use of the *Paraphrase* for many years. He stressed the desirability of such a translation because of the frequency with which reference was made to the work. While he had made some adverse criticisms of Locke's reliance on philosophical presuppositions, he clearly regarded the *Paraphrase* as one of the most important commentaries on the Epistles.[4]

The German translator of the *Paraphrase*, Johann Georg Hofmann (1724-72), took a different attitude to it from that of Michaelis. Although he recognized its merits, he regarded it as a threat to orthodoxy. He gave an account of what he believed to be the work's main errors,[5] and added copious notes of his own, most of which were corrective rather than explanatory. Sometimes he substituted his own paraphrase for Locke's; for it was his intention to prevent his readers from being led astray by Locke's heresies. A German

[1] Christoph Wolle, *Commentatio Philologica de Parenthesi Sacra* (Leipzig, 1726), p. 11.

[2] Johann Christoph Wolf, *Curae Philologicae et Criticae* (4 vols.: Hamburg, 1737-41), iii. 3, 35, 36, 37, 365, 415, 511, etc.; iv. 66, 105, 165.

[3] Siegmund Jakob Baumgarten, *Auslegung der beiden Briefe an die Korinther* (Halle, 1761), pp. 14, 644; *Auslegung der Epistel an die Römer* (Halle, 1749), pp. 16, 341; *Nachrichten von merkwürdigen Büchern*, viii (1755), 101-21; x (1756), 386-9.

[4] Johann David Michaelis in *Johann Locke, Paraphrastische Erklärung und Anmerkungen über S. Pauli Briefe an die Galater, Korinther, Römer und Epheser*, trans. and ed. by Johann Georg Hofmann (Frankfurt am Main, 1768-9), pt. i, pp. iii-xii. Michaelis had already translated works by Peirce and Benson into Latin: James Peirce, *Paraphrasis et Notae Philologicae atque Exegeticae in Epistolam ad Hebraeos* (Halle, 1747); George Benson, *Paraphrasis et Notae Philologicae atque Exegeticae in Epistolam S. Iacobi* (Halle, 1746). A collection of Benson's paraphrases and notes was translated into German under the title *Paraphrastische Erklärung und Anmerkungen einiger Bücher des Neuen Testaments* (Leipzig, 1761).

[5] Hofmann in Locke, *Paraphrastische Erklärung*, pt. i, pp. (ii-xiii).

translation of the paraphrase and notes on Romans appeared a few years later, providing further evidence of interest in the work.[1] Although the nineteenth-century scholars, Tholuck and Meyer, made frequent reference to him,[2] it was in the eighteenth century that Locke's *Paraphrase* exercised its greatest influence in Germany. And Michaelis, who esteemed the work highly, was himself an important figure in the development of biblical criticism.

In the late nineteenth and in the twentieth centuries the *Paraphrase* has not been mentioned with as much frequency as before. Yet it has not been forgotten. An Italian translation of the Preface was published in 1919.[3] A variety of scholars have recognized the importance of the *Paraphrase* in the history of biblical criticism, and special attention has been paid to it by Pahl and Schouls.[4] It was in the eighteenth and early nineteenth centuries, however, that the work had its most powerful influence. During that period it held its own as one of the leading commentaries on Paul's Epistles in Britain and America. Among biblical scholars it received widespread recognition. Some of them praised it, and others spoke of it adversely. But it was regarded as a book to be reckoned with. Having made his mark in other spheres of thought, Locke had succeeded in making a powerful impact as an interpreter of Paul.

[1] *Paraphrase des Briefes Pauli an die Römer* (Frankfurt and Leipzig, 1773).

[2] Friedrich August Gottreu Tholuck, *Auslegung des Briefes Pauli an die Römer* (Berlin, 1824); Heinrich August Wilhelm Meyer, *Kritisch-exegetischer Kommentar über das Neue Testament* (Göttingen, 1832-59).

[3] *Saggio su l'intendimento delle Epistole di S. Paolo*, trans. with introductory note by Francesco A. Ferrari (Lanciano, 1919).

[4] Gretchen Graf Pahl, 'John Locke as Literary Critic and Biblical Interpreter', pp. 137-57, 270-2; P. A. Schouls, *The Imposition of Method*, pp. 219-51. See also R. I. Aaron, *John Locke* (3rd edn. Oxford, 1971), pp. 295-6; Romeo Crippa, *Studi sulla coscienza etica e religiosa del Seicento. Esperienza e libertà in J. Locke* (Milan, 1960), p. 155; Alexander Campbell Fraser, *Locke* (Edinburgh and London, 1890), pp. 262-3; Werner Georg Kümmel, *The New Testament: The History of the Investigation of its Problems*, trans. by S. McLean Gilmour and Howard C. Kee (Nashville and New York, 1972), pp. 3-4, 414; H. McLachlan, *The Religious Opinions of Milton, Locke, and Newton* pp. 93-6; Henning Graf Reventlow, *Bibelautorität und Geist der Moderne* (Göttingen, 1980), p. 446; Luigi Salvatorelli, 'From Locke to Reitzenstein. The Historical Investigation of the Origins of Christianity', *Harvard Theological Review*, xxii (1929), 264-5. Other works on Locke's theological views are mentioned in Christophersen, *Bibliographical Introduction*, pp. 129-31.

IV. TEXTUAL MATTERS[1]

The Copy-Text

(i) *The Preface and Ephesians*. The copy-text for the Preface and the paraphrase and notes on Ephesians is the first edition, which appeared in 1707. No manuscript is available of these parts of the *Paraphrase*, and the second time they appeared in print was in the first collected edition of Locke's *Works* in 1714. No edition apart from that of 1707 can be seriously considered as the copy-text for these parts of the work.

(ii) *1 and 2 Corinthians; Romans*. A choice of copy-text for the paraphrase and notes on the Corinthian Epistles and Romans had to be made between the Bodleian manuscript and the first edition, which in the case of 1 and 2 Corinthians was published in 1706 and in the case of Romans in 1707. Certain features of the first edition would favour its use as the copy-text. Its style of spelling, capitalization, and punctuation conforms more closely than that of the manuscript to the style found in the works of Locke published during his own lifetime. The spelling is more modern, the capitalization more frequent, and the punctuation more plentiful in the first edition than in the manuscript. Since Locke allowed other works of his to be printed with these formal features, it could be argued that he intended, or at least expected, similar treatment to be given to the *Paraphrase*. On the other hand, the manuscript has powerful claims to be chosen as copy-text. While the first edition appeared after Locke's death, the manuscript has the decided advantage of having been wholly written in his own hand. It is impossible to be sure that the first edition would have met in all respects with his approval.

Moreover, a considerable number of changes made by him in the manuscript are absent from the first edition, which still contains the words deleted from the manuscript. Probably Locke did not have time before his death to inform the printer about these alterations, which include the insertion of additional notes as well as other extensive changes. There are, of course, numerous other differences between the manuscript and the first edition, but most of them consist of comparatively minor variations in wording or differences in formal features; and many of these may be the result of the copyist's

[1] This part results from close collaboration between the editor and the late General Editor, Peter Nidditch.

or the printer's errors, or even of their attempts to make corrections. Some of the differences which do not correspond to manuscript alterations are more substantial, and may well have been made by Locke only in the printer's copy of the manuscript. But the nature of those alterations to the Bodleian manuscript which are absent from the first edition suggests that the manuscript contains Locke's final revision of the work.[1] There is therefore a strong case for selecting it as the copy-text.

It would be possible to adopt a third solution to the problem of choosing a basic text. A composite edition could be produced which followed the Bodleian manuscript as far as the actual words are concerned, but conformed to the first edition in formal features such as spelling, capitalization, and, where it did not affect the meaning, punctuation. It might be argued that Locke would have intended, or at least expected, the manuscript to be printed in such a way.

It has been decided that, on balance, the most appropriate method for the historico-critical edition in the Clarendon Edition of the Works of John Locke is to make the Bodleian manuscript the copy-text in a thoroughgoing and uniform way, i.e. in its formal as well as its material features, for the Corinthian Epistles and Romans. Further, because of its unique position among Locke's papers, the text of this manuscript should be made more readily accessible: the *Paraphrase* is the only longer work by Locke of which the major part survives in manuscript. The Bodleian manuscript is not a preliminary draft. It contains Locke's final text, and also provides evidence of the final alterations which he made. While several copies of the first edition are available in libraries, the manuscript is by the nature of things found only in one place. Its transcription in this present edition makes it more widely available, in accordance with the policy of the Clarendon Locke, which aims at doing this in general for Locke's manuscripts. Moreover, this particular manuscript is in a very fragile condition, and parts of it have already seriously deteriorated. It is important to make sure that its text is preserved for posterity.

(iii) *Galatians*. A more complex problem is presented by Galatians than by the Corinthian Epistles and Romans. This part of the *Paraphrase* was already in the hands of the publisher before Locke's death, and he had seen some, if not all, of the proofs of it.[2] Its first

[1] See Appendix XII for a list of the relevant passages.

[2] See above, p. 6.

edition, therefore, which was published in 1705, might appear to have a better claim than the first printing of the Corinthian Epistles and Romans to be chosen as copy-text. Since only a few of Locke's changes in the Bodleian manuscript of Galatians have not been incorporated into the first edition, and since Locke himself had seen the proofs, it might be argued that the published work conveys his intentions in both material and formal features. But such a case is difficult to maintain. As Awnsham Churchill remarked in a letter to Locke,[1] the proofs were in a foul condition. Even though steps may have been taken before publication to remedy its defects, the first edition of Galatians leaves much to be desired. Footnotes are misplaced, and frequently fail to appear on the same page as the verses of paraphrase to which they refer. The footnote signs are often thoroughly confused. There are obvious errors in printing. It is not surprising that in 1706 a second edition of Galatians was published, which remedied many of these defects and presented the work in a format similar to that used for the Corinthian Epistles, Romans, and Ephesians. In spite of the proofs having been seen by Locke, the faults of the first edition are such that it has even less claim than the first edition of the Corinthian Epistles and of Romans to be used as the copy-text. These negative considerations reinforce the positive reasons, mentioned under (ii) above, for selecting the Bodleian manuscript as copy-text for Galatians.

(iv) *The Authorized Version*. Apart from the first four verses of Romans, the Authorized Version is not transcribed in the Bodleian manuscript, although it is printed in the first edition of Locke's work on all five Epistles. Its presence in the first edition of the paraphrase and notes on Galatians, which Locke had seen in proof, is evidence of his intention to include it in his published work. Although he may not have approved of all the details of the proofs, it is likely that his wish was being carried out in a matter as important and conspicuous as the inclusion of the Authorized Version. It has therefore been decided to include the version in this present edition. The copy-text for this part of the work is the first edition of Locke's work on 1 and 2 Corinthians, Romans, and Ephesians, and the second edition of his work on Galatians.

This text frequently differs in formal features from the first edition (1611) of the Authorized Version. These differences include capitalization, spelling, punctuation, and the use of roman type instead of

[1] *Corr.* viii. 380. See above, p. 6.

the first edition's black-letter. There are also material differences from the first edition. For example, in 1 Cor. VII.18 the *Paraphrase* reads 'become circumcised' where the 1611 edition reads 'be circumcised'; and in 1 Cor. XIV.23 the *Paraphrase* has 'one place', where the 1611 edition has 'some place'.

In this present edition it has been decided to use the first edition of the *Paraphrase* as the copy-text of the Authorized Version of 1 and 2 Corinthians, Romans, and Ephesians. In most of its material differences from the 1611 edition it is in agreement with one or more of the numerous seventeenth- or early eighteenth-century printings; and in most respects it is in material agreement with the 1703 Holy Bible, printed in London by Charles Bill and the Executrix of Thomas Newcomb, who were printers to Queen Anne. This present edition has not been made to conform to the 1703 printing in formal features, but where the *Paraphrase* is not in agreement with any earlier printing that has been consulted, it has been emended to agree with the 1703 edition. There is no certainty that the printer of the first edition of the *Paraphrase* used this or a similar printing of the Authorized Version; but, at any rate, it was available when the *Paraphrase* went to the press.

No attempt has been made to conform to modern printings of the Authorized Version. For example, in 2 Cor. XI.26, where modern printings have the word 'journeyings', both the 1703 Bible and the copy-text (as well as the 1611 edition) have 'journeying'; and even though it is an inaccurate translation, the latter has been retained, because it was printed in many editions available at the time when the *Paraphrase* was published.

A special difficulty arises with Galatians. The Authorized Version in the first edition of Locke's paraphrase and notes on that Epistle makes use of italics, both for proper names and for words which have no literal equivalent in the Greek text. The latter procedure goes back to the 1611 edition, where roman type was used for this purpose, the rest of the words being in black-letter. This first edition of Locke's Galatians is by no means in complete agreement with the 1611 edition in its choice of words to be treated in this way; nor does it agree fully in its italicization with any other edition of the Authorized Version which has been inspected. It has been decided to use the second edition of the paraphrase and notes on Galatians as the copy-text for the Authorized Version. This edition has the virtue of being consistent with the first edition of Locke's work on the other

Epistles, in that, with few exceptions it dispenses with the use of italics.

The Treatment of the Manuscript

The Bodleian manuscript, which is the copy-text for Locke's paraphrase and notes on Galatians, 1 and 2 Corinthians, and Romans, is transcribed in this present edition with the following modifications.

Silent Changes. Contractions have been expanded, e.g. 'y^{e}' to 'the', 'y^{t}' to 'that', 'ag^{n}' to 'again', 'wth' to 'with', 'w^{ch}' to 'which', '-m^{t}' to '-ment', and '-con' to '-tion'. Ampersands have been expanded to 'and', and '&c' to 'etc.'. Some abbreviations have been written in full, e.g. 'N T' as 'New Testament', 'S S' as 'Sacred Scripture' or 'Sacred Scriptures', and 'v.' as 'ver.' (as is usual in the early editions) for 'verse' or 'verses'. Single quotation marks have been used even when the manuscript has double quotation marks. If the manuscript does not use them at the end of a quotation, they have been supplied. In conformity with the procedure of the manuscript, they have been placed at the beginning of each line of a quotation. Underlined words have been italicized, except for Greek words, which have been letter-spaced. Words with double underlining have been printed in italicized capitals. Section headings and the headings 'Contents' and 'Paraphrase' have been regularized. Verse-numbers for the paraphrase have been inserted interlineally, although they are in the margins of the manuscript. Chapter-numbers have been inserted at appropriate places in both the paraphrase and the notes. Where the absence of punctuation in the manuscript might cause difficulty to a reader, an upper point (Greek colon) '·' has been inserted, but such points have not been inserted at the end of paragraphs. Stops which are likely to have been caused by the resting of a pen have been omitted, as have occasional dashes which appear to serve no other purpose than the filling of a blank space. Catchwords at the foot of a page or a column have not been transcribed. The lineation of the manuscript has not been preserved. The headword denoting the Epistle and chapter-number at the top of each page of the manuscript has not been reproduced, but appropriate chapter- and verse-numbers, together with the title of each Epistle, have been supplied. Cross-reference numbers which indicate extra additions to the manuscript have been omitted, and footnote signs have been regularized. The heading 'Notes' has been omitted. Locke's notes are printed at the foot of the page, although in the manuscript they sometimes come at the end of a section.

Ambiguities in the Manuscript. It is not always clear whether Locke intended to write a stop or a comma, and often a subjective decision has to be made about the matter. Lightly written stops placed below the line have normally been transcribed as commas, but stops on the line have been transcribed as stops, even though they appear to fulfil the function of a comma in modern punctuation. Sometimes Locke has written a full stop where a question mark would have been expected, but in these cases too his punctuation has been preserved. There are various other ambiguities. It is not always clear whether words like 'them selves', 'him self', and 'an other' are written as two words or one. Sometimes it is difficult to distinguish an 'e' from an 'o'. In many instances it is not clear whether the initial letter of a word is intended as a capital or as lower case; this ambiguity is especially frequent with the letters 'c', 'e', 'k', 'm', 'n', 'o', 'p', 's', 'u', 'v', 'w', and 'y'. In such matters an editorial decision has been made without comment.

Yet another cause of uncertainty is the lack of clarity in some of the script. Deterioration of the manuscript has caused some of the writing to grow faint or to be smudged, although no doubt some of these defects go back to Locke himself. When words have been conjectured because of this lack of clarity, a record has been made in the manuscript notes. On occasions when words have been particularly hard to decipher, the first edition has been consulted. But any conjecture takes into account the apparent length of words and the formal characteristics of the manuscript.

Furthermore, some contractions can have more than one meaning. 'Y^e' can mean 'the' or 'ye', and 'y^r' can mean 'your' or 'their'. Usually the meaning is clear from the context, and the contraction has been expanded without comment. But cases of real ambiguity are mentioned in either the manuscript notes or the textual notes.

Recorded Changes. Any departure from the manuscript, apart from silent changes mentioned, has been recorded in the textual notes. The manuscript is adhered to except where it seems clearly not to represent Locke's intention. Obvious misspellings have been corrected, but where Locke could conceivably be preserving an older form of spelling, his text has been reproduced. If Hebrew, Greek, and Latin words are misspelt, they also are corrected. If the same word is mistakenly written twice in succession, the error is rectified. All these corrections are recorded in the textual notes, except for a few instances where Locke has failed to cancel part of a larger deletion and the matter has been recorded in the manuscript notes. No attempt has been made to achieve consistency of punctuation after numbers in scripture references or after abbreviations. Locke's inconsistency in these matters has been preserved. But sometimes punctuation which confuses the sense has been changed.

Greek Breathings and Accents. Breathings, accents, and iota subscripts are silently altered or supplied to conform to modern practices in the printing of Classical and Hellenistic Greek. In the seventeenth and eighteenth centuries the treatment of grave and acute accents and the positioning of accents over diphthongs varied greatly, as can be seen from an examination of books as diverse as Walton's Polyglot Bible, Lightfoot's publications, Le Clerc's edition of Erasmus, and the paraphrases and notes by Peirce and Benson.

In his manuscript Locke normally disagrees with the modern practice of accenting ancient Greek texts in the following respects. When the first two letters of a word are a diphthong, he places the accent and breathing over the first, not the second, of the letters. He usually accents the last syllable of a word as a grave, even when it is followed by a punctuation mark. But he is not consistent, and conforms on some occasions to the procedure accepted in modern editions.

Hebrew Pointing. Sometimes Locke points Hebrew words, and sometimes he leaves them unpointed. His variation in practice has been retained in this edition but pointing has been silently corrected. The Hebrew has been changed when it has been misspelt, and such changes have been recorded in the textual notes.

Textual Notes for Galatians, 1 and 2 Corinthians, and Romans. A register of variants is given in the textual notes, in which the Bodleian manuscript is collated with the first edition (Galatians, 1705; 1 Corinthians, 1706; 2 Corinthians, 1706; Romans, 1707) and the second edition (Galatians, 1706). No attempt is made to collate formal differences of spelling, capitalization, and punctuation, or of differences in the style of footnote signs. When the first and second editions contain misspellings or inverted letters, no record is made of them unless they could be misunderstood as other words. The following matters, however, are recorded in the textual notes.

(i) All differences between this present edition and the manuscript, except those mentioned above on Silent Changes.

(ii) Differences in actual wording between the manuscript and the first and second editions.

(iii) Differences of spelling between the manuscript and the first and second editions, where (and only where) they could lead to a misunderstanding.

(iv) Differences of punctuation between the manuscript and the first and second editions, where (and only where) they might imply a difference of meaning.

(v) Differences of italicization between the manuscript and the first and second editions, where (and only where) they might lead to a different understanding of the precise length of a biblical quotation.

(vi) Differences in the use of a footnote sign, when it is used in one of the collated texts to explain a word in a different verse from that which it explains in another. If a sign explains a different word in the same verse from that which it explains in another text, no record has been made, unless the difference would affect the understanding of the note. No attempt has been made to record all the errors in the footnote signs in the first edition of Galatians, where there is widespread confusion over the matter.

(vii) Differences of Greek spelling, breathings, and accents between the manuscript and the first and second editions only where they might give rise to a misunderstanding. Accents and breathings have been silently regularized in the chosen readings but not in rejected ones.

The first collected edition, *The Works of John Locke* (1714), is mentioned only where it supports an editorial reading against both the manuscript and the collated editions. The same use would have been made of the third edition (1708) of Galatians, if need had arisen.

Register of Locke's own Changes in the Manuscript. Apart from the most trifling matters, Locke's own changes in his manuscript have been recorded in the manuscript notes. Included in these notes is a record of the additions, deletions, and alterations which he made. Some of these changes affect only one or two words. Others are more extensive. Sometimes a whole page is deleted. Sometimes lengthy additions are made, some of them interlinear and others in the margins. The signs used in these notes are explained in a later section.

The Treatment of the First Edition of the Preface, Ephesians, and the Authorized Version of all Five Epistles

The copy-text for the Preface, Ephesians, and the Authorized Version text of all five Epistles is the first edition. The copy-text is reproduced in this present edition with the following modifications.

Silent Changes. Ampersands have been lengthened to 'and', and '&c.' to 'etc.'. The long 's' has been replaced by the normal modern form. Section numbers are adapted to conform to the pattern maintained throughout this present edition. Single quotation marks are used, even though they are normally double in the copy-text. Although the copy-text does not use quotation marks at the end of a quotation, they are supplied in this edition. In conformity with the procedure of the copy-text, quotation marks are placed at the beginning of each line of a quotation. Verse-numbers for the paraphrase have been inserted interlineally, although they are in the margins of the copy-text. Chapter-numbers have been inserted at appropriate places in both the paraphrase and the notes. The Authorized Version precedes the paraphrase in each section, although in the copy-text the biblical text and the paraphrase are in parallel columns. In the Authorized Version text of this edition each verse begins a new line, regardless of the varying practice of the different parts of the copy-text. Chapter-numbers are inserted at the beginning of each chapter and each section or part of a section. The practice in the copy-text of beginning the Contents, the Paraphrase, and the Authorized Version text of each section or part of a section with a word or words completely or partially capitalized is disregarded, as is the same practice at the beginning of the Preface and Ephesians. The heading 'Notes', used frequently by Locke, has been silently omitted. Catchwords at the foot of a page or column have not been reproduced, nor has the lineation of the copy-text been preserved. Greek accentuation has been revised to conform to modern printing practice. Italics in the Authorized Version text have been romanized.

Recorded Changes. Any departure from the copy-text, apart from the silent changes mentioned above, has been recorded in the textual notes. The copy-text is adhered to except where it clearly seems to misrepresent Locke's intention. Obvious misspellings have been corrected, in Hebrew, Greek, and Latin as well as in English.

Textual Notes for the Preface, Ephesians, and the Authorized Version Text of all Five Epistles. The textual notes contain a register of the above-mentioned recorded changes for these parts of the work. No attempt is made to collate the copy-text with other editions. The first collected edition (1714) is sometimes mentioned if it supports an editorial reading against the copy-text. The 1703 Authorized Version and the Authorized Version in the first edition of the paraphrase and notes on Galatians are also quoted in support of departures from the copy-text. Accents and breathings of Greek words have been silently regularized in the chosen readings but not in rejected ones.

Signs and Abbreviations used in the Manuscript, Textual, and Explanatory Notes, and in the Text and Appendices

The following signs and abbreviations are used:

L	The Bodleian Manuscript (Galatians, 1 and 2 Corinthians, Romans)
1	The First Edition
2	The Second Edition (Galatians only)
W	The First Collected Edition
1703	*The Holy Bible*, 2 vols. Printed by Charles Bill and the Executrix of Thomas Newcomb, Printers to Queen Anne. London, 1703.
edit.	editorial
ital.	in italic type, or, in the case of the manuscript, underlined
rom.	in roman type, or, in the case of the manuscript, not underlined
alt.	alteration
]	end of quoted expression from text
|	separation sign between annotations of variants
/	end-of-line marker
ˋ ˊ	interlineation and/or marginal insertion
[ ]	deletion
⟦ ⟧	cancellation by superimposition of correction
ạ.	the sign ‘a’ is conjectural and the next sign is indecipherable
⟨ ⟩	editorial insertion
{ }	editorial omission

The upper point ‘·’ is used as an editorial stop.

Editorial comments in manuscript and textual notes are printed in italics. In the textual notes '*edit.*' indicates that the reading is editorial. In cases where the chosen reading diverges from the copy-text but is supported by a printed edition, the abbreviation '*edit.*' is not used, but the reading is silently conformed to the formal characteristics of the copy-text. For example, the textual note on the paraphrase of 1 Cor. VI.8 is:

VI.8 father⟨s⟩] 1 | father L

In this case, although the first edition actually reads 'Fathers', the reading 'fathers' has been adopted in conformity with the formal features of the manuscript. It should also be noted that, in accordance with the same policy, a footnote sign where the inclusion is supported by a printed edition may not be the actual sign found in that edition. Moreover, in the case of a reading which has not been adopted, the textual notes give the formal features found in the first of the authorities quoted in its support.

Occasionally the sign '*1st*' or '*2nd*' precedes a word in the textual notes. These signs indicate the first or second occurrence of the word in the relevant verse or note or section (a, b, c, etc.).

In the manuscript notes the annotation '*no caret*' indicates the absence of a caret beneath an interlineation; but if the interlineation replaces a deletion, the annotation is not used. When an incomplete word is deleted, an attempt is usually made to conjecture the complete word. For example, the manuscript note on 1 Cor. VIII.7, Para., reads:

VIII.7 [ph⟨ansie⟩] imaginations of the phansie

This means that Locke wrote 'ph', intending to complete the word as 'phansie', but deleted the two letters and wrote 'imaginations of the phansie'. A more complex example is the manuscript note on Rom. VII.9, Para., which reads:

VII.9 [s⟦ṭṛẹ⟨ngth⟩⟧ịṇ] sin got life and strength

This means that Locke wrote 'stre', intending to complete the word as 'strength'. He then altered the letters 'tre' to 'in', making the word 'sin'. Next he deleted 'sin' and wrote 'sin got life and strength'. The note also indicates that the letters 'tre' and the alteration of them to 'in' are not completely clear or certain.

When a manuscript note shows a deletion appearing within a deletion, the shorter deletion will have been made before the longer. When a deletion appears within an interlineation, it will have been made after the interlineation. When an interlineation appears within a deletion, it will have been made before the deletion. And when an interlineation appears within an interlineation, it will have been made after the longer one.

The editorial insertion signs ⟨ ⟩ are used to signify the insertion of words, letters, numbers, and footnote signs which are not present in the manuscript. In the parts of the *Paraphrase* where the Bodleian manuscript is the copy-text, the insertion signs are used in the text as well as in editorial notes. The signs [ ] indicate deletions only in manuscript notes. In the text they are Locke's brackets.

Nine of the Appendices to this present edition give transcriptions of material from Locke's papers which is relevant to the study of the *Paraphrase*. The signs and abbreviations used in the transcription of this material and the accompanying manuscript notes are the same as those used in the treatment of the Bodleian manuscript of the *Paraphrase*.

In the explanatory notes of this present edition there are numerous transcriptions of Locke's entries in his interleaved Bible and Testaments and his New Testament notebook. No attempt has been made to give an account of the alterations made by Locke to this material. But occasionally the above-mentioned signs and abbreviations have been introduced to indicate editorial additions, deletions, and conjectures.

The signs and abbreviations used for the manuscript notes of this edition have been derived from those employed by Peter Nidditch in his edition of *Draft A of Locke's Essay Concerning Human Understanding*. The signs and abbreviations used for the textual notes have been derived from those employed by the same editor in his edition of Locke's *Essay*. The principles on which the manuscript and textual notes have been developed are based on those outlined by Nidditch in his introductions to the two works mentioned.[1] These principles have been modified because of the particular needs of this edition of the *Paraphrase*, in which both manuscript and textual notes are provided for the same work. Moreover, no attempt is made to provide a comprehensive record of formal variants for the *Paraphrase*, as Nidditch does for the *Essay*. The textual notes in this present edition contain a record of what Nidditch describes as material variants together with a limited selection of what he describes as formal variants.

[1] Peter H. Nidditch in John Locke, *An Essay Concerning Human Understanding* (Oxford, 1975), pp. xxxvii-liii, and *Draft A of Locke's Essay Concerning Human Understanding* (Sheffield, 1980), pp. 5-20; cf. also his edition of *Draft B of Locke's Essay Concerning Human Understanding* (Sheffield, 1982).

Signs introduced into the Text

The signs 'a', 'b', 'c', etc. have been introduced above the line in certain passages in order to facilitate the process of reference in the manuscript, textual, and explanatory notes. They are purely arbitrary, editorial insertions, made for reference purposes only. They do not indicate the precise words on which a note comments but the passage within which the words are to be found. The signs are only introduced for longer units of material. They are also employed in the Appendices.

In the Preface to the *Paraphrase* a different system of reference signs is used. The letters 'a', 'b', 'c', etc. are used to identify the words on which a textual note comments, and arabic numerals are used to identify the words on which an explanatory note comments.

V. EXPLANATORY NOTES

Explanatory notes, printed at the end of each volume, comment on various matters of interest in the *Paraphrase*. They make available a large amount of the material included by Locke in those parts of his interleaved Bible and Testaments and his notebook which deal with the Epistles to the Galatians, Corinthians, Romans, and Ephesians. Sometimes Locke repeats the material almost verbatim in either his paraphrase or his notes. More often the influence on the wording is limited to a few words. In many cases the thought of Locke's work appears to have been influenced by entries from his interleaved volumes and his notebook, even where there is little or no verbal similarity. At other times an entry is given because it represents a viewpoint from which Locke dissented. Entries which neither support nor dissent from positions taken by Locke are generally not reproduced in these explanatory notes, unless they are of interest because they show that Locke has been studying a writer of special importance.

When an entry is assigned by Locke to a particular writer or book, this fact is mentioned in the explanatory notes. But this is no guarantee that Locke's entry contains a verbatim quotation from the source mentioned. Often, even when the entry is in Latin, it is not an exact quotation. Entries range from verbatim reproductions to summaries in Locke's own words. If an entry has no name attached to it, but is in fact an allusion to an excerpt from a particular author, that fact is mentioned. If no author is mentioned in the explanatory note, it is likely that the entry represents Locke's own views, especially if it consists of a synopsis or introduction for an Epistle. When the letters 'JL' appear in an entry, they usually indicate that he is giving expression to his own opinions.

The explanatory notes also make reference to other writings by Locke, indicating similarities or differences of thought between them and the *Paraphrase*, and also pointing out similarities in the use of language. Reference is made to other writers whose views are likely to have been known to Locke. In this way it is possible to see how on particular points of interpretation he agreed or disagreed with other scholars and theologians who were influential in his day. In writing his *Paraphrase* Locke reflected on many issues which are not mentioned in entries in his interleaved Bible or Testaments or in his notebook. The explanatory notes attempt to illuminate the background to Locke's thought on these matters.

Among the writers frequently mentioned in the explanatory notes are commentators whose works he actually possessed: Erasmus (*Annotationes*),[1] Vorstius, Crellius, Grotius, Hammond, Lightfoot, Walker, Le Clerc, and Whitby. Reference has also been made to commentaries not known to have been possessed by Locke. These writings include Erasmus's *Paraphrases*, Luther's commentary on Galatians,[2] and the commentaries of Calvin and Beza. Since these works were highly influential in sixteenth- and seventeenth-century England, many of the views expressed in them are likely to have been known to Locke, whether or not he had actually read them. When allusion is made to commentaries, it does not follow that he was always directly aware of the writers' opinions on the points under discussion. But it does follow that the interpretations given in those works were current in Locke's day.

VI. REFERENCES

References in this present edition to Locke's paraphrase of particular verses of the Epistles are of the form, 1 Cor. X.16, Para. and Rom. IV.24, Para. References to his notes in the *Paraphrase* are of the form, Rom. VI.2*a and Eph. II.15(*p*)e. 'Contents' passages are referred to not by the section number but by the chapter and verse numbers of the section, e.g. 1 Cor. III.1-IV.20, Contents, c.

[1] Locke had access to this work in his copy of *Critici Sacri*. See above, p. 15.

[2] Of all Luther's commentaries and similar works on the scriptures the one on Galatians (*In Epistolam S. Pauli ad Galatas Commentarius*, 1535) was the best known in Locke's England.

References to Locke's other writings are to E. S. de Beer's edition of his *Correspondence* (1976-), Peter Nidditch's edition of his *Essay Concerning Human Understanding* (1975) and of *Draft A* (1980) and *Draft B* (1982) of that Essay, Wolfgang von Leyden's edition of his *Essays on the Law of Nature* (1954), John C. Biddle's edition of his paper on 'Infallibility' (1977), Philip Abrams's edition of his *Two Tracts on Government* (1967), Peter Laslett's second edition of his *Two Treatises of Government* (1967), and the twelfth edition of his *Works* (1824). 'MS Locke' refers to his papers in the Bodleian Library.

Corr. is an abbreviation for Correspondence, and *Essay* for *Essay Concerning Human Understanding*. 'LL no.' indicates the number of a work in the catalogue of books owned by Locke, compiled by John Harrison and Peter Laslett, *The Library of John Locke*.

When the views of commentators are mentioned, page numbers are not usually recorded. Unless it is otherwise stated, their views are to be found in their comments on the passage under discussion. When a writer is responsible for more than one work on an Epistle, the following abbreviations are used. Erasmus (*Ann.*) refers to that writer's *Annotationes*, and Erasmus (*Para.*) to his *Paraphrases*. As far as Galatians, Romans, and Ephesians are concerned, Crellius (*Comm.*) refers to his *Commentarius*, and Crellius (*Para.*) to his *Paraphrasis*. Since Crellius wrote a commentary but no paraphrase on 1 Corinthians, no such distinction has to be made for his work on that Epistle. It should be noted that Crellius's commentary on Galatians was based on his spoken lectures and actually written by Jonas Schlichtingius. Le Clerc (*Supp.*) refers to his *A Supplement to Dr. Hammond's Annotations on the New Testament*, and Le Clerc (NT) to his *Le Nouveau Testament*. Whitby (*Add.*) refers to his *Additional Annotations to the New Testament*, while the simple allusion 'Whitby' refers to the first edition of his *A Paraphrase and Commentary on all the Epistles of the New Testament*. References to Lightfoot, unless otherwise stated, are to his *Horae Hebraicae et Talmudicae* (*Hebrew and Talmudical Exercitations*) on the passage under discussion.

References to Henry Hammond's *Paraphrase and Annotations* are to the 1845 edition; those to Obadiah Walker's *Paraphrase and Annotations* are to the 1702 edition; and those to the *Racovian Catechism* are to Thomas Rees's translation. For the problem of identifying the source of the references to Pierre Allix, see above, p. 14.

LL nos. 309, 2862, 2864 are Locke's interleaved volumes. MS Locke f. 30 is his notebook. See Appendix X.

BIBLIOGRAPHY

THE works listed in this bibliography are those to which reference has been made in this edition of the *Paraphrase*. If a work is included by Harrison and Laslett, *The Library of John Locke*, in their catalogue of works owned by him, its number in that catalogue is given below, prefixed by the abbreviation 'LL no.'.

AARON, RICHARD I. *John Locke*. 3rd edn. Oxford, 1971.

AARSLEFF, HANS. 'The State of Nature and the Nature of Man in Locke.' In *John Locke: Problems and Perspectives*, pp. 99-136. Edited by John W. Yolton. Cambridge, 1969.

ABRAMS, PHILIP. *See* Locke, John, *Two Tracts on Government*.

AINSWORTH, HENRY. *Annotations upon the Five Bookes of Moses, the Booke of the Psalmes, and the Song of Songs*. London, 1639. LL no. 41.

ALLESTREE, RICHARD. *See* Walker, Obadiah.

BARNES, ANNIE. *Jean Le Clerc (1657–1736) et la République des Lettres*. Paris, 1938.

BARRINGTON, JOHN SHUTE, first Viscount Barrington. *Miscellanea Sacra*. 2 vols. London, 1725.

BAUMGARTEN, SIEGMUND JAKOB. *Auslegung der beiden Briefe an die Korinther*. Halle, 1761.

—— *Auslegung der Epistel an die Römer*. Halle, 1749.

—— *See Nachrichten von merkwürdigen Büchern*.

—— *See* Peirce, James, *Paraphrasis*.

BAXTER, RICHARD. *A Paraphrase on the New Testament, with Notes Doctrinal and Practical*. London, 1685.

BAYLE, PIERRE. *Dictionaire historique et critique*. 4 vols. Rotterdam, 1697. LL no. 237.

BEER, E. S. DE. *See* Locke, John, *Correspondence*.

BENSON, GEORGE. *A Paraphrase and Notes on St. Paul's Epistle to Philemon. Attempted in Imitation of Mr. Locke's Manner*. London, 1731.

—— *A Paraphrase and Notes on St. Paul's Ist Epistle to the Thessalonians. In Imitation of Mr. Locke's Manner*. London, 1731.

—— *A Paraphrase and Notes on St. Paul's IId Epistle to the Thessalonians. In Imitation of Mr. Locke's Manner*. London, 1732.

—— *A Paraphrase and Notes on the Epistles of St. Paul to Philemon, Ist Thessalonians, IId Thessalonians, Ist Timothy, Titus, IId Timothy. Attempted in Imitation of Mr. Locke's Manner*. London, 1734.

—— *A Paraphrase and Notes on the Seven (Commonly Called) Catholic Epistles . . . Attempted in Imitation of Mr. Locke's Manner*. London, 1749.

BENSON, GEORGE. *Paraphrasis et Notae Philologicae atque Exegeticae in Epistolam S. Iacobi*. Translated and edited by J. D. Michaelis. Preface by S. J. Baumgarten. Halle, 1746.

—— *Paraphrastische Erklärung und Anmerkungen einiger Bücher des Neuen Testaments*. Leipzig, 1761.

BEZA, THEODORE. *Annotations Maiores in Novum Domini Nostri Jesu Christi Testamentum*. New and revised edn. 1594.

Bibliothèque choisie. Edited by Jean Le Clerc. 27 vols. and index vol. Amsterdam, 1703-13, 1718.

Bibliothèque universelle et historique. Edited by Jean Le Clerc. 25 vols. and index vol. Amsterdam, 1686-93, 1718. For vols. i-xxiv see LL no. 332.

BIDDLE, JOHN. *The Apostolical and True Opinion Concerning the Holy Trinity*. London, 1691. LL no. 336.

—— *The Faith of One God . . . Asserted and Defended in Several Tracts*. London, 1691 (described also by Locke as *Doctrin in Several Peices*). LL no. 3007.

BIDDLE, JOHN C. *John Locke on Christianity: his Context and Text*. Ann Arbor, Mich., 1972.

—— 'John Locke's Essay on Infallibility: Introduction, Text and Translation.' *Journal of Church and State*, xix (1977). 301-27.

BIRCH, THOMAS. *The Life of Mrs. Catharine Cockburn*. In Catharine Cockburn, *Works*, i, pp. i-xlviii. London, 1751.

BLOUNT, CHARLES. *Miscellaneous Works*. London, 1695. LL no. 353.

BOLD, SAMUEL. *Some Considerations on the Principal Objections and Arguments which have been Publish'd against Mr. Locke's Essay*. London, 1699. LL no. 384.

BOLINGBROKE, HENRY ST. JOHN, first Viscount. *The Philosophical Works*. 5 vols. London, 1754-77.

BOSSUET, JACQUES BÉNIGNE. *Doctrinae Catholicae . . . Expositio*. Antwerp, 1678. LL no. 398.

BOYLE, ROBERT. *Some Considerations Touching the Style of the Holy Scriptures*. London, 1661.

BROWN, JERRY WAYNE. *The Rise of Biblical Criticism in America 1800–1870*. Middletown, Conn., 1965.

BURNET, THOMAS. *Remarks upon an Essay Concerning Humane Understanding*. London, 1697. LL no. 1794.

—— *Second Remarks upon an Essay Concerning Humane Understanding*. London, 1697. LL no. 1795.

—— *The Theory of the Earth*. 2 vols. London, 1684. Vol. i, LL no. 534.

—— *Third Remarks upon an Essay Concerning Humane Understanding*. London, 1699. LL no. 1799.

BURNS, NORMAN T. *Christian Mortalism from Tyndale to Milton*. Cambridge, Mass., 1972.

BURTHOGGE, RICHARD. *Christianity a Revealed Mystery*. London, 1702. LL no. 542.

—— *An Essay upon Reason, and the Nature of Spirits*. London, 1694. LL no. 538.

—— *Of the Soul of the World; and of Particular Souls*. London, 1699. LL no. 541.

CALVIN, JOHN. *Corpus Reformatorum*. Vols. lxxvii-lxxxiii: *Commentarii in*

Epistolas Novi Testamenti. Sermons sur divers textes des Épîtres du Nouveau Testament. Brunswick, 1892-6.

—— *Institutio Christianae Religionis*. Geneva, 1585, LL no. 570; edited by Theodore Beza, Leyden, 1654, LL no. 571.

CAPPELLUS, JACOBUS. *Observationes in Novum Testamentum*. Amsterdam, 1657. LL no. 581.

CAPPELLUS, LUDOVICUS. *Historia Apostolica*. Amsterdam, 1657. LL no. 581.

—— *Spicilegium post Messem*. Amsterdam, 1657. LL no. 583.

Catechesis Ecclesiarum Polonicarum. Irenopolis, sc. Amsterdam, 1659, LL no. 878; Stauropolis, sc. Amsterdam, 1680, LL no. 879.

CHANNING, WILLIAM ELLERY. *Works*. Boston, Mass., 1896.

CHILLINGWORTH, WILLIAM. *The Religion of Protestants*. 4th edn. London, 1674, LL no. 685; 5th edn. London, 1684, LL no. 686.

CHRISTOPHERSEN, H. O. *A Bibliographical Introduction to the Study of John Locke*. Oslo, 1930.

CLAGETT, WILLIAM. *Eleven Sermons . . . And a Paraphrase with Notes upon the First, Second, Third, Fourth, Fifth, Seventh, and Eighth Chapters of St. John*. London, 1693.

—— *A Paraphrase, with Notes, and a Preface, upon the Sixth Chapter of St. John*. London, 1686.

CLARKE, SAMUEL. *A Paraphrase on the Gospel of St. John*. London, 1703. LL no. 734.

—— *A Paraphrase on the Gospel of St. Matthew*. London, 1701. LL no. 732.

—— *A Paraphrase on the Gospels of St. Mark and St. Luke*. London, 1702. LL no. 733.

COCKBURN (*née* TROTTER), CATHARINE. *A Defence of the Essay of Human Understanding*. London, 1702. LL no. 1801.

—— *Works*. Edited by Thomas Birch. 2 vols. London, 1751.

COKE, THOMAS. *A Commentary on the Holy Bible*. 6 vols. London, 1801-3.

COLLINS, ANTHONY. Letters to Pierre Desmaizeaux. British Library Add. MS 4282, fos. 159, 192.

The Confession of Faith together with the Larger and Lesser Catechisms Composed by the Reverend Assembly of Divines Sitting at Westminster. 3rd edn. London, 1688. LL no. 140.

COOLE, BENJAMIN. *Some Brief Observations on the Paraphrase and Notes of the Judicious John Locke relating to the Women's Exercising their Spiritual Gifts in the Church*. Cited in Josiah Martin, *A Letter to the Author of Some Brief Observations*, London, 1716.

—— *Reflections on a Letter to the Author of Some Brief Observations*. London, 1717.

CRADOCK, SAMUEL. *A Brief and Plain Exposition and Paraphrase of the Whole of the Book of the Revelation*. London, 1696.

CRANSTON, MAURICE. *John Locke: a Biography*. London, 1957.

CRELLIUS, JOHANNES. *Liber de Deo et eius Attributis et . . . de Uno Deo Patre Libri Duo*. Amsterdam?, 1642? LL no. 877.

—— *Opera Omnia Exegetica*. 2 vols. in 1. Eleutheropolis, sc. Amsterdam, 1656. LL no. 876.

CRIPPA, ROMEO. *Studi sulla coscienza etica e religiosa del Seicento. Esperienza e libertà in J. Locke*. Milan, 1960.

Critici Sacri. 9 vols. London, 1668; new edn. 9 vols. Amsterdam, 1698, LL no. 886.

CROUS, ERNST. *Die religionsphilosophischen Lehren Lockes und ihre Stellung zu dem Deismus seiner Zeit*. Halle, 1910.

CUDWORTH, RALPH. *A Discourse Concerning the True Notion of the Lords Supper*. 3rd edn. London, 1676. LL no. 897.

—— *The True Intellectual System of the Universe*. London, 1678. LL no. 896.

CURCELLAEUS, STEPHANUS. *Opera Theologica*. Amsterdam, 1675. LL no. 902.

DAY, WILLIAM. *A Paraphrase and Commentary upon the Epistle of Saint Paul to the Romans*. London, 1666.

DESCARTES, RENÉ. *Opera Philosophica*. 3rd edn. Amsterdam, 1658. LL no. 601a.

DIEU, LUDOVICUS DE. *Animadversiones*. Leyden, 1646.

—— *Critica Sacra*. Amsterdam, 1693.

DODDRIDGE, PHILIP. *The Family Expositor*. 6 vols. London, 1739-56.

DUNN, JOHN. *The Political Thought of John Locke*. Cambridge, 1969.

EDWARDS, JOHN. *Socinianism Unmask'd*. London, 1696. LL no. 1026.

—— *Some Thoughts Concerning the Several Causes and Occasions of Atheism*. London, 1695. LL no. 1024.

EPISCOPIUS, SIMON. *Opera Theologica*, 2nd edn. 2 vols. London, 1678. LL no. 1060.

ERASMUS, DESIDERIUS. *Opera Omnia*. Edited by Jean Le Clerc. 10 vols. in 11. Leyden, 1703-6. Vol. vi: *Novum Testamentum ... cui subjectae sunt singulis paginis Annotationes*. Vol. vii: *Paraphrases in Novum Testamentum*.

EUSEBIUS PAMPHILI. *Ecclesiastica Historia*. Paris, 1659. LL no. 1076. (Often entitled *Historia Ecclesiastica*.)

FELL, JOHN. (Ed.) *Novi Testamenti Libri Omnes*. Oxford, 1675. LL no. 2865.

—— *See* Walker, Obadiah.

FELTON, HENRY. *The Resurrection of the Same Numerical Body, and its Reunion to the Same Soul*. Oxford, 1725.

FILMER, Sir ROBERT. *Patriarcha*. London, 1680. LL no. 1122.

—— *Patriarcha and Other Political Works*. Edited by Peter Laslett. Oxford, 1949.

FLEETWOOD, WILLIAM. *An Essay upon Miracles*. London, 1701. LL no. 1140.

FOSTER, HERBERT D. *Collected Papers*. New York, 1929.

FOWLER, EDWARD. *The Principles and Practices of Certain Moderate Divines of the Church of England*. 2nd edn. London, 1671 (described by Locke as *The principles and practices of Latitudinarians*). LL no. 1163.

FOX, ADAM. *John Mill and Richard Bentley*. Oxford, 1954.

FOX BOURNE, H. R. *The Life of John Locke*. 2 vols. London, 1876.

FRASER, ALEXANDER CAMPBELL. *Locke*. Edinburgh and London, 1890.

GODEAU, ANTOINE. *Paraphrase sur les Épistres de Saint Paul et sur les Épistres Canoniques*. New edn. Paris, 1650.

GODWIN, THOMAS. *Moses and Aaron. Civil and Ecclesiastical Rites Used by the Ancient Hebrews*. 7th edn. London, 1655. LL no. 1281a.

Grallae. Franeker, 1646. LL no. 1306.

GROTIUS, HUGO. *Annotationes in Novum Testamentum*. Vol. ii. Paris, 1646 (described by Locke as *Annotationes in Acta Apostolorum et Epistolas Apostolicas*). LL no. 1337.

—— *Defensio Fidei Catholicae de Satisfactione Christi*. Leyden, 1617.

HAMMOND, HENRY. *Of Fundamentals in a Notion referring to Practise*. London, 1654.

—— *Novum Testamentum... cum Paraphrasi et Annotationibus*. Translated with notes by Jean Le Clerc. 2 vols. Amsterdam, 1698-9. LL no. 1382.

—— *A Paraphrase and Annotations upon all the Books of the New Testament*. London, 1653; new edn. 4 vols. Oxford, 1845.

—— *A Practical Catechisme*. Oxford, 1645.

HAMPTON, BENJAMIN. *The Existence of the Human Soul after Death*. London, 1711.

HARRISON, JOHN and LASLETT, PETER. *The Library of John Locke*. 2nd edn. Oxford, 1971.

HEFELBLOWER, S. G. *The Relation of John Locke to English Deism*. Chicago, 1918.

HELMONT, FRANCISCUS MERCURIUS VAN. *Seder Olam, sive Ordo Seculorum*. Leyden?, 1693. LL no. 1416a.

HERBERT, EDWARD, first Baron Herbert of Cherbury. *De Veritate*. Paris, 1624.

HERTLING, GEORG FREIHERR VON. *John Locke und die Schule von Cambridge*. Freiburg im Breisgau, 1892.

HIGGINS-BIDDLE, JOHN C. *See* Biddle, John C.

HILL, CHRISTOPHER. *Antichrist in Seventeenth-Century England*. London, 1971.

—— *Milton and the English Revolution*. London, 1977.

The History of the Works of the Learned. 13 vols. London, 1699-1712; 14 vols. London, 1737-43.

HOBBES, THOMAS. *Leviathan*. London, 1651. LL no. 1465.

—— *The Questions Concerning Liberty, Necessity, Chance*. London, 1656.

HOLDSWORTH, WINCH. *A Defence of the Doctrine of the Resurrection of the Same Body*. London, 1727.

—— *A Sermon Preached... on Easter Monday, 1719*. Oxford, 1720.

HORATIUS FLACCUS, Q. *Œuvres en latin et en françois avec des remarques critiques et historiques par M. Dacier*. 10 vols. Paris, 1691. LL no. 1505.

JENKIN, ROBERT. *Remarks on Some Books Lately Publish'd. viz. Mr. Basnage's History of the Jews. Mr. Whiston's Eight Sermons. Mr. Locke's Paraphrase and Notes on St. Paul's Epistles. Mr. Le Clerc's Bibliothèque Choisie*. London, 1709.

JOHNSON, MERWYN S. *Locke on Freedom*. Austin, Texas, 1978.

Journal de Trévoux (ou Mémoires pour l'histoire des sciences et des beaux-arts). Trévoux and Paris, 1701-67.

KELLEY, MAURICE. *See* Milton, John, *The Complete Prose Works*.

KEMP, J. *Reason, Action and Morality*. London, 1964.

KING, PETER, first Lord King, Baron of Ockham. *An Enquiry into the Constitution, Discipline, Unity, and Worship... of the Primitive Church*. London, 1691. LL no. 1636.

KING, PETER, first Lord King, Baron of Ockham. *The History of the Apostles Creed with Critical Observations on its Several Articles*. London, 1702. LL no. 1637.

KING, PETER, seventh Lord King, Baron of Ockham. *The Life and Letters of John Locke*. New edn. London, 1858.

KNATCHBULL, Sir NORTON. *Animadversiones in Libros Novi Testamenti*. 3rd edn. Oxford, 1677. LL no. 1645.

KÜMMEL, WERNER GEORG. *The New Testament: the History of the Investigation of its Problems*. Translated by S. McLean Gilmour and Howard C. Kee. Nashville and New York, 1972.

KUTSCH, E. 'Kapitel- und Verseinteilung in der Bibel.' *Die Religion in Geschichte und Gegenwart*. 3rd edn. Tübingen, 1956-65, iii. 1141-2.

LAMPRECHT, STERLING P. *The Moral and Political Philosophy of John Locke*. New York, 1918.

LARDNER, NATHANAEL. *Works*. 10 vols. London, 1838.

LASLETT, PETER. *See* Filmer, Sir Robert, *Patriarcha and Other Political Works*.

—— *See* Harrison, John, and Laslett, Peter.

—— *See* Locke, John, *Two Treatises of Government*.

LECHLER, GOTTHARD VICTOR. *Geschichte des englischen Deismus*. Stuttgart and Tübingen, 1841.

LE CLERC, JEAN. *Ars Critica*. 2 vols. Amsterdam, 1697. LL no. 769.

—— *Défense des sentimens de quelques théologiens de Hollande sur l'histoire critique du Vieux Testament*. Amsterdam, 1686. LL no. 755.

—— *The Harmony of the Evangelists*. London, 1701. LL no. 775.

—— *Le Nouveau Testament . . . traduit sur l'original grec. Avec des remarques . . . par Jean Le Clerc*. 2 vols. Amsterdam, 1703. LL no. 2879.

—— Letters to Pierre Desmaizeaux. British Library Add. MS 4282, fo. 107.

—— *Sentimens de quelques théologiens de Hollande sur l'histoire critique du Vieux Testament*. Amsterdam, 1685. LL no. 754.

—— *A Supplement to Dr Hammond's Paraphrase and Annotations on the New Testament*. London, 1699. LL no. 772.

—— *See Bibliothèque choisie*.

—— *See Bibliothèque universelle et historique*.

—— *See* Erasmus, Desiderius, *Opera Omnia*.

—— *See* Hammond, Henry, *Novum Testamentum*, etc.

LE MOYNE, STEPHANUS. *Varia Sacra*. 2 vols. Leyden, 1685. LL no. 2061.

LEYDEN, WOLFGANG VON. *See* Locke, John, *Essays on the Law of Nature*.

LIGHTFOOT, JOHN. *Horae Hebraicae et Talmudicae. Impensae I. In Chorographiam . . . II. In Evangelium S. Matthaei*. Cambridge, 1658. LL no. 1747a.

—— *Horae Hebraicae et Talmudicae Impensae in Epistolam Primam S. Pauli ad Corinthios*. Paris, 1677. LL no. 1747.

—— *Opera Omnia*. 2 vols. Rotterdam, 1686. LL no. 1745.

—— *Works*. 2 vols. London, 1684. LL no. 1748.

LIGHTFOOT, JOSEPH BARBER. *Saint Paul's Epistle to the Galatians*. 10th edn. London, 1890.

LIMBORCH, PHILIP VAN. *Theologia Christiana*. Amsterdam, 1686. LL no. 1754; 2nd edn. Amsterdam, 1695. LL no. 1757.

LOCKE, JOHN. *The Correspondence of John Locke*. Edited by E. S. de Beer. 8 vols. Oxford, 1976- .

—— *Draft A of Locke's Essay Concerning Human Understanding*. Edited by Peter H. Nidditch. Sheffield, 1980.

—— *Draft B of Locke's Essay Concerning Human Understanding*. Edited by Peter H. Nidditch. Sheffield, 1982.

—— *An Essay Concerning Human Understanding*. Edited by Peter H. Nidditch. Oxford, 1975. Paperback edn. Oxford, 1979.

—— *An Essay for the Understanding of St. Paul's Epistles, by Consulting St. Paul Himself*. London, 1707.

—— *Essays on the Law of Nature*. Translated and edited by Wolfgang von Leyden. Oxford, 1954.

—— 'Infallibility'. *See* Biddle, John C., 'John Locke's Essay on Infallibility: Introduction, Text, and Translation'.

—— Manuscripts. References to MS Locke are to the collection of Locke's papers in the Bodleian Library.

—— *Œuvres diverses de M. Locke*. New edn. 2 vols. Amsterdam, 1732.

—— *Over den brief van Paulus aan de Romeinen*. Amsterdam, 1768.

—— *A Paraphrase and Notes on the Epistle of St. Paul to the Ephesians*. London, 1707.

—— *A Paraphrase and Notes on the Epistle of St. Paul to the Galatians*. London, 1705; 2nd edn. London, 1706; 3rd edn. London, 1708; another 3rd edn. London, 1718.

—— *A Paraphrase and Notes on the Epistle of St. Paul to the Romans*. London, 1707.

—— *A Paraphrase and Notes on the Epistles of St. Paul to the Galatians, I and II Corinthians, Romans, Ephesians, To which is Prefix'd, an Essay for the Understanding of St. Paul's Epistles, by Consulting St. Paul Himself*. London, 1707; 2nd edn. London, 1709. For details of the contents of these editions see Introduction, pp. 8-9. Further editions of the work were published in England and Ireland during the eighteenth century. An American edition was published in Cambridge, Mass., in 1832.

—— *A Paraphrase and Notes on the First Epistle of St. Paul to the Corinthians*. London, 1706; another edn. London, 1718.

—— *A Paraphrase and Notes on the Second Epistle of St. Paul to the Corinthians*. London, 1706.

—— *Paraphrase des Briefes Pauli an die Römer*. Frankfurt and Leipzig, 1773.

—— *Paraphrastische Erklärung und Anmerkungen über S. Pauli Briefe an die Galater, Korinther, Römer und Epheser*. Translated and edited by J. G. Hofmann. Preface by J. D. Michaelis. Frankfurt am Main, 1768-9.

—— *Saggio su l'intendimento delle Epistole di S. Paolo*. Translated with introductory note by Francesco A. Ferrari. Lanciano, 1919.

—— *Two Tracts on Government*. Translated and edited by Philip Abrams. Cambridge, 1967.

—— *Two Treatises of Government*. Edited by Peter Laslett. 2nd edn. Cambridge, 1967.

—— *Works*. 3 vols. London, 1714; 12th edn. 9 vols. London, 1824.

LONG, PHILIP. *A Summary Catalogue of the Lovelace Collection of the Papers of John Locke in the Bodleian Library* (Oxford Bibliographical Society Publications, new series, vol. viii). Oxford, 1959.

LORD, HENRY. *A Display of Two Forraigne Sects in the East Indies*. London, 1630. LL no. 1807.

LUPTON, WILLIAM. *The Resurrection of the Same Body*. Oxford, 1711.

LUTHER, MARTIN. *Werke*. Vol. xl, pt. i (Weimar, 1911), pp. 1-691; pt. ii (Weimar, 1914), pp. 1-181: *In Epistolam S. Pauli ad Galatas Commentarius* (1535).

MCGIFFERT, A. C. *Protestant Thought before Kant*. New York, 1911.

MACKNIGHT, JAMES. *A New Literal Translation from the Original Greek of all the Apostolical Epistles, with a Commentary, and Notes, Philological, Critical, Explanatory, and Practical*. 2nd edn. 3 vols. Edinburgh, 1795.

MCLACHLAN, H. *The Religious Opinions of Milton, Locke, and Newton*. Manchester, 1941.

MCLACHLAN, H. JOHN. *Socinianism in Seventeenth Century England*. London, 1951.

MACLEAN, KENNETH. *John Locke and English Literature of the Eighteenth Century*. New Haven, Conn., 1936.

MANUEL, FRANK E. *A Portrait of Isaac Newton*. Revised edn. Cambridge, Mass., 1979.

MARTIN, JOSIAH. *A Letter to the Author of Some Brief Observations*. London, 1716.

—— *A Vindication of Women's Preaching, as well from Holy Scripture and Antient Writings as from the Paraphrase and Notes of the Judicious John Locke*. London, 1717.

MEDE, JOSEPH. *Works*. 2 vols. London, 1664. LL no. 1952.

Mémoires pour l'histoire des sciences et des beaux-arts. See *Journal de Trévoux*.

METZGER, BRUCE M. *The Text of the New Testament*. 2nd edn. Oxford, 1968.

MEYER, HEINRICH AUGUST WILHELM. *Kritisch-exegetischer Kommentar über das Neue Testament*. Göttingen, 1832-59.

MILNER, JOHN. *An Account of Mr. Lock's Religion*. London, 1700. LL no. 1802b.

MILTON, JOHN. *The Complete Prose Works of John Milton*. Edited by Maurice Kelley. New Haven, Conn., 1953- .

—— *Paradise Lost*. London, 1669. LL no. 1993.

MORE, HENRY. *Opera Omnia*. 3 vols. London, 1675-9.

Nachrichten von merkwürdigen Büchern. Edited by Siegmund Jakob Baumgarten. 20 vols. Halle, 1748-58.

NAPIER, JOHN. *A Plaine Discovery of the Whole Revelation of Saint John*. Edinburgh, 1593.

NEWTON, Sir ISAAC. *The Correspondence of Isaac Newton*. Edited by H. W. Turnbull, J. F. Scott, A. Rupert Hall, and Laura Tilling. 7 vols. Cambridge, 1959-77.

NIDDITCH, PETER H. *See* Locke, John, *Draft A*, etc.

—— *See* Locke, John, *Draft B*, etc.

—— *See* Locke, John, *Essay Concerning Human Understanding*.

Nouvelles de la République des Lettres. Amsterdam, 1684-1710, 1716-18. (For some vols. see LL no. 2099.)

NYE, STEPHEN. *The Agreement of the Unitarians with the Catholic Church*. London, 1697. LL no. 3021.

O'HIGGINS, JAMES. *Anthony Collins, the Man and his Works*. The Hague, 1970.

PAHL, GRETCHEN GRAF. 'John Locke as Literary Critic and Biblical Interpreter', in *Essays Critical and Historical Dedicated to Lily B. Campbell*. Berkeley and Los Angeles, 1950, pp. 137-57, 270-3.

PALEY, WILLIAM. *A View of the Evidences of Early Christianity in Three Parts; and the Horae Paulinae*. Cambridge, 1849.

PASCAL, BLAISE. *Pensées*. Lyons, 1675, LL no. 2222a; new edn. Paris, 1678, LL no. 2222.

PATRICK, SIMON. *Jesus and the Resurrection Justified by Witnesses in Heaven and in Earth*. 2 vols. London, 1677. LL no. 2235.

PEARSON, JOHN. *Opera Posthuma Chronologica*. London, 1688. LL no. 2243.

PEIRCE, JAMES. *A Paraphrase and Notes on the Epistle of St. Paul to the Colossians. With an Appendix upon Ephesians iv. 8*. London, 1725.

—— *A Paraphrase and Notes on the Epistle of St. Paul to the Philippians. To which are added Two Dissertations: one on Gal. iv. 21–v. 1; the other on Matt. ii. 13–15*. London, 1725.

—— *A Paraphrase and Notes on the Epistles of St. Paul to the Colossians, Philippians, and Hebrews: after the Manner of Mr. Locke . . . with a Paraphrase and Notes on the Three Last Chapters of the Hebrews . . . by Joseph Hallett, Jr*. London, 1733.

—— *Paraphrasis et Notae Philologicae atque Exegeticae in Epistolam ad Hebraeos*. Translated and edited by J. D. Michaelis. Halle, 1747.

POOLE, MATTHEW. *Synopsis Criticorum*. 5 vols. London, 1669-76. LL no. 2369.

POPPLE, WILLIAM. *A Rational Catechism*. London, 1687.

PRIESTLEY, JOSEPH. *The Theological and Miscellaneous Works*. 25 vols. in 26. London, 1817-32.

The Racovian Catechism. Translated and edited by Thomas Rees. London, 1818. A translation of *Catechesis Ecclesiarum Polonicarum*, Stauropolis sc. Amsterdam, 1680.

RAWES, WILLIAM. *The Gospel Ministry of Women, under the Christian Dispensation, Defended from the Scripture and from the Writings of John Locke, Josiah Martin*, etc. London, 1801.

REES, THOMAS. *See The Racovian Catechism*.

REVENTLOW, HENNING GRAF. *Bibelautorität und Geist der Moderne*. Göttingen, 1980.

Sacrosancti et Oecumenici Concilii Tridentini . . . Canones et Decreta. Cologne, 1615. LL no. 2981.

SALVATORELLI, LUIGI. 'From Locke to Reitzenstein. The Historical Investigation of the Origins of Christianity.' *Harvard Theological Review*, xxii (1929), 263-369.

SARRAU, CLAUDE. *Epistolae*. Orange, 1654.

SCAINO, ANTONIO. *Paraphrasis in Omnes S. Pauli Epistolas, cum Adnotationibus*. Venice, 1589.

SCHMID, SEBASTIAN. *In Divi Pauli ad Colossenses Epistolae* [sic] *Commentatio . . . Paraphrases in Capita VII–XI Epistolae ad Romanos* etc. Hamburg, 1696.

SCHOULS, PETER A. *The Imposition of Method. A Study of Descartes and Locke*. Oxford, 1980.

SCOTT, THOMAS. *The Holy Bible*. 6 vols. New York, 1810-12.

SELDEN, JOHN. *Table-Talk*. 2nd edn. London, 1696. LL no. 2609.

SIMON, RICHARD. *Histoire critique des principaux commentateurs du Nouveau Testament*. Rotterdam, 1693 (described by Locke as *Histoire Critique du Nouveau Testament Tom. 3*). LL no. 2677.

—— *Histoire critique des versions du Nouveau Testament*. Rotterdam, 1690 (described by Locke as *Histoire Critique du Nouveau Testament Tom. 2*). LL no. 2676.

—— *Histoire critique du texte du Nouveau Testament*. Rotterdam, 1689 (described by Locke as *Histoire Critique du Nouveau Testament Tom. 1*). LL no. 2675.

—— *Histoire critique du Vieux Testament*. Paris, 1680, LL no. 2673a; new edn. Rotterdam, 1685, LL no. 2673.

SOCINUS, FAUSTUS. *Opera Omnia*. 2 vols. Irenopolis, sc. Amsterdam, 1656. LL no. 2712.

SPENCER, JOHN. *De Legibus Hebraeorum Ritualibus et earum Rationibus*. Cambridge, 1685. LL no. 2740.

SPINOZA, BARUCH. *Tractatus Theologico-Politicus*. Amsterdam, 1674. LL no. 2743.

STILES, EZRA. *The Literary Diary of Ezra Stiles*. 3 vols. New York, 1901.

STILLINGFLEET, EDWARD. *An Answer to Mr. Cressy's Epistle Apologetical*. London, 1675.

—— *The Bishop of Worcester's Answer to Mr Lockes Second Letter*. London, 1698. LL no. 2790.

STUART, MOSES. *A Commentary on the Epistle to the Romans*. Andover, Mass., 1832.

TAYLOR, JEREMY. *Ductor Dubitantium*. 2 vols. London, 1660.

—— *Works*. 15 vols. London, 1839.

TAYLOR, JOHN. *A Paraphrase with Notes on the Epistle to the Romans*. London, 1745.

—— *The Scripture Doctrine of Original Sin*. London, 1740.

THOLUCK, FRIEDRICH AUGUST GOTTREU. *Auslegung des Briefes Pauli an die Römer*. Berlin, 1824.

THOMAS, CECIL K. *Alexander Campbell and his New Version*. St. Louis, 1958.

TILLOTSON, JOHN. *Sermons*. 4 vols. London, 1688-94. LL no. 2910.

—— *Works*. 3 vols. London, 1752.

TOLAND, JOHN. *Christianity Not Mysterious*. London, 1696. LL no. 2935.

TROTTER, CATHARINE. *See* Cockburn, Catharine.

TUCK, RICHARD. *Natural Rights Theories, their Origin and Development*. Cambridge, 1979.

TULLY, JAMES. *A Discourse on Property*. Cambridge, 1980.

TURRETIN, JEAN ALPHONSE. *Opera Omnia*. 3 vols. Leeuwarden and Franeker, 1774-6.

USSHER, JAMES. *Annales Veteris et Novi Testamenti*. 3rd edn. Bremen, 1686. LL no. 3028.

VITRINGA, CAMPEGIUS. *De Synagoga Vetere*. Franeker, 1696. LL no. 3098.

VOLKELIUS, JOHANNES. *De Vera Religione*. Amsterdam?, 1642? LL no. 3103.

VORSTIUS, CONRADUS. *Commentarius in Epistolas Apostolicas*. Amsterdam, 1631. LL no. 3106.

VOSSIUS, ISAAC. *Appendix ad Librum de LXX Interpretibus*. The Hague, 1663. LL no. 3114.

WALKER, OBADIAH. *A Paraphrase and Annotations upon all St Pauls Epistles*. 'Done by Several Eminent Men at Oxford. Corrected and Improved by the late Right Reverend and Learned Bishop Fell.' 3rd edn. London, 1702, LL no. 1103; another edn. edited by W. Jacobson, Oxford, 1852. (A 1708 edition ascribes the work to Abraham Woodhead, Richard Allestree, and Obadiah Walker.)

WALTON, BRIAN (ed.). *Biblia Sacra Polyglotta*. 6 vols. London, 1655-7. LL no. 324.

WAPLE, EDWARD. *The Book of the Revelation Paraphrased*. London, 1693.

WATSON, RICHARD. *Works*. 13 vols. London, 1846.

WATTS, ISAAC. *Horae Lyricae*. 3rd edn. London, 1715.

Westminster Confession. See *The Confession of Faith*, etc.

WETTSTEIN, JOHANN JACOB. (ed.) *Novum Testamentum Graecum*. 2 vols. Amsterdam, 1751-2.

WHISTON, WILLIAM. *An Essay on the Revelation of Saint John*. Cambridge, 1706.

—— *Sermons and Essays upon Several Subjects*. London, 1709.

WHITBY, DANIEL. *A Paraphrase and Commentary on all the Epistles of the New Testament*. London, 1700. LL no. 3149.

—— *A Paraphrase and Commentary on the New Testament*. 2 vols. London, 1703. LL no. 3150.

—— *Additional Annotations to the New Testament*. London, 1710.

WILBUR, EARL MORSE. *A History of Unitarianism in Transylvania, England, and America*. Boston, Mass., 1964.

WILLIAMS, GEORGE H. *The Radical Reformation*. Philadelphia, 1962.

WOLF, JOHANN CHRISTOPH. *Curae Philologicae et Criticae*. 4 vols. Hamburg, 1737-41.

WOLLE, CHRISTOPH. *Commentatio Philologica de Parenthesi Sacra*. Leipzig, 1726.

WOODHEAD, ABRAHAM. *See* Walker, Obadiah.

WRIGHT, CONRAD. *The Liberal Christians: Essays on American Unitarian History*. Boston, Mass., 1970.

YOLTON, JOHN W. *Locke and the Compass of the Human Understanding*. Cambridge, 1970.

YOLTON, JOHN W. (ed.). *John Locke: Problems and Perspectives*. Cambridge, 1969.

A PARAPHRASE AND NOTES ON THE EPISTLES OF ST PAUL TO THE GALATIANS, 1 AND 2 CORINTHIANS ROMANS, EPHESIANS,

TO WHICH IS PREFIXED

AN ESSAY FOR THE UNDERSTANDING OF ST PAUL'S EPISTLES BY CONSULTING ST PAUL HIMSELF

THE PREFACE

AN ESSAY FOR THE UNDERSTANDING OF ST PAUL'S EPISTLES BY CONSULTING ST PAUL HIMSELF

THE PREFACE

To go about to explain any of St. Paul's *Epistles, after so great a Train of Expositors and Commentators, might seem an Attempt of Vanity, censurable for its Needlessness, did not the daily and approv'd Examples of pious and learned Men justify it.*[1] *This may be some Excuse for me to the Publick, if ever these following Papers should chance to come abroad: But to my self, for whose Use this Work was undertaken, I need make no Apology. Though I had been conversant in these Epistles, as well as in other Parts of Sacred Scripture, yet I found that I understood them not; I mean the doctrinal and discursive parts of them: Though the practical Directions, which are usually drop'd in the latter Part of each Epistle, appear'd to me very plain, intelligible, and instructive.*

I did not, when I reflected on it, very much wonder that this part of Sacred Scripture had Difficulties in it, many Causes of Obscurity did readily occur to me. The Nature of Epistolary Writings in general, disposes the Writer to pass by the mentioning of many Things, as well known to him to whom his Letter is address'd, which are necessary to be laid open to a Stranger, to make him comprehend what is said: And it not seldom falls out, that a well Penn'd Letter which is very easy and intelligible to the Receiver, is very obscure to a Stranger, who hardly knows what to make of it. The Matters that St. Paul *writ about, were certainly things well known to those he writ to, and which they had some peculiar Concern in, which made them easily apprehend his Meaning, and see the Tendency and Force of his Discourse. But we having now at this distance no Information of the Occasion of his writing, little or no Knowledge of the Temper and Circumstances those he writ to were in, but what is to be gather'd out of the Epistles themselves, it is not strange that many things in them lie conceal'd to us, which no doubt they who were concern'd in the Letter understood at first sight. Add to this, that in many places 'tis manifest he answers Letters sent, and Questions propos'd to him, which if we had, would much better clear those Passages that relate to them, than all the learned Notes of Criticks and Commentators, who in after-times fill us with their Conjectures; for very often, as to the Matter in hand, they are nothing else.*[2]

The Language wherein these Epistles are writ, are another; and that no small occasion of their Obscurity to us now:[a] *The Words are* Greek; *a Language dead many Ages since: A Language of a very witty volatile People, Seekers after Novelty, and abounding with Variety of Notions and Sects, to which they applied the Terms of their common Tongue with great Liberty and Variety: And yet this makes but one small part of the Difficulty in the Language of these Epistles; there is a Peculiarity in it, that much more obscures and perplexes the Meaning of these Writings, than what can be occasion'd by the Looseness and Variety of the Greek Tongue. The Terms are* Greek, *but the Idiom or Turn of the Phrases may be truly said to be* Hebrew *or* Syriack.[1] *The Custom and Familiarity of which Tongues do sometimes so far influence the Expressions in these Epistles, that one may observe the Force of the Hebrew Conjugations, particularly that of* Hiphil *given to Greek Verbs, in a way unknown to the* Grecians *themselves.*[2] *Nor is this all; the Subject treated of in these Epistles is so wholly new, and the Doctrines contained in them so perfectly remote from the Notions that Mankind were acquainted with, that most of the important Terms in it have quite another Signification from what they have in other Discourses: So that putting all together, we may truly say, that the New Testament is a Book written in a Language peculiar to it self.*

To these Causes of Obscurity common to St. Paul, *with most of the other Penmen of the several Books of the New Testament, we may add those that are peculiarly his, and owing to his Stile and Temper. He was, as 'tis visible, a Man of quick Thought, warm Temper,*[3] *mighty well vers'd in the Writings of the Old Testament, and full of the Doctrine of the New: All this put together, suggested Matter to him in abundance on those Subjects which came in his way: So that one may consider him when he was writing, as beset with a Crowd of Thoughts, all striving for Utterance. In this Posture of Mind it was almost impossible for him to keep that slow Pace, and observe minutely that Order and Method of ranging all he said, from which results an easie and obvious Perspicuity. To this Plenty and Vehemence of his may be imputed those many large Parentheses which a careful Reader may observe in his Epistles.*[4] *Upon this account also it is, that he often breaks off in the Middle of an Argument, to let in some new Thought suggested by his own Words; which having pursued and explained as far as conduced to his present Purpose, he reassumes again the Thread of his Discourse, and goes on with it, without taking any notice that he returns again to what he had been before saying, though sometimes it be so far off, that it may well have slipt out of his Mind, and requires a very attentive Reader to observe, and so bring the disjointed Members together, as to make up the Connection, and see how the scatter'd Parts of the Discourse hang together in a coherent well-agreeing Sense,*[5] *that makes it all of a Piece.*

Besides the disturbance in perusing St. Paul'*s Epistles, from the Plenty and Vivacity of his Thoughts, which may obscure his Method, and often hide his Sense from an unwary, or over-hasty Reader; the frequent changing of the Personage he speaks in, renders the Sense very uncertain, and is apt to mislead one that has not some Clue to guide him; sometimes by the Pronoun* I, *he means himself; sometimes any Christian; sometimes a Jew, and sometimes any Man,* etc. *If speaking of himself in the first Person Singular has so various meanings; his use of the first Person Plural is with a far greater Latitude, sometimes designing himself alone, sometimes those with himself whom he makes Partners to the Epistle;*

sometimes with himself[a] *comprehending the other Apostles, or Preachers of the Gospel, or Christians*: *Nay, sometimes he in that way speaks of the Converted* Jews, *other times of the Converted* Gentiles, *and sometimes of others, in a more or less extended Sense, every one of which varies the meaning of the Place, and makes it to be differently understood. I have forborn to trouble the Reader with Examples of them here. If his own Observation hath not already furnished him with them, the following Paraphrase and Notes I suppose will satisfie him in the point.*[1]

In the current also of his Discourse, he sometimes drops in the Objections of others, and his Answers to them, without any Change in the Scheme of his Language, that might give Notice of any other speaking besides himself. This requires great Attention to observe, and yet if it be neglected or overlook'd, will make the Reader very much mistake, and misunderstand his Meaning, and render the Sense very perplex'd.

These are intrinsick difficulties arising from the Text it self, whereof there might be a great many other named, as the uncertainty, sometimes, who are the Persons he speaks to, or the Opinions or Practices which he has in his Eye, sometimes in alluding to them, sometimes in his Exhortations and Reproofs. But those above mentioned being the chief, it may suffice to have opened our Eyes a little upon them, which, well examin'd, may contribute towards our Discovery of the rest.

To these we may subjoyn two external Causes that have made no small increase of the Native and Original Difficulties that keep us from an easie and assur'd Discovery of St. Paul'*s Sense, in many parts of his Epistles, and those are,*

First, The dividing of them into Chapters and Verses,[2] *as we have done, whereby they are so chop'd and minc'd, and as they are now Printed, stand so broken and divided, that not only the Common People take the Verses usually for distinct Aphorisms, but even Men of more advanc'd Knowledge in reading them, lose very much of the strength and force of the Coherence, and the Light that depends on it. Our Minds are so weak and narrow, that they have need of all the helps and assistances can be procur'd, to lay before them undisturbedly, the Thread and Coherence of any Discourse; by which alone they are truly improv'd and lead into the Genuine Sense of the Author. When the Eye is constantly disturb'd with loose Sentences, that by their standing and separation, appear as so many distinct Fragments; the Mind will have much ado to take in, and carry on in its Memory an uniform Discourse of dependent Reasonings, especially having from the Cradle been used to wrong Impressions concerning them, and constantly accustom'd to hear them quoted as distinct Sentences, without any limitation or explication of their precise Meaning from the Place they stand in, and the Relation they bear to what goes before, or follows. These Divisions also have given occasion to the reading these Epistles by parcels and in scraps, which has farther confirm'd the Evil arising from such partitions. And I doubt not but every one will confess it to be a very unlikely way to come to the Understanding of any other*

Letters, to read them Peicemeal, a Bit to day, and another Scrap to morrow, and so on by broken Intervals; Especially if the Pause and Cessation should be made as the Chapters the Apostles Epistles are divided into do end sometimes in the middle of a Discourse, and sometimes in the middle of a Sentence. It cannot therefore but be wondred, that that should be permitted to be done to Holy Writ, which would visibly disturb the Sense, and hinder the Understanding of any other Book whatsoever. If Tully'*s Epistles*[1] *were so printed, and so used, I ask whither they would not be much harder to be understood, less easy and less pleasant to be read by much than now they are?*

How plain soever this Abuse is, and what Prejudice soever it does to the Understanding of the Sacred Scripture, yet if a Bible was printed as it should be, and as the several Parts of it were writ, in continued Discourses where the Argument is continued, I doubt not but the several Parties would complain of it, as an Innovation, and a dangerous Change in the publishing those holy Books. And indeed those who are for maintaining their Opinions, and the Systems of Parties by Sound of Words, with a Neglect of the true Sense of Scripture, would have reason to make and foment the Outcry. They would most of them be immediately disarm'd of their great Magazine of Artillery wherewith they defend themselves, and fall upon others, if the Holy Scripture were but laid before the Eyes of Christians in its due Connection and Consistency, it would not then be so easy to snatch out a few Words, as if they were separate from the rest, to serve a Purpose, to which they do not at all belong, and with which they have nothing to do. But as the matter now stands, he that has a mind to it, may at a cheap rate be a notable Champion for the Truth, that is, for the Doctrines of the Sect that Chance or Interest has cast him into. He need but be furnished with Verses of Sacred Scripture, containing Words and Expressions that are but flexible (as all general obscure and doubtful ones are) and his System that has appropriated them to the Orthodoxie of his Church, makes them immediately strong and irrefragable Arguments for his Opinion. This is the Benefit of loose Sentences, and Scripture crumbled into Verses, which quickly turn into independent Aphorisms. But if the Quotation in the Verse produc'd, were consider'd as a part of a continued coherent Discourse, and so its Sense were limited by the Tenour of the Context, most of these forward and warm Disputants would be quite strip'd of those, which they doubt not now to call Spiritual Weapons, and they would have often nothing to say that would not shew their Weakness, and manifestly fly in their Faces. I crave leave to set down a Saying of the Learned and Judicious Mr. Selden,[2] *'In interpreting the Scripture, says he, many do as if a Man should see one have Ten 'Pounds, which he rekon'd by* 1, 2, 3, 4, 5, 6, 7, 8, 9, 10. *meaning Four was but 'four Unites, and five five Unites,* etc. *and that he had in all but Ten Pounds: 'The other that sees him, takes not the Figures together, as he doth, but picks here 'and there; and thereupon reports that he had five Pounds in one Bag, and six 'Pounds in another Bag, and nine Pounds in another Bag,* etc. *when as in truth 'he has but ten Pounds in all. So we pick out a Text here and there, to make it serve 'our turn; whereas if we take it altogether, and consider what went before, and 'what followed after, we should find it meant no such thing.' I have heard sober Christians very much admire why ordinary illiterate People, who were Professors, that shew'd a Concern for Religion, seem'd much more conversant in St.* Paul's *Epistles, than in the plainer, and as it seem'd to them much more intelligible Parts of the New Testament; They confessed that tho' they read St.* Paul's *Epistles with their best Attention, yet they generally found them too hard to be master'd, and they labour'd in vain so far to reach the Apostle's Meaning all along in the Train of what he said, as to read them with that Satisfaction that arises from a feeling that we understand and fully comprehend the Force and Reasoning of an Author; and therefore they could not imagin what those saw in them, whose Eyes they thought not much better than their own. But the Case was plain, These sober inquisitive Readers had a mind to see nothing in St.* Paul's *Epistles but just what he meant; whereas those others of a quicker and gayer Sight could see in them what they pleased. Nothing is more acceptable to Phansie than plyant Terms and Expressions that are not obstinate, in such it can find its account with Delight, and with them be illuminated, Orthodox, infallible at pleasure, and in its own way. But where the Sense of the Author goes visibly in its own Train, and the Words, receiving a determin'd Sense from their Companions and Adjacents, will not consent to give Countenance and Colour to what is agreed to be right, and must be supported at any rate, there Men of establish'd Orthodoxie do not so well find their Satisfaction. And perhaps if it were well examin'd, it would be no very extravagant Paradox to say, that there are fewer that bring their Opinions to the Sacred Scripture to be tried by that infallible Rule, than bring the Sacred Scripture to their Opinions, to bend it to them, to make it as they can a Cover and Guard of them.*[1] *And to this Purpose its being divided into Verses, and brought as much as may be into loose and general Aphorisms, makes it most useful and serviceable. And in this lies the other great Cause of Obscurity and Perplexedness, which has been cast upon St.* Paul's *Epistles from without.*

St. Paul's *Epistles, as they stand translated in our English Bibles, are now by long and constant Use become a part of the English Language, and common Phraseology, especially in Matters of Religion; This every one uses familiarly, and thinks he understands, but it must be observed, that if he has a distinct meaning when he uses those Words and Phrases, and knows himself what he intends by them, it is alway according to the Sense of his own System, and the Articles or Interpretations of the Society he is engaged in. So that all this Knowledge and Understanding which he has in the Use of these Passages of Sacred Scripture, reaches no farther than this, that he knows (and that is very well) what he himself says, but thereby knows nothing at all what St.* Paul *said in them. The Apostle writ not by that Man's System, and so his Meaning cannot be known by it. This being the ordinary way of understanding the Epistles, and every Sect being perfectly Orthodox in its own Judgment: What a great and invincible Darkness must this cast upon St.* Paul's *Meaning to all those of that way, in all those Places where his Thoughts and Sense run counter to what any Party has espoused for Orthodox; as it must unavoidably to all but one of the different Systems, in all those Passages that any way relate to the Points in Controversie between them.*

This is a Mischief which, however frequent and almost natural, reaches so far, that it would justly make all those who depend upon them, wholly diffident of Commentators, and let them see, how little Help was to be expected from them in relying on them for the true Sense of the Sacred Scripture, did they not take care to help to cozen themselves, by choosing to use and pin their Faith on such Expositors as explain the Sacred Scripture in favour of those Opinions that they before hand have voted Orthodox, and bring to the Sacred Scripture not for Trial, but Confirmation. No Body can think that any Text of St. Paul'*s Epistles has two contrary Meanings, and yet so it must have to two different Men, who taking two Commentators of different Sects for their respective Guides into the Sense of any one of the Epistles, shall build upon their respective Expositions. We need go no further for a Proof of it, than the Notes of the two Celebrated Commentators on the New Testament, Dr.* Hammond *and* Beza,[1] *both Men of Parts and Learning, and both thought by their Follower's Men mighty in the Sacred Scriptures. So that here we see the hopes of great Benefit and Light from Expositors and Commentators, is in a great part abated, and those who have most need of their Help, can receive but little from them, and can have very little Assurance of reaching the Apostle's Sense by what they find in them, whilst Matters remain in the same State they are in at present. For those, who find they need Help, and would borrow Light from Expositors, either consult only those who have the good luck to be thought sound and Orthodox, avoiding those of different Sentiments from themselves in the great and approved Points of their Systems, as dangerous and not fit to be medled with; or else with Indifferency look into the Notes of all Commentators promiscuously. The first of these take Pains only to confirm themselves in the Opinions and Tenents they have already, which whether it be the way to get the true Meaning of what St.* Paul *deliver'd, is easy to determin. The others with much more Fairness to themselves, tho with reaping little more Advantage (unless they have something else to guide them into the Apostle's Meaning than the Comments themselves) seek Help on all hands, and refuse not to be taught by any one, who offers to enlighten them in any of the dark Passages. But here tho they avoid the Mischief which the others fall into, of being confin'd in their Sense, and seeing nothing but that in St.* Paul'*s Writings, be it right or wrong; yet they run into as great on the other side, and instead of being confirm'd in the meaning, that they thought they saw in the Text, are distracted with an hundred, suggested by those they advised with; and so instead of that one Sense of the Scripture which they carried with them to their Commentators, return from them with none at all.*

This indeed seems to make the Case desperate: For if the Comments and Expositions of pious and learned Men cannot be depended on, whether shall we go for Help? To which I answer, I would not be mistaken, as if I thought the Labours of the Learned in this Case wholly lost, and fruitless. There is great Use and Benefit to be made of them, when we have once got a Rule to know which of their Expositions, in the great Variety there is of them, explains the Words and Phrases according to the Apostle's Meaning. Till then 'tis evident, from what is above said, they serve for the most part to no other Use, but either to make us find our own Sense, and not his in St. Paul'*s Words; or else to find in them no settled Sense at all.*

Here it will be ask'd, how shall we come by this Rule you mention? Where is that Touchstone to be had, that will shew us whether the Meaning we our selves put, or take as put by others upon St. Paul'*s Words in his Epistles, be truly his Meaning or no? I will not say the way which I propose, and have in the following Paraphrase follow'd, will make us infallible in our Interpretations of the Apostle's Text: But this I will own, that till I took this way, St.* Paul'*s Epistles to me, in the ordinary way of reading and studying them, were very obscure Parts of Scripture, that left me almost every where at a loss; and I was at a great Uncertainty in which of the contrary Senses, that were to be found in his Commentators, he was to be taken. Whether what I have done has made it any clearer and more visible now, I must leave others to judge. This I beg leave to say for my self, that if some very sober judicious Christians, no Strangers to the Sacred Scriptures, nay learned Divines of the Church of* England, *had not professed that by the Perusal of these following Papers, they understood the Epistles better much than they did before, and had not with repeated Instances pressed me to publish them,* [1] *I should not have consented they should have gone beyond my own private Use, for which they were at first designed, and where they made me not repent my Pains.*

If any one be so far pleased with my Endeavours, as to think it worth while to be informed, what was the Clue I guided my self by through all the dark Passages of these Epistles, I shall minutely tell him the Steps by which I was brought into this way, that he may judge whether I proceeded rationally, upon right Grounds or no, if so be any thing in so mean an Example as mine may be worth his notice.

After I had found by long Experience, that the reading of the Text and Comments in the ordinary way proved not so successful as I wish'd to the end propos'd, I began to suspect that in reading a Chapter as was usual, and thereupon sometimes consulting Expositors upon some hard Places of it, which at that time most affected me, as relating to Points then under Consideration in my own Mind, or in Debate amongst others, was not a right Method to get into the true Sense of these Epistles. I saw plainly, after I began once to reflect on it, that if any one now should write me a Letter, as long as St. Paul'*s to the* Romans, *concerning such a Matter as that is, in a Stile as Foreign, and Expressions as dubious as his seem to be, if I should divide it into fifteen or sixteen Chapters, and read of them one to day, and another to morrow,* etc. *it was ten to one I should never come to a full and clear Comprehension of it. The way to understand the Mind of him that writ it, every one would agree, was to read the whole Letter through from one end to the other, all at once, to see what was the main Subject and Tendency of it: or if it had several Views and Purposes in it, not dependent one of another, nor in a Subordination to one chief Aim and End, to discover what those different Matters were, and where the Author concluded one, and began another; and if there were any Necessity of dividing the Epistle into Parts, to make the Boundaries of them.*

In Prosecution of this Thought, I concluded it necessary, for the understanding of any one of St. Paul'*s Epistles, to read it all through at one Siting, and to observe as well as I could the Drift and Design of his writing it. If the first reading gave me some Light, the second gave me more; and so I persisted on reading constantly the whole Epistle over at once, till I came to have a good general View of the Apostle's main Purpose in writing the Epistle, the chief Branches of his Discourse wherein he prosecuted it, the Arguments he used, and the Disposition of the whole.*

This, I confess, is not to be obtained by one or two hasty Readings; it must be repeated again and again, with a close Attention to the Tenour of the Discourse, and a perfect Neglect of the Divisions into Chapters and Verses. On the contrary, the safest way is to suppose, that the Epistle has but one Business, and one Aim, till by a frequent Perusal[1] *of it, you are forced to see there are distinct independent Matters in it, which will forwardly enough shew themselves.*

It requires so much more Pains, Judgment and Application, to find the Coherence of obscure and abstruse Writings, and makes them so much the more unfit to serve Prejudice and Pre-occupation when found, that it is not to be wondered that St. Paul'*s Epistles have with many passed rather for disjointed, loose pious Discourses,*[2] *full of Warmth and Zeal, and Overflows of Light, rather than for calm strong coherent Reasonings, that carried a Thread of Argument and Consistency all through them.*

But this muttering of lazy or ill disposed Readers, hindered me not from persisting in the Course I had began; I continued to read the same Epistle over and over, and over again, till I came to discover, as appeared to me, what was the Drift and Aim of it, and by what Steps and Arguments St. Paul *prosecuted his Purpose. I remembred that St.* Paul *was miraculously called to the Ministry of the Gospel, and declared to be a chosen Vessel;*[3] *that he had the whole Doctrine of the Gospel from God by immediate Revelation, and was appointed to be the Apostle of the* Gentiles, *for the propagating of it in the Heathen World.*[4] *This was enough to perswade me, that he was not a Man of loose and shattered Parts, uncapable to argue, and unfit to convince those he had to deal with. God knows how to choose fit Instruments for the Business he employs them in. A large Stock of Jewish Learning he had taken in at the Feet of* Gamaliel,[5] *and for his Information in Christian Knowledge, and the Mysteries and Depths of the Dispensation of Grace by Jesus Christ, God himself had condescended to be his Instructer and Teacher. The Light of the Gospel he had received from the Fountain and Father of Light himself, who, I concluded, had not furnished him in this extraordinary manner, if all this plentiful Stock of Learning and Illumination had been in danger to have been lost, or proved useless, in a jumbled and confused Head; nor have laid up such a Store of admirable and useful Knowledge in a Man, who for want of Method and Order, Clearness of Conception, or Pertinency in Discourse, could not draw it out into Use with the greatest Advantages of Force and Coherence. That he knew how to prosecute his Purpose with Strength of Argument and close Reasoning, without incoherent Sallies, or the intermixing of things foreign to his Business, was evident to me from several Speeches of his recorded in the* Acts: *And it was hard to think that a Man that could talk with so much Consistency and Clearness of Conviction, should not be able to write without Confusion, inextricable Obscurity, and perpetual Rambling. The Force, Order and Perspicuity of those Discourses could not be denied to be very visible. How then came it that the like was thought much wanting in his Epistles? and of this there appear'd to me this plain Reason: The Particularities of the History in which these Speeches are inserted, shew St.* Paul'*s end in Speaking, which being seen, casts a Light on the whole, and shews the Pertinency of all that he says. But his Epistles not being so circumstantiated; there being no concurring History that plainly declares the Disposition St.* Paul *was in, what the Actions, Expectations, or Demands of those to whom he writ, required him to speak to, we are no where told. All this and a great deal more necessary to guide us into the true meaning of the Epistles, is to be had only from the Epistles themselves, and to be gather'd from thence with stubborn Attention, and more than common Application.*

This being the only safe Guide (under the Spirit of God, that dictated these Sacred Writings) that can be rely'd on, I hope I may be excused, if I venture to say, that the utmost ought to be done to observe and trace out St. Paul'*s Reasonings; to follow the Thread of his Discourse in each of his Epistles; to shew how it goes on still directed with the same View, and pertinently drawing the several Incidents towards the same Point. To understand him right, his Inferences should be strictly observed; and it should be carefully examined from what they are drawn, and what they tend to. He is certainly a coherent, argumentative, pertinent Writer, and Care I think should be taken in expounding of him, to shew that he is so. But tho I say he has weighty Aims in his Epistles, which he steadily keeps in his Eye, and drives at in all that he says, yet I do not say that he puts his Discourses into an artificial Method, or leads his Reader into a Distinction of his Arguments, or gives them notice of new Matter by Rhetorical or study'd Transitions. He has no Ornaments borrow'd from the Greek Eloquence; no Notions of their Philosophy mix'd with his Doctrine to set it off. The* inticing Words of Man's Wisdom, *whereby he means all the studied Rules of the Grecian Schools, which made them such Masters in the Art of Speaking, he, as he says himself,* I Cor. 2. 4. *wholly neglected. The Reason whereof he gives in the next Verse, and in other places. But tho Politeness of Language, Delicacy of Stile, Fineness of Expression, laboured Periods, artificial Transitions, and a very methodical ranging of the Parts with such other Imbellishments as make a Discourse enter the Mind smoothly, and strike the Phansie at first hearing, have little or no place in his Stile, yet Coherence of Discourse, and a direct Tendency of all the Parts of it, to the Argument in hand, are most eminently to be found in him. This I take to be his Character, and doubt not but he will be found to be so upon diligent Examination. And in this if it be so, we have a Clue, if we will take the Pains to find it, that will conduct us with Surety through those seemingly dark Places, and imagined Intricacies in which Christians have wander'd so far one from another, as to find quite contrary Senses.*

Whether a superficial Reading, accompanied with the common Opinion of his invincible Obscurity, has kept off some from seeking in him the Coherence of a Discourse tending with close strong reasoning to a Point; Or a seemingly more honourable Opinion of one that had been wrap'd up into the Third Heaven, as if from a Man so warm'd and illuminated as he had been, nothing could be expected but Flashes of Light, and Raptures of Zeal, hinder'd others to look for a Train of Reasoning, proceeding on regular and cogent Argumentation from a Man rais'd above the ordinary pitch of Humanity to an higher and brighter way of Illumination; Or else whether others were loth to beat their Heads about the Tenor and Coherence in St. Paul'*s Discourses, which if found out, possibly might set him at a manifest and irreconcileable Difference with their Systems, 'tis certain that whatever hath been the Cause, this way of getting the true Sense of St.* Paul'*s Epistles, seems not to have been much made use of, or at least so throughly pursued as I am apt to think it deserves.*

For, granting that he was full stor'd with the Knowledge of the things he treated of: For he had Light from Heaven, it was God himself furnished him, and he could not want: Allowing also that he had Ability to make use of the Knowledge had been given him for the end for which it was given him, viz. *the Information, Conviction, and Conversion of others; and accordingly that he knew how to direct his Discourse to the Point in hand, we cannot widely mistake the Parts of his Discourse imploy'd about it, when we have any where found out the Point he drives at: Where-ever we have got a View of his Design, and the Aim he proposed to himself in Writing, we may be sure that such or such an Interpretation does not give us his genuine Sense, it being nothing at all to his present purpose. Nay among various Meanings given a Text, it fails not to direct us to the best, and very often to assure us of the true. For it is no Presumption, when one sees a Man arguing for this or that Proposition, if he be a sober Man, Master of Reason or common Sense, and takes any care of what he says, to pronounce with Confidence in several Cases, that he could not talk thus or thus.*

I do not yet so magnifie this Method of studying St. Paul'*s Epistles, as well as other Parts of Sacred Scripture, as to think it will perfectly clear every hard Place, and leave no Doubt unresolved. I know Expressions now out of use, Opinions of those times, not heard of in our days, Allusions to Customs lost to us, and various Circumstances and Particularities of the Parties,*[1] *which we cannot come at,* etc. *must needs continue several Passages in the dark now to us at this distance, which shon with full Light to those they were directed to. But for all that the studying of*

St. Paul'*s Epistles in the way I have proposed, will, I humbly conceive, carry us a great length in the right understanding of them, and make us rejoyce in the Light we receive from those most useful Parts of Divine Revelation, by furnishing us with visible Grounds that we are not mistaken, whilst the Consistency of the Discourse, and the Pertinency of it to the Design he is upon, vouches it worthy of our great Apostle. At least I hope it may be my Excuse for having indeavoured to make St.* Paul *an Interpreter to me of his own Epistles.*[1]

To this may be added another Help which St. Paul *himself affords us towards the attaining the true meaning contained in his Epistles. He that reads him with the Attention I propose, will easily observe, that as he was full of the Doctrine of the Gospel, so it lay all clear and in order open to his view. When he gave his Thoughts Utterance upon any Point, the Matter flow'd like a Torrent, but 'tis plain 'twas a Matter he was perfectly Master of: he fully possess'd the entire Revelation he had receiv'd from God, had throughly digested it; all the Parts were formed together in his Mind into one well contracted harmonious Body. So that he was no way at Uncertainty, nor ever in the least at a loss concerning any Branch of it. One may see his Thoughts were all of a piece in all his Epistles, his Notions*[2] *were at all times uniform, and constantly the same, tho his Expressions very various. In them he seems to take great Liberty. This at least is certain, that no one seems less tied up to a Form of Words. If then having by the Method before proposed got into the Sense of the several Epistles, we will but compare what he says, in the Places where he treats of the same Subject, we can hardly be mistaken in his Sense, nor doubt what it was, that he believed and taught concerning those Points of the Christian Religion. I know it is not unusual to find a Multitude of Texts heaped up for the maintaining of an espoused Proposition, but in a Sense often so remote from their true Meaning, that one can hardly avoid thinking that those who so used them, either sought not or valued not the Sense; and were satisfied with the Sound where they could but get that to favour them. But a verbal Concordance leads not always to Texts of the same meaning; trusting too much thereto, will furnish us but with slight Proofs in many Cases, and any one may observe how apt that is to jumble together Passages of Scripture not relating to the same Matter, and thereby to disturb and unsettle the true meaning of Holy Scripture. I have therefore said that we should compare together Places of Scripture treating of the same Point. Thus indeed one part of the Sacred Text could not fail to give light unto another. And since the Providence of God hath so order'd it, that St.* Paul *has writ a great Number of Epistles, which tho upon different Occasions, and to several Purposes, yet are all confined within the Business of his Apostleship, and so contain nothing but Points of Christian Instruction, amongst which he seldom fails to drop in, and often to inlarge on the great and distinguishing Doctrines of our holy Religion; which, if quitting our own Infallibility in that Analogy of Faith*[3] *which we have made to our selves, or have implicitly adopted from some other, we would carefully lay together, and diligently compare and study, I am apt to think would give us St.* Paul'*s System in a clear and indisputable Sense, which every one must acknowledge to be a better Standard to interpret his Meaning by, in any obscure and doubtful Parts of his Epistles, if any such should still remain, than the System, Confession, or Articles of any Church or Society of Christians yet known, which however pretended to be founded on Scripture, are visibly the Contrivances of Men*[1] *(fallible both in their Opinions and Interpretations) and as is visible in most of them, made with partial Views, and adapted to what the Occasions of that time, and the present Circumstances they were then in, were thought to require for the Support or Justification of themselves. Their Philosophy also has its part in mis-leading Men from the true Sense of the Sacred Scripture. He that shall attentively read the Christian Writers after the Age of the Apostles, will easily find how much the Philosophy they were tinctured with, influenced them in their Understanding of the Books of the Old and New Testament. In the Ages wherein Platonism prevailed, the Converts to Christianity of that School, on all occasions, interpreted Holy Writ according to the Notions they had imbib'd from that Philosophy.*[2] Aristotle'*s Doctrine had the same effect in its turn, and when it degenerated into the Peripateticism of the Schools, that too brought its Notions and Distinctions into Divinity, and affixed them to the Terms of the Sacred Scripture.*[3] *And we may see still how at this day every ones Philosophy regulates every ones Interpretation of the Word of God. Those who are possessed with the Doctrine of Aerial and Ætherial Vehicles,*[4] *have thence borrowed an Interpretation of the Four first Verses of* 2 Cor. 5. *without having any Ground to think that St.* Paul *had the least Notion of any such Vehicles. 'Tis plain that the teaching of Men Philosophy, was no part of the Design of Divine Revelation*; *but that the Expressions of Scripture are commonly suited in those Matters to the Vulgar Apprehensions and Conceptions of the Place and People where they were delivered. And as to the Doctrine therein directly taught by the Apostles, that tends wholly to the seting up the Kingdom of Jesus Christ in this World, and the Salvation of Mens Souls, and in this 'tis plain their Expressions were conformed to the Ideas and Notions which they had received from Revelation, or were consequent from it. We shall therefore in vain go about to interpret their Words by the Notions of our Philosophy, and the Doctrines of Men deliver'd in our Schools. This is to explain the Apostles*[a] *meaning by what they never thought of whilst they were writing, which is not the way to find their Sense in what they deliver'd, but our own, and to take up from their Writings not what they left there for us, but what we bring along with us in our selves. He that would understand St.* Paul *right, must understand his Terms in the Sense he uses them, and not as they are appropriated by each Man's particular Philosophy, to Conceptions that never enter'd the Mind of the Apostle. For Example, he that shall bring the Philosophy now taught and receiv'd to the explaining of* Spirit, Soul, *and* Body, *mentioned* I Thess. 5.[b] 23. *will I fear hardly reach St.* Paul'*s Sense, or represent to himself the Notions St.* Paul *then had in his Mind.*[5] *That is what we should aim at in reading him, or any other Author, and 'till we from his Words paint his very Ideas and Thoughts in our Minds, we do not understand him.*

In the Divisions I have made, I have indeavour'd the best I could to govern my self by the Diversity of Matter. But in a Writer like St. Paul, *it is not so easie always to find precisely where one Subject ends, and another begins. He is full of the Matter he treats and writes with Warmth,*[1] *which usually neglects Method, and those Partitions and Pauses which Men educated in the Schools of Rhetoricians usually observe. Those Arts of Writing St.* Paul, *as well out of Design as Temper, wholly laid by: The Subject he had in hand, and the Grounds upon which it stood firm, and by which he inforced it, was what alone he minded, and without solemnly winding up one Argument, and intimating any way that he began another, let his Thoughts, which were fully possess'd of the Matter, run in one continued Train, wherein the Parts of his Discourse were wove one into another. So that it is seldom that the Scheme of his Discourse makes any Gap; and therefore without breaking in upon the Connection of his Language, 'tis hardly possible to separate his Discourse, and give a distinct View of his several Arguments in distinct Sections.*

I am far from pretending Infallibility in the Sense I have any where given in my Paraphrase or Notes; That would be to erect my self into an Apostle, a Presumption of the highest Nature in any one that cannot confirm what he says by Miracles. I have for my own Information sought the true Meaning as far as my poor Abilities would reach. And I have unbiassedly imbraced what upon a fair Enquiry appear'd so to me. This I thought my Duty and Interest in a Matter of so great Concernment to me. If I must believe for my self, it is unavoidable that I must understand for my self. For if I blindly and with an Implicit Faith take the Pope's Interpretation of the Sacred Scripture, without examining whether it be Christ's Meaning, 'tis the Pope I believe in, and not in Christ; 'tis his Authority I rest upon; 'tis what he says I imbrace: For what 'tis Christ says, I neither know nor concern my self. 'Tis the same thing when I set up any other Man in Christ's place, and make him the Authentique Interpreter of Sacred Scripture to my self. He may possibly understand the Sacred Scripture as right as any Man, but I shall do well to examin my self, whether that which I do not know, nay (which in the way I take) I can never know, can justifie me in making my self his Disciple, instead of Jesus Christ's,[a] *who of Right is alone and ought to be my only Lord and Master:*[2] *and it will be no less Sacrilege in me to substitute to my self any other in his room, to be a Prophet, to me, than to be my King or Priest.*

The same Reasons that put me upon doing what I have in these Papers done, will exempt me from all Suspition of imposing my Interpretation on others. The Reasons that lead me into the Meaning which prevail'd on my Mind, are set down with it;[b] *as far as they carry Light and Conviction to any other Man's Understanding, so far I hope my Labour may be of some Use to him;*[c] *beyond the Evidence it carries with it, I advise him not to follow mine, nor any Man's Interpretation. We are all Men liable to Errors, and infected with them; but have this sure way to preserve our selves every one from danger by them, if laying aside Sloth, Carelessness, Prejudice, Party, and a Reverence of Men, we betake our selves in earnest to the Study of the way to Salvation,*[1] *in those holy Writings wherein God has reveal'd it from Heaven, and propos'd it to the World, seeking our Religion where we are sure it is in Truth to be found, comparing spiritual things with spiritual things.*[2]

A PARAPHRASE AND NOTES ON THE EPISTLE OF ST PAUL TO THE GALATIANS

THE EPISTLE OF ST PAUL TO THE GALATIANS

SYNOPSIS

[a]The subject and designe of this Epistle of St Paul is much what the same with that of his Epistle to the Romans but treated in some what a different manner. The business of it is to dehort and hinder the Galatians from bringing themselves under the bondage of the Mosaical law

[b]St Paul himself had planted the Churches of Galatia and therefore refering (as he does Ch. I.8.9) to what he had before taught them, does not in this Epistle lay down at large to them the doctrine of the Gospel as he does in that to the Romans, who haveing been converted to the Christian faith by others, [c]he did not know how far they were instructed in all those particulars, which on the occasion where on he writ to them it might be necessary for them to understand. And therefore he sets before them a large and comprehensive view of the Cheif heads of the Christian religion

[d]He also deales more roundly with his disciples the Galatians than, we may observe, he does with the Romans to whom he being a stranger writes not in so familiar a stile, nor in his reproofs and exhortations uses so much the tone of a master as he does to the Galatians

[e]St Paul had converted the Galatians to the faith and erected several churches among them in the year of our Lord 51 between which and the year 57 wherein this Epistle ,was writ, the disorders following were got into those Churches

[f]1° Some zealots for the Jewish constitution had very near perswaded them out of their Christian liberty and made them willing to submit to circumcision and all the ritual observances of the Jewish Church as necessary under the gospel. Ch I.7. III.3. IV.9.10.21. V.1.2.6.9.10

[g]2°Their dissensions and disputes in this matter had raised great animositys amongst them to the disturbance of their peace, and the seting them at Strife one with an other. Ch. V.6.13-15

[h]The reforming them in these two points seems the main business of this Epistle, where in he endeavours to establish them in a resolution to stand firm in the freedom of the Gospel, which exempts them from the bondage of the Mosaical law: And labours to reduce them to a sincere love and affection one to an other. which he concludes with an exhortation to liberality and general beneficence espetialy to their teachers Ch. VI.6-10. [i]These being the matters he had in his mind to write to them about he seems here as if he had donne. But upon mentioning ver. 11 what a long letter he had writ to them with his own hand, the former argument concerning circumcision which filled and warmd his mind broke out again into what we find ver. 12-17.

SECTION I

The year of our Lord 57
of Nero.3.
From Ephesus

Ch. I.1-5
Introduction

CONTENTS

[a]The general view of this Epistle plainly shews St Pauls cheif designe in it to be to keep the Galatians from hearkening to those Judaizing Seducers who had almost perswaded them to be circumcised. These perverters of the Gospel of Christ as St Paul himself cals them ver. 7 had as may be gatherd from ver. 8. and 10. and from Ch. V.11. [b]and other passages of this epistle made the Galatians beleive that St Paul himself was for circumcision. Till St Paul had set them right in this matter and convinced them of the falshood of this aspersion it was in vain for him by other arguments to attempt the reestablishing the Galatians in the Christian liberty and truth which he had preachd to them. [c]The removeing therefore of this calumnie was his first endeavour and to that purpose this Introduction different from what we find in any other of his epistles is marvelously well adapted. He declares here at the entrance very expresly and emphatically that he was not sent by men of their errands, [d]Nay that Christ in sending him did not soe much as convey

his Apostolick power to him by the ministry or intervention of any man, but that his commission and instructions were all entirely from God and Christ himself by immediate revelation. This of it self was an argument sufficient to induce them to beleive 1° That what he taught them when he first preachd the gospel to them was the truth, and that they ought to stick firm to that. [e]2°That he changed not his doctrine whatever might be reported of him. He was Christs chosen officer and had noe dependence on mens opinions, nor regard to their authority or favour in what he preachd and therefore 'twas not likely he should preach one thing at one time and an other thing at an other

[f]Thus this preface is very proper in this place to introduce what he is goeing to say concerning himself, and addes force to his discourse and the account he gives of him self in the next section

TEXT

I.1. Paul an Apostle (not of men, neither by man, but by Jesus Christ, and God the Father who raised him from the dead.)

2. And all the brethren which are with me unto the Churches of Galatia:

3. Grace be to you, and Peace from God the Father, and from our Lord Jesus Christ:

4. Who gave himself for our Sins, that he might deliver us from this present evil world, according to the will of God and our Father.

5. To whom be glory for ever and ever, Amen.

PARAPHRASE

I.1 Paul (an Apostle not of men* to serve their ends or carry on their designes, nor receiveing his call or commission by the intervention of any man,* to whom he might be thought to owe any respect or deference on that account; but immediately from Jesus Christ and from god the father who raised him up from the dead) 2 and all the bretheren that are with me, unto the Churches* of Galatia. 3 Favour

I.1* [a]Οὐκ ἀπ' ἀνθρώπων *not of men*. i e not sent by men at their pleasure or by their authority; not instructed by men what to say or doe, as we see Timothy and Titus were when sent by St Paul and Judas and Silas sent by the church of Jerusalem. οὐδὲ δι' ἀνθρώπου. [b]i e His choise and separation to his ministry and Apostleship was so wholy an act of God and Christ that there was no intervention of any thing done by any man in the case as there was in the election of Matthias. All this we may see explaind at large ver. 10-12 and ver. 16.17. and Ch II.6-9

2* *Churches of Galatia*. This was an evident seale of his Apostleship to the Gentiles since in no bigger a country then Galatia a smal Province of the lesser Asia he had in noe long stay amongst them planted several distinct churches

3* *Peace*· The wishing of *Peace* in the Scripture language is the wishing of all manner of good.

be to you and peace* from God the father and from our Lord Jesus Christ [4]who gave him self for our sins that he might take us out of this present evil world* according to the will and good pleasure of god and our father [5]to whom be glory for ever and ever. Amen

SECTION II

Ch. I.6-II.21

CONTENTS

[a]We have above observed that St Pauls first endeavours in this Epistle was to Satisfie the Galatians that the report spread of him that he preached circumcision was false. Til this obstruction that lay in his way was removed, it was to no purpose for him to go about to disswade them from Circumcision though that be what he principaly aims at in this epistle. [b]To shew them that he promoted not Circumcision he cals their hearkening to those who perswaded them to be circumcised their being *removed from him*, and those that so perswaded them *perverters of the gospel of Christ*. He farther assures them that the gospel which he preachd every where was that [c]and that onely which

4* [a]ὅπως ἐξέληται ἡμᾶς ἐκ τοῦ ἐνεστῶτος αἰῶνος πονηροῦ *That he might take us out of this present evil world* or *age*· So the Greek words signifie. whereby it can not be thought that St Paul meant that Christians were to be immediately removed into the other world. [b]Therefore ἐνεστὼς αἰών must signifie some thing else than *present world* in the ordinary import of those words in English. Αἰὼν οὗτος. 1 Cor II.6.8 and in other places plainly signifies the Jewish nation under the Mosaical constitution. And it suits very well with the Apostles designe in this epistle that it should doe so here. God has in this world but one kingdome and one people. [c]That Kingdome whilst the law stood and the Nation of the Jews under the Mosaical constitution were the people of god was called αἰὼν οὗτος *this age* or as it is commonly translated *this world*, to which αἰὼν ἐνεστώς *the present world* or *age* here answers. [d]But the Kingdom of god which was to be under the Messiah wherein the œconomie and constitution of the Jewish Church and the nation it self that in opposition to Christ adhered to it was to be laid aside is in the New Testament called αἰὼν μέλλων *the world* or *age to come*. [e]So that Christs *takeing them out of the present world* may without any violence of the words be understood to signifie his seting them free from the Mosaical constitution. This is suitable to the designe of this Epistle, and what St Paul has declared in many other places. See Col II.14-17. and 20 which agrees to this place and Rom VII.4.6. [f]The law is said to be *contrary to us* Col. II.14 and to work wrath Rom IV.15 and St Paul speaks very deminishingly of the ritual parts of it in many places: But yet if all this may not be thought sufficient to justify the applying of the Epithet πονηρός *evil* to it [g]that scruple will be removed if we take ἐνεστὼς αἰών *this present world* here.for the Jewish constitution and nation together in which sense it may very well be caled *evil*, though the Apostle, [h]out of his wonted tenderness to his nation, forbears to name them openly, and uses a doubtfull expression, which might comprehend the heathen world also though he cheifly pointed at the Jews

he had received by immediate revelation from Christ, and no contrivance of man, nor did he vary it to please men: That would not consist with his being a servant of Christ: And he expresses such a firm adherence to what he had received from Christ [d]and had preachd to them that he pronounces an anathema upon him self or any other man or angel that should preach any thing else to them. To make out this to have been all along his conduct he gives an account of him self for many years backwards even from the time before his conversion. [e]wherein he shews that from a zealous persecuteing Jew he was made a Christian and an Apostle by immediate revelation and that haveing no communication with the Apostles or with the Churches of Judea or any man for some years he had no thing to preach but what he had received by immediate revelation. [f]Nay when 14 years after he went up to Jerusalem it was by revelation, and there communicated the Gospel which he preachd to the Gentiles Peter James and John approved of it without addeing any thing, but admitted him as their fellow Apostle· So that in all this he was guided by no thing but divine revelation [g]which he inflexibly stuck to so far that he openly opposed St Peter for his Jewdaizeing at Antioch All which account of him self tends clearly to shew that St Paul made not the least step towards complying with the Jews in favour of the law or did out of regard to man deviate from the doctrine he had received by revelation from God.

[h]All the parts of this section and the narrative conteined in it manifestly concenter in this as will more fully appear as we goe through them and take a closer view of them, which will shew us that the whole is so skilfully managed and the parts so gently slid into that it is a strong but not seemingly laboured justification of himself from the imputation of preaching up Circumcision.

TEXT

I.6. I marvel that ye are so soon removed from him that called you into the grace of Christ, unto another gospel:

7. Which is not another; but there be some that trouble you, and would pervert the Gospel of Christ.

8. But though we or an angel from heaven preach any other gospel unto you, than that which we have preached unto you, let him be accursed.

9. As we said before, so say I now again, if any man preach any other gospel unto you than that ye have received, let him be accursed.

10. For do I now perswade men, or God? or do I seek to please men? for if I yet pleased men, I should not be the servant of Christ.

11. But I certifie you, brethren, that the gospel which was preached of me, is not after man.

12. For I neither received it of man, neither was I taught it, but by the Revelation of Jesus Christ.

13. For ye have heard of my conversation in time past, in the Jews religion, how that beyond measure I persecuted the Church of God, and wasted it:

14. And profited in the Jews religion, above many my equals in mine own nation, being more exceedingly zealous of the traditions of my fathers.

15. But when it pleased God who separated me from my mother's womb, and called me by his grace,

16. To reveal his Son in me, that I might preach him among the Heathen; immediately I conferred not with flesh and blood:

17. Neither went I up to Jerusalem, to them which were Apostles before me, but I went into Arabia, and returned again unto Damascus.

18. Then after three years I went up to Jerusalem to see Peter, and abode with him fifteen days.

19. But other of the apostles saw I none, save James the Lords brother.

20. Now the things which I write unto you, behold, before God, I lie not.

21. Afterwards I came into the regions of Syria and Cilicia:

22. And was unknown by face unto the Churches of Judea, which were in Christ.

23. But they had heard only, That he which persecuted us in times past, now preacheth the faith which once he destroyed.

24. And they glorified God in me.

II.1. Then fourteen years after, I went up again to Jerusalem, with Barnabas, and took Titus with me also.

2. And I went up by revelation, and communicated unto them that gospel which I preach among the Gentiles, but privately to them which were of reputation, lest by any means I should run, or had run in vain.

3. But neither Titus, who was with me, being a Greek, was compelled to be circumcised:

4. And that because of false brethren unawares brought in, who came in privily to spy out our liberty, which we have in Christ Jesus, that they might bring us into bondage:

5. To whom we gave place by subjection, no not for an hour; that the truth of the gospel might continue with you.

6. But of these, who seemed to be somewhat, (whatsoever they were, it maketh no matter to me: God accepteth no mans person) for they who seemed to be somewhat, in conference added nothing to me.

7. But contrariwise, when they saw that the Gospel of the uncircumcision was committed unto me, as the Gospel of the circumcision was unto Peter;

8. (For he that wrought effectually in Peter to the apostleship of the circumcision, the same was mighty in me towards the Gentiles)

9. And when James, Cephas, and John, who seemed to be pillars, perceived the grace that was given unto me, they gave to me and Barnabas the right hands of fellowship; that we should go unto the heathen, and they unto the circumcision.

10. Only they would that we should remember the poor; the same which I also was forward to do.

11. But when Peter was come to Antioch, I withstood him to the face, because he was to be blamed.

12. For before that certain came from James, he did eat with the Gentiles: but when they were come, he withdrew, and separated himself, fearing them which were of the circumcision.

13. And the other Jews dissembled likewise with him; insomuch that Barnabas also was carried away with their dissimulation.

14. But when I saw that they walked not uprightly, according to the truth of the gospel, I said unto Peter before them all, If thou, being a Jew, livest after the manner of Gentiles, and not as do the Jews, why compellest thou the Gentiles to live as do the Jews?

15. We who are Jews by nature, and not sinners of the Gentiles,

16. Knowing that a man is not justified by the works of the law, but by the faith of Jesus Christ, even we have believed in Jesus Christ; that we might be justified by the faith of Christ, and not by the works of the law: for by the works of the law shall no flesh be justified.

17. But if while we seek to be justified by Christ, we our selves also are found sinners, is therefore Christ the minister of sin? God forbid.

18. For if I build again the things which I destroyed, I make my self a transgressour.

19. For I through the law am dead to the law, that I might live unto God.

20. I am crucified with Christ: Nevertheless I live; yet not I, but Christ liveth in me: and the life which I now live in the flesh, I live by the faith of the Son of God, who loved me, and gave himself for me.

21. I do not frustrate the grace of God: for if righteousness come by the law, then Christ is dead in vain.

PARAPHRASE

[I.6] I cannot but wonder that you are so soon* removed from me† who

I.6* [a] *So soon*. The first place we find Galatia mentioned is Act XVI.6 and therefore St Paul may be supposed to have planted these churches there in his journey mentioned Act XVI which was anno Domini 51. He visited them again after he had been at Jerusalem Act. XVIII.21-23 *Anno Domini* 54. From thence he returnd to Ephesus and staid there above two years. [b]dureing which time this Epistle was writ, so that counting from his last visit this letter was writ to them within two or three year from the time he was

 [*See p. 126 for n. I.6* cont. and n. I.6†*]

called you into the Covenant of Grace which is in Christ unto an other
sort of Gospel which is not altogether an other. [7]Which is not oweing
to any thing I have done or any thing else* but onely this, that you are
troubled by a certain sort of men who would overturne the Gospel of
Christ by makeing circumcision and the keeping of the law necessary†
under the Gospel. [8]But if even I my self or an angel from heaven
should preach any thing to you for gospel different from the gospel I
have preachd unto you let him be accursed. [9]I say it again to you· if any
one under pretence of the gospel preach any other thing to you than
what you have received from me let him be accursed.⟨*⟩ [10]For can it
be doubted of me after haveing don and sufferd so much for the
gospel of Christ whether I doe now* at this time of day make my

last with them and had left them confirmed in the doctrine he had taught them, and therefore he might with reason wonder at their forsakeing him so soon and that gospel he had converted them to.

† *from him that called you*· These words plainly point out him self, but then one might wonder how St Paul came to use them. Since it would have sounded better to have said *removed from the gospel I preachd to you to an other gospel* than *removed from me that preachd to you to an other gospel*. But if it be rememberd that St Pauls designe here is to vindicate him self from the aspersion cast on him that he preachd circumcision no thing could be more suitable to that purpose than this way of expresseing him self

7* [a]ὃ οὐκ ἔστιν ἄλλο I take to signifie *which is not any thing else*. The words themselves, the context, and the business the Apostle is upon here, doe all concur to give these words the sense I have taken them in for 1° If ὃ had referd to εὐαγγέλιον it would have been more natural to have kept to the word ἕτ(ε)ρον and not have changed it into ἄλλο. [b]2° It can scarce be supposed by any one who reads what St Paul says in the following words of this ver. and the two adjoyning; and also Ch: III.4. and V.2-4 and 7 that St Paul should tell them, that what he would keep them from *is not an other gospel*. 3° It is suitable to St Pauls designe here to tell them that to their being *removed to an other gospel* noe body else had contributed, but it was wholy oweing to those Judaizeing Seducers.

† see Act XV.1.5.23.24

9* *Accursed*· Though we may look upon the repetition of the *anathema* here to be for the addeing of force to what he says, yet we may observe that by joyning himself with an angel in the foregoeing ver. he does as good as tell them that he is not guilty of what deserves it, by skilfully insinuateing to the Galatians that they might as well suspect an Angel might preach to them a gospel different from his. i e a false gospel, as that he him self should: and then in this ver. lays the *anathema* wholy and soly upon the Judaizing seducers.

10* [a]Ἄρτι *now* and ἔτι *yet* cannot be understood without a reference to some thing in St Pauls past life. What that was which he had particularly then in his mind we may see by the account he gives of himself in what immediately follows. (viz) That before his conversion he was imploid by men in their designes and made it his business to please them, as may be seen Act IX.1.2. [b]But when god called him, he received his commission and instruction from him alone, and set immediately about it without consulting any man whatsoever, preaching that and that onely which he had received from Christ. So that it would be sensless folly in him and no less than the forsakeing his master Jesus Christ, [c]if he should *now* as was reported of him mix any thing of men's with the pure doctrine of the gospel which he had received immediately by revelation from Jesus

court† to men or seek the favour of god.† If I had hitherto* made it my business to please men I should not have been the servant of Christ nor taken up the profession of the Gospel. [11]But I certifie you, Brethren, that the gospel which has been every where* preachd by me is not such as is pliant to humane interest or can be accomodated to the pleaseing of men. [12](For I neither received it from man, nor was I taught it by any one as his scholer) but it is the pure and unmixed immediate revelation of Jesus Christ to me. [13]To satisfie you of this, my behaviour whilst I was of the Jewish religion is soe well known that I need not tell you how excessive violent I was in persecuteing the Church of god, and destroyed it all I could; [14]and that being carried on by an extraordinary zeal for the traditions of my forefathers I out stripd many students of my owne age and nation in Judaisme. [15]But when it pleased god (who seperated* me from my mothers womb and by his espetial favour called† me to be a Christian and a preacher of the gospel) [16]to reveal his son to me that I might preach him among the Gentiles I there upon applyd not my self to any man* for advice what to doe.† [17]Neither went I up to Jerusalem to those who were Apostles before me to see whether they approved my doctrine, or to have farther instruction from them· But I went immediately* into

Christ to please the Jews after he had so long preachd onely that, and had to avoid all appearance or pretence of the contrary so carefully shund all communication with the Churches of Judea; [d]and had not till a good while after and that very spareingly conversed with any and those but a few of the Apostles them selves some of whom he openly reproovd for their Judaizeing. Thus the narrative subjoynd to this verse explains the *Now* and *yet* in it, and all tends to the same purpose.

† Πείθω *perswad* in our translation, is sometimes used for makeing application to any one to obtein his goodwill or friendship and hence Act XII.20 πείσαντες Βλάστον is translated *haveing made Blastus their friend*, The sense here is the same which the 1 Thess: II.4 he expresses in these words οὐχ ὡς ἀνθρώποις ἀρέσκοντες ἀλλὰ τῷ θεῷ. *not as pleasing men but god*.

11* Τὸ εὐαγγελισθὲν ὑπ' ἐμοῦ *which has been preachd by me*· This being spoken indefinitely must be understood in general *every where*. And so is the import of the foregoeing verse.

15* *Seperated* This may be understood by Jer. I.5

† Called. The history of this call see Act. IX.1. etc.

16* *Flesh and blood* is used for *man*· See Eph. VI.12

† *For advice*· This and what he says in the following ver. is to evidence to the Galatians the full assurance he had of the truth and perfection of the gospel which he had received from Christ by immediate revelation; and how little he was disposed to have any regard to the pleaseing of men in preaching it, that he did not so much as communicate or advise with any of the Apostles about it, to see whether they approved of it.

17* [a]εὐθέως *immediately* though placed just before οὐ προσανεθέμην *I conferred not* yet it is plain by the sense and the designe of St Paul here that it principaly relates to *I went*

Arabia, and from thence returned again to Damascus. [18]Then after
three years* I went up to Jerusalem to see Peter and abode with him
fiveteen days. [19]But other of the Apostles saw I none but James the
brother of our Lord. [20]These things that I write to you I call god to
witness are all true, there is noe falshood in them. [21]Afterwards I came
into the regions of Syria and Cilicia. [22]But with the Churches of
Christ* in Judea I had had noe communication· they had not soe much
as seen my face† [23]onely they had heard that I who formerly persecuted the churches of Christ did now preach the gospel which I
once endeavourd to suppress and extirpate· [24]And they glorified god
upon my account. [II.1]Then fourteen years after I went up again to Jerusalem with Barnabas and took Titus also with me· [2]And I went up by
revelation and there laid before them⟨*⟩ the Gospel which I preach to
the Gentiles, But privately to those who were of note and reputation
amongst them, least the pains that I have already taken† or should
take in the gospel should be in vain‡ [3]But though I communicated the

into Arabia, his departure into *Arabia* presently upon his conversion before he had consulted with any body being made use of to shew that the gospel he had received by immediate revelation from Jesus Christ was compleat, [b]and sufficiently instructed and inabled him to be a preacher and apostle to the Gentiles without borrowing any thing from any man in order thereunto noe not from any of the Apostles noe one of whom he saw till three years after

18* *Three years*. i e from his conversion

22* *In Christ* i e Beleiveing in Christ. see Rom XVI.7

† This which he soe particularly takes notice of does noe thing to the prooveing that he was a true Apostle, but serves very well to shew that in what he preachd he had no communication with those of his own nation, nor took any care to please the Jews.

II.2* [a]*I communicated*. The conference he had in private with the Cheif of the Church of Jerusalem concerning the gospel which he preachd among the Gentiles seems not to have been barely concerning the doctrine of their being free from the law of Moses. That had been openly and hotly disputed at Antioch, [b]and was known to be the business they came about to Jerusalem. but it is probable it was to explain to them the whole doctrine he had received by revelation, by the fulness and perfection whereof (For it is said ver. 6 that in that conference they added noe thing to it) and by the miracles he had don in confirmation of it (see ver. 8) they might see and own what he preachd to be the truth, [c]and him to be one of themselves both by commission and doctrine, as indeed they did. αὐτοῖς *them* signifies those at Jerusalem· κατ' ἰδίαν δὲ τοῖς δοκοῦσι are exegetical and shew the particular manner and persons and import nempe privatim eminentioribus. Twas enough to his purpose to be owned by those of greatest authority and so we see he was by James Peter and John ver. 9. [d]and therefore it was safest and best to give an account of the Gospel he preachd in private to them and not publiquely to the whole church. See Act. XXI.18-33

† *Runing* St Paul uses for *takeing pains* in the Gospel. See ⟨Phil⟩. II.16. A metaphor I suppose taken from the Olympick games to express his utmost endeavours to prevail in propagateing the gospel.

‡ [a]*In vain*· He seems here to give two reasons why at last after 14 years he communicated to the Cheif of the Apostles at Jerusalem the Gospel that he preachd to the Gentiles, when as he shews to the Galatians he had formerly declined all communication with the convert Jews. 1° he seems to intimate that he did it by revelation. [b]2° He gives an other reason. viz

gospel which I preachd to the Gentiles to the eminent men of the
Church at Jerusalem yet neither* Titus who was with me being a
Greek was forced to be circumcised 4Nor* did I yeild any thing one
moment by way of subjection† to the law to those false brethren
who by an unwary admittance were slyely crept in to spie out our
liberty from the law which we have under the gospel that they
might bring us into bondage‡ to the law: 5But I stood my ground
against it that the truth* of the gospel might remain† among you.

that if he had not communicated as he did with the leading men there, and satisfied them concerning his doctrine and mission, his opposers might unsetle the churches he had or should plant by urgeing that the Apostles knew not what it was that he preachd, nor had ever owned it for the gospel or him for an Apostle. [c]Of the readiness of the Judaizing seducers to take any such advantage against him he had lately an Example in the church of Corinth.

3* [a]οὐκ ἠναγκάσθη is rightly translated *was not compelled* a plain evidence to the Galatians that the circumciseing of the convert Gentiles was noe part of the gospel which he laid before these men of note as what he preachd to the Gentiles For if it had Titus must have been circumcised for noe part of his gospel was blamed or alterd by them ver. 6· [b]Of what other use his mentioning this of Titus here can be but to shew to the Galatians that what he preachd conteined no thing of circumciseing the convert Gentiles, it is hard to find. If it were to shew that the other Apostles and church at Jerusalem dispensed with circumcision and other ritual observances of the Mosaical law, that was needless, [c]for that was sufficiently declared by their decree Act XV, which was made and communicated to the churches before this Epistle was writ as may be seen Act XVI.4. Much less was this of Titus of any force to prove that St Paul was a true Apostle, if that were what he was here labouring to justifie. [d]But considering his aim here to be the clearing himself from a report that he preachd up circumcision there could be noe thing more to his purpose than this instance of Titus whom uncircumcised as he was he took with him to Jerusalem, uncircumcised he kept with him there, and uncircumcised he took back with him when he returned. [e]This was a strong and pertinent instance to perswade the Galatians, that the report of his preaching Circumcision was a meer aspersion.

⟨4⟩* οὐδέ *Neither* in the 3d ver. according to proprietie of speech ought to have a *Nor* to answer it which is the οὐδέ *Nor* here which so taken answers the proprietie of the Greek, and very much clears the sense· οὐδὲ Τίτος ἠναγκάσθη οὐδὲ πρὸς ὥραν εἴξαμεν, *Neither was Titus compelled nor did we yeild to them a moment*

† [a]Τῇ ὑποταγῇ *by subjection*. The point that those false brethren contended for was that the law of Moses was to be kept· see Act XV.5· St Paul who on other occasions was so complaisant that to the Jews he became as a Jew; to those under the law as under the law (See 1 Cor IX.19-22) yet when subjection to the law was claimd as due in any case he would not yeild the least matter· [b]this I take to be his meaning of οὐδὲ εἴξαμεν τῇ ὑποταγῇ. for where compliance was desired of him upon the account of expedience and not of subjection to the law we doe not find him stiff and inflexible as may be seen Act XXI.18-26 which was after the writeing of this epistle

‡ *Bondage*· What this *bondage* was See Act. XV 1.5.10

5* *The truth of the gospel*· By it he means here the doctrine of freedom from the law, and so he cals it again ver. 14 and ch: III.1. IV.16 V.7.

† *might remain among you*. Here he tells the reason himself why he yeilded not to those Judaizeing false brethren: It was that the true doctrine which he had preachd to the Gentiles of their freedom from the law might stand firm: A convinceing argument to the Galatians that he preachd not circumcision

4.5 [a]*And that. To whom*· There appears a manifest difficulty in these two verses, which

6a But* as for those† who were realy‡ men of eminency and value, what they were here to fore it matters not at all to me god accepts not the person of any man but communicates the gospel to whom he pleases as

has been observed by most interpreters and is by several ascribed to a redundancie, which some place in δέ in the begining of ver. 4 and others to οἷς in the begining of ver. 5. [b]The relation between οὐδέ ver. 3 and οὐδέ ver. 5 methinks puts an easy end to the doubt by shewing St Pauls sense to be that he *neither* circumcised Titus *Nor* yeilded in the least to the false brethren· He haveing told the Galatians that upon his laying before the men of most authority in the Church at Jerusalem the doctrine which he preachd Titus was not circumcised, [c]he as a farther proof of his not preaching circumcision tels them how he caried it towards the false brethren whose design it was to bring the convert Gentiles into subjection to the law. *And* or *moreover* (for so δέ often signifies) says he *in regard to the false brethren* etc [d]which way of entrance on the matter would not admit of οὐδέ after it to answer οὐδέ ver. 3 which was already writ, but without οἷς the negation must have been expressed by οὐκ as any one will perceive who attentively reads the Greek original. [e]And thus οἷς may be allowed for an Hebrew Pleonasme and the reason of it to be the preventing the former οὐδέ to stand alone to the disturbance of the sense.

6* [a]He that considers the begining of this ver. Ἀπὸ δὲ τῶν δοκούντων with regard to the Διὰ δὲ τοὺς ψευδαδέλφους in the begining of the 4th ver. will easily be induced by the Greek idiom to conclude that the author by these beginings intimates a plain distinction of the matter seperately treated of in what follows each of them [b](viz) what passed between the False brethren and him conteined in ver. 4 and 5 and what passed between the Cheif of the brethren and him conteined ver. 6-10 And therefore some (and I think with reason) introduce this ver. with these words *Thus we behaved our selves towards the false brethren: But* etc:

† [a]Every body sees that here is something to be supplied to make up the sense. Most commentators that I have seen adde these words *I learned noe thing*. But then that enervates the reason that follows *For in conference they added no thing to me* giveing the same thing as a reason for it self and makeing St Paul talk thus *I learnt no thing of them: for they taught me nothing*. [b]But it is very good reasoning and suited to his purpose that it was noe thing at all to him how much those great men were formerly in Christs favour; This hinderd not but that God who was no respecter of persons might reveale the gospel to him also, as 'twas evident he had don and that in its ful perfection [c]For those great men the most eminent of the Apostles had nothing to adde to it or except against it. This was proper to perswade the Galatians that he no where in his preaching receded from that doctrine of freedom from the law which he had preachd to them and was satisfied was the truth even before he had conferred with these Apostles. [d]The bare supplying of οἱ in the begining of the verse takes away the necessity of any such addition. Examples of the like elleipses we have Mat XXVII.9 where we read ἀπὸ υἱῶν for οἱ ἀπὸ υἱῶν and John XVI.17 ἐκ τῶν μαθητῶν for οἱ ἐκ τῶν μαθητῶν [e]and so here takeing ἀπὸ τῶν δοκούντων to be for οἱ ἀπὸ τῶν δοκούντων all the difficulty is removed and St Paul haveing in the foregoeing verse ended the narrative of his deportment towards the false brethren he here begins an account of what passed between him and the cheif of the Apostles

‡ [a]τῶν δοκούντων εἶναί τι our tran⟨s⟩lation renders *who seemd to be some what*. which however it may answer the words, yet to an English ear it carrys a diminishing and ironical sense contrary to the meaning of the Apostle who speaks here of those for whom he had a real esteem and were truly of the first rank [b]for it is plain by what follows that he means Peter James and John. Besides οἱ δοκοῦντες being taken in a good sense ver. 2d and translated *those of reputation* the same expression should have been kept to in rendering ver. 6 and ⟨9⟩ where the same terme occurs again three times and may be presumed in the same sense that it was at first used in ver. 2

he has done to me by revelation without their help [b]for in their conference with me they added no thing to me, they taught me no thing new nor that Christ had not taught me before nor had they any thing to object against what I preachd to the Gentiles. [7]But on the contrary James Peter and John who were of reputation and justly esteemd to be pillars perceiveing that the gospel* which was to be preachd to the Gentiles was committed to me. as that which was to be preachd to the Jews was committed to Peter. [8](For he that had wrought powerfully* in Peter to his executǫing the office of an Apostle to the Jews, had also wrought powerfully in me in my application and Apostleship to the Gentiles). [9]And knowing* the favour that was bestowed on me gave me and Barnabas the right hand† of fellowship that we should preach the Gospel to the Gentiles, and they to the Children of Israel. [10]All that they proposed was that we should remember to make collections among the gentiles for the poor Christians of Judea which was a thing that of my self I was forward to.

[11]But when Peter came to Antioch I openly opposed* him to his

⟨7⟩* [a]Peter James and John who 'tis manifest by ver. 9 are the persons here spoken of, seem of all the Apostles to have been most in esteem and favour with their master dureing his conversation with them on earth. See Mar V.37 IX.2. XIV.33. 'But yet that', *says St Paul*, 'is of noe moment now to me. [b]The gospel, which I preach, and which god, 'who is no respecter of persons has been pleased to commit to me by imm⟨e⟩diate 'revelation, is not the less true, nor is there any reason for me to recede from it in a title. 'For these men of the first rank could find no thing to adde alter or gainsay in it.' [c]This is suitable to St Pauls designe here to let the Galatians see that as he in his cariage had never favoured circumcision so neither had he any reason by preaching circumcision to forsake the doctrine of liberty from the law which he had preachd to them as a part of that gospel which he had received by revelation.

8* 'Ενεϱγήσας *workeing in* may be understood here to signifie both the operation of the spirit upon the mind of St Peter and St Paul in sending them the one to the Jews the other to the Gentiles; and also the holy ghost bestowed on them whereby they were enabled to doe miracles for the confirmation of their doctrine. In neither of which St Paul as he shews was inferior, and so had as authentique a seale of his mission and doctrine.

9* [a]καί *And* copulates γνόντες *knowing* in this ver. with ἰδόντες *seeing* ver. 7. and makes both of them to agreé with the nominative case to the verb ἔδωκαν *gave* which is no other but *James Cephas* and *John* and so justifies my transfering those names to ver. 7. for the more easy construction and understanding of the text, [b]though St Paul defers the nameing of them till he is, as it were against his will, forced to it before he end his discourse

† The giveing the right hand was a symbol amongst the Jews as well as other nations of accord and admitting men into fellowship

11* [a]*I opposed him·* from this opposition to St Peter which they suppose to be before the Council at Jerusalem some would have it that this Epistle to the Galatians was writ before that council, as if what was don before the Council could not be mentioned in a letter writ after the Council. [b]They also contend that this journey mentioned here by St Paul was not that wherein he and Barnabas went up to that council to Jerusalem but

face. For indeed he was to be blamed. [12]For he conversd there familiarly with the Gentiles and eat with them till some Jews came thither from James, then he withdrew and seperated from the Gentiles for fear of those who were of the circumcision· [13]And the rest of the Jews joynd also with him in this hypocrisie, insomuch that Barnabas him self was carried away with the stream and dissembled as they did. [14]But when I saw they conformed not their conduct to the truth* of the gospel I said unto Peter before them all. If thou being a Jew takest the liberty some times to live after the manner of the Gentiles not keeping to those rules which the Jews observe why doest thou constrain the Gentiles to conforme themselves to the rites and manner of liveing of the Jews? [15]We who are by nature Jews borne under the instruction and guidance of the law* gods peculiar people, and not of the unclean and profligate race of the Gentiles abandond to sin and death, [16]knowing that a man cannot be justified by the deeds of the law but soly by faith in Jesus Christ, even we have put ourselves upon beleiveing on him and imbraced the profession of the gospel for the attainment of justification by faith in Christ and not by the works of the law: [17]But if we who seek to be justified in Christ even we our selves also are found unjustified sinners,* (for such are all those who are under the law

that mentioned Act XI.30 but this with as little ground as the former· The strongest reason they bring is that if this journey had been to the council, and this letter after that council [c]St Paul would not certainly have omitted to have mentioned to the Galatians that decree. To which I answer 1° The mention of it was superfluous for they had it already see Act XVI.4. 2° The mentioning of it was impertinent to the designe of St Pauls narrative here. [d]For it is plain that his aim in what he relates here of him self and his past actions is to shew that haveing received the gospel from Christ by immediate revelation he had all along preachd that and noething but that, every where. so that he could not be supposed to have preachd circumcision, or by his cariage to have shewn any subjection to the law. [e]All the whole narrative following being to make good what he says Ch I.11. That the gospel which he preachd was not accommodated to the humoring of men; nor did he seek to please the Jews (who were the men here meant) in what he taught. [f]Takeing this to be his aim, we shall find the whole account he gives of himself from that 11 ver. of Ch I to the end of this II to be very clear and easie and very proper to invalidate the report of his preaching circumcision.

14* [a]'Αλήθεια τοῦ εὐαγγελίου *The truth of the Gospel* is put here for that freedom from the law of Moses which was a part of the true doctrine of the gospel· For it was in no thing else ⟨but⟩ their undue and timerous observeing some of the Mosaical rites that St Paul here blames St Peter and the other Judaizing converts at Antioch. [b]In this sense he uses the word *truth* all along through this epistle, as Ch II.5.14. III.1. V.7. insisting on it that this doctrine of freedome from the law was the true gospel.

15* φύσει 'Ιουδαῖοι *Jews by nature·* What the Jews thought of themselves in contradistinction to the Gentiles see Rom II.17-23

17* [a]*Sinners·* Those who are under the law haveing once transgressed remain always sinners unalterably so in the eye of the law which excludes all from justification. The

which admits of noe remission nor justification), is Christ therefore the minister of sin? is the dispensation by him a dispensation of sin and not of righteousness? Did he come into the world that those who beleive in him should still remain sinners i e under the guilt of their sins without the benefit of justification? By no means. [18]And yet certain it is, if I who quitted the law* to put my self under the gospel. put my self again under the law I make my self a transgressor, I reassume again the guilt of all my transgressions which by the termes of that covenant of workes I cannot be justified from. [19]For by the tenor of the law* it self I by faith in Christ am discharged† from the law that I might be appropriated‡ to god and live acceptably to him in his kingdom which he has now set up under his son. [20]I a member of Christs body am crucified* with him, but though I am thereby dead to the law, I never the less live, yet not I but Christ liveth in me i.e the life which I now live in the flesh is upon noe other principle nor under any other

Apostle in this place argues thus 'We Jews who are by birth gods holy people and not as 'the profligate Gentiles abandond to all manner of pollution and uncleaness, [b]not being 'nevertheless able to attain righteousness by the deeds of the law have beleived in 'Christ that we might be justified by faith in him· But if even we who have betaken our 'selves to Christ for justification are our selves found to be unjustified sinners, liable 'still to wrath. as all under the law, to which we subject our selves, are, what deliverance 'have we from sin by Christ? [c]None at all: We are as much concluded under sin and 'guilt as if we did not beleive in him, So that by joyning him and the law together for 'justification, we shut our selves out from justification, which cannot be had under the 'law; and make Christ the minister of sin and not of justification, which god forbid.'

18* Whether this be a part of what St Paul said to St Peter or whether it be addressed to the Galatians St Paul by speakeing it in his own name plainly declares that if he sets up the law again he must necessarily be an offender: whereby he strongly insinuates to the Galatians that he was no promoter of circumcision, espetialy when what he says Ch: V.2-4 is added to it.

19* *By the tenor of the law it self·* See Rom III.21. Gal III 24.25. IV.21 etc

† Being *dischargd from the law* St Paul expresses by *dead to the law·* Compare Rom VI.14 with VII.4

‡ [a]*Live to god·* What St Paul says here seems to implye that liveing under the law was to live not acceptably to god, a strange doctrine certainly to the Jews and yet it was true now under the gospel. For god haveing put his Kingdom in this world wholy under his son when he raised him from the dead, all who after that would be his people in his kingdom were to live by no other law but the Gospel which was now the law of his kingdom. [b]And hence we see god cast off the Jews, because sticking to their old constitution they would not have this man reign over them· So that what St Paul says here is in effect this. 'By beleiveing in Christ I am discharged from the Mosaical law that I may wholy 'conforme my self to the rule of the Gospel. which is now the law which must be owned 'and observed by all those who as gods people will live acceptably to him.' [c]This I think is visibly his meaning though the accustomeing himself to Antitheses may possibly be the reason why after haveing said *I am dead to the law* he expresses his puting him self under the gospel by *liveing to god*

20* *Crucified with Christ·* See this explaind Rom: VII.4 and VI.2-14.

law but that of faith in the son of god† who loved me and gave himself for me. [21]And in so doeing I avoid frustrateing the grace of god. I accept of the grace* and forgiveness of god as it is offerd through faith in Christ in the gospel: But if I subject my self to the law as still in force under the gospel I doe in effect frustrate grace. For if righteousness be to be had by the law then Christ died to noe purpose, there was noe need of it†

SECTION III

Ch. III.1-5

CONTENTS

By the account St Paul has given of him self in the foregoeing section the Galatians being furnishd with evidence sufficient to clear him in their minds from the report of his preaching circumcision, he comes now the way being thus opend directly to oppose their being circumcised and subjecting them selves to the law· The first argument he uses is that they received the holy ghost and the gifts of miracles by the Gospel and not by the law.

TEXT

III.1. O foolish Galatians, who hath bewitched you, that you should not obey the truth, before whose Eyes Jesus Christ hath been evidently set forth, crucified among you?

2. This only would I learn of you, Received ye the Spirit by the works of the law, or by the hearing of faith?

3. Are ye so foolish? Having begun in the spirit, are ye now made perfect by the flesh?

4. Have ye suffered so many things in vain? If it be yet in vain.

5. He therefore that ministreth to you the Spirit, and worketh miracles among you, doth he it by the works of the law, or by the hearing of faith?

† i e The whole management of my self is conformable to the doctrine of the gospel of justification in Christ alone and not by the deeds of the law· This and the former ver. seems to be spoken in opposition to St Peters owning a subjection to the law of Moses by his walking mentioned ver. 14

21* *Grace of god*. See Ch I.6.7 to which this seems here opposed

† *In vain*· Read this explaind in St Pauls own words Ch. V.3-6

PARAPHRASE

[III.1]O ye foolish Galatians who hath cast a mist before your eyes that you should not keep to the truth,* of the gospel, you to whom the suffering and death of Christ† upon the cross hath been by me soe lively represented as if it had been actualy don in your sight. [2]This one thing I desire to know of you did you receive the miraculous gifts of the spirit by the workes of the law or by the gospel preachd to you? [3]Have you so little understanding that haveing begun in the reception of the spiritual doctrine of the gospel,* you hope to be advanced to higher degrees of perfection, and to be compleated by the law?* [4]Have you suffered so many things in vain, if at least you will render it in vain by falling off from the profession of the pure and uncorrupted doctrine of the gospel and apostatiseing to Judaisme? [5]The gifts of the holy ghost that have been conferred upon you have they not been conferred on you as Christians professeing faith in Jesus Christ and not as observers of the law? And hath not he* who hath conveyd these gifts to you, and don miracles amongst you don it as a preacher and professor of the Gospel, the Jews who stick in the law of Moses being not able by virtue of that to doe any such thing?

SECTION IV

Ch. III.6-18

CONTENTS

His next argument against Circumcision and subjection to the law

III.1* *Obey the truth*. i e Stand fast in the liberty of the Gospel *Truth* being used in this Epistle as we have already noted Ch II.14 for the doctrine of being free from the law which St Paul had deliverd to them. The reason whereof he gives Ch: V.3-5

† [a]St Paul mentions no thing to them here but *Christ crucified* as knowing that when formerly he had preachd Christ crucified to them he had shewn them, that by Christs death on the cross beleivers were set free from the law, and the covenant of workes was removed to make way for that of Grace. This we may find him inculcateing to his other Gentile converts. [b]see Eph. II.15.16. Col: II.14.20. And accordingly he tels the Galatians Ch: V.2.4 that if by circumcision they put themselves under the law, they were fallen from grace, and Christ should profit them nothing at all. Things which they are supposed to understand at his writeing to them.

3* It is a way of speaking very familiar to St Paul in opposeing the law and the gospel to call the Law *flesh* and the gospel *spirit*· The reason whereof is very plain to any one conversant in his Epistles.

5* *He*· The person meant here by ὁ ἐπιχορηγῶν *he that ministreth* and Ch. I.6 by ὁ καλ⟨έ⟩σας *he that called*, is plainly St Paul himself, though out of modesty he declines nameing himself.

is that the children of Abraham entitled to the inheritance and blesseing promised to Abraham and his seed, are so by faith and not by
being under the law, which brings a curse upon those who are under it

TEXT

III.6. Even as Abraham believed God, and it was accounted to him for righteousness.

7. Know ye therefore, that they which are of Faith, the same are the Children of Abraham.

8. And the Scripture foreseeing that God would justifie the Heathen through faith, preached before the gospel unto Abraham, saying, In thee shall all nations be blessed.

9. So then they which be of faith, are blessed with faithful Abraham.

10. For as many as are of the works of the law, are under the curse: for it is written, Cursed is every one that continueth not in all things which are written in the book of the law to do them.

11. But that no man is justified by the law in the sight of God, it is evident: for, the just shall live by faith.

12. And the law is not of faith: but, The man that doth them shall live in them.

13. Christ hath redeemed us from the curse of the law, being made a curse for us: for it is written, Cursed is every one that hangeth on a tree:

14. That the blessing of Abraham might come on the Gentiles through Jesus Christ; that we might receive the promise of the Spirit through faith.

15. Brethren, I speak after the manner of men; Though it be but a mans covenant, yet if it be confirmed, no man disannulleth or addeth thereto.

16. Now to Abraham and his seed were the promises made. He saith not, And to seeds, as of many; but as of one, And to thy seed, which is Christ.

17. And this I say, that the covenant that was confirmed before of God in Christ, the law which was four hundred and thirty years after, cannot disanul, that it should make the promise of none effect.

18. For if the inheritance be of the law, it is no more of promise: but God gave it to Abraham by promise.

PARAPHRASE

III.6 But to proceed. As Abraham beleived in god and it was
accounted to him for righteousness 7 so know ye that those who are of
faith i e who relye upon god and his promises of grace and not upon
their own performances, they are the children of Abraham who shall
inherit 8 and this is plain in the Sacred Scripture. For it being in the
purpose of god to justifie the Gentiles by faith he gave Abraham

a foreknowledg of the gospel in these words* *In thee all the nations of the earth shall be blessed·* [9]So that they who are of* faith are blessed† with Abraham who beleived; [10]But as many as are of* their works of the law are under the† curse. For it is written‡ *cursed is every one who remaineth not in all things which are written in the book of the law to doe them*. [11]But that noe man is justified by the law in the sight of god is evident for *the just shall live by faith*.* [12]But the law says not soe, the law gives not life to those who beleive* but the rule of the law is *He that doth them shall live in them*.† [13]Christ hath redeemed us from the curse of the law being made a curse for us. For it is written* *cursed is every one that hangeth on a tree* [14]That the blesseing* promised to Abraham might come on the Gentiles through Jesus Christ; that we who are Christians might by beleiveing receive the spirit that was promised†

[15]Brethren this is a known and allowed rule in humane affairs that a promise or compact, though it be barely a mans covenant, yet if it be once ratified soe it must stand noebody can render it void or make any alteration in it. [16]Now to Abraham and his seed were the promises

III.8* Gen XII.3

9.10* *Of faith* and *of the works of the law*. See explaind Rom III.26. note. Spoken as of two races of men the one as the genuin posterity of Abraham heirs of the promise, the other not.

† *Blessed* and *under the curse·* Here again there is another division (viz) into the *blessed* and those *under the curse* whereby is meant such as are in a state of life or acceptance with god, or such as are exposed to his wrath and to death· see Deutr: XXX.19

10‡ *Written* Deut. XXVII.26

11* Hab: II.4

12* See Act XIII.39

† Lev: ⟨XVIII.5⟩

13* Deut XXI.23

14* *Blesseing*. That Blesseing ver. 8.9.14 Justification ver. 11 Righteousness ver. 21 Life ver. 11.12.21. Inheritance ver. 18 Being the children of god ver. 26 are in effect all the same on the one side, and *the Curse* ver. 13 the direct contrary on the other side is so plain in St Pauls discourse here that noebody who reads it with the least attention will be in any doubt about it

† [a]*Promised·* St Pauls argument, to convince the Galatians that they ought not to be circumcised or submit to the law, from their haveing received the spirit from him upon their receiveing the gospel which he preachd to them ver. 2. and 5. stands thus. The Blesseing promised to Abraham and to his seed was wholy upon the account of faith ver. 7. [b]There were not different seeds who should inherit the promise, The one by the works of the law, and the other by faith. For there was but one seed which was Christ ver. 16, and those who should claim in and under him by faith. Among those there was noe distinction of Jew and Gentile. They and they onely who beleived were all one and the same true seed of Abraham, and heirs according to the promise ver. 28.29. [c]And therefore the promise made to the people of god of giveing them the spirit under the Gospel was performed onely to those who beleived in Christ; a clear evidence that it was not by puting themselves under the law, but by faith in Jesus Christ, that they were the people of God, and heirs of the promise.

made. God doth not say *and to seeds** as if he spoke of more seeds than one, that were entitled to the promise upon different accounts, but onely of one sort of men who upon one sole account were that seed of Abraham. which was alone meant and concerned in the promise soe that *unto thy seed*† designed Christ and his mistical body‡ i e Those that become members of him by faith. [17]This therefore I say that the law which was not till 430 years after cannot disanul the covenant that was long before made and ratified to Christ, by god so as to set aside the promise. [18]For if the right to the inheritance be from the workes of the law it is plain that it is not founded in the promise, to Abraham as certainly it is. For the inheritance was a donation and free gift of god setled on Abraham and his seed by promise.

SECTION V

Ch. III.19-25

CONTENTS

In answer to this objection, *To what then serveth the law?* he shews them, That the law was not contrary to the promise; But since all men were guilty of transgression ver. 22 the law was added to shew the Israelites, the fruit and inevitable consequence of their sin, and thereby the necessity of betakeing themselves to Christ; But as soon as men have received Christ, they have attained the end of the law, and so are no longer under it· This is a farther argument against circumcision

TEXT

III.19. Wherefore then serveth the law? It was added because of transgressions, till the seed should come, to whom the promise was made; and it was ordained by angels in the hand of a mediator.

20. Now a mediator is not a mediator of one; but God is one.

21. Is the law then against the promises of God? God forbid: for if there had been a law given which could have given life, verily righteousness should have been by the law.

16* *And to seeds*. By *seeds* St Paul here visibly means the οἱ ἐκ πίστεως *Those of faith* and the οἱ ἐξ ἔργων νόμου *Those of the works of the law* spoken of above ver. 9.10 as two distinct seeds or descendants claiming from Abraham.

† *And to thy seed·* See Gen XII.7. Repeated again in the following Chapters.

‡ *mystical body·* See ver. 27

22. But the Scripture hath concluded all under sin, that the promise by faith of Jesus Christ might be given to them that believe.

23. But before faith came, we were kept under the law, shut up unto the faith which should afterwards be revealed.

24. Wherefore the law was our school-master to bring us unto Christ, that we might be justified by faith.

25. But after that faith is come, we are no longer under a school-master.

PARAPHRASE

III.19a If the blessing and inheritance be setled on Abraham and Beleivers as a free gift by promise, and was not to be obteined by the deeds of the law, to what purpose then was the law? It was added because the Israelites the posterity of Abraham were transgressors* as well as other men, [b]to shew them their sins and the punishment and death they incurred by them, till Christ should come who was that seed into whom both Jews and Gentiles ingrafted by beleeving, become the people of god and children of Abraham, that seed to which the promise was made. And the law was Ordained by Angels in the hand of a mediator† Whereby it is manifest that the law could not disanul the promise, 20 Because a mediator is a mediator between two partys concerned. but god is but one* of those concerned in the

III.19* That this is the meaning of *because of transgression* the following part of this section shews wherein St Paul argues to this purpose. The Jews were sinners as well as other men ver. 22· The law denounceing death to all sinners could save none ver. 21 but was thereby useful to bring men to Christ that they might be justified by faith. ver. 24· See Ch. II.15.16

† *mediator*· See Deut. V.5. Lev. XXVI.46. where it is said the law was made between god and the children of Israel *by the hand of Moses*

20* [a]*But god is one*· To understand this ver. we must cary in our minds what St Paul is here doeing and that from ver. 17 is manifest he is proveing that the law could not disanul the promise, and he does it upon this known rule that a covenant or promise once ratified can not be altered or di⟨s⟩anulled by any other, but both the partys concerned. [b]Now says he God is but one of the partys concerned in the promise, the Gentiles and Israelites together made up the other. ver. 14. But Moses at the giveing the law was a Mediator onely between the I⟨s⟩raelites and god, And therefore could not transact any thing to the disanulling the promise which was between god and the Israelits and Gentiles together, [c]Because God was but one of the partys to that Covenant; The other which was the Gentiles as well as Israelites Moses appeard or transacted not for. And so what was don at Mount Sinay by the Mediation of Moses could not affect a covenant made between partys whereof one onely was there. [d]How necessary it was for St Paul to adde this we shall see if we consider that without it, his argument of 430 years distance would have been deficient and hardly conclusive. For if both the partys concernd in the promise had transacted by Moses the Mediator, (as they might if none but the Nation of the Israelites had been concerned in the promise made by god to Abraham) [e]they might by mutual consent have altered or set asid the former promise as well four hundred years as four days after. That which hindered it

promise. [21]If then the promised inheritance come not to the seed of Abraham by the law, is the law opposite by the curse it denounces against transgressors to the promises that god made of blesseing to Abraham? No by noe means· For if there had been a law given which could have put* us into a state of life certainly righteousness should have been by law·† [22]But we find the quite contrary by the Scripture which makes noe distinction betwixt Jew and Gentile in this respect, but has shut up together all mankind* Jews and Gentiles under sin† and guilt that the blesseing‡ which was promised to that which is Abrahams true and intended seed by faith§ in Christ might be given to those who beleive· [23]But before Christ and the doctrine of justification by faith* in him came we Jews were shut up as a company of prisoners together under the custody and inflexible rigor of the law unto the comeing of the Messiah when the doctrine of justification by faith in him should be revealed. [24]So that the law by its severity served as a schoolmaster to bring us to Christ that we might be justified by faith. [25]But Christ being come and with him the doctrine of justification by faith we are set free from this schoolmaster there is no longer any need of him.

was, that at Moses's Mediation at Mount Sinai God who was but one of the partys to the Promise was present: But the other party Abrahams seed consisting of Israelites and Gentiles together was not there, [f]Moses transacted for the Nation of the Israelites alone, The other Nations were not concerned in the Covenant made at Mount Sinay, as they were in the promise made to Abraham and his seed which therefore could not be di⟨s⟩anulled without their consent. For that both the promise to Abraham and his seed and the Covenant with Israel at Mount Sinai was National is in it self evident.

21* ζωοποιῆσαι *Put into a state of life*· The Greek word signifies to *make alive*· St Paul considers al men here as in a mortal state, and to be put out of that mortal state into a state of life he cals being *made alive*· This he says the Law could not doe because it could not confer righteousness

† ἐκ νόμου *by law*. i e by workes or obedience to that law, which tended towards righteousness as well as the promise but was not able to reach or confer it· See Rom VIII.3 i e Frail men were not able to attain righteousness by an exact conformity of their actions to the law of righteousness.

22* τὰ πάντα *All*, is used here for *All men*. The Apostle Rom. III.9 and 19 expresses the same thing by πάντας *all men* and πᾶς ὁ κόσμος *all the world*, But speaking in the next verse here of the Jews in particular he says *We* meaning those of his own nation as is evident from ver. 24.25

† *under sin*. i e rank them all together as one guilty race of sinners. See this proved Rom III.9. I.18. etc: To the same purpose of puting both Jews and Gentiles into one state St Paul uses συνέκλεισε πάντας. *hath shut them up all together* Rom XI.32

‡ The thing *promised* is in this chapter sometimes called *blesseing* ver. 9.14. some times *inheritance* 18. Sometimes *Justification* ver. 11.24 Sometimes righteousness ver. 21 and sometimes *life* 11.21

§ *By faith*· See ver. 14

23* *Justification by faith*· See ver. 24

SECTION VI

Ch. III.26-29

CONTENTS

As a farther argument to disswade them from Circumcision he tels the Galatians that by faith in Christ all whether Jews or Gentiles are made the children of god, and soe they stood in noe need of Circumcision

TEXT

III.26. For ye are all the children of God by faith in Christ Jesus.

27. For as many of you as have been baptized into Christ, have put on Christ.

28. There is neither Jew nor Greek, there is neither bond nor free, there is neither male nor female: for ye are all one in Christ Jesus.

29. And if ye be Christs, then are ye Abrahams seed, and heirs according to the promise.

PARAPHRASE

III.26 For ye are all* the children of God by faith in Christ Jesus. 27 For
as many of you as have been baptised into Christ have put on* Christ.
28 There is noe distinction of Jew or Gentile; of bond or free; of male or
female. For ye are all one body makeing up one person in Christ Jesus·
29 And if ye are all one* in Christ Jesus ye are the true one seed of
Abraham, and heirs according to the promise

III.26* *All*. i e Both Jews and Gentiles

27* [a]*Put on Christ·* This, which at first sight may seem a very bold metaphor, if we consider what St Paul has said ver. 16 and 26 is admirably adapted to express his thoughts in a few words, and has a great grace in it. He says ver. 16 that *the seed* to which the promise was made *was but one and that one was Christ*: [b]And ver. 26 he declares that *by faith in Christ they all become the sons of god*. To lead them into an easie conception how this is done he here tels them, that by takeing on them the profession of the Gospel *they have*, as it were, *put on Christ*, soe that to god now lookeing on them there appears no thing but Christ. [c]They are as it were coverd all over with him, as a man is with the clothes he hath put on. And hence he says in the next verse that *they are all one in Christ Jesus*, as if there were but that one person.

29* The Clermont Copy reads εἰ δὲ ὑμεῖς εἷς ἐστε ἐν Χριστῷ Ἰησοῦ. *And if ye are one in Christ Jesus* more suitable as it seems to the Apostles argument. For ver. 28 he says *they are all one in Christ Jesus*, from whence the inference in the following words of the Clermont copy is natural *And if ye be one in Christ Jesus, then are ye Abrahams seed and heirs according to the promise*.

SECTION VII

Ch. IV.1-11

CONTENTS

[a]In the first part of this section he farther shews that the law was not against the promise in that the Child is not disinherited by being under Tutors. But the cheif designe of this section is to shew that though both *Jews* and *Gentiles* were intended to be the children of god and heirs of the promise by faith in Christ, [b]yet they both of them were left in bondage, the *Jews* to the law. ver. 3; and the *Gentiles* to false gods ver. 8 till Christ in due time came to redeem them both; and therefore it was folly in the Galatians being redeemd from one bondage, to goe backwards and put them selves again in a state of bondage, though under a new master.

TEXT

IV.1. Now I say, that the heir as long as he is a child, differeth nothing from a servant, tho he be lord of all;

2. But is under tutors and governours, until the time appointed of the father.

3. Even so we, when we were children, were in bondage under the elements of the world:

4. But when the fulness of the time was come, God sent forth his Son made of a woman, made under the law,

5. To redeem them that were under the law, that we might receive the adoption of sons.

6. And because ye are sons, God hath sent forth the Spirit of his Son into your hearts, crying, Abba, Father.

7. Wherefore thou art no more a servant, but a son; and if a son, then an heir of God through Christ.

8. Howbeit, then when ye knew not God, ye did service unto them which by nature are no gods.

9. But now after that ye have known God, or rather are known of God, how turn ye again to the weak and beggarly elements, whereunto ye desire again to be in bondage?

10. Ye observe days, and months, and times, and years.

11. I am afraid of you, lest I have bestowed upon you labour in vain.

PARAPHRASE

[IV.1]Now I say that the heir as long as he is a Child differeth noething from a bond man* though he be Lord of all [2]but is under tutors and guardians until the time prefixed by his father. [3]So we* Jews whilst we were Children were in bondage under the law† [4]But when the time appointed for the comeing of the Messiah was accomplished, God sent forth his son made of a woman, and subjected to the law, [5]that he might redeem those who were under the law and set them free from it, that we who beleive might be put out of the state of bond men into that of sons. [6]Into which state of sons it is evident that you Galatians who were heretofore Gentiles are put, for as much as god hath sent forth his spirit* into your hearts which inables you to crye Abba father [7]So that thou art noe longer a bond-man but a son: and if a son, then an heir* of God, or of the promise of god through Christ· [8]But then. i e before ye were made the sons of god by faith in Christ now under the

IV.1* *Bond-man·* so δοῦλος signifies and unless it be so translated ver. 1.7.8 *bondage* ver. 3.7 will scarce be understood by an English reader, but St Pauls sense will be lost to one who by *servant* understands not one in a state of *bondage*

3* *We·* 'Tis plain St Paul speaks here in the name of the *Jews* or Jewish Church, which though gods peculiar people, yet was to passe its nonage (so St Paul cals it) under the restraint and tutorage of the law, and not to receive the possession of the promised inheritance till Christ came.

† *The law* he cals here στοιχεῖα τοῦ κόσμου. *Elements* or *rudiments of the world*. Because the observances and discipline of the law which had restraints and bondage enough in it led them not beyond the things of this world into the possession or tast of their spiritual and heavenly inheritance.

6* [a]The same argument of proveing their sonship from their haveing the *Spirit* St Paul uses to the Romans Rom: VIII.16. And he that will read 2 Cor IV 17-V.6 and Eph I.11-14 will find that the Spirit is lookd on as the seale and assurance of the inheritance of life to those who *have received the adoption of sons* as St Paul speaks here ver. 5. [b]The force of the argument seems to lie in this, that as he that hath the spirit of a man in him has an evidence that he is the son of a man, so he that hath the spirit of god has thereby an assurance that he is the son of god. Conformable here unto the opinion of the *Jews* was, that the Spirit of god was given to none but them selves, [c]they alone being the people or children of god, for god cals the people of Israel his son Exod IV.22.23. And hence we see that when to the astonishment of the *Jews* the Spirit was given to the *Gentiles* the *Jews* no longer doubted that the inheritance of eternal life was also conferred on the Gentiles. Compare Act X 44-48 with Act XI.15-18

7* [a]St Paul from the Galatians haveing received the spirit (as appears Ch III.2) argues that they are the sons of god without the law, and consequently heirs of the promise without the law. For says he ver. 1-6 the Jews themselves were fain to be redeemd from the bondage of the law by Jesus Christ, that as sons they might attain to the inheritance. [b]But you Galatians says he have by the spirit that is given you by the ministry of the gospel an evidence that god is your father, and being sons are free from the bondage of the law, and heirs without it. The same sort of reasoning St Paul uses to the Romans VIII.14-17

Gospel ye not knowing god were in bondage to those who were in truth no gods. [9]But now that ye know god, yea rather that ye are known and taken into favour* by him how can it be that you who have been put out of a state of bondage into the freedom of sons should goe backwards, and be willing to put your selves under the weak† and beggarly† elements of the world into a state of bondage⟨‡⟩ again? [10]Ye observe days. and months and times, and years in compliance with the Mosaical institution. [11]I begin to be afraid of you, and to be in doubt whether all the pains I have taken about you to set you at liberty in the freedom of the gospel will not prove lost labour

SECTION VIII

Ch. IV.12-20

CONTENTS

He presses them with the remembrance of the great kindness they had for him when he was amongst them, and assures them that they have no reason to be alienated from him, Though that be it which the Judaizeing Seducers aim at.

TEXT

IV.12. Brethren, I beseech you, be as I am; for I am as ye are: ye have not injured me at all.

13. Ye know how through infirmity of the flesh, I preached the gospel unto you at the first.

9⟨*⟩ *Known·* It has been before observed how apt St Paul is to repeat his words though something varied in their signification· We have here an other instance of it. Haveing said, *ye have known God* he subjoyns, *or rather are known of him* in the Hebrew latitude of the word *known* in which language it sometimes signifies *knowing* with choise and approbation. See Amos III.2. 1 Cor VIII.3.

† The law is here called *weak* because it was not able to deliver a man from bondage and death into the glorious liberty of the sons of god. Rom VIII.1-3. And it is called *beggarly* because it kept men in the poor estate of pupils from the full possession and enjoyment of the inheritance. ver. 1-3

‡ [a]The Apostle makes it matter of astonishment how they who had been in bondage to false gods haveing been once set free could endure the thought of parting with their liberty, and of returning into any sort of bondage again even under the mean and beggarly rudiments of the Mosaical institution, which was not able to make them sons and instate them in the inheritance. [b]For St Paul ver. 7 expresly opposes bondage to sonship, so that all who are not in the state of Sons are in the state of bondage. Πάλιν *again* cannot here refer to στοιχεῖα *elements* which the Galatians had never been under hitherto. but to *bondage*, which he tels them ver. 8 they had been in to false gods

14. And my temptation which was in my flesh ye despised not, nor rejected; but received me as an Angel of God, even as Christ Jesus.

15. Where is then the Blessedness you spake of? for I bear you record, that if it had been possible, ye would have plucked out your own eyes, and have given them to me.

16. Am I therefore become your enemy, because I tell you the truth?

17. They zealously affect you, but not well; yea, they would exclude you, that you might affect them.

18. But it is good to be zealously affected always in a good thing, and not only when I am present with you.

19. My little children, of whom I travail in birth again until Christ be formed in you:

20. I desire to be present with you now, and to change my voice, for I stand in doubt of you.

PARAPHRASE

[IV.12]I beseech you Brethren Let you and I be as if we were all one. Think your selves to be very me; as I in my own mind put no difference at all between you and my self. You have don me noe manner of injury; [13]On the contrary ye know that through infirmity of the flesh I heretofore preachd the Gospel to you, [14]and yet ye dispised me not for the trial I underwent in the flesh,* you treated me not with contempt and scorne: But you received me as an Angel of God, yea as Jesus Christ him self. [15]What benedictions* did you then power out upon me? For I bear you witness had it been practicable you would have pulled out your very eyes and given them me. [16]But is it so that I am become your enemie* in continueing to tell you the truth? [17]They who would make you of that mind shew a warmth of affection to you; But it is not well. For their business is to exclude me, that they might get into your affection. [18]It is good to be well and warmely affected towards a good man* at all times, and not barely when I am present

IV.14* [a]What this *weakness* and *tryal in the flesh* was since it has not pleased the Apostle to mention it is impossible for us to know: but may be remarked here as an instance once for all of that unavoidable obscurity of some passages in Epistolary writeings without any fault in the auther. [b]For some things necessary to the understanding of what is writ are usualy of course and justly omitted because already known to him the letter is writ to, and it would be sometimes ungraceful, oftentimes superfluous particularly to mention them.

15* The context makes this sense of the words so necessary and visible, that it is to be wonderd how any one could overlook it.

16* *your enemie·* See Ch. I.6

18⟨*⟩ [a]That by καλῷ he here means a person and himself the scope of the context evinces. In the six preceding verses he speaks onely of himself and the change of their

with you [19]my little children, for whom I have again the pains of a woman in child-birth till Christ be formed in you.* i e till the true doctrine of Christianity be setled in your minds. [20]But I would willingly be this very moment with you. and change* my discourse as I should find occasion, For I am at a Stand about you and know not what to think of you

SECTION IX

Ch. IV.21-V.1

CONTENTS

He exhorts them to stand fast in the liberty with which Christ hath made them free, shewing those who are so zealous for the law, that if they mind what they read in the law, they will there find, that the children of the promise or of the new Jerusalem were to be free; but the children after the flesh, of the earthly Jerusalem, were to be in bondage, and to be cast out, and not to have the inheritance.

affection to him since he left them. There is noe other thing mentioned as peculiarly deserveing their affection to which the rule given in this verse could refer. [b]He had said ver. 17 ζηλοῦσιν ὑμᾶς *they affect you* and ἵνα αὐτοὺς ζηλοῦτε *that you might affect them*, this is onely of persons, and therefore ζηλοῦσθαι ἐν καλῷ which immediately follows may best be understood of a person, [c]else the following part of the verse though joynd by the copulative καί *and* will make but a disjoynted sense with the preceding. But there can be noe thing plainer nor more coherent than this which seems to be St Pauls sense here. *You were very affectionate to me when I was with you.* [d] *You are since estranged from me, it is the artifice of the seducers that have cooled you to me. But if I am the good man you took me to be you will doe well to continue the warmth of your affection to me when I am absent and not to be well affected towards me onely when I am present among you.* [e]Though this be his meaning, yet the way he has taken to express it is much more elegant, modest and gracefull. Let any one read the original and see whether it be not so.

19* [a]If this verse be taken for an entire sentence by it self it will be a parenthesis and that not the most necessary or congruous that is to be found in St Pauls epistles or δέ *But* must be left out as we see it is in our translation· [b]But if τεκνία μου *my little children* be joynd on by apposition to ὑμᾶς *You* the last word of the foregoing verse and so the two verses 18 and 19 be read as one sentence the 20 ver. with δέ *But* in it, follows very naturally. [c]But as we now read it in our English bible δέ *But* is forced to be left out, and the 20th ver. stands alone by it self without any connection with what goes before or follows.

20* [a]'Αλλάξαι φωνήν *to change the voice* seems to signifie the speakeing higher or lower, changeing the tone of the voice suitably to the matter one delivers. v.g whether it be advice, or commendation, or reproof etc: for each of these have their distinct voyces. [b]St Paul wishes him self with them that he might accomodate him self to their present condition and circumstances which he confesses himself to be ignorant of and in doubt about

TEXT

IV.21. Tell me, ye that desire to be under the law, do ye not hear the law?

22. For it is written, that Abraham had two Sons; the one by a bond-maid, the other by a free-woman.

23. But he who was of the bond-woman, was born after the flesh: but he of the free-woman was by promise.

24. Which things are an allegory; for these are the two covenants; the one from the mount Sinai, which gendreth to bondage, which is Agar.

25. For this Agar is mount Sinai in Arabia, and answereth to Jerusalem which now is, and is in bondage with her children.

26. But Jerusalem which is above, is free, which is the Mother of us all.

27. For it is written, Rejoyce thou barren that bearest not; break forth and cry, thou that travailest not: for the desolate hath many more Children than she which hath an Husband.

28. Now we brethren, as Isaac was, are the Children of promise.

29. But as then he that was born after the flesh, persecuted him that was born after the Spirit, even so it is now.

30. Nevertheless, what saith the scripture? Cast out the bond-woman and her son: for the son of the bond-woman shall not be heir with the son of the free-woman.

31. So then, brethren, we are not children of the bond-woman, but of the free.

V.1. Stand fast therefore in the liberty wherewith Christ hath made us free, and be not intangled again with the yoke of bondage.

PARAPHRASE

[IV.21]Tell me you that would so fain be under the law doe you not acquaint your selves with what is in the law either by reading* it or hearing it read in your assemblies. [22]For it is there Written* Abraham had two sons one by a bond-maid the other by a free woman: [23]but he that was of the bond-woman was borne according to the flesh in the ordinary course of nature; but he that was of the free woman Abraham had by virtue of the promise after he and his wife were past the hopes of an other Child. [24]These things have an allegorical meaning· For the two women are the two covenants, the one of them delivered from mount Sinai and is represented by Agar who produces her issue into

IV.21* The vulgat has after some Greek MSS *Read*

22* *Written there* viz Gen XVI.15. XXI.1. The term *Law* in the foregoing ver. comprehends the five books of Moses

bondage [25](For Agar is mount Sinai in Arabia) and answers to Jerusalem that now is, and is in bondage with her Children. [26]But the heavenly Jerusalem which is above and answers to Sarah the mother of the promised seed is free, the mother of us all, both Jews and Gentiles, who beleive. [27]For it was of her that it is written* *Rejoyce thou barren that bearest not; break out into loud acclamations of joy thou that hast not the travails of Child birth, for more are the Children of the desolate then of her that hath an husband*. [28]And 'tis we my brethren who, as Isaack was, are the Children of promise. [29]But as then Ismael who was borne in the ordinary course of nature persecuted Isaac who was borne by an extraordinary power from heaven working miraculously:* So is it now. [30]But what Saith the Scripture* *Cast out the bond woman and her son. For the son of the bond-woman shal not share the inheritance with the son of the freewoman*· [31]So then, Brethren, we who beleive in Christ are not the Children of the bondwoman; but of the free:* [V.1]Stand fast therefore in the liberty wherewith Christ hath made you free and doe not put on again a yoke of bondage by puting your selves under the law.

SECTION X

Ch. V.2-13

CONTENTS

[a]It is evident from ver. 11 that the better to prevail with the Galatians to be circumcised it had been reported that St Paul himself preachd up circumcision. St Paul without takeing express notice of this calumnie Ch I.6-II 21 gives an account of his past life in a large train of particulars which all concur to make such a character of him [b]as renders it very incredible that he should ever declare for the circumcision of the Gentile Converts or for their submission to the law.

27* *Written* (viz.) Isai: LIV.1

29* ὁ κατὰ σάρκα γεννηθείς *born after the flesh* and τὸν κατὰ πνεῦμα *born after the spirit*. These expressions have in the original brevity with regard to the whole view wherein St Paul uses them an admirable beauty and force which cannot be reteined in a paraphrase.

30* *Scripture* (viz) Gen: XXI.10

31* The Apostle by this alegorical history shews the Galatians that they who are sons of Agar. i e under the law given at mount Sinai are in bondage, and intended to be cast out, the inheritance being designed for those onely who are the free borne sons of god under the spiritual covenant of the gospel. And thereupon he exhorts them in the following words to preserve themselves in that state of freedom.

Haveing thus prepared the minds of the Galatians to give him a fair hearing as a fair man ζηλοῦσθαι ἐν καλῷ, he goes on to argue against their subjecting them selves to the law: [c]And haveing established their freedom from the law by many strong arguments he comes here at last openly to take notice of the report had been raised of him that he preached circumcision, and directly confutes it

[d]1° By positively denounceing to them him self very solemnly that they who sufferd themselves to be circumcised put them selves into a perfect legal state, out of the covenant of grace and could receive no benefit by Jesus Christ ver. 2-4

[e]2° By assureing them that he and those that followed him expected justification onely by faith. ver. 5.6

3° By telling them that he had put them in the right way, and that this new perswasion came not from him that converted them to Christianity. ver. 7.8

[f]4° By insinuateing to them that they should agree to passe judgment on him that troubled them with this doctrine ver. 9.10

5° By his being persecuted for opposeing the circumcision of the Christians. For this was the great offence which stuck with the Jews. even after their conversion ver. 11

6° By wishing those cut off that trouble them with this doctrine ver. 12.

[g]This will, I doubt not, by who ever weighs it be found a very skilful management of the argumentative part of this Epistle which ends here. For though he begins with sapping the foundation on which the Judaizing seducers seem to have laid their main stress. (viz) the report of his preaching circumcision, [h]yet he reserves the direct and open confutation of it to the end, and so leaves it with them that it may have the more forceible and lasting impression on their minds.

TEXT

V.2. Behold, I Paul say unto you, that if ye be circumcised, Christ shall profit you nothing.

3. For I testifie again to every man that is circumcised, that he is a debter to do the whole law.

4. Christ is become of no effect unto you, whosoever of you are justified by the law; ye are fallen from grace.

5. For we through the Spirit wait for the hope of righteousness by faith.

6. For in Jesus Christ, neither circumcision availeth any thing, nor uncircumcision, but faith which worketh by love.

7. Ye did run well, who did hinder you, that ye should not obey the truth?

8. This perswasion cometh not of him that calleth you.

9. A little leaven leaveneth the whole lump.

10. I have confidence in you through the Lord, that you will be none otherwise minded: but he that troubleth you, shall bear his judgment, whosoever he be.

11. And I, brethren, if I yet preach circumcision, why do I yet suffer persecution? then is the offence of the cross ceased.

12. I would they were even cut off which trouble you.

13. For, brethren, ye have been called unto liberty.

PARAPHRASE

[V.2]Take notice that I Paul* who am falsly reported to preach up circumcision in other places say unto you, that if you are circumcised Christ shall be of noe advantage to you. [3]For I repeat here again what I have always preachd, and solemnly testifie to every one who yeilds to be circumcised in compliance with those who say that now under the gospel he cannot be saved without it,* that he is under an obligation to the whole law, and bound to observe and performe every title of it. [4]Christ is of noe use to you, who seek justification by the law. whosoever doe soe be ye what ye will ye are fallen from the covenant of Grace. [5]But I* and those who with me are true Christians, we who follow the truth of the gospel† the doctrine of the spirit of god have noe other hope of justification but by faith in Christ. [6]For in the state of the Gospel under Jesus the Messiah 'tis neither circumcision nor uncircumcision that is of any moment; All that is available is faith alone working by Love.* [7]When you first enterd into the profession of

V.2* Ἴδε, ἐγὼ Παῦλος *Behold I Paul* I the same Paul who am reported to preach circumcision μαρτύρομαι πάλιν παντὶ ἀνθρώπῳ ver. 3 *Witnesse again*, continue my testimony, *to every man* to you and all men. This so emphatical way of speaking may very well be understood to have regard to what he takes notice ver. 11 to be cast upon him (viz) his preaching circumcision, and is a very significant vindication of himself.

3* *Cannot be saved·* This was the ground upon which the Jews and Jewdaizing Christians urged circumcision· see Act: XV.1.

5* *We·* 'Tis evident from the context that St Paul here means himself. But *we* is a more graceful way of speakeing than *I* though he be vindicateing himself alone from the imputation of seting up circumcision.

† *Spirit·* The law and the gospel opposed under the titles of *flesh* and *Spirit* we may see Ch: III.3 of this Epistle· The same opposition it stands in here to *the law* in the foregoing ver. points out the same signification.

6* *which worketh by love·* This is added to repress the animosities which were amongst them, probably raised by this question about circumcision. See ver. 13-15

the gospel you were in a good way and went on well· who has put a stop to you, and hinderd you that you keep no longer to the truth of the Christian doctrine? [8]This perswasion that it is necessary for you to be circumcised cometh not from him* by whose preaching you were called to the profession of the gospel. [9]Remember that a little leaven leaveneth the whole lump; the influence of one man* enterteind among you may mislead you all: [10]I have confidence in you that by the help of the Lord, you will be all of this same mind⟨*⟩ with me; and consequently he that troubles you shall fall under the censure he deserves for it† who ever he be. [11]But as for me Brethren if I at last am become a preacher of Circumcision, why am I yet persecuted?* If it be so that the Gentile converts are to be circumcised and so subjected to the law the great offence of the gospel in relying soly on a crucified† saviour for salvation is removed. [12]But I am of an other mind and wish that they may be cut off who trouble you about this matter, and they shall be cut off· [13]For Brethren ye have been called by me unto liberty.

8* [a]This expression of *him that called* or *calleth you* he used before Ch. I.6 and in both places means him self, and here declares that this πεισμονή (whether taken for *perswasion* or for *subjection* as it may be in St Pauls stile considering πείθεσθαι in the end of the foregoing ver.) came not from him, for he called them to liberty from the law and not subjection to it· [b]see ver. 13. *You were goeing on well in the liberty of the Gospel· who stopd you? I you may be sure had noe hand in it· I you knew called you to liberty and not to subjection to the law and therefor you can by noe means suppose that I should preach up circumcision·* Thus St Paul argues here

9* By this and the next ver. it looks as if all this disorder arose from one man

10* [a] *Will not be otherwise minded·* Will beware of this Leaven so as not to be put into a ferment nor shaken in your liberty, which you ought to stand fast in, and to secure it I doubt not (such confidence I have in you) will with one accord cast out him that troubles you. [b]For as for me you may be sure I am not for circumcision, in that the Jews continue to persecute me. This is evidently his meaning, though not spoken out, but managed warily with a very skilfull and moveing insinuation. For as he says himself IV.20 he knew not at that distance what temper they were in.

† κρίμα *Judgment* seems here to mean expulsion by a Church censure· see ver. 12· We shall be the more inclined to this if we consider that the Apostle uses the same argument of *a little leaven leaveneth the whole lump* 1 Cor. V.6 where he would perswade the Corinthians to purge out the Fornicator

11* *Persecution·* The *Persecution* St Paul was still under was a convinceing argument that he was not for circumcision and subjection to the law, For it was from the Jews upon that account that at this time rose all the persecution which the Christians suffered as may be seen through all the history of the Acts. Nor are there wanting clear footsteps of it in several places of this Epistle besides this here, as Ch III.4 VI.12.

† Offence of the cross. see VI.12–14

SECTION XI

Ch. V.13-26

CONTENTS

From the mention of liberty which he tels them they are called to under the gospel he takes a rise to caution them in the use of it. and so exhorts them to a spiritual or true Christian life, shewing the difference and contrarietie between that and a carnal life or a life after the flesh.

TEXT

V.13 (*cont.*). Only use not liberty for an occasion to the flesh, but by love serve one another.

14. For all the law is fulfilled in one word, even in this; Thou shalt love thy neighbour as thy self.

15. But if ye bite and devour one another, take heed that ye be not consumed one of another.

16. This I say then, Walk in the Spirit, and ye shall not fulfil the lust of the flesh.

17. For the flesh lusteth against the Spirit, and the Spirit against the flesh: and these are contrary the one to the other; so that ye cannot do the things that ye would.

18. But if ye be led by the Spirit, ye are not under the law.

19. Now the works of the flesh are manifest, which are these, Adultery, fornication, uncleanness, lasciviousness,

20. Idolatry, witchcraft, hatred, variance, emulations, wrath, strife, seditions, heresies,

21. Envyings, murders, drunkenness, revellings, and such like: of the which I tell you before, as I have also told you in time past, that they which do such things, shall not inherit the Kingdom of God.

22. But the fruit of the Spirit is love, joy, peace, long suffering, gentleness, goodness, faith,

23. Meekness, temperance: against such there is no law.

24. And they that are Christ's, have crucified the flesh, with the affections and lusts.

25. If we live in the Spirit, let us also walk in the Spirit.

26. Let us not be desirous of vain glory, provoking one another, envying one another.

PARAPHRASE

V.13 (*cont.*) Though the gospel to which ye are called be a state of libertie
from the bondage of the law, yet pray take great care you doe not
mistake that libertie, nor think it affords you an oportunity in the
abuse of it to satisfie the lusts of the flesh but serve* one an other in
Love. 14 For the whole law concerning our duty to others is fulfild in
observeing this one precept* *Thou shalt love thy neighbour as thy self*.
15 But if you bite and tear one an other take heed that you be not
destroid and consumed by one an other. 16 This I say to you conduct
your selves by the light that is in your minds* and doe not give your
selves up to the lusts of the flesh to obey them in what they put you
upon. 17 For the inclinations and desires of the flesh are contrary to
those of the spirit: And the dictates and inclinations of the spirit are
contrary to those of the flesh; so that under these contrary impulses
you doe* not doe the things that you propose to your selves.† 18 But if

V.13* Δουλεύετε *Serve* has a greater force in the Greek than our English word *serve* does in the common acceptation of it express. For it signifies the opposite to ἐλευθερία *freedom*. And so the Apostle elegantly informes them that though by the gospel they are called to a state of *liberty* from the law yet they were still as much bound and subjected to their brethren in all the offices and dutys of love and good will as if in that respect they were their vassals and bondmen.

14* Lev. XIX.18

16* That which he here and in the next ver. cals *Spirit* he cals Rom VII.22 *the inward man* 23 *the law of the mind* 25 *the mind*

17* *Doe not*· so it is in the Greek, and ours is the onely translation that I know which renders it *can not*

16.17† [a]There can be no thing plainer than that the State St Paul discribes here in these two verses, he paints out more at large Rom VII.17 etc: speakeing there in the person of a Jew. This is very evident that St Paul supposes two principles in every man which draw him different ways. The one he cals *flesh*, the other *spirit*. [b]These, though there be other appellations given them, are the most common and usual names given them in the New Testament: By *flesh* is meant all those vitious, and irregular appetites, inclinations, and habitudes whereby a man is turnd from his obedience to that eternall law of right, the observance whereof god always requires and is pleased with. [c]This is very properly called *Flesh*, This bodily state being the sourse from which all our deviations from the strait rule of rectitude doe for the most part take their rise, or else doe ultimately terminate. On the other side *Spirit* is that part of a man which is endowed with light from god to know and see what is righteous, just, and good. and which being consulted and hearkend to is always ready to direct and prompt to that which is good. [d]The *Flesh* then in the gospel language is that principle which inclines and carrys men to ill; the *Spirit* that principle which dictates what is right and inclines to good. But because by prevailing custome and contrary habits this principle was very much weakened and almost extinct in the Gentiles. [e]See Eph IV.17–21· he exhorts them to be *renewed in the spirit of their minds* ver. 23 and to *put off the old man*. i e Fleshly corrupt habits and to put on the *new man* which he tels them ver. 24 is created *in righteousness and true holyness*. This is also called *renewing of the mind* Rom XII.2. *renewing of the inward man* 2 Cor IV.16. which is don by the assistance of the Spirit of God Eph. III.16.

you give your selves up to the conduct of the gospel* by faith in Christ, ye are not under the law† [19]Now the works of the flesh as is manifest are these· Adultery, Fornication, Uncleaness, Lasciviousness, [20]Idolatry, Witchcraft* Enmities, Quarrels, Emulations, Animosities, Strife, Seditions, Sects. [21]Envyings, Murders Drunkenness Revellings* and such like concerning which I forewarne you now as here to fore I have done, that they who doe such things shall not inherit the Kingdom of god. [22]But on the other side the fruit of the Spirit is Love, peace, Long suffering, Sweetness of disposition. Beneficence, Faithfulness, [23]Meekness, Temperance. Against these and the like there is no law. [24]Now they who belong* to Christ, and are his members have crucified the flesh† with the affections and lusts thereof. [25]If our life then (our flesh haveing been crucified) be as we profess by the spirit, where by we are alive from that estate of sin we were dead in before, let us regulate

18* [a]This is plainly the sense of the Apostle who teaches all along in the former part of this Epistle, and also that to the Romans that those who put themselves under the Gospel are not under the law. The question then that remains is onely about the phrase *led by the spirit*. [b]And as to that it is easie to observe how natural it is for St Paul haveing in the two foregoeing verses more than once mentioned the *Spirit*, to continue the same word though some what varied in the sense. In St Pauls phraseologie as the irregularities of appetite, and the dictates of right reason are opposed under the titles of *flesh* and *Spirit* as we have seen: So the covenant of workes, and the covenant of grace; [c]Law, and Gospel are opposed under the titles of *flesh* and *Spirit*· 2 Cor III.6.8 he cals the Gospel *Spirit* and Rom. VII 5 *In the flesh* signifies in the legal state. But we need goe no farther than Ch III.3 of this very epistle to see the law and the gospel opposed by St Paul under the titles of *flesh* and *Spirit*. [d]The reason of thus useing the word *spirit* is very apparent in the doctrine of the New Testament. which teaches that those who receive Christ by faith, with him receive his spirit, and its assistance against the flesh. See Rom VIII.9-11· Accordingly for the attaining of Salvation St Paul joyns together beleif of the truth and sanctification of the Spirit ⟨2⟩ Thess II.13. [e]And so *Spirit* here may be taken for the *spirit of their minds* but renewed and strengthened by the spirit of god· See Eph III.16. IV.23

† The reason of this assertion we may find Rom VIII 14 viz Because *they who are led by the spirit of god* are *the sons of god* and so heirs and free without the law as he argues here. Ch III and IV

20* φαρμακεία signifies either *witchcraft* or *poisoning*

21* κῶμοι *Revellings* were amongst the Greeks disorderly spending of the night in feasting with a licentious indulgeing to wine, good cheer, musick, danceing etc:

24* Oἱ τοῦ Χριστοῦ *Those who are of Christ* are the same with *those who are led by the spirit* ver. 18 and are opposed to *those who live after the flesh* Rom VIII.13 Where it is said conformably to what we find here, they *through the spirit mortifie the deeds of the body*.

† [a]*Crucified the flesh*· That principle in us from whence spring vitious inclinations and actions, is, as we have observed above, called sometimes the *flesh*, sometimes the *old man*· The subdueing and mortifieing of this evil principle, so that the force and power, where with it used to rule in us, is extinguished. [b]the Apostle by a very engageing accomodation to the death of our Saviour, cals *crucifying the old-man* Rom. VI.6. *Crucifying the flesh* here. *Puting off the body of the sins of the flesh* Col II.11 *Puting of the old man* Eph IV.⟨2⟩2 Col III.8.9. It is also called *mortifying the members which are on the earth* Col III.5. *Mortifying the deeds of the body* Rom VIII.13.

our lives and actions by the light and dictates of the spirit. [26]Let us not be led by an itch of vain-glory to provoke one an other or to envie one an other.*

SECTION XII

Ch. VI.1-5

CONTENTS

He here exhorts the Stronger to gentleness and meekness towards the weak

TEXT

VI.1. Brethren, if a man be overtaken in a fault, ye which are spiritual, restore such an one in the spirit of meekness; considering thy self, lest thou also be tempted.

2. Bear ye one anothers burdens, and so fulfil the law of Christ.

3. For if a man think himself to be something, when he is nothing, he deceiveth himself.

4. But let every man prove his own work, and then shall he have rejoycing in himself alone, and not in another.

5. For every man shall bear his own burden.

PARAPHRASE

[VI.1]Brethren if a man by frailty or surprise fall into a fault doe you who are eminent in the church for knowledg practise and gifts* raise him up again and set him right with gentleness and meekness considering that you your selves are not out of the reach of temptation. [2]Beare with one an others infirmities and help to support each other under your burdens* and so fulfill the law of Christ† [3]For if any one

26* Whether the *vain-glory* and *envying* here were about their spiritual gifts, a fault which the Corinthians were guilty of as we may see at large 1 Cor XII.XIII.XIV, or upon any other occasion and so conteined in ver. 15 of this Chapter. I shall not curiously examin: either way the sense of the words will be much what the same, and accordingly this verse must end the V or begin the VI. Chapter.

VI.1* πνευματικοί *Spiritual* in 1 Cor III.1 and XII.1 taken together has this sense

2* See a parallel exhortation 1 Thess. V.14 which will give light to this. as also Rom XV.1.

† [a]See John XIII 34.35. X⟨V⟩.12. There were some among them very zealous for the observation of the Law of Moses· St Paul here puts them in mind of a law which they were under and were obleiged to observe viz *the law of Christ*. And he shews them how to do it (viz) by helping to bear one an others burdens, and not increaseing their burdens

be conceited of himself as if he were something, a man of weight fit to prescribe to others when indeed he is not he dec⟨e⟩iveth himself. [4]But let him take care that what he himself doth be right and such as will bear the test and then he will have matter of glorying* in him self and not in an other. [5]For every one shall be accountable onely for his own actions

SECTION XIII

Ch. VI.6-10

CONTENTS

St Paul haveing laid some restraint upon the authority and forwardness of the teachers and leading men amongst them, who were as it seems more ready to impose on the Galatians what they should not, than to help them forward in the practise of gospel obedience, he here takes care of them in respect of their maintenance and exhorts the Galatians to liberality towards them, and in general towards all men espetialy Christians

TEXT

VI.6. Let him that is taught in the word, communicate unto him that teacheth, in all good things.

by the observances of the Levitical law. [b]Though the Gospel contein the law of the Kingdom of Christ yet I doe not remember that St Paul any where cals it *the Law of Christ* but in this place where he mentions it in opposition to those who thought a law so necessary that they would retain that of Moses under the Gospel.

4* [a]καύχημα I think should have been translated here *glorying* as καυχήσ⟨ω⟩νται is ver. 13. the Apostle in both places meaning the same thing (viz) glorying in an other in haveing brought him to circumcision and other ritual observances of the Mosaical law. For thus St Paul seems to me to discourse in this section. [b]'Brethren there are some among 'you that would bring others under the ritual observances of the Mosaical law. a yoke 'which was too heavy for us and our fathers to bear. They would doe much better to 'ease the burdens of the weak; this is suitable to the law of Christ which they are under, 'and is the law which they ought strictly to obey. [c]If they think because of their spiritual 'gifts that they have power to prescribe in such matters, I tell them that they have not 'but doe deceive themselves. Let them rather take care of their own particular actions, 'that they be right and such as they ought to be. [d]This will give them matter of glorying 'in themselves, and not vainly in others, as they doe when they prevail with them to be 'circumcised. For every man shall be answerable for his own actions.' Let the Reader judg whether this does not seem to be St Pauls view here, and suit with his way of writeing?

"Εχειν καύχημα is a phrase whereby St Paul signifies *to have matter of glorying* and to that sense it is rendered Rom IV.2.

7. Be not deceived; God is not mocked: for whatsoever a man soweth, that shall he also reap.

8. For he that soweth to his flesh, shall of the flesh reap corruption: but he that soweth to the Spirit, shall of the Spirit reap life everlasting.

9. And let us not be weary in well doing: for in due season we shall reap, if we faint not.

10. As we have therefore opportunity, let us do good unto all men, especially unto them who are of the houshold of faith.

PARAPHRASE

[VI.6]Let him that is taught the doctrine of the Gospel freely communicate the good things of this world to him that teaches him. [7]Be
not deceived. God will not be mocked. For as a man soweth* so also
shall he reap. [8]He that lays out the stock of good things he has, onely
for the satisfaction of his own bodily necessitys, conveniencys or
pleasures, shall at the harvest find the fruit and product of such husbandry to be corruption* and perishing: But he that lays out his
worldly substance according to the rules dictated by the spirit of god
in the gospel shall of the spirit reap life everlasting. [9]In doeing thus
what is good and right let us not wax weary for in due season when the
time of harvest comes we shall reap if we continue on to doe good, and
flag not. [10]Therefore as we have oportunityes let us doe good unto all
men, espetialy to those who profess faith in Jesus Christ i e the
Christian religion.

SECTION XIV

Ch. VI.11-18

CONTENTS

One may see what lay upon St Pauls minde in writeing to the Galatians by what he inculcates to them here even after he had finished his letter. The like we have taken notice of in the last chapter to the Romans. He here winds up all with an admonition to the Galatians of a different end and aim they had to get the Galatians circumcised from what he had in preaching the gospel.

VI.7* *Soweth*· A metaphor used by St Paul for mens laying out their worldly goods. See 2 Cor IX.6. etc:

8* Rom VIII.13. II.12.

TEXT

VI.11. Ye see how large a letter I have written unto you with mine own hand.

12. As many as desire to make a fair shew in the flesh, they constrain you to be circumcised; only lest they should suffer persecution for the cross of Christ.

13. For neither they themselves who are circumcised keep the law; but desire to have you circumcised, that they may glory in your flesh.

14. But God forbid that I should glory save in the cross of our Lord Jesus Christ, by whom the world is crucified unto me, and I unto the world.

15. For in Christ Jesus neither circumcision availeth any thing, nor uncircumcision, but a new creature.

16. And as many as walk according to this rule, peace be on them, and mercy, and upon the Israel of God.

17. From henceforth let no man trouble me; for I bear in my body the marks of the Lord Jesus.

18. Brethren, the grace of our Lord Jesus Christ be with your spirit, Amen.
¶Unto the Galatians, written from Rome.

PARAPHRASE

VI.11 You see how long a letter I have writ to you with my own hand.*
12 They who are willing to carry it so fairly in the ritual part* of the law,
and to make ostentation of their compliance there in, constrain you to
be circumcised onely to avoid persecution for owning their dependence for salvation soly on a crucified Messiah† and not on the
observance of the law. 13 For even they themselves who are circumcised doe not keep the law But they will have you to be circumcised
that this mark in your flesh may afford them matter of glorying and of
recommending them selves to the good opinion of the Jews. 14 But as
for me, what ever may be said of me,* God forbid that I should glory
in any thing, but in haveing Jesus Christ who was crucified, for my
sole Lord and Master whom I am to obey and depend on which I so
entirely doe without regard to any thing else that I am wholy dead to

VI.11* St Paul mentions the *writeing with his own hand* as an argument of his great concern for them in the case. For it was not usual for him to write his Epistles with his own hand, but to dictate them to others who writ them from his mouth. See Rom XVI.22. 1 Cor XVI.21.

12* *In the flesh*. i e In the ritual observances of the law which Heb. IX.10. are called δικαιώματα σαρκός. see Note Rom II.26

† See V.11

14* See V.11

the world and the world dead to me and it has noe more influence on me than if it were not. [15]For as to the obteining a share in the Kingdom of Jesus Christ and the privileges and advantages of it neither circumcision nor uncircumcision such outward differences in the flesh availe any thing, but the new creation wherein by a through change a man is disposed to righteousness and true holyness in good works.*
[16]And on all those who walk by this rule, (viz) that it is the new Creation alone and not circumcision that availeth under the gospel, peace and mercy shall be on them they being that Israel which are truly the people of god·* [17]From hence forth let no man give me trouble by questions or doubt whether I preach circumcision or no. Tis true I am circumcised. But yet the marks I now bear in my body are the markes of Jesus Christ that I am his. The markes of the stripes which I have received from the Jews, and which I still bear in my body for preaching Jesus Christ are an evidence that I am not for circumcision. [18]Brethren the grace of our Lord Jesus Christ be with your Spirit. Amen.

15* See Eph: II.10. IV.24

16* [a]St Paul haveing in the foregoeing ver. asserted that it is the new creation alone that puts men into the Kingdom of Christ and into the possession of the privileges there of this ver. may be understood also as assertory rather than as a prayer unless there were a verb that expressed it; Espetialy considering that he writes this Epistle to incourage them to refuse circumcision. [b]To which end the assureing them that those who doe so shall have peace and mercy from god is of more force than to tell them that he prays that they may have peace and mercy. And for the same reason I understand the *Israel of God* to be the same with *those who walk by this rule* though joynd with them by the Copulative καί *And*. A way of Speaking not very unusual

A PARAPHRASE AND NOTES ON THE FIRST EPISTLE OF ST PAUL TO THE CORINTHIANS

THE FIRST EPISTLE OF ST PAUL TO THE CORINTHIANS

SYNOPSIS

[a]St Pauls first comeing to Corinth was anno Christi 52 where he first applied him self to the Synagogue Act XVIII.4. But finding them obstinate in their opposition to the Gospel he turnd to the Gentils ver. 6 out of whom this church at Corinth seems cheifly to be gatherd as appears Acts XVIII and 1 Cor XII.2.

[b]His stay here was about two years as appears from Acts XVIII.11.18 compared: In which time it may be concluded he made many converts, for he was not idle there, nor did he use to stay long in a place where he was not incouraged by the success of his ministry. [c]Besides what his soe long abode in this one citty and his indiffatigable labour every where might incline one to presume of the number of converts he made in that Citty, the Scripture it self Act XVIII.10 gives sufficient evidence of a numerous church gatherd there

[d]Corinth it self was a Rich merchant town; The inhabitants Greeks. A people of quick parts and inquisitive. 1 Cor I.22 but naturaly vain and conceited of themselves

These things considered may help us in some measure the better to understand St Pauls Epistles to this church which seems to be in greater disorder then any other of the Churches which he writ to.

[e]This Epistle was writ to the Corinthians Anno Christi 57 between two and three years after St Paul had left them· In this interval there was got in amongst them a new Instructor a Jew by nation who had raised a faction against St Paul. With this party, whereof he was the Leader, this false Apostle had gaind great authority, soe that they admired and gloried in him with an apparent disesteem and diminishing of St Paul.

[f]Why I suppose the opposition to be made to St Paul in this church by one Party under one Leader I shall give the reasons that make it probable to me as they come in my way goeing through these two Epistles which I shall leave to the reader to judg without positively determining on either side and therefor shall as it happens speak of

these opposers of St Paul sometimes in the singular and sometimes in the plural number

[g]This at least is evident that the main designe of St Paul in this Epistle is to support his own authority dignity and credit with that part of the church which stuck to him; to vindicate him self from the aspersions and calumnies of the opposite party; To lessen the credit of the cheif and leading men in it by intimateing their miscariages and shewing their noe cause of glorying or being gloried in, [h]that soe withdrawing their party from the admiration and esteem of those their leaders he might breake the faction, and puting an end to the division might reunite them with the uncorrupted part of the church that they might all unanimously submit to the authority of his divine mission and with one accord receive and keep the doctrine and directions he deliverd to them.

[i]This is the whole subject from Ch I.10 to the end of the VI. In the remaining part of this Epistle he answers some questions they proposed to him. and resolves some doubts, not without a mixture, on all occasions, of reflections on his opposers and of other things, that may tend to the breaking of their Faction

SECTION I

Anno Christi 57
Neronis 3

Ch. I.ver.1-9

TEXT

I.1. Paul called to be an apostle of Jesus Christ, through the will of God, and Sosthenes our brother.

2. Unto the church of God which is at Corinth, to them that are sanctified in Christ Jesus, called to be Saints, with all that in every place call upon the name of Jesus Christ our Lord, both theirs and ours.

3. Grace be unto you, and Peace from God our Father, and from the Lord Jesus Christ.

4. I thank my God always on your behalf, for the grace of God, which is given you by Jesus Christ;

5. That in every thing ye are enriched by him in all utterance, and in all knowledge:

6. Even as the testimony of Christ was confirmed in you.

7. So that ye come behind in no Gift; waiting for the coming of our Lord Jesus Christ:

8. Who shall also confirm you unto the end, that ye may be blameless in the day of our Lord Jesus Christ.

9. God is faithful, by whom ye were called unto the fellowship of his Son Jesus Christ our Lord.

INTRODUCTION

[I.1]Paul an Apostle of Jesus Christ called to be soe by the will of god*
and Sosthenes† our brother in the Christian faith, [2]to the church of god
which is at Corinth to them that are seperated from the rest of the world
by faith in Christ Jesus,* called to be Saints, with all that are every
where called by the name of Jesus Christ† their Lord‡ and ours;
[3]Favour and peace be unto you from god our father and from the Lord
Jesus Christ.
[4]I thank god always on your behalf for the favour of god which is
bestowed on you through Jesus Christ, [5]soe that by him you are
inriched with all knowledg and utterance and all extraordinary gifts [6]as
at first by those miraculous gifts the Gospel of Christ was confirmed
among you, [7]soe that in noe spiritual gift are you short or deficient*
waiting for the comeing⟨†⟩ of our Lord Jesus Christ, [8]who also shall
confirme you unto the end, that in the day of the Lord Jesus Christ there
may be noe charge against you. [9]For god who has called you unto the

I.1* St Paul in most of his Epistles mentions his being *called to be an Apostle by the will of god* which way of speaking being peculiar to him we may suppose him there in to intimate his extraordinary and miraculous call Act IX and his receiveing the gospel by immediate revelation Gal I.11.12. For he doubted not of the will and providence of god governing all things

† Act XVIII.17.

2* [a]Ἡγιασμένοις ἐν Χριστῷ Ἰησοῦ *Sanctified in Christ Jesus* does not signifie here whose lives are pure and holy for there were many amongst those he writ to who were quite other wise but *sanctified* signifies seperate from the common state of mankind to be the people of god and to serve him. [b]The heathen world had revolted from the true god to the service of Idols and false gods: see Rom I.18-25· The Jews being separated from this corrupted mass to be the peculiar people of god were called *Holy* Exod XIX.5.6. Num XV.40 and they being cast off the professors of Christianity were seperated to be the people of god and became holy 1 Pet II.9.10

† Ἐπικαλούμενοι ὄνομα Χριστοῦ. *that are called Christians* these Greek words being a periphrasis for Christian, as is plain from the design of this verse· But he that is not satisfied with that may see more proofs of it in Dr Hammond upon the place

‡ What the Apostle means by *Lord* when he attributes it to Christ. vid. VIII.6

7* Vid 2 Cor XII.12.13

† That the opinion at that time was that Christs comeing was at hand I think may be gatherd from this and several other passages in St Pauls Epistles. See Rom XIII.11.12. 1 Cor VII.29.31

fellowship of his son Jesus Christ our Lord may be relyd on for what is to be done on his side

SECTION II

Ch. I.10-VI.20

[a]There were great disorders in the Church of Corinth caused cheifly by a faction raised there against St Paul· The partisans of the faction mightily cried up, and gloried in their leaders who did all they could to disparage St Paul and lessen him in the esteem of the Corinthians. [b]St Paul makes it his business in this section to take off the Corinthians from sideing with, and glorying in this pretended Apostle, whose followers and scholars they professed them selves to be, and to reduce them into one body as the Scholars of Christ united in a beleif of the gospel which he had preachd to them, and in an obedience to it, [c]without any such distinction of masters or Leaders from whom they denominated them selves. He also here and there intermixes a justification of himself against the aspersions which were cast upon him by his opposers. How much St Paul was set against their Leaders may be seen 2 Cor. XI.13-15

[d]The arguments used by St Paul to break the opposite faction and put an end to all divisions amongst them being various we shall take notice of them under their several heads as they come in the order of his discourse

SECTION II. NO. 1

Ch. I.10-16

CONTENTS

St Pauls first argument is. That in Christianity they all had but one Master viz Christ, And therefor were not to fall into partys denominated from distinct teachers as they did in their Schools of philosophie.

TEXT

I.10. Now I beseech you, brethren, by the name of our Lord Jesus Christ, that ye all speak the same thing, and that there be no divisions among you; but that ye be perfectly joined together in the same mind, and in the same judgment.

11. For it hath been declared unto me of you, my brethren, by them which are of the house of Chloe, that there are contentions among you.

12. Now this I say, that every one of you saith, I am of Paul; and I of Apollos, and I of Cephas, and I of Christ.

13. Is Christ divided? was Paul crucified for you? or were ye baptized in the name of Paul?

14. I thank God that I baptized none of you, but Crispus and Gaius:

15. Lest any should say that I had baptized in mine own name.

16. And I baptized also the houshold of Stephanas: besides, I know not whether I baptized any other.

PARAPHRASE

[I.10]Now I beseech you Brethren by the name* of our Lord Jesus
Christ that ye hold the same doctrine and that there be noe divisions
amongst you; but that ye be framed togeather into one entire body
with one mind, and one affection. [11]For I understand my Brethren* by
some of the house of Cloe that there are quarrels and dissensions
amongst you, [12]soe that ye are all fallen into partys ranking your selves
under different Leaders and Masters, one saying I am of Paul, an
other, I of Apollos, I of Cephas, I of Christ. [13]Is Christ, who is our only
head and master divided? Was Paul crucified for you? Or were you
baptised into* the name of Paul? [14]I thank god that I baptised none of
you but Crispus and Gaius, [15]lest any one should say I had baptised
into my own name. [16]I baptised also the house hold of Stephanas·
Farther I know not whether I baptised any other for Christ sent me
not to Baptise

I.10* [a]Of whom the whole family in heaven and earth is, and ought to be, named. If any one has thought St Paul a loose writer it is only because he was a loose reader. He that takes notice of St Pauls designe shall find that there is not a word scarce, [b]or expression that he makes use of but with relation and tendency to his present main purpose. As here intending to abolish the names of Leaders they distinguishd them selves by, he beseeches them by the *name* of Christ, a forme that I doe not remember he else where uses

11* Brethren, a name of union and freindship used here twice togeather by St Paul in the entrance of his perswasion to them to put an end to their divisions

13* Εἰς properly signifies *into*· Soe the French translate it here. The phrase βαπτισθ(ῆ)ναι εἰς *to be baptised into any ones name* or *into any one* is solemnly by that ceremony to enter him self a disciple of him into whose name he is baptised with profession to receive his doctrine and rules and submit to his authority. a very good argument here why they should be called by noe ones name but Christs.

SECTION II. NO. 2

Ch. I.17-31

CONTENTS

The next argument of St Paul to stop their followers from glorying in these false Apostles is that neither any advantage of Extraction, nor skil in the learning of the Jews nor in the philosophie and Eloquence of the Greeks was that for which god chose men to be preachers of the gospel. Those whom he made choise of for overturning the mighty and the learned were mean, plain ill⟨i⟩terate men

TEXT

I.17. For Christ sent me not to baptize, but to preach the gospel: not with wisdom of words, lest the cross of Christ should be made of none effect.

18. For the preaching of the cross is to them that perish, foolishness: but unto us which are saved, it is the power of God.

19. For it is written, I will destroy the wisdom of the wise, and will bring to nothing the understanding of the prudent.

20. Where is the wise? where is the scribe? where is the disputer of this world? hath not God made foolish the wisdom of this world?

21. For after that, in the wisdom of God, the world by wisdom knew not God, it pleased God by the foolishness of preaching to save them that believe.

22. For the Jews require a sign, and the Greeks seek after wisdom:

23. But we preach Christ crucified, unto the Jews a stumbling block, and unto the Greeks, foolishness;

24. But unto them which are called, both Jews and Greeks, Christ, the power of God, and the wisdom of God.

25. Because the foolishness of God is wiser than men; and the weakness of God is stronger than men.

26. For ye see your calling, brethren, how that not many wise men after the flesh, not many mighty, not many noble are called.

27. But God hath chosen the foolish things of the world, to confound the wise; and God hath chosen the weak things of the world, to confound the things which are mighty;

28. And base things of the world, and things which are despised, hath God chosen, yea, and things which are not, to bring to nought things that are:

29. That no flesh should glory in his presence.

30. But of him are ye in Christ Jesus, who of God is made unto us wisdom, and righteousness, and sanctification, and redemption:

31. That according as it is written, He that glorieth, let him glory in the Lord.

PARAPHRASE

[I.17]But to preach the Gospel not with learned and eloquent harangues lest thereby the virtue and efficacy of Christs sufferings and death should be overlooked and neglected if the stress of our persuasion should be laid on the learning and quaintness of our preaching. [18]For the plain insisting on the death of a crucified Saviour is by those who perish received as a foolish contemptible thing, though to us who are saved it be the power of god, [19]conformable to what is prophesied by Isayah. I will destroy the wisdome of the wise, and I will bring to noething the understanding of the prudent. [20]Where is the philosopher skild in the wisdom of the Greeks? where the Scribe* studied in the learning of the Jews? where the professor of humane arts and Sciences? Hath not God renderd all the learning and wisdome of this world foolish and useless for the discovery of the truths of the Gospel? [21]For since the world by their natural parts and improvements in what with them passed for wisdome acknowledgd not the one only true god, though he had manifested himself to them in the wise contrivance and admirable frame of the visible works of the creation, it pleased god by the plain, and (as the world esteems it) foolish doctrine of the gospel to save those who receive and beleive it: [22]Since both* the Jews demand extraordinary signes and miracles and

I.20* [a]*Scribe* was the title of a learned man amongst the Jews; one versed in their law and rites which was the study of their Doctors and Rabbis. It is likely the false Apostle soe much concerned in these 2 Epistles to the Corinthians who was a Jew pretended to something of this kind, and magnified him self there upon. [b]Otherwise it is not probable that St Paul should name to the Corinthians a sort of men not much known or valued amongst the Greeks. This therefor may be supposd to be said to take off their glorying in their false Apostle

22* [a]Ἐπειδὴ καί *since both*· These words used here by St Paul are not certainly idle and insignificant and therefor I see not how they can be omitted in the translation· Ἐπειδὴ is a word of reasoning and if minded will lead us into one of St Pauls reasonings here which the neglect of this word makes the reader overlooke. [b]St Paul in the 21 verse argues thus in general. 'Since the world by their natural parts and improvements did 'not attain to a right and saveing knowledg of god; God by the preaching of the Gospel 'which seems foolishness to them was pleased to communicate that knowledg to those 'who beleived.'

[c]In the three following verses he repeats the same reasoning a little more expresly applied to the people he had here in his view viz Jews and Greeks and his sense seems to be this. 'Since the Jews to make any doctrine goe down with them require extraordi'nary signes of the *power* of god to accompany it; [d]and noething will please the nice 'palates of the Learned Greeks but *wisdome*, though our preaching of a crucified 'Messiah be a Scandal to the Jews, and foolishness to the Greeks, yet we have what they 'both seek, for both Jew and Gentil when they are called find the Messiah, whom we 'preach to be the *power* of god and the *wisdom* of god'

the Greeks seek wisdome: [23]But I have noething else to preach to them but Christ crucified, a doctrine offensive to the hopes and expectation of the Jews, and foolish to the acute men of learning, the Greeks; [24]it is to those both Jews and Greeks (when they are converted) Christ the power of god and Christ the wisdome of god. [25]Because that which seems foolishnesse in those* who come from god surpasses the wisdom of men; and that which seems weakness in those sent by god surpasses the power of men. [26]For reflect upon your selves Brethren and you may observe that there are not many of the wise and learned men, not many men of power or of birth among you that are called. [27]But god hath chosen the foolish men* in the account of the world to confound the wise. and god hath chosen the weak men of the world to confound the mighty: [28]The mean men* of the world and contemptible has god chosen; and those that are of noe account, are noe thing† to displace those that are, [29]that soe there might be noe room or pretence for any one to glory in his presence. [30a]Natural Humane abilities parts or wisdome could never have reachd this way to happiness: tis to his wisdom alone that ye owe the contrivance of it: to his revealeing it that ye owe the knowledg of it: [b]and tis from him alone that you are in Christ Jesus, whom god has made unto us Christians wisdom, and righteousness, and sanctification and redemption, which is all the dignity and preeminency, all that is of any value amongst us Christians, [31]that as it is written he that glorieth should glory only in the Lord

25.27.28* He that will read the context cannot doubt but that St Paul, by what he expresses in these verses in the neuter gender, means persons the whole argument of the place being about persons and their glorying. and not about things

28† [a]Τὰ μὴ ὄντα. *Things that are not* I think may well be understood of the Gentils, who were not the people of god, and were counted as noe thing by the Jews; and we are pointed to this meaning by the words καταισχύνῃ and καταργήσῃ by *the foolish* and *weak things* i e by simple illiterate and mean men god would *make ashamd* the learned philosophers and great men of the nations. [b]but by the μὴ ὄντα, *the things that are not* he would *abolish the things that are*, as in effect he did abolish the Jewish Church by the Christian taking in the Gentils to be his people in the place of the rejected Jews who till then were his people.

[c]This St Paul mentions here, not by Chance, but pursuant to his main designe to stop their glorying in their false Apostle who was a Jew, by shewing that whatever that head of the faction might claim under that pretence (as it is plain he did stand upon it. v. 2 Cor XI.21.22), [d]he had not any the least title to esteem or respect upon that account since the Jewish nation was laid aside. and god had chosen the Gentiles to take their place and to be his church and people instead of them vid: note Ch. II.6· there one may see who are the καταργούμενοι the Abolishd whom god says here he will abolish

SECTION II. NO. 3⟨a⟩

Ch. II.1-5

CONTENTS

Farther to keep them from glorying in their Leaders he tells them that as the preachers of the Gospel of gods chooseing were mean and illiterate men soe the gospel was not to be propagated nor men to be established in the faith by humane learning and eloquence but by the Evidence it had from the Revelation conteined in the old Testament and from the power of god accompanying and confirming it with miracles

TEXT

II.1. And I, brethren, when I came to you, came not with excellency of speech, or of wisdom, declaring unto you the testimony of God.

2. For I determined not to know any thing among you, save Jesus Christ, and him crucified.

3. And I was with you in weakness, and in fear, and in much trembling.

4. And my speech, and my preaching was not with enticing words of mans wisdom, but in demonstration of the Spirit, and of power:

5. That your faith should not stand in the wisdom of men, but in the power of God.

PARAPHRASE

[II.1] And I brethren when I came and preachd the gospel to you. I did not endeavour to set it off with any ornaments of rhetorique or the mixture of humane learning or philosophie but plainly declared it to you as a doctrine comeing from god revealed and attested* by him.

II.1* [a]Τὸ μαρτύριον τοῦ θεοῦ. *The testimony of god* i e what god hath revealed and testifies in the old testament: The Apostle here declares to the Corinthians that when he brought the gospel to them he made noe use of any humane science improvement or skil; no insinuations of Eloquence; [b]no philosophical speculations, or ornaments of humane learning appeard in any thing he said, to perswade them: All his arguments were, as he tels them ver. 4 from the revelation of the spirit of god in the predictions of the old testament and the miracles which he Paul did among them, that their faith ⟨m⟩ight be built wholy upon the spirit of god, and not upon the abilities and wisdome of man. [c]Though μαρτύριον τοῦ θεοῦ *The testimony of god* agrees very well with so much of St Pauls meaning as relates to his founding his preaching on the testimony of god, yet those copys which read μυστήριον *mystery* for μαρτύριον *testimony* seem more perfectly to correspond with St Pauls sense in the whole latitude of it. [d]For though he ownes the doctrine of the gospel dictated by the spirit of god to be conteined in the Scriptures of the old Testament and builds upon that revelation. yet he every where teaches that it

[2]For I resolved to owne or shew no other knowledg among you but the knowledg* or doctrine of Jesus Christ and of him crucified. [3]All my cariage among you had nothing in it but the appearance of weakness and humility and fear of offending you.* [4]Neither did I in my discourses, or preaching make use of any humane art of perswasion to inveagle you: But the doctrin of the gospel which I proposed I confirmed and inforced by what the spirit* had revealed and demonstrated of it in the old testament, and by the power* of god accompanying it with miraculous operations, [5]that your faith might have its foundation not in the wisdome and endowments of men but in the power of god*

SECTION II. NO. 3⟨b⟩

Ch. II.6-16

CONTENTS

The next argument the Apostle uses to shew them that they had noe reason to glory in their teachers is that the knowledg of the gospel was

remained a secret there, not understood till they were lead into the hidden evangelical meaning of those passages [e]by the comeing of Jesus Christ and the assistance of the spirit in the times of the Messiah and then published to the world by the preachers of the gospel. And therefore he cals it, espetialy that part of it which relates to the Gentiles almost everywhere μυστήριον Mystery. See particularly Rom XVI.25.26

2* St Paul who was himself a learned man espetialy in the Jewish knowledg, haveing in the foregoeing chapter told them that neither the Jewish learning nor Grecian Sciences give a man any advantage as a minister of the gospel he here reminds them that he made no shew or use of either when he planted the gospel amongst them, intimateing thereby that those were not things for which their teachers were to be valued or followed.

3* St Paul by thus seting forth his own modest and humble behaviour amongst them reflects on the contrary cariage of their false Apostle which he describes in words at length 2 Cor XI 20.

4* [a]There were two sorts of arguments where with the Apostles confirmed the gospel. The one was the revelations made concerning our saviour by types and figures and prophesies of him under the law: The other in miracles and miraculous gifts accompanying the first preachers of the gospel in the publishing and propagateing of it. [b]The later of these St Paul here calls *power* the former in this Chapter he termes *spirit*. so ver. ⟨13⟩ 14 *things of the spirit of god*, and *spiritual things* are things which are revealed by the spirit of god, and not discoverable by our natural faculties.

⟨5⟩* Their faith being built wholy on divine revelation and miracles, whereby all humane abilitys were shut out there could be no reason for any of them to boast them selves of their teachers or value them selves upon their being the followers of this or that preacher. which St Paule hereby obviates

not attainable by our natural parts however they were improved by arts and philosophie, but was wholy oweing to Revelation.

TEXT

II.6. Howbeit we speak wisdom among them that are perfect: yet not the wisdom of this world; nor of the princes of this world, that come to nought.

7. But we speak the wisdom of God in a Mystery, even the hidden wisdom which God ordained before the world unto our glory.

8. Which none of the princes of this world knew: for had they known it, they would not have crucified the Lord of glory.

9. But as it is written, Eye hath not seen, nor ear heard, neither have entred into the heart of man, the things which God hath prepared for them that love him.

10. But God hath revealed them unto us by his Spirit: for the Spirit searcheth all things; yea, the deep things of God.

11. For what man knoweth the things of a man, save the spirit of man which is in him? even so the things of God knoweth no man, but the Spirit of God.

12. Now we have received, not the spirit of the world, but the Spirit which is of God; that we might know the things that are freely given to us of God.

13. Which things also we speak, not in the words which mans wisdom teacheth, but which the holy Ghost teacheth; comparing spiritual things with spiritual.

14. But the natural man receiveth not the things of the Spirit of God: for they are foolishness unto him; neither can he know them, because they are spiritually discerned.

15. But he that is spiritual, judgeth all things, yet he himself is judged of no man.

16. For who hath known the mind of the Lord, that he may instruct him? but we have the mind of Christ.

PARAPHRASE

II.6 Howbeit that which we preach is wisdome and known to be soe among those who are throughly instructed in the Christian religion and take it upon its true principles* but not the wisdome† of this

II.6* [a]*Perfect* here is the same with Spiritual ver. 15 i e one that is so perfectly well apprised of the divine nature and originall of the Christian religion that he sees and acknowledges it to be all a pure revelation from god, and not in the least the product of humane discovery parts or learning, [b]and so deriveing it wholy from what god hath taught by his Spirit in the Sacred Scriptures allows not the least part of it to be ascribd to the skil or abilities of men as authors of it but received as a doctrine comeing from god alone. [c]And thus *perfect* is opposed to *Carnal* Ch. III.1.3. i e such *babes* in Christianity such weak and mistaken Christians that they thought the gospel was to be managed as humane arts and sciences amongst men of the world, and those were better instructd

 [*See p. 174 for n. II.6* cont. and n. II.6†*]

world‡ nor of the princes§ or great men of this world‡ who will quickly be brought to nought.¶ [7]But we speak the wisdome of

and were more in the right who followed this master or teacher rather than an other, [d]and so glorying in being the scholers one of St Paul and an other of Apollos fell into divisions and partys about it, and vaunted one over an other, whereas in the school of Christ all was to be built on the authority of god alone and the revelation of his Spirit in the Sacred Scriptures

† *Wisdome of this world* i e the knowledg arts and sciences attainable by mans natural parts and faculties. such as mans wit could find out cultivate and improve· *or of the princes of this world*. i e such doctrines arts and sciences as the princes of the world approve incourage and endeavour to propagate

‡ Αἰὼν οὗτος which we translate. *This world* seems to me to signifie commonly if not constantly in the New Testament that State which dureing the Mosaical constitution men either Jews or Gentiles were in, as contradistinguished to the Evangelical state or constitution which is commonly called Αἰὼν μέλλων or ἐρχόμενος. *The world to come*

§ [a]Though by Ἄρχοντες τοῦ αἰῶνος τούτου may here be understood the *princes* or great men *of this world* in the ordinary sense of these words yet he that well considers ver. 28 of the foregoeing Ch: and ver. 8 of this Ch: may find reason to think that the Apostle here principaly designes the rulers and great men of the Jewish nation. [b]If it be objected that there is little ground to think that St Paul by the wisdom he disownes should mean that of his owne nation which the Greeks of Corinth (whom he was writeing to), had little acquainta⟨n⟩ce with: and had very little esteem for, [c]I reply that to understand this right and the pertinency of it we must remember that the great designe of St Paul in writeing to the Corinthians was to take them off from the respect and esteem that many of them had for a false Apostle that was got in among them, and had there raised a faction against St Paul. [d]This pretended Apostle tis plain from 2 Cor. XI.22 was a Jew, and as it seems 2 Cor V 16.17 valued himself upon that account, and possibly boasted him self to be a man of note, either by birth, or alliance, or place, or learning among that people, who counted themselves the holy and illuminated people of god, and therefore to have a right to sway among these new heathen converts. [e]To obviate this claim of his to any authority St Paul here tells the Corinthians that the wisdom and learning of the Jewish nation lead them not into the knowledg of the wisdom of god. i e the gospell revealed in the old testament, evident in this [f]that it was their rulers and Rabbis who stifly adhereing to the notions and prejudices of their nation had crucified Jesus the Lord of glory and were now them selves with their state and religion upon the point to be swept away and abolished. 'Tis to the same purpose that 2d Cor. ⟨V⟩.16-19 he tels the Corinthians, that he *knows noe man after the flesh* i e that he acknowledges noe dignity of birth or descent or outward national privileges. [g]The old things of the Jewish constitution are past and gon· who ever is in Christ and enterd into his kingdome is in a new creation where in all things are new, all things are from god, no right, no claim, or preference derived to any one from any former institution, but every ones dignity consists soly in this, that god had reconciled him to him self, not imputeing his former trespasses to him

¶ [a]τῶν καταργουμένων, *who are brought to nought*. i.e who are vanishing. If *the wisdome of this world and of the princes of this world* be to be understood of the wisdome and learning of the world in general as contradistinguished to the doctrine of the gospel, [b]then the words are added to shew what folly it is for them to glory as they doe in their teachers when all that worldly wisdom and learning and the great men the supporters of it would quickly be gon where as all true and lasting glory came onely from Jesus Christ the Lord of glory· [c]But if these words are to be understood of the Jews as seems most consonant both to the main designe of the Epistle and to St Pauls expressions here. Then his telling them that the *princes* of the Jewish nation *are brought to nought* is to take them off

god* conteined in the mysterious and obscure prophesies of the old Testament† which has been therein concealed and hid though it be what god predetermined in his own purpose before the Jewish constitution‡ to the glory§ of us who now understand and preach it. [8]which

from glorying in their Judaizing false Apostle, [d]since the authority of the rulers of that nation in matters of religion was now at an end, and they with all their pretences and their very constitution it self were upon the point of being abolished and swept away for haveing rejected and crucified the Lord of glory

7* [a]*Wisdome of god* is used here for the doctrine of the gospel comeing immediately from god by the revelation of his spirit and in this Ch: is set in opposition to all knowledg discoverys and improvements whatsoever attainable by humane industry parts and study, all which he calls *the wisdome of the world* and *mans wisdome*. [b]Thus distinguishing the knowledg of the gospel which was derived wholy from revelation and could be had noe other way, from all other knowledg whatsoever.

† [a]What the spirit of god had revealed of the gospel dureing the times of the law was soe little understood by the Jews in whose sacred writeings it was conteined that it might well be called the *wisdome of god in a mystery* i e declared in obscure prophesies and mysterious expressions and types. [b]Though this be undoubtedly so as appears by what the Jews both thought and did when Jesus the Messiah, exactly answering what was foretold of him, came amongst them, yet by *the wisdome of god in mystery where in it was hid though purposed by god before the setling of the Jewish œconomie* St Paul seems more particularly to mean what the Gentiles and consequently the Corinthians were more particularly concerned in [c](viz) gods purpose of calling the Gentiles to be his people under the Messiah, which though revealed in the old testament yet was not in the least understood till the times of the gospel and the Preaching of St Paul the Apostle of the Gentiles which therefore he so frequently and peculiarly cals a *mystery*. [d]The reading and compareing Rom XVI 25.26. Eph. III.3-9. VI.19.20 Col. I.26.27. II.1-8. IV.3.4. will give light to this. To which give me leave to observe upon the use of the word *Wisdome* here that St Paul speakeing of gods calling the Gentiles can not in mentioning it forbear expressions of his admiration of the great and incomprehensible wisdom of god therein. See Eph. III 8.10. Rom XI.33

‡ [a]Πρὸ τῶν αἰώνων signifies properly *before the ages* and I think it may be doubted whether these words *before the world* doe exactly render the sense of the place· that αἰών or αἰῶνες, should not be translated *The World* as in many places they are, I shall give one convinceing instance among many that might be brought. viz Eph III.9 compared with Col: I.26· [b]The words in Col: are τὸ μυστ⟨ή⟩ριον τὸ ἀποκεκρυμμένον ἀπὸ αἰώνων, thus renderd in the English translation *which hath been hidden from ages*· But in Eph: III.9 a parallel place the same words τοῦ μυστ⟨η⟩ρίου τοῦ ἀποκεκρυμμένου ἀπὸ τῶν αἰώνων are translated *The mystery which from the begining of the world hath been hid* [c]wheras it is plain from Col. I.26 ἀπὸ τῶν αἰώνων· does not signifie the Epoch or commencement of the concealment but those from whom it was concealed. Tis plain the Apostle in ver. 6 of this 2d Chap to the Corinthians immediately preceding and ver. 8th immediately following this which we have before us speaks of the Jews, [d]and therefore πρὸ τῶν αἰώνων here may be well understood to mean *Before the ages of the Jews*. and so ἀπ' α⟨ἰ⟩ώνων *from the ages of the Jews* in the other two mentioned texts. Why αἰῶνες in these and other places as Luk. I.70 and Act. III.21 and else where should be appropriated to the Ages of the Jews may be oweing to their counting by Ages or Jubilies vid: Dr Burthogge in his judicious treatise *Christianity a revealed Mystery*. c. 2. p. 17

§ [a]St Paul opposes here the true *glory* of Christian preachers and beleivers to the *glorying* which was amongst the Corinthians in the eloquence, learning or any other quality of their factious Leaders. for St Paul in all his expressions has an eye on his main

none of the Rulers amongst the Jews understood for if they had they would not have crucified the Lord Christ who has in his hands the disposeing of all true glory. [9]But they knew it not, as it is written eye hath not seen, nor ear heard, nor have the things, that god hath prepared for them that love him, enterd into the heart of man or thoughts of man. [10]But these things which are not discoverable by mans natural faculties and powers god hath revealed to us by his spirit which searcheth out all things even the deep counsels of god which are beyond the reach of our abilities to discover. [11]For as noe man knoweth what is in the mind of an other man but only the spirit of the man himself that is in him, soe much less doth any man know or can discover the thoughts and counsels of god but only the Spirit of god. [12]But we* have received not the spirit of the world† but the Spirit which is of god that we might know, what things are in the purpose of god out of his free bounty to bestow upon us, [13]which things we not only know but declare also, not in the language and learning taught by humane Eloquence and Philosophi, but in the language and expressions which the holy ghost teacheth in the revelations conteined in the holy Scriptures, compareing one part of revelation* with an other· [14]But a man who hath noe other help but his own natural faculties how

purpose as if he should have said Why doe you make divisions by glorying in your distinct teachers as you doe upon account of their parts learning or other endowments. [b]The true glory of a minister and disciple that god has ordaind him to is to be an expounder preacher and beleiver of those revealed truths and purposes of god which though conteined in the Sacred Scriptures of the old testament were not understood in former ages. this is all the glory that belongs to us gospel consorts. [c]this we have from Christ the Lord of all power and glory. and this is enough, it far excelling what either Jews or Gentiles had any expectation of from what they gloried in ver. 9. Thus St Paul takes away all matter of Glorying from the fals Apostle and his factious folowers among the Corinthians. That the ministration of the Gospel was more glorious than that of the law in St Pauls account see 2 Cor III 6-11

12* [a]*We* the true Apostles or rather *I·* for though he speaks in the plural number to avoid ostentation as it might be interpreted, yet he is here justifying him self and shewing the Corinthians that none of them had reason to forsake and slight him to follow and cry up their false Apostle· [b]and that he speaks of himself is plain from the next verse where he saith *we speak not in the words which mans wisdome teacheth* the same which he says of himself Chap: I. ver. 17 *I was sent to preach not with wisdom of words* and Ch: II. ver. 1 *I came to you not with excellency of speech or of wisdom*

† As he puts *princes of this world* ver. 6 and 8 for the rulers of the Jews soe here he puts *spirit of the world* for the notions of the Jews. that worldly Spirit where with they interpreted the old testament and the prophesies of the Messiah and his Kingdom. which spirit in contradistinction to the spirit of god which the Roman converts had receivd, he cals *the Spirit of bondage* Rom VIII.15

13* Tis plain the *spiritual things* he here speaks of are the unsearchable counsels of god revealed by the spirit of god which therefor he cals *spiritual things*

much soever improved by humane arts and sciences cannot receive the truths of the gospel which are made known by an other principle onely viz the spirit of god revealeing them and therefor seem foolish and absurd to such a man, nor can he by the bare use of his natural faculties and the principles of humane reason ever come to the knowledg of them because it is by the studying of divine revelation alone that we can attain the knowledg of them: [15]But he that lays his foundation in divine revelation* can judg what is and what is not the doctrine of the gospel and of salvation: he can judg who is and who is not a good minister and preacher of the word of god: But others who are bare animal* men that goe not beyond the discoverys made by the natural faculties of humane understanding without the help and study of revelation cannot judg of such an one whether he preaches right and well or noe. [16]For who by the bare use of his natural parts can come to know the mind of the Lord in the designe of the gospel soe as to be able to instruct him* [the spiritual man] in it? But I who renounceing all humane learning and knowledg in the case take all that I preach from divine revelation alone I am sure that therein I have the mind of Christ: And therefor there is noe reason why any of you should prefer other teachers to me; glory in them who oppose and vilifie me; and count it an honour to goe for their scholers and bee of their party.

SECTION II. NO. 4

Ch. III.1-IV.20

CONTENTS

[a]The next matter of boasting which the faction made use of to give the preeminence and preference to their Leader above St Paul seems to have been this that their new teacher had lead them farther and

15* ψυχικός the *animal* man and πνευματικός the *spiritual* man are opposed by St Paul in ⟨ver.⟩ 14 and 15 the one signifieing a man that has noe higher principles to build on than those of natural reason, the other a man that founds his faith and religion on divine revelation.

16* [a]αὐτόν *him* refers here to *spiritual man* in the former verse and not to *Lord* in this. For St Paul is shewing here, not that a *natural man* and a meer philosopher can not instruct Christ, this noe body pretending to be a Christian could owne; [b]but that a man by his bare natural parts not knowing the mind of the Lord could not instruct, could not judg, could not correct a preacher of the gospel who built upon revelation as he did and therefor 'twas certain that he had the mind of Christ given them a deeper insight into the mysterys of the gospel than St Paul had donne. [b]To take away their glorying on this account St Paul tells them, that they were carnal, and not capable of those more advanced truths, or any thing beyond the first principles of Christianity which he had taught them; and though an other had come and watered what he had planted, [c]yet neither planter nor waterer could assume to himself any glory from thence, because it was god alone that gave the increase. But what ever new doctrines they might pretend to receive from their magnified new Apostle yet noe man could lay any other foundation in a Christian Church but what he St Paul had laid viz that Jesus is the Christ; [d]and therefor there was noe reason to glory in their teachers; because upon this foundation they possibly might build false or unsound doctrines, for which they should receive noe thanks from god, though continuing in the faith they might be saved. [e]Some of the particular hey and stubble which this Leader brought into the Church at Corinth he seems particularly to point at Ch. III.16.17 viz their defileing the church by reteining and as it may be supposed patronizeing the Fornicator who should have been turned out. v: Ch. V.7.13. [f]He further addes that these extolled heads of their party were at best but men and none of the church ought to glory in men for Even Paul and Apollos and Peter and all the other preachers of the gospel were for the use benefit and glory of the church as the church was for the glory of Christ.

[g]Moreover he shews them that they ought not to be puffed up upon the account of these their new Teachers to the undervalueing of him though it should be true that they had learned more from them than from him self for these reasons

[h]1 Because all the preachers of the Gospel are but Stewards of the mysterys of god; and whither they have been faithfull in their Stewardship cannot be now known; And therefor they ought not to be some of them magnified and extolled and others depressed and blamed by their hearers here till Christ their Lord came [i]and then he knowing how they have behaved themselves in their ministry will give them their due prayses· Besides these Stewards have noe thing but what they have received and therefor noe glory belongs to them for it

[j]2 Because if these Leaders were (as was pretended) Apostles, Glory and honour and outward affluence here was not their portion, the Apostles being destined to want, contempt and persecution

[k]3 They ought not to be honourd, followed and gloried in as

Apostles because they had not the power of miracles which he intended shortly to come and shew they had not

TEXT

III.1. And I, brethren, could not speak unto you as unto spiritual, but as unto carnal, even as unto babes in Christ.

2. I have fed you with milk, and not with meat: for hitherto ye were not able to bear it, neither yet now are ye able.

3. For ye are yet carnal: for whereas there is among you envying, and strife, and divisions, are ye not carnal, and walk as men?

4. For while one saith, I am of Paul, and another, I am of Apollos, are ye not carnal?

5. Who then is Paul, and who is Apollos, but ministers by whom ye believed, even as the Lord gave to every man?

6. I have planted, Apollos watered; but God gave the increase.

7. So then, neither is he that planteth any thing, neither he that watereth: but God that giveth the increase.

8. Now he that planteth, and he that watereth, are one: and every man shall receive his own reward, according to his own labour.

9. For we are labourers together with God: ye are Gods husbandry, ye are Gods building.

10. According to the grace of God which is given unto me, as a wise master-builder I have laid the foundation, and another buildeth thereon. But let every man take heed how he buildeth thereupon.

11. For other Foundation can no man lay, than that is laid, which is Jesus Christ.

12. Now if any Man build upon this foundation, gold, silver, precious stones, wood, hay, stubble:

13. Every mans work shall be made manifest. For the day shall declare it, because it shall be revealed by fire; and the fire shall try every mans work, of what sort it is.

14. If any mans work abide which he hath built thereupon, he shall receive a reward.

15. If any mans work shall be burnt, he shall suffer loss: but he himself shall be saved; yet so, as by fire.

16. Know ye not that ye are the temple of God, and that the Spirit of God dwelleth in you?

17. If any man defile the temple of God, him shall God destroy: for the temple of God is holy, which temple ye are.

18. Let no man deceive himself: if any man among you seemeth to be wise in this world, let him become a fool, that he may be wise.

19. For the wisdom of this world is foolishness with God: for it is written, He taketh the wise in their own craftiness.

20. And again, The Lord knoweth the thoughts of the wise, that they are vain.

21. Therefore let no man glory in men: for all things are yours:

22. Whether Paul, or Apollos, or Cephas, or the world, or life, or death, or things present, or things to come; all are yours:

23. And ye are Christ's; and Christ is Gods.

IV.1. Let a man so account of us, as of the ministers of Christ, and stewards of the mysteries of God.

2. Moreover it is required in stewards, that a man be found faithful.

3. But with me it is a very small thing that I should be judged of you, or of mans judgment: yea, I judge not mine own self.

4. For I know nothing by my self, yet am I not hereby justified: but he that judgeth me is the Lord.

5. Therefore judge nothing before the time, until the Lord come, who both will bring to light the hidden things of darkness, and will make manifest the counsels of the hearts: and then shall every man have praise of God.

6. And these things, brethren, I have in a figure transferred to my self, and to Apollos for your sakes: that ye might learn in us, not to think of men above that which is written, that no one of you be puffed up for one against another.

7. For who maketh thee to differ from another? and what hast thou that thou didst not receive? now if thou didst receive it, why dost thou glory, as if thou hadst not received it?

8. Now ye are full, now ye are rich, ye have reigned as kings without us: and I would to God ye did reign, that we also might reign with you.

9. For I think that God hath set forth us the apostles last, as it were appointed to death. For we are made a spectacle unto the world, and to angels, and to men.

10. We are fools for Christs sake, but ye are wise in Christ: we are weak, but ye are strong; ye are honourable, but we are despised.

11. Even unto this present hour we both hunger, and thirst, and are naked, and are buffeted, and have no certain dwelling-place;

12. And labour working with our own hands: being reviled, we bless: being persecuted, we suffer it:

13. Being defamed, we intreat: we are made as the filth of the world, and are the off-scouring of all things unto this day.

14. I write not these things to shame you, but as my beloved sons I warn you.

15. For though you have ten thousand instructers in Christ, yet have ye not many fathers: for in Christ Jesus I have begotten you through the gospel.

16. Wherefore I beseech you, be ye followers of me.

17. For this cause have I sent unto you Timotheus, who is my beloved son,
and faithful in the Lord, who shall bring you into remembrance of my ways
which be in Christ, as I teach every where in every church.
18. Now some are puffed up as though I would not come to you.
19. But I will come to you shortly, if the Lord will, and will know, not the
speech of them which are puffed up, but the power.
20. For the kingdom of God is not in word, but in power.

PARAPHRASE

[III.1a]And I brethren found you soe given up to pride and vainglory in affectation of learning and philosophical knowledg* that I could not speake to you as Spiritual† i e as to men not wholy depending on philosophie and the discoverys of natural reason; as to men who had resigned them selves up in matters of religion to revelation and the knowledg which comes onely from the spirit of god [b]But as to Babes who yet reteined a great many childish and wrong notions about it· [2a]This hinderd me that I could not goe soe far as I desired in the mysterys of the christian religion but was fain to content my self with instructing you in the first principles* and more obvious and easie doctrines of it: [b]I could not apply my self to you as to spiritual men that could compare spiritual things† with spiritual one part of scripture with an other and thereby understand the more advanced truths revealed by the spirit of god, discerning true from false doctrines, good and usefull from evil‡ and vain opinions· A further discovery of

III.1* vid Ch: I.22. III.18

† [a]Here σαρκικός *carnal* is opposed to πνευματικός *spiritual* in the same sense that ψυ(χ)ικός *natural* or *animal* is opposed to πνευματικός *spiritual*. Ch II.14 as appears by the explication which St Paul himself gives here to σαρκικός carnal. [b]For he makes the *Carnal* to be all one with *Babes in Christ* ver. 1. i e such as had not their understandings yet fully opened to the true grounds of the Christian religion but reteined a great many childish thoughts about it as appeared by their divisions. one declareing for the doctrine of his master Paul another for that of his master Apollos which if they had been *spiritual*. [c]i e had looked upon the doctrine of the gospel to have come solely from the spirit of god, and to be had only from Revelation they could not have done. For then all humane mixtures of any thing derived either from Paul or Apollos or any other man had been wholy excluded. But they in these divisions professed to hold their religion one from one man and an other from an other and were there upon divided into partys. [d]This he tells them was to be *carnal* and περιπατεῖν κατὰ ἄνθρωπον to be led by principles purely humane i e to found their religion upon mens natural parts and discoverys whereas the gospel was wholy built upon divine revelation and noe thing else and from thence alone those who were πνευματικοί took it.

2* That this is the meaning of the Apostles metaphor of milk and Babes see Heb V.12–14

† vid: Ch. II.13

‡ vid: Heb. V.14

the truths and mysterys of Christianity depending wholy on revelation you were not able to bear then, nor are you yet able to bear; [3]because you are carnal* full of envyings and strife and factions upon the account of your knowledg and the orthodoxie of your particular partys.* [4]For whilst you say one I am of Paul, and another I am of Apollos* are ye not carnal and manage yourselves in the conduct both of your minds and actions according to barely humane principles and doe not as spiritual men acknowledg all that information and all those gifts where with the ministers of Jesus Christ are furnishd for the propagation of the gospel to come solely from the spirit of god. [5a]What then are any of the preachers of the Gospel that you should glory in them and divide into partys under their names? Who for Example is Paul, or who Apollos? What are they else but bare ministers by whose ministry according to those several abilitys and gifts which god has bestowed upon each of them ye have received the gospel· [b]They are onely servants imploid to bring unto you a religion derived intirely from divine revelation wherein humane abilities or wisdome had noe thing to doe. The preachers of it are onely instruments by whom this doctrine is conveyed to you, which whether you looke on it in its original it is not a thing of humane invention or discovery, [c]or whether you look upon the gifts of the teachers who instruct you in it, all is entirely from god alone and affords you not the least ground to attribut any thing to your teachers. [6]For example I planted it amongst you and Apollos waterd it but noe thing can from thence be ascribed to either of us, there is noe reason for your calling your selves some of Paul and others of Apollos. [7]For neither the planter nor the waterer have any power to make it take root and grow in your hearts, they are

3* κατ' ἄνθρωπον speaking *according to man* signifies speaking according to the principles of natural reason in contradistinction to revelation vid 1 Cor. IX.8. Gal I.11 and soe *walkeing according to man* must here be understood

4* [a]From this 4th verse compared with Ch: IV.6 it may be noe improbable conjecture that the division in this church was only into two opposite partys whereof the one adhered to St Paul: The other stood up for their head a false Apostle who opposed St Paul. For the Apollos whom St Paul mentions here was one (as he tells us Vers 6) who came in and waterd what he had planted. [b]i e when St Paul had planted a church at Corinth this Apollos got into it and pretended to instruct them farther and boasted in his performances amongst them which St Paul takes notice of again 2 Cor X.15.16. Now the Apollos that he here speaks of he himself tells us Ch IV.6 was an other man under that borrowed name. [c]Tis true St Paul in his Epistles to the Corinthians generaly speaks of that his opposer in the plural number But it is to be remembred that he speaks soe of himself too. which as it was the less invidious way in regard of himself. soe it was the softer way towards his opposer though he seems to intimate plainly that it was one Leader that was set up against him as noe thing in that respect, the growth and success is oweing to god alone· [8]The planter and the waterer on this account are all one neither of them to be magnified or preferd before the other, they are but instruments concurring to the same end, and therefor ought not to be distinguished and set in opposition one to an other or cried up as more deserveing one than an other. [9]We the preachers of the Gospel are but labourers imploid by god, about that which is his work. and from him shall receive reward hereafter every one according to his own labour, and not from men here, who are liable to make a wrong estimate of the labours of their teachers, prefering those who doe not labour togeather with god, who doe not cary on the designe or worke of god in the gospel, or perhaps doe not cary it on equally with others, who are undervalued by them. [10]Ye who are the church of god are gods building, in which I, according to the skil and knowledg which god of his free bounty has been pleased to give me, and therefor ought not to be to me or any other matter of glorying, as a skilfull architect have laid a sure foundation [11]which is Jesus the Messiah the sole and onely foundation of Christianity besides which noe man can lay any other. But though noe man who pretends to be a preacher of the gospel can build upon any other foundation, yet you ought not to cry up your new instructer* who has come† and built upon the foundation that I laid for the doctrines he builds there on, as if there were noe other minister of the gospel but he. [12]For tis possible a man may build upon that true foundation wood, hey, and stubble, things that will not bear the test when the trial by fire at the last day* shall come· [13]at that day every mans work shall be tried and discoverd of what sort it is. [14]If what he hath taught be sound and good and will stand the triall as silver and gold and pretious stones abide in the fire he shall be rewarded for his labour in the gospel: [15]But if he hath introduced false or unsound doctrines into Christianity he shall be like a man whose building being of wood hey and stubble is consumed by the fire, all his pains in building is lost, and his worke consumed and gon. though he him self should escape and be saved. [16]I told you that ye are gods building* yea more than that· ye are the temple of god in which his spirit dwelleth· [17]if any man* by corrupt doctrine or discipline

11* v Ch. IV 15

† In this he reflects on the false Apostle. v 2 Cor X 15 16

⟨12⟩* When the *day* of trial and recompense shall be. see Ch: IV.5 where he speaks of the same thing

16* vid ver. 9

17* [a]It is not incongruous to think that by *any man* here St Paul designes one particular man viz the false Apostle who tis probable by the strength of his party supporting

defileth* the temple of god he shall not be saved with loss as by fire: but
him will god destroy for the temple of god is holy which temple ye are.
[18]Let noe man deceive him self by his success in carying his point·* If
any one seemeth to him self or others wise† in worldly wisdome soe as
to pride himself in his parts and dexterity incompasseing his ends let
him renounce all his natural and acquired parts, all his knowledg and
ability, that he may become truly wise in imbraceing and owneing noe
other knowledg but the simplicity of the gospel. [19]For all other wisdom,
all the wisdom of the world is foolishness with god For it is written· he
taketh the wise in their own craftyness: [20]and again the Lord knoweth
the thoughts of the wise that they are vain. [21]Therefor let none of you
glory in any of your teachers for they are but men· [22a]For all your
teachers whither Paul or Apollos or Peter even the Apostles them
selves, nay all the world and even the world to come, all things are yours
for your sake and use; as you are Christs subjects of his kingdom for his
glory and Christ and his Kingdom for the glory of god. [b]Therefor if all
your teachers and soe many other greater things are for you and for your
sakes, you can have noe reason to make it a glory to you, that you belong
to this or that particular teacher amongst you. [23]Your true glory is that
you are Christs and Christ and all his are gods, and not that you are this
or that mans scholer or Follower. [IV.1]As for me I pretend not to set up a
school amongst you and as a Master to have my scholars denominated
from me. No let noe man have higher thoughts of me than as a minister
of Christ imploid as his Steward to dispense the truths and doctrines of
the gospel which are the mysteries which god wraped up. in types and
obscure predictions where they have lain hid till by us his Apostles
he now reveals them. [2]Now that which is principally required and
regarded in a Steward is that he be faithfull in dispenseing what is

and reteining the Fornicator mentioned Ch V in the Church, had defiled it, [b]Ch: V.6 which may be the reason why St Paul soe often mentions Fornication in this Epistle and that in some places with particular Emphasis as Ch V 9. VI.13-20. most of the disorders in this church we may look on as oweing to this false Apostle, [c]which is the reason why St Paul sets him self soe much against him in both these Epistles and makes almost the whole business of them to draw the Corinthians off from this Leader, judging, as 'tis like, that this church could not be reformed as long as that person was in credit and had a party among them

18* What it was where in the Craftiness of the person mentiond had appeard, it was not necessary for St Paul writeing to the Corinthians who knew the matter of fact to particularise; to us therefor it is left to guess and possibly we shall not be much out if we take it to be the keeping the Fornicator from censure soe much insisted on by St Paul Ch.V

† That by σοφός here the Apostle means a cuning man in business is plain from his quotation in the next verse where the wise spoken of are the crafty

committed to his charge. [3]But as for me I value it not if I am censured by some of you or by any man, as not being a faithfull steward: Nay as to this I pass noe judgment on my self. [4]For though I can truly say that I know noething by my self yet am I not hereby justified to you But the Lord whose Steward I am at the last day will pronounce sentence on my behaviour in my stewardship and then you will know what to think of me. [5]Then judg not either me or others before the time; untill the Lord come, who will bring to light the dark and secret counsels of mens hearts in preaching the gospel, and then shall every one have that prayse that estimate set upon him by god him self which he truly deserves. But praise ought not to be given them before the time by their hearers who are ignorant fallible men. [6a]On this occasion I have chosen to name Apollos and my self* as the magnified and opposed heads of distinct factions amongst you, not that we are soe, but out of respect to you, that I might offend noe body by nameing them; and that you may learn by us, of whom I have written† that we are but planters, waterers. and Stewards, [b]not to think of the ministers of the Gospel above what I have written to you of them, that you be not puffed up each party in the vain glory of their one extolled Leader to the crying down and contempt of any other who is well esteemd of by others. [7]For what maketh one to differ from an other? or what gifts of the Spirit, what knowledg of the Gospel has any Leader amongst you, which he received not as intrusted to him of god, and not acquired by his own abilitys? [8a]And if he received it as a Steward, why does he glory in that which is not his own? However you are mightily satisfied with your present state, you now are full, you now are rich, and abound in every thing you desire, you have noe need of me, [b]but have reigned like princes without me, and I wish you did truly reigne, that I might come and share in the protection and prosperity you enjoy now you are in your kingdome. [9]For I being made an Apostle last of all, it seems to me as if I were brought last* upon the stage to be in my sufferings and death a spectacle to the world and to angels and to men. [10]I am a fool for Christs sake, but you manage your Christian concernes with wisdome. I am weak and in a suffering condition* you are strong and flourishing; you are honourable but I am dispised, [11]even to this present hour I both

IV.6* vid Ch: III.4

† vid: Ch. III.6.9. Ch: IV.1

9* The Apostle seems here to allude to the custome of bringing those last upon the theater who were to be destroid by wild beasts

10* Soe he uses the word weakness often, in his Epistles to the Corinthians, applied to him self vid 2 Cor XII.10

hunger and thirst and want clothes and am buffeted wandering without
house or home and maintain my self with the labour of my hands:
[12]Being reviled I bless: Being persecuted I suffer patiently: [13]Being
defamed I intreat: I am made as the filth of the world and the ofscouring
of all things unto this day. [14]I write not these things to shame you: But as
a father to warn ye my children that ye be not the devoted zealous partizans and followers of such whose cariage is not like this; under whom,
however you may flatter your selves, in truth you doe not reigne: but on
the contrary are domineerd over and fleeced by them.* [15]I warn you I
say as your father· For how many teachers soever you may have you can
have but one father, It was I that begot you in Christ. i e I converted you
to Christianity; [16]Wherefore I beseech you be ye followers of me·* [17]To
this purpose I have sent my beloved Son Timothy to you who may be
relyd upon, he shall put you in mind and informe you how I behave my
self every where in the ministry of the gospel*

[18]Some indeed are puffed up and make their boasts as if I would not
come to you. [19]But I intend god willing to come shortly and then will
make trial not of the rhetorique or talkeing of those boasters but of what
miraculous power of the holy ghost is in them. [20]For the doctrine and
prevalency of the gospel, the propagation and support of Christs Kingdome by the conversion and establishment of beleivers does not consist
in talkeing, nor in the fluency of a glib tongue and a fine discourse; but
in the miraculous operations of the holy ghost.

SECTION II. NO. 5

Ch. IV.21-VI.20

CONTENTS

[a]Another means which St Paul makes use of to bring off the

14* Vid 2 Cor XI.20. St Paul here from ver. 8 to 17 by giveing an account of his own cariage gently rebukes them for following men of a different Character and exhorts them to be followers of him self

16* This he presses again Ch: XI.1. and tis not likely he would have proposd him self over and over again to them to be followed by them had the question and contest amongst them been only whose name they should have borne his or their new Teachers· His proposeing him self therefor thus to be followed must be understood in direct opposition to the false Apostle who mislead them and was not to be sufferd to have any credit or followers amongst them.

17* This he does to shew that what he taught them and pressed them to was not in a pique against his opposer; but to convince them that all he did at Corinth was the very same and noe other then what he did every where as a faithfull steward and minister of the Gospel.

Corinthians from their false Apostle and to stop their veneration of him and their glorying in him, is by representing to them the fault and disorder was committed in that Church by not judging and expelling the Fornicator which neglect, as may be guessed, was oweing to that faction

[b]1 Because it is natural for a faction to support and protect an offender that is of their side

2 From the great fear St Paul was in whither they would obey him in Censureing the offender as appears by the second Epistle. Which he could not fear but from the opposite faction. They who had preservd their respect to him being sure to follow his orders.

[c]3 From what he says Ch: IV.16. After he had told them ver. 6 of that Chapter that they should not be puffed up for any other against him, for soe the whole scope of his discourse here imports, he beseeches them to be his followers. i e leaveing their other guides to follow him in punishing the offender. [d]For that we may conclude from his immediately insisting on it soe earnestly, he had in his view, when he beseeches them to be Followers of him; and consequently that they might joyn with him, and take him for their Leader, Ch. V.3.4 he makes himself by his Spirit, as his proxie, the president of their assembly to be convened for the punishing that criminal

[e]4 It may further be suspected, from what St Paul says Ch. VI.1, that the opposite party to stop the Church censure pretended that this was a matter to be judgd by the civil magistrate: nay possibly from what is said ver. 6 of that Chapter it may be gathered, that they had got it brought before the heathen judg; or at least from ver. 12 that they pleaded, [f]that what he had donne was lawfull and might be justified before the Magistrate. For the judging spoken of Ch. VI must be understood to relate to the same matter that it does Ch: V. it being a continuation of the same discourse and argument [g]As is easy to be observed by any one who will read it without regarding the divisions into Chapters and verses, whereby ordinary people (not to say others) are often disturbed in reading the holy Scripture and hinderd from observeing the true sense and coherence of it. The whole VI Chapter is spent in prosecuteing the business of the Fornicator began in the V. [h]That this is soe is evident from the later end as well as begining of the VI Chapter. And therefor what St Paul says of *lawfull* VI.12 may without any violence be supposed to be said, in answer to some, who might have alledgd in favour of the Fornicator, that what he had done was *lawful* and might be justified by the laws of

the country which he was under. [i]Why else Should St Paul subjoyn soe many arguments (wherewith he concludes this VI Ch: and this subject) to prove the Fornication in question to be by the law of the gospel a great sin, and consequently fit for a Christian Church to censure in one of its members, However it might passe for *lawfull* in the esteem and by the laws of the gentils?

[j]There is one objection which at first sight seems to be a strong argument against this supposition that the fornication here spoken of was held lawfull by the Gentils of Corinth and that possibly this very case had been brought before the magistrate there and not condemned. [k]The objection seems to lie in these words. Ch V.1 *There is Fornication heard of amongst you and such Fornication as is not named amongst the Gentils that one should have his fathers wife*. But yet I conceive the words duely considerd have noething in them contrary to my supposition.

[l]To clear this I take liberty to say, it cannot be thought that this man had his fathers wife, whilst by the laws of the place she actualy was his fathers wife. for then it had been μοιχεία adultery, and soe the Apostle would have called it, which was a crime in Greece. nor could it be tolerated in any civil Societie, that one man should have the use of a woman whilst she was an other mans wife, i e an other mans right and possession.

[m]The case therefore here seems to be this. The woman had parted from her husband; which it is plain from Ch. VII.10.11.13. at Corinth women could doe. For if by the law of that country a woman could not divorce herself from her husband the Apostle had there in vain bid her not leave her husband

[n]But however known and allowed a practise it might be amongst the Corinthians for a woman to part from her husband, yet this was the first time it was ever known that her husbands own son should mary her. This is that which the Apostle takes notice of in these words *Such a Fornication as is not named amongst the Gentils*· [o]Such a Fornication this was, soe little known in practise amongst them, that it was not soe much as heard named or spoken of by any of them. But whither they held it unlawfull that a woman soe separated should mary her husbands son when she was looked upon to be at liberty from her former husband and free to mary whom she pleased that the Apostle says not. [p]This indeed he declares that by the law of Christ a womans leaveing her husband and marying another is unlawfull Ch. VII.11. and this womans marying her husbands son he

declares Ch. V.1 (the place before us) to be Fornication, a peculiar sort of Fornication. whatever the Corinthians or their law might determin in the case: [q]And therefor a Christian church might and ought to have censured it within them selves, it being an offence against the rule of the Gospel, which is the law of their society· And they might and should have expelled this fornicator out of their Society, for not submitting to the laws of it, notwithstanding that the civil laws of the country, and the judgment of the heathen magistrate might acquit him. [r]Suitable here unto it is very remarkable that the arguments that St Paul uses, in the close of this discourse Ch. VI.13-20 to prove Fornication unlawfull are all drawn Soley from the Christian institution. v.g That our bodys are made for the Lord ver. 13. That our bodys are members of Christ ver. 15. [s]That our bodys are the temples of the holy ghost ver. 19. That we are not our own but bought with a price ver. 20. all which arguments concerne Christians onely; And there is not in all this discourse against Fornication one word to declare it to be unlawfull by the law of nature to man kind in general. [t]That was altogeather needless, and besides the Apostles purpose here, where he was teaching and exhorting Christians what they were to doe as Christians within their own Society by the law of Christ. [u]which was to be their rule and was sufficient to obleige them whatever other laws the rest of mankind observed or were under. Those he professes here Ch: V.12.⟨13⟩ not to meddle with nor to judg. For haveing noe authority among them he leaves them to the judgment of god under whose government they are.

[v]These considerations afford ground to conjecture that the faction which opposed St Paul had hinderd the church of Corinth from censureing the Fornicator, and that St Paul shewing them their miscariage herein aims thereby to lessen the credit of their Leader by whose influence they were drawn into it. [w]For as soon as they had unanimously shewn their obedience to St Paul in this matter we see his severity ceases and he is all softness and gentleness to the Offender 2 Cor II.5-8 and he tells them in express words ver. 9 that his end in writeing to them of it was to try their obedience. [x]To which let me adde that this supposition though it had not all the evidence for it, which it has, yet being suited to St Pauls principal designe in this Epistle and helping us the better to understand these two chapters may deserve to be mentioned

TEXT

IV.21. What will ye? shall I come unto you with a rod, or in love, and in the spirit of meekness?

V.1. It is reported commonly that there is fornication among you, and such fornication as is not so much as named amongst the Gentiles, that one should have his fathers wife.

2. And ye are puffed up, and have not rather mourned, that he that hath done this deed, might be taken away from among you.

3. For I verily as absent in body, but present in spirit, have judged already, as though I were present, concerning him that hath so done this deed;

4. In the name of our Lord Jesus Christ, when ye are gathered together, and my spirit, with the power of our Lord Jesus Christ,

5. To deliver such an one unto Satan for the destruction of the flesh, that the spirit may be saved in the day of the Lord Jesus.

6. Your glorying is not good: know ye not that a little leaven leaveneth the whole lump?

7. Purge out therefore the old leaven, that ye may be a new lump, as ye are unleavened. For even Christ our passover is sacrificed for us.

8. Therefore let us keep the feast, not with old leaven, neither with the leaven of malice and wickedness; but with the unleavened bread of sincerity and truth.

9. I wrote unto you in an epistle, not to company with fornicatours.

10. Yet not altogether with the fornicatours of this world, or with the covetous, or extortioners, or with idolaters; for then must ye needs go out of the world.

11. But now I have written unto you, not to keep company, if any man that is called a brother be a fornicatour, or covetous, or an idolater, or a railer, or a drunkard, or an extortioner, with such an one, no not to eat.

12. For what have I to do to judge them also that are without? do not ye judge them that are within?

13. But them that are without, God judgeth. Therefore put away from among your selves that wicked person.

VI.1. Dare any of you, having a matter against another, go to law before the unjust, and not before the saints?

2. Do ye not know that the saints shall judge the world? and if the world shall be judged by you, are ye unworthy to judge the smallest matters?

3. Know ye not that we shall judge angels? how much more things that pertain to this life?

4. If then ye have judgments of things pertaining to this life, set them to judge who are least esteemed in the church.

5. I speak to your shame. Is it so, that there is not a wise man amongst you? no not one that shall be able to judge between his brethren?

6. But brother goeth to law with brother, and that before the unbelievers.

7. Now therefore there is utterly a fault among you, because ye go to law one with another: why do ye not rather take wrong? why do ye not rather suffer your selves to be defrauded?

8. Nay, you do wrong and defraud, and that your brethren.

9. Know ye not that the unrighteous shall not inherit the kingdom of God? be not deceived: neither fornicatours, nor idolaters, nor adulterers, nor effeminate, nor abusers of themselves with mankind,

10. Nor thieves, nor covetous, nor drunkards, nor revilers, nor extortioners, shall inherit the kingdom of God.

11. And such were some of you: but ye are washed, but ye are sanctified, but ye are justified in the name of the Lord Jesus, and by the Spirit of our God.

12. All things are lawful unto me, but all things are not expedient: all things are lawful for me, but I will not be brought under the power of any.

13. Meats for the belly, and the belly for meats: but God shall destroy both it and them. Now the body is not for fornication, but for the Lord; and the Lord for the body.

14. And God hath both raised up the Lord, and will also raise up us by his own power.

15. Know ye not, that your bodies are the members of Christ? shall I then take the members of Christ, and make them the members of an harlot? God forbid.

16. What, know ye not that he which is joined to an harlot, is one body? for two (saith he) shall be one flesh.

17. But he that is joined unto the Lord is one spirit.

18. Flee fornication. Every sin that a man doeth, is without the body: but he that committeth fornication, sinneth against his own body.

19. What, know ye not that your body is the temple of the holy Ghost which is in you, which ye have of God, and ye are not your own?

20. For ye are bought with a price: therefore glorifie God in your body, and in your spirit, which are Gods.

PARAPHRASE

[IV.21] I purposed to come unto you. But what would you have me doe? Shall I come to you with a rod to chastise you? or with kindness and a peaceable disposition of* mind? [V.1] In short it is commonly reported

IV.21* He that shall carefully read 2 Cor I.20-II.11 will easily perceive that this last verse here of this IV Ch: is an introduction to the severe act of discipline which St Paul was goeing to exercise amongst them though absent as if he had been present. And therefore this verse ought not to have been separated from the following Chapter as if it belongd not to that discourse.

that there is Fornication* among you and such Fornication as is not
known† ordinarily among the Heathen, that one should have his
fathers wife, 2 and yet ye remain puffed up though it would better have
become you to have been dejected for this scandalous fact amongst
you and in a mournful sense of it to have removed the offender out of
the Church. 3 For I truly though absent in body yet as present in spirit
have thus already judgd, as if I were personally with you, him that
committed this fact. 4 When in the name of the Lord Jesus ye are
assembled, and my spirit i e my vote as if I were present makeing one
by the power of our Lord Jesus Christ 5 deliver the offender up to
Sathan, that being put thus into the hands and power of the devil his
body may be afflicted and brought down that his soule may be saved
when our Lord Jesus comes to judg the world. 6 Your glorying* as you
doe in a Leader who drew you into this scandalous indulgence† in
this case is a fault in you, ye that are knowing know ye not that a little
leaven leaveneth the whole‡ lump? 7 Therefore laying by that deference and veneration ye had for those Leaders you gloryed in turn out
from among you that Fornicator that the church may receive noe taint
from him that you may be a pure new lump or Societie free from such
a dangerous mixture which may corrupt you· For Christ our pasover is
slain for us, 8 therefore let us, in commemoration of his death, and our
deliverance by him, be a holy people to him*

V.1* [a]The writers of the new Testament seem to use the Greek word πορνεία which we translate Fornication in the same sense that the Hebrews used זנות which we also translate Fornication though it be certein both these words in Sacred Scripture have a larger sense than the word Fornication has in our language [b]for זנות amongst the Hebrews signified *Turpitudinem* or *Rem Turpem*, uncleaness or any flagitious scandalous crime, but more espetialy the uncleaness of unlawfull copulation and Idolatry; and not precisely Fornication in our sense of the word. i e the unlawful mixture of an unmaried couple

† [a]*Not known*. That the marrying of a son-in-law and a mother-in-law was not by the Roman laws prohibited we have an instance in *Tully*: but yet it was lookd on as so scandalous and infamous that it never had any countenance from practise. [b]His words in his oration *pro Cluentio* Section IV are so agreeable to the present case that it may not be amiss to set them down. *Nubit genero Socrus, nullis auspitiis, nullis auctoribus, funestis ominibus omnium. O mulieris scelus incredibile: et praeter hanc unam, in omni vita inauditum*!

6* Glorying is all along in the begining of this Epistle spoken of the preference they gave to their new Leader in opposition to St Paul

† If their Leader had not been guilty of this miscariage it had been out of St Pauls way here to have reproved them for their glorying in him. But St Paul is a close writer and uses not to mention things where they are impertinent to his subject

‡ What reason he had to say this vid: 2 Cor XII.21——Grex totus in agris unius scabie cadit et porrigine porci

7 and 8* In these two verses he alludes to the Jews cleansing their houses at the feast of the pasover from all leaven the symbol of corruption and wickedness

[9]I wrote to you before that you should not keep company with
Fornicators. [10]You are not to understand by it as if I meant that you
are to avoid all unconverted heathens, that are Fornicators or
coviteous or rapaceous or Idolaters: for then you must goe out of the
world. [11]But that which I now write unto you is that you should not
keep company, noe nor eat with a Christian by profession, who is
lascivious, coviteous, idolatrous, a rayler, drunkard, or rapacious.
[12]For what have I to doe to judg those who are out of the church? Have
ye not a power to judg those who are members of your church? [13]But
as for those who are out of the church leave them to god, to judg them
belongs to him: Therefore doe ye what is your part; remove that
wicked one the Fornicator out of the church. [VI.1]Dare any one of you
haveing a controversie with an other bring it before an heathen* judg
to be tried, and not let it be decided by Christians?* [2]Know ye not that
Christians shall judg the world, and if the world shall be judgd by you,
are ye unworthy to judg ordinary small matters? [3]Know ye not that we
Christians have power over evil spirits? how much more over the little
things relateing to this animal life? [4]If then ye have at any time controversies among you concerning things pertaining to this life let the
partys contending choose arbitrators* in the church i e out of Church
members. [5]Is there not among you, I speak it to your shame a wise*
man whom ye can think able enough to refer your controversies to?
[6]But one Christian goeth to law with an other and that before the
unbeleivers in the heathen courts of justice: [7]Nay verily it is a failure
and defect in you that you so far contest matters of right one with
another as to bring them to trial or ju⟨d⟩gment. Why doe ye not rather
suffer losse and wrong? [8]But it is plain by the mans haveing his
father⟨s⟩ wife that ye are guilty of doeing wrong* one to an other and

VI.1* ἅγιοι *saints* is put for Christians· ἄδικοι *unjust* for Heathens

4* [a]*Least esteemed*· the word in the original is ἐξουθενημένους· Amongst the Jews there was *con⟨s⟩essus triumviralis authenticus* who had authority and could hear and determin causes ex officio, There was an other *consessus triumviralis* which were chosen by the partys· these though they were not *authentici* yet could judg and determine the causes referd to them. [b]These were those which St Paul cals here ἐξουθενημένους *Judices non authenticos* i.e Referees chosen by the partys. See *de Dieu*. That St Paul does not mean by it here *those who are least esteemd* is plain from the next following verse

5* *Wise man* σοφός· If St Paul uses this word in the sense of the Synagoge it signifyes one ordaind a Rabbi and so capacitated to be a judg for such were called *Wise men*. If in the sense of the Greek schools then it signifies a man of learning study and parts. if it be taken in the latter sense it may seem to be with some reflection on their pretending to wisdom

8* [a]That the wrong here spoken of was the Fornicators takeing and keeping his fathers wife the words of St Paul 2 Cor: VII.12 instanceing this very wrong are stick not to doe injustice even to your Christian brethren. [9]Know ye not that the transgressors of the law of Christ shall not inherit the kingdom of god? Deceive not your selves. neither Fornicators, nor Idolaters, nor adulterers, nor effeminate, nor abusers of them selves with mankind, [10]nor theives, nor coviteous, nor drunkards, nor revilers, nor extortioners shall inherit the Kingdom of god. [11]And such were some of you, but your past sins are washed away and forgiven you upon your receiveing of the gospel by baptisme: But ye are sanctified.* i e ye are members of Christs church which consists of Saints, and have made some advances in the reformation of your lives† by the doctrine of Christ confirmed to you by the extraordinary operations of the holy ghost

[12]But* supposeing fornication were in it self as lawfull as eating promiscuously all sorts of meat that are made for the belly on purpose to be eaten yet I would not so far indulge either custome or my appetite as to bring my body thereby into any disadvantageous state of subjection.† As in eating and drinking though meat be made

a sufficient evidence. And it is not wholy improbable there had been some hearing of this matter before a heathen judg. or at lest talked of· [b]which if supposed, will give a great light to this whole passage, and sev⟨e⟩ral others in these Chapters. For thus visibly runs St Pauls argument Ch V.12 13 Ch. VI.1.2.3 etc coherent and easy to be understood if it stood togeather as it should and were not chopd in peices by a division into two Chapters. [c]Ye have a power to judg those who are of your church· therefor put away from among you that Fornicator. You doe ill to let it come before a heathen magistrate. Are you, who are to judg the world and angels, not worthy to judg such a matter as this?

11* ἡγιάσθητε, *sanctified*. i e have remission of your sins, So *sanctified* signifies Heb X.10 and 18 compared. He that would perfectly comprehend and be satisfied in the meaning of this place let him read Heb: IX.X particularly IX.13-23

† ἐδικαιώθητε. *Ye are become just*. i e are reformd in your lives. see it soe used Rev: XXII.11

12* [a]St Paul haveing, upon occasion of injustice amongst them particularly in the matter of the Fornicator, warned them against that and other sins that exclude men from salvation, he here reassumes his former argument about fornication and by his reasoning here it looks as if some among them had pleaded that fornication was lawful. [b]To which he answers that granting it to be so, yet the lawfulness of all wholesome food reachd not the case of Fornication, and shews by several instances (as particularly the degradeing the body and makeing what in a Christian is the member of Christ, the member of an harlot) [c]that fornication upon several accounts might be so unsuitable to the state of a Christian man that a Christian societie might have reason to animadvert upon a Fornicator though fornication migh⟨t⟩ pass for an indifferent action in an other man.

† [a]*Expedient* And *Brought under power* in this ver. seem to refer to the two parts of the following ver. the first of them to eating in the first part of the 13 ver. and the later of them to fornication in the later part of the 13 ver. To make this the more intelligible it may be fit to remark that St Paul here seems to obviat such a sort of reasoning as this in behalf of the Fornicator. [b]'All sorts of meats are lawfull to Christians who are set free 'from the law of Moses and why are they not soe in regard of women who are at their

purposely for the belly and the belly for meat yet because it may not be expedient† for me I will not in so evidently a lawfull thing as that goe to the utmost bounds of my liberty [13a]though there be noe danger that I should thereby bring any lasting dammage upon my belly since god will speedily put an end both to belly and food. But the case of the body in reference to women is far different from that of the belly in reference to meats. For the body is not made to be joynd to a woman,* much less to be joynd to an harlot in Fornication, [b]as the belly is made for meat and then to be put an end to when that use ceases. But the body is for a much nobler purpose and shall subsist when the belly and food shall be destroid; The body is for our Lord Christ to be a member of him, as our Lord Christ has taken a body† that he might partake of our nature and be our head· [14]so that as god has already raised him up and given him all power soe he will raise us up likewise who are his members to* the partakeing in the nature of his glorious

'own disposal?' To which St Paul replyes 'Though my belly was made onely for eating 'and all sorts of meat were made to be eaten and so are lawfull for me, [c]yet I will abstein 'from what is lawfull if it be not convenient for me, though my belly will be certain to 'recei⟨v⟩e no prejudice by it which will affect it in the other world since god will there 'put an end to the belly and all use of food. But as to the body of a Christian the case is 'quite otherwise. [d]That was not made for the enjoyment of women; but for a much 'nobler end, to be a member of Christs body and so shall last for ever and not be 'destroid as the belly shall be. Therefore supposeing Fornication to be lawfull in it self I 'will not so debase and subject my body and doe it that prejudice, as to take that which 'is a member of Christ and make it the member of an harlot. this ought to be had in 'detestation by all Christians.'

[e]The context is so plain in the case that interpreters allow St Paul to discourse here upon a supposition of the lawfulness of Fornication. Nor will it appear at all strange that he does soe if we consider the argument he is upon. He is here convinceing the Corinthians that though Fornication were to them an indifferent thing and were not condemned in their country more than eating any sort of meat [f]yet there might be reasons why a Christian society might punish it in their own members by church censures and expulsion of the guilty. Conformably hereunto we see in what follows here that all the arguments used by St Paul against Fornication are brough⟨t⟩ from the incongruity it hath with the state of a Christian as a Christian, [g]but no thing is said against it as a fault in a man as a man, no plea used that it is a sin in all men by the law of Nature. A Christian society without entering into that enquiry or goeing so far as that had reason to condemn and censure it as not comporting with the dignity and principles of that religion which was the foundation of their societie

13* *Woman*. I have put in this to make the Apostles sense understood the easier. For he argueing here as he does upon the supposition that fornication is in it self lawfull Fornication in these words must mean the supposed lawfull enjoyment of a woman· otherwise it will not answer the foregoeing instance of the belly and eating

† *And the Lord for the Body*. See Heb II.5–18

14* [a]Διὰ τῆς δυνάμεως αὐτοῦ *To his power*. The context and designe of St Paul here strongly incline one to take διά here to signifie as it does 2 Pet I.3 *to* and not *by*. St Paul is here makeing out to the Corinthian converts that they have a power to judg. He tels

body and the power he is vested with in it. [15]Know ye not, you who are so knowing, that our bodys are the members of Christ? Will you then take the members of Christ and make them the members of an Harlot? [16]What! Know ye not that he who is joynd to an harlot is one body with her? for two, saith god, shall be united into one flesh: [17]but he who is joynd to the Lord is one with him by that one spirit that unites the members to the head, which is a nearer and stricter union, whereby what indignity is done to the one equaly affects the other. [18]Flee fornication, all other sins that a man commits debase onely the soule, but are in that respect as if they were done out of the body, the body is not debased, suffers noe loss of its dignity by them. but he who committeth fornication sinneth against the end for which his body was made, degradeing his body from the dignity and honour it was designed to, makeing that the member of an harlot which was made to be a member of Christ. [19]What· know ye not* that your body is the temple of the holy ghost that is in you, which body you have from god, and soe it is not your own to bestow on harlots. [20]Besides ye are bought with a price viz the pretious bloud of Christ, and therefore are not at your own disposal: but are bound to glorifie god with both body and soule. For both body and soule are from him and are gods.

them that they shall judg the world ver. 2. [b]And that they shall judg angels much more then things of this life ver. 3. And for their not judging he blames them, and tels them 'tis a lessening to them not to exercise this power ver. 7. And for it he gives a reason in this ver. viz that Christ is raised up into the power of god and so shall they be. Unless it be taken in this sense this ver. seems to stand alone here. [c]For what connection has the mention of the resurrection in the ordinary sense of this ver. with what the Apostle is saying here but raiseing us up with bodys to be members of his glorious body and to partake in his power in judging the world· this addes a great honour and dignity to our bodys, and is a reason why we should not debase them into the members of an harlot.

[d]These words also give a reason of his saying *he would not be brought under the power of any thing* ver. ⟨12⟩ (viz) 'Shall I whose body is a member of Christ and shall be raised 'to the power he has now in heaven suffer my body to be a member and under the 'power of an harlot? that I will never doe, let fornication in it self be never so lawfull.'

[e]If this be not the meaning of St Paul here I desire to know to what purpose it is that he so expresly declares that the belly and meat shall be destroyd. and does so manifestly put an opposition between the body and the belly ver. 13.

19* This question *Know ye not?* is repeated six times in this one chapter, which may seem to cary with it a just reproach to the Corinthians who had got a new and better instructor than himself in whom they soe much gloried. and may not unfitly be thought to set on his Irony Ch: IV.10 where he tells them they are *wise*.

SECTION III

Ch. VII.1-40

CONTENTS

[a]The cheif business of the foregoeing chapters we have seen to be the lessening the false Apostles credit and the extinguishing that faction. What follows is in answer to some questions they had proposed to St Paul. This section conteins conjugal matters, wherein he disswades from mariage those who have the gift of continence· [b]But mariage being appointed as a remedie against fornication, those, who cannot forbear, should mary and render to each other due benevolence. Next he teaches that converts ought not to forsake their unconverted mates insoe much as Christianity changes noe thing in mens civil estate. but leaves them under the same obligations they were tied by before. And last of all he gives directions about marying or not marying their daughters.

TEXT

VII.1. Now concerning the things whereof ye wrote unto me: it is good for a man not to touch a woman.

2. Nevertheless, to avoid fornication, let every man have his own wife, and let every woman have her own husband.

3. Let the husband render unto the wife due benevolence: and likewise also the wife unto the husband.

4. The wife hath not power of her own body, but the husband: and likewise also the husband hath not power of his own body, but the wife.

5. Defraud you not one the other, except it be with consent for a time, that ye may give your selves to fasting and prayer; and come together again, that satan tempt you not for your incontinency.

6. But I speak this by permission, and not of commandment.

7. For I would that all men were even as I my self: but every man hath his proper gift of God, one after this manner, and another after that.

8. I say therefore to the unmarried and widows, It is good for them if they abide even as I.

9. But if they cannot contain, let them marry: for it is better to marry than to burn.

10. And unto the married I command, yet not I, but the Lord, Let not the wife depart from her husband:

11. But and if she depart, let her remain unmarried, or be reconciled to her husband: and let not the husband put away his wife.

12. But to the rest speak I, not the Lord, If any brother hath a wife that believeth not, and she be pleased to dwell with him, let him not put her away.

13. And the woman which hath an husband that believeth not, and if he be pleased to dwell with her, let her not leave him.

14. For the unbelieving husband is sanctified by the wife, and the unbelieving wife is sanctified by the husband: else were your children unclean; but now are they holy.

15. But if the unbelieving depart, let him depart. A brother or a sister is not under bondage in such cases: but God hath called us to peace.

16. For what knowest thou, O wife, whether thou shalt save thy husband? or how knowest thou, O man, whether thou shalt save thy wife?

17. But as God hath distributed to every man, as the Lord hath called every one, so let him walk: and so ordain I in all churches.

18. Is any man called being circumcised? let him not become uncircumcised: is any called in uncircumcision? let him not become circumcised.

19. Circumcision is nothing, and uncircumcision is nothing, but the keeping of the commandments of God.

20. Let every man abide in the same calling wherein he was called.

21. Art thou called being a servant? care not for it; but if thou mayst be made free, use it rather.

22. For he that is called in the Lord, being a servant, is the Lord's freeman: likewise also he that is called being free, is Christ's servant.

23. Ye are bought with a price, be not ye the servants of men.

24. Brethren, let every man wherein he is called, therein abide with God.

25. Now concerning virgins, I have no commandment of the Lord: yet I give my judgment as one that hath obtained mercy of the Lord to be faithful.

26. I suppose therefore, that this is good for the present distress, I say, that it is good for a man so to be.

27. Art thou bound unto a wife? seek not to be loosed. Art thou loosed from a wife? seek not a wife.

28. But and if thou marry, thou hast not sinned; and if a virgin marry, she hath not sinned: nevertheless, such shall have trouble in the flesh; but I spare you.

29. But this I say, brethren, the time is short. It remaineth, that both they that have wives, be as though they had none;

30. And they that weep, as though they wept not; and they that rejoice, as though they rejoiced not; and they that buy, as tho they possessed not;

31. And they that use this world, as not abusing it: for the fashion of this world passeth away.

32. But I would have you without carefulness. He that is unmarried, careth for the things that belong to the Lord, how he may please the Lord:

33. But he that is married, careth for the things that are of the world, how he may please his wife.

34. There is difference also between a wife and a virgin: the unmarried woman careth for the things of the Lord, that she may be holy, both in body and in spirit: but she that is married, careth for the things of the world, how she may please her husband.

35. And this I speak for your own profit, not that I may cast a snare upon you, but for that which is comely, and that you may attend upon the Lord without distraction.

36. But if any man think that he behaveth himself uncomely toward his virgin, if she pass the flower of her age, and need so require, let him do what he will, he sinneth not: let them marry.

37. Nevertheless, he that standeth stedfast in his heart, having no necessity, but hath power over his own will, and hath so decreed in his heart, that he will keep his virgin, doth well.

38. So then, he that giveth her in marriage, doth well: but he that giveth her not in marriage, doth better.

39. The wife is bound by the law as long as her husband liveth: but if her husband be dead, she is at liberty to be married to whom she will; only in the Lord.

40. But she is happier if she so abide, after my judgment: and I think also that I have the Spirit of God.

PARAPHRASE

VII.1 Concerning those things that ye have writ to me about I answer it is most convenient not to have to doe with a woman; 2 But because every one cannot forbear therefor they that cannot contein should both men and women each have their owne peculiar husband and wife to avoid fornication. 3 And those that are maried for the same reason are to regulate them selves by the disposition and exigency of their respective mates, and therefor let the husband render to the wife that benevolence* which is her due, and soe like wise the wife to the husband and vice versa

4 For the wife has not power or dominion over her own body to refuse the husband when he desires, but this power and right to her body is in the husband. And on the other side the husband has not the power and dominion over his own body to refuse the wife when she shews an inclination, but this power and right to his body when she has occasion is in the wife.* 5 Doe not in this matter be wanting one to

VII.3* Εὔνοια *Benevolence* signifies here that complaisance and compliance which every maried couple ought to have for each other when either of them shews an inclination to conjugal injoyments.

4* The woman (who in all other rights is inferior) has here the same power given her over the mans body, that the man has over hers. The reason whereof is plain. Because if

an other unless it be by mutual consent for a short time, that ye may wholy attend to acts of devotion when ye fast upon some solemn occasion, and when this time of solemn devotion is over return to your former freedome and conjugal societie, least the devil takeing advantage of your inability to contein should tempt you to a violation of the marriage bed. [6]As to marying in general I wish that you were all unmaried as I am, but this I say to you by way of advice, not of command. [7]Every one has from god his own proper gift some one way and some an other whereby he must govern himself. [8]To the u⟨n⟩maried and widows I say it as my opinion that it is best for them to remain unmaried as I am. [9]But if they have not the gift of continency let them mary, for the inconveniencys of mariage are to be preferd to flames of lust.

[10]But to the maried I say not by way of counsel from my self but of command from the Lord that a woman should not leave her husband: [11]But if she has separated her self from him let her return and be reconciled to him again or at least let her remain unmaried. And let not the husband put away his wife. [12]But as to others 'tis my advice not a commandement from the Lord That if a Christian man hath an heathen wife that is content to live with him let him not break company with her* and dissolve the mariage: [13]And if a christian woman hath an heathen husband that is content to live with her, let her not break company with him* and dissolve the mariage. [14]You need have noe scruple concerning this matter. for the heathen husband or wife in respect of conjugal duty can be noe more refused than if they were Christian. for in this case the unbeleiveing husband is sanctified* or made a Christian as to his issue in his wife, and the wife sanctified in her husband: If it were not soe the children of such parents would be unclean* i e in the state of Heathens· but now are they holy.* i e born members of the Christian church. [15]But if the unbeleiveing party will

she had not her man, when she had need of him; as well as the man his woman when he had need of her, mariage would be noe remedy against fornication.

12 and 13* 'Αφιέτω the Greek word in the original signifying *put away* being directed here in these two verses both to the man and the woman, seems to intimate the same power and same act of dismis⟨s⟩ing in both, and therefor ought in both places to be translated alike.

14* [a]'Ηγίασται *sanctified* ἅγια *holy* and ἀκάθαρτα *unclean* are used here by the Apostle in the Jewish sense. The Jews calld all that were Jews *holy* and all others they called *unclean*. Thus *proles genita extra sanctitatem* was a child begot by parents whilst they were yet heathens; [b]*Genita intra sanctitatem* was a child begot by parents after they were proselyts. This way of speaking St Paul transfers from the Jewish into the Christian church, calling all that are of the Christian Church *saints* or *holy* by which reason all that were out of it were *unclean*· see Note Ch. I.2

separate let them separate. A christian man or woman is not inslaved in such a case, only it is to be remembred that it is incumbent on us, whom god in the gospel has called to be Christians, to live peacably with all men as much as in us lieth and therefore the Christian husband or wife, is not to make a breach in the family by leaveing the unbeleiveing party who is content to stay. [16]For what knowest thou o woman but thou mayest be the means of converting and soe saveing thy unbeleiveing husband if thou continuest peaceably as a loveing wife with him? Or what knowest thou o man but after the same maner thou mayst save thy wife? [17]On this occasion let me give you this general rule. Whatever condition god has alloted to any one of you let him continue and goe on contentedly in the same* state wherein he was called not looking on him self as set free from it by his conversion to Christianity. And this is noe more than what I order in all the churches. [18]For example was any one converted to Christianity being circumcised, let him not become uncircumcised: was any one called being uncircumcised, let him not be circumcised. [19]Circumcision or uncircumcision are noe thing in the sight of god, but that which he has a regard to is an obedience to his commands. [20]Christianity gives not any one any new privilege to change the state or put off* the obligations of civil life which he was in before. [21]Wert thou called being a slave, think thy self not the less a Christian for being a slave: but yet prefer freedom to slavery if thou canst obtein it. [22]For he that is converted to Christianity being a bond-man is

17* ὡς signifies here not the manner of his calling, but the state and condition of life he was in when called, and therefore οὕτω must signifie the same too as the next verse shews

⟨20⟩* [a]Μενέτω *Let him abid*· 'tis plain from what immediatly follows, that this is not an absolute command; but only signifies that a man should not think him self discharged, by the priviledg of his Christian state and the franchises of the Kingdom of Christ which he was enterd into, [b]from any ties or obligations he was in as a member of the civil societie. And therefore for the setling a true notion thereof in the mind of the reader it has been thought convenient to give that, which is the Apostles sense to verse 17, 20, and 24 of this Chapter in words some what different from the Apostles. [c]The thinking themselves freed by Christianity, from the ties of Civil Societie and government was a fault it seems that these Christians were very apt to run into. For St Paul, for the preventing their thoughts of any change of any thing of their civil state upon their imbraceing Christianity thinks it necessary to warne them against it three times in the compass of seven verses, and that in the forme of a direct command not to change their condition or state of life. [d]whereby he intends that they should not change upon a presumption that Christianity gave them a new or peculiar liberty soe to doe. For notwithstanding the Apostles positively bidding them remain in the same condition in which they were at their conversion, yet it is certain it was lawfull for them as well as others to change, where it was lawfull for them to change without being Christians

Christs Freed-man:* And he that is converted being a free man, is Christs bond-man under his command and dominion. [23]Ye are bought with a price* and soe belong to Christ, be not, if you can avoid it, slaves to any body. [24]In whatsoever state a man is called in the same he is to remain notwithstanding any priviledges of the gospel, which gives him noe dispensation or exemption from any obligation he was in before to the laws of his country.

[25]Now concerning virgins* I have noe express command from Christ to give you: but I tell you my opinion as one whom the Lord has been gratiously pleased to make credible† and soe you may trust and rely on in this matter. [26]I tell you therefore that I judg a single life to be convenient because of the present streights of the church; and that it is best for a man to be unmaried. [27]Art thou in the bonds of wedlock? seek not to be loosed: Art thou loosed from a wife? seek not a wife· [28](But if thou maryest thou sinnest not: or if a virgin mary she sins not. But those that are maryed shall have worldly troubles. But I spare you by not representing to you how little enjoyment Christians are like to have from a maried life in the present state of things, and soe I leave you the liberty of marying. [29]But give me leave to tell you that the time for enjoying husbands and wives is but short* But be that as it will this is certain. that those who have wives should be as if they had them not, and not set their hearts upon them: [30]And they that weep as if they wept not: and they that rejoyce as if they rejoyced not: and they that buy, as if they possessed not: All these things should be done with

22* Ἀπελεύθερος In Latin *Libertus* signifies not simply a *free man* but one who haveing been a slave has had his freedom given him by his master.

23* [a]Slaves were bought and sold in the market as cattle are and soe by the price paid there was a proprietie acquired in them. This therefore here is a reason for what he advised ver. 21 that they should not be slaves to men, because Christ had paid a price for them and they belongd to him. [b]The slavery he speaks of is civil slavery, which he makes use of here to convince the Corinthians, that the civil ties of mariage were not dissolvd by a mans becomeing a Christian since Slavery it self was not and in general in the next verse he tells them, that noething in any mans civil estate or rights is altered by his becoming a Christian.

25* [a]By *Virgins* tis plain St Paul here means those of both sexes who are in a celibate state· Tis probable he had formerly disswaded them from mariage in the present state of the church. This it seems they were uneasy under ver. 28. and 35 and therefore sent some questions to St Paul about it and particularly what then should men doe with their daughters. [b]Upon which occasion ver. 25-37 he gives directions to the unmaried about their marying or not marying and in the close ver. 38 answers to the parents about marying their daughters, And then ver. 39 and 40 he speaks of widows.

† In this sense he uses πιστὸς ἄνθρωπος, and πιστὸς λόγος 2 Tim. II.2. and 11

29* Said possibly out of a prophetical foresight of the approaching persecution under Nero

resignation and a Christian indifferency. [31]And those who use this
world should use it without an over relish of it* without giveing them
selves up to the enjoyment of it. For the Scene of things is always
changeing in this world, and noething can be relyed on in it†· [32]All
the reason why I disswade you from mariage is that I would have you
free from anxious cares. He that is unmaried, has time and liberty to
minde things of religion how he may please the Lord: [33]But he that is
maried is taken up with the cares of the world how he may please his
wife. [34]The like difference there is between a maried woman and a
maid. She that is unmaried has oportunity to mind the things of religion, that she may be holy in mind and body: but the maried woman
is taken up with the cares of the world how to please her husband.
[35]This I say to you for your particular advantage not to lay any con-
straint* upon you; but to put you in a way where in you may most
suitably, and as best becomes Christianity, apply your selves to the
study and dutys of the gospel without distraction. [36]But if any one
thinks that he carys not himself as becomes him to his virgin if he lets
her pass the flower of her age unmaried, and need so requires, let him
doe as he thinks fit, he sins not if he mary her. [37]But whoever is setled
in a firm resolution of mind, and finds him self under noe necessity of
marying, and is master of his own will or is at his own disposal, and
has soe determined in his thoughts that he will keep his virginity* he

31* καταχρώμενοι does not here signify *abuseing* in our English sense of the word; but *intently useing*

† All from the begining of 28 ver. to the end of this 31 ver. I think may be lookd on as a Parenthesis

35* Βρόχος which we translate a *snare* signifies a cord. which possibly the Apostle might, according to the language of the Hebrew school, use here for binding, and then his discourse runs thus. Though I have declared it my opinion that it is best for a virgin to remain unmaried yet I *bind* it not. i e. I doe not declare it to be unlawfull to mary.

37* [a]Παρθένον *Virgin* seems used here for the virgin state and not the person of a virgin; whither there be examples of the like use of it I know not and therefore I propose it as my conjecture upon these grounds

[b]1 Because the resolution of mind here spoken of must be in the person to be maryed, and not in the father that has the power over the person concernd, for how will the firmness of mind of the father hinder fornication in the child who has not that firmness.

[c]2 The necessity of maryage can onely be judgd of by the persons themselves: A father cannot feel the childs flames which make the need of mariage. The persons themselves onely know whither they burn or have the gift of continence.

[d]3 Ἐξουσίαν ἔχει περὶ τοῦ ἰδίου θελήματος *hath the power over his own will*. must signifie, either *can govern his own desires, is master of his own will*· But this can not be meant here, because it is sufficiently expressed before by ἑδραῖος τῇ καρδίᾳ *stedfast in heart* and afterwards too by κέκρι(κ)εν ἐν χαρδίᾳ *decreed in heart*: [e]Or must signifie *has the disposal of himself* i e is free from the fathers power of disposeing their children in maryage. For

chooses the better† side. [38]Soe then he that marrieth* doth well. but he that marryeth* not doth better. [39]It is unlawfull for a woman to leave her husband as long as he lives; but when he is dead she is at liberty to marry or not marry as she pleases and to whom she pleases, which virgins cannot doe being under the disposal of their parents: onely she must take care to marry as a Christian fearing god. [40]But in my opinion she is happier if she remain a widow, and permit me to say that whatever any among you may think or say of me I have the spirit of god soe that I may be relyed on in this my advice that I doe not mislead you.

SECTION IV

Ch. VIII.1-13

CONTENTS

[a]This section is concerning the eating things offered to Idols where in one may guess. by St Pauls answer, that they had writ to him that they knew their Christian liberty herein that they knew that an Idol was noe thing and therefor that they did well to shew their knowledg of the nullity of the heathen gods and their disregard of them by eating promiscuously and without scrupule things offered to them. [b]Upon which the designe of the Apostle here seems to be, to take down their

I think the words should be translated, *hath a power concerning his own will*. i e concerning what he willeth. [f]For if by it St Paul meant a power over his own will, one might think he would have expressed that thought as he does Ch: IX.12 and Rom IX.21 without περί or by the preposition ἐπί as it is Luke IX.1

[g]4 Because. if *keep his virgin* had here signified, keep his children from marying, the expression had been more natural to have used the word τέκνα which signifies both sexes than παρθένος which belongs only to the female. If therefore παρθένος be taken abstractly for virginity the precedent Verse must be understood thus. [h]*But if any one think it a shame to pass the flower of his age unmaried, and he find it necessary to mary, let him doe as he pleases· he sins not. Let such mary*. I confess it is hard to bring these two verses to the same sense and both of them to the designe of the Apostle here without takeing the words in one or both of them very figuratively. [i]St Paul here seems to obviate an objection that might be made against his disswasion from mariage viz that it might be an indecency one should be guilty of if one should live unmaried past ones prime and afterwards be forced to mary; [j]To which he answers that noebody should abstain upon the account of being a Christian but those who are of steady resolutions, are at their own disposal, and have fully determind it in their own minds

† καλῶς here as in ver. 1.8, and 26 signifies not simply good but preferable

38* Παρθένος being taken in the sense before mentioned, it is necessary in this verse to follow the copies which read γαμίζων *marrying*, for ἐκγαμίζων, *giveing in marriage*

opinion of their knowledg by shewing them that notwithstanding all the knowledg they presumed on and were puffed up with yet the eating of those sacrifices did not recommend them to god. vid: ver. 8 and that they might sin in their want of charity by offending their weak brother. [c]This seems plainly from ver. 1-3 and 11.12 to be the designe of the Apostles answer here, and not to resolve the case of eating things offered to Idols in its full latitude. For then he would have prosecuted it more at large here, and not have deferred the doeing of it to Chap: X where under an other head he treats of it more particularly

TEXT

VIII.1. Now as touching things offered unto idols, we know that we all have knowledge. Knowledge puffeth up, but Charity edifieth.

2. And if any man think that he knoweth any thing, he knoweth nothing yet as he ought to know.

3. But if any man love God, the same is known of him.

4. As concerning therefore the eating of those things that are offered in sacrifice unto idols, we know that an idol is nothing in the world, and that there is none other God but one.

5. For though there be that are called gods, whether in heaven or in earth, (as there be gods many, and lords many)

6. But to us there is but one God, the Father, of whom are all things, and we in him; and one Lord Jesus Christ, by whom are all things, and we by him.

7. Howbeit there is not in every man that knowledge: for some with conscience of the idol unto this hour, eat it as a thing offered unto an idol; and their conscience being weak, is defiled.

8. But meat commendeth us not to God: for neither if we eat, are we the better; neither if we eat not, are we the worse.

9. But take heed lest by any means this liberty of yours become a stumbling block to them that are weak.

10. For if any man see thee which hast knowledge, sit at meat in the idols temple, shall not the conscience of him which is weak be emboldned to eat those things which are offered to idols:

11. And through thy knowledge shall the weak brother perish, for whom Christ died?

12. But when ye sin so against the brethren, and wound their weak conscience, ye sin against Christ.

13. Wherefore if meat make my brother to offend, I will eat no flesh while the world standeth, lest I make my brother to offend.

PARAPHRASE

VIII.1 As for things offered up unto Idols it must not be questioned but that every one of you, who stand soe much upon your knowledg, knows that the imaginary gods to whom the Gentils sacrifice are not in reality gods but meer fictions, but with this pray remember that such a knowledg or opinion of their knowledg swels men with pride and vanity· But Charity it is, that improves and advances men in Christianity*

2 (But if any one be conceited of his own knowledg as if Christianity were a science for speculation and dispute he knows noe thing yet of Christianity as he ought to know it. 3 But if any one love god and consequently his neighbour for gods sake such an one is made to know* or has got true knowledg from god himself. 4 To the question then of eating things offerd to Idols. I know as well as you that an Idol, i e that the fictitious gods, whose images are in the heathen temples, are noe real beings in the world; and there is in truth noe other but one god. 5 For though there be many imaginary nominal gods both in heaven and earth* as are indeed all their many gods and many Lords which are merely titular; 6 yet to us Christians there is but one god the father and author of all things to whom alone we address all our worship and service, and but one Lord viz Jesus Christ by whom all things come from god to us, and by whom we have access to the father) 7 For notwithstanding all the great pretences to knowledg that are amongst you every one doth not know that the gods of the

VIII.1* To continue the thread of the Apostles discourse the 7th ver. must be read as joynd on to the 1st and all between looked on as a Parenthesis

3* Ἔγνωσται. *is made to know* or *is taught*. The Apostle tho writeing in Greek yet often uses the Greek verbs according to the Hebrew conjugations. soe Ch: XIII.12 ἐπιγνώσομαι which according to the Greek proprietie signifies *I shall be known* is used for *I shall be made to know*· and soe Gal IV 9 γνω(σ)θέντες is put to signifie *being taught*

5* [a] *In heaven and earth*· The heathen had supreme soveraigne gods whom they supposed eternal remaining always in the heavens· these were called θεοί *gods*. They had besides another order of inferior gods, *gods upon earth* who by the will and direction of the heavenly gods governed terrestrial things, and were the mediators between the supreme heavenly gods and men, without whom there could be noe communication between them. [b]These were called in Scripture *Baalim*. i.e *Lords* and by the Greeks Δαίμονες· To this the Apostle alluds here saying though there be in the opinion of the heathen *gods many*. i e. many celestial soveraigne gods in heaven. And *Lords many*. i e many Baalim or Lord-Agents and presidents over earthly things, [c]yet to us Christians there is but one soveraigne god the father, of whom are all things and to whom as supreme we are to direct all our services; And but one Lord-Agent Jesus Christ by whom are all things that came from the father to us and through whom alone we find access unto him. Mede Disc on 2 Pet II.1.

heathens are but imaginations of the phansie, mere noe thing, some to
this day conscious to themselves that they think those Idols to be real
deities, eat things sacrificed to them as sacrificed to real dieties,
whereby doeing that which they in their consciences not yet
suffi⟨ci⟩ently enlightened think to be unlawfull, are guilty of sin.
[8]Food of what kind soever makes not god regard us.* For neither if in
knowledg and full perswasion that an Idol is noe thing,† we eat things
offered to Idols, doe we thereby adde any thing to our Christianity: Or
if not being soe well informed, we are scrupulous and forbear, are we
the worse Christians, or are lessened by it.‡ [9]But this you Knowing
men ought to take espetiall care of, That the power or freedom you
have to eat be not made such an use of as to become a stumbling-
block to weaker Christians who are not convinced of that liberty. [10]For
if such an one shall see thee, who hast this knowledg of thy liberty, to
sit feasting in an Idol temple, shall not his weake conscience not
throughly instructed in the matter of Idols be drawn in by thy example
to eat what is offered to Idols though he in his conscience doubts of its
lawfulness? [11]And thus thy weak brother, for whom Christ died, is
destroid by thy knowledg wherewith thou justifiest thy eating. [12]But
when you sin thus against your brethren, and wound their weak
consciences you sin against Christ. [13]Wherefore if meat make my
brother offend I will never more eat flesh to avoyd makeing my
brother offend.

SECTION V

Ch. IX.1-27

CONTENTS

[a]St Paul had preached the gospel at Corinth about two years, in all which time he had taken noe thing of them. 2 Cor XI.7-9· This by some of the opposite faction, and particularly, as we may suppose, by their leader, was made use of to call in question his Apostleship 2 Cor XI 5.6. [b]For why if he were an Apostle should he not use the power of

8* οὐ παρίστησι *sets us not before god* i e to be taken notice of by him.

† *noe thing*. i e. a bare fiction of the mind and is really either noe thing at all, or at least as much as noe thing in respect of any alteration it can make in the things offerd to it.

‡ It cannot be supposed that St Paul in answer to a letter of the Corinthians should tell them that *if they eat things offerd to Idols they were not the better or if they eat not they were not the worse* unless they had expressed some opinion of good in eating.

an Apostle to demand maintenance where he preachd. In this section St Paul vindicates his Apostleship And in answer to these enquirers gives the reason why though he had a right to maintenance yet he preached gratis to the Corinthians. [c]My answer says he to these Inquisitors is that though as being an Apostle I know that I have a right to maintenance as well as Peter or any other of the Apostles, who all have a right as is evident from reason and from Scripture, yet I neither have nor shall make use of my priviledg amongst you for fear that if it cost you any thing that should hinder the effect of my preaching. [d]I would neglect noe thing that might promote the gospel. For I doe not content my self with doeing barely what is my duty. for by my extraordinary call and commission it is now incumbent on me to preach the gospel. But I endeavour to excell in my ministry and not to execute my commission overtly and just enough to serve the turn. [e]For if those who in the Agonistick games aiming at victory to obtein onely a corruptible crown deny them selves in eating and drinking and other pleasures, How much more does the eternal crown of glory deserve that we should doe our utmost to obtein it? to be as carefull in not indulgeing our bodys, in denying our pleasures, in doeing every thing we could in order to get it as if there were but one that should have it? [f]Wonder not therefor if I haveing this in view neglect my body, and those outward conveniencyes that I as an Apostle sent to preach the gospel might claim and make use of: wonder not that I prefer the propagateing of the gospel and makeing of converts, to all care and regard of my self.

This seems the designe of the Apostle and will give light to the following discourse which we shall now take in the order St Paul writ it.

TEXT

IX.1. Am I not an apostle? am I not free? have I not seen Jesus Christ our Lord? are not you my work in the Lord?

2. If I be not an apostle unto others, yet doubtless I am to you: for the seal of mine apostleship are ye in the Lord.

3. Mine answer to them that do examine me, is this,

4. Have we not power to eat and to drink?

5. Have we not power to lead about a sister a wife as well as other apostles, and as the brethren of the Lord, and Cephas?

6. Or I only and Barnabas, have not we power to forbear working?

7. Who goeth a warfare any time at his own charges? who planteth a vineyard, and eateth not of the fruit thereof? or who feedeth a flock, and eateth not of the milk of the flock?

8. Say I these things as a man? or saith not the law the same also?

9. For it is written in the law of Moses, Thou shalt not muzzle the mouth of the ox that treadeth out the corn. Doth God take care for oxen?

10. Or saith he it altogether for our sakes? for our sakes, no doubt, this is written: that he that ploweth should plow in hope; and that he that thresheth in hope, should be partaker of his hope.

11. If we have sown unto you spiritual things, is it a great thing if we shall reap your carnal things?

12. If others be partakers of this power over you, are not we rather? Nevertheless, we have not used this power; but suffer all things, lest we should hinder the gospel of Christ.

13. Do ye not know that they which minister about holy things, live of the things of the temple? and they which wait at the altar, are partakers with the altar?

14. Even so hath the Lord ordained, that they which preach the gospel, should live of the gospel.

15. But I have used none of these things. Neither have I written these things, that it should be so done unto me: for it were better for me to die, than that any man should make my glorying void.

16. For though I preach the gospel, I have nothing to glory of: for necessity is laid upon me; yea, wo is unto me, if I preach not the gospel.

17. For if I do this thing willingly, I have a reward: but if against my will, a dispensation of the gospel is committed unto me.

18. What is my reward then? verily that when I preach the gospel, I may make the gospel of Christ without charge, that I abuse not my power in the gospel.

19. For though I be free from all men, yet have I made my self servant unto all, that I might gain the more.

20. And unto the Jews, I became as a Jew, that I might gain the Jews; to them that are under the law, as under the law, that I might gain them that are under the law;

21. To them that are without law, as without law, (being not without law to God, but under the law to Christ) that I might gain them that are without law.

22. To the weak became I as weak, that I might gain the weak: I am made all things to all men, that I might by all means save some.

23. And this I do for the gospels sake, that I might be partaker thereof with you.

24. Know ye not that they which run in a race, run all, but one receiveth the prize? so run that ye may obtain.

25. And every man that striveth for the mastery, is temperate in all things: now, they do it to obtain a corruptible crown, but we an incorruptible.

26. I therefore so run, not as uncertainly: so fight I, not as one that beateth the air:

27. But I keep under my body, and bring it into subjection: lest that by any means when I have preached to others, I my self should be a cast-away.

PARAPHRASE

[IX.1]Am I not an Apostle? And am I not at liberty* as much as any other of the Apostles to make use of the privilege due to that office? Have I not had the favour to see Jesus Christ our Lord after an extraordinary manner? And are not you your selves, whom I have converted, an evidence of the success of my imployment in the gospel? [2]If others should question my being an Apostle, you at least can not doubt of it. Your conversion to Christianity is as it were a seal set to it to make good the truth of my Apostleship. [3]This then is my answer to those who set up an inquisition upon me. [4]Have not I a right to meat and drink where I preach? [5]Have not I and Barnabas a power to take along with us in our travelling to propagate the gospel a Christian woman* to provide our conveniencys and be serviceable to us as well as Peter, and the brethren of the Lord, and the rest of the Apostles? [6]Or is it I onely and Barnabas who are excluded from the privilege of being maintained without workeing? [7]who goes to the warr any where and serves as a soldier at his own charges? Who planteth a vinyard and eateth not of the fruit thereof? Who feedeth a flock and eateth not of the milk? [8]This is allowed to be reason, that those who are soe imploid should be maintained by their imployments, and soe likewise a preacher of the Gospel. But I say not this barely upon the principles of humane reason, Revelation teaches the same thing in the law of Moses, [9]where it is said, thou shalt not muzzle the mouth of the ox that treadeth out the corne. Doth god take care to provide soe particularly for oxen by a law? [10]Noe certainly· it is said particularly for our sakes and not for oxen, that he who sows may sow in hope of enjoying the fruits of his labour at harvest and may then thresh out and eat the corn he hoped for. [11]If we have sowed to you spiritual things in preaching the gospel to you, is it unreasonable that we should expect a little meat and drink from you, a little share of your carnal things? [12]If any partake of this power over you* why not we much rather? But

IX.1* It was a law amongst the Jews not to receive alms from the Gentils.

5* There were not in those parts as among us Innes where travellers might have their conveniencies. And strangers could not be accomodated with necessarys unlesse they had some body with them to take that care and provide for them· They who would make it their business to preach and neglect this must needs suffer great hardships.

12*· [a]For τῆς ἐξουσίας I should incline to read τῆς οὐσίας If there be as Vossius Says any MSS to authorize it, and then the words will run thus *If any partake of your substance·*

I made noe use of it, but bear with any thing that I may avoid all
hindrance to the progress of the gospel. [13]Doe ye not know that they
who in the temple serve about holy things live upon those holy things?
And they who wait at the altar are partakers with the altar? [14]Soe has
the Lord ordained, that they who preach the gospel, should live of the
gospel. [15]But though as an Apostle and preacher of the gospel I have
as you see a right to maintenance, yet I have not taken it. Neither have
I written this to demand it. For I had rather perish for want than be
deprived of what I glory in. viz preaching the gospel freely. [16]For if I
preach the gospel I doe barely my duty but have noe thing to glory in,
for I am under an obligation and command to preach* [17]And wo be to
me if I preach not the gospel. which if I doe willingly I shall have a
reward: If unwillingly the dispensation is never the lesse intrusted to
me and ye ought to hear me as an Apostle. [18]How therefore doe I make
it turn to account to my self. Even thus. If I preach the gospel of Christ
of free cost, soe that I exact not the maintenance I have a right to by
the gospel. [19]For being under noe obligation to any man I yet subject
my self to every one, to the end that I may make the more converts to
Christ. [20]To the Jews and those under the law of Moses I became as a
Jew and one under that law, that I might gain the Jews and those
under the law: [21]To those without the law of Moses I applyd my self as
one not under that law (not indeed as if I were under noe law to god
but as obeying and following the law of Christ) that I might gain those
who were without the law. [22]To the weak I became as weak, that I
might gain the weak. I became all things to all men, that I might leave
noe lawfull thing untried whereby I might save people of all sorts.
[23]And this I doe for the gospels sake that I my self may share in the
benefits of the gospel. [24]Know ye not that they who run a race run not
lazily, but with their utmost force: they all indeavour to be first,
because there is but one that gets the prize. It is not enough for you to
run, but soe to run that ye may obtein, which they cannot doe who
runing onely because they are bid, doe not run with all their might.
[25]They who propose to themselves the geting the garland in your
games readily submit themselves to severe rules of exercise and
abstinence, and yet theirs is but a fadeing transitory crown, that which

This better suits the foregoeing words, and needs not the addition of the word *this* to be inserted in the translation, [b]which with difficulty enough makes it refer to a power which he was not here speaking of but stands eight verses off. besides in these words St Paul seems to glance at what they sufferd from the false Apostle who did not only pretend to power of maintenance but did actualy devour them. vid 2 Cor XI.20

16* vid Act. XXII.15-21

we propose to our selves is everlasting, and therefore deserves that we should endure greater hardships for it I therefor soe run as not to leave it to uncertainty. [26]I doe what I doe not as one who fences for exercise or ostentation; [27]But I realy and in earnest keep under my body and entirely inslave it to the service of the gospel, without allowing any thing to the exigences of this animal life. which may be the least hindrance to the propagation of the gospel, least that I who preach to bring others into the kingdome of heaven should be disapproved of and rejected my self.

SECTION VI. NO. 1

Ch. X.1-22

CONTENTS

[a]It seems by what he here says as if the Corinthians had told St Paul that the temptations and constraints they were under of goeing to their heathen neighbours feasts upon their sacrifices were soe many and soe great, that there was noe avoiding it: and therefore they thought they might goe to them without any offence to god or danger to them selves, [b]since they were the people and church of god, purged from sin by Baptisme, and fenced against it by partakeing of the body and bloud of Christ in the Lords supper. To which St Paul answers, that notwithstanding their baptisme and partakeing of that spirituall meat and drink, yet they, as well as the Jews of old did, might sin and draw on themselves destruction from the hand of god; [c]That eating of things that were known and owned to be offerd to Idols, was partakeing in the idolatrous worship; and therefore they were to prefer even the danger of persecution before such a compliance, for god would find a way for them to escape.

TEXT

X.1. Moreover, brethren, I would not that ye should be ignorant, how that all our fathers were under the cloud, and all passed through the sea;

2. And were all baptized unto Moses in the cloud, and in the sea;

3. And did all eat the same spiritual meat;

4. And did all drink the same spiritual drink: (for they drank of that spiritual Rock that followed them: and that Rock was Christ)

5. But with many of them God was not well pleased: for they were overthrown in the wilderness.

6. Now these things were our examples to the intent we should not lust after evil things, as they also lusted.

7. Neither be ye idolaters, as were some of them; as it is written, The people sat down to eat and drink, and rose up to play.

8. Neither let us commit fornication, as some of them committed; and fell in one day three and twenty thousand.

9. Neither let us tempt Christ, as some of them also tempted, and were destroyed of serpents.

10. Neither murmur ye, as some of them also murmured, and were destroyed of the destroyer.

11. Now all these things happened unto them for ensamples: and they are written for our admonition, upon whom the ends of the world are come.

12. Wherefore let him that thinketh he standeth, take heed lest he fall.

13. There hath no temptation taken you, but such as is common to man: but God is faithful, who will not suffer you to be tempted above that ye are able; but will with the temptation also make a way to escape, that ye may be able to bear it.

14. Wherefore my dearly beloved, flee from idolatry.

15. I speak as to wise men: judge ye what I say.

16. The cup of blessing which we bless, is it not the communion of the blood of Christ? The bread which we break, is it not the communion of the body of Christ?

17. For we being many are one bread, and one body: for we are all partakers of that one bread.

18. Behold Israel after the flesh: are not they which eat of the sacrifices, partakers of the altar?

19. What say I then? that the idol is any thing, or that which is offered in sacrifice to idols is any thing?

20. But I say, that the things which the Gentiles sacrifice, they sacrifice to devils, and not to God: and I would not that ye should have fellowship with devils.

21. Ye cannot drink the cup of the Lord, and the cup of devils: ye cannot be partakers of the Lords table, and of the table of devils.

22. Do we provoke the Lord to jealousie? are we stronger than he?

PARAPHRASE

X.1 I would not have you ignorant, Brethren, that all our fathers the whole congregation of the children of Israel at their comeing out of Egypt were all to a man under the cloud and all passed through the sea.

[2]and were all by this baptisme* in the cloud and passeing through the
water initiated into the Mosaical institution and government by these
two miracles of the cloud and the sea· [3]And they all eat the same meat
which had a typical and spiritual signification. [4]And they all drank the
same spiritual typical drink which came out of the rocke and followed
them· which rocke typified Christ. All which were typical representations of Christ as well as the bread and wine which we eat and drink in
the Lords supper are typical representations of him. [5]But yet though
every one of the children of Israel that came out of Egypt were thus
solemnly seperated from the rest of the profane idolatrous world and
were made gods peculiar people sanctified and holy every one of them
to him self and members of his church: nay though they did all*
partake of the same meat and the same* drink which did typicaly
represent Christ, yet they were not thereby priviledged from sin but
great numbers of them provoked god and were destroid in the wilderness for their disobedience. [6]Now these things were set as patterns to
us, that we warned by these examples should not set our minds a longing as they did after meats* that would be safer let alone: [7]Neither be
ye Idolaters as were some of them; as it is written· the people sat down
to eat and to drink and rose up to play:* [8]Neither let us committ fornication as some of them committed and fell in one day three and
twenty thousand: [9]Neither let us provoke Christ as some of them provoked. and were destroyed of serpents: [10]Neither murmur ye as some
of them murmured and were destroyed of the destroyer·* [11]Now

X.2* The Apostle calls it Baptisme which is the initiateing ceremony into both the Jewish and Christian Church: And the *cloud* and *sea* both being noe thing but water are well suited to that typical representation, And that the children of Israel were washd with rain from the cloud may be collected from Psal: LXVIII.9

5* [a]It may be observed here that St Paul speaking of the Israelites uses the word πάντες *all* five times in the four foregoeing verses besides that he carefully says τὸ αὐτὸ βρῶμα *the same* meat and τὸ αὐτὸ πόμα the *same* drink, which we cannot suppose to be donne by chance, but emphatically to signifie to the Corinthians, [b]who probably presumed too much upon their baptisme and eating the Lords supper as if that were enough to keep them right in the sight of god, that though the Israelites *all to a man* eat the *very same* spiritual food. and *all to a man* drank the *very same* spiritual drink, yet they were not *all to a man* preservd but many of them for all that sinned and fell under the avengeing hand of god in the wilderness

6* κακῶν *evil things*· The fault of the Israelites which this place refers to seems to be their longing for flesh Num: XI which cost many of them their lives: And that which he warns the Corinthians of here is their great propension to the Pagan Sacrifice feasts

7* *play* i e danse. feasting and danseing usualy accompanied the heathen sacrifices

10* 'Ολοθρευτο⟨ῦ⟩. *Destroyer* was an angel that had the power to destroy mentioned Exod XII.23. Heb. XI.28

all these things* happened to the Jews for examples and are written for our admonition upon whom the ends of the ages† are come. [12]Wherefore taught by these examples let him that thinks him self safe by being in the church and partakeing of the Christian Sacraments take heed least he fall into sin and soe destruction from god overtake him. [13]Hitherto the temptations you have met with have been but light and ordinary. If you should come to be pressed harder, god, who is faithfull and never forsakes those who forsake not him, will not suffer you to be tempted above your strength but will either enable you to bear the persecution or open you a way out of it. [14]Therefore my beloved take care to keep off from Idolatry and be not drawn to any approaches near it by any temptation or persecution whatsoever. You are satisfied that you want not knowledg.* [15]And therefor as to knowing men I appeale to you, and make you judges of what I am goeing to say in the case. [16]They who drink of the cup of Blesseing* which we bless in the Lords supper, doe they not thereby partake of the benefits purchased by Christs bloud shed for them upon the cross which they here symbolically drink? And they who eat of the bread broken† there doe they not partake in the sacrifice of the body of Christ, and professe to be members of him. [17]For by eating of that bread we though many in number are all united and make but one body, as many grains of corne are united into one loaf. [18]See how it is among the Jews who are outwardly according to the flesh by circumcision the people of god. Among them they who eat of the sacrifice are partakers of gods table the altar, have fellowship with him, and share in the benefit of

11* It is to be observed that all these instances mentioned by the Apostle of destruction which came upon the Israelites who were in covenant with god and partakers in those typical sacraments above mentioned, were occasiond by their luxurious appetites about meat and drink; by fornication; and by Idolatry. sins which the Corinthians were inclined to, and which he here warns them against

† [a]Soe I think τὰ τέλη τῶν αἰώνων should be rendered, and not contrary to grammar *the end of the world*· Because it is certain that τέλη and συντέλεια τοῦ αἰῶνος or τῶν αἰώνων cannot signifie every where as we render it *the end of the world* which denotes but one certain period of time, for the world can have but one end [b]whereas those words signifie in different places different periods of time as will be manifest to any one who will compare these texts where they occur viz Mat XIII 39.40 XXIV.3 XXVIII.20 1 Cor X.11 Heb: IX.26. It may be worth while therefore to consider whether αἰών hath not ordinarily a more natural signification in the new Testament by standing for a considerable length of time passeing under some one remarkable dispensation.

⟨14⟩* vid VIII.1

16* *Cup of blesseing* was a name given by the Jews to a cup of wine which they solemnly drank in the passover, with thanksgiveing

† This was also taken from the custome of the Jews in the passeover to break a cake of unlevened bread

the sacrifice as if it were offered for them. [19]Doe not mistake me as if I hereby said that the Idols of the gentils are gods in reality. Or that the things offered to them change their nature, and are any thing really different from what they were before soe as to affect us in our use of them,* [20]noe, but this I say that the things which the Gentils sacrifice they sacrifice to Devils and not to god; and I would not that you should have fellowship and be in league with divils, as they who by eating of the things offered to them enter into covenant alliance and friendship with them: [21]You cannot eat and drink with god as friends at his table in the Eucharist, and entertain familiarity and friendship with devils, by eating with them, and partakeing of the sacrifices offered to them:* you cannot be Christians and Idolaters too: nor, if you should endeavour to joyn these inconsistent rites, will it availe you any thing. For your partakeing in the Sacraments of the Christian church, will noe more exempt you from the anger of god and punishment due to your Idolatry, than the eating of the spiritual food and drinking of the spiritual rock kept the baptised Israelites, who offended god by their Idolatry or other sins from being destroid in the wilderness. [22]Dare you then being espoused to Christ, provoke the Lord to Jealousy by idolatry which is spiritual whordome? Are you stronger than hee, and able to enter the list with the almighty

SECTION VI. NO. 2

Ch. X.23-XI.1

CONTENTS

[a]We have here an other of his arguments against things offered to Idols wherein he shews the danger might be in it from the scandal it might give supposeing it a thing lawfull in it self. He had formerly treated of this subject Ch: VIII soe far as to let them see that there was noe good noe virtue in eating things offered to Idols, not with standing they knew that Idols were noe thing, [b]and they might think that their free eating without scruple shewd that they knew their freedom in the

19* This is evident from what he says ver. 25.27. that things offered to Idols may be eaten, as well as any other meat, soe it be without partakeing in the Sacrifice and without Scandal.

21* Tis plain by what the Apostle says that the thing he speaks against here is their assisting at the heathen Sacrifices or at least at the feasts in their temples upon the Sacrifice which was a federal right.

gospel, that they knew that Idols were in reality noe thing and therefore they slighted and disregarded them and their worship as noe thing; but that there might be evil in eating by the offence it might give to weak Christians who had not that knowledg, [c]He here takes up the argument of Scandal again and extends it to Jews and Gentils. vid: ver. 32 And shews that it is not enough to justifie them in any action that the thing they doe is in it self lawfull, unless we seek in it the glory of God and the good of others

TEXT

X.23. All things are lawful for me, but all things are not expedient: all things are lawful for me, but all things edifie not.

24. Let no man seek his own: but every man anothers wealth.

25. Whatsoever is sold in the shambles, that eat, asking no question for conscience sake.

26. For the earth is the Lords, and the fulness thereof.

27. If any of them that believe not, bid you to a feast, and ye be disposed to go; whatsoever is set before you, eat, asking no question for conscience sake.

28. But if any man say unto you, This is offered in sacrifice unto idols, eat not, for his sake that shewed it, and for conscience sake. For the earth is the Lords, and the fulness thereof.

29. Conscience I say, not thine own, but of the others: for why is my liberty judged of another mans conscience?

30. For, if I by grace be a partaker, why am I evil spoken of for that for which I give thanks?

31. Whether therefore ye eat or drink, or whatsoever ye do, do all to the glory of God.

32. Give none offence, neither to the Jews, nor to the Gentiles, nor to the church of God:

33. Even as I please all men in all things, not seeking mine own profit, but the profit of many, that they may be saved.

XI.1. Be ye followers of me, even as I also am of Christ.

PARAPHRASE

[X.23]Farther supposeing it lawfull to eat things offered to Idols yet all things that are lawfull are not expedient. Things that in themselves are lawfull for me, may not tend to the edification of others, and soe may be fit to be forborne. [24]Noe one must seek barely his owne private particular interest alone but let every one seek the good of others also. [25]Eat whatever is sold in the shambles without any enquiry or scruple–whither it had been offered to any Idol or noe: [26]For the earth and all there in are the good creatures of the true god given by him to men for their use. [27]If an heathen invite you to an entertainment and you goe, eat whatever is set before you without makeing any question or scruple about it. whither it had been offered in sacrifice or noe. [28]But if any one say to you this was offered in sacrifice to an Idol, eat it not, for his sake that mentioned it, and for conscience sake·* [29]conscience, I say, not thine own, (for thou knowest thy liberty and that an Idol is noe thing) but the conscience of the other. For why is my liberty by my ill use of it judgd i e in effect condemned by an other mans co⟨n⟩science as if I allowed Idolatry:⟨*⟩ [30]And if I with thanksgiveing partake of what is lawfull for me to eat why doe I order the matter soe that I am ill spoken of for that which I blesse god for?* [31]Whether therefore ye eat or drink or whatever you doe let your care and aime be the glory of god. [32]Give noe offence to the Jews* by giveing them occasion to think that Christians are permitted to worship heathen Idols; Nor to the gentils† by giveing them occasion to think that you allow their Idolatry by partakeing of their sacrifices; Nor to weak members of the church‡ of god, by drawing them by your example to eat of things offered to Idols of the lawfulness whereof they are not fully satisfied. [33]As I myself doe who abridg my self of many conveniencys of life to comply with the different judgments of men and gain the good opinion of others, that I may be instrumental to the Salvation of as many as is possible. [XI.1]Immitate herein my example as I doe that of our Lord Christ who neglected himself for the Salvation of others.*

X.28* The repetition of these words. *For the earth is the Lords and the fulness thereof* does soe manifestly disturb the sense that the Syriac, Arabic, Vulgat and French translations have omitted them, and are justifyed in it by the Alexandrian and some other Greek copys

29* The ill effect of a Christians eating what the heathen that invited him told him had been offerd to an idol was the countenance this use of his liberty might be interpreted to give to Idolatry, and therefore in that sense κρίνεται must here be understood. And so much βλασφημοῦμαι in the next verse. viz il spoken of as allowing Idolatry

30* vid. Rom XIV.6.16

32* The Jews ill speakeing of the Christians on this account I suppose are meant. ver. 30.

† The conscience of the Gentiles confirmd in their Idolatry. ver. 29.

‡ And the weak Christians offended VIII.10

XI.1* [a]vid. Rom XV.3. This vers: seems to belong to the precedent wherein he had proposed himself as an example and therefor this verse should not be cut off from the former chapter. In what St Paul says in this and the preceding verse taken togeather we may suppose he makes some reflection on the false Apostle whom many of the Corinthians followed as their Leader. [b]At least it is for St Pauls justification that he proposes himself to be followed noe farther than as he sought the good of others and not his own, and had Christ for his pattern v. Ch. IV.16

SECTION VII

Ch. XI.2-16

CONTENTS

St Paul commends them for observeing the orders he had left with them, and uses arguments to justifie the rule he had given them that women should not pray or prophesie in their assemblyes uncovered. which it seems there was some contention about, and they had writ to him to be resolved in it

TEXT

XI.2. Now I praise you, brethren, that you remember me in all things, and keep the ordinances, as I delivered them to you.

3. But I would have you know, that the head of every man is Christ; and the head of the woman, is the man; and the head of Christ, is God.

4. Every man praying or prophesying, having his head covered, dishonoureth his head.

5. But every woman that prayeth, or prophesieth with her head uncovered, dishonoureth her head: for that is even all one as if she were shaven.

6. For if the woman be not covered, let her also be shorn: but if it be a shame for a woman to be shorn or shaven, let her be covered.

7. For a man indeed ought not to cover his head, forasmuch as he is the image and glory of God: but the woman is the glory of the man.

8. For the man is not of the woman: but the woman of the man.

9. Neither was the man created for the woman: but the woman for the man.

10. For this cause ought the woman to have power on her head, because of the angels.

11. Nevertheless, neither is the man without the woman, neither the woman without the man in the Lord.

12. For as the woman is of the man, even so is the man also by the woman: but all things of God.

13. Judge in your selves: is it comely that a woman pray unto God uncovered?

14. Doth not even nature it self teach you, that if a man have long hair, it is a shame unto him?

15. But if a Woman have long hair, it is a glory to her: for her hair is given her for a covering.

16. But if any man seem to be contentious, we have no such custom, neither the churches of God.

PARAPHRASE

XI.2 I commend you Brethren for remembring all my orders and for reteining those rules I delivered to you when I was with you. [3]But for your better understanding what concernes women* in your assemblys

XI.3* [a]This about women seeming as difficult a passage as most in St Pauls Epistles I crave leave to premise some few considerations which I hope may conduce to the clearing of it.

[b]1° It is to be ob⟨s⟩erved that it was the custome, for women, who appeared in publik, to be vailed. ver. 13-16. Therefore it could be noe question at all, whether they ought to be veyled when they assisted at the prayers and prayses in the publik assemblys: or if that were the thing intended by the Apostle it had been much easier, shorter, and plainer for him to have said, that women should be coverd in the assemblys.

[c]2° It is plain that this covering the head in women is restraind to some particular actions which they performed in the assembly expressed by the words *praying* and *prophesieing* ver. 4 and 5. which whatever they signifie, must have the same meaning when applyd to the women in the 5th ver. that they have when applyd to the men in the 4th ver.

[d]It will possibly be objected. If women were to be vailed in the assemblys, let those actions be what they will, the women joyning in them were still to be veyled

Answer· This would be plainly soe if their interpretation were to be followed, who are of opinion that by *praying* and *prophesieing* here, [e]was meant to be present in the assembly and joyning with the congregation in the prayers that were made, or hymns that were sung, or in hearing the reading and exposition of the holy Scriptures there. But against this, that the hearing of preaching or prophesieing, was never called *preaching* or *prophesying* is soe unanswerable an objection, that I think there can be noe reply to it

[f]The case in short seems to be this. The men prayed and prophesyed in the assemblys, and did it with their heads uncovered. The women also some times prayd and prophesyed too in the assemblys, which when they did they thought dureing their performing that action they were excused from being veyled, and might be bearheaded or at least open faced as well as the men. This was that which the Apostle restrains in them, and directs that though they prayd or prophesied they were still to remain veyled

[g]3° The next thing to be considered is what is here to be understood by *praying* and *prophesying*. And that seems to me to be the performing of some particular publick action in the assembly by some one person, which was for that time peculiar to that person and whilst it lasted the rest of the assembly silently assisted. [h]For it cannot be supposed that when the Apostle says a man praying or prophesying that he means an action performed in common by the whole congregation, or if he did what pretence could that give the women to be unveyled more dureing the performance of such an action than at any other time? [i]A woman must be veyled in the assembly, what pretence then or claim could it give her to be unveyled that she joynd with the rest of the assembly in the prayer that some one person made? such a praying as this could give noe more ground for her being unveyled, [j]than her being in the assembly could be thought a reason for her being unveyld. The same may be said of prophesying when understood to signify a womans joyning with the congregation in singing the prayses of god. But if the woman prayed as the mouth of the assembly etc: then it was like she might think she might have the privilege to be unveyled.

[k]*Praying* and *prophesying* as has been shewn signifying here the doeing some peculiar action in the assembly whilst the rest of the congregation only assisted, let us in the next place examin what that action was. As to *prophesying* the Apostle in express words tels us Ch. ⟨XIV⟩.3 and 12 that it was speaking in the assembly. The same is evident as to

you are to take notice that Christ is the head to which every man is subjected, and the man is the head to which every woman is subjected and that the head or superior to Christ him self is god. [4]Every man

praying, that the Apostle means by it praying publickly with an audible voyce in the congregation vid Ch XIV 14-19

[l]4° It is to be observed that whither any one prayd or prophesyed they did it alone the rest remaining silent Ch: XIV.27-33. Soe that even in these extraordinary prayses which any one sung to god by the immediate motion and impulse of the holy ghost, which was one of the actions called prophesying they sung alone. [m]And indeed how could it be otherwise? For who could joyn with the person soe prophesying in things dictated to him alone by the holy ghost which the others could not know till the person prophesying uttered them?

[n]5° Prophesying as St Paul tels us Ch: XIV.3 was speaking unto others to edification exhortation, and comfort: But every speaking to others to any of those ends was not prophesying but only then when such speaking was a spiritual gift performed by the immediate and extraordinary motion of the holy ghost vid. Chap: XIV.1.12.24.30· [o]For example singing prayses to god was called prophesying: but we see when Saul prophesyed the spirit of god fel upon him and he was turned into an other man 1 Sam X.6. Nor doe I think any place in the New Testament can be produced wherein prophesying signifyes bare reading of the Scripture or any other action performed without a supernatural impulse and assistance of the spirit of god. [p]This we are sure that the prophesying which St Paul here speaks of is one of the extraordinary gifts given by the spirit of god. vid Cha: XII.10. Now that the spirit of god and the gift of prophesie should be powerd out upon women as well as men in the time of the gospel is plain from Acts. II.17. and then where could be a fitter place for them to utter their prophesies in than the Assemblys?

[q]It is not unlikely what one of the most learned and sagacious of our interpreters of Scripture (Mr Mede Disc. 16) suggests upon this place viz that Christian women might out of a vanity incident to that Sex propose to them selves and affect an imitation of the preists and prophitesses of the gentils, who had their faces uncovered when they utterd their oracles or officiated in their sacrifices: [r]But I cannot but wonder that that very acute writer should not see that the bare being in the assembly could not give a Christian woman any pretence to that freedom. None of the Bacchai or Pythiai quited their ordinary modest guise, but when she was as the poets express it *Rapta* or *plena Deo* possesd and hurried by the spirit she served. [s]And soe possibly a Christian woman when she found the spirit of god powerd out upon her as *Joel* expresses it exciteing her to pray or sing prayses to god, or discover any truth immediately revealed to her might think it convenient for her better uttering of it to be uncovered, [t]or at least to be noe more restraind in her liberty of shewing her self than the femal preists of the heathens were when they deliverd their oracles. But yet even in these actions the Apostle forbids the women to unveyle themselves

[u]St Pauls forbidding women to speak in the assemblys will probably seem a strong argument against this: But when well considered will perhaps prove none. There be two places where the Apostle forbids women to speak in the church 1 Cor XIV.34.35 and 1 Tim. II 11.12. He that shall attentively read and compare these togeather may observe that the silence injoynd the women is for a mark of their subjection to the male sex: [v]And therefore what in the one is expressed by *keeping silence and not speaking but being under obedience*, in the other is called *being in silence with all subjection not teaching nor usurping authority over the man*. The women in the churches were not to assume the personage of Doctors, or speak there as teachers, this caryed with it the appearance of superiority, and was forbidden. [w]Nay they were not soe much as to aske questions there or to enter into any sort of conference. This shews a kind of equality, and was also

that prayeth or prophesieth i e by the gift of the Spirit of god speaketh in the church for the edifying exhorting and comforting of the congregation haveing his head covered dishonoureth Christ his head, by appearing in a garb not becomeing the authority and dominion which god through Christ has given him over all the things of this world, the covering of the head being a mark of subjection: [5]But on the contrary a woman praying or prophesying in the church with her head uncovered dishonoureth the man who is her head by appearing in a garb that disowns her subjection to him. For to appear bareheaded in publick is all one as to have her hair cut off, which is the garb and dress of the other sex and not of a woman. [6]If therefore it be unsuitable to the female sex to have their hair shorne or shaved off let her for the same reason be covered. [7]A man indeed ought not to be veyled because he is the image and representative of god in his dominion over the rest of the world, which is one part of the glory of god: [8]But the woman who was made out of the man, made for him, and in subjection to him, is matter of glory to the man. [9]But the man not being made out of the woman, nor for her, but the woman made out of, and for the man, [10]she ought for this reason to have a vaile on her head in token of her subjection, because of the

forbidden. But yet though they were not to speak in the church in their own names or as if they were raised by the franchises of Christianity to such an equality with the men [x]that where knowledg or presumption of their own abilitys emboldened them to it they might take upon them to be teachers and instructers of the congregation or might at least enter into questionings and debates there. [y]This would have had too great an air of standing upon even ground with the men, and would not have well comported with the subordination of the sex. But yet this subordination which god for orders sake had instituted in the world hinderd not [z]but that by the supernatural gifts of the spirit he might make use of the weaker sex to any extraordinary function when ever he thought fit, as well as he did of the men. But yet when they thus either prayd or prophesied by the motion and impulse of the holy-ghost care was taken that whilst they were obeying god who was pleasd by his spirit to set them a speaking, [aa]the subjection of their sex should not be forgotten, but owned and preserved by their being covered. The Christian religion was not to give offence by any appearance or suspition that it took away the subordination of the sexes and set the women at liberty from their natural subjection to the men. [bb]And therefore we see that, in both these cases, the aim was to maintain and secure the confessed superiority and dominion of the man and not permit it to be invaded soe much as in appearance. Hence the arguments in the one case for covering and in the other for silence are all drawn from the natural superiority of the man and the subjection of the woman. [cc]In the one the woman, without an extraordinary call was to keep silent, as a mark of her subjection: In the other where she was to speak by an extraordinary call and commission from god she was yet to continue the profession of her subjection in keeping her self covered. [dd]Here by the way it is to be observed that there was extraordinary praying to god by the impulse of the Spirit, as well as speaking unto men for their edification exhortation and comfort. Vid Chap XIV.15. Rom VIII.26. Jude 20. These things being premised let us follow the thread of St Pauls discourse

Angels.* [11]Nevertheless the sexes have not a being one without the other, neither the man without the woman, or the woman without the man, the Lord soe ordering it. [12]For as the first woman was made out of the man, soe the race of men ever since is continued and propagated by the female sex: but they and all other things had their being and original from god. [13]Be you your selves judges whither it be decent for a woman to make a prayer to god in the church uncovered. [14]Does not even nature, that has made and would have the distinction of sexes preserved, teach you, that if a man wear his hair long and dressed up after the manner of women it is misbecomeing and dishonourable to him? [15]But to a woman, if she be curious about her hair in haveing it long and dresseing her self with it, it is a grace and commendation since her hair is given her for a covering. [16]But if any shew himself to be a lover of contention* we the Apostles have noe such custome, nor any of the churches of god.

SECTION VIII

Ch. XI.17-34

CONTENTS

[a]One may observe from several passages in this Epistle that several Judaical customs were crept into the Corinthian Church. This church being of St Pauls own planting, who spent two years at Corinth in forming it, it is evident these abuses had their rise from some other teacher who came to them after his leaveing them which was about five years before his writeing this Epistle. [b]These disorders therefore may with reason be ascribed to the head of the faction that opposed St Paul, who as has been remarked was a Jew and probably Jewdaized. And that tis like was the foundation of the great opposition between him and St Paul and the reason why St Paul labours soe earnestly to destroy his credit amongst the Corinthians, this sort of men being very busy very troublesome and very dangerous to the gospel, as may be seen in other of St Pauls Epistles, particularly that to the Gallatians

[c]The celebrateing the Passover amongst the Jews, was plainly the eating of a meal distinguished from other ordinary meales by several peculiar ceremonies. Two of these ceremonys were eating of bread

10* What the meaning of these words is I confesse I doe not understand
16* Why may not this *any one* be understood of the false Apostle here glanced at?

solemnly broken and drinking a cup of wine called the cup of Blesseing. These two our Saviour transferd into the Christian Church, to be used in their assemblys for a commemoration of his death and sufferings. [d]In celebrateing this institution of our Saviour the Judaizing Corinthians followed the Jewish custom of eating their Passover: They eat the Lords supper as a part of their meal bringing their provisions into the assembly, where they eat divided into distinct companys, some feasting to excess, whilst others ill provided were in want. [e]This eating thus in the publik assembly, and mixing the Lords supper with their ordinary meale as a part of it, with other disorders and indecencys accompanying it, is the matter of this section. These innovations he tells them here he as much blames, as in the begining of this Chapter he commends them for keeping to his directions in some other things.

TEXT

XI.17. Now in this that I declare unto you, I praise you not, that you come together not for the better, but for the worse.

18. For first of all, when ye come together in the church, I hear that there be divisions among you; and I partly believe it.

19. For there must be also heresies among you, that they which are approved, may be made manifest among you.

20. When ye come together therefore into one place, this is not to eat the Lords supper.

21. For in eating every one taketh before other, his own supper: and one is hungry, and another is drunken.

22. What, have ye not houses to eat and to drink in? Or despise ye the church of God, and shame them that have not? what shall I say to you? shall I praise you in this? I praise you not.

23. For I have received of the Lord, that which also I delivered unto you, that the Lord Jesus, the same night in which he was betrayed, took bread:

24. And when he had given thanks, he brake it, and said, Take, eat; this is my body, which is broken for you: this do in remembrance of me.

25. After the same manner also he took the cup, when he had supped, saying, This cup is the new testament in my blood: this do ye, as oft as ye drink it, in remembrance of me.

26. For as often as ye eat this bread, and drink this cup, ye do show the Lords death till he come.

27. Wherefore, whosoever shall eat this bread, and drink this cup of the Lord unworthily, shall be guilty of the body and blood of the Lord.

28. But let a man examine himself, and so let him eat of that bread, and drink of that cup.

29. For he that eateth and drinketh unworthily, eateth and drinketh damnation to himself, not discerning the Lords body.

30. For this cause many are weak and sickly among you, and many sleep.

31. For if we would judge our selves, we should not be judged.

32. But when we are judged, we are chastened of the Lord, that we should not be condemned with the world.

33. Wherefore my brethren, when ye come together, to eat, tarry one for another.

34. And if any man hunger, let him eat at home; that ye come not together unto condemnation. And the rest will I set in order when I come.

PARAPHRASE

XI.17 Though what I said to you concerning womens behaviour in the
Church, was not without commendation of you, yet this that I am now
goeing to speak to you of is without praising you: because you soe
order your meetings in your assemblys that they are not to your
advantage but harm. 18 For first I hear that when you come togeather in
the church you fall into partys and I partly beleive it, 19 because there
must be divisions and factions amongst you that those who Stand firm
upon trial may be made manifest amongst you· 20 You come together
tis true in one place and there you eat but yet this makes it not to be
the eating of the Lords supper. 21 For in eating you eat not together but
every one takes his own supper one before an other·* 22 Have ye not
houses to eat and drink in at home for sati⟨s⟩fying your hunger and

XI.21* [a]To understand this we must observe

1° That they had sometimes meetings on purpose onely for eating the Lords supper. ver. 33

2° That to those meetings they brought their own suppers ver. 21

[b]3° That though every ones supper were brought into the common assembly yet it was not eat in common, but every one fell to his own supper apart as soon as he and his supper were there ready for one an other, without staying for the rest of the company or communicateing with them in eating ver. 21.33

[c]In this St Paul blames three things espetially

1° That they eat their common food in the assembly, which was to be eaten at home in their houses ver. 22.34

2° That though they eat in the common meeting place yet they eat seperately every one his own supper a part, Soe that the plenty and excesse of some shamd the want and penury of others ver. 22. [d]Hereby also the divisions amongst them were kept up ver. 18 they being as soe many separated and divided societys not as one united body of Christians commemorateing their common head as they should have been in celebrateing the Lords supper Ch. X.16.17.

[e]3° That they mixed the Lords supper with their own, eating it as a part of their ordinary meale, when they made not that discrimination between it and their common food as they should have donne ver. 29

thirst? Or have ye a contempt for the church of god, and take a pleasure
to put those out of countenance, who have not wherewithall to feast
there as you doe? What is it I said to you, that I praise you* for reteining
what I deliverd to you? in this occasion indeed I praise you not for it.
[23]For what I received concerning this institution from the Lord himself
that I deliverd unto you when I was with you and it was this. viz That the
Lord Jesus in the night wherein he was betraid, took bread and haveing
given thanks brake it, and said· [24]take· eat· this is my body which is
broken for you, this doe in remembrance of me. [25]Soe likewise he took
the cup also, when he had supped, saying. This cup is the new testament in my blood, this doe ye as often as ye doe it, in remembrance of
me. [26]Soe that the eating of this bread and the drinking of this cup of the
Lords supper is not to satisfie hunger and thirst but to shew forth the
Lords death till he comes· [27]Insoemuch that he who eats this bread and
drinks this cup of the Lord in an unworthy manner* not suitable to that
end shall be guilty of a misuse of the body and blood of the Lord.† [28]By
this institution therefore of Christ let a man examin him self* and

22* He here plainly refers to what he has said to them ver. 2 where he praised them for remembring him in all things, and for reteining τὰς παραδόσεις καθὼς παρέδωκα, what he had *delivered* to them. This commendation he here retracts for in this matter of eating the Lords supper they did not retein ὃ παρέδωκα ver. 23 what he had *deliverd* to them which therefore in the immediately following words he repeats and delivers to them again.

27* [a]'Αναξίως *Unworthily*. Our Saviour in the institution of the Lords supper tells the Apostles that the bread and the cup were sacramentaly his body and blood, and that they were to be eaten and drunk in remembrance of him, which as St Paul interprets it ver. 26 was to shew forth his death till he came. [b]Whoever therefore eat and drank them soe as not solemnly to shew forth his death followed not Christs institution but used them *unworthily*. i e not to the end to which they were instituted· This makes St Paul tell them ver. 20 that their comeing togeather to eat it as they did. [c]viz the sacramental bread and wine promiscuously with their other food as a part of their meal and that though in the same place yet not all together at one time and in one company was not the eating of the Lords supper

† Ἔνοχος ἔσται shall be liable to the punishment due to one who makes a wrong use of the sacramentall body and blood of Christ in the Lords supper. What that punishment was vid. ver. 30

28* [a]St Paul, as we have observed, tells the Corinthians ver. 20 That to eat it after the manner they did was not to eat the Lords supper. He tells them also ver. 29 That to eat it without a due and discriminateing regard had to the Lords body (for soe he cals the sacramental bread and wine as our Saviour did in the institution) [b]by seperateing the bread and wine from the common use of eating and drinking for hunger and thirst was to eat unworthily. To remedie their disorders, herein he sets before them Christs own institution of this Sacrament, that in it they might see the manner and end of its institution. and by that every one might examin his own comportment herein whither it were conformable to that institution and suited to that end. [c]In the account he gives of Christs institution we may observe that he particularly remarks to them, that this eating and drinking was noe part of common eating and drinking for hunger and thirst: but according to that† let him eat of this bread and drink of this cup. 29 For he who eats and drinks after an unworthy maner without a due respect had to the Lords body in a discriminateing* and purely sacramental use of the bread and wine that represent it draws punishment† on him self by soe doeing. 30 And hence it is that many among you are weak

was instituted in a very solemn manner after they had supped and for an other end viz to represent Christs body and blood, and to be eaten and drunk in remembrance of him; or as St Paul expounds it. to shew forth his death. [d]An other thing which they might observe in the institution was. that this was donne by all who were present united together in one company at the same time. All which put together shews us what the examination here proposed is. For the designe of the Apostle here being to reforme what he found fault with in their celebrateing the Lords supper, [e]'tis by that alone we must understand the directions he gives them about it, if we will suppose he talked pertinently to this captious and touchy people, whom he was very desirous to reduce from the irregularitys they were run into in this matter, as well as several others. [f]And if the account of Christs institution be not for their examining their cariage by it and adjusting it to it to what purpose is it here? The examination therefore proposd was noe other but an examination of their maner of eating the Lords supper by Christs institution to see how their behaviour herein comported with the institution and the end for which it was instituted. [g]Which further appears to be soe by the punishment annexed to their miscariages here in, which was infirmitys sickness and temporal death with which god chastened them that they might not be condemned with the unbeleiving world ver. 30.32. For if the unworthiness here spoke of were either unbeleif or any of those sins which are usualy made the matter of examination 'tis to be presumed the Apostle would not wholy have passed them over in silence: [h]This at lest is certain that the punishment of these sins is infinitely greater than that which god here inflicts on unworthy receivers whither they who are guilty of them received the sacrament or noe.

† [a]καὶ οὕτως· These words as to the letter are rightly translated *and so*: But that translation I imagin leaves generally a wrong sense of the place in the mind of an English Reader. For in ordinary speakeing these words *Let a man examin and soe let him eat* are understood to import the same with these. [b]*Let a man examin and then let him eat*· as if they signified noe more but that examination should precede and eating follow, which I take to be quite different from the meaning of the Apostle here, whose sense the whole designe of the context shews to be this: *I here set before you the Institution of Christ· by that let a man examin his cariage*, καὶ οὕτως, *and according to that let him eat*; *Let him conforme the maner of his eating to that*

29* [a]Μὴ διακρίνων. *Not discriminateing*. Not puting a difference between the sacramental bread and wine (which St Paul with our Saviour cals christs body) and other bread and wine in the solemn and separate use of them. The Corinthians as has been remarkd eat the Lords supper in and with their own ordinary supper, [b]where by it came not to be sufficiently distinguished (as became a religious and Christian observance soe solemnly instituted.) from common eating for bodily refreshment. nor from the Jewish Paschal supper and the bread broken and the cup of blesseing used in that. Nor did it in this way of eating it in seperate companys as it were in private familys shew forth the Lords death [c]as it was designed to doe by the concurrence and communion of the whole assembly of Christians joyntly united in the partakeing of bread and wine in a way peculiar to them with reference soly to Jesus Christ. This was that as appears by this place, which St Paul as we have already explained cals *eating unworthily*

† *Damnation* by which our translation renders κρίμα is vulgarly taken for eternal damnation in the other world whereas κρίμα here signifies punishment of an other nature as appears by ver. 30.32.

and sick and a good number are gon to their graves. [31]But if we would discriminate* our selves i e by our discriminateing use of the Lords supper, we should not be judged.† i e punished by god· [32]But being punished by the Lord we are corrected* that ⟨w⟩e may not be condemned hereafter with the unbeleiveing world. [33]Wherefor my brethren when you have a meeting for celebrateing the Lords supper stay for one an other that you may eat it all together as partakers all in common of the Lords table without division or distinction. [34]But if any one be hungry let him eat at home to satisfie his hunger, That soe the disorder in these meetings may not draw on you the punishment above mentioned. What else remains to be rectifyed in this matter I will set in order when I come

SECTION IX

Ch. XII.1-XIV.40

CONTENTS

[a]The Corinthians seem to have enquired of St Paul what order of precedency and preference men were to have in their assemblys in regard of their spiritual gifts. Nay if we may guess by his answer the question they seem more particularly to have proposd was whether those who had the gift of tongues ought not to take place and speak first and be first heard in their meetings. [b]Concerning this there seems to have been some strife maligning and disorder amongst them as may be collected from Ch XII 21-25 XIII.4.5. XIV.40

To this St Paul answers in these three Chapters as followeth

[c]1° That they had all been heathen Idolaters and soe being denyers of Christ were in that state none of them *spiritual*· But that now being Christians and owning Jesus to be the Lord, (which could not be done without the Spirit of god⟨)⟩ they were all πνευματικοί *spiritual* and soe

31* [a]Διακρίνειν does noe where that I know signifye to *judg* as it is here translated but always signifies to *distinguish* or *discriminate*, and in this place has the same signification and means the same thing that it does ver. 29. [b]He is little versed in St Pauls writeings who has not observed how apt he is to repeat the same word he had used before to the same purpose though in a different and sometimes a pretty hard construction: as here he applys διακρίνειν to the persons discriminateing as in the 29 ver. to the thing to be discriminated though in both places it be put to denote the same action.

† Ἐκρινόμεθα here signifies the same that κρίμα does ver. 29

32* παιδευόμεθα properly signifies to be corrected as scholers are by their master for their good.

there was noe reason for one to undervalue another as if he were not spiritual as well as himself. Ch. XII.1-3

[d]2° That though there be diversity of gifts yet they are all by the Same Spirit, from the same Lord and the same God workeing them all in every one according to his good pleasure. Soe that in this respect also there is no difference nor precedency, noe occasion for any ones being puffed up or affecting priority upon account of his gifts Ch. XII.4-11.

[e]3° That the diversity of gifts is for the use and benefit of the church which is Christs body wherein the members (as in the natural body) of meaner functions are as much parts and as necessary in their use to the good of the whole and therefor to be honourd as much as any other. [f]The union they have as members in the same body makes them all equaly share in one an others good and evil; gives them a mutual esteem and concerne one for an other, and leaves noe room for contests or divisions amongst them about their gifts, or the honour and place due to them upon that account XII.12-⟨31⟩

[g]4° That though gifts have their excellency and use and those who have them may be zelous in the use of them, yet the true and sure way for a man to get an excellency and preference above others is the enlargeing himself in Charity and excelling in that, without which a Christian with all his spiritual gifts is noe thing–XIII.1-13

[h]5° In the comparison of Spiritual gifts he gives those the precedency which edifie most: And in particular prefers prophesieing to tongues. Ch: XIV:1-40

SECTION IX. NO. 1

Ch. XII.1-3

TEXT

XII.1. Now concerning spiritual gifts, brethrén, I would not have you ignorant.

2. Ye know that ye were Gentiles, carried away unto these dumb idols, even as ye were led.

3. Wherefore I give you to understand, that no man speaking by the Spirit of God, calleth Jesus accursed: and that no man can say that Jesus is the Lord, but by the holy Ghost.

PARAPHRASE

XII.1 As to spiritual men or men assisted and acted by the spirit* I shall informe you for I would not have you be ignorant. 2You your selves know that you were heathens ingaged in the worship of stocks and stones dumb sensless Idols by those who were then your leaders. 3aWhere upon let me tell you that noe one who opposes Jesus Christ or his religion has the spirit of god.* And whoever is brought to own Jesus to be the Messiah the Lord† does it by the holy-ghost·* And therefor upon account of haveing the spirit you can none of you lay any claim to superiority; [b]or have any pretence to slight any of your brethren as not haveing the spirit of god as well as you· For all that own our Lord Jesus Christ and beleive in him doe it by the spirit of god i e can doe it upon noe other ground but revelation comeing from the spirit of god.

SECTION IX. NO. 2

Ch. XII.4-11

CONTENTS

Another consideration which St Paul offers against any contention for superiority or pretence to precedency upon account of any spiritual gift is that those distinct gifts are all of one and the same spirit by the same Lord, wrought in every one by god alone and all for the profit of the church.

XII.1* [a]Πνευματικῶν *Spiritual*. we are warranted by a like use of the word in several of places of St Pauls Epistles as Ch. II.15. XIV.37 of this Epistle; and Gall: VI.1. to take it here in the masculine gender standing for persons and not gifts· And the context obleiges us to understand it so. [b]For if we will have it stand for gifts and not persons, the sense and coherence of these three first verses will be very hard to be made out. Besides there is evidence enough in several parts of it [c]that the subject of St Pauls discourse here is πνευματικοί persons endowed with spiritual gifts contending for precedency in consideration of their gifts· vid ver. 13 etc of this Ch: and to what purpose else says he Ch. XIV.5 *Greater* is he that prophesieth than he that speaketh with tongues?

3* This is spoken against the Jews who pretended to the holy-ghost and yet spoke against Jesus Christ and denyd that the holy ghost was ever given to the gentils vid Act. X.45. Whether their Judaizing false Apostle were at all glanced at in this may be considered.

† Lord. What is meant by Lord. see Note Ch. VIII.⟨5⟩

TEXT

XII.4. Now there are diversities of gifts, but the same Spirit.

5. And there are differences of administrations, but the same Lord.

6. And there are diversities of operations, but it is the same God, which worketh all in all.

7. But the manifestation of the Spirit is given to every man to profit withal.

8. For to one is given by the Spirit, the word of wisdom; to another the word of knowledge by the same Spirit;

9. To another faith by the same Spirit; to another the gifts of healing by the same Spirit;

10. To another the working of miracles; to another prophesie; to another discerning of spirits; to another divers kinds of tongues; to another the interpretation of tongues.

11. But all these worketh that one and the self same Spirit, dividing to every man severally as he will.

PARAPHRASE

[XII.4]Be not mistaken by the diversity of gifts, for though there be diversity of gifts amongst Christians yet there is noe diversity of Spirits, they all come from one and the same spirit. [5]Though there be diversitys of offices in the church, yet all the officers* have but one Lord. [6]And though there be various influxes* whereby Christians are enabled to doe extraordinary things yet it is the same god that works† all these extraordinary gifts in every one that has them. [7]But the way or gift where in every one, who has the spirit, is to shew it, is given him not for his private advantage or honour* but for the good and advantage of the church. [8]For instance to one is given by the spirit the word of wisdome* or the revelation of the gospel of Jesus Christ in the full latitude of it such as was given to the Apostles; to an other by the same spirit the knowledg† of the true sense and true meaning of the

XII.5* These different offices are rĕcond up ver. 28 etc.

6* What these ἐνεϱγήματα were see ver. 8-11

† [a]They were very properly called ἐνεϱγήματα–*inworkings* because they were above all humane power, men of themselves could doe noe thing of them at all but it was god as the Apostle tells us here who in these extraordinary gifts of the holy ghost did all that was done, it was the effect of his immediate operation, as St Paul assures us in that parallel place Phil: II.13. [b]In which Ch: ver. 3 and ver. 14 we find that the Philippians stood a little in need of the same advice which St Paul soe at large presses here upon the Corinthians

7* vid Rom XII.3-8

8* σοφία. The doctrine of the gospel is more than once in the begining of this epistle called the *wisdome* of god

† Γνῶσις is used by St Paul for such a *knowledg* of the law and the prophets.

holy Scriptures of the old testament for the explaining and confirmation of the Gospel; [9]To an other by the same spirit is given an undoubting perswasion* and steadfast confidence of performing what he is goeing about; To an other the gift of cureing diseases by the same spirit. [10]To an other the workeing of miracles; to an other prophesie;* To an other the discerning by what spirit men did any extraordinary operation; to an other diversity of languages; To an other the interpretation of languages. [11]All which gifts are wrought in beleivers by one and the same spirit distributing to every one in particular as he thinks fit.

SECTION IX. NO. 3

Ch. XII.12-30

CONTENTS

From the necessarily different functions in the body and the strict union nevertheless of the members adapted to those different functions in a mutual sympathie and concerne one for another St Paul here farther shews that there ought not to be any Strife or division amongst them about precedency and preference upon account of their distinct gifts.

TEXT

XII.12. For as the body is one, and hath many members, and all the members of that one body, being many, are one body: so also is Christ.

9* [a]In this sense πίστις *faith* is some times taken in the new testament particularly Ch. XIII.2. It is difficult I confess to difine the precise meaning of each word which the Apostle uses in the 8.9 and 10 verses here. But if the order which St Paul observes in enumerateing by 1st. 2d. 3d the three first officers set down ver. 28 [b]viz *first Apostles. secondly prophets. thirdly Teachers*. have any relation or may give any light to these three gifts which are set down in the first place here. viz *Wisdom. Knowledg* and *Faith* we may then properly understand by σοφία *wisdome* the whole doctrine of the gospel as communicated to the Apostles. [c]By γνῶσις *knowledg* the gift of understanding the mystical sense of the Law and the prophets: and by πίστις *faith* that assurance and confidence in delivering and confirming the doctrine of the gospel, which became διδασκάλους *Doctors* or *Teachers*. [d]This at least I think may be presumed that since σοφία and γνῶσις have λόγος joynd to them and it is said. *the word of wisdome* and *the word of knowledg*· wisdom and knowledg here signifie such gifts of the mind as are to be imploid in Preaching

10* *Prophesie* comprehends these three things· prediction; singing by the dictate of the spirit; and understanding and explaining the mysterious hidden sense of Sacred Scripture by an immediate illumination and motion of the spirit. as we have already shewn. And that the prophesying here spoke of was by immediate revelation vid XIV.29-31

13. For by one Spirit are we all baptized into one body, whether we be Jews or Gentiles, whether we be bond or free; and have been all made to drink into one Spirit.

14. For the body is not one member, but many.

15. If the foot shall say, Because I am not the hand, I am not of the body; is it therefore not of the body?

16. And if the ear shall say, Because I am not the eye, I am not of the body; is it therefore not of the body?

17. If the whole body were an eye, where were the hearing? If the whole were hearing, where were the smelling?

18. But now hath God set the members, every one of them in the body, as it hath pleased him.

19. And if they were all one member, where were the body?

20. But now are they many members, yet but one body.

21. And the eye cannot say unto the hand, I have no need of thee: nor again, the head to the feet, I have no need of you.

22. Nay, much more those members of the body which seem to be more feeble are necessary.

23. And those members of the body, which we think to be less honourable, upon these we bestow more abundant honour, and our uncomely parts have more abundant comeliness.

24. For our comely parts have no need: but God hath tempered the body together, having given more abundant honour to that part which lacked:

25. That there should be no schism in the body; but that the members should have the same care one for another.

26. And whither one member suffer, all the members suffer with it: or one member be honoured, all the members rejoice with it.

27. Now ye are the body of Christ, and members in particular.

28. And God hath set some in the church, first apostles, secondarily prophets, thirdly teachers, after that miracles, then gifts of healings, helps, governments, diversities of tongues.

29. Are all apostles? are all prophets? are all teachers? are all workers of miracles?

30. Have all the gifts of healing? do all speak with tongues? do all interpret?

PARAPHRASE

XII.12 For as the body being but one hath many members, and all the members of the body though many yet make but one body, soe is Christ in respect of his mistical body the church. 13 For by one spirit we are all baptised into one church and are thereby made one body without any preeminence to the Jew* above the Gentil to the free

XII.13* [a]The nameing of the Jews here with the Gentils and seting them both on the same level when converted to Christianity may probably be done here by St Paul with

above the bond man: And the bloud of Christ which we all partake of in the Lords supper makes us all have one life, one spirit, as the same blood diffused through the whole body communicates the same life and spirit to all the members· [14] For the body is not one sole member but consists of many members all vitaly united in one common Sympathie and usefulness. [15] If any one have not that function or dignity in the Church which he desires he must not therefore declare that he is not of the church· [16] he does not thereby cease to be a member of the church. [17] There is as much need of several and distinct gifts and functions in the church as there is of different senses and members in the body, and the meanest and least honourable would be missed if it were wanting, and the whole body would suffer by it: [18] Accordingly god hath fitted several persons as it were soe many distinct members to several offices and functions in the church by proper and peculiar gifts and abilitys which he has bestowd on them according to his good pleasure. [19] But if all were but one member what would become of the body? there would be noe such thing as a humane body. Noe more could the church be edified and framed into a growing lasting societie if the gifts of the spirit were all reduced to one. [20] But now by the various gifts of the spirit bestowed on its several members it is as a well organized body wherein the most eminent member cannot despise the meanest. [21] The eye cannot say to the hand I have noe need of thee: nor the head to the feet I have noe need of you. [22] It is soe far from being soe, that the parts of the body that seem in them selves weak are never the lesse of absolute necessity. [23] And those parts which are thought least honourable we take care always to cover with the more respect, and our least gracefull parts have thereby a more studyed and adventitious comelyness, [24] For our comely parts have noe need of any borrowed helps or ornaments; [25] But god hath soe contrived the Symmetry of the body, that he hath added honour to those parts that might seem naturally to want it, that there might be noe disunion noe schisme in the body, but that the members should all have the same care and concerne one for an other, [26] and all equally partake and share in the harme or honour that is done to any one of them in particular. [27] Now in like manner you are by your particular gifts each of you in his peculiar station and aptitude members of the

reference to the false Apostle who was a Jew, and seems to have claimed some preeminence as due to him upon that account [b] whereas among the members of Christ which all make but one body there is noe superiority or other distinction, but as by the several gifts bestowed on them by god they contribute more or less to the edification of the Church

body of Christ which is the Church, [28]Wherein god hath set first some Apostles, Secondly prophets, thirdly teachers, next workers of miracles, then those who have the gift of healing, helpers,* Governors.† and such as are able to speak diversity of tongues. [29]Are all Apostles? Are all prophets? Are all teachers? Are all workers of miracles? [30]Have all the gift of healing? Doe all speake diversity of tongues? Are all interpreters of tongues?

SECTION IX. NO. 4

Ch. XII.31-XIII.13

CONTENTS

[a]St Paul haveing in the foregoeing Number to put a stop to their emulation upon account of their gifts told them that though their gifts were various yet being all of the same spirit, their Lord one and the same and one and the same god that wrought all things in all of them, and that those gifts were given for the common good of the whole: [b]And also haveing shewd that they being in Christ as the different member⟨s⟩ of one body it was impossible that every one of them should have the most honourable function and soe it was absurd to strive for precedency upon account of their gifts; [c]he here tels them that since they did seeke preeminence there was a way to that and that he would shew them· and soe fals in to this admirable description and encomium of Charity conteined in the XIII Ch:

TEXT

XII.31. But covet earnestly the best gifts: And yet shew I unto you a more excellent way.

XIII.1. Though I speak with the tongues of men and of angels, and have not charity, I am become as sounding brass, or a tinkling cymbal.

2. And though I have the gift of prophesie, and understand all mysteries, and all knowledge; and tho I have all faith, so that I could remove mountains, and have no charity, I am nothing.

28* Ἀντιλήψεις *Helps* Dr Lightfoot takes to be those who accompanied the Apostles, were sent up and down by them in the service of the Gospel and baptized those that were converted by them

†κυβερνήσεις to be the same with discerning of spirits ver. 10

3. And though I bestow all my goods to feed the poor, and though I give my body to be burned, and have not charity, it profiteth me nothing.

4. Charity suffereth long, and is kind; charity envieth not; charity vaunteth not it self, is not puffed up,

5. Doth not behave it self unseemly, seeketh not her own, is not easily provoked, thinketh no evil,

6. Rejoiceth not in iniquity, but rejoiceth in the truth:

7. Beareth all things, believeth all things, hopeth all things, endureth all things.

8. Charity never faileth: but whether there be prophesies, they shall fail; whether there be tongues, they shall cease; whether there be knowledge, it shall vanish away.

9. For we know in part, and we prophesie in part.

10. But when that which is perfect is come, then that which is in part shall be done away.

11. When I was a child, I spake as a child, I understood as a child, I thought as a child: but when I became a man, I put away childish things.

12. For now we see through a glass darkly; but then face to face: now I know in part; but then shall I know even as also I am known.

13. And now abideth faith, hope, charity, these three; but the greatest of these is charity.

PARAPHRASE

XII.31 You make your gifts matter of emulation and have contests among you which of them are best and ought to have the preference:*

XII.31* [a]That this is the Apostles meaning here, is plain in that there was an emulation amongst them and a strife for precedency on account of the several gifts they had (as we have already observed from several passages in this section) which made them in their assemblys desire to be heard first. [b]This was the fault the Apostle was here correcting and tis not likely he should exhort them all promiscuously to seek the principal and most eminent gifts at the end of a discourse wherein he had been demonstrateing to them by the example of the humane body that there ought to be diversity of gifts and functions in the church; [c]but that there ought to be noe schisme emulation or contest amongst them upon the account of the exercise of those gifts. that they were all usefull in their places, and noe member was at all to be the less honoured or valued for the gift he had though it were not one of those of the first rank. [d]And in this sense the word ζηλοῦν is taken in the next Ch: ver. 4 where St Paul pursueing the same argument exhorts them to mutual charity good will and affection which he assures them is preferable to any gifts whatsoever

[e]Besides to what purpose should he exhort them to *Covet earnestly the best gifts* when the obteining of this or that gift did not at all lie in their desires or indeavours, the Apostle having just before told them ver. 11 that *the spirit divides those gifts to every man severally as he will*, and those he writt to had their allotment already. [f]He might as reasonably, according to his own doctrine in this very Chapter, bid the foot covet to be the hand, or the ear to be the eye. Let it be rememberd therefore to rectifie this that St Paul says ver. 17 of this Chapter. *If the whole body were the eye where were the hearing?* etc: [g]St

And I (notwithstanding what I have said to restrain your emulation)
will yet shew you a way to excelling.⟨†⟩
[XIII.1] If I speak all the languages of men and Angels* and yet have not
charity to make use of them entirely for the good and benefit of others
I am noe better than a sounding brass or noysy cymbal,† which fills
the ears of others without any advantage to its self by the sound it
makes· [2] And if I have the gift of prophesie and see in the law and the
prophets all the mysteries* conteind in them, and comprehend all the
knowledg they teach: And if I have faith to the highest degree and
power of miracles soe as to be able to remove mountains.† and have
not charity I am noe thing I am of noe value: [3] And if I bestow all I have
in releif of the poor, and give my self to be burnt, and have not Charity
it profits me noe thing. [4] Charity is long suffering, is gentle and
benigne without emulation, insolence, or being puffed up, [5] is not
ambitious, nor at all self interessed, is not sharp upon others failings
or inclined to ill interpretations. [6] Charity rejoyces with others when
they doe well, [7] and when any thing is amiss is troubled and covers
their failings· Charity beleives well, hopes well of every one, and
patiently bears with every thing.* [8] Charity will never cease as a thing

Paul does not use to cross his own designe, nor contradict his own reasoning. But says he, pursuant to his argument, though you contest for what you can not have, (viz) that every ones gift should be τὸ ⟨κ⟩ϱεῖττον such as should passe for the best and carry the precedency; [h] there is yet a way to attain to preference and preeminency that is Charity and good will to his fellow members. That ⟨κ⟩ϱείττονα here is put for such gifts as gave the persons that had them preeminency in the church appears also from ver. 2 and 3 of the next Chapter where St Paul haveing mentioned the gifts of tongues and prophesie etc: he does not say, [i] compareing them with charity, that they are, or profit, nothing, but says οὐδέν εἰμι and οὐδὲν ὠφελοῦμαι, I that have and exercise them, without Charity am noe thing, am of noe value· am not at all advanced by them.

†καθ' ὑπεϱβολὴν ὁδόν Beza translates *iter ad excellentiam*· the Greek words signifie *a way according to excelleing*. i e that allows emulation and striveing to excelle and have the precedency

XIII.1* *Tongues of Angels* are mentioned here according to the conception of the Jews

† A *cymbal* consisted of two large hollowed plates of brass with broad brims, which were strooke one against an other to fill up the symphonie in great consorts of Musick, they made a great deep sound but had scarce any varietie of musicall notes.

2* [a] Any predictions relateing to our saviour. or his doctrine or the times of the gospel conteind in the old testament in types or figurative and obscure expressions not understood before his comeing and being revealed to the world, St Paul calls *mysterys* as may be seen all through his writeings. [b] Soe that *mystery* and *knowledg* are terms here used by St Paul to signifi truths concerning Christ to come conteined in the old testament and *prophesie* the understanding of the types and prophesies conteining those truths, soe as to be able to explain them to others.

† To *remove mountains* is to doe what is next to impossible

7* May we not suppose that in this discription of Charity St Paul intimates and tacitly reproves their contrary carriage in their emulation and contests about the dignity and preference of their spiritual gifts?

out of use, but the gifts of prophesie and tongues and the knowledg whereby men look into and explain the meaning of the scriptures the time will be when they will be laid aside as noe longer of any use, [9]for the knowledg we have now in this state and the explication we give of Scripture is short partial and defective; [10]But when hereafter we shall be got into the state of accomplishment and perfection wherein we are to remain in the other world there will noe longer be any need of these imperfecter ways of information where by we arive at but a partial knowledg here. [11]Thus when I was in the imperfect state of Childhood I talkd, I understood, I reasoned after the imperfect manner of a child: but when I came to the state and perfection of manhood I laid aside those childish ways. [12]Now we see but by reflection the dimn and as it were enigmatical representation of things: but then we shall see, things directly and as they are in themselves as a man sees another when they are face to face. Now I have but a superficial partial knowledg of things, but then I shall have an intuitive comprehensive knowledg of them, as I my self am known and lie open to the view of superior seraphick beings, not by the obscure and imperfect way of deductions and reasoning. [13]But then even in that state Faith, hope, and Charity will remain But the greatest of the three is Charity.

SECTION IX. NO. 5

Ch. XIV.⟨1-40⟩

CONTENTS

St Paul in this Chapter concludes his answer to the Corinthians concerning spiritual men and their gifts, and haveing told them that those were most preferable that tended most to edification and particularly shewn that prophesie was to be preferd to tongues he gives them directions for the decent orderly and profitable exercise of their gifts in their assemblys

TEXT

XIV.1. Follow after ˈcharity, and desireˈ spiritual gifts, but rather that ye may prophesie.

2. For he that speaketh in an unknown tongue, speaketh not unto men, but unto God: for no man understandeth him; howbeit in the spirit he speaketh mysteries.

3. But he that prophesieth, speaketh unto men to edification, and exhortation, and comfort.

4. He that speaketh in an unknown tongue, edifieth himself: but he that prophesieth edifieth the church.

5. I would that ye all spake with tongues, but rather that ye prophesied: for greater is he that prophesieth, than he that speaketh with tongues, except he interpret, that the church may receive edifying.

6. Now brethren, if I come unto you speaking with tongues, what shall I profit you, except I shall speak to you either by revelation, or by knowledge, or by prophesying, or by doctrine?

7. And even things without life giving sound, whether pipe or harp, except they give a distinction in the sounds, how shall it be known what is piped or harped?

8. For if the trumpet give an uncertain sound, who shall prepare himself to the battel?

9. So likewise you, except ye utter by the tongue words easie to be understood, how shall it be known what is spoken? for ye shall speak into the air.

10. There are, it may be, so many kinds of voices in the world, and none of them is without signification.

11. Therefore if I know not the meaning of the voice, I shall be unto him that speaketh, a barbarian; and he that speaketh shall be a barbarian unto me.

12. Even so ye, forasmuch as ye are zealous of spiritual gifts, seek that ye may excel to the edifying of the church.

13. Wherefore let him that speaketh in an unknown tongue, pray that he may interpret.

14. For if I pray in an unknown tongue, my spirit prayeth, but my understanding is unfruitful.

15. What is it then? I will pray with the spirit, and I will pray with the understanding also: I will sing with the spirit, and I will sing with the understanding also.

16. Else when thou shalt bless with the spirit, how shall he that occupieth the room of the unlearned, say Amen at thy giving of thanks, seeing he understandeth not what thou sayest?

17. For thou verily givest thanks well, but the other is not edified.

18. I thank my God, I speak with tongues more than you all:

19. Yet in the church I had rather speak five words with my understanding, that by my voice I might teach others also, than ten thousand words in an unknown tongue.

20. Brethren, be not children in understanding: howbeit, in malice be ye children, but in understanding be men.

21. In the law it is written, With men of other tongues, and other lips will I speak unto this people: and yet for all that will they not hear me, saith the Lord.

22. Wherefore tongues are for a sign, not to them that believe, but to them that believe not: but prophesying serveth not for them that believe not, but for them which believe.

23. If therefore the whole church be come together into one place, and all speak with tongues, and there come in those that are unlearned, or unbelievers, will they not say that ye are mad?

24. But if all prophesie, and there come in one that believeth not, or one unlearned, he is convinced of all, he is judged of all:

25. And thus are the secrets of his heart made manifest; and so falling down on his face he will worship God, and report that God is in you of a truth.

26. How is it then, brethren? when ye come together, every one of you hath a psalm, hath a doctrine, hath a tongue, hath a revelation, hath an interpretation. Let all things be done to edifying.

27. If any man speak in an unknown tongue, let it be by two, or at the most by three, and that by course; and let one interpret.

28. But if there be no interpreter, let him keep silence in the church; and let him speak to himself, and to God.

29. Let the prophets speak two or three, and let the other judge.

30. If any thing be revealed to another that sitteth by, let the first hold his peace.

31. For ye may all prophesie one by one, that all may learn, and all may be comforted.

32. And the spirits of the prophets are subject to the prophets.

33. For God is not the author of confusion, but of peace, as in all churches of the saints.

34. Let your women keep silence in the churches: for it is not permitted unto them to speak; but they are commanded to be under obedience, as also saith the law.

35. And if they will learn any thing, let them ask their husbands at home: for it is a shame for women to speak in the church.

36. What? came the word of God out from you? or came it unto you only?

37. If any man think himself to be a prophet, or spiritual, let him acknowledge that the things that I write unto you, are the commandments of the Lord.

38. But if any man be ignorant, let him be ignorant.

39. Wherefore, brethren, covet to prophesie, and forbid not to speak with tongues.

40. Let all things be done decently, and in order.

PARAPHRASE

XIV.1 Let your endeavours, let your pursuit therefore be after Charity· not that you should neglect* the use of your spiritual gifts espetialy

XIV.1* [a]ζηλοῦτε τὰ πνευματικά. That ζηλοῦν does not signifie to *covet* or *desire* nor can be understood to be soe used by St Paul in this section I have already shewn

the gift of prophesie· [2]For he that speaks in an unknown tongue* speaks
to god alone but not to men· For nobod⟨y⟩ understands him; the things
he utters by the spirit in an unknown tongue are mysterys things not
understood by those who hear them. [3]But he that prophesieth* speaks
to men who are exhorted and comforted thereby and helpd forwards in
religion and piety: [4]He that speaks in an unknown tongue* edifies

Ch. XII.31. That it has here the sense that I have given it is plain from the same direction concerning spiritual gifts repeted ver. 39 in these words [b]ζηλοῦτε τὸ προφητεύειν καὶ τὸ λαλεῖν γλώσσαις μὴ κωλύετε, the meaning in both places being evidently this, That they should not neglect the use of their spiritual gifts, espetialy they should in the first place cultivate and exercise the gift of prophesying but yet should not wholy lay aside the speaking with variety of tongues in their assemblys. [c]It will perhaps be wonderd why St Paul should imploy the word ζηλοῦν in soe unusual a sense but that will easily be accounted for if what I have remarked Ch. XIV.15 concerning St Pauls custome of repeating words be remembred. But besides what is familiar in St Pauls way of writeing, we may find a particular reason for his repeating the word ζηλοῦν here though in a some what unusual signification. [d]He haveing by way of reproof told them that they did ζηλοῦν τα χαρίσματα τὰ ⟨κ⟩ρείτ⟨τ⟩ονα had an emulation or made a stir about whose gifts were best and were therefore to take place in their assemblys, to prevent their thinking that ζηλοῦν might have too harsh a meaning [e](for he is in all this epistle very tender of offending them and therefor sweetens all his reproofs as much as possible) he here takes it up again and uses it more than once in a way that approves and advises that they should ζηλοῦν πνευματικά, whereby yet he means noe more but that they should not neglect their spiritual gifts: He would have them use them in their assemblys but yet in such method and order as he directs.

2* [a]He who attentively reads this section about spir⟨i⟩tual men and their gifts may find reason to imagin that it was those who had the gift of tongues who caused the disorder in the Church at Corinth, by their forwardness to speak and striveing to be heard first and soe takeing up too much of the time in their assemblys in speakeing in unknown tongues. [b]For the remedying this disorder and better regulateing of this matter amongst other things they had recourse to St Paul. He will not easily avoid thinking soe who considers

1° That the first gift, which St Paul compares with Charity Ch: XIII, and extremly undervalues in comparison of that divine virtue, is the gift of tongues. [c]As if that were the gift they most affected to shew and most valued themselves upon, as indeed it was in it self most fited for ostentation in their assemblys of any other, if any one were inclined that way: And that the Corinthians in their present state were not exempt from emulation vanity and ostentation is very evident.

2° [d]That Ch XIV wher St Paul compares their spiritual gifts one with another, the first nay and onely one that he debases and depreciates in comparison of others is the gift of tongues which he discourses of for above 20 verses together in a way fit to abate a too high esteem and a too excessive an use of it in their assemblys, [e]which we can not suppose he would have done had they not been guilty of some such miscariages in the case whereof the 24th ver. is not without an intimation.

3° When he comes to give directions about the exercise of their gifts in their meetings this of tongues is the onely one that he restrains and limits ver. 27.28

3* what is meant by prophesying see Ch: XII.10

4* By γλώσσῃ unknown *tongue* Dr Lightfoot in this Chapter understands the Hebrew tongue which, as he observes, was used in the synagogue in reading the Sacred Scripture, in praying, and in preaching. If that be the meaning of *Tongue* here it suits

himself alone, but he that prophesieth edifieth the church. [5]I wish that ye had all the gift of tongues, but rather that ye all prophesied, for greater is he that prophesieth than he that speaks with tongues unless he interprets what he delivers in an unknown tongue, that the church may be edified by it: [6]For example should I apply my self to you in a tongue you knew not, what good should I doe you unlesse I interpreted to you what I said, that you might understand the revelation, or knowledg, or prophesie, or doctrine* conteined in it? [7]Even inanimate instruments of sound as pipe or harp are not made use of to make an insignificant noise but distinct notes expresseing mirth or mourning or the like are plaid upon them whereby the tune and composure is understood. [8]And if the trumpet sound not some point of warr that is understood the soldier is not thereby instructed what to doe; [9]soe likewise ye unlesse with the tongue which you use ye utter words of a clear and known signification to your hearers, you talke to the wind for your auditors understand noe thing that you say. [10]There is a great number of significant languages in the world, I know not how many, every nation has its own, [11]if then I understand not an others language and the force of his words I am to him when he speaks a barbarian, and what ever he says is all gibbrish to me, [12]And soe is it with you· ye are barbarians to one an other as far as ye speak to one an other in unknown tongues. But since there is emulation amongst you concerning spiritual gifts seeke to abound in the exercise of those which tend most to the edification of the church. [13]Wherefore let him that speaks an unknown tongue pray soe as that he may interpret what he says. [14]For if I pray in the congregation in an unknown tongue my spirit tis true accompanys my words which I understand and soe my

well the Apostles designe which was to take them off from their Jewish false Apostle, who probably might have incouraged and promoted the speaking of Hebrew in their assemblys.

6* [a]'Tis not to be doubted but these four distinct termes used here by the Apostle had each its distinct signification in his mind and intention, whither what may be collected from these Epistles may sufficiently warrant us to understand them thus in the following significations I leave to the judgment of others. [b]1° 'Αποκάλυψις *Revelation*· some thing revealed by god immediately to the person: vid. ver. 30. 2°γνῶσις. *Knowledg*. The understanding the mystical and evangelical sense of passages in the old testament relateing to our saviour and the gospel. 3° προφητεία *Prophesie*· An inspired hymn vid: ver. 26. [c]4° Διδαχή *Doctrine*: Any truth of the gospel concerning faith or maners. But whither this or any other precise meaning of these words can be certainly made out now, it is perhaps of noe great necessity to be over curious, It being enough for the understanding the sense and argument of the Apostle here, to know that these terms stand for some intelligible discourse tending to the edification of the church, though of what kind each of them was in particular we certainly know not.

spirit prays* but my meaning is unprofitable to others who understand not my words. [15]What then is to be done in the case? why, I will when moved to it by the spirit pray in an unknown tongue but soe that my meaning* may be understood by others i e I will not doe it but when there is some body by to interpret.† And soe I will also doe in singing‡ I will sing by the spirit in an unknown tongue but I will take care that the meaning of what I sing shall be understood by the assistants. And thus ye should all doe in all like cases· [16]For if thou by the impulse of the spirit givest thanks to god in an unknown tongue which all understand not how shall the hearer who in this respect is unlearned, and being ignorant in that tongue knows not what thou sayest, how shall he say amen? How shall he joyn in the thanks which he understands not? [17]Thou indeed givest thanks well, but the other is not at all edified by it. [18]I thank god I speak with tongues more than you all, [19]but I had rather speak in the church five words that are understood that I might instruct others also then in an unknown tongue ten thousand that others understand not. [20]My Brethren be not in understanding children* who are apt to be taken with the novelty or strangeness of things: In temper and disposition be as children void of malice† but in matters of understanding be ye perfect men and use your understandings. [21]Be not soe zealous for the use of

14* This is evident from ver. 4th where it is said *he that speaketh with a tongue edifies him self*.

15* [a]I will not pretend to justifie this interpretation of τῷ νοΐ by the exact rules of the Greek idiom But the sense of the place will I think bear me out in it. And, as there is occasion often to remark, he must be little versed in the writeing of St Paul who does not observe that when he has used a terme [b]he is apt to repete it again in the same discourse in a way peculiar to himself and some what varied from its ordinary signification. Soe haveing here in the foregoeing verse used νοῦς for the sentiment of his own mind, which was unprofitable to others when he praid in a tongue unknown to them, and opposed it to πνεῦμα. [c]which he used there for his own sense accompanying his own words intelligible to himself when by the impulse of the spirit he praid in a foraigne tongue, he here in this verse continues to use praying τῷ πνεύματι and τῷ νοΐ in the same opposition the one for praying in a strange tongue which his own mind alone understood and accompanied: [d]the other for praying soe as that the meaning of his mind in those words he utterd was made known to others. soe that they were also benefited. This use of πνεύματι is farther confirmed in the next verse: and what he means by νοΐ here: he expresses by διὰ νοός. ver. 19 and there explains the meaning of it.

† For soe he orders in the use of an unknown tongue ver. 27

‡ Here it may be observed that as in their publick prayer one praid and the others held their peace, soe it was in their singing at least in that singing which was of extempory hymns by the impulse of the spirit.

20* vid Rom XVI.19 Eph IV.13–15

† By κακία *malice* I think is here to be understood all sorts of ill temper of mind contrary to the gentleness and innocence of childhood and in particular their emulation and strife about the exercise of their gifts in their assemblys.

unknown tongues in the church· they are not soe proper there: It is written in the law·* with men of other tongues and other lips will I speak unto this people and yet for all that will they not hear me sayth the Lord. [22]Soe that you see the speaking of strange tongues miraculously is not for those who are already converted but for a signe to those who are unbeleivers: But prophesie is for beleivers and not for unbeleivers, and therefore fitter for your assemblys. [23]If therefore when the church is all come together you should all speake in unknown tongues. and men unlearned or unbeleivers, should come in, would they not say that you are mad? [24]But if ye all prophesie and an unbeleiver or ignorant man come in· the discourses he hears from you reaching his conscience and the secret thoughts of his heart, [25]he is convinced and wrought upon, and soe falling down worships god and declares that god is certainly amongst you. [26]What then is to be done brethren? When ye come together every one is ready.* one with a psalme, an other with a doctrine, an other with a strange tongue, an other with a revelation, an other with interpretation. Let all things be done to edification [27]even though* any one speak in an unknown tongue which is a gift that seems least intended for edification.† Let but two or three at most at any one meeting speak in an unknown

21* The books of Sacred Scripture deliverd to the Jews by divine revelation under the law before the time of the gospel which we now call the old Testament are in the writeings of the New Testament called Sometimes *The law the prophets and the psalms* as Luk XXIV.44. Sometimes *the law and the prophets* as Acts XXIV.14· And sometimes they are all comprehended under this one name *The Law* as here, for the passage cited is in Isayah

26* [a]Tis plain by this whole discourse of the Apostles that there were contentions and emulations amongst them for precedency of their gifts, and therefor I think ἕκαστος ἔχει may be renderd *every one is ready with.* as impatient to be first heard. [b]If there were noe such disorder amongst them there would have been noe need for the regulations given in the end of this verse and the 7 verses following espetialy ver. 31 and 32 where he tels them they may all prophesie one by one, and that the motions of the spirit were not soe ungovernable as not to leave a man master of himself. [c]He must not think himself under a necessity of speaking as soon as he found any impulse of the spirit upon his mind

27* [a]St Paul has said in this Chapter as much as conveniently could be said to restrain their speaking in unknown tongues in their assemblys, which seems to be that wherein the vanity and ostentation of the Corinthians was most forward to shew it self. [b]It is not says he a gift intended for the edification of beleevers, however since you will be exerciseing it in your meetings let it always be soe orderd that it may be for edification. Εἴτε I have renderd *although*. Soe I think it is sometimes used, but noe where as I remember simply for *if* as in our translation, [c]nor will the sense here bear *whither* which is the common signification of εἴτε. And therefore I take the Apostles sense to be this· You must doe noething but to edification, though you speak in an unknown tongue even an unknown tongue must be made use of in your assemblys only to edification

† vid. ver. 2 and 4

tongue and that seperately one after an other and let there be but one
interpreter:‡ [28]But if there be noebody present that can interpret let
not any one use his gift of tongues in the congregation, but let him
silently within him self speak to him self and to god. [29]Of those who
have the gift of prophesie let but two or 3 speak at the same meeting
and let the others examin and discuss it. [30]But if dureing their debate
the meaning of it be revealed to one that sits by let him that was dis-
courseing of it before give off. [31]For ye may all prophesie one after an
other that all may in their turns be hearers and receive exhortation
and instruction. [32]For the gifts of the holy ghost are not like the possession of the heathen priests, who are not masters of the spirit that
possesses them. But Christians however fild with the holy-ghost are
masters of their own actions, can speak or hold their peace as they see
occasion, and are not hurried away by any compulsion. [33]It is therefore noe reason for you to speake more than one at once, or to inter-
rupt one an other because you find your selves inspired and moved by
the spirit of god. For god is not the author of confusion and disorder,
but of quietness and peace. And this is what is observed in all the
Churches of god. [34]As to your women let them keep silence in your
assemblys for it is not permitted them to discourse there or pretend to
teach, that does noe way suit their state of subjection appointed them
in the law. [35]But if they have a mind to have any thing explained to
them that passes in the church let them for their information aske
their husbands at home for it is a shame for women to discourse and
debate with men publiquely in the congregation*

[36]What· doe you pretend to give laws to the church of god or to a
right to doe what you please amongst your selves as if the gospel began
at Corinth and issueing from you was communicated to the rest of the
world or as if it were communicated to you alone of all the world· [37]If
any man amongst you think that he hath the gift of prophesie and
would passe for a man knowing in the revealed will of god* let him

‡ The rule of the Synagogue was. In the law let one read and one interpret. In the prophets Let one read and two interpret. In Esther ten may read and ten interpret. Tis not improbable that some such disorder had been introduced into the church of Corinth by their Judaizeing false Apostle which St Paul would have an end put to.

34·35* Why I apply this prohibition of speakeing only to reasoning and purely voluntary discourse, but suppose a liberty left women to speak where they had an immediate impulse and revelation from the spirit of god. vid Ch: XI.3· In the synagogue it was usual for any man that had a mind, to demand of the teacher a farther explication of what he had said: but this was not permitted to the women.

37* Πνευματικός. *A spiritual man* In the sense of St Paul, is one who founds his knowledg in what is revealed by the spirit of god, and not in the bare discoverys of his natural reason and parts. vid. Ch. II 15.

acknowledg that these rules which I have here given are the commandements of the Lord. [38]But if any man* be ignorant that they are soe I have noe more to say to him. I leave him to his ignorance· [39]To conclude brethren· Let prophesie have the preference in the exercise of it;* but yet forbid not the speaking unknown tongues. [40]But whither a man prophesies or speaks with tongues, whatever spiritual gift he exercises in your assemblys let it be done without any indecorum or disorder.

SECTION X

Ch. XV.1-58

CONTENTS

After St Paul (who had taught them another doctrine) had left Corinth some among them denyd the Resurrection of the dead. This he confutes by Christs resurrection, which the number of witnesses yet remaining that had seen him put past question besides the constant inculcateing of it by all the Apostles every where. From the resurrection of Christ thus established he infers the resurrection of the dead, Shews the order they shall rise in and what Sort of bodys they shall have.

TEXT

XV.1. Moreover, brethren, I declare unto you the gospel which I preached unto you, which also you have received, and wherein ye stand;

2. By which also ye are saved, if ye keep in memory what I preached unto you, unless ye have believed in vain.

3. For I delivered unto you first of all, that which I also received, how that Christ died for our sins according to the scriptures:

4. And that he was buried, and that he rose again the third day according to the scriptures:

5. And that he was seen of Cephas, then of the twelve.

38* By the *any man* mentiond in this and the foregoeing verse St Paul seems to intimate the false Apostle who pretended to give laws amongst them and as we have observed may well be supposd to be the author of these disorders, whom therefor St Paul reflects on and presses in these three verses

39* ζηλοῦν in this whole discourse of St Paul taken to refer to the exercise and not to the obteining the gifts to which it is joynd will direct us right in understanding St Paul and make his meaning very easy and intelligible.

6. After that, he was seen of above five hundred brethren at once: of whom the greater part remain unto this present, but some are fallen asleep:

7. After that, he was seen of James; then of all the apostles.

8. And last of all he was seen of me also, as of one born out of due time.

9. For I am the least of the apostles, that am not meet to be called an apostle, because I persecuted the church of God.

10. But by the grace of God, I am what I am: and his grace which was bestowed upon me, was not in vain; but I laboured more abundantly than they all: yet not I, but the grace of God which was with me.

11. Therefore whether it were I or they, so we preach, and so ye believed.

12. Now if Christ be preached that he rose from the dead, how say some among you, that there is no resurrection of the dead?

13. But if there be no resurrection of the dead, then is Christ not risen.

14. And if Christ be not risen, then is our preaching vain, and your faith is also vain.

15. Yea, and we are found false witnesses of God; because we have testified of God, that he raised up Christ: whom he raised not up, if so be that the dead rise not.

16. For if the dead rise not, then is not Christ raised:

17. And if Christ be not raised, your faith is vain; ye are yet in your sins.

18. Then they also which are fallen asleep in Christ, are perished.

19. If in this life only we have hope in Christ, we are of all men most miserable.

20. But now is Christ risen from the dead, and become the first fruits of them that slept.

21. For since by man came death, by man came also the resurrection of the dead.

22. For as in Adam all die, even so in Christ shall all be made alive.

23. But every man in his own order: Christ the first-fruits, afterward they that are Christs, at his coming.

24. Then cometh the end, when he shall have delivered up the kingdom to God, even the Father; when he shall have put down all rule, and all authority and power.

25. For he must reign till he hath put all enemies under his feet.

26. The last enemy that shall be destroyed, is death.

27. For he hath put all things under his feet. But when he saith all things are put under him, it is manifest that he is excepted which did put all things under him.

28. And when all things shall be subdued unto him, then shall the Son also himself be subject unto him that put all things under him, that God may be all in all.

29. Else what shall they do which are baptized for the dead, if the dead rise not at all? why are they then baptized for the dead?

30. And why stand we in jeopardy every hour?

31. I protest by your rejoycing which I have in Christ Jesus our Lord, I die daily.

32. If after the manner of men I have fought with beasts at Ephesus, what advantageth it me, if the dead rise not? let us eat and drink, for to morrow we die.

33. Be not deceived: Evil communications corrupt good manners.

34. Awake to righteousness, and sin not; for some have not the knowledge of God: I speak this to your shame.

35. But some man will say, How are the dead raised up? and with what body do they come?

36. Thou fool, that which thou sowest is not quickned except it die.

37. And that which thou sowest, thou sowest not that body that shall be, but bare grain, it may chance of wheat, or of some other grain.

38. But God giveth it a body as it hath pleased him, and to every seed his own body.

39. All flesh is not the same flesh: but there is one kind of flesh of men, another flesh of beasts, another of fishes, and another of birds.

40. There are also celestial bodies, and bodies terrestrial: but the glory of the celestial is one, and the glory of the terrestrial is another.

41. There is one glory of the sun, and another glory of the moon, and another glory of the stars; for one star differeth from another star in glory.

42. So also is the resurrection of the dead. It is sown in corruption, it is raised in incorruption:

43. It is sown in dishonour, it is raised in glory: It is sown in weakness, it is raised in power:

44. It is sown a natural body, it is raised a spiritual body. There is a natural body, and there is a spiritual body.

45. And so it is written, The first man Adam was made a living soul, the last Adam was made a quickning spirit.

46. Howbeit, that was not first which is spiritual, but that which is natural; and afterward that which is spiritual.

47. The first man is of the earth, earthy: the second man is the Lord from heaven.

48. As is the earthy, such are they also that are earthy: and as is the heavenly, such are they also that are heavenly.

49. And as we have born the image of the earthy, we shall also bear the image of the heavenly.

50. Now this I say, brethren, that flesh and blood cannot inherit the kingdom of God; neither doth corruption inherit incorruption.

51. Behold, I shew you a mystery; we shall not all sleep, but we shall all be changed,

52. In a moment, in the twinkling of an eye, at the last trump (for the

trumpet shall sound) and the dead shall be raised incorruptible, and we shall be changed.

53. For this corruptible must put on incorruption, and this mortal must put on immortality.

54. So when this corruptible shall have put on incorruption, and this mortal shall have put on immortality, then shall be brought to pass the saying that is written, Death is swallowed up in victory.

55. O death, where is thy sting? O grave, where is thy victory?

56. The sting of death is sin; and the strength of sin is the law.

57. But thanks be to God, which giveth us the victory, through our Lord Jesus Christ.

58. Therefore my beloved brethren, be ye stedfast, unmoveable, always abounding in the work of the Lord, forasmuch as ye know that your labour is not in vain in the Lord.

PARAPHRASE

XV.1 In what I am now goeing to say to you brethren I make known to
you noe other gospel than what I formerly preachd to you, and you
received and have hitherto professed and by which alone you are to be
saved. 2 This you will find to be soe, if you retain in your memorys
what it was that I preachd to you. which you certainly doe, unless you
have taken up the Christian name and profession to noe purpose. 3 For
I deliverd to you, and particularly insisted on this which I had
received viz. that Christ died for our sins according to the Scriptures;
4 and that he was buried and that he was raised again the third day
according to the Scriptures; 5 and that he was seen by Peter; 6 Afterwards by the twelve Apostles, and after that by above five hundred
Christians at once, of whom the greatest part remain alive to this day,
but some of them are deceased; 7 Afterwards he was seen by James;
and after that by all the Apostles. 8 Last of all he was seen by me also as
by one borne before my time.* 9 For I am the least of the Apostles not
worthy the name of an Apostle because I persecuted the church of
god. 10 But by the free bounty of god I am what it hath pleased him to
make me: And this favour which he hath bestowed on me hath not
been altogether fruitless, for I have labourd in preaching of the gospel
more than all the other Apostles* which yet I doe not ascribe to any

XV.8* An abortive birth that comes before its time which is the name St Paul gives him self here is usualy suddain and at unawares and is also weak and feeble scarce deserveing to be called or counted a man. The former part agrees to St Pauls being made a Christian and an Apostle. Though it be in regard of the later that in the following verse St Paul cals himself abortive.

10* St Paul drops in this commendation of himself to keep up his credit in the Church of Corinth where there was a faction labouring to discredit him

thing of my self but to the favour of god which accompanied me. [11]But whither I or the other Apostles preached this was that which we preached; and this was the faith ye were baptised into viz that Christ died and rose again the third day. [12]If therefore this be soe, If this be that which has been preachd to you viz that Christ has been raised from the dead; how comes it that some* amongst you say as they doe that there is noe resurrection of the dead? [13]And if there be noe resurrection of the dead, then even Christ himself is not risen: [14]And if Christ be not risen our preaching is idle talk, and your beleiveing it is to noe purpose. [15]And we who pretend to be witnesses for god and his truth shall be found liars bearing witness against god and his truth affirming that he raised Christ, whom in truth he did not raise, if it be soe that the dead are not raised. [16]For if the dead shall not be raised neither is Christ raised. [17]And if Christ be not risen your faith is to noe purpose, your sins are not forgiven but you are still liable to the punishment due to them. [18]And they also who died in the beleif of the gospel. are perished and lost· [19]If the advantages we expect from Christ are confined to this life and we have noe hope of any benefit from him in an other life hereafter we Christians are the most miserable of all men. [20]But in truth Christ is actualy risen from the dead and is become the firstfruits* of those who were dead. [21]For since by man came death, by man came also the resurrection of the dead or restauration to life. [22]For as the death that all men suffer is oweing to Adam soe the life that all shall be restored to again is procured them by Christ. [23]But they shall return to life again not all at once but in their proper order· Christ the first-fruits is already risen: Next after him shall rise those who are his people his church and this shall be at his second comeing. [24]After that shall be the day of Judgment. which shall bring to a conclusion and finish the whole dispensation to the race and posterity of Adam in this world. when Christ shall have

12* [a]This may well be understood of the head of the contrary faction and some of his scholers

1° because St Paul introduces this confutation by asserting his mission which these his opposers would bring in question

[b]2° because he is soe careful to let the Corinthians see he maintains not the doctrine of the resurrection in opposition to these their new leaders, It being the doctrine he had preachd to them at their first conversion before any such false Apostle appeard among them and mislead them about the resurrection. [c]Their false Apostle was a Jew and in all appearance Jewdaized, May he not also be suspected of Saducisme? For 'tis plain he with all his might opposed St Paul. which must be from some main difference in opinion at the bottom. for there are noe footsteps of any personal provocation

20* The first fruits was a smal part which was first taken and offered to god and sanctified the whole mass which was to follow

deliverd up the kingdome to god and the father, which he shall not doe till he hath destroid all empire power and authority that shall be in the world besides. [25]For he must reigne till he has totaly subdued and brought all his enemies into subjection to his Kingdom· [26]The last enemy that shall be destroid is death· [27]For god hath subjected all things to Christ but when it is said all things are subjected, it is plain that he is to be excepted who did subject all things to him. [28]But when all things shall be actualy reduced under subjection to him then even the son himself. i e Christ and his whole kingdome he and all his subjects and members shall be subjected to him that gave him this kingdome and universal dominion that god may immediately governe and influence all: [29]Else* what shall they do who are baptized for the dead† and why doe we venture our lives continually? [30]As to my self I am exposed, villefied treated soe that I die dayly. [31]and for this I call to witness your glorying against me in which I really glory as comeing on me for our Lord Jesus Christs sake· [32]And particularly to what purpose did I suffer my self to be exposed to wild beasts at Ephesus if the dead rise not? If there be noe resurrection 'tis wiser a great deale to preserve our selves as long as we can in a free injoyment of all the pleasures of this life, for when death comes as it shortly will there is an end of us forever. [33]Take heed that ye be not mislead by such discourses for evil communication is apt to corrupt even good minds. [34]Awake from such dreams as tis fit you should, and give not your selves up sinfully to the enjoyments of this life. For there are some* Atheistical people among you. This I say to make you ashamd. [35]But possibly it will be asked. How comes it that men dead are raised? And with what kind of bodys doe they come?* Shall they have at the

29* [a]*Else* here relates to ver. 20. where it is said *Christ is risen*. St Paul haveing in that verse mentioned Christ being the first-fruits from the dead takes occasion from thence now that he is upon the Resurrection, to informe the Corinthians of several particularitys relateing to the resurrection [b]which might inlighten them about it and could not be known but by revelation· Haveing made this excursion in the eight preceding verses he here in the 29th reassumes the thread of his discourse and goes on with his arguments for beleiveing the Resurrection.

† What this baptizeing for the dead was I confess I Know not: but it seems by the following verses to be something wherein they exposed them selves to the danger of death.

34* May not this probably be said to make them ashamd of their leader whom they were soe forward to glory in? For tis not unlikely that their questioning. and denying the Resurrection came from their new Apostle who raisd such opposition against St Paul

35* [a]If we will allow St Paul to know what he says, it is plain from what he answers that he understands these words to contein two questions. 1° How comes it to pass that dead men are raised to life again· would it not be better they should live on; why doe they die to live again? [b]2° With what bodys shall they return to life? To both these he

resurrection such bodys as they have now? 36 Thou fool Does not dayly
experience teach thee that the seed which thou sowest corrupts and
dies before it springs up and lives again? 37 That which thou sowest is
the bare grain of wheat or barely, or the like, but the body which it has
when it rises up is different from the seed that is sown. 38 For it is not
the seed that rises up again but a quite different body such as god hath
thought fit to give it, viz. a plant of a particular shape and size which
god has appointed to each sort of seed. 39 And soe likewise it is in
animals· there are different kinds of flesh·* for the flesh of men is of
one kind; the flesh of cattle is of another kind: That of fish is different
from them both: and the flesh of birds is of a peculiar sort different
from them all. 40 To look yet farther into the difference of bodys· There
be both heavenly and earthly bodys, but the beauty and excellency of
the heavenly bodys is of one kind. and that of earthly bodys of an
other. 41 The sun moon and stars have each of them their particular
beauty and brightness and one star differs from another in glory·
42 And soe shall the resurrection of the dead* be· 43 That which is sown

distinctly answers viz That those who are raised to an heavenly state shall have other bodys: and next that it is fit that men should die, death being noe improper way to the attaining other bodys· [c]This he shews there is soe plain and common an instance of in the sowing of all seeds that he thinks it a foolish thing to make a difficulty of it: and then proceeds to declare that as they shall have other so they shall have better bodys than they had before viz spiritual and incorruptible

39* The scope of the place makes it evident that by *Flesh* St Paul here means bodys viz That god has given to the several sorts of animals bodys in shape texture and organization very different one from an other as he has thought good, and soe he can give to men at the resurrection bodys of very different constitutions and qualitys from those they had before.

42* [a]*The resurrection of the dead* here spoken of is not the resurrection of all man kind in common but only the resurrection of the Just: This will be evident to any one who observes that St Paul having ver. 22 declared that all men shall be made alive again tells the Corinthians ver. 23 that it shall not be all at once but at several distances of time. [b]First of all Christ rose: Afterwards next in order to him the saints should all be raised. which resurrection of the Just is that which he treats and gives an account of to the end of this discourse and chapter. and soe never comes to the resurrection of the wicked which was to be the third and last in order. [c]Soe that from the 23 ver. to the end of this chapter all that he says of the resurrection is a discription onely of the resurrection of the Just though he cals it here by the general name of the resurrection of the dead. That this is soe there is soe much evidence that there is scarse a verse from the 41 to the end that does not evince it

[d]1° What in this resurrection is raised St Paul assures us ver. 43 is raised in glory but the wicked are not raised in glory.

2° He says. *we* (speakeing in the name of all that shall be then raised) shall bear the image of the heavenly Adam ver. 49 which cannot belong to the wicked. [e]*We* shall all be changd that by puting on incorruptibility and immortality death may be swallowed up of victory which god giveth *us* through our Lord Jesus Christ ver. 51.52.53.54.57 which cannot likewise belong to the damned. And therefore *we* and *us* here must be under-in this world* and comes to die is a poor weak contemptible corruptible thing. When it is raised again it shall be powerfull glorious and incorruptible. [44]The body we have here surpasses not the animal

stood to be spoken in the name of the dead that are Christs who are to be raised by them selves befor the rest of mankind.

[f]3° He says ver. 52 that when the dead are raised they who are alive shall be changed in the twinkleing of an eye. Now that these *dead* are onely the dead in Christ which shall rise first and shall be caught up in the clouds to meet the Lord in the air is plain from 1 Thess. IV.16.17.

[g]4° He teaches ver. 54 that by this Corruptible's putting on incorruption is brought to pass the saying, that death is swallowed up of victory. But I think noe body will say that the wicked have victory over death: yet that according to the Apostle here belongs to all those whose corruptible bodys have put on incorruption: [h]which therefore must be onely those that rise the second in order. From whence it is clear that their resurrection alone is that which is here mentioned and discribed

5° A farther proof whereof is ver. 56.57. In that their sins being taken away the sting whereby death kils is taken away: [i]And hence St Paul says god has given *us* the victory which is the same *us* or *we* who should bear the image of the heavenly Adam ver. 49. And the same *We* who should *all* be changed ver. 51.52. All which places can therefore belong to none but those who are Christs who shall be raised by themselves the second in order before the rest of the dead

[j]Tis very remarkable what St Paul says in this 51 ver. We shall not *all* sleep but we shall *all* be changed in the twinkleing of an eye. The reason he gives for it ver. 53 is because this corruptible thing must put on incorruption, and this mortal thing must put on immortality. [k]How? Why by putting off flesh and blood by an instantaneous change because as he tels us ver. 50 flesh and blood cannot inherit the kingdom of god, and therefore to fit beleivers for that kingdom, those who are alive at Christs comeing shall be changed in the twinkling of an eye, [l]and those that are in their graves shall be changed likewise at the instant of their being raised and soe *all* the whole collection of the saints all the members of Christs body shall be put into a state of incorruptibility ver. 52. in a new sort of bodys

[m]Takeing the resurrection here spoken of to be the resurrection of all the dead promiscuously St Pauls reasoning in this place can hardly be understood. But upon a supposition that he here describes the resurrection of the Just onely that resurrection which as he say⟨s⟩ ver. 23, is to be next after Christs and separate from the rest, [n]there is noe thing can be more plain natural and easy than St Pauls reasoning, and it stands thus. Men alive are flesh and blood, the dead in the graves are but the remains of corrupted flesh and blood, but flesh and blood cannot inherit the kingdom of god; neither corruption inherit incorruption i e immortality. [o]therefor to make all those who are Christs capable to enter into his eternall kingdom of life, as well those of them who are alive, as those of them who are raised from the dead shall all in the twinkleing of an eye be *all* changed and their corruptible shall put on incorruption and their mortal shall put on immortality, and thus god gives them the victory over death through their lord Jesus Christ. [p]This is in short St Paul argueing here and the account he gives of the resurrection of the blessed. But how the wicked who were afterwards to be restored to life were to be raised, and what was to become of them he here say⟨s⟩ noe thing, as not being to his present purpose which was to assure the Corinthians by the resurrection of Christ, [q]of a happy resurrection to beleivers and thereby to incourage them to continue stedfast in the faith which had such a reward. That this was his designe may be seen by the begining of his discourse ver. 12-21. and by the conclusion ver. 58 in these words. [r]*Wherefore my beloved brethren be ye stedfast unmoveable always abounding in the worke of the Lord forasmuch as ye know that your labour is not in vain in the Lord*. Which words shew that

 [*See p. 254 for n. XV.42* cont. and n. XV.43**]

nature, at the resurrection it shall be spiritual. There are both animal*
and spiritual bodys· 45 And soe it is written· The first man Adam was
made a liveing soul i e made of an animal constitution indowed with
an animal life· the second Adam was made of a spiritual constitution
with a power to give life* to others· 46 Howbeit the spiritual was not
first but the animal and afterwards the spiritual· 47 The first man was of
the earth made up of dust or earthy particles. the second man is the
Lord from heaven. 48 Those who have noe higher an extraction than
barely from the earthy man they like him have barely an animal life or
constitution. But those who are regenerate and borne of the heavenly
seed are, as he that is heavenly, spiritual and immortal· 49 And as in the
animal corruptible mortal state we were born in we have been like him
that was earthy soe also shall we who at the resurrection partake of

what he had been speaking of in the immediately preceding verses, viz, their being changd and the puting on of incorruption and immortality [s]and their haveing thereby the victory through Jesus Christ was what belongd soly to the Saints as a reward to those who remaind stedfast and abounded in the work of the Lord.

[t]The like use of the like though shorter discourse of the resurrection where in he describes only that of the blessed he make⟨s⟩ to the Thessalonians 1 Thess: IV.13-18. which he concludes thus: *Wherefore comfort one an other with these words*.

[u]Nor is it in this place alone that St Paul cals the resurrection of the Just by the general name of the resurrection of the dead. He does the same Phil: III.11. where he speaks of his sufferings and of his indeavours if by any means he might attain unto the resurrection of the dead. [v]whereby he can not mean the resurrection of the dead in general which since as he has declared in this very chapter ver. 22 all men both good and bad shall as certainly partake of as that they shall all die· there needs noe indeavours to attain to it. [w]Our saviour likewise speaks of the resurrection of the Just in the same general terms of *the resurrection* Mat XXII.30 and *the resurrection from the dead* Luk XX 35 by which is meant onely the resurrection of the Just as is plain from the context

43* The time that man is in this world affixed to this earth is his being sown and not when being dead he is put in the grave as is evident from St Pauls own words. For dead things are not sown, seeds are sown being alive, and die not till after they are sown. Besides he that will attentively consider what follows will find reason from St Pauls argueing to understand him so.

44* [a]Σῶμα ψυχικόν which in our bibles is translated *natural body* should I think more suitably to the propriety of the Greek and more confor⟨m⟩able to the Apostles meaning be translated *Animal body*· For that which St Paul is doeing here is to shew that as we have animal bodys now (which we derived from Adam) endowed with an animal life [b]which unless suported with a con⟨s⟩tant supply of food and air will fail and perish and at last, doe what we can, will dissolve and come to an end. Soe at the resurrection we shall have from Christ the second Adam *spiritual bodys* which shall have an essential and naturaly inseperable life in them [c]which shall continue and subsist perpetualy of itself without the help of meat drink or air or any such forain support without decay or any tendency to a dissolution· of which our Saviour speaking Luk XX.35 says. *They who shall be accounted worthy to* obtain that world and the resurrection from the dead can not die any more for they are equall to the angels. i e are of an Angelical nature and constitution

45* vid Phil III.21

a spiritual life from Christ be made like him the Lord from heaven heavenly. i e live as the spirits in heaven doe without the need of food or nourishment to support it, and without infirmitys decay and death. injoying a fixed stable unfleeting life. [50]This I say to you Brethren to satisfie those that aske with what bodys the dead shall come, that we shall not at the resurrection have such bodys as we have now· For flesh and blood cannot enter into the kingdom which the saints shall inherit in heaven: Nor are such fleeting corruptible things as our present bodys are fitted to that state of immutable incorruptibility. [51]To which let me adde what has not been hitherto discoverd. viz that we shall not all die but we shall all be changed [52]in a moment in the twinkleing of an eye at the sounding of the last trumpet. for the trumpet shall sound and the dead shall rise, and as many of us beleivers as are then alive shall be changed. [53]For this corruptible frame and constitution* of ours must put on incorruption and from mortal become immortal. [54]And when we are got into that state of incorruptibility and immortality then shall be fulfilled what was foretold in these words· Death is swallowed up of victory i e Death is perfectly subdued and exterminated by a complete victory over it soe that there shall be noe death any more. [55]Where o Death is now that power whereby thou deprivest

53* [a]Tὸ φ⟨θ⟩αϱτὸν τοῦτο *this corruptible* and τὸ θνητὸν τοῦτο *This mortal* have not here σῶμα *body* for their substantive as some imagin but are put in the neuter gender absolute and stand to represent νεκϱοί as appears by the immediately preceding ver. and also ver. 42. οὕτω καὶ ἀνάστασις τῶν νεκϱῶν σπείϱεται ἐν φθοϱᾷ *soe is the resurrection of dead persons· it is sown in corruption*. [b]i e Mortal corruptible men are sown being corruptible and weak. Nor can it be thought strange or strained that I interpret φθαϱτόν and θνητόν as adjectives of the Neuter gender to signifie persons, when in this very discourse the Apostle uses two adjectives in the neuter gendre to signifie the persons of Adam and Christ in such a way as makes it impossible to understand them other wise. [c]The words no farther off than ver. 46 are these ἀλλὰ οὐ πϱῶτον τὸ πνευματικὸν ἀλλὰ τὸ ψυχικὸν ἔπειτα τὸ πνευματικόν. The like way of speaking we have Mat I.20 Luk I.35. in both which places the p⟨e⟩rson of our Saviour is expressed by adjectives of the neuter gender, to any one of all which places I doe not think any one will adde the substantive σῶμα body to make out the sense. [d]That then which is meant here being this. that this mortal man shall put on immortality, and this corruptible man incorruptibility any one will easily find an other nominative case to σπείϱεται *is sown* and not σῶμα body when he considers the sense of the place, where in the apostles purpose is to speak of νεκϱοί *mortal men* being dead and raised again to life and made immortal. [e]Those with whom grammatical construction and the nominative case weighs so much may be pleased to read this Passage in Virgil

Linquebant dulces animas. aut aegra trahebant
Corpora ____________ aeniad: l. 3. ver. 140.

[f]where by finding the nominative case to the two verbs in it he may come to discover that personality as contradistinguishd both to body and soule may be the nominative case to verbs.

men of life? What is become of the dominion of the grave whereby they were deteined prisoners there.* [56]That which gives death the power over men is sin, and tis the law by which sin has this power· [57]But thanks be to god who gives us deliverance and victory over death the punishment of sin by the law through our Lord Jesus Christ who has deliverd us from the rigor of the law. [58]Wherefore my beloved brethren continue stedfast and unmoveable in the Christian faith. all ways abounding in your obedience to the precepts of Christ and in those dutys which are requird of us by our Lord and Saviour· Knowing that your labour will not be lost. whatsoever you shall doe or suffer for him will be aboundantly rewarded by eternal life.

SECTION XI

Ch. XVI. 1-4

CONTENTS

He gives directions concerning their contribution to the poor Christians at Jerusalem

TEXT

XVI. 1. Now concerning the collection for the saints, as I have given order to the churches of Galatia, even so do ye.

2. Upon the first day of the week, let every one of you lay by him in store, as God hath prospered him, that there be no gatherings when I come.

3. And when I come, whomsoever you shall approve by your letters, them will I send to bring your liberality unto Jerusalem.

4. And if it be meet that I go also, they shall go with me.

PARAPHRASE

[XVI.1]As to the Collection for the converts to Christianity who are at Jerusalem I would have you doe as I have directed the Churches of Galatia. [2]Let every one of you according as he thrives in his calling lay a side some part of his gain by it self which the first day of the week let him put into the common treasury* of the church that there may be

55* This has something the air of a song of triumph which St Paul breaks out into Upon a view of the Saints victory over death in a State where in death is never to have place any more

XVI.2* θησαυρίζων seems used here in the sense I have given it· For tis certain that the Apostle directs that they should every Lords day bring to the congregation what

noe need of any gathering when I come. [3]And when I come those whom you shall approve of, will I send with letters* to Jerusalem to carry thither your benevolence. [4]Which if it deserves that I also should goe they shall goe along with me.

SECTION XII

Ch. XVI.5-12

CONTENTS

He gives them an account of his own, Timothies and Apollos's intention of comeing to them.

TEXT

XVI.5. Now I will come unto you, when I shall pass through Macedonia: (for I do pass through Macedonia)

6. And it may be that I will abide, yea, and winter with you, that ye may bring me on my journey, whithersoever I go.

7. For I will not see you now by the way, but I trust to tarry a while with you, if the Lord permit.

8. But I will tarry at Ephesus until Pentecost.

9. For a great door and effectual is opened unto me, and there are many adversaries.

10. Now if Timotheus come, see that he may be with you without fear: for he worketh the work of the Lord, as I also do.

11. Let no man therefore despise him: but conduct him forth in peace, that he may come unto me: for I look for him with the brethren.

12. As touching our brother Apollos, I greatly desired him to come unto you with the brethren: but his will was not at all to come at this time; but he will come when he shall have convenient time.

their charity had laid a side the foregoeing week, as their gains came in, that there it might be put into some publick box appointed for that purpose or officers hands. For if they onely laid it aside at home there would neverthe lesse be need of a collection when he came

3* [a]δοκιμά(σ)ητε, δι' ἐπιστολῶν τούτους πέμψω this pointing that makes δι' ἐπιστολῶν belong to πέμψω and not to δοκιμάσητε the Apostles sense justifies. He telling them here that finding their collection ready when he came he would write by those they should think fit to send it by, [b]or goe himself with them if their present were worthy of it. There needed no approbation of their messengers to him by their letters when he was present: And if the Corinthians by their letters approved of them to the Saints at Jerusalem how could St Paul say he would send them

PARAPHRASE

XVI.5 I will come unto you when I have been in Macedonia for I intend
to take that in my way: 6 And perhaps I shall make some stay, nay winter,
with you. That you may bring me goeing on my way whethersoever I
goe. 7 For I doe not intend just to call in upon you as I pass by: but I hope
to spend some time with you, if the Lord permit· 8 But I shall stay at
Ephesus till Pentecost i e Whitsontide. 9 For now I have a very fair and
promiseing oportunity given me of propagateing the gospel though
there be many opposers.

10 If Timothy come to you pray take care that he be easy and without
fear amongst you. for he promotes the work of the Lord in preaching
the gospel even as I doe. 11 Let noe body therefor dispise him but treat
him kindly, and bring him goeing that he may come unto me for I
expect him with the brethren

12 As to brother* Apollos I have earnestly endeavourd to prevaile with
him to come to you with the brethren† but he has noe mind to it at all at
present. He will come however when there shall be a fit occasion

SECTION XIII

Ch. XVI.13-24

CONTENTS

The Conclusion. where in St Paul according to his custom leaves with them some which he thinks most necessary exhortations and sends particular greetings.

TEXT

XVI.13. Watch ye, stand fast in the faith, quit you like men, be strong.

14. Let all your things be done with charity.

15. I beseech you, brethren, (ye know the house of Stephanas, that it is the first fruits of Achaia, and that they have addicted themselves to the ministry of the saints)

16. That ye submit your selves unto such, and to every one that helpeth with us and laboureth.

XVI.12* There be few perhaps who need to be told it, yet it may be convenient here once for all to remarke that in the Apostles time *Brother* was the ordinary compellation that Christians used to one an other

† The *Brethren* here mentioned seem to be Stephanas and those other who with him came with a message or letter to St Paul from the church of Corinth. by whom he returned this Epistle in answer.

17. I am glad of the coming of Stephanas, and Fortunatus, and Achaicus: for that which was lacking on your part they have supplied.

18. For they have refreshed my spirit and yours: therefore acknowledge ye them that are such.

19. The churches of Asia salute you. Aquila and Priscilla salute you much in the Lord, with the church that is in their house.

20. All the brethren greet you. Greet ye one another with an holy kiss.

21. The salutation of me Paul with mine own hand.

22. If any man love not the Lord Jesus Christ, let him be Anathema, Maranatha.

23. The grace of our Lord Jesus Christ be with you.

24. My love be with you all in Christ Jesus. Amen.

PARAPHRASE

XVI.13 Be upon your guard. Stand firme in the faith. Behave your selves
like men with courage and resolution, 14 and whatever is donne amongst
you either in your publick assemblys or elsewhere let it all be done with
affection and good will one to an other*

15 You know the house of Stephanas that they were the first converts
of Achaia, and have all along made it their business to minister to the
saints, 16 to such I beseech you to submit your selves: Let such as with us
labour to promote the gospel be your leaders. 17 I am glad that Stephanas Fortunatus and Achaicus came to me: because they have supplied
what was deficient on your side. 18 For by the account they have given
me of you they have quieted my mind and yours too* Therefore have a
regard to such men as these. 19 The Churches of Asia salute you. and soe
doe Aquila and Priscilla with much Christian affection, with the church
that is in their house. 20 All the brethren here salute you. 21 Salute one
another with an holy kiss. That which followeth is the salutation of me
Paul with my own hand. 22 If any one be an enemie to the Lord Jesus
Christ and his gospel, let him be accursed or devoted to destruction.*
The Lord cometh to execute vengeance on him. 23 The favour of the
Lord Jesus Christ be with you. 24 My love be with you all in Christ Jesus.
Amen.

XVI.14* His main designe being to put an end to the faction and division which the false Apostle had made amongst them tis noe wonder that we find unity and Charity soe much and soe often pressed in this and the second Epistle

18* Viz. By removeing those suspitions and fears that were on both sides

22* This being soe different a sentence from any of those writ with St Pauls own hands in any of his other Epistles may it not with probability be understood to mean the false Apostle? to whom St Paul imputes all the disorders of this church and of whom he speaks not much less severely 2 Cor XI.13-15

A PARAPHRASE AND NOTES ON THE SECOND EPISTLE OF ST PAUL TO THE CORINTHIANS

2 CORINTHIANS

Anno Christi 57
Neronis 3

SYNOPSIS

[a]St Paul haveing writ his first Epistle to the Corinthians to trye as he says himself Chap: II.9 what power he had still with that Church wherein there was a great faction against him which he was attempting to break, was in pain till he found what success it had. II.12.13. VII.5. [b]But when he had by Titus received an account of their repentance upon his former letter; of their submission to his orders; and of their good disposition of mind towards him, he takes courage, speaks of him self more freely and justifies himself more boldly as may be seen I.12. II.14-VI.10. X.1-XIII.10· [c]And as to his opposers he deals more roundly and sharply with them than he had done in his former Epistle as appears from II.17. IV.2-5 V.12. VI.11-16 XI.11 XII.15.

[d]The observation of these particulars may possibly be of use to give us some light for the better understanding of this second Epistle· Espetially if we adde that the main business of this as of his former Epistle is to take off the people from the new Leader they had got who was St Pauls opposer, and wholy to put an end to the faction and disorder which that false Apostle had caused in the Church of Corinth. He also in this Epistle stirs them up again to a liberal contribution to the poor saints at Jerusalem

[e]This Epistle was writ in the same year not long after the former

SECTION I

Ch. I.1.2

TEXT

I.1. Paul an apostle of Jesus Christ by the will of God, and Timothy our brother, unto the church of God which is at Corinth, with all the saints which are in all Achaia:

2. Grace be to you, and peace from God our Father, and from the Lord Jesus Christ.

INTRODUCTION

I.1 Paul an Apostle of Jesus Christ by the will of god and Timothy our Brother* to the Church of god which is in Corinth with all the Christians that are in all Achaia† 2 Favour and peace be to you from god our father and from the Lord Jesus Christ

SECTION II

Ch. I.3-VII.16

CONTENTS

This first part of this 2d Epistle of St Paul to the Corinthians is spent in Justifying himself against several imputations from the opposite faction· And seting himself right in the opinion of the Corinthians. The particulars whereof we shall take notice of in the following numbers.

SECTION II. NO. 1

Ch. I.3-14

CONTENTS

[a]He begins with Justifying his former letter to them which had afflicted them vid VII.7.8 by telling them that he thanks god for his deliverance out of his afflictions because it inables him to comfort them by the example both of his affliction and deliverance [b]acknowledging the obligation he had to them and others for their prayers and thanks for his deliverance which he presumes they could not but put

I.1* [a]*Brother* i e either in the common faith, and soe, as we have already remarked he frequently calls all the converted as Rom I.13 and in other places. or *Brother* in the work of the ministry vid. Rom XVI.21. I Cor ⟨XVI⟩ 10. [b]To which we may adde that St Paul may be supposed to have given Timothy the title of *Brother* here for dignitys sake, to give him a reputation above his age amongst the Corinthians, to whom he had before sent him with some kind of authority to rectifie their disorders. [c]Timothy was but a yonge man when St Paul writ his first epistle to him as appears 1 Tim. IV.12 which Epistle by the consent of all was writ to Timothy after he had been at Corinth and in the opinion of some very learned men not less than 8 years after [d]and therefor his calling him brother here and joyning him with himself in writeing this Epistle may be to let the Corinthians see that though he were soe yonge who had been sent to them yet it was one whom St Paul thought fit to treat very much as an Equal

† Achaia the country wherein Corinth stood

up for him since his conscience bears him witness (which was his comfort) that in his cariage to all men and to them more espetially he had been direct and sincere without any self or carnal interest and [c]that what he writ to them had noe other designe but what lay open and they read in his words and did also acknowledg, and he doubted not but they should alway acknowledg, part of them acknowledging also that he was the man they gloried in as they shall be his glory in the day of the Lord. [d]From what St Paul says in this section (which if read with attention will appear to be writ with a turn of great insinuation) it may be gathered that the opposite faction indeavourd to evade the force of the former Epistle by suggesting that what ever he might pretend St Paul that was a cunning artificial self-interested man had some hidden designe in it which accusation appears in other parts also of this Epistle as IV.2.5

TEXT

I.3. Blessed be God, even the Father of our Lord Jesus Christ, the Father of mercies, and the God of all comfort;

4. Who comforteth us in all our tribulation, that we may be able to comfort them which are in any trouble, by the comfort wherewith we our selves are comforted of God.

5. For as the sufferings of Christ abound in us, so our consolation also aboundeth by Christ.

6. And whether we be afflicted, it is for your consolation and salvation, which is effectual in the enduring of the same sufferings which we also suffer: or whether we be comforted, it is for your consolation and salvation.

7. And our hope of you is stedfast, knowing that as you are partakers of the sufferings, so shall ye be also of the consolation.

8. For we would not, brethren, have you ignorant of our trouble which came to us in Asia, that we were pressed out of measure, above strength, insomuch that we despaired even of life:

9. But we had the sentence of death in our selves, that we should not trust in our selves, but in God which raiseth the dead.

10. Who delivered us from so great a death, and doth deliver: in whom we trust that he will yet deliver us:

11. You also helping together by prayer for us, that for the gift bestowed upon us by the means of many persons, thanks may be given by many on our behalf.

12. For our rejoicing is this, the testimony of our conscience, that in simplicity and godly sincerity, not with fleshly wisdom, but by the grace of God, we have had our conversation in the world, and more abundantly to you-wards.

13. For we write none other things unto you, than what you read or acknowledge, and I trust you shall acknowledge even to the end.

14. As also you have acknowledged us in part, that we are your rejoicing, even as ye also are ours in the day of the Lord Jesus.

PARAPHRASE

[I.3]Blessed be the god* and father of our Lord Jesus Christ the father
of mercys and god of all consolation. [4]who comforteth me in all my
tribulations, that I may be able to comfort them* who are in any
trouble by the comfort which I receive from him. [5]Because as I have
suffered aboundantly for Christ, soe through Christ I have been abundantly comforted. [6]And both these for your advantage. For my affliction is for your consolation and releif,* which is effected by a patient
endureing those sufferings whereof you see an example in me: And
again when I am comforted it is for your consolation and releif who
may expect the like from the same compassionate god and father,
[7]upon which ground I have firm hopes as concerning you being
assured that as you have had your Share of sufferings soe ye shall like
wise have of Consolation. [8]For I would not have you ignorant Brethren of the load of the afflictions in Asia that were beyond measure
heavy upon me and beyond my strength soe that I could see noe way
of escapeing with life. [9]But I had the sentence of death in my self that I
might not trust in my self but in god, [10]who can restore to life even
those who are actualy dead, who delivered me from soe eminent a
danger of death, who doth deliver, and in whom I trust he will yet
deliver me· [11]you also joyning the assistance of your prayers for me so
that thanks may be returned by many for the deliverance p⟨ro⟩cured
me by the prayers of many persons. [12]For I cannot doubt of the
prayers and concerne of you and many others for me since my glorying is this viz the testimony of my own conscience that in plainess of
heart and sincerity before god, not in fleshly wisdome* but by the
favour of god directing me† I have behaved my self towards all men
but more particularly towards you. [13]For I have noe designe, noe

I.3* That this is the right translation of the Greek here see Eph. I.3. and 1 Pet. I.3 where the same words are soe translated and that it is their true meaning see Eph. I.17

4* He means here the Corinthians who were troubled for their miscariage towards him vid. VII.7

6* σωτηρία *releif* rather than *Salvation* which is understood of deliverance from death and hell, but here it signifies onely deliverance from their present sorrow.

12* What *fleshly wisdome* is may be seen Ch. IV.2.5

† This ἀλλ᾽ ἐν χάριτι θεοῦ *But in the favour of god* is the same with ἀλλὰ χάρις θεοῦ ἡ σὺν ἐμοί *The favour of god that is with me*. i e by gods favourable assistance

meaning in what I write to you but what lies open and is legible in what you read, and you your selves cannot but acknowledg it to be soe and I hope you shall always acknowledg it to the end: [14]as part of you have already acknowledgd that I am your glory* as you will be mine at the day of judgment when being my scholars and converts ye shall be saved.

SECTION II. NO. 2

Ch. I.15-II.17

CONTENTS

[a]The next thing St Paul justifies is his not comeing to them: St Paul had promised to call on the Corinthians in his way to Macedonia, but failed. This his opposers would have to be from Levity in him, or a mind that regulated it self wholy by carnal interest vid ver. 17· [b]To which he answers that god himself haveing confirmed him amongst them by the unction and earnest of his spirit in the ministry of the gospel of his son whom he Paul had preachd to them steadily the same, without any the least variation or unsaying any thing he had at any time deliverd, [c]they could have no ground to suspect him to be an unstable uncertain man that would play fast and loose with them and could not be depended on in what he said to them. This is what he says I.15-22

In the next place he with a very solemn asseveration professes that it was to spare them that he came not to them· This he explains I.23-II.11.

[d]He gives an other reason II.12.13 why he went on to Macedonia without comeing to Corinth as he had purposed and that was the uncertainty he was in by the not comeing of Titus, what temper they were in at Corinth. Haveing mentioned his journey to Macedonia he takes notice of the success which god gave to him there and every-where: [e]declareing of what consequence his preaching was both to the salvation and condemnation of those who received or rejected it: pro-fessing again his sincerity and disinteressedness, not without a severe reflection on their false Apostle. [f]All which we find in the following

14* *That I am your glory* whereby he signifies that part of them which stuck to him and owned him as their teacher, in which sense *glorying* is much used in these Epistles to the Corinthians upon the occasion of the several partisans boasting some that they were of Paul and others of Apollos.

verses viz II.14-17. and is all very suitable and pursuant to his designe in this Epistle. which was to Establish his authority and credit amongst the Corinthians.

TEXT

I.15. And in this confidence I was minded to come unto you before, that you might have a second benefit:

16. And to pass by you into Macedonia, and to come again out of Macedonia unto you, and of you to be brought on my way toward Judea.

17. When I therefore was thus minded, did I use lightness? or the things that I purpose, do I purpose according to the flesh, that with me there should be yea, yea, and nay, nay?

18. But as God is true, our word toward you, was not yea and nay.

19. For the Son of God, Jesus Christ, who was preached among you by us, even by me, and Silvanus, and Timotheus, was not yea and nay, but in him was yea.

20. For all the promises of God in him are yea, and in him amen, unto the glory of God by us.

21. Now he which stablisheth us with you in Christ, and hath anointed us is God:

22. Who hath also sealed us, and given the earnest of the Spirit in our hearts.

23. Moreover, I call God for a record upon my soul, that to spare you I came not as yet unto Corinth.

24. Not for that we have dominion over your faith, but are helpers of your Joy: for by faith ye stand.

II.1. But I determined this with my self, that I would not come again to you in heaviness.

2. For if I make you sorry, who is he then that maketh me glad, but the same which is made sorry by me?

3. And I wrote this same unto you, lest when I came, I should have sorrow from them of whom I ought to rejoice, having confidence in you all, that my joy is the joy of you all.

4. For out of much affliction and anguish of heart, I wrote unto you with many tears; not that you should be grieved, but that ye might know the love which I have more abundantly unto you.

5. But if any have caused grief, he hath not grieved me, but in part: that I may not overcharge you all.

6. Sufficient to such a man is this punishment which was inflicted of many.

7. So that contrariwise ye ought rather to forgive him, and comfort him, lest perhaps such a one should be swallowed up with overmuch sorrow.

8. Wherefore I beseech you, that ye would confirm your love towards him.

9. For to this end also did I write, that I might know the proof of you, whether ye be obedient in all things.

10. To whom ye forgive any thing, I forgive also: for if I forgave any thing, to whom I forgave it, for your sakes forgave I it, in the person of Christ;

11. Lest satan should get an advantage of us: for we are not ignorant of his devices.

12. Furthermore, when I came to Troas to preach Christ's gospel, and a door was opened unto me of the Lord,

13. I had no rest in my spirit, because I found not Titus my brother: but taking my leave of them, I went from thence into Macedonia.

14. Now thanks be to God, which always causeth us to triumph in Christ, and maketh manifest the savour of his knowledge by us in every place.

15. For we are unto God a sweet savour of Christ, in them that are saved, and in them that perish.

16. To the one we are the savour of death unto death; and to the other the savour of life unto life: and who is sufficient for these things?

17. For we are not as many, which corrupt the word of God: but as of sincerity, but as of God, in the sight of God speak we in Christ.

PARAPHRASE

[I.15]Haveing this perswasion (viz) of your love and esteem of me, I purposed to come unto you ere this that you might have a second gratification* [16]and to take you in my way to Macedonia, and from thence return to you again, and by you be brought on in my way to Judea. [17]If this fell not out soe as I purposed; Am I therefore to be condemned of fickleness? or am I to be thought an uncertain man that talkes forwards and backwards, one that has noe regard to his word any farther than may suit his carnal interest? [18]But god is my witness that what you have heard from me has not been uncertain, deceitfull or variable. [19]For Jesus Christ the Son of god who was preachd among you by me and Silvanus and Timotheus was not sometimes one thing and sometimes an other but has been shewn to be uniformly one and the same in the counsel or revelation of god. [20](for all the promises of god doe all consent and stand firme in him) to the glory of god by my preaching. [21]Now it is god who establishes me with you for the

I.15* By the word χάρις which our bibles translate *benefit* or *grace* tis plain the Apostle means his being present among them a second time without giveing them any greif or displeasure. He had been with them before almost two years togeather with satisfaction and kindness. He intended them an other visit but it was he says that they might have the like gratification. i e the like satisfaction in his company a second time which is the same he says 2 Cor II.1

preaching of the gospel who has anoynted* [22]and also sealed* me and given me the earnest† of his spirit in my heart.

[23]Moreover I call god to witness and may I die if it be not soe that it was to spare you that I came not yet to Corinth. [24]Not that I pretend to such a dominion over your faith. as to require you to beleive what I have taught you without comeing to you, when I am expected there to maintain and make it good. For 'tis by that faith you stand. But I forbore to come as one concerned to preserve and help forwards your joy which I am tender of, and therefore declined comeing to you whilst I thought you in an estate that would require severity from me that would trouble you.* [II.1]I purposed in my self, tis true, to come to you again but I resolvd too it should be without bringing sorrow with me* [2]For if I greive you, who is there when I am with you to comfort me but these very persons whom I have discomposed with greif? [3]And this

21* *Anoynted* i e set apart to be an Apostle by an extraordinary cal. Preists and prophets were set apart by anoynting as well as Kings

22* *Sealed* i e by the miraculous gifts of the holy ghost, which are an evidence of the truths he brings from god as a seale is of a letter

† [a]*Earnest* of eternal life for of that the spirit is mentioned as a pledg in more places than one vid 2 Cor. V.5 Eph. I.13.14· All these are arguments to satisfie the Corinthians that St Paul was not, nor could be a shuffleing man that minded not what he said but as it served his turne

[b]The reasoning of St Paul ver. 18-22 whereby he would convince the Corinthians that he is not a fickle unsteady man that says and unsays as may suit his humor or interest being a little obscure by reason of the shortness of his stile here [c]which has left many things to be supplied by the reader to connect the parts of the argumentation and make the deduction clear· I hope I shall be pardond if I endeavour to set it in its clear light for the sake of Ordinary readers

'[d]God hath set me apart to the ministry of the Gospel by an extraordinary call; has 'attested my mission by the miraculous gifts of the holy ghost and given me the earnest 'of eternal life in my heart by his spirit. and hath confirmd me amongst you in preaching 'the gospel, [e]which is all uniforme and of a peice as I have preached it to you without 'triping in the least and thereby to the glory of god have shewn that all the promises 'concurr and are unalterably certain in Christ, [f]I therefore haveing never falterd in any 'thing I have said to you and haveing all these attestations of being under the special 'direction and guidance of god himself who is unalterably true cannot be suspected of 'dealeing doubly with you in any thing relateing to my ministry.'

24* [a]It is plain St Pauls doctrine had been opposed by some of them at Corinth vid: 1 Cor: XV.12; his Apostleship questioned 1 Cor IX 1.2. 2 Cor XIII.3: He himself triumphed over as if he durst not come 1 Cor IV.18 they saying his letters were weighty and powerfull; but his bodily presence weak and his speech contemptible 2 Cor X.10· [b]This being the state his reputation was then in at Corinth. and he haveing promised to come to them 1 Cor XVI.5 he could not but think it necessary to excuse his failing them by reasons that should be both convinceing and kind such as are conteined in this verse in the sense given of it.

II.1* That this is the meaning of this verse, and not that he would not come to them in sorrow a second time, is past doubt, since he had never been with them in sorrow a first time. vid 2 Cor I.15

very thing* which made you sad I writ to you not comeing my self, on
purpose that when I came I might not have sorrow from those from
whom I ought to receive comfort, haveing this beleif and confidence
in you all, that you all of you make my joy and satisfaction soe much
your own that you would remove all cause of disturbance before I
came· [4]For I writ unto you with great sadness of heart and many tears,
not with an intention to greive you, but that you might know the over-
flow of tenderness and affection which I have for you. [5]But if the
Fornicator has been the cause of greif I doe not say he has been soe to
me, but in some degree to you all. that I may not lay load on him,* [6]the
correction he hath received from the majority of you is sufficient in
the case, [7]Soe that on the contrary* it is fit rather that you forgive and
comfort him, least he† should be swallowed up by an excesse of
sorrow. [8]Wherefore I beseech you to confirm your love to him which I
doubt not of. [9]For this also was one end of my writeing to you viz to
have a trial of you and to know whither you are ready to obey me in all
things. [10]To whom you forgive any thing, I also forgive. For if I have
forgiven any thing, I have forgiven it to him for your sakes by the
authority and in the name of Christ [11]that we may not be over-reached
by Sathan for we are not ignorant of his wiles

[12]Furthermore being arived at Troas because Titus whom I
expected from Corinth with news of you was not come I was very

3* [a]καὶ ἔγραψα ὑμῖν τοῦτο αὐτό. *And I writ to you this very thing*. That ἔγραψα *I writ* relates here to the first Epistle to the Corinthians is evident because it is soe used in the very next verse and again a little lower ver. 9. [b]What therefore, is it in his first Epistle which he here cals τοῦτο αὐτό *this very thing* which he had writ to them? I answer the punishment of the Fornicator. This is plain by what follows here to ver. 11 espetialy if it be compared with 1 Cor IV.21-V.8 [c]For there he writes to them to punish that person, whom if he St Paul had come himself before it was done, he must have come, as he cals it, with a rod, and have himself chastised: [d]But now that he knows that the Corinthians have punishd him in compliance to his letter and he had had this triall of their obedience, he is soe far from continueing the severity, that he writes to them to forgive him and take him again into their affection.

5* St Paul being satisfied with the Corinthians for their ready complyance with his orders in his former letter to punish the fornicator intercedes to have him restored and to that end lessens his fault and declares however he might have caused greif to the Corinthians yet he had caused none to him

7* Τοὐναντίον *On the contrary* here has noe thing to refer to but ἐπιβαρῶ *overcharge* in the 5th ver. which makes that to belong to the forni⟨cator as⟩ I have explained it.

† [a]ὁ τοιοῦτος *such an one* meaning the Fornicator. It is observable how tenderly St Paul deals with the Corinthians in this Epistle, for though he treats of the Fornicator from the 5th to the 10th ver. inclusively, yet he never mentions him under that or any other disobleigeing title; [b]but in the soft and inoffensive terms of *any one* or *such an one*. And that possibly may be the reason why he says μὴ ἐπιβαρῶ indefinitely without nameing the person it relates to.

uneasy* there in soe much that I made not use of the oportunity which was put into my hands by the Lord of preaching the gospel of Christ, for which I came thither, [13]I hastily left those of Troas and departed thence to Macedonia. [14]But thanks be to god in that he always makes me triumph every where* through Christ, gives me success in preaching the gospel, and spreads the knowledg of Christ by me. [15]For my ministry and labour in the gospel is a service or sweet smelling sacrifice to god through Christ both in regard of those that are saved and those that perish: [16]to the one, my preaching is of ill savour unacceptable and offensive, by their rejecting whereof they draw death on themselves; and to the other being as a sweet savour acceptable they thereby receive eternal life. And who is sufficient for these things?* and yet, as I said, my service in the gospel is well-pleaseing to god. [17]For I am not as several* are who are Hucksters of the word of god preaching it for gain: But I preach the gospel of Jesus Christ in Sincerity. I speak as from god himself, and I deliver it as in the presence of god.

SECTION II. NO. 3

Ch. III.1-VII.16

CONTENTS

[a]His speaking well of himself (as he did sometimes in his first Epistle and with much more freedome in this) which as it seems had been objected to him amongst the Corinthians: His plainess of Speech: And his sincerity in preaching the gospell, are the things which he cheifly justifies in this section many ways. [b]We shall observe his arguments as they come, in the order of St Pauls discourse in which are mingled with great insinuation many expressions of an overflowing kindness to the Corinthians, not without some exhortations to them.

12* How uneasy he was and upon what account see Ch VII 5-16. It was not barely for Titus's absence but for want of the news he brought with him VII.7.

14* *Who makes me triumph every where*. i e in the success of my preaching in my journey to Macedonia, and also in my victory at the same time at Corinth over the false Apostles my opposers that had raised a faction against me amongst you. This I think is St Pauls meaning and the reason of his useing the word *triumph* which implys contest and victory, though he places that word soe as modestly to cover it.

16* vid III.5.6

17* This I think may be understood of the false Apostle

TEXT

III.1. Do we begin again to commend our selves? or need we, as some others, epistles of commendation to you, or letters of commendation from you?

2. Ye are our epistle written in our hearts, known and read of all men:

3. Forasmuch as ye are manifestly declared to be the epistle of Christ, ministred by us, written not with ink, but with the Spirit of the living God; not in tables of stone, but in fleshly tables of the heart.

4. And such trust have we through Christ to Godward.

5. Not that we are sufficient of our selves to think any thing as of our selves: but our sufficiency is of God.

6. Who also hath made us able ministers of the new testament, not of the letter, but of the spirit: for the letter killeth but the spirit giveth life.

7. But if the ministration of death written and engraven in stones, was glorious, so that the children of Israel could not stedfastly behold the face of Moses, for the glory of his countenance, which glory was to be done away;

8. How shall not the ministration of the spirit be rather glorious?

9. For if the ministration of condemnation be glory, much more doth the ministration of righteousness exceed in glory.

10. For even that which was made glorious, had no glory in this respect, by reason of the glory that excelleth.

11. For if that which is done away was glorious, much more that which remaineth is glorious.

12. Seeing then that we have such hope, we use great plainness of speech.

13. And not as Moses, which put a vail over his face, that the children of Israel could not stedfastly look to the end of that which is abolished.

14. But their minds were blinded: for until this day remaineth the same vail untaken away, in the reading of the old testament; which vail is done away in Christ.

15. But even unto this day, when Moses is read, the vail is upon their heart.

16. Nevertheless, when it shall turn to the Lord, the vail shall be taken away.

17. Now the Lord is that Spirit: and where the Spirit of the Lord is, there is liberty.

18. But we all with open face, beholding as in a glass the glory of the Lord, are changed into the same image, from glory to glory, even as by the Spirit of the Lord.

IV.1. Therefore seeing we have this ministry, as we have received mercy we faint not:

2. But have renounced the hidden things of dishonesty, not walking in craftiness, nor handling the word of God deceitfully, but by manifestation of the truth, commending our selves to every mans conscience in the sight of God.

3. But if our gospel be hid, it is hid to them that are lost:

4. In whom the god of this world hath blinded the minds of them which believe not, lest the light of the glorious gospel of Christ, who is the image of God, should shine unto them.

5. For we preach not our selves, but Christ Jesus the Lord; and our selves. your servants for Jesus sake.

6. For God who commanded the light to shine out of darkness, hath shined in our hearts, to give the light of the knowledge of the glory of God, in the face of Jesus Christ.

7. But we have this treasure in earthen vessels, that the excellency of the power may be of God, and not of us.

8. We are troubled on every side, yet not distressed; we are perplexed, but not in despair;

9. Persecuted, but not forsaken; cast down, but not destroyed.

10. Always bearing about in the body, the dying of the Lord Jesus, that the life also of Jesus might be made manifest in our body.

11. For we which live, are alway delivered unto death for Jesus sake, that the life also of Jesus might be made manifest in our mortal flesh.

12. So then death worketh in us, but life in you.

13. We having the same spirit of faith, according as it is written, I believed, and therefore have I spoken: we also believe, and therefore speak;

14. Knowing that he which raised up the Lord Jesus, shall raise up us also by Jesus, and shall present us with you.

15. For all things are for your sakes, that the abundant grace might, through the thanksgiving of many, redound to the glory of God.

16. For which cause we faint not, but though our outward man perish, yet the inward man is renewed day by day.

17. For our light affliction, which is but for a moment, worketh for us a far more exceeding and eternal weight of glory;

18. While we look not at the things which are seen, but at the things which are not seen: for the things which are seen, are temporal; but the things which are not seen are eternal.

V.1. For we know, that if our earthly house of this tabernacle were dissolved, we have a building of God, an house not made with hands, eternal in the heavens.

2. For in this we groan earnestly, desiring to be cloathed upon with our house which is from heaven:

3. If so be, that being cloathed, we shall not be found naked.

4. For we that are in this tabernacle do groan, being burdened: not for that we would be uncloathed, but cloathed upon, that mortality might be swallowed up of life.

5. Now he that hath wrought us for the self-same thing, is God, who also hath given unto us the earnest of the Spirit.

6. Therefore we are always confident, knowing that whilst we are at home in the body, we are absent from the Lord:

7. (For we walk by faith, not by sight)

8. We are confident, I say, and willing rather to be absent from the body, and to be present with the Lord.

9. Wherefore we labour, that whether present or absent we may be accepted of him.

10. For we must all appear before the judgment-seat of Christ, that every one may receive the things done in his body, according to that he hath done, whether it be good or bad.

11. Knowing therefore the terror of the Lord, we perswade men; but we are made manifest unto God, and I trust also are made manifest in your consciences.

12. For we commend not our selves again unto you, but give you occasion to glory on our behalf, that you may have somewhat to answer them which glory in appearance, and not in heart.

13. For whether we be besides our selves, it is to God: or whether we be sober, it is for your cause.

14. For the love of Christ constraineth us, because we thus judge, that if one died for all, then were all dead:

15. And that he died for all, that they which live, should not henceforth live unto themselves, but unto him which died for them, and rose again.

16. Wherefore henceforth know we no man after the flesh: yea, though we have known Christ after the flesh, yet now henceforth know we him no more.

17. Therefore if any man be in Christ, he is a new creature: old things are past away, behold, all things are become new.

18. And all things are of God, who hath reconciled us to himself by Jesus Christ, and hath given to us the ministry of reconciliation;

19. To wit, that God was in Christ, reconciling the world unto himself, not imputing their trespasses unto them; and hath committed unto us the word of reconciliation.

20. Now then we are ambassadours for Christ, as though God did beseech you by us: we pray you in Christs stead, be ye reconciled to God.

21. For he hath made him to be sin for us, who knew no sin; that we might be made the righteousness of God in him.

VI.1. We then as workers together with him, beseech you also, that ye receive not the grace of God in vain.

2. (For he saith, I have heard thee in a time accepted, and in the day of salvation have I succoured thee: behold, now is the accepted time; behold, now is the day of salvation)

3. Giving no offence in any thing, that the ministery be not blamed:

4. But in all things approving our selves as the ministers of God, in much patience, in afflictions, in necessities, in distresses,

5. In stripes, in imprisonments, in tumults, in labours, in watchings, in fastings,

6. By pureness, by knowledge, by long suffering, by kindness, by the holy Ghost, by love unfeigned,

7. By the word of truth, by the power of God, by the armour of righteousness, on the right hand and on the left,

8. By honour and dishonour, by evil report and good report: as deceivers, and yet true;

9. As unknown, and yet well known; as dying, and behold, we live; as chastened, and not killed;

10. As sorrowful, yet alway rejoicing; as poor, yet making many rich; as having nothing, and yet possessing all things.

11. O ye Corinthians, our mouth is open unto you, our heart is enlarged.

12. Ye are not straitned in us, but ye are straitned in your own bowels.

13. Now for a recompense in the same, (I speak as unto my children) be ye also enlarged.

14. Be ye not unequally yoked together with unbelievers: for what fellowship hath righteousness with unrighteousness? and what communion hath light with darkness?

15. And what concord hath Christ with Belial? or what part hath he that believeth with an infidel?

16. And what agreement hath the temple of God with idols? for ye are the temple of the living God; as God hath said, I will dwell in them, and walk in them; and I will be their God, and they shall be my people:

17. Wherefore come out from among them, and be ye separate, saith the Lord, and touch not the unclean thing; and I will receive you,

18. And will be a father unto you, and ye shall be my sons and daughters, saith the Lord almighty.

VII.1. Having therefore these promises (dearly beloved) let us cleanse our selves from all filthiness of the flesh and spirit, perfecting holiness in the fear of God.

2. Receive us: we have wronged no man, we have corrupted no man, we have defrauded no man.

3. I speak not this to condemn you: for I have said before, that you are in our hearts to die and live with you.

4. Great is my boldness of speech toward you, great is my glorying of you: I am filled with comfort, I am exceeding joyful in all our tribulation.

5. For when we were come into Macedonia, our flesh had no rest, but we were troubled on every side; without were fightings, within were fears.

6. Nevertheless, God that comforteth those that are cast down, comforted us by the coming of Titus:

7. And not by his coming only, but by the consolation wherewith he was comforted in you, when he told us your earnest desire, your mourning, your fervent mind toward me; so that I rejoyced the more.

8. For though I made you sorry with a letter, I do not repent, though I did repent: for I perceive that the same epistle made you sorry, though it were but for a season.

9. Now I rejoyce, not that ye were made sorry, but that ye sorrowed to repentance: for ye were made sorry after a godly manner, that ye might receive damage by us in nothing.

10. For godly sorrow worketh repentance to salvation not to be repented of: but the sorrow of the world worketh death.

11. For behold, this self same thing that ye sorrowed after a godly sort, what carefulness it wrought in you, yea, what clearing of your selves, yea, what indignation, yea, what fear, yea, what vehement desire, yea, what zeal, yea, what revenge: in all things ye have approved your selves to be clear in this matter.

12. Wherefore though I wrote unto you, I did it not for his cause that had done the wrong, nor for his cause that suffered wrong, but that our care for you in the sight of God might appear unto you.

13. Therefore we were comforted in your comfort: yea, and exceedingly the more joyed we for the joy of Titus, because his spirit was refreshed by you all.

14. For if I have boasted any thing to him of you, I am not ashamed; but as we spake all things to you in truth, even so our boasting which I made before Titus is found a truth.

15. And his inward affection is more abundant toward you, whilst he remembreth the obedience of you all, how with fear and trembling you received him.

16. I rejoyce therefore that I have confidence in you in all things.

PARAPHRASE

III.1 Doe I begin again to Commend my self?* or need I, as some,† commendatory letters to or from you? 2 You are my commendatory epistle written in my heart known and read by all men. 3 I need noe other commendatory letter but that, you being manifested to be the commendatory epistle of Christ written on my behalf not with ink but with the spirit of the liveing god, not on tables of Stone but of the heart διακονηθεῖσα ⟨ὑφ'⟩ ἡμῶν, whereof I was the amanuensis. i e your conversion was the effect of my ministry* 4 And this so great

III.1* This is a plain indication that he had been blamed amongst them for commending himself

† Seems to intimate that their false Apostle had got him self recommended to them by letters and soe had introduced himself into that Church.

3* [a]The sense of St Paul in this 3d ver: is plainly this. That he needed noe letters of commendation to them, but that by their conversion and the gospel written not with ink but with the spirit of god in the tables of their hearts and not in tables of stone by his ministry [b]was as clear an evidence and testimony to them of his mission from Christ as the law writ in tables of stone was an evidence of Moses's mission, soe that he St Paul

confidence* have I through Christ in god. [5]Not as if I were sufficient
of my self to recon* upon any thing as of my self but my sufficiency my
ability to performe any thing is wholy from god, [6]who has fitted and
enabled me to be a minister of the new Testament not of the letter*
but of the spirit. for the letter kils† but the spirit gives life. [7]But if the
ministry of the law written in stone which condems to death were soe
glorious to Moses that his face shone soe that the children of Israel
could not steadily behold the brightness of it which was but temporary and was quickly to vanish.* [8]How can it be otherwise but that

needed noe other recommendation. This is what is to be understood by this verse unless we will make *the tables of stone* to have noe signification here. [c]But to say as he does that the Corinthians being writ upon in their hearts not with ink but with the spirit of god by the hand of St Paul was Christs commendatory letter of him [d]being a pretty bold expression liable to the exception of the captious part of the Corinthians· he to obviate all imputation of vanity or vain-glory herein immediately subjoyns what follows in the next verse

4⟨,5⟩* [a]As if he had said. But mistake me not as if I boasted of my self. This soe great boasting that I use is only my confidence in god through Christ. For it was god that made me minister of the gospel, that bestowed on me the ability for it; and whatever I performe in it is wholy from him

[b]Πεποίθησις *Trust* a milder word for *boasting* for soe St Paul uses it Ch: X.7 compared with ver. 8 where also λογίζεσθαι ver. 7. is used as here for counting upon ones self· St Paul also uses πέποιθας for *thou boastest* Rom II.19 which will appear if compared with ver. 17· [c]But if λογίσασθαι shall rather be thought to signifie here, to discover by reasoning, then the Apostles sense will run thus· 'Not as if I were sufficient of my selfe by the 'strength of my own natural parts or abilitys to attain the knowledg of the gospel truths 'that I preach but my ability herein is all from god'. [d]But in whatever sense λογίσασθαι is here taken 'tis certain τι which is translated *any thing* must be limited to the subject in hand viz the gospel that he preached to them.

6* [a]οὐ γράμματος ἀλλὰ πνεύματος. *Not of the letter but of the Spirit*. By expresseing himself as he does here St Paul may be understood to intimate that *the new Testament* or *covenant* was also though obscurely held forth in the law. [b]For he says he was constituted a minister πνεύματος *of the Spirit* or spiritual meaning of the law which was Christ (as he tels us him self ver. 17.) and giveth life, whilst the *letter* killeth. But both *letter* and *spirit* must be understood of the same thing, viz *the letter* of the law, and *the spirit* of the law. [c]And in fact we find St Paul truly a minister of the spirit of the law, espetialy in his epistle to the Hebrews where he shews what a spiritual sense ran through the Mosaical institution and writeings

† *The letter kils*. i e pronounceing death, without any way of remission, on all transgressors leaves them under an irrevocable sentence of death. But the spirit i e Christ ver. 17 who is a quickening spirit. 1 Cor XV.45. giveth life

7* [a]καταργουμένη *done away* is applied here to the shineing of Moses's face; and to the law ver. 11 and 13. in all which places it is used in the present tense and has the signification of an adjective standing for temporary or of a duration whose end was determined [b]and is opposed to τῷ μένοντι. *that which remaineth*. i e that which is lasting and hath noe predetermined end set to it, as ver. 11 where the gospel dispensation is called τὸ μένον *that which remaineth*· [c]This may help us to understand ἀπὸ δόξης εἰς δόξαν ver. 18 *from glory to glory* which is manifestly opposed to δόξ⟨α⟩ καταργουμένη the *glory done away* of this verse, And so plainly signifies a continued lasting glory of the

the ministry of the spirit which giveth life should confer more glory and
luster on the ministers of the gospel? [9]For if the ministration of condemnation were glory, the ministry of justification* in the gospel doth
certainly much more exceed in glory. [10]Though even the glory that
Moses's ministration had, was noe glory in comparison of the far more
excelling glory of the gospel ministry* [11]Farther if that which is temporary and to be done away were deliverd with glory how much rather
is, that which remains without being done away, to appear in glory.*
[12]Wherefore haveing such hope* we use great freedom and plainess of
speech: [13]And not as Moses who put a vail over his face, doe we vaile the
light soe that the obscurity of what we deliver hinders* the children of

ministers of the gospel: [d]which as he tels us there consisted in their being changed into the image and clear representation of the Lord him self, as the glory of Moses consisted in the transitory brightness of his face which was a faint reflection of the glory of god appearing to him in the mount.

9* Διακονία τῆς δικαιοσύνης *The ministration of righteousness*. Soe the ministry of the gospel is called, because by the gospel a way is provided for the Justification of those who have transgressed: But the law has noe thing but rigid condemnation for all transgressors and therefore is called here *the ministration of condemnation*.

10* [a]Though the shewing that the ministry of the gospel is more glorious than that of the law be what St Paul is upon here, thereby to justifye himself if he has assumed some authority and commendation to him self in his ministry and Apostleship; [b]yet in his thus ind⟨u⟩striously placeing the ministry of the Gospel in honour above that of Moses may he not possibly have an eye to the Jewdaizeing false Apostle of the Corinthians. to let them see what litle regard was to be had to that ministration in comparison of the ministry of the gospel?

11* Here St Paul mentions an other preeminency and superiority of glory in the gospel over the law viz that the law was to cease and be abolished but the gospel to remain and never be abolished.

12* [a]*Such hope*. That St Paul by these words means the soe honourable employment of an Apostle and minister of the gospel or the glory belonging to his ministry in the gospel is evident by the whole foregoeing comparison which he has made which is all a long between διακονία *the ministry* of the law and of the gospel, and not between the law and the gospel themselves. [b]The calling of it *hope* insted of glory here where he speaks of his own haveing of it, is the language of modestie, which more particularly suited his present purpose. For the conclusion which in this verse he draws from what went before, plainly shews the Apostles designe in this discourse to be the justifying his speaking freely of himself and others, his argument amounting to thus much. [c]'Haveing 'therefore soe honourable an imployment as is the ministry of the gospel, which far 'exceeds the ministry of the law in glory, though even that gave soe great a luster to 'Moses's face, that the children of Israel could not with fixed eyes look upon him, I as 'becomes one of such hopes, in such a post as sets me above all mean considerations 'and compliances, use great freedom and plainess of speech in all things that concerne 'my ministry'

13* [a]Πρὸς τὸ μὴ ἀτενίσαι. etc *That the children of Israel could not steadfastly look* etc· St Paul is here justifyeing in him self and other ministers of the gospel, the plainess and openess of their preaching which he had asserted in the immediately preceding verse. [b]These words therefore here must of necessity be understood not of Moses, but of the ministers of the gospel. viz that it was not the obscurity of their preaching, not any thing

Israel from seeing in the law, which was to be done away, Christ who was the end† of the law: [14a]But their not seeing it is from the blindness of their own minds: For unto this day the same vail remains upon their understandings in reading of the old Testament which vayle is done away in Christ. [b]i e. Christ now he is come soe exactly answers all the types prefigurations and predictions of him in the old Testament that presently upon turning our eyes upon him he visibly appears to be the person designed and all the obscurity of those passages concerning him which before were not understood is taken away and ceases. [15]Nevertheless even until now when the writeings of Moses are read the vayl* remains upon their hearts, they see not the spiritual and Evangelical truths conteined in them. [16]But when their heart shall turn to the Lord and laying by prejudice and aversion shall be willing to receive the truth the vayl shall be taken away and they shall plainly see him to be the person spoken of and intended.* [17]But the Lord is the spirit* whereof we are ministers and they who have this spirit they have liberty† soe that they speak openly and freely. [18]But we all the faithfull ministers of the new

veyled in their way of proposeing the gospel which was the cause why the children of Israel did not understand the law to the bottom and see Christ the end of it in the writeings of Moses. [c]What St Paul says in the next verse *But their minds were blinded: for until this day remaineth the same vail untaken away* plainly determin the words we are upon to the sense I have taken them in. For what sense is this? [d]*Moses put a vail over his face soe that the children of Israel could not see the end of the law; but their minds were blinded: for the vail remains upon them untill this day*. But this is very good sense and to St Pauls purpose viz 'We the ministers of the gospel speak plainly and openly and put noe vail upon our 'selves [e]as Moses did whereby to hinder the Jews from seeing Christ in the law: But that 'which hinders them is a blindness on their minds, which has been always on them and 'remains to this day.' [f]This seems to be an obviateing an objection which some among the Corinthians might make to his boasting of soe much plainess and clearness in his preaching. viz if you preach the gospel and Christ conteind in the law with such a shineing clearness and evidence how comes it that the Jews are not converted to it? [g]His reply is 'Their unbeleif comes not from any obscurity in our preaching but from a 'blindness which rests upon their minds to this day, which shall be taken away when 'they turn to the Lord.'

† vid Rom X:2-4

15* St Paul possibly alludes here to the custome of the Jews which continues still in the Synagogue that when the law is read they put a vail over their faces

16* When this shall be see Rom XI.25-27

17* ὁ δὲ κύριος τὸ πνεῦμά ἐστι. *But the Lord is that Spirit·* These words relate to ver. 6 where he says that he is a minister not of the letter of the law, not of the outside and literal sense but of the mystical and spiritual meaning of it which here he tels us is Christ.

† *There is liberty*. Because the spirit is given onely to sons, or those that are free. see Rom. VIII.15. Gal IV.6.7.

Testament not vailed* but with open countenances as mirors reflecting the glory of the Lord are changed into his very image by a continued succession of glory as it were streaming upon us from the Lord who is the Spirit who gives us this clearness and freedom. [IV.1]Seeing therefore I am intrusted with such a ministry as this according as I have received great mercy, being extraordinarily and miraculously called when I was a persecutor, I doe not fail* nor flag, I doe not

18* [a]St Paul justifies his freedome and plainess of speech by his being made by god himself a minister of the gospel which is a more glorious ministry than that of Moses in promulgateing the law. This he does from ver. 6 to ver. 12 inclusively. [b]From thence to the end of the Chapter he justifies his liberty of speakeing in that he as a minister of the gospel being illuminated with greater and brighter rays of light than Moses, was to speak (as he did) with more freedome and clearness than Moses had done. [c]This being the scope of St Paul in this place tis visible that all from these words *who put a vaile upon his face* ver. 13 to the begining of ver. 18 is a parenthesis, which being laid aside, the comparison between the ministers of the gospel and Moses stands clear

[d]'Moses with a vayl coverd the brightness and glory of god which shone in his coun-'tenance: But we the ministers of the gospel with open countenances κατοπτριζόμενοι 'reflecting as mirors the glory of the Lord' soe the word κατοπτριζόμενοι must signifie here, [e]and not *beholding as in a miror*. because the comparison is between the ministers of the Gospel and Moses and not between the ministers of the gospel and the Children of Israel. Now the action of *Beholding* was the action of the children of Israel but of *Shineing or refle⟨c⟩ting the glory received in the mount* was the action of Moses [f]and therefore it must be some thing answering that in the ministers of the gospel wherein the comparison is made. as is farther manifest in an other express part of the comparison between the vailed face of Moses ver. 13. and the open face of the ministers of the gospel in this verse. [g]The face of Moses was vailed that the bright shineing or glory of god remaining on it or reflected from it might not be seen and the faces of the ministers of the gospel are open that the bright shineing of the gospel or the glory of Christ may be seen. [h]Thus the justness of the comparison stands fair and has an easy sense, which is hard to be made out if κατοπτριζόμενοι be translated *Beholding as in a glass*.

[i]Τὴν αὐτὴν εἰκόνα μεταμορφούμεθα *we are changed into that very image*. i e The reflection of the glory of Christ from us is soe very bright and clear that we are changed into his very image, whereas the light that shone in Moses's countenance was but a faint reflection of the glory which he saw when god shewd him his back parts Exod XXXIII.23

[j]Ἀπὸ δόξης εἰς δόξαν *from glory to glory* i e with a continued influx and renewing of glory, in opposition to the shineing of Moses's face which decaid and disappeard in a little while: ver. 7.

[k]Καθάπερ ἀπὸ κυρίου πνεύματος. *as from the Lord the spirit*. i e as if this irradiation of light and glory came immediatly from the sourse of it the Lord himself who is that Spirit whereof we are the ministers ver. 6 which giveth life and liberty ver. 17.

[l]This liberty he here speaks of ver. 17 is παρρησία *liberty of speech* mentioned ver. 12 the subject of St Pauls discourse here, as is farther manifest from what immediately follows in the six first verses of the next chapter wherein an attentive reader may find a very clear comment on this 18 ver. we are upon, which is there explaind in the sense we have given of it.

IV.1* [a]οὐκ ἐκκακοῦμεν *we faint not* is the same with πολλῇ παρρησίᾳ χρώμεθα *we use great plainess of speech* ver. 12 of the foregoeing Chapter and signifies in both places the clear plain direct disinterested preaching of the gospel, which is what he means in that figurative way of speaking in the former chapter, [b]especialy the last verse of it, and

behave my self unworthily in it nor misbecomeing the honour and dignity of such an imployment. [2]But haveing renounced all unworthy and indirect* designes which will not bear the light, free from craft and from playing any deceitful tricks in my preaching the word of god I recommend my self to every ones conscience onely by makeing plain* the truth which I deliver as in the presence of god. [3]But if the gospel which I preach be obscure and hidden it is soe onely to those who are lost, [4]in whom being unbeleivers the god of this world* has blinded their minds† soe that the glorious‡ brightness of the light of the gospel of Christ who is the image of god can not enlighten them. [5]For I seek not my own glory or secular advantage in preaching, but only the propagateing of the gospel of the Lord Jesus Christ, professeing my self your servant for Jesus's sake. [6]For god who made light to shine out of darkness hath enlightend also my dark heart who before saw not the end of the law that I might communicate the knowledg and light of the glory of god which shines in the face* of Jesus Christ. [7]But yet we to whom this treasure of knowledg the gospel of Jesus

which he more plainly expresses in the 5 or 6 first verses of this. The whole business of the first part of this Epistle being, as we have already observed, to justifie to the Corinthians his behaviour in his ministry [c]and to convince them that in his preaching the gospel he hath been plain clear open and candid, without any hidden designe or the least mixture of any concealed secular interest

2* Ἀπειπάμεθα τὰ κρυπτὰ τῆς αἰσχύνη⟨ς⟩ *have renounced the hidden things of dishonesty*, and τῇ φανερώσει τῆς ἀληθείας *by manifestation of the truth*· These expressions explain ἀνακεκαλυμ⟨μ⟩ένῳ προσώπῳ *with open face* Ch: III.⟨18⟩

4* *The god of this world*. i e The Devil soe called. because the men of the world worshiped and obeyd him as their god

† ἐτύφλωσε τὰ νοήματα *Blinded their minds* answers ἐπωρώθη τὰ νοήματα *their minds were blinded* Ch: III.14. And the 2d and 3d verse of this explain the 13th and 14th verses of the preceding chapter.

‡ δόξα *glory* here as in the former Chapter is put for shining and brightness soe that εὐαγγέλιον τῆς δόξης τοῦ Χριστοῦ is the brightness or clearness of the doctrine wherein Christ is manifested in the gospel

6* [a]This is a continuation still of the Alegory of Moses and the shineing of his face etc: soe much insisted on in the foregoeing Chapter. For the explication whereof give me leave to adde here one word more to what I have said upon it already. Moses by approaching to god in the mount had a communication of *glory* or *light* from him [b]which iradiated from his face when he discended from the mount. Moses put a vail over his face to hide this *light* or *glory*, for both those names St Paul uses in this and the foregoeing Chapter for the same thing. [c]But the *glory* or *light* of the knowledg of god more fully and clearly communicated by Jesus Christ is said here to *shine in his face* and in that respect it is that Christ in the foregoeing verse is called by St Paul *the image of god*, and the Apostles are said in the last verse of the pricedent chapter, [d]to be *transformed into the same image from glory to glory* i e by their large and clear communications of the knowledg of god in the gospel they are said to be transformed into the same image and to represent as mirors the glory of the Lord and to be as it were the image of Christ, as Christ is (as we are told here ver. 4) the image of god

Christ is committed to be propagated in the world are but fraile men, that so the exceeding great power that accompanys it may appear to be from god and not from us. [8]I am pressed on every side, but doe not shrink: I am perplexed, but yet not soe as to dispond: [9]persecuted, but yet not left to sink under it: thrown down but not slain: [10]Carrying about every where in my body the mortification i e a representation of the sufferings of the Lord Jesus, that also the life of Jesus risen from the dead may be made manifest by the energie that accompanies my preaching in this frail body. [11]For as long as I live I shall be exposed to the danger of death for the sake of Jesus that the life of Jesus risen from the dead may be made manifest by my preaching and sufferings in this mortal flesh of mine. [12]Soe that the preaching of the gospel procures sufferings and danger of death to me, but to you it procures life. i e the energie of the spirit of Christ whereby he lives in, and gives life to those who beleive in him. [13]Never the less though suffering and death accompany the preaching of the gospel, yet haveing the same spirit of faith that David had when he said I beleive therefore have I spoken, I also beleiving therefore speak, [14]knowing that he who raised up the Lord Jesus shall raise me up also by Jesus and present me with you to god· [15a]For I doe and suffer all things for your sakes that the exuberant favour of god may abound by the thanksgiveing of a greater number to the glory of god. i e. I indeavour by my sufferings and preac⟨h⟩ing to make as many converts as I can that soe the more partakeing of the mercy and favour of god [b]of which there is a plentiful and inexhaustible store the more men may give thanks unto him. It being more for the glory of god that a greater number should give thanks and prayse to him. [16]For which reason I faint* I flag not but though my bodily strength decay yet the vigor of my mind is dayly renewed. [17]For the more my sufferings are here in propagateing the gospel which at worst are but transient and light the more will they procure me an exceedingly far greater addition of that glory* in heaven which is solid and eternal [18]I haveing no regard to the visible things of this world but to the invisible things of the other. For the

16* *I faint not*. what this signifies we have seen ver. 1. Here St Paul gives an other proof of his sincerity in his ministry, and that is the sufferings and danger of death which he dayly incurs by his preaching the gospel. And the reason why those sufferings and dangers deter him not nor make him at all flag he tells them is the assurance he has that god through Christ will raise him again and reward him with immortalitie in glory· this argument he pursues IV.7–V.9.

17* *Weight of glory*· What an influence St Pauls Hebrew had upon his Greek is every where visible. כב⟨ד⟩ in Hebrew signifies to be *heavy* and to be *glorious*· In the Greek St Paul joyns them and says *weight of glory*

things that are seen are temporal but those that are not seen eternal.
[V.1]For I know that if this my body which is but as a tent for my sojourn-
ing here upon earth for a short time were dissolved I shall have an
other of a divine original which shall not, like buildings made with
mens hands, be subject to decay but shall be eternal in the heaven.
[2]For in his tabernacle* I groan earnestly desireing, without puting off
this mortal earthly body by death, to have that celestial body super-
induced, [3]If soe be the comeing* of Christ shall overtake me in this
life before I put off this body. [4]For we that are in the body groan under
the pressures and inconveniencys that attend us in it, which yet we are
not therefore willing to put off. but had rather without dying have it
changed* into a celestial immortal body, that so this mortal state may
be put an end to by an immediate entrance into an immortal life.
[5]Now it is god who prepares and fits us for this immortal state, who
also gives us the spirit as a pledg* of it. [6]Wherefore being always
undaunted* and knowing that whilst I dwell or sojourn in this body I
am absent from my proper home which is with the Lord [7](for I regulate my conduct not by the injoyment of the visible things of this
world. but by my hope and expectation of the invisible things of the
world to come) [8]I with boldness* preach the gospel, prefering in my
choice the quiting this habitation to get home to the Lord· [9]wherefore

V.2* vid. ver. 4

3* That the Apostle lookd on the comeing of Christ as not far off appears by what he says 1 Thess. IV 15-V.6· which Epistle was written some years before this. See also to the same purpose 1 Cor. I.7. VII.29.31. X.11 Rom XIII.11.12 Heb X.37

4* [a]The same that he had told them in the first Epistle XV.51 should happen to those who should be alive at Christs comeing. This I must own is noe very easy passage, whither we understand by γυμνοί, *naked* as I doe here the state of the dead unclothed with immortal bodys 'till the resurrection. [b]which sense is favourd by the same word 1 Cor XV.37. or whither we understand the *clotheing upon*, which the Apostle desires, to be those immortal bodys which souls shall be clothed with at the resurrection· which sense of *clotheing upon* seems to be favourd by 1 Cor XV.53 54, [c]and is that which one should be inclined to, were it not accompanied with this difficulty viz that then it would follow that the wicked should not have immortal bodys at the resurrection. [d]For what ever it be that St Paul here means by being *clothed upon*: it is some thing that is peculiar to the saints, who have the spirit of god, and shall be with the Lord in contradistinction to others as appears from the following verses and the whole tenor of this place

5* The spirit is mentioned in more places than one as the pledg and earnest of immortality; more particularly Eph. I.13.14 which compared with Rom VIII.23 shews that the inheritance whereof the spirit is the earnest is the same which the Apostle speaks of here viz. the possession of immortall bodys

6.8* [a]θαρροῦντες and θαρροῦμεν *we are confident* signifie in these two verses the same that οὐκ ἐκκακοῦμεν *we faint not* does Ch: IV.1. and 16. i e I goe on undauntedly without flaging· preaching the gospel with sincerity, and direct plainess of speech. [b]This conclusion which he draws here from the consideration of the resurrection and immortality is the same that he makes upon the same ground Ch. IV.14.16.

I make this my onely aim whither staying* here in this body or de-
parting* out of it so to acquit my self as to be acceptable to him·† [10]For
we must all appear before the judgment seat of Christ that every one
may receive according to what he has done in the body* whither it be
good or bad. [11]Knowing therefore this terrible judgment of the Lord I
preach the gospel perswading men to be Christians. And with what
integrity I discharge that duty is manifest to god, and I trust you also
are convinced of it in your consciences. [12]And this I say not that I
commend* my self again· But that I may give you an occasion not to be
ashamd of me but to glory on my behalf haveing wherewithall to reply
to those who make a shew of glorying in outward appearance without
doeing soe inwardly in their hearts·† [13]For* if I am besides my

9* [a]Εἴτε ἐνδημοῦντες εἴτε ἐκδημοῦντες. *whither staying in the body or goeing out of it* i e whither I am to stay longer here, or suddainly to depart. This sense the foregoeing verse leads us to and what he says in this verse that he endeavours. (w⟨h⟩ither ἐνδημ⟨εῖ⟩ν or ἐκδημ⟨εῖ⟩ν) *to be well pleaseing to the lord*. [b]i e doe what is well pleaseing to him shews that neither of these words can signifie here his being with Christ in heaven. For when he is there the time of indeavouring to approve himself is over.

† [a]St Paul from IV.12 to this place has, to convince them of his uprightness in his ministry, been shewing that the hopes and sure expectation he had of eternal life kept him steady and resolute in an open sincere preaching of the gospel without any tricks or deceitfull artifice· [b]In which his argument stands thus·'Knowing that god who raised up 'Christ will raise me up again, I without any fear or consideration of what it may draw 'upon me preach the gospel faithfully makeing this account that the momentaneous 'afflictions which for it I may suffer here, which are but slight in comparison of the 'eternal things of an other life, [c]will exceedingly increase my happyness in the other 'world. where I long to be. And therefore death which brings me home to Christ is noe 'terror to me, all my care is that whither I am to stay longer in this body, or quickly to leave 'it, liveing or dyeing I may approve my self to Christ in my ministry.' [d]In the next two verses he has an other argument to fix in the Corinthians the same thoughts of him and that is the punishment he shall receive at the day of judgment if he should neglect to preach the gospel faithfully and not indeavour sincerely and earnestly to make converts to Christ

10* Τὰ διὰ τοῦ σώματος. *dureing the bodily state*. vid Rom IV.11

12* [a]From this place, and several other in this epistle it cannot be doubted but that his speaking well of himself had been objected to him as a fault· And in this lay his great difficulty how to deale with this people. If he answerd noe thing to what was talkd of him his silence might be interpreted guilt and confession: [b]If he defended him self he was accused of vanity self commendation and folly. Hence it is that he uses soe many reasons to shew that his whole cariage was upon principles far above all worldly considerations: and tells them here once for all that the account he gives of himself is onely to furnish them who are his freinds and stuck to him, with matter to justifie themselves in their esteem of him and to reply to the contrary faction

† This may be understood of the Leaders of the opposite faction who as tis manifest from X.7.15. XI.12.22.23 pretended to something that they gloried in, though St Paul assures us they were satisfied in conscience that they had noe solid ground of glorying

13* [a]St Paul from the 13 ver. of this Chapter to Chap VI.12 gives an other reason for his disinterested carriage in preaching the gospel and that is his love to Christ who by his death haveing given him life who was dead, he concludes that in gratitude he ought

self† in speaking as I doe of my self it is between god and me, he must judg, men are not concerned in it, nor hurt by it: Or if I doe it soberly and upon good ground. If what I profess of my self be in reality true, it is for your sake and advantage· [14]For tis the love of Christ constraineth me judging as I doe that if Christ died for all then all were dead; [15]And that if he died for all his intention was, that they, who by him have attaind to a state of life, should not any longer live to them selves alone seekeing onely their own private advantage; but should imploy their lives in promoteing the gospel and kingdome of Christ who for them died and rose again, [16]Soe that from hence forth I have noe regard to any one according to the flesh.* i e for being circumcised or a Jew. For if I my self have gloried in this that Christ himself was circumcised as I am, and was of my blood and nation, I doe soe now noe more any longer. [17]Soe that if any one be in Christ it is as if he were in a new creation* where in all former mundane relations, considerations and interests† are ceased and at an end, all things in that state are new to him, [18]and he owes his very being in it and the advantages he therein enjoys not in the least measure to his birth extraction or any legal

not to live to himself any more. [b]He therefore being as in a new creation had now no longer any regard to the things or persons of this world but being made by god a minister of the gospel he minded onely the faithfull discharge of his duty in that Ambassay and pursuant thereunto took care that his behaviour should be such as he discribes VI.3-10

† *Besides my self*. i e. in speakeing well of my self in my own justification. He that observes what St Paul says Ch: XI.1 and 16-21. XII.6 and 11 will scarce doubt but that the speaking of himself as he did was by his enemys called glorying, and imputed to him as folly and madness.

16* This may be supposed to be said with reflection on their Jewish false Apostle who gloried in his circumcision, and perhaps that he had seen Christ in the flesh, or was some way related to him.

17* [a]Gal VI.14 may give some light to this place: To make this 16th and 17th ver. coherent to the rest of St Pauls discourse here, they must be understood in reference to the false Apostle against whom St Paul is here justifying himself, and makes it his main business in this as well as the former Epistle to shew that what that false Apostle gloried in was noe just cause of boasting. [b]Pursuant to this design of sinking the authority and credit of that false Apostle St Paul in these and the following verses dexterously insinuates these two things. 1° That the ministry of reconciliation being committed to him, they should not forsake him to hearken to and follow that pretender. [c]2° That they being in Christ and the new Creation should, as he does, not know any man in the flesh, not esteem or glory in that false Apostle because he might perhaps pretend to have seen our Saviour in the flesh or have heard him, or the like. κτίσις signifies *creation* and is so translated Rom VIII 22

† Τὰ ἀρχαῖα *old things* perhaps may here mean the Jewish œconomie for the false Apostle was a Jew, and as such assumed to himself some authority probably by right of blood and priviledge of his nation vid. 2 Cor XI.21.22. But that, St Paul here tels them, now under the gospel is all antiquated and quite out of dores

observances or priviledges but wholy and soly to god alone [19]recon-
cileing the world to himself by Jesus Christ and not imputeing their
trespasses to them. And therefore I whom god hath reconciled to him
self, and to whom he hath given the ministry and committed the word
of this reconciliation [20]as an Ambassador for Christ, as though god did
by me b⟨e⟩seech you. I pray you in Christs stead be ye reconciled to
god. [21]For god hath made him subject to sufferings and death the
punishment and consequence of sin as if he had been a sinner though
he were guilty of noe sin, that we in and by him might be made righteous by a righteousness imputed to us by god. [VI.1]I therefore workeing
together with him beseech you also that you receive not the favour of
god in the gospel preachd to you, in vain* [2](For he sayth· I have heard
thee in a time accepted, and in the day of Salvation have I succord
thee: behold now is the accepted time: behold now is the day of salvation) [3]giveing noe offence to any one in any thing that the ministry be
not blamed: [4]But in every thing approveing my self as becomes the
minister of god by much patience in afflictions, in necessitys, in
streights, [5]in stripes, in imprisonments. in being tossed up and down,
in labours, in watchings, in fastings; [6]By a life undefiled; by knowledg;
by long suffering; by the gifts of the holy ghost; by love unfeigned; [7]by
preaching the gospel of truth sincerely; by the power of god assisting
my ministry; by uprightness of mind, wherewith I am armed at all
points both to doe and to suffer; [8]by honour and disgrace; by good and
bad report, as a deceiver,* and yet faithfull; [9]as an obscure unknown
man, but yet known and owned; as one often in danger of death, and
yet behold I live; as chastened, but yet not killed; [10]as sorrowfull, but
yet always rejoyceing; as poor, yet makeing many rich; as haveing noe
thing, and yet possessing all things.

[11]O ye Corinthians my mouth is opened to you, my heart is
enlarged* to you: [12]my affection my tenderness my compliance for you
is not streight or narrow. 'Tis your own narrowness makes you uneasy.
[13]Let me speak to you as a father to his children, in return doe you
likewise enlarge your affection and deference to me: [14]Be ye not

VI.1* *Receive the grace of god in vain* the same with *beleiveing in vain* 1 Cor XV 2. i e receiveing the doctrine of the gospel for true and professing Christianity without persisting in it or performing what the gospel requires

8* *Deceiver* a title 'tis like he had received from some of the opposite faction at Corinth vid. XII.16

11* Another argument St Paul makes use of to justifie and excuse his plainess of speech to the Corinthians, is the great affection he has for them, which he here breaks out into an expression of in a very pathetical manner This with an exhortation to separat from Idolaters and unbeleivers is what he insists on from this place to VII.16

associated with unbeleivers, have noe thing to doe with them in their vices or worship·* for what fellowship hath righteousness with unrighteousness? what communion hath light with darkness? [15]what concord hath Christ with Belial?* or what part hath a beleiver with an unbeleiver? [16]what agreement hath the temple of god with Idols? For ye are the temple of the liveing god, as god hath said· I will dwell in them, among them will I walk, and I will be their god, and they shal be my people. [17]Wherefore come out from among them, and be separate· saith the Lord, and touch not the unclean thing, and I will receive you to me, [18]and I will be a father, and ye shall be my sons and daughters· saith the Lord almighty. [VII.1]Haveing therefore these promises (dearly beloved) let us cleanse our selves from the defilement of all sorts of sins whither of body or mind endeavouring after perfect holyness in the fear of god. [2]Receive me, as one to be harkend to as one to be followed, as one that hath done noething to forfeit your esteem. I have wrongd noe man: I have corrupted noe man: I have defrauded noe man·* [3]I say not this to reflect on your cariage towards me,* for I have already assured you that I have soe great an affection for you that I could live and die with you. [4]But in the transport of my joy I use great liberty of speech towards you: But let it not be thought to be of ill will, for I boast much of you: I am filled with comfort and my joy abounds exceedingly in all my afflictions· [5]For when I came to Macedonia I had no respit from continual trouble that beset me on every side· From without I met with strife and opposition in preaching the gospel. And within I was filled with fear upon your account least the false Apostle continueing his credit and faction amongst you should pervert you from the simplicity of the gospel.* [6]But god who comforteth those who are cast down comforted me by the comeing of Titus, [7]not barely by his presence but by the comfort I received from you by him, when he acquainted me with your great desire of conforming your selves to my orders; your trouble for any neglects you have been guilty of towards me; the great warmth of your affection and concerne for me; soe that I rejoyced the more for my past fears, [8]haveing writ to you a letter, which I repented of: but now doe not repent of, perceiveing that though that letter greived you, it made you sad but for a short time: [9]But now I rejoyce, not that you were made sorry. but

14* vid: VII.1

15* *Belial* is a general name for all the false gods worshiped by the Idolatrous Gentils

VII.2* This seems to insinuate the contrary behaviour of their false Apostle

3* vid I Cor IV.3. 2 Cor X.2. XI.20.21: XIII.3

5* vid Ch: XI.3

that you were made sorry to repentance. For this proved a beneficial sorrow acceptable to god, that in noe thing you might have cause to complain that you were dammaged by me. [10]For godly sorrow worketh repentance to salvation not to be repented of: But sorrow riseing from worldly interest worket⟨h⟩ death. [11a]In the present case marke it, that godly sorrow which you had what carefulness it wrought in you to* conform your selves to my orders. ver. 15, yea, what clearing your selves from your former miscariages; yea what indignation against those who led you into them; [b]yea what fear to offend me,† yea what vehement desire of satisfying me; yea what zeale for me; yea what revenge against your selves for haveing been soe misled. you have shewn your selves to be set right‡ and be as you should be in every thing by this cariage of yours·§ [12]If therefore I wrote unto you concerning the Fornicator. It was not for his sake that had done, nor his that had sufferd the wrong but principally that my care and concerne for

11* St Paul writeing to those who knew the temper they were in, and what were the objects of the several passions which were raised in them doth both here and in the 7 ver. forbear to mention by and to what they were moved, out of modesty and respect to them. This is necessary for the information of ordinary readers to be supplied as can be best collected from the main designe of the Apostle in these two Epistles and from several passages giveing us light in it.

† vid. ver. 15.

‡ [a]*clear* This word answers very well ἁγνός in the Greek: but then to be *clear* in English is generaly understood to signifie not to have been guilty; which could not be the sense of the Apostle, he haveing charged the Corinthians so warmly in his first epistle. [b]His meaning must therefore be that they had now resolved on a contrary course, and were so far clear. i e. were set right and in good disposition again as he discribes it in the former part of this verse.

§ [a]And therefore I think ἐν τῷ πράγματι may best be renderd *in fact* i e. by your sorrow, your fear, your indignation, your zeale etc: I think it cannot well be translated *in this matter* understanding thereby the punishment of the Fornicator· For that was not the matter St Paul had been speakeing of, [b]but the Corinthians sideing with the false apostle against him was the subject of the preceding part of this and of the 3 or 4 foregoeing chapters where in he justifies him self against their slanders and invalidats the pretences of the adverse party. [c]This is that which lay cheifly upon his heart and which he labours might and main both in this and the former epistle to rectifie as the foundation of all the disorders amongst them. And consequently is the matter where in he rejoyces to find them all set right. [d]Indeed in the immediately following ver. he mentions his haveing writ to them concerning the fornicator, but it is onely as an argument of his kindness and concerne for them; But that what was the great cause of his rejoyceing, what it was that gave him the great satisfaction, [e]was the breaking the faction and the reuniteing them *all* to himself which he expresses in the word *All* emphatically used ver. 13 and 15 and from thence he concludes thus ver. 16· *I rejoyce therefore that I have confidence in you in all things*· His mind was now at rest, [f]the partizans of his opposer the false Apostle haveing forsaken that Leader whom they had soe much gloried in, and being all now come over to St Paul. he doubted not but all would goe well, and soe leaves off the subject he had been upon in the seven foregoeing Chapters. viz the Justification of himself with here and there reflections on that false Apostle.

you might be made known to you as in the presence of god. [13]Therefore I was comforted in your comfort· But much more exceedingly rejoyced I in the joy of Titus because his mind was set at ease by the good disposition he found you all in towards me:* [14]So that I am not ashamed of haveing boasted of you to him. For as all that I have said to you is truth, so what I said to Titus in your commendation he has found to be true, [15]whereby his affection to you is aboundantly increased, he carrying in his mind the universal obedience of you all unanimously to me and the manner of your receiveing him with fear and trembleing. [16]I rejoyce therefore that I have confidence in you in all things.

SECTION III

Ch. VIII.1-IX.15

CONTENTS

The Apostle haveing imploid the 7 foregoeing Chapters in his own justification in the close whereof he expresses the great satisfaction he had in their being all united again in their affection and obedience to him, he in the two next chapters exhorts them espetialy by the example of the churches of Macedonia to a liberal contribution to the poor Christians in Judea.

TEXT

VIII.1. Moreover brethren, we do you to wit of the grace of God bestowed on the churches of Macedonia:

2. How that in a great trial of affliction, the abundance of their joy, and their deep poverty abounded unto the riches of their liberality.

3. For to their power (I bear record) yea, and beyond their power, they were willing of themselves,

4. Praying us with much intreaty, that we would receive the gift, and take upon us the fellowship of the ministring to the saints.

5. And this they did, not as we hoped, but first gave their own selves to the Lord, and unto us by the will of God.

6. Insomuch that we desired Titus, that as he had begun, so he would also finish in you the same grace also.

7. Therefore as ye abound in every thing, in faith, in utterance, and know-

13* vid. ver. 15

ledge, and in all diligence, and in your love to us; see that ye abound in this grace also.

8. I speak not by commandment, but by occasion of the forwardness of others, and to prove the sincerity of your love.

9. For ye know the grace of our Lord Jesus Christ, that though he was rich, yet for your sakes he became poor, that ye through his poverty might be rich.

10. And herein I give my advice: for this is expedient for you who have begun before, not only to do, but also to be forward a year ago.

11. Now therefore perform the doing of it; that as there was a readiness to will, so there may be a performance also out of that which you have.

12. For if there be first a willing mind, it is accepted according to that a man hath, and not according to that he hath not.

13. For I mean not that other men be eased, and you burdened:

14. But by an equality, that now at this time your abundance may be a supply for their want, that their abundance also may be a supply for your want, that there may be equality,

15. As it is written, He that had gathered much, had nothing over; and he that had gathered little, had no lack.

16. But thanks be to God, which put the same earnest care into the heart of Titus for you.

17. For indeed he accepted the exhortation, but being more forward, of his own accord he went unto you.

18. And we have sent with him the brother, whose praise is in the gospel, thoroughout all the churches:

19. (And not that only, but who was also chosen of the churches to travel with us with this grace, which is administred by us to the glory of the same Lord, and declaration of your ready mind)

20. Avoiding this, that no man should blame us in this abundance, which is administred by us:

21. Providing for honest things, not only in the sight of the Lord, but also in the sight of men.

22. And we have sent with them our brother, whom we have often times proved diligent in many things, but how much more diligent, upon the great confidence which I have in you.

23. Whether any do enquire of Titus, he is my partner, and fellow helper concerning you: or our brethren be enquired of, they are the messengers of the churches, and the glory of Christ.

24. Wherefore shew ye to them, and before the churches the proof of your love, and of our boasting on your behalf.

IX.1. For as touching the ministring to the saints, it is superfluous for me to write to you.

2. For I know the forwardness of your mind, for which I boast of you to

them of Macedonia, that Achaia was ready a year ago; and your zeal hath provoked very many.

3. Yet have I sent the brethren, lest our boasting of you should be in vain in this behalf; that, as I said, ye may be ready:

4. Lest haply if they of Macedonia come with me, and find you unprepared, we (that we say not, you) should be ashamed in this same confident boasting.

5. Therefore I thought it necessary to exhort the brethren, that they would go before unto you, and make up before hand your bounty, whereof ye had notice before, that the same might be ready as a matter of bounty, and not as of covetousness.

6. But this I say, He which soweth sparingly, shall reap also sparingly: and he which soweth bountifully, shall reap also bountifully.

7. Every Man according as he purposeth in his heart, so let him give; not grudgingly, or of necessity: for God loveth a cheerful giver.

8. And God is able to make all grace abound towards you; that ye always having all sufficiency in all things, may abound to every good work:

9. (As it is written, He hath dispersed abroad; he hath given to the poor: his righteousness remaineth for ever.

10. Now he that ministreth seed to the sower, both minister bread for your food, and multiply your seed sown, and increase the fruits of your righteousness)

11. Being enriched in every thing to all bountifulness, which causeth through us thanksgiving to God.

12. For the administration of this service, not only supplieth the want of the saints, but is abundant also by many thanksgivings unto God;

13. (Whiles by the experiment of this ministration, they glorifie God for your professed subjection unto the Gospel of Christ, and for your liberal distribution unto them, and unto all men)

14. And by their prayer for you, which long after you, for the exceeding grace of God in you.

15. Thanks be unto God for his unspeakable gift.

PARAPHRASE

VIII.1 Moreover brethren I make known to you the gift* which by the
grace of god is given in the churches of Macedonia 2(viz.) that amidst
the afflictions* they have been much tried with, they have with
exceeding cheerfulness and joy made their very low estate of poverty

VIII.1* Χάρις which is translated *grace* is here used by St Paul for *gift* or *liberality* and is soe used ver. 4.6.7.9.19 and 1 Cor. XVI 3. It is called also χάρις θεοῦ the *gift of god* because god is the cause and procurer of it moveing their hearts to it. vid. IX.15. And δεδομένην ἐν cannot signifie *bestowed on* but *given by*

2* How ill disposed and rough to the Christians the Macedonians were may be seen Act. XVI and XVII

yeild a rich contribution of liberality, [3]being forward of them selves (as I must bear them witness) to the utmost of their power nay and beyond their power, [4]earnestly intreating me to receive their contribution, and be a partner with others in the charge of conveying and distributeing it to the saints. [5]And in this they out did my expectation who could not hope for so large a collection from them. But they gave themselves first to the Lord, and to me to dispose of what they had according as the good pleasure of god should direct. [6]Insomuch that I was moved to perswade Titus, that as he had begun so he would also see this charitable contribution caried on among you till it was perfected [7]that as you excell in every thing abounding in faith, in well speakeing, in knowledg, in every good quality and in your affection to me ye might abound in this act of charitable liberality also. [8]This I say to you not as a command from god, but on occasion of the great liberality of the churches of Macedonia and to shew the world a proof of the genuine noble temper of your love.* [9]For ye know the munificence* of our Lord Jesus Christ, who being rich made himself poor for your sakes, that you by his poverty might become rich. [10]I give you my opinion in the case because it becomes you soe to doe, as haveing began not only to doe something in it but to shew a willingness to it above a year agoe. [11]Now therefore apply your selves to the doeing of it in earnest, so that as you undertook it readily, soe you would as readily performe it out of what you have. [12]For every mans charity is accepted by god according to the largeness and willingness of his

8* [a]Τὸ τῆς ὑμετέρας ἀγάπης. γνήσιον δοκιμάζων. *shewing the world a proof of the genuine temper of your love*. Thus I think it should be renderd. St Paul who is soe careful all along in this epistle to shew his esteem and good opinion of the Corinthians takeing all occasions to speake and presume well of them, whereof we have an eminent example in these words *ye abound in your love to us* in the immediately preceding verse, [b]he could not in this place soe far forget his designe of treating them very tenderly now they were newly returnd to him, as to tell them that he sent Titus for the promoteing their contribution to make a trial of the *sincerity of their love*, this had been but an ill expression of that *confidence* which VII.16 he tells them, he has *in them in all things*. [c]Takeing therefore as without violence to the words one may δοκιμάζων for *drawing out a proof* and γνήσιον for *genuine* the words very well express St Pauls obleigeing way of stiring up the Corinthians to a liberal contribution as I have understood them. For St Pauls discourse to them breifly stands thus. [d]'The great liberality of the poor Macedonians Made me send 'Titus to you to carry on the collection of your Charity which he had begun that you 'who excel in all other virtues might be eminent also in this. But this I urge not as a 'command from god, but upon occasion of others liberality lay before you an oportunity 'of giveing the world a proof of the genuine temper of your charity which like that of 'your other virtues loves not to come behind that of others'

9* Τὴν χάριν the *grace* rather the *Munificence*, the signification where in St Paul uses χάρις over and over again in this chapter and is translated *gift*. ver. 4

heart in giveing and not according to the narrowness of his fortune. [13]For my meaning is not that you should be burdened to ease others; [14]but that at this time your aboundance should make up what they through want came short in, that in an other occasion their abundance may supply your deficiency, that there may be an equality· [15]As it is written, He that had much, had noe thing over and he, that had little, had noe lack. [16]But thanks be to god who put into the heart of Titus the same concerne for you, [17]who not onely yeilded to my exhortation* but being more than ordinary concerned for you of his own accord went unto you. [18]with whom I have sent the Brother* who has praise through all the churches for his labour in the gospel [19](and not that onely, but who was also chosen of the churches to accompany me in the carrying this collection, which service I undertook for the glory of our Lord and for your incouragement to a liberal contribution) [20]to prevent any aspersion might be cast on me by any one on occasion of my medleing with the management of soe great a sum, [21]and to take care by haveing such men joynd with me in the same trust, that my integrity and credit should be prese⟨r⟩ved not onely in the sight of the Lord; but also in the sight of men. [22]With them I have sent our Brother of whom I have had frequent experience in sundry affairs, to be a forward active man; but now much more earnestly intent by reason of the strong perswasion he has of your contributeing liberally. [23]Now whither I speake of Titus, he is my partner, and one who with me promotes your interests; or the two other Brethren sent with him, they are the messengers of the churches of Macedonia by whom their collect is sent, and are promoters of the glory of Christ. [24]give therefor to them. and by them to those churches a demonstration of your love, and a justification of my boasting of you. [IX.1]For as touching the releif of the poor Christians in Jerusalem it is needless for me to write to you. [2]For I know the forwardness of your minds which I boasted of on your behalf to the Macedonians that Achaia* was ready a year agoe, and your zeale in this matter hath been a spur to many others. [3]Yet I have sent these Brethren that my boasting of you may not appear to be vain and groundless in this part: [4]But that you may as I said have your collection ready lest if perchance the Macedonians should come with me and find it not ready, I (not to say you) should be ashamd in this

17* vid. ver. 6

18* This Brother most take to be St Luke. who now was and had been a long while St Pauls companion in his travels

IX.2* Achaia. i e the Church of Corinth which was made up of the inhabitants of that town and of the circumjacent parts of Achaia. Vid Ch. I.1.

matter whereof I have boasted· [5]I thought it therefore necessary to put
the brethren upon goeing before unto you to prepare things by a
timely notice before hand that your contribution may be ready as a
free benevolence of yours and not as a nigardly gift extorted from you.
[6]This I say, he who soweth spareingly shall reap also spareingly; and
he who soweth plentifully shall also reap plentifully. [7]Soe give as you
find your selves disposed every one in his own heart, not grudgingly as
if it were wrung from you. For god loves a cheerfull giver. [8]For god is
able to make every charitable gift* of yours redound to your advantage, that you haveing in every thing always a fulness of plenty ye may
abound to every good work [9](as it is written· he hath scattered, he hath
given to the poor, and his liberality* remaineth forever. [10]Now he that
supplys seed to the sower and bread for food: supply and multiply
your stock of seed† and increase the fruit of your liberality.*) [11]enrichd
in every thing to all beneficence which by me as instrumental in it
procureth thanksgiveing to god. [12]For the performance of this service
doth not onely bring supply to the wants of the saints, but reacheth
farther even to god himself by many thanksgiveings [13](whilst they
haveing such a proof of you in this your supply glorify god for your
professed subjection to the gospel of Christ and for your liberality in
communicateing to them and to all men) [14]and to the procureing their
prayers for you they haveing a great inclination towards you because
of that gratious gift of god bestowed on them by your liberality.
[15]Thanks be to god for this his unspeakable gift

SECTION IV

Ch. X.1–XIII.10

CONTENTS

St Paul haveing finished his exhortation to liberality in their collect for the Christians at Jerusalem, he here resumes his former argument and prosecutes the main purpose of this Epistle, which was totaly to

8⟨*⟩ χάρις *grace* rather *charitable gift* or *liberality* as it signifies in the former Chapter, and as the context determins the sense here

9 and 10* Δικαιοσύνη. *Righteousness* rather *Liberality* for soe δικαιοσύνη in scripture language often signifies, and so Mat VI.1 for ἐλεημοσύνην *alms* some copys have δικαιοσύνην *liberality* and so Joseph Mat: I 19 is caled δίκαιος *just* i e *benigne*.

⟨10⟩† σπόρον *seed sown* rather your *seed and seed plot*. i e. increase your plenty to be laid out in charitable uses

reduce and put a final end to the adverse faction (which seems not yet to be entirely extinct) by bringing the Corinthians wholy off from the false Apostle they had adhered to: And to reestablish him self and his authority in the minds of all the members of that church. And this he does by the steps conteined in the following numbers.

SECTION IV. NO. 1

Ch. X.1-6

CONTENTS

He declares the extraordinary power he hath in preaching the gospel and to punish his opposers amongst them

TEXT

X.1. Now I Paul my self beseech you, by the meekness and gentleness of Christ, who in presence am base among you, but being absent am bold toward you.

2. But I beseech you, that I may not be bold when I am present, with that confidence wherewith I think to be bold against some which think of us, as if we walked according to the flesh.

3. For though we walk in the flesh, we do not war after the flesh:

4. (For the weapons of our warfare are not carnal, but mighty through God, to the pulling down of strong holds.)

5. Casting down imaginations, and every high thing that exalteth it self against the knowledge of God, and bringing into captivity every thought to the obedience of Christ:

6. And having in a readiness to revenge all disobedience, when your obedience is fulfilled.

⟨PARAPHRASE⟩

[X.1]Now I the same Paul who am (as tis said amongst* you) base and mean when present with you, but bold towards you when absent beseech you by the meekness and gentleness† of Christ. [2]I beseech you I say that I may not when present among you be bold after that

X.1* vid: ver. 10

† St Paul thinking it fit to forbear all severity till he had by fair means reduced as many of the contrary party as he could to a full submission to his authority (vid. ver. 6) begins here his discourse by conjureing them by the meekness and gentleness of Christ as an example that might excuse his delay of exemplary punishment on the ring-leaders and cheif offenders without giveing them reason to think it was for want of power.

manner I have resolvd to be bold towards some who count that in my conduct and ministry I regulate my self wholy by carnal considerations. [3]For though I live in the flesh yet I doe not carry on the work of the gospel (which is a warfare) according to the flesh [4](For the weapons of my warfare are not fleshly* but such as god hath made mighty to the pulling down of strong holds. i e what ever is made use of in opposition) [5]beating down humane reasonings and all the touring and most elevated superstructures raised thereon by the wit of men against the knowledg of god as held forth in the gospel captivateing all their notions and bringing them into subjection to Christ; [6]and haveing by me in a readiness power wherewithall to punish and chastise all disobedience when you* who have been misled by your false Apostle withdrawing your selves from him shall returne to a perfect obedience

SECTION IV. NO. 2

Ch. X.7-18

CONTENTS

St Paul examins the false Apostles pretensions and compares his own with his performances

TEXT

X.7. Do ye look on things after the outward appearance? if any man trust to himself, that he is Christs, let him of himself think this again, that as he is Christs, even so are we Christs.

8. For though I should boast somewhat more of our authority, (which the

4* What the ὅπλα σαρκικά the *Carnal weapons* and those other opposed to them which he cals δυνατὰ τῷ θεῷ *mighty through god* are, may be seen if we read and compare 1 Cor I.23.24 II.1.2.4.5 12.13, 2 Cor IV.2.6

6* [a]Those whom he speaks to here are the Corinthian converts to whom this epistle is written. Some of these had been drawn into a faction against St Paul. These he had been and was endeavouring to bring back to that obedience and submission which the rest had continued in to him as an Apostle of Jesus Christ· [b]The Corinthians of these two sorts are those he means when he says to them Ch. II.3. VII 13.15 *you all* i e all ye Christians of Corinth: and Achaia. For he that had raised the faction amongst them and given soe much trouble to St Paul was a Stranger and a Jew. vid XI.22 Crept in amongst them after St Paul had gatherd and establishd that Church 1 Cor III.6.10. 2 Cor X.15.16 [c]of whom St Paul seems to have noe hopes XI.13-15 and therefor him he every where threatens 1 Cor IV.19, and here particularly ver. 6. and 11, to make an example of him and his adherents (if any were soe obstinate to stick to him) when he had brought back again all the Corinthians that he could hope to prevail on

Lord hath given us for edification, and not for your destruction) I should not be ashamed:

9. That I may not seem as if I would terrifie you by letters.

10. For his letters (say they) are weighty and powerful, but his bodily presence is weak, and his speech contemptible.

11. Let such an one think this, that such as we are in word by letters, when we are absent, such will we be also in deed when we are present.

12. For we dare not make our selves of the number, or compare our selves with some that commend themselves: but they measuring themselves by themselves, and comparing themselves amongst themselves are not wise.

13. But we will not boast of things without our measure, but according to the measure of the rule which God hath distributed to us, a measure to reach even unto you.

14. For we stretch not our selves beyond our measure, as though we reached not unto you; for we are come as far as to you also, in preaching the gospel of Christ:

15. Not boasting of things without our measure, that is, of other mens labours; but having hope when your faith is increased, that we shall be enlarged by you, according to our rule abundantly.

16. To preach the gospel in the regions beyond you, and not to boast in another mans line of things made ready to our hand.

17. But he that glorieth, let him glory in the Lord.

18. For not he that commendeth himself is approved, but whom the Lord commendeth.

PARAPHRASE

X.7 Doe ye judg of men by the outward appearance of things? Is it by such measures you take an estimate of me and my adversary? If he has confidence in himself that he is Christs. i e assumes to himself the authority of one imploid and commissioned by Christ,* Let him on the other side count thus with himself that as he is Christs soe I also am Christs. 8 Nay if I should boastingly say something more* of the authority and power, which the Lord has given me for your edification and not for your destruction,† I should not be put to shame.‡ 9 But that I may not seem to terrifie you by letters, as is objected to me by some, 10 who say that my letters are weighty and powerfull; but my bodily presence weake; and my discourse contemptible. 11 Let him that says so recon upon this, that such as I am in word by letters when

X.7* vid XI.23

8* *more* vid XI.23

† Another reason insinuated by the Apostle for his forbearing severity to them

‡ *I should not be put to shame*. i e the truth would justifie me in it

I am absent such shall I be also in deed when present. [12]For I dare not
be soe bold* as to rank or compare my self with some who vaunt
themselves. But they measureing them selves within themselves† and
compareing them selves with them selves doe not understand·‡ [13]But I
for my part will not boast of my self in what has not been measured
out or alloted to me* i e I will not goe out of my owne province to seek
matter of commendation, but proceeding orderly in the province
which god hath measured out and alloted to me I have reachd even
unto you. i e I preachd the gospel in every country as I went till I came
as far as to you· [14]For I doe not extend my self farther than I should, as
if I had skipd over other countrys in my way, without proceeding
gradualy to you, no for I have reachd even unto you in preaching of
the gospel in all countrys as I passed along* [15]not extending my boasting* beyond my own bounds into provinces not alloted to me, nor
vaunting my self of any thing I have done in anothers labour.† i e in

12* This is spoken Ironically.

† [a]ἐν ἑαυτοῖς *amongst them selves* rather *within themselves*. For in all likelyhood the faction and opposition against St Paul was made by one person as we have before observed. For though he speaks here in the plural number, which is the softer and decenter way in such cases, [b]yet we see in the foregoeing verse he speaks directly and expresly as of one person. and therefore ἐν ἑαυτοῖς may most consonantly to the Apo⟨s⟩tles meaning here be understood to signifie *within them selves* i e with what they find in them selves. [c]The whole place shewing that this person made an estimate of himself onely by what he found in himself and thereupon preferd himself to St Paul, without considering what St Paul was or had done.

‡ *Doe not understand* that they ought not to intrude them selves into a church planted by another man and there vaunt themselves, and set themselvs above him that planted it, which is the meaning of the 4 next verses.

13* Ἄμετρα here and in the ver. 15. doth not signifie immense or immoderate, but some thing that hath not been measured out and alloted to him; some thing that is not commited to him, nor within his province.

14* This seems to charge the false pretended Apostle who had caused all this disturbance in the church of Corinth, that without being appointed to it; without preaching the gospel in his way thither as became an Apostle he had crept into the Church of Corinth.

15* *Boasting* i e intermedleing or assumeing to my self authority to medle, or honour for medleing.

15.16† [a]Here St Paul visibly taxes the false Apostle for comeing into a church converted and gathered by an other and there pretending to be somebody and to rule all. This is an other thing that makes it probable, that the opposition made to St Paul was but by one man that had made him self the head of an opposite faction. [b]For it is plain it was a Stranger who came thither after St Paul had planted this church, who pretending to be more an Apostle than St Paul, with greater illumination, and more power, set up against him to governe that church, and withdraw the Corinthians from following St Paul, his rules and doctrine. [c]Now this can never be supposed to be a combination of men who came to Corinth with that designe. nor that they were different men that came thither seperately, each seting up for him self. For then they would have fallen out one with an other as well as with St Paul: and in both cases St Paul must have spoken of a church planted by an other mans pains.‡ But haveing hope that your faith increasing my province will be inlarged by you yet farther, [16]so that I may preach the gospel to the yet unconverted countrys beyond you and not take glory to my self from an other mans province where all things are made ready to my hand† [17]But he that will glory let him glory or seek prayse from that which is committed to him by the Lord or in that which is acceptable to the Lord. [18]For not he who commends himself does thereby give a proof of his authority or mission; but he whom the Lord commends by the gifts of the holy-ghost*

SECTION IV. NO. 3

Ch. XI.1-6

CONTENTS

He shews that their pretended Apostle bringing to them noe other Saviour or Gospel; nor confering greater power of miracles then he [St Paul] had done, was not to be preferd before him

TEXT

XI.1. Would to God you could bear with me a little in my folly; and indeed bear with me.

2. For I am jealous over you with godly jealousie: for I have espoused you to one husband, that I may present you as a chaste virgin to Christ.

3. But I fear, lest by any means, as the serpent beguiled Eve through his subtility, so your minds should be corrupted from the simplicity that is in Christ.

4. For if he that cometh, preacheth another Jesus whom we have not preached, or if ye receive another spirit, which ye have not received, or another gospel, which ye have not accepted, ye might well bear with him.

5. For I suppose I was not a whit behind the very chiefest apostles.

6. But though I be rude in speech, yet not in knowledge; but we have been throughly made manifest among you in all things.

them in a different way from what he does now. [d]The same character and cariage is given to them all through out both these Epistles· and 1 Cor III.10 he plainly mentions one man. That thus seting up to be a preacher of the gospel amongst those that were already Christians was looked upon by St Paul to be a fault we may see Rom XV.20.

15‡ vid Rom. XV.20

18* Tis of these weapons of his warfare that St Paul speaks in this chapter: And tis by them that he intends to trie which is the true Apostle when he comes to them.

PARAPHRASE

XI.1 Would you could bear me a little in my folly,* and indeed doe bear with me. 2 For I am jealous over you with a jealousy that is for god. For I have fited and prepared you for one alone to be your husband (viz) that I might deliver you up a pure virgin to Christ. 3 But I fear lest some way or other, as the serpent beguiled Eve by his cunning soe your minds should be debauchd from that singleness which is due to Christ.* 4 For if this intruder who has been a Leader amongst you, can preach to you an other Saviour, whom I have not preachd; or if you receive from him other or greater gifts of the spirit, than those you received from me; or an other gospel than what you accepted from me, you might well bear with him and allow his pretensions of being a new and greater Apostle. 5 For as to the Apostles of Christ I suppose I am not a whit behind the Cheifest of them. 6 For though I am but a mean speaker, yet I am not without knowledg, but in every thing have been made manifest unto you i e to be an Apostle

SECTION IV. NO. 4

Ch. XI.7–15

CONTENTS

He justifies him self to them in his haveing taken noe thing of them.

XI.1* *Folly*· soe he modestly calls his speaking in his own defence.

3* [a]'Απλότητος τῆς εἰς τὸν Χριστόν. *The simplicity that is in* rather *towards Christ* Answers to ἑνὶ ἀνδρὶ Χριστῷ *to one husband Christ* in the immediatly foregoeing verse. For ἑνί *one* is not put there for noe thing, but makes the meaning plainly this· [b]'I have 'formed and fitted you for one person alone, one husband who is Christ. I am concerned 'and in care that you may not be drawn aside from that submission that obedience that 'temper of mind that is due singly to him. [c]for I hope to put you into his hands possessed 'with pure virgin thoughts wholy fixed on him not divided nor roveing after any other, 'that he may take you to wife and marry you to himself for ever·' Tis plain their perverter who opposed St Paul was a Jew as we have seen. 'Twas from the Jews from whom of all professing Christianity St Paul had most trouble and opposition· [d]For they haveing their hearts set upon their old religion indeavourd to mix Judaisme and Christianity together. We may suppose the case here to be much the same with that which he more fully expresses in the Epistle to the Galatians particularly Gal I.6-12. IV.9-11 and 16-21 V.1-13. [e]The meaning of this place here seems to be this. 'I have taught you the gospel alone in its 'pure and unmixed simplicity by which onely you can be united to Christ: But I fear lest 'this your new Apostle should draw you from it, and that your minds should not stick to 'that Singly [f]but should be corrupted by a mixture of Judaisme.' After the like manner St Paul expresses Christians being delivered from the law and their freedom from the ritual observances of the Jews by being married to Christ Rom VII.4 which place may give some light to this

There had been great talk about this, and objections raised against St Paul there upon vid 1 Cor IX.1-3· As if by this he had discovered him self not to be an Apostle: to which he there answers, and here touches it again and answers an other objection, which it seems was made (viz) that he refused to receive maintenance from them out of unkindness to them.

TEXT

XI.7. Have I committed an offence in abasing my self that you might be exalted, because I have preached to you the Gospel of God freely?

8. I robbed other Churches, taking wages of them to do you service.

9. And when I was present with you and wanted, I was chargeable to no man: for that which was lacking to me, the brethren which came from Macedonia supplied: and in all things I have kept my self from being burdensome unto you, and so will I keep my self.

10. As the truth of Christ is in me, no man shall stop me of this boasting in the regions of Achaia.

11. Wherefore? because I love you not? God knoweth.

12. But what I do, that I will do, that I may cut off occasion from them which desire occasion, that wherein they glory, they may be found even as we.

13. For such are false apostles, deceitful workers, transforming themselves into the Apostles of Christ.

14. And no marvel; for satan himself is transformed into an angel of light.

15. Therefore it is no great thing if his ministers also be transformed as the ministers of righteousness; whose end shall be according to their works.

PARAPHRASE

XI.7 Have I committed an offence* in abaseing my self to work with my hands neglecting my right of maintenance due to me as an Apostle, that you might be exalted in Christianity, because I preached the gospel of god to you gratis? 8 I robd other churches takeing wages of them to doe you service: And being with you, and in want I was chargeable to not a man of you. 9 For the brethren who came from Macedonia supplied me with what I needed: And in all things I have kept my self from being burdensome to you, and soe will I continue to doe. 10 The truth and sincerity I owe to Christ is in what I say to you

XI.7* The adverse party made it an argument against St Paul as an evidence that he was noe Apostle since he took not from the Corinthians maintenance 1 Cor IX.1-3· An other objection raised against him from hence was, that he would receive noe thing from them because he loved them not. 2 Cor XI.11· This he answers. here by giveing another reason for his soe doeing. A third allegation was that it was onely a Crafty trick in him to Catch them 2 Cor XII.16 which he answers there

(viz)· This boasting of mine shall not in the regions of Achaia be stopd
in me. [11]Why so? Is it because I love you not? For that god can be my
witness, he knoweth. [12]But what I doe and shall doe* is that I may cut
off all occasion from those, who, if I took any thing of you. would be
glad of that occasion to boast that in it they had me for a pattern and
did noe thing but what even I my self had done. [13]For these are false*
Apostles, deceitfull labourers in the gospel haveing put on the
counterfet shape and outside of Apostles of Christ: [14]And no marvel
for Satan himself is sometimes transformed into an Angel of light.
[15]Therefore it is not strange if soe be his ministers are disguised so, as
to appear ministers of the gospel: whose end shall be according to
their works.

SECTION IV. NO. 5

Ch. XI.16-33

CONTENTS

He goes on in his justification reflecting upon the cariage of the false Apostle towards the Corinthians 16-21. He compares him self with the false Apostle in what he boasts of as being an Hebrew 21.22 Or minister of Christ 23 and here St Paul enlarges upon his labours and sufferings

TEXT

XI.16. I say again, Let no man think me a fool; if otherwise, yet as a fool receive me, that I may boast my self a little.

17. That which I speak, I speak it not after the Lord, but as it were foolishly in this confidence of boasting.

18. Seeing that many glory after the flesh, I will glory also.

19. For ye suffer fools gladly, seeing ye your selves are wise.

20. For ye suffer if a man bring you into bondage, if a man devour you, if a man take of you, if a man exalt himself, if a man smite you on the face.

21. I speak as concerning reproach, as though we had been weak: howbeit, wherein soever any is bold (I speak foolishly) I am bold also.

12* καὶ ποιήσω, *that I will doe* rather *and will doe*· soe the words stand in the Greek and doe not refer to ver. 10 as a profession of his resolution to take noe thing of them; but to ver. 11 to which it is joynd. shewing that his refuseing any reward from them was not out of unkindness but for an other reason.

13* They had questioned St Pauls Apostleship 1 Cor. IX. because of his not takeing maintenance of the Corinthians. He here directly declars them to be noe true Apostles

22. Are they Hebrews? so am I: are they Israelites? so am I: are they the seed of Abraham? so am I:

23. Are they ministers of Christ? (I speak as a fool) I am more: in labours more abundant, in stripes above measure, in prisons more frequent, in deaths oft.

24. Of the Jews five times received I forty stripes save one.

25. Thrice was I beaten with rods, once was I stoned, thrice I suffered shipwrack; a night and a day I have been in the deep:

26. In journeying often, in perils of waters, in perils of robbers, in perils by mine own countrey men, in perils by the heathen, in perils in the city, in perils in the wilderness, in perils in the sea, in perils among false brethren;

27. In weariness and painfulness, in watchings often, in hunger and thirst, in fastings often, in cold and nakedness.

28. Besides those things that are without, that which cometh upon me daily, the care of all the churches.

29. Who is weak, and I am not weak? who is offended, and I burn not?

30. If I must needs glory, I will glory of the things which concern mine infirmities.

31. The God and Father of our Lord Jesus Christ, which is blessed for evermore, knoweth that I lie not.

32. In Damascus the governour under Aretas the king kept the city of the Damascenes with a garrison, desirous to apprehend me:

33. And through a window in a basket was I let down by the wall, and escaped his hands.

PARAPHRASE

XI.16 I say again let noe man think me a fool that I speak so much of my self. or at lest if it be a folly in me bear with me as a fool, that I too as well as others* may boast my self a little. 17 That which I say on this occasion is not by command from Christ but as it were foolishly in this matter of boasting.* 18 Since many glory in their circumcision or extraction* I will glory also. 19 For ye bear with fools easily being your selves wise* 20 For you bear with it if a man bring you into bondage*

XI.16* vid. ver. 18

17* vid XII.11

18* *After the flesh*· what this glorying *after the flesh* was in particular here vid ver. 22 (viz) being a Jew by discent.

19* Spoken Ironically, for their bearing with the insolence and coviteousness of their false Apostle

20* [a]The *bondage* here meant was subjection to the will of their false Apostle as appears by the following particulars of this verse, and not subjection to the Jewish rites. For if that had been St Paul was soe zealous against it [b]that he would have spoke more plainly and warmly as we see in his Epistle to the Galatians, and not have touched it thus only by the by slightly in a doubtfull expression. Besides it is plain no such thing was yet attempted openly, onely St Paul was afraid of it vid ver. 3.

i e domineer over you and use you like his bond men; If he make a prey
of you; If he take or extort presents or a salary from you; If he be
elevated and high amongst you; If he smite you on the face, i e. treat you
contumeliously. [21] I speak according to the reproach has been cast upon
me as if I were weak, i e destitute of what might support me in dignity
and authority, equal to this false Apostle as if I had not as fair pretences
to power and profit amongst you as he. [22] Is he* an Hebrew i e by
language an Hebrew? so am I: Is he an Israelite, truly of the Jewish
nation and bred up in that religion? so am I: Is he of the seed of
Abraham realy descended from him, and not a proselyte of a forain
extraction? soe am I. [23] Is he a minister of Jesus Christ? (I speak in my
foolish way of boasting) I am more soe. In toilsome labours I surpasse
him: In stripes I am exceedingly beyond him·* In prisons I have been
oftener; and in the very jaws of death more than once. [24] Of the Jews I
have five times received forty stripes save one: [25] Thrice was I whipd
with rods: Once was I stoned: Thrice Shipwracked: I have passed a
night and a day in the sea: [26] In journyings often: In perils by water; in
perils by robbers; in perils from my own country men; in perils from the
heathen; in perils in the citty; in perils in the country; in perils at sea; in
perils amongst false brethren; [27] In toile and trouble and sleepless
nights often; in hunger and thirst; in fastings often; in cold and nakedness. [28] Besides these troubles from without, the disturbance that comes
dayly upon me from my concerne for all the churches. [29] Who is a weak
Christian in danger through frailty or ignorance to be mislead whose
weakness I doe not feel and suffer in as if it were my own? who is actualy
mislead for whom my zeale and concerne does not make me uneasy as if
I had a fire in me? [30] If I must be compelled* to glory† I will glory of

22* [a] *Is he an Hebrew?* Haveing in the foregoeing verse spoke in the singular number I have been fain to continue on the same number here though different from that in the text, to avoid an inconsistency in the paraphrase which could not but shock the reader. [b] But this I would be understood to doe without imposeing my opinion on any body or pretending to change the text; But as an expositor to tell my reader that I think, that though St Paul says *they* he means but one, as often when he says *We* he means onely himself· the reason whereof I have given else where.

23* [a] 'Εν πληγαῖς ὑπερβαλλόντως *In stripes above measure*, rather. *In stripes exceeding*. For these words as the other particulars of this verse ought to be taken comparatively with reference to the false Apostle with whom St Paul is compareing him self in the ministry of the gospel. [b] Unless this be understood soe there will seem to be a disagreeable tautologie in the following verses, which, takeing these words in a comparative sense, are proofs of his saying· *in stripes I am exceedingly beyond him for of the Jews five times* etc

30* *Compelled* vid XII.11

† By καυχᾶσθαι which is translated sometimes to *glory* and sometimes to *Boast* the Apostle all along where he applys it to him self means noe thing, but the mentioning

those things which are of my weak and suffering side. [31]The god and
father of our Lord Jesus Christ, who is blessed for ever knoweth that I
lie not. [32]In Damascus the governor under Aretas the king, who kept
the town with a garison being desireous to apprehend me, [33]I was
through a window let down in a Basket and escaped his hands

SECTION IV. NO. 6

Ch. XII.1–11

CONTENTS

He makes good his Apostleship by the Extraordinary visions and revelation. which he had received

TEXT

XII.1. It is not expedient for me doubtless to glory: I will come to visions and revelations of the Lord.

2. I knew a man in Christ, above fourteen years ago (whether in the body I cannot tell; or whether out of the body, I cannot tell: God knoweth) such an one caught up to the third heaven.

3. And I knew such a man (whether in the body, or out of the body, I cannot tell: God knoweth)

4. How that he was caught up into paradice, and heard unspeakable words, which it is not lawful for a man to utter.

5. Of such an one will I glory: yet of my self I will not glory, but in mine infirmities.

6. For though I would desire to glory, I shall not be a fool; for I will say the truth: but now I forbear, lest any man should think of me above that which he seeth me to be, or that he heareth of me.

7. And lest I should be exalted above measure through the abundance of the revelations, there was given to me a thorn in the flesh, the messenger of satan to buffet me, lest I should be exalted above measure.

8. For this thing I besought the Lord thrice, that it might depart from me.

9. And he said unto me, My Grace is sufficient for thee: for my strength is made perfect in weakness. Most gladly there fore will I rather glory in my infirmities, that the power of Christ may rest upon me.

10. Therefore I take pleasure in infirmities, in reproaches, in necessities, in persecutions, in distresses for Christ's sake: for when I am weak, then am I strong.

some commendable action of his without vanity or ostentation but barely upon necessity on the present occasion.

11. I am become a fool in glorying, ye have compelled me: for I ought to have been commended of you: for in nothing am I behind the very chiefest apostles, though I be nothing.

PARAPHRASE

XII.1 If I must be forced to glory* for your sakes for me it is not expedient, I will come to visions and revelations of the Lord· 2 I knew a man* by the power of Christ above 14 years agoe caught up into the third heaven, whither the entire man body and all or out of the body in an extasie I know not; god knows. 3 And I know such an one* whither in the body or out of the body I know not; god knows, 4 that he was caught up into Paradise and there heard what is not in the power of man to utter. 5 Of such an one I will glory· But my self I will not mention with any boasting unless in things that carry the marks of weakness and shew my sufferings. 6 But if I should have a mind to glory in other things I might doe it without being a fool for I would speak noe thing but what is true, haveing matter in abundance·* But I forbear lest any one should think of me beyond what he sees me or hears commonly reported of me· 7 And that I might not be exalted above measure by reason of the abundance of reveleations that I had there was given me a thorn in the flesh* the messenger of Satan to buffet me, that I might not be over much elevated. 8 Concerning this thing I besought the Lord thrice that it might depart from me; 9 And he said· my favour is sufficient for thee. For my power exerts it self and its sufficiency is seen the more perfectly the weaker thou thy self art. I therefore most willingly choose to glory rather in things that shew my weakness than in my abundance of glorious revelations, that the power of Christ may the more visibly be seen to dwell in me. 10 Wherefore I have satisfaction in weaknesses, in reproaches, in necessitys, in persecutions, in distresses for Christs sake. For when I, lookd upon in my outward State, appear weak, then by the power of Christ, which dwelleth in me, I am found to be strong. 11 I am become foolish in glorying thus: But it is you who have forced me to it. For I ought to have been

XII.1* Εἰ καυχᾶσθαι δεῖ. *If I must glory* is the reading of some copys and is justified by ver. 30 of the foregoeing Chapter, by the vulgare translation, and by the Syriac much to the same purpose: and suiting better with the context renders the sense clearer

2 and 3* modestly speaking of himself in a third person

6* vid. ver. 7

7* *Thorn in the flesh*· what this was in particular St Paul haveing thought fit to conceale it is not easy, for those who came after, to discover; nor is it much material

commended by you. since in noe thing came I behind the cheifest of the Apostles, though in my self I am noe thing.

SECTION IV. NO. 7

Ch. XII.12.13

CONTENTS

He continues to justifie him self to be an Apostle by the miracles he did and the supernatural gifts he bestowd amongst the Corinthians

TEXT

XII.12. Truly the signs of an apostle were wrought among you in all patience, in signs, and wonders, and mighty deeds.

13. For what is it wherein ye were inferiour to other churches, except it be that I my self was not burdensome to you? forgive me this wrong.

PARAPHRASE

XII.12 Truly the signes where by an Apostle might be known were wrought among you by me in all patience* and submission under the difficultys I there met with, in miraculous wonderfull and mighty works performd by me. 13 For what is there which you were any way Shortend in, and had not equally with other churches* except it be that I my self was not burdensome to you. Forgive me this injury.

SECTION IV. NO. 8

Ch. XII.14-21

CONTENTS

He farther justifies himself to the Corinthians by his passed disinterestedness and his continued kind intentions to them

TEXT

XII.14. Behold, the third time I am ready to come to you; and I will not be

XII.12* This may well be understood to reflect on the haughtyness and plenty where in the false Apostle lived amongst them

13* vid 1 Cor. I.4-7

burdensome to you: for I seek not yours, but you: for the children ought not to lay up for the parents, but the parents for the children.

15. And I will very gladly spend and be spent for you, though the more abundantly I love you, the less I be loved.

16. But be it so, I did not burden you: nevertheless being crafty, I caught you with guile.

17. Did I make a gain of you by any of them whom I sent unto you?

18. I desired Titus, and with him I sent a brother: did Titus make a gain of you? walked we not in the same spirit? walked we not in the same steps?

19. Again, think you that we excuse our selves unto you? we speak before God in Christ: but we do all things, dearly beloved, for your edifying.

20. For I fear, lest when I come I shall not find you such as I would, and that I shall be found unto you such as ye would not: lest there be debates, envyings, wraths, strifes, back-bitings, whisperings, swellings, tumults:

21. And lest when I come again, my God will humble me among you, and that I shall bewail many which have sinned already, and have not repented of the uncleanness, and fornication, and lasciviousness which they have committed.

PARAPHRASE

XII.14 Behold this is the third time I am ready to come unto you. But I will not be burdensome to you. For I seek not what is yours but you: For 'tis not expected nor usual that children should lay up for their parents, but parents* for their children. 15 I will gladly lay out what ever is in my possession or power; nay even wear out and hazard my self for your souls* though it should soe fall out that the more I love you the less I should be beloved by you† 16 Be it soe as some suggest, that I was not burdensome to you, but it was in truth out of cunning with a designe to catch you with that trick, drawing from you by others what I refused in person. 17 In answer to which I aske, Did I by any one of those I sent unto you make a gain of you? 18 I desired Titus to goe to you, and with him I sent a brother. Did Titus make a gain of you? Did not they behave themselves with the same temper that I did amongst you? Did we not walk in the same steps. i e neither they nor I received any thing from you. 19 Again* doe not upon my mentioning my sending

XII.14* vid 1 Cor IV.14.15

15* vid. 2 Tim. II.10

† vid Ch VI 12.13

19* [a]He had before given the reason, Ch I.23 of his not coming to them, with the like asseveration that he uses here. If we trace the thread of St Pauls discourse here we may observe that haveing concluded the justification of him self and his Apostleship by his past actions, ver. 13 [b]he had it in his thoughts to tell them how he would deale with the

of Titus to you think that I apologize for my not comeing my self I speak as in the presence of god, and as a Christian· there is noe such thing: In all my whole cariage towards you, beloved, all that has been done has been done onely for your edification. Noe there is noe need of an Apologie for my not comeing to you sooner. [20]For I fear when I doe come I shall not find you such as I would; and that you will find me such as you would not: I am afraid that among you there are disputes, envyings, animositys, strifes, backbiteings, whisperings swellings of mind disturbances. [21]And that my god when I come to you again will humble me amongst you, and I shall bewail many who have formerly sinned, and have not yet repented of the uncleaness, fornication, and lasciviousness where of they are guilty.

SECTION IV. NO. 9

Ch. XIII.1-10

CONTENTS

He reassumes what he was goeing to say Ch. XII.14 and tels them how he intends to deale with them when he comes to them· And assures them, that however they question it he shall be able by miracles to give proof of his authority and commission from Christ.

false Apostle and his adherents when he came as he was ready now to doe. And therefore solemnly begins ver. 14 with *Behold* and tells them now *the third time* he was ready to come to them, [c]to which joyning (what was much upon his mind) that he would not be burdensome to them when he came, this suggested to his thoughts an objection (viz) that this personal shiness in him was but cunning, for that he designed to draw gain from them by other hands. [d]From which he clears him self by the instance of Titus and the brother whom he had sent together to them who were as far from receiveing any thing from them as he himself. Titus and his other messenger being thus mentioned, he thought it necessary to obviate an other suspition that might be raised in the minds of some of them, [e]as if he mentioned the sending of those two, as an Apologie for his not comeing himself. This he disclaims utterly. And to prevent any thoughts of that kind solemnly protests to them, that in all his cariage to them, he had done noe thing but for their edification nor had any other aim in any of his actions but purely that. [f]And that he forbore comeing merely out of respect and goodwill to them. Soe that all from *Behold this third time I am ready to come to you* ver. 14 to *This third time I am comeing to you* Ch: XIII.1 must be lookd on as an incident discourse that fell in occasionaly though tending to the same purpose with the rest. [g]A way of writeing very usual with our Apostle, and with other writers who abound in quickness and variety of thoughts as he did. Such men are often by new matter riseing in their way put by from what they were goeing. and had begun to say, [h]which therefore they are fain to take up again and continue at a distance which St Paul does here after the interposi⟨ti⟩on of eight verses. Other instances of the like kind may be observed in other places of St Pauls writeings

TEXT

XIII.1. This is the third time I am coming to you: in the mouth of two or three witnesses shall every word be established.

2. I told you before, and foretel you as if I were present the second time, and being absent, now I write to them which heretofore have sinned, and to all other, that if I come again I will not spare:

3. Since ye seek a proof of Christ speaking in me, which to youward is not weak, but is mighty in you.

4. For though he was crucified through weakness, yet he liveth by the power of God: for we also are weak in him, but we shall live with him by the power of God toward you.

5. Examine your selves, whether ye be in the faith, prove your own selves: know ye not your own selves, how that Jesus Christ is in you, except ye be reprobates?

6. But I trust that ye shall know that we are not reprobates.

7. Now I pray to God that ye do no evil; not that we should appear approved, but that ye should do that which is honest, though we be as reprobates.

8. For we can do nothing against the truth, but for the truth.

9. For we are glad when we are weak, and ye are strong: and this also we wish, even your perfection.

10. Therefore I write these things being absent, lest being present I should use sharpness, according to the power which the Lord hath given me to edification, and not to destruction.

PARAPHRASE

XIII.1 This is now the third time I am comeing to you. And when I come I shall not spare you, haveing proceeded according to our saviours rule, and endeavoured by fair means first to reclaim you, before I come to the last extremity: 2 And of this my former epistle where in I applied my self to you. and this where in I now as if I were present with you foretell those who have formerly sinned, and all the rest to whom being now absent I write, that when I come I will not spare you. I say these two letters are my witnesses according to our Saviours rule which says· in the mouth of two or three witnesses every word shall be established* 3 Since you demand a proof of my mission

XIII.2* [a] *In the mouth of two or three witnesses shall every word be established*. These words seem to be quoted from the law of our Saviour Mat. XVIII.16 and not from the law of Moses in Deuteronomy not onely because the words are the same with those in St Matthew but from the likeness of the case. [b]In Deutronomy the rule given concerns onely judicial trials: In St Matthew it is a rule given for the management of perswation used for the reclaiming an offender by fair means before comeing to the utmost extremity and of what I deliver that it is dictated by Christ speaking in me. who must be acknowledged not to be weak to you ward but has given sufficient marks of his power amongst you. [4]For though his crucifixion and death were with appearance* of weakness, yet he liveth with the manifestation* of the power of god appearing in my punishing you. [5]You examin me whither I can by any miraculous operation give a proof that Christ is in me: Pray examin your selves whither you be in the faith; make a trial upon your selves whither you your selves are not some what destitute of proofs.⟨*⟩ or are you soe little acquainted with your selves as not to know whither Christ be in you? [6]But if you doe

which is the case of St Paul here: In Deuteronomy The Judg was to hear the witnesses Deut: XVII 6. XIX.15· [c]In St Matthew the party was to hear the witnesses Mat XVIII.17. which was also the case of St Paul here. The witnesses which he means that he made use of to perswade them being his two Epistles. That by witnesses he means his two epistles is plain from his way of expresseing himself here [d]where he carefully sets down his telling them twice (viz) *before* in his former epistle Ch. IV.19 and now a *second time* in his second epistle. And also by these words ὡς παρὼν τὸ δεύτερον, *As if I were present* with you *a second time*. By our Saviours rule the offended person was to goe twice to the offender. [e]And therefore St Paul says *as if I were with you a second time*, counting his letters as two personal applications to them as our Saviour directed should be done before comeing to rougher means. Some take the witnesses to be the three messengers by whom his first epistle is supposed to be sent. [f]But this would not be according to the method prescribd by our saviour in the place from which St Paul takes the words he uses· For there were noe witnesses to be made use of in the first application. neither if those had been the witnesses meant would there have been any need for St Paul soe carefully and expresly to have set down, [g]ὡς παρὼν τὸ δεύτερον, *as if present a second time*, words which in that case would be superfluous. Besides, those three men are noe where mentioned to have been sent by him to perswade them, nor the Corinthians required to hear them, [h]or reproved for not haveing done it: and lastly they could not be better witnesses of St Pauls endeavours twice to gain the Corinthians by fair means before he proceeded to severity, than the Epistles themselves

4* [a]Ἐξ ἀσθενείας *through weakness* ἐκ δυνάμεως θεοῦ *by the power of god* I have renderd *with appearance of weakness* and *with the manifestation of the power of god*, which I thinke the sense of the place, and the style of the Apostle will justifie. St Paul sometimes uses the Greek prepositions in a larger sense than that tongue ordinarily allows. [b]Farther it is evident that ἐξ joynd to ἀσθενείας has not a causal signification, and therefore in the antithesis ἐκ δυνάμεως θεοῦ it cannot be taken causally. And it is usual for St Paul in such cases to continue the same word, though it happen some times seemingly to carry the sense another way. [c]In short the meaning of the place is this. 'Though Christ in his 'crucifixion appeared weak and despicable, yet he now lives to shew the power of god 'in the miracles and mighty works which he does: So I though I by my sufferings and 'infirmitys appear weak and contemptible yet shall I live to shew the power of god in 'punishing you miraculously.'

5.6.7* [a]Ἀδόκιμοι translated here *Reprobates* 'tis plain in these three verses has noe such signification, Reprobation being very remote from the argument the Apostle is here upon but the word ἀδόκιμος is here used for one that cannot give proof of Christ being in him; [b]one that is destitute of a supernatural power. for thus stands St Pauls discourse ver. ⟨3.⟩ Ἐπεὶ δοκιμὴν ζητεῖτε ver. 6. γνώσεσθε ὅτι οὐκ ἀδόκιμοί ἐσμεν. *Since you seek a proof ye shall know that I am not destitute of a proof*

not know your selves whither you can give proofs or noe yet I hope you shall know that I am not unable to give proofs* of Christ in me. [7]But I pray to god that you may doe noe evil, wishing not for an oportunity to shew my proofs* but that you doeing what is right I may be as if I had noe proofs* noe supernatural power. [8]For though I have the power of punishing supernaturally I cannot shew this power upon any of you unlesse it be that you are offenders and your punishment be for the advantage of the gospel. [9]I am therefore glad when I am weak and can inflict noe punishment upon you, and you are soe strong i e clear of faults, that ye cannot be touched. For all the power I have is onely for promoteing the truth of the gospel· whoever are faithfull and obedient to that, I can doe noething to; I cannot make examples of them by all the extraordinary power I have if I would. Nay this also I wish even your perfection. [10]These things therefore I write to you being absent that when I come I may not use severitie according to the power which the Lord hath given me for edification not for destruction

SECTION V

Ch. XIII.11–14

TEXT

XIII.11. Finally, brethren, farewell: be perfect, be of good comfort, be of one mind, live in peace; and the God of love and peace shall be with you.

12. Greet one another with an holy kiss.

13. All the saints salute you.

14. The grace of the Lord Jesus Christ, and the love of God, and the communion of the holy Ghost, be with you all. Amen.

CONCLUSION

[XIII.11]Finaly Brethren farewell. Bring your selves into one well united firm unjaring society:* Be of good comfort: Be of one mind: Live in peace and the god of love and peace shall be with you. [12]Salute one an other with a holy kiss. [13]All the saints Salute you. [14]The grace of our Lord Jesus Christ, and the love of god, and the communion of the holy ghost be with you all.

Amen

XIII.11* The same that he exhorts them to in the begining of the first Epistle Ch: I. ver. 10

MANUSCRIPT NOTES

For an explanation of signs and abbreviations, and for a discussion of the transcription of the manuscript, see Introduction, pp. 78–81, 83–6.

GALATIANS

SYNOPSIS

a	`of St Paul′ (*cf. next note*)
a	[his] [St Pauls] `his′ Epistle
e	`and erected . . . among them′ (*mostly in margin*)
f	[law] Jewish Church
i	[ịṇṭẹṇ⟨ded⟩] had in his mind
i	`ḥạḍ′ donne

Section I: I.1-5

CONTENTS

	[Paraphrase] Contents
a	per[verts]`verters′
f	[ịṇṭṛọḍụçṭion] `preface′

PARAPHRASE

I.1	raised [up] him up
I.4	[us] our sins
I.4	th⟦ẹ⟧is [ṣẹçụḷaṛ ụṣẹ of this ẉọṛld (*all appears to be a superimposed correction*)] `present evil′ world
I.4	[our] god and our`father

NOTES

I.1*b	[Hịṣ ẉạs not onely designed] His choise
I.4*f	[Though] ⟦t⟨he⟩⟧The law [ḅẹ] `is′ said to be
I.4*f	speaks [very deminishingly of the ṛitual part of it, yet it may be doubted whether upon any of these accounts he would cal the Mosaical constitution abstractly considerd πονηρός and] {speaks} very . . . parts of it (*cf. textual note ad loc.*)
I.4*f	justify[ing]
I.4*g	⟦F̣⟨or⟩⟧for

Section II: I.6-II.21

CONTENTS

b	⟦ḥịṣ⟧that [opinion of] `he promoted not´
b	th⟦ọse⟧em that

PARAPHRASE

I.7	that [that whẹṇ] you
I.7	`who´
I.7	[o]the[r] [Mosaical rites] `keeping of the law´ (*in margin*)
I.8	`my self´
I.8	`for´ (*in left margin at top of fo. 205^{r}, and also catchword at bottom of fo. 204^{v}*)
I.10	[thought] `doubted´ (*in margin*) of me [that]
I.10	[that] `whether´ I [should] `doe´
I.10	court† to men [†]
I.11	⟦ḅ⟨rethren⟩⟧Brethren
I.13	[with ex⟨cessive⟩] how excessive
I.14	[ṛẹçẹịvẹd frọṃ] `of´ my forefathers
I.14	[many] many students
I.20	⟦F̣⟨alshood⟩⟧falshood
I.22	face [*̣] †
II.2	preach[ḍ] (*cf. textual note ad loc.*)
II.2	⟦ṛ⟨eputation⟩⟧note and reputation
II.2	taken [*̣] †
II.3-4	[[ṃy] the doctrine I preachd to the eminent men] {of the Church} [of Jẹṛụsalem yet I .... was so far from any cọṃpliaṇce] {to please men} [that I neither sufferd* Titus who was with me being a Greek to be circumcised in consideration of] `the gospel ... [a] `one´ moment ḅy ... ḷaw to´ (*in margin*)
II.4	`to the law´ (*in margin*)
II.5	[Nor* did I to thọse false breṭhren give way in the least or [pay any deference] [`yẹịḷḍ ṭọ them´] (*in margin*) [`........´] so much as f̣ọṛ a moment `yẹịḷḍ ṭọ ṭḥẹṃ ạṣ ọwṇịṇg ạṇy any subjection to the law.´] (owning ... law. *in margin*): But I
II.5	`against it´
II.6a	⟦ọf⟧as `for´ those
II.6a	revelation [...... and that .... that]
II.6b	had `they´
II.11	*Paragraph-break marker precedes* But; *cf. textual note ad loc.*

II.11	I opẹṇly
II.14	some times to live [some times]
II.17	their sins [fọrẹstated]
II.18	[so it will ⟨be⟩] certain it is, if I [*]
II.18	'all' my [former] transgressions
II.20	[dead.] thereby dead

NOTES

I.9*	*This entire note is an insertion;* 9* . . . of the *anathema is at the foot of the main column and* here to . . . seducers. *is in the margin*
I.9*	⟦8⟧9*
I.10*b	But [from the time that] 'when'
I.10*c	[avoided] shund
I.10*d	[opposed in their compliạṇçẹ with the ⟨law⟩] reproovd for their Judaizeing
I.10*d	tends 'to' (*no caret*)
I.10†	οὐ⟦κ⟧χ 'ὡς'
I.22*	'i e' (*no caret*)
I.22†	[Shewṣ] serves very well to shew
II.2*b	[they] 'he' had don
II.2*c	both *is a superimposed correction*
II.2*c-d	κατ' ἰδιάν . . . Act. XXI.18-33 *is an insertion (*τοῖς δοκοῦσι . . . 33 *in margin*). See . . . 33 *may have been inserted later than the rest; cf. textual note on II.2*d.*
II.2*c	to be owned by [ṣọṃẹ] those
II.2*d	18 [etc] -33
II.2‡c	the[iṛ] readiness
II.2‡c	[that] 'any such'
II.2‡c	Corinth [and in the Churches of Galatia as appears by his Epistles to the Corinthians and by thiṣ here to the Gạlatians which were writ about the same time. And it seems probable by what we find in this Epistle Ch. I.6. II.5.14. III.1 as if some had said that what he preachd was an other gospel and not the truth].
II.3*a	*compelled* [though in the Paraphrase which is intended to give what one conceives to be St Pauls meaning you find *I sufferd not* · The word ἠναγκάσθη *compelled* forbids us not to suppose that there were some endeavours towards it and then that it was St Paul that hindered it· The 9th ver. seems to import it Bụṭ yet St Paul who always uses the softest way of speakeing might choose to say [Ṇẹ⟨ither⟩]

Titus was not compelled ṭọ *ḅẹ circuṃçịṣẹḍ* rather than *I suffered him not to be circumcisẹd*] 'a plain . . . [ṛạṭḥẹṛ] Titus . . . alṭẹṛd by them ver. ḍ' (of the convert . . . ver. 6 *in margin*)

II.3*b — shew [hoẉ] to the Galatians [how averse he had been to] 'that . . . no thing of'

II.3*c — [dẹçl⟨ared⟩] communicated

II.4* — [very ṃụçh] answers . . . very much

II.4†b — for where . . . epistle *is an insertion,* for where *at the end of the line in the main column, and* compliance . . . epistle *in the margin*

II.5* — [f̣⟨reedom⟩] doctrine of freedom

II.5† — [opposed Titus's being circumcised, and] yeilded not

II.4, 5b — *neither* [ḷọọḳḍ] circumcised

II.4, 5c — caried 'it'

II.6*a — Διὰ

II.6*a — [ṭhạ⟨t⟩] to conclude that

II.6*a — [makes a plain distinction] intimates a plain distinction

II.6*b — (viz) [what] what

II.6†a — ⟦ḅ⟨ut⟩⟧But

II.6†b — [to] and suited to

II.6†e — haveing . . . [ḥaveing] ended

II.6†e — [most] cheif

II.7*c — *After the end of this note the following paragraph is deleted:*

[7* Though the Gospel that was revealed to St Paul was the same covenant of grace in all the parts of it which was preachd by St Peter and the other Apostles yet may not this way of expresseing himself here *The gospel of the uncircumcision* and *The Gospel of the circumcision* give us occasion to consider whether an exemption of the Gentile converts from the observances of the law might not ḅẹ more plainly and expresly revealed to St Paul than it haḍ been to the other Apostles of the Circumcision. who were therefore as we see not altogether so clear and forward in the case· That which seemṣ a little to look this way is St Pauls emphaticaly mentioning *HIS gospel* ịṇ ṃọṛẹ places than ọne That ọf Rom XVI.{33}⟨25⟩ deserves our ṇọṭẹ *Now to him that is of power to establish you according to my gospel* In which place we may observe that *establishing them according to his gospel* was the establishing them in an assurance of their freedom from the law; and upon the like occasion of Gods free grace to the Gentiles it is that he intrọḍụçes the mention of *HIS gospel* in most other places.]

II.8* — [here] *workeing in* . . . here

II.9*a	ˋno′ other
II.9*b	ˋas′ (*no caret*)
II.11*e	[ịṇ] (who were the men here meant) in
II.17*a	⟦Ṣ⟨inners⟩⟧17* *Sinners*
II.17*a	{from} all [after] ˋfrom′ justification (*cf. textual note ad loc.*)
II.17*b	[ẉ⟨e⟩] even we who [seek to be justified by] ˋhave betaken our selves to′ Christ ˋfor justification′
II.17*b-c	what [doe we else, but [by makeing the] make Christ contribute to our being in a state of sin and death.] ˋdeliverance . . . not of justification, {w}′ (*all after* deliverance *in margin*) which
II.19‡a	under [the power ⟨of⟩] his son
II.20†	[withḥ] in opposition

Section III: III.1-5

PARAPHRASE

III.1	[ọf bọṭ⟨h⟩ . . . . . before the sight of Christ crucified] of the gospel
III.1	suffering[s] (*cf. textual note ad loc.*)
III.1	[before yọụṛ ẹy⟨es⟩] in your sight
III.5	upon you [and the miracles don amongst you] . . . and don miracles amongst you

Section IV: III.6-18

PARAPHRASE

III.10	of* their (ir *inserted*) (*cf. textual note ad loc.*)
III.13	redeemed ⟦ṃẹṇ⟧us
III.14	[promise] spirit that was promised
III.16	[He] ˋGod′
III.17	ˋlong before made and′ ratified to [god] Christ, [lo⟨ng before⟩] ˋby god′
III.18	ˋthe′ (*no caret*) right
III.18	ˋto Abraham′ as certainly it is. For [god gave] the inheritance [to Abraham] was a [free] donation and free gift

NOTES

III.9, 10*	[. . . . . . .] the one
III.14*	⟦Ạ⟨re⟩⟧are
III.14*	[ọ⟨ne⟩] the one
III.14*	[. . . . . of . . . . . .] be in any doubt about it
III.16*	[ạṣ] spoken

Section V: III.19-25

CONTENTS

	the[ṃ] Israelites

PARAPHRASE

III.19a	what [what]
III.19b	`their sins and´ the punishment and death they incurred by the⟦ir⟧m [sins]
III.19b	[ṛẹceiṿẹd] `ingrafted´
III.19b	o⟦ṛ⟧f `god and´ (*in margin*)
III.19b	⟦Ṇọẉ⟧Whereby
III.19b	dịsaṇụḷ the pṛomise
III.21	opposite ⟦ṭọ⟧by
III.21	[by] which [life] could . . . life
III.21	by [thẹ] law†
III.22	[has] makes . . . and [*̣] Gentile . . . but has
III.22	[thẹ cọṇṣẹqụẹnce ọf ṣịn dẹạth] (*probably a superimposed correction*) guilt
III.22	blesseing [*̣]
III.23	Jews [*] [†]
III.23	[pr⟨isoners⟩] as a company of prisoners
III.23	[the] `the´ law

NOTES

III.19*	⟦t⟨he⟩⟧The law
III.20*a	⟦. .⟧17 is manifest [is] h⟦is⟧e is proveing
III.20*a	[but] by any other [person], but
III.20*c	a covenant [a covenant]
III.20*d	[on one side to them] to Abraham
III.20*e	Moses`'s´
III.20*e	present; [The other `Party´ was not there. nor [ḅẹ⟨ing⟩] Moses tra⟨n⟩sacted not long it being both [I⟨sraelites⟩] Gentiles and Israelites] But the other party `Abrahams seed´ . . . Gentiles
III.20*f	`the´ (*no caret*) Nation
III.20*f	.`and his seed´ which
III.20*f	⟦ịṇ⟧is in it self
III.22*	[which signifies] *All*, is

Section VI: III.26-9

PARAPHRASE

III.28	o⟦f⟧r free

NOTES

III.27*a	in ⟦in⟧ a few (*cf. textual note ad loc.*)

Section VII: IV.1-11

PARAPHRASE

IV.6	inables] s *inserted*
IV.6	father [*]
IV.7	Christ [*̣]
IV.8	[mục̣ḥ] under
IV.9	`ye´ are known
IV.9	[should] be willing
IV.11	begin to [begin to]

NOTES

IV.6*a	`ver. 5´
IV.9‡a	[just] matter

Section VIII: IV.12-20

PARAPHRASE

IV.18-19	you [:] my (*alt. of* My; *cf. textual note ad loc.*)
IV.20	⟦I⟧But `I´

NOTES

IV.18*b	[ạṇḍ] this . . . and
IV.18*c	`more´ ,
IV.18*d	`*onely*´
IV.18*e	w⟦ọṛḍṣ⟧ay he has [ụṣẹḍ] `taken´ (*in margin*) to express it [much] is much
IV.19*a	epistles ⟦ạṇḍ⟧or
IV.19*a	[English] translation
IV.20*a	hig`h´er
IV.20*a	[tọ⟨ne⟩] the tone
IV.20*b	⟦.⟧St Paul

Section IX: IV.21-V.1

PARAPHRASE

IV.21	2⟦2⟧1
IV.22	⟦..⟧there
IV.22	Abraham had two sons] *underlining deleted*

NOTES

IV.21*	has [has]
IV.22*	`*there*´
IV.27*	⟦I⟨sai:⟩⟧ *Written* (viz.) Isai:
IV.29*	[him that was] *born after the spirit*
IV.31*	gospel⟦,⟧.

Section X: V.2-13

CONTENTS

a	`without´
f	[th⟨at⟩] on him that

PARAPHRASE

V.2	fa`l´sly
V.3	[testifie again to every one] repeat here again . . . testifie to every one
V.5	w⟦ḥ⟨o⟩⟧e who
V.6	[under] `in´ . . . under
V.6	`Jesus´
V.6	; (*inserted*) All (*alt. of* all)
V.6	available [ṇọẉ] is
V.7	`has´
V.10	Lord, [that] you
V.11	[yet preach circumcision] at last . . . Circumcision
V.11	[the great offence of the gospel] `and so subjected . . . [ọṇ] soly on . . . salvation´ (*in margin*)
V.12	[were even] `may be´

NOTES

V.5*	*I* [*̣]
V.8*a	⟦ịṇ⟧Ch. . . . in
V.8*a-b	[see ver. 13] for he . . . see ver. 13
V.10*a	[and] `nor´ shaken
V.10*b	`warily´

V.10†	[ạ censure] expulsion by a Church censure· ⟦ver.⟧see ver. 12
V.11*	[thẹ] subjection to the law
V.11†	*This entire note appears to be an insertion*

Section XI: V.13-26

XI. [.....]

PARAPHRASE

V.19	manifest[ly]
V.20-1	[Ṃ⟨urders·⟩] Animosities . . . Murders
V.21	[of which] concerning which
V.24	[They] Now they
V.26	[by ostentation to] or to

NOTES

V.16, 17†e	*'of' the mind*
V.18*a	[of] to the Romans
V.20*	'either' (*cf. textual note ad loc.*)
V.24*	*'flesh'*

Section XII: VI.1-5

PARAPHRASE

VI.1	⟦ạṇḍ⟧or surprise
VI.1	fa⟦ụḷ⟨t⟩⟧ll into a fault
VI.1	[more advanced in the knowledg and practise of [thẹ] Christianity* with meekness and gentleness [..] reduce him into the right way and into [thẹ] your church communion] eminent . . . meekness

NOTES

VI.1*	'in' (*no caret*)
VI.4*a	th⟦i⟨s⟩⟧us . . . this
VI.4*a	Paul[e]
VI.4*a	[intend] 'discourse'
VI.4*b	to'o'

Section XIII: VI.6-10

PARAPHRASE

VI.7	[what] as
VI.9	[time] season when the ⟦ḥạ⟨rvest⟩⟧time of harvest

VI.9 — [ịf] and flag

Section XIV: VI.11-18

PARAPHRASE

VI.12 — observance[ṣ] (*cf. textual note ad loc.*)
VI.14 — `it´ (*in margin*) has
VI.15 — [the privileges and advantages which they partake in who are] a share . . . advantages
VI.15 — `Jesus´
VI.17 — [trouble] `give´ me trouble
VI.17 — preach [up]

NOTES

VI.11* — his [own] mouth
VI.16*a — [best] [`better´] be understood
VI.16*a — [than] `rather than´
VI.16*b — `*those*´ (*in margin*) *who walk*
VI.16*b — ⟦ạ⟧A [noe very unusual] way of Speaking `not very unusual´ (*no caret*) (*cf. textual note ad loc.*)

1 CORINTHIANS

SYNOPSIS

c — [in preaching the Gospel] every where might in[ḍụç̣ẹ ỵọụ] `cline´ one (*cf. textual note ad loc.*)
d — [Citty] merchant toẉn
d — [th⟦is⟧em] this church
d — the⟦ṛẹ⟧n
d — [one] `other´
e — faction [and sett him self at the head of a party] . . . party
e — of St Paul.] *followed by paragraph-break marker*
f — th⟦ịṣ⟧ẹ opposition
f — reasonṣ
g — authority [and] dignity and
g — [false Apostles and their adherents] `opposite party´; To (*alt. of* to)
g — [heads of the opposite faction] `cheif and leading men in it´
h — the[ịṛ] admiration . . . [them] those their leaders
h — division [in the church]
h — [in the obedience that with one accord they might adhere to the doctrine and discipline (*last three words previously underlined*)] that they might . . . receive and [acquiesce in]

	\`keep′ the doctrine and [directions he had or should] [\`ordinances′] \`directions he⟨s⟩
i	[on the false Apostles] \`on his opposers′ (*in margin*) and [the] \`of′ other

Section I: I.1-9

On fo. 102v are the following deletions:

[1 [Epis⟨tle⟩] Corinthians

1 Section [Ch] I Ch: 1-9

The introduction

[1]Paul an Apostle of Jesus Christ called to be soe by the will of god* and Sosthenes† unto the Church of god which is at Corinth to them that are separated]

[1* St Paul in most of his Epistles mentions his being *called to be an Apostle by the will of god* [a way] which way of speakeing being peculiar to him we may suppose him therein to intimate his extraordinary and miraculous call. v: Act. IX And his receiveing the Gospel by immediate Revelation. Gal. I.11.12

† Sosthenes. v. Act XVIII.17.]

INTRODUCTION

I.4-5	[given you by] \`bestowed on you through′ Jesus Christ, [that in every thing you are inrichd by him] soe that ⟦in⟧by him
I.7	\`short or′ deficient* [or unprovided]
I.8	of[*]

NOTES

I.1*	[doub⟨ted⟩]/doubted
I.2*a	\`here′ whose li⟦f⟧ves are [⟦very⟧ pure] pure
I.2*a-b	state [to the service of god as those who professed Christianity were] \`of mankind to (*from* to *in margin*) . . . to ⟦serv⟨ice⟩⟧the service of Idols ⟦or⟧and . . . mass [were] to be . . . were called . . . 9.10′

Section II: I.10-VI.20

b	th⟦ese⟧is pretended Apostle[s]
b	[as] \`into′ one
b	in a beleif [and obedience] . . . and in an obedience
c	[those [false Apostles] \`of the contrary faction′] \`his

opposers′ ([`of . . . faction′] *and* `his opposers′ *in margin*) (*cf. next paragraph in text*)

c th⟦ọse⟧eir Leaders

d w⟦hich⟧e

Section II. No. 1: I.10-16

CONTENTS

Conten⟦ce⟧ts
⟦under⟧ denominated `from′ (*in margin*) distinct teachers

PARAPHRASE

I.12 Leaders `and′ Masters (*cf. textual note ad loc.*)

NOTES

I.10*a [⟦ḥạṣ⟧ ịṣ ṣọ] is only
I.10*b `a forme . . . uses′ (*in margin and at foot of page*)
I.11* th⟦ịṣ⟧e entrance

Section II. No. 2: I.17-31

CONTENTS

Conten⟦ce⟧ts (*inserted title*)
sto⟦ỵ⟧p
chose [any one] `men′ to be [a] preachers of the gospel. Those [that he sent were quite otherwise qualified, and those qualifications were not of use in preaching the gospel] `[those] whom he made . . . men′ (*in margin*)

PARAPHRASE

I.17 learned and [learned] `eloquent′ (*in margin*) harangues
I.17 Christs (*final* s *may have been added by someone other than Locke*)
I.17 `if′ the stress of our persuasion `should′ (*in margin*) be[ing] laid on the [oratory and] learning
I.19 `the understanding′ (*in margin*)
I.20 [knowledg] `wisdom′ of the Greeks
I.20 [versed] `studied′
I.20 `learning and′ wisdome
I.22 [For] `Since both*′
I.22 [want eloquent and learned discourses of philosophie and humane knowledg] `seek wisdome′
I.23 [ṃẹṇ ạc̣ụte] acute men

I.24-5 [though] 'it is' to those [[who are called] 'very men called' to the understanding and beleif of it] both Jews and Greeks [it be when called Christ] (when they are converted) Christ the power of god and 'Christ' the wisdome of god. Because [whatsoever comes from god how much soever mistaken men may think of it the power and wisdome of it far] 'that which . . . by ⟦G⟨od⟩⟧god' surpasses the [utmost] power [and wisdom] of [the ablest] men

I.26 there 'are' not many [men] of the wise and learned men

I.27 chosen 'the' foolish

I.28 are [counted as] 'of noe account, are' noe thing† to [bring to nought] 'displace' those that are [thought very considerable]

I.30a-b [Tis not of your own power] 'Natural Humane abilities' parts or wisdome [but of god alone that ye are converted to gospel and ⟦ṭḥẹ⟧ṭṛụẹ faith and are thereby] 'could . . . you are' (*in margin*)

I.30b 'all that is of any value'

fo. 105ʳ ends with the words Where is the *from the paraphrase of I.20. fo. 106ᵛ continues with the words* philosopher skild. *fo. 105ᵛ is blank and fo. 106ʳ contains the following deletion of paraphrase for I.13–20:*

[was Paul crucified for you? or were ye baptised into* the name of Paul*? I thank god that I baptised none of you but Crispus and Gajus, lest any one should say I had baptised into my own name. I baptised also the household of Stepanas. (*followed by paragraph-break marker*)

Farther I know not whether I baptised any other: for Christ sent me not to baptise; but to preach the Gospel; not with learned and eloquent discourses, lest thereby the virtue and efficacy of Christs sufferings and death should be overlookd and neglected, the stress of our perswasion being laid upon the oratory of our preaching. For the plain insisting on the death of a crucified Saviour is by those who perish receivd only as a foolish contemptible thing; though [those] 'to us' who are saved. [find in] it 'be' (*no caret*) the power of god; conformable to what is prophesied by Isayah. I will destroy the wisdome of the wise, and I will bring to noe thing the understanding of the prudent. Where is the [man of learning and letters, knowing]]

Then follows this deleted note on I.13:

[13 Εἰς properly signifies *into* and soe the French translate it here. The phrase [to be] ⟦bapti⟨sed⟩⟧ βαπτισθ{ε}⟨ῆ⟩ναι *to be baptised into any one*, or *into any ones name* is solemny by that ceremony to enter [and pṛọfess] him self a [13* . . . disciples to . . . . . . Chṛịṣṭ] disciple of him into whose name he is baptised, with profession to receive his doctrine and rules and submit to his authority v. Ch. X.2 an argument why they should be called by noe ones name but Christs]

In the margin of the page the following words are inserted and then deleted:

[Section II N. 2

I.17-31

St Pauls first argument is that neither the learning of the Jews or Greeks fited or enabled any one to preach the gospel neither had god chosen such to it]

NOTES

I.20*a	`amongst the Jews;´
I.20*a	these `2´ (*no caret*) Epistles
I.20*a	pretended `to´ something
I.22*a	Pauls `reasonings´ (*in margin*)
I.22*a	[makes the reader overlooḳ] makes the reader overlooke
I.22*b	the [former] `21´ verse[s]
I.22*c	he [ḅẹ] had here
I.22*d	but [what they call] *wisdome*
I.25, 27, 28*	[28* He that will read the context cannot doubt but] 25. 27. 28* He . . . doubt but
I.25, 27, 28*	verses [ḅ⟨y⟩] in
I.28†a	⟦Ḅ⟨y⟩⟧by *the foolish*
I.28†a	`simple´
I.28†b	[take] `abolish . . . taking´ (*in margin*)
I.28†c	`not by Chance, bụt´ (*in margin*)
I.28†c	preteṇc⟦ẹḍ⟧e
I.28†d	upon that . . . abolish] *inserted* (account . . . abolish *in margin*)

Section II. No. 3a: II.1-5

CONTENTS

Conten⟦ce⟧ts

NOTES

II.1*b	revelation of th⟦at⟧e spirit
II.1*c	[testimony] preaching on the testimony
II.2*	Paul `who´
II.4*a	[.. ... b⟨y⟩] concerning
II.4*b	`14´

II.4*b	[*of god*] `*of god*, . . . *things*´ (*in margin*)
II.5*	[them] any of them

Section II. No. 3b: II.6-16

PARAPHRASE

II.7	[ḥiḍ] `conteined´
II.7	[god ordained] `has been . . . predetermined [ạṇḍ] in his own purpose´ (and hid . . . purpose *in margin*)
II.7	[to the glory§ of us who now understand and preach it ạgạịṇ*] to the glory[*]§ of us who `now´ understand and preach it
II.8	[the] none of the
II.10	out [and] all
II.12	what [is] `things are´
II.13	[but] not in the language and [stile] `learning´ taught [in the schools of Orators and Philosophers by the masters of Oratory and philosophie which are the learning and wisdom of humane original.] `by humane Eloquence and Philosophi´ (*in margin*)
II.13	the [revealeing them] `revelations conteined in the holy Scriptures´ (*in margin*)
II.13	other[*]
II.14	[doctrine of t⟨he⟩] truths of the
II.14	[only] by an other principle onely
II.14	⟦ḥịṣ⟧the bare `use of his´
II.14	`and the principles . . . ever´
II.16	`come to´ know the mind of [god] the Lord
II.16	`to instruct . . . mind of Christ´ (*in margin*) {by his natural wisdom to instruct and rectifie the spiritual* man· But I am sure I have the spirit of Christ whereby I know his mind, his doctrine⟦:⟧;} And (*cf. textual note ad loc.*)

NOTES

II.6*b	skil or abilities] or *is catchword*
II.6†	[n]*or*
II.6‡	[constitution which is commonly caḷḷẹḍ αἰὼν μέλλων or ἐρχόμενος *The world to come*.] constitution which is . . . *come*
II.6§b	`there is little ground to think that´
II.6§b	nation [with whom] `which´ (*in margin*)
II.6§b	esteem for [them or their learning]

II.6§c	among [,] them
II.6¶a	\`*to´ nought*
II.6¶b	true [glory] and lasting glory
II.7*a	\`the´ (*no caret*) revelation
II.7*a	Ch: [is] is
II.7†c	⟦uṇ⟨der⟩⟧in the old testament
II.7†d	III [.] 8.
II.7‡a	do⟦es⟧e (*cf. textual note ad loc.*)
II.7‡a	the sense of the place (*that phrase may have been added after next deletion, which occurs on next page of MS*) [the sense of it. αἰῶνες ịṇ the new testament seems often to import several considerable durations of time in ẉḥịçḥ man kind or at least the church of god was under different dispensations. Thus we may ţạķẹ the time before the floud. from the flọụd to the law. under the law. and under the gospel to be αἰῶνẹς Ḅụţ]
II.7‡a	instance[s]
II.7‡c	[ţịṃẹ] \`commencement´ of the concealment but th⟦e⟧ose [pẹŗşọņş] from whom it was concealed. [And soe αἰῶνες is to be understood in several other places.]
II.7‡c-d	Tis plain the . . . p. 17] *inserted* (Apostle . . . p. 17 *in margins*)
II.7‡c	⟦.⟧8th
II.7§	[*̣]§
II.7§a	{a} Christian [ţọ ţḥẹ] \`preachers and beleivers to the´ (*cf. textual notes ad loc.*)
II.7§a	amongst [them] \`the Corinthians´
II.7§a	\`as if he should have said´
II.7§a-c	\`Why doe . . . 6-̣1̣1̣´ (*in margins*)
II.7§a	by [extolling and] glorying [\`ạş you said´] in
II.7§a	\`upon account . . . endowmentş´ (*no caret*)
II.7§b	minister [ọf the gospel is] \`and disciple´ that . . . \`is to´ be an expounder [and] preacher \`and beleiver´
II.7§b	of [his] \`god´ which
II.7§b-c	[glory enough and] all the glory that belongs to us [ministers of the] gospel [and] \`consorts´ (as *is written in the margin before* ministers)
II.7§c	[and it is greatẹŗ] and this is enough
II.7§c	\`ver. 9´
II.7§c	[see] in Şţ Pauls account see
II.12*a	plụŗạl
II.12*b	and that] and *is catchword*
II.12*b	*we* [*teach*] *speak . . . teacheth*
II.12*b	sạys

II.12*b	*Ị ẉas*
II.12*b	[words] *speech*
II.12†	*th⟦e⟧is world (cf. textual note ad loc.)*
II.12†	here] *catchword*
II.16*a	[the] *spiritual*
II.16*a	not that [the] \`a´
II.16*b	[without the revelation of the scriptu⟨re⟩] by his bare . . . Lord
II.16*b	built [ạḷḷ]

Section II. No. 4: III.1-IV.20

CONTENTS

	Conten⟦ce⟧ts
a	the [. . .] faction
a	Leader[s]
a	[th⟦ese⟧is] \`their new´ (*in margin*) teacher[s]
b	cap[e]able
e	th⟦ese⟧is Leader[s]
h-i	cạṃẹ and (*inserted after next deletion*) [\`cạṃẹ and´] (*in margin*)
k	\`be´ honourd

PARAPHRASE

III.1a	[whọḷy] \`as to men [ḅụṭ] who had´ resigned
III.1b-2b	[This hinderd me that I could not gọẹ [. . . . .] \`so far as I ḍẹsired´ in the mysterys of the Christian religion [thẹṛẹ fọṛẹ] \`but was fạin to content my self with´ instructing you] {in̄ the} [\`more obvious and easy´ first principles \`ạṇḍ doctrins´ of it; and \`I could not apply my self to you´] \`But as to . . . my self to you´ (*in margin*) (*the deleted insertions have no carets*)
III.2b	\`mọre advanced´
III.2b	[thereby] discerning
III.2b	opinions[*]
III.4	\`doe´ not as spiritual men [according to what has been revealed by] [\`ṭḥạṭ ṃẹạṇịṇg ạḷḷ ṭḥẹịr . .´] \`[who] acknowledg . . . the spirit of god´ (*in margin*) {the spirit of god} (*cf. textual note ad loc.*)
III.5a	[under their names?] \`under . . . gospel´ (*in margin*)
III.5b	[ministers,] servants
III.5b	[and] which [you received and beleived according ṭọ that

measure of faith which god gave to each of you soe that] whether you looke on ⟦the⟧it [doctrine of the gospel]

III.5c upon [it in the reception you gave it even the faith whẹṛẹwith you received it, it is the gift of god, and there is noe room in either of these considerations to attribute (*latter word is a superimposed correction*) any thing to your selvẹs or] `the gifts . . . your teachers´ {your teachers} (*cf. textual note ad loc.*)

III.8 neither `of them´

III.9 `his´ work. . . . [every one of us] receive [his] reward . . . every one

III.9 ⟦.⟧cary on

III.11 `noe man´ can

III.11 `who has . . . I laid´ (*in margin*)

III.14 ⟦and⟧as

III.17 `or discipline´

III.18 `by his success´

III.22a are `yours´ for

IV.1 [lye] `have lain´

IV.4 `whose Steward I am´

IV.4 `sentence´

IV.5 [thọsẹ ẉḥọ] `shall . . . him [which] by god him self which he´ (*in margin*) truly deserves [prayse shall receive it of him].

IV.6a have `chosen to´ (*in margin*) name[d] (*cf. textual note ad loc.*)

IV.6b the [.] crying

IV.7 [from the free gift] `as intrusted to him´ of god

IV.8b I (*inserted*) wish [ṭṛụḷy] you did `truly´ (*cf. textual note ad loc.*)

IV.8b prosperity [of] `you enjoy now you are in´

IV.14 `to´ warn

IV.14 f`l´atter

IV.14 truth [,]

IV.15 `I warn . . . your father´

IV.19 make[*]

IV.19 `miraculous´ power of the [`miraculous´ (*in margin*)] holy g`h´ost

IV.20 doctrine `and prevalency´

IV.20 n *in* nor *is badly smudged, but probably not deleted*

IV.21 *After IV.20 a few words (perhaps intended for the paraphrase of IV.21) are deleted, beyond decipherment.*

NOTES

III.1†a-b [† Here πνευματικός *Spiritual* is opposed to σαρκικός *carnal* as Ch II.14 it is to ψ{ε}υχικός *natural* or rather *animal*. Soe that here we have three sorts of men 1 *Carnal* or such as are sẹṛṿẹd by fleshly passions and interests. 2 *animal*. i e such as seek wisdome or a way to happyness only by the guidance of their own natural parts without any supernatural light comeing from the spirit of god. i e by reason without revelation by philosophie without scripture. 3 *Spiritual* i e Such as [sọụght] `seek′ their direction to happyness not in the dictates of natural reason and philosophie but in the revelations of the spirit of god in the holy Scriptures] `† Here σαρκικός *carnal* is opposed to πνευματ[...] ικός . . . which [ḍẹṣc̣ṛịption] St Paul . . . such as had′ (*in margins*) (*cf. textual note on III.1**)

III.1†b-c — `not their understandings . . . divisions. [ịṇṭọ p̣ạṛṭỵṣ ọṇe declare/] `one declare/′ -ing for `the′ (*no caret*) doctrine . . . upon the doctrine of the′ (*in margin*)

III.1†c-d — gospel to have come . . . [ψυ{κ}⟨χ⟩ι⟨κοί⟩] πνευματικο[ς]ί took it. (*written in main columns after deletion recorded in next manuscript note had been made*)

III.2*, III.2†, III.2‡ — *These notes replace the following deletions (from the left main column of fo.* 115^{v}*):*

[2† That this is the meaning of the apostles metaphor of *Milk* and *Babes* may be seen Heb V 12-14
* vid Ch. II.13
‡ vid Heb V.14]

III.3* — [Ị ạṃ] speaking `*according to man*′

III.3* — [here applied to walkẹing] and soe *walkeing*

III.17* — 1⟦6̣⟧7*

III.17*b — `Ch: V.6′ (*in margin; cf. textual note ad loc.*)

III.18* — insịṣṭed ọn

IV.6† — 1 [and]

IV.16* — `only′ whose [scholars] `name′ they [should be⟨ar⟩] `should have borne′ (*latter in margin*)

IV.16* — [borne] sufferd to have any (*latter four words inserted*) `credit . . . amongst them.′ (*in margin*)

Section II. No. 5: IV.21-VI.20

CONTENTS

Conten⟦ce⟧ts

a — [the] St Paul

a — was oweing [was oweing]

d — `to be′ convened

f — matter `that′ (*cf. textual note ad loc.*)

g — [the holy Scripture is in many places miserably mangled to the noe smal interruption of the sense and disturbance of the reader] `ordinary people . . . Scriptur⟦es⟧e . . . coherence of it′ (others . . . it *in margin*)

h under⟦,⟧.

i th⟦at⟧e Fornication

j ⟦F̣⟨irst⟩⟧first

j `very′

o unlaw`full′

u [had or] observed or were under. Those [who were without]

PARAPHRASE

IV.21 *Although it is written in the main column, the paraphrase of this verse appears to have been added later. Also, the heading* Paraphrase *has been deleted to make way for the inserted material, and has been rewritten higher in the column* .

IV.21 [⟦Paraphrase⟧ you but what] you. But what (*see previous note*)

IV.21-V.1 [commonly reporteḍ that there is fornication . . . you and such* . . . . commonly] (*the deletion is itself a superimposed correction*) `with kindness . . . commonly′ reported . . . Heathen

V.3 ⟦ḅụṭ⟧yet

V.3 `thus′ (*in margin*)

V.5 [in the day of] `when′ our Lord Jesus

V.6 [yọụṛ] `a′ Leader

V.6 `ye that . . . leaven[eṭḥ] leaveneth the whole‡ lump?[†]′ (*in margin*)

VI.2 `world, and if the′ (*in margin*)

VI.4 [partys in things] `[jurisdiction] at any time . . . concerning things′ (at . . . things *in margin*)

VI.5 among you, `I speak it to your shame′ [who stand soe much upon your wisdome, one] `a′ wise* man (*cf. textual note ad loc.*)

VI.6 `in′ (*no caret*) the heathen [. . . . .] courts

VI.7 [there are any] `you so far′ contest[s] [concerning] matters of right [amongst you at all] `one . . . ju⟨d⟩gment′ (to trial or ju⟨d⟩gment *in margin*)

VI.8 `even′

VI.11 forgiven [†]

VI.12-15 *Between the paraphrase of VI.11 and that of VI.12 the following is deleted:*

[[12]But supposeing fornication were in it self lawfull.* In things that are lawfull to me I will not goe to the utmost

bounds of my liberty because it may not be expedient: In things that are lawfull to me I will not soe far indulge either custome or appetite as not to abstain in many cases:
[13]As in eating and drinking: [For] though [though the Belly be made onely for eating and] meat be made purposely for the belly, and the belly for meat, yet I will not be inslaved to any lawfull pleasure in eating and drinking. For though the belly were made only for eating and food onely to be eaten yet the time will be when god will put an end to the use of the belly and food: But the body which shall remain still was not made purposly that a man might be joynd to a woman* much lesse that in fornication he might be joynd to a Harlot: but it was made for our Lord Christ to be a member of him as Christ our Lord was made with a body that he might partake of our nature and be our head,
[14]soe that as god has already raised him up, soe he will raise us up likewise who are his members that our bodys may be like unto his glorious body and subsist even [when the belly and food shall be destroid*]. [15]Know ye not ⟦†̣†̣⟧
you that are soe well instructed that our bodys are the members of Christ? will you then take the members of Christ and make them]

VI.13a [Though Fornication should as you pretend be lawfull yet I would abstain rather than] For the body

VI.13b that [end] `use´

VI.13b [made] for a much nobler [end] purpose [which shall give it ạṇ endless duration in ṭḥẹ ọṭḥẹṛ ẉọṛld] `and shall . . . destroid´ (subsist . . . destroid *in margin*); The body is [made] for

VI.14 [lik⟨ewise⟩] already . . . likewise

VI.14 ⟦p̣⟨artake⟩⟧ the partakeing

NOTES

IV.21* *This entire note is in the margin*

IV.21* [censure] act of discipline

V.1* ⟦[1* ....⟧Chap to the eig⟨h⟩th and th⟨e⟩] `1*´ (*in margin*)

V.1† *This entire note is in the margin*

V.1†a [ạmọṇg] `ḅy´ the Roman[s] `laws´

V.1†a `yet´ it was lookd on

V.1†a [ignominious] `infamous´

V.1†b [what St Paul says here] `the present case´

V.6† [ḅẹẹṇ]/been guilty

VI.4*a-b `4* *Least* . . . authority [from superior c̣ọụṛṭṣ] and . . . cals here´ (*in margin*)

VI.4*b [4*] ἐξουθενημένους [`ị ẹ´] *Judices non authenticos* [de Dieu] i.e . . . `See´ *de Dieu*

VI.5* *This entire note is in the margin*

VI.5* `σοφός´ (*no caret; cf. textual note ad loc.*)

VI.5* ⟦ra⟨bbi⟩⟧Rabbi

VI.5* parts [amongst them. I incline to take it in the fọṛṃẹṛ sense].

VI.5* latter `sense´

VI.5* reflection [ṭọ] `on´

VI.8*a ⟦2̣⟧the [Cor VII.12] words . . . 2 Cor: VII.12

VI.8*a or at lest talked of (*in direction-line*)

VI.8*b `coherent and´

VI.11* *This entire note is in the margin*

VI.11* *sa`n´ctified*. i e

VI.11† [R⟦om⟧ev:] `Rev:´ (*in margin*)

VI.12*, VI.13*, VI.14* *Between notes VI.11* and VI.12* the following notes, which explain deleted paraphrase material for VI.12–14, are deleted:*

[12* St Paul haveing, upon occasion of injustice amongst them particularly in the matter of Fornication, warned them against these and other sins that exclude men from Salvation. he reassumes his former argument about Fornication in Particular, and by his reasoning here it looks as if some among them had pleaded that Fornication was lawfull: To which St Paul replys that it is not expedient to goe to the utmost bounds of what is lawful; And besides Fornication in a Christian is a degradeing the body makeing what is the member of Christ the member of an Harlot.

13* I have put in these words to make the Apostles sense the easier understood. For [upon the supposition he [is] argue⟦ing⟧s here of [fọṛṇịc̣ạṭịọṇ being lawful] `the fornication ḥere spoken of´ (*in margin*)] `he argueing here as he does upon a supposition that `ṭḥẹ´ fornication ⟦ẉạṣ⟧here spoken of was lawful´ (he . . . lawful *in margin*), *Fornication* in these words *the body is not for Fornication* must mean the lawful enjoyment of a woman otherwise it will [ṭọ] not answer the foregoeing instance of the belly and eating

14* vid Heb II.5-18]

VI.12*a against th⟦ịṣ⟧at

VI.12*c	\`a´ Christian man
VI.12*c	[ça̦u̦se] \`reason´ (*in margin*) to [....] animadvert
VI.12†b	made [for] to be
VI.12†c	\`of a Christian´
VI.12†d	be [[ț⟨he⟩]a] a member
VI.12†d	take (*alt. of* make) that which \`is´
VI.12†d-e	Christians.' [The cont⟨ext⟩] (*new paragraph*) The context
VI.12†e	eating [[&]and] any
VI.12†g	[contrary to the nature and constitution] not comporting with the dignity and principles
VI.12†g	foundation] *catchword*
VI.13*	lawfull [thȩ l̦⟨awfull⟩] Fornication ... lawfull
VI.13†	*This entire note is in the margin*
VI.14*a	[i̦n̦⟨cline⟩] strongly incline

Section III: VII.1-40

CONTENTS

	Conten[ce]ts
b	[thȩi̦r̦ n̦⟨ot⟩] marying or not marying

PARAPHRASE

VII.2	Should both ... [should] each
VII.3	like wise \`the wife´ ... and (*inserted*) vice versa
VII.5	th[ȩ]is time
VII.5	[y̦o̦u̦r̦]the [chastity] \`marriage bed´ (*in margin*)
VII.6	[but] not
VII.12	\`let him´
VII.12	h[i̦ș]er
VII.14	sc\`r´uple
VII.14	[and] \`or´ wife [can be] in respect ... can be
VII.14	\`as to his issue´
VII.15	that \`it is incumbent on us, whom´ god in the gospel [cals us Christians] has called to be [\`..´] Christians (to be *has been deleted, then restored by subscript dots*)
VII.15	[if] is not to [break with husband or wife and] make a breach in the family
VII.17	[In] Whatever ... contentedly in
VII.26	[celibate] \`a single life´
VII.28	s[ȩ]ins
VII.31	in it[*]†
VII.36	[daughter] \`virgin´ (*in margin*)

NOTES

VII.3*	injoyments. [unlawfull copulation and Idolatry and not precisely Fornication in our sense of the word. i e the unlawfull mixture of any unmaried couple.]
VII.14*a	others they] *latter is catchword*
VII.14*b	‘were’ proselyts
VII.14*b	see Note Ch. I.2] *perhaps inserted*
VII.20*b	therefore [for]/for
VII.20*d	‘new or’
VII.20*d	[not] remain
VII.23*b	which he] *latter inserted*
VII.25*a	[advịşed them against] ‘disswaded them from’ (*in margin*)
VII.25*a	‘ver. 28. and 35’ (*in margin*)
VII.31†	{3⟦2̣⟧1[*̣]}†
VII.31†	[2̣8̣ (*a superimposed correction*)] 28 ver. to the [beginin⟨g⟩] end
VII.37*a	παϱθένο[ς]ν ‘*Virgin*’ (*cf. textual note ad loc.*)
VII.37*b	[to be maryed] concernd
VII.37*d	‘*hath the power over his own will.*’
VII.37*d	before ‘by’
VII.37*f	[it were] ‘by it St Paul meant’
VII.37*f	‘Ch: IX.12 and’
VII.37*i	[might] should be guilty
VII.37*j	[resolved] ‘fully determind’

Section IV: VIII.1-13

CONTENTS

Conten⟦ce⟧ts

PARAPHRASE

VIII.1	of [our] ‘their’ knowledg
VIII.1	‘it is, that’ (*in margin*)
VIII.4	‘i e’ (*in margin*)
VIII.6	father ⟦f̣ṛọṃ⟧ and author
VIII.7	[ph⟨ansie⟩] imaginations of the phansie
VIII.7	deities (*alt. of dieties*), eat
VIII.10	hast ⟦ṣụç̣ḥ⟧this
VIII.12	[weak] brethren . . . weak consciences

NOTES

VIII.5*b	‘*gods many*. i e.’

VIII.5*c [to] 'from' the father [from] 'to' us
VIII.8* 'i e'
VIII.8† *This entire note is probably an insertion; cf. textual note ad loc.*
VIII.8‡ 'a' letter

Section V: IX.1-27

CONTENTS

Conten⟦ce⟧ts
a '2 Cor XI.5.6'
c-f My answer . . . write it.] *inserted* (these Inquisitors . . . write it. *in margins*)

PARAPHRASE

IX.7 goes [ạt] to . . . at
IX.7 [and] 'a' vin⟦e⟧yard and
IX.9 [Th] Doth
IX.12 any [others] partake
IX.12 ⟦we⟧I made noe use of [this] it
IX.12 [.] avoid
IX.16 [barely] preach the gospel[!] I doe barely
IX.17 [For if my zeal for the gospel cary me willingly beyond what is absolutely necessary in preaching it, I have some cause of glorying and may expect a reward] which if . . . reward
IX.18 therefore [shall] 'doe'
IX.20-1 ⟦that⟧the law: To
IX.22 whereby 'I might'
IX.23 'my self'

NOTES

IX.5* ⟦4⟧5*
IX.12*b 'refer,' (*no caret*) to a power [. . . . .]
IX.12*b speaking 'of' (*no caret*)
IX.12*b vid 2 Cor XI.20] *runs into the margin*

Section VI. No. 1: X.1-22

X.1-[XX.] ⟦1⟧22.

CONTENTS

Conten⟦ce⟧ts
c [That though it were lawfull to goe to those feasts yet it

might not be convenient or not for edification;] That eating of things [offered to Idols]

c escape[; And finaly that in all that they did they should aime at the glory of god and good of their neighbour].

PARAPHRASE

X.2 'and the sea' (*in margin*)
X.11 'for examples . . . admonition'
X.11 ages [*̣]†
X.16 be[come] members
X.18 [Consider the children of Israel according to the flesh: They] 'See how . . . them they' (*in margin*)
X.18 sacrifice [ạṇḍ]
X.20 [[Devils] 'Daemons' and not] 'Devils and not' (*in margin*)
X.22 [resist him when he lets loose his fury against you?] enter . . . almighty (*cf. textual note ad loc.*)

NOTES

X.5*a meat] *catchword*
X.5*b the '*very*' *same* spiritual food
X.5*b [eat] 'drank'
X.5*b wilderness] *catchword*
X.6* [Those] *evil*
X.11* 1⟦9⟧1*
X.11†b dispensation. [such αἰῶνες we may take to be. The time 'before the (*rest of insertion in margin*) floud, the time from the floud to the promise to Abraham, the time' that the Israelites were under the promise before the law, the time under the law. The Christian church under the promise of ạ kingdome. The Christian Church under the enjoyment of that kingdome, one of these αἰῶνες begining at Christs 1st comeing the other at his 2d comeing.]
X.16* passover] *first* s *inserted*
X.16† *This entire note is an insertion* (of the Jews . . . bread *in margin*)
X.21* says [in that verse]

At the foot of fo. 139[v], the page on which Section VI. No. 1 ends, is deleted the following material. It is very similar to that part of note X.11† which is written on fo. 138[v]. It was probably written too far ahead, deleted, and rewritten on fo. 138[v].

[that τέλη and συντέλεια τοῦ αἰῶνος or τῶν αἰώνων which we every where translate *the end of the world* doe not signifie every where one and the same time as will appear by compareing the places where they occur. viz Mat

XIII 39.40 XXIV 3. XXVIII.20 1 Cor X.11. Heb IX ?26 and therfore αἰών cannot signifie the world, which can have but one end, and the end of the world designe but one certain period of time. I aske therefore whether αἰών in the new testament may not be supposed commonly to signifie a certain considerable length of time under a certain dispensation such αἰῶνες we may take to be the state of the Israelites under the promise before the law; The state of the Israelites under the law: The state of the Christian church under the promise of a kingdome the state of the Church under the injoyment of that kingdome at Christs second comeing]

Section VI. No. 2: X.23-XI.1

CONTENTS

	Conten⟦ce⟧ts
c	'not' enough

PARAPHRASE

X.27	[any] makeing any
X.29	[should I use my liberty soe that an other mans (*latter* s *added*) [should ịṇ cọṇscience thịṇk Ị offended] 'be brought within the judgment or conscience* of'] 'is my . . . effect [effect] . . . Idolatry' (*latter insertion in margin*) (*cf. textual note ad loc.*)
X.31	[give god the glory of the right over his creatures by your giveing thanks] let . . . god
X.32	[Christians] members of the church

NOTES

X.29*	*This entire note is in the margin; cf. textual note ad loc.*
X.29*	[th⟨e⟩] a Christians
X.29*	[it] 'this use of his liberty'
X.29*	give ['couṇtenạṇce']
X.30*	*This entire note may have been inserted; cf. textual note ad loc.*
X.32*	*This entire note is in the margin; cf. textual note ad loc.*
X.32†	*This entire note is in the margin; cf. textual note ad loc.*
X.32‡	*This entire note is in the margin; cf. textual note ad loc.*

Section VII: XI.2-16

CONTENTS

Conten⟦ce⟧ts
⟦gị⟨ves⟩⟧uses

PARAPHRASE

XI.3	to [whom] Christ
XI.4	[supremacy] \`dominion´
XI.8	to ⟦hịṃ⟧the \`man´
XI.11	⟦ḍọẹ⟧have not [subsist or procreate] \`a being´
XI.12	ever since . . . propagated [ẹỵẹṛ since]
XI.13	⟦ṭḥạṭ⟧for
XI.15	[credit, to her] [\`ornament´] \`commendation´ (*latter words in margin*)

NOTES

XI.3*e	meant] *catchword*
XI.3*e	prayers \`that´
XI.3*f	their [their] performing
XI.3*f	\`and directs´
XI.3*h	unveyled [.]
XI.3*k	pḷace
XI.3*l	pray⟦ẹṛṣ⟧seṣ
XI.3*n	\`exhortation,´ (*in margin*)
XI.3*o-p	spirit of [gọḍ Ị ạṃ] \`god. This we are´ (*in margin*) sure
XI.3*p	\`here´ speaks of [in this Epistle]
XI.3*q	learned [and] and
XI.3*q	Scripture* \`*Mr Mede Disc. 16´ (*in margin. See textual note ad loc.*)
XI.3*q	uncovered [. . . . . (*about five words*)] \`when they´ (*in margin*) utterd
XI.3*w	[sort] \`kind´
XI.3*w	or [upon] as
XI.3*x	[p⟨owers⟩] abilitys
XI.3*z	\`to any extraordinary function´
XI.3*z	taken \`that´
XI.3*dd	[by] to god by

Section VIII: XI.17-34

CONTENTS

d	\`divided´ into (to *is an insertion*)
e	meale [food]

PARAPHRASE

XI.18	\`when´
XI.18	partys [and contentions]

XI.19	'there must be' (*in margin*) divisions and factions [must arise]
XI.21	For [every one] in eating . . . but every one
XI.26	[Fọṛ] Soe that
XI.27	[thịṣ] this bread
XI.27	suitabl⟦y⟧e to that end [is guilty] 'shall be guilty of a misuse'
XI.29	[that] who
XI.29	[unworth⟨yly⟩] 'after an' unworthy[ly] maner
XI.29	[reverend] 'purely sacramental'
XI.31	[singled out or distinguished* ḅy i e by the haṇḍ oḟ gọḍ ịṇflịçting diseases and death on thọse who doe not duely discriminate the Lords body] judged
XI.32	condemned hereafter [condemned]
XI.34	That soe [that]

NOTES

XI.27*b	'ver. 20' (*in margin*)
XI.27†	[shall] ἔσται shall
XI.27†	[use of the] 'use of the sacramen'tall'' (*in margin*)
XI.27†	'in the Lords' (*in margin*)
XI.27†	supper . . . 30] *inserted*
XI.28*b	[them] 'the bread and wine' (*in margin*)
XI.28*d	'this was donne by' (*in margin*)
XI.28*e-f	[as several others.] 'as several others. And . . . here?' (*in margin*)
XI.28†b	*that let* {*him*} *'a man'* (*smudge may be caret*) *examin* (*cf. textual note ad loc.*)
XI.29*b	çọmpanys
XI.31*a	translạṭẹḍ ḅụṭ ạlways
XI.31*b	discriminateing (*overlaps into margin*)
XI.31*b	discriminated (*overlaps into margin*)

Section IX: XII.1-XIV.40

Section IX [. .]
XII.1-[. . . . . . .] XIV.40

CONTENTS

b	[fṛọṃ Çḥ:] 'from Ch XII 21-25' (*in margin*)
b	[2̣1̣.] 40
e	a⟦s⟧re as

g though [.................... in the uṣe of the gifts] `gifts . . . use of them' (who . . . use of them *in margin*)

g [Çḥ ....]-XIII.1 [..]-13 (*cf. textual note ad loc.*)

h XI⟦ỊỊ⟧V: 1[4̣]-40

Section IX. No. 1: XII.1-3

PARAPHRASE

XII.1 [ạçted] assisted and acted

XII.3a [informe] `tell'

XII.3b i e . . . god. (*These words are in the main column, but may have been added, since they are crammed into a small space above the line which ends the paraphrase for this section*)

NOTES

XII.1*a pẹṛṣons and not giftṣ· Ạṇḍ ṭḥẹ

XII.1*c [for precedency] for precedency

XII.1*c [Ch XII 13 etc:] `ver. 13 etc of this Ch:' (*in margin*)

XII.3* Ạçt

Section IX. No. 2: XII.4-11

CONTENTS

`any' contention `for superiority'
account of [of]
[all] those
[ạḷḷ ọf thẹṃ] wrought

PARAPHRASE

XII.5 o⟦ff⟨ices⟩⟧f offices

XII.6 [supeṛṇạṭụṛạḷ operations] `influxes'

XII.7 [is] `has' the spirit, is

XII.8 [ạ faculty to explain and/and convinceingly ḷạy before others in the consistency beauty and symmetry of its parts the general systeme of the gospel of Jesus Christ] the revelation . . . Jesus Christ

XII.8 [espetialy] of the old testament

XII.10 `by' what spirit

XII.12-13 *The following has been deleted from this section. An almost identical paraphrase of these verses is to be found in Section IX. No. 3.*
[[12]For as the body being but one hath many members, and all the members of the body though many yet make but one body: soe is Christ in respect of his mystical body the

church. [13]For by one Spirit we are all baptised into one
church and are thereby made one body without any
preeminency to the Jew* above the Gentil; to the free
above the bondman, And the bloud of Christ which we all
partake of in the Eucharist makes us all have one life one
spirit as the same bloud [circulateing] diffused through
the whole body communicates the same life and spirit to
all the members]

NOTES

XII.6†a	[in⟨workings⟩] ἐνεργήματα–*inworkings*
XII.6†a	\`of themselves′ (*in margin*)
XII.6†b	\`and ver. 14′ (*in margin*)
XII.7*	*This entire note is in the margin*
XII.8†	[*]†
XII.9*a	\`*faith*′ (*in margin*)
XII.9*a	\`particularly Ch. XIII.2′
XII.9*a	[by] \`in′ enumerateing by
XII.9*b	may then
XII.9*b	\`*wisdome*′
XII.9*c	[the] \`*knowledg* the′ (*in margin*) gift
XII.9*c	[[[that]]faith] \`*faith* that′ (*in margin*) assurance
XII.10*	*This entire note is an insertion*
XII.10*	motion of the spirit. [.........] as

Section IX. No. 3: XII.12-30

XII.1[[3]]2-[31]30 (*cf. textual note ad loc.*)

PARAPHRASE

XII.12	\`as′
XII.12	[hath many members] hath many members
XII.19	the[se] gifts
XII.27	are [memb⟨ers⟩] by . . . members
XII.31	*The following paraphrase of the verse has been deleted. A different paraphrase of the verse is given in Section IX. No. 4.* [But ye contest one with an other whose particular gift is best and most preferable* But I \`will′ shew you \`thereby′ (*no caret*) a most excellent way viz mutuall goodwill affection and charity] (*cf. textual note on XII.30*)

NOTES

XII.28* [baptisẹd thọsẹ ẉhọ] were sent up and (sent up and *restored after their deletion*) . . . baptized `those that . . . them´ (*in margin*)

Section IX. No. 4: XII.31-XIII.13

XII [I,1-13] `31-XIII.13 [. .]´ (*cf. textual note ad loc.*)

CONTENTS

The whole of this Contents passage is an insertion (mostly marginal), replacing:

[Sṭ Paul haveing told the Corinthians in the last words of the precedent Chapter that he would shew them a more ẹxçẹllent way than the emulous produceing of their gifts in the assembly, he in this chapter tells them that this more excellent way is Charity which he at large explains and shews the excellency of.] (*cf. textual note ad loc.*)

a [given] their Lord . . . given

b absurd [that every one of them should have the most ḥọṇọụṛạḅḷẹ function]

PARAPHRASE

XII.31 `You make . . . excelling.´ (*largely in margin*)

XII.31 [there is yet I owne] I (notwithstanding . . . emulation)

XIII.1 [ṭḥ⟨ough⟩] If I

XIII.1 [but like] [b⟦ṛạ⟨ss⟩⟧ụṭ] noe better . . . brass

XIII.10 [perfection all these imperfecter ẉạys of `iṇfọṛṃạṭịọṇ ạṇḍ´ kṇọẉing ṣḥạḷḷ ḅẹ done away.] accomplishment . . . information

NOTES

XII.31*a `is plain´

XII.31*a section) [ạṇḍ] `which made ṭḥẹṃ´

XII.31*a desir⟦ḍ⟧ẹ to be heard

XII.31*b where `in´

XII.31*e *every* [ọṇẹ ạṣ ḥẹ ẉịḷḷ] *man severally as he will*

XII.31*g-h But says . . . his fellow] *apparently an insertion; cf. textual note on XII.31*g–i*

XII.31*g [every one] `you´ can not . . . every ones

XII.31*h-i `members. . . . adyạnced by them.´ (*in margin; cf. textual note on XII.31*g–i*)

XII.31† *This entire note is in the margins; cf. textual note ad loc.*

XII.31† `*a way*´
XIII.1† had] *catchword*
XIII.2*b Soe that *mystery* and] *apparently an insertion*
XIII.2*b `*knowledg* . . . others.´ (*in margin*)
XIII.2† *This entire note is in the margin*
XIII.2† doe

Section IX. No. 5: XIV.1-40

CONTENTS

answer

PARAPHRASE

XIV.2 [The things he says are unintelligible mysteries which he speaks by the spirit But he that speaks in an unknown tongue speaks to god alone but not to me for noebody understands him the things he says are [`unintelligible´] mysteries which he speaks by the spirit and are unintelligible to others. and soe] the things . . . not understood by those who hear them

XIV.3 [by the influence and impulse of the Spirit opens and explains the scriptures] `prophesieth*´ (*in margin*)

XIV.7 `as´ [cornet] pipe

XIV.8 `sound´

XIV.9 `which´

XIV.10 [different] `significant´

XIV.11 [an other man and] I understand not [one] an others language[s]

XIV.11 [our] `his´ words [naturaly]

XIV.15 take care that the meaning

XIV.15 the assistants

XIV.16 thou by the

XIV.16 how shall the hearer

XIV.19 [ten thousand] in an unknown tongue{*} ten thousand

XIV.20 [children in understanding who speak often without understanding or [without] unintelligibly without make-ing their meaning understood, but in disposition and temper being children without malice or spleen but speak with understanding as men doe] in understanding children* [who are forward to speak without being understood little minding the information of their hearers] `who are apt to be taken with the novelty or strangeness of things´ (*in margin*)

XIV.20	\`and use your understandings´
XIV.22	spẹạking
XIV.23	[with] \`in unknown´
XIV.24	[thẹ⟨n⟩] come
XIV.26	interpretation [*]
XIV.26	\`to edification´
XIV.27	interpreter: [*]\`‡´
XIV.29	[consider] examin
XIV.33	be⟦gị⟨ning⟩⟧cause
XIV.36	your sel⟦f⟧ves
XIV.37	prophesie[s] (*cf. textual note ad loc.*)
XIV.39	forbid not [ạṇy ọṇẹ]

NOTES

XIV.1*c	Ch. [X̣IV 3ị] \`XIV.15 concerning St Pauls custome of repeating words´ (*in margin*)
XIV.1*d	[maḳẹ] had an emulation or made
XIV.1*e	meanṣ
XIV.2*a	[section] this section
XIV.2*e	3° . . . 28] *perhaps an insertion; the writing overlaps into the margin*
XIV.2*e	ṭọṇgụes
XIV.3*	*This entire note, which explains the marginal insertion* prophesieth *in the paraphrase, may be an insertion*
XIV.6*a	thụṣ \`in the following significations´
XIV.15*a	[ọḅṣẹṛṿẹ] \`remark´
XIV.15*b	ṛẹpete
XIV.15*b	\`used´
XIV.15*b	sẹṇtiment
XIV.15*c	which ḥẹ used
XIV.15*c	sẹṇse
XIV.15*c	whẹṇ
XIV.15*c	use pṛạyịṇg
XIV.15*c-d	his own . . . utterd was] *many letters and the punctuation are decayed*
XIV.15‡	hẹld
XIV.20*	*This entire note is an insertion. It runs on from the end of note XIV.20†. For change of order, see textual note ad loc.*
XIV.26*a	ẹṃulations
XIV.27*a	shẹẉ
XIV.27*b	[sịmply fọṛ *if*] as I remember simply for *if*
XIV.27*c	[tọ ẹḍịfịçạṭion] in your assemblys only to edification

XIV.27‡ `would´ (*in margin*)

XIV.38* [ṭẉọ] foregoeing verse[s]

XIV.39* `and´ not `to the´ (*latter in margin*)

Section X: XV.1-58

CONTENTS

thụs

PARAPHRASE

XV.1-3 *Many letters and some punctuation marks are decayed*

XV.10 favour [and] of

XV.12 hạs bẹẹn rạịṣẹḍ fṛọṃ

XV.15 [rise] `are´ not raised

XV.21 since *is written at the end of the line in clearer script and may be an insertion*

XV.21 came also [came]

XV.23 shall [shall] rise those who `are´

XV.24 [put ạṇ end] bring to a conclusion

XV.31 ọn ṃẹ

XV.32 ḍẹạd

XV.32 wiṣẹr

XV.35 [ạṛẹ dead ṃẹṇ] `comes . . . dead are´

XV.35 ạṣ

XV.36 ḍạyly

XV.36 [...... ạẉạỵ,] `corrupts and´ dies [ạṇḍ c̣ẹạṣẹṣ ṭọ ḅẹ ẉḥạṭ it ẉạṣ]

XV.37 [pḷạṇṭẹṣṭ in the ẹạṛth] `sowest´

XV.41 stạṛṣ ḥave ẹạch

XV.41 stạṛ dịffẹṛs

XV.43 [ḷạịḍ ịṇ ṭḥẹ gṛ⟨ave⟩] `sown . . . die´

XV.44 [laid in the grave] `we have here´ surpasse⟦d⟧s

XV.44 spiritual[*] bodys

XV.50 you Brethren to satisfie [yọụ] those

XV.54 noe [ṃọṛẹ] death any more

XV.57 `who has . . . law´

NOTES

XV.8* 8* Aṇ ạḅọṛṭịvẹ biṛth ṭḥạṭ comẹṣ bẹfọre ịṭṣ ṭime ẉḥịc̣ḥ is ṭḥẹ

XV.8* mạdẹ

XV.8* fọḷḷọwing vẹṛṣẹ

XV.12*a [ḅỵ] `Ṣt Paul´ introduces this confutation by

XV.12*a thẹse

XV.12*b	\`such´
XV.29*b	inligḥṭẹṇ theṃ
XV.29*b	ṃạḍẹ ṭḥịṣ ẹxc̣ụrsion in the ẹịgḥṭ
XV.29*b	29ṭḥ rẹạssụṃẹs
XV.34*	3⟦*̣⟧4̣*
XV.34*	thẹṃ
XV.35*	*This entire note is in the margin*
XV.35*a	\`to´ contein
XV.35*b	attaining other bodyṣ
XV.39*	[tḥạt] viz That
XV.42*a	ạṭ several
XV.42*b	Just ịṣ
XV.42*b	\`treats and´ (*in margin*)
XV.42*b	ḅẹ the third
XV.42*c	dead⟦,̣⟧. [which ẹxplạinṣ] That
XV.42*e	\`ḥẹṛẹ´
XV.42*i	*us* or *we* w⟦ḥịc̣ḥ⟧ho
XV.42*j	*all* [ạḷḷ] sleep
XV.42*k	[ẉẹṛ⟨e⟩] are alive
XV.42*o	make \`all´
XV.42*o	shall \`ạḷḷ´ (*cf. textual note ad loc.*)
XV.42*q	ṭọ continue
XV.42*v	\`ạṣ´ that
XV.43*	*This entire note is in the margin*
XV.44*a	[ẹṇḍ⟨owed⟩] [fọṛṃ⟨ed⟩] [and] endowed
XV.44*c	[of] perpetualy of
XV.44*c	[says] \`speȧking´ (*in margin*) Luk XX.35 says
XV.44*c	[attain] obtain
XV.53*	*This entire note is an insertion*
XV.53*a	\`τοῦτο *this*´ *corruptible* (*cf. textual note ad loc.*)
XV.53*b	\`the´ persons [when]
XV.53*f	\`both´ (*cf. textual note ad loc.*)

Section XI: XVI.1-4

NOTES

XVI.2*	[or·off⟨icers⟩] appointed . . . or officers
XVI.3*a	[πεψω] πέμψω this
XVI.3*b	[⟦ṭḥẹṃ⟧him] himself
XVI.3*b	th⟦ẹỵ⟧ẹ Corinthians (*in margin*)
XVI.3*b	[send them] \`say´ he would send them

Section XII: XVI.5-12

PARAPHRASE

XVI.8 `stay´ (*in margin*)

Section XIII: XVI. 13-24

CONTENTS

`according to his custom´ leaves with `them´ (*cf. textual note ad loc.*)

PARAPHRASE

XVI.18 ⟦y̤o̤ṳ⟧me of you
XVI.18 too·* [so by removeing]
XVI.18 men[s]
XVI.24 ⟦t̤o̤⟧b̤e̤ `with´ you all [f̤o̤ṛ] `in´ Christ Jesus [sake]. [Amen.]/Amen. (*cf. textual note ad loc.*)

NOTES

XVI.22* *This entire note is written in smaller characters than the others in this section, and may be an insertion*
XVI.22* `2 Cor´ (*in margin*)

2 CORINTHIANS

SYNOPSIS

a [he] `it´ had
b g`o´od
c VI.[1̤2̤]11
d [in opposition to] `who was´ St Pauls opposer

Section I: I.1-2

NOTES

I.1*b supposed [here]
I.1*d Equal *is in the margin, but is probably part of the original text*
I.1† *This entire note appears to be an insertion*

Section II: I.3-VII.16

CONTENTS

`of St Paul´
`And seting . . . Corinthians´

Section II. No. 1: I.3-14

CONTENTS

The first fifteen lines and the first two words of the sixteenth line of these Contents (fo. 169^r-v) have been deleted. The deleted passage begins with the words [He begins it with justifying his former]. *Nearly all the rest of the deletion is indecipherable except for the final words, which are* [no occasion through out the whole Epistle to express a great tenderness for and esteem of them.].

The entire Contents as they now stand are an insertion, written in margins.

b	[of thẹṃ] direct

PARAPHRASE

I.5	[by] through
I.6	[preservation] [⸢deliverance⸣] ˋreleif,*′ which
I.6	iṭ ịṣ for your c̣ọṇṣọḷation and [ḍẹḷịṿẹṛạṇc̣ẹ] ˋreleif′ who
I.6	liḳẹ f̣roṃ the ṣạme
I.7	wḥịc̣ḥ gṛounḍ Ị
I.7	shạḷḷ liḳẹ wise hạṿe
I.8	woụḷḍ ṇọt ḥạṿẹ ỵọu igṇọṛạnt
I.8	afflictionṣ
I.11	[you also joyning] you also joyning
I.13	noe designe, [⟦ṇọ⟧ịṇ] noe meaning in
I.14	[⸢g̣lory being′ (*in margin*)] glory (*deleted, and subsequently restored by the insertion of stops under each letter*)

NOTES

I.3*	ṭṛạṇslation oḟ the Greek ḥẹṛẹ ṣẹẹ
I.3*	ˋand 1 Pet. I.3′
I.3*	wordṣ
I.3*	and that . . . 17] *inserted*
I.4*	4*
I.6*	*This entire note is in the margin*
I.14*	ˋwhich′ stuck to him and [gloried in] ˋowned′ (*in margin*) him

Section II. No. 2: I.15-II.17

CONTENTS

d	[. . . . .] ˋwas the′ (*in margin*) uncertainty
f	[All which we find] All which we find
f	⟦wạ⟨s⟩⟧is all

PARAPHRASE

I.15	a [my company the testimony of my kindness,] {a} second [time*] 'gratification*' (*cf. textual note ad loc.*)
I.18	[God is faithfull and may be .... that] But god
I.24	[ẉhọ ạṃ] 'as one' concerned
I.24	forwards (s *inserted*) your joy which I [desire] 'am tender of', and therefore [would ⟨not⟩] declined
II.2	[there] 'with you'
II.3	sad[*̣]
II.5	'I doẹ not say' (*inserted after next del.*) he has [not]
II.5	[I say this] that I may
II.9	'to obey me'
II.14	god [who] 'in that . . . Christ,' gives
II.14	by me[[,]]. [and makes me triumph every where*]
II.16	well/-pleaseing

NOTES

I.15*	*This entire note is in the margin*
I.21*	2[[2]]1*
I.21*	[for] to be
I.21*	as well as Kings *appears to be an insertion*
I.22*	2[[.]]2*
I.22†c	left [ọụt]
I.22†e	[certif⟨ied⟩] certain
II.5*	*This entire note is in the margin*
II.7*	[..] forni⟨cator as⟩ (⟨cator as⟩ *is supplied where the MS has been damaged*)
II.14*	*The line above this note consists of the following deletion:* [14* *Every where**]

Section II. No. 3: III.1-VII.16

Above the beginning of this section: [[[çḥ, II.ị-VIII.]] Section II.]

PARAPHRASE

III.1	as some† [doe],
III.3	[Nay you are manifested to be the Epistle of Christ which by my ministry is written not with ink but with the spirit of the liveing god not in tables of Stone but in the fleshy tables of your hearts i e your conversịọṇ by my] I need . . . conversion was the effect of my ministry

III.7 ministry[*̣] of the law[*̣] `written in stone′ which condems `to death′

III.7 `steadily behold′ thẹ ḅṛightness

III.8 [gospel] `spirit′

III.8 gospel?[*̣]

III.9 of condemnation [ọṛ of the lạẉ ẉhẹṛẹḅy all] were [c̣ọṇdẹṃṇẹd] glory, the ministry of [gospel] justification* in the gospel

III.11 [gḷọṛiọ⟨us⟩] deliverd with glory

III.11 [⟦ṛẹṃạịṇ⟧ạppẹạṛ] `appear′

III.14b `now he is come′

III.18 [brightness] clearness

IV.1 [am not remiss in the execution of it] doe not behave . . . it

IV.2 `from′ playing

IV.6 [spṛẹạd ṭ⟨he⟩] communicate the

IV.7 power ⌈of god⌉

IV.15b [mẹn] may give

IV.17 a⟦ṛẹ⟧t wors⟦ẹ⟧t are

V.5 `it is′ god who {is} prepare⟦ịṇg⟧s and fit⟦ịṇg⟧s (*cf. textual note ad loc.*)

V.5 `also′ (*in margin*)

V.6 `or sojourn′ (*in margin*)

V.9 [staying] staying

V.12 ṃạy

V.14 love of [god] Christ

V.14 `dead;′ (*in margin*)

V.16 `was′ (*no caret*) ọf

V.18 [has noe thing to doe with any thing ḅụṭ ẉḥạṭ is from god] `owes his [being in it and ạḷḷ the benefịṭs he enjoyṣ in it and receives from it ṭọ god alone] very being . . . god alone′

V.20 f⟦ṛọṃ⟧oṛ Christ

VI.6 giftṣ

VI.6 unfeig[h]ned

VI.12 streight[ẹṇẹḍ]

VI.14 [and] `or′

VI.16 [Lord] liveing god

VII.7 `your′ affection

VII.13 [by] `in′ your comfort

VII.13 [whose] because his mind

NOTES

III.3*a `of St Paul in′

III.3*b 'St Paul'

III.3*c hand] *catchword*

III.3*c [being a pretty bold expression] w⟦ẹṛẹ⟧as Christs

III.4, 5*a ⟦B⟨ut⟩⟧As if he had said.⟦.⟧ But

III.4, 5*b [confi⟨dence⟩] *Trust* [may not unfitly here be translated] 'a milder word for' *boasting*

III.4, 5*b [λογισμοί ver. 5 and] λογίζεσθαι ver. 7. [are] 'is' used

III.4, 5*c-d 'But if . . . preached to them.' (*in margin*)

III.6*c [he every where abounding in applications of passages in the law to Jesus Christ] espetialy

III.7*a κα'τα'ργουμένη

III.7*a ⟦ṭọ⟧and 'to' (*in margin*) the law

III.7*b [ạṣ ṿẹṛ ver. 1̣1̣] *that which remaineth* . . . as ver. [thẹ] 11

III.7*c '*from glory to glory*' (*in margin*)

III.10*b [may] in his thus . . . may

III.10*b [institution] ministration in [ṛẹgạṛd] comparison of

III.11* preeminency [which] and superiority of glory 'in the gospel'

III.12*a 'between' διακονία '*the*' *ministry*

III.13† *This entire note is in the margin*

III.13† [4] 2-4

III.16* *This entire note is in the margin*

III.17* [π⟨νεῦμα⟩] τὸ πνεῦμά

III.17† *This entire note is an insertion*

III.18*c 'the' begining

III.18*f-h [Besides ạṇ ọṭḥẹṛ ẹx̣p̣ṛẹss pạṛṭ ọf the comparison is between ạ vayld and an open face the one attributed to Moses ver. 13 the other to the ministers of the gospel in this verse. Now the action *beholding* was the action of the children of Israel but of *shineing* or reflecting the glory received in the mount was the action of Moses and therefor tis something answering that in the ministers ọf̣ the gospel wherein the çọṃpạṛiṣọṇ is] as is farther . . . comparison

III.18*i *th⟦ẹ⟧at very*

III.18*l [thẹ πα̣⟨ρρησία⟩] παρρησία

IV.1*a *greạt plainess*

IV.2* [and] explain

IV.4‡ *This entire note is in the margin*

IV.6*d 'as Christ' (*in margin*)

IV.16* V.9. *is in the right margin, overlapping from the right main column, and is probably part of the original text*

IV.17* *This entire note is in the margin*

V.3* That *is a superimposed correction*
V.3* lookd ⟦ṭọ⟧on
V.3* appẹars
V.3* `15-V.6′
V.3* `Rom . . . X.37′ (*in margin*)
V.4*b [X̣. . :] `XV′.53
V.5* speaḳṣ ọf
V.6, 8*a [iṇ] *we are confident* signifie in
V.6, 8*b `the resurrection and′
V.9*a [*ṛẹṇdẹṛ ḥịṃṣẹḷf ạpp̣ṛọṿẹḍ*] *be well pleaseing*
V.9†a [ẉịṇ] convince ([ẉịṇ] *is a superimposed correction*)
V.9†b `momentaneous′
V.9†d [ẹṇsuṛẹ] fix ([ẹṇsuṛẹ] *is a superimposed correction*)
V.10* *This entire note is in the margin; cf. textual note ad loc.*
V.17*a Apostle [ạṇḍ ḥịṣ pạṛṭị⟨zans⟩] gloried
V.17*b verses] *catchword*
V.17*c heard `him′
V.17*c κτίσις . . . VIII 22 *is an insertion* (*all except* κτίσις *is in margin*)
V.17† St *is a superimposed correction*
VI.1* [*Iṇ ṿạịṇ*] *Receive . . . in vain*
VII.11* `by and to′ (*in margin*)
VII.11§b invalidat⟦ẹing⟧s
VII.11§c `to′ (*perhaps with caret*) rectifie

Section III: VIII.1-IX.15

IX.1⟦1⟧5

PARAPHRASE

Paraphrase] *inserted*
VIII.6 [whereby*̣] `Insomuch that′
VIII.7 `act of′
VIII.8-9 [Fọṛ yẹ ḳṇọẉ] This I say . . . For ye know
VIII.8 [make trial of the] shew the
VIII.8 `genuine′
VIII.12 [a willing mind when it ẉạṣ] `every mans charity [is accepted]′ ịs accepted
VIII.12 `by god′ (*in margin*)
VIII.12 according to [what ạ man hạs, and not according to what he has not] `the largeness . . . fortune′
VIII.14 throug`h′
IX.10 supplys seed to the sower [supply you with] `and′ bread for

food: [and ạḷṣọ] `supply and' multiply [ṭḥẹ] `your stock of' seed [ṭḥạṭ yọụ have ṣọẉṇ]†

IX.13 [supply] subjection

IX.13 [Christ] Christ

NOTES

VIII.1* `And δεδομένον . . . *given by'* *is an insertion*

VIII.8*d ⟦.⟧who excel

IX.2* [ṣṭọọd] was made up

IX.9 and 10* `i e' (*in margin; cf. textual note ad loc.*)

Section IV. No. 1: X.1-6

X.1-6

CONTENTS

`in preaching the gospel ạṇḍ' to punish (ạṇḍ *is badly smudged. It is not clear whether it is meant to be deleted or not*)

PARAPHRASE

X.1 ạṃ (ạs ṭis

X.1 ḅọḷḍ

X.2 [conclude] `count'

X.2 [[by] `according to' the corrupt and inordinate desires of the flesh,* ọṛ ṭḥạṭ I ṃạṇạge my self by ẉọṛḷḍly inteṛẹṣtṣ ọṛ the indiṛẹçt arts of hụṃạṇe life.] `wholy by carnal considerations.' (*in margin*)

X.3 [by humạṇẹ artifice ọṛ ạṇỵ sụçḥ fḷẹṣḥḷỵ ṃẹạṇs] according to the flesh

X.4 not [such ẉẹạk things as flesh and blood] fleshly* but such as [çọṃẹịṇg fṛọṃ] god [are by his assistance] `hath made' mighty

X.4 [all] strong holds

X.5 `by the wit of men' against the knowledg of god [ḅỵ ṭḥẹ ẉịṭ ọf ṃẹṇ] as held forth in the gospel

NOTES

X.1† disçọụṛṣẹ by çọnjureing

X.1† meeḳṇẹss

X.1† ẹxçụse

X.1† *After this note the following is deleted:*

[[.] 3.4* That by [*ẉạḷḳing accọṛding to thẹ fḷẹsh*]

warring after the flesh And *Carnal weapons* expressions which the Apostle uses in these [tḥṛẹẹ] two verses noe thing is meant but bare humane arts and acquisitions such as lẹạṛning, eloquence, address ṃạnagement, cunning, etc and not the corrupt and vitious inclinations of the flesh is manifest from what he opposes to theṣẹ ver. 4 5. and 6. (viz) the supernatural ạṇḍ miraculous powers of the ḥọly ghost accompanying his preaching, where by he çọụld subdue all that stood in opposition. That this is the meaning of this place is fạrther evident from what follows. in this Chapter where he insists more]

X.4*	*This entire note is in the margin*
X.4*	[ạṛẹ] and those . . . *throug`h´ god* are
X.6*a-b	Cọrinthian[s whom ḥẹ endẹạvọụrs to ḅṛiṇg back again to their former obedience. And tis these Corinthian[s] converts he ṃẹạns when he says to them *You all* Ch II.3, VII.13.15 (viz) the pẹṛṣọṇs he writes tọ] converts . . . Achaia
X.6*a	ạgạiṇṣt
X.6*b	[Ị̈Ṿ] III.6
X.6*c	[ḥọpẹṣ] `hopes XI.13-1ṣ´ (*in margin*)

Section IV. No. 2: X.7-18

PARAPHRASE

X.8	⟦ṣạ⟨y⟩⟧boastingly say
X.8	ṣḥaṃe
X.9	lẹṭṭẹrs
X.9-10	[ṭḥạṭ] by some, who say that
X.12	selves[‡̣] doe
X.13	or alloted `to´ me
X.13	w⟦ịḷḷ⟧hich
X.18	him-/`-self´ (*in margin*)

NOTES

X.8*	*This entire note is in the margin*
X.8†	[8̣]†
X.12†a	[ṃạḍẹ] agains̀t
X.12‡	⟦ạḅ⟨ove⟩⟧and set themselvs above
X.12‡	⟦ṇ⟨ext⟩⟧4 next
X.13*	[ṇọṭ] `not´ signifie immens⟦ẹṛ⟧e

X.15, 16†a	15.16 *is an insertion, partly in margin*
X.15, 16†a	[ḥẹạḍ] man that . . . head
X.15, 16†c	sẹṭịṇg
X.15, 16†d	mentions [ḥịṃ ṭọ ḅẹ]
X.15, 16†d	\`thụș seting . . . XV.20. [And perhaps 'tis hard to find that preaching of the gospel is any where used in the New Testament for any thing but declareing ụṇto those who were not yet converted to Christianity]´ (*in margin*)
X.15‡	*This entire note is in the margin; cf. textual note ad loc.*

Section IV. No. 3: XI.1-6

PARAPHRASE

XI.2	⟦ạș⟧with
XI.4	[who is now your leader] who has been a Leader amongst you
XI.5	[Christs] \`the´ Apostles of Christ

NOTES

XI.3*f	*The following is in the margin:* \`but [should be corrupted by the doctrin of Judaisme] (*latter words are a superimposed correction*) should be . . . freedom \`from´ . . . light to this´

Section IV. No. 4: XI.7-15

7-1⟦6⟧5

PARAPHRASE

XI.9	Ḟọṛ

NOTES

XI.12*	refuṣẹịṇg ạny
XI.12*	ọụṭ of
XI.13*	directḷy ḍeclars

Section IV. No. 5: XI.16-33

1⟦7⟧6-33

CONTENTS

16-2⟦9⟧1

PARAPHRASE

XI.16 [ḥẹṛẹ] bear
XI.18 [outward priviledges and advantages] [ˋbeing circumcised ˊ] ˋtheir circumcision or extraction ˊ*
XI.22 bre[a]d
XI.22 pros⟦y⟧elyte
XI.30 ˋare ˊ

NOTES

XI.20*a [ḷạẉ] ṛịtes
XI.22*b [ḅụṭ] be understood
XI.23*a-b ˋto the false . . . etc ˊ (*in margin*)
XI.23*a ˋis ˊ compareing

Section IV. No. 6: XII.1-11

PARAPHRASE

XII.5 [this man] ˋsuch an one ˊ
XII.5 [ọf] my self I [shạll ṣạy ṇọẹ thịṇg] will not . . . boasting
XII.5 unless [ṭḥạṭ]
XII.6 ˋhave a mind to ˊ
XII.6 wịṭhout [ạp̣p̣ẹạṛịṇg] ˋbeing ˊ a [ỵạịṇ] fool
XII.6 noe thing ḅụt
XII.6 forḅeaṛ
XII.9 ˋmost willingly ˊ
XII.10 [considerd] ˋlookd upon ˊ in my [self, am] ˋoutward State ˊ (*in margin*), ˋappear ˊ

NOTES

XII.1* [If I must (*latter only partially deleted*)] *If I must*
XII.1* [the] ver.

Section IV. No. 7: XII.12-13

PARAPHRASE

XII.13 we⟦ṇ⟨t⟩⟧re

Section IV. No. 8: XII.14-21

PARAPHRASE

XII.18 they [and I] behave
XII.18 ˋthat I did ˊ
XII.19 Christian (*foll. by short gap*)/

NOTES

XII.15*	vid. *appears to be an insertion*
XII.19*a	\`ver. 13′
XII.19*c	[hạḍ] \`designed to′ draw[ṇ] gain
XII.19*c	[Titus and the brother] other hands
XII.19*d	who w⟦ạṣ⟧ere
XII.19*h	[other instạṇçẹṣ whereof may be found in other Episṭḷẹs of St Paulṣ writing which .... will be ...... Ģạḷạṭịạṇṣ ạṇḍ Ŗọṃạṇṣ] \`Other instances ... writeings′ (*the words* whereof ... Ŗọṃạṇṣ *are a superimposed correction*)

Section IV. No. 9: XIII.1-10

CONTENTS

assures \`them′

PARAPHRASE

XIII.3	but has given sufficient [but has given suffi⟨cient⟩]
XIII.4	crucifi[ct]\`x′ion
XIII.5	\`whither you your selves′
XIII.8	[miracles] \`punishing supernaturally′

NOTES

XIII.2*a	[ṭạḳẹṇ] quoted
XIII.2*b	[ỊX̣] Deut: XVII
XIII.2*e	as ⟦ş⟨hould⟩⟧our Saviour directed should
XIII.2*e-f	⟦Ḅ⟨ut⟩⟧to be sent. But
XIII.2*g	wo⟦ụ⟨ld⟩⟧ṛḍṣ which in that case would
XIII.2*g	the⟦ṣẹ⟧ṃ, \`nor the′ Corinthians
XIII.4*a	[as suitable to] \`which I thinke′ (*in margin*) the sense ... will justifie
XIII.4*c	[ịṇ] by my sufferings

TEXTUAL NOTES

For an explanation of signs and abbreviations, and for a discussion of textual matters, see Introduction, pp. 74-86.

THE PREFACE

p. 103[a]	*now*:] W | *now* 1
p. 105[a]	*himself*] W | *himself*, 1
p. 114[a]	*Apostles*] W | *Apostle's* 1
p. 114[b]	5.] W | 5 1
p. 115[a]	*Christ's*] W | *Christ* 1
p. 115[b]	*it*;] W | *it*, 1
p. 115[c]	*him;*] *edit.* | *him*, 1

GALATIANS

In 1 *and* 2, *but not in* L, *the following is included after the title-page of the part of the work dealing with Galatians. The text of* 1 *is reproduced, but* 2 *differs from it only in formal features.*

THE PUBLISHER TO THE READER

There is nothing certainly of greater concernment to the Peace of the Church in general, nor to the direction and edification of all Christians in particular, than a right understanding of the Holy Scripture. This consideration has set so many Learned and Pious Men amongst us of late Years upon Expositions, Paraphrases and Notes on the Sacred Writings; that the Author of these hopes the fashion may excuse him for endeavouring to add his Mite, believing, that after all that has been done by those great Labourers in the Harvest, there may be some Gleanings left, whereof he presumes he has an Instance Ch. III. *v*.20. *and some other Places of this Epistle to the* Galatians, *which he looks upon not to be the hardest of* St. Paul'*s. If he has given a Light to any obscure Passage, he shall think his pains well imploy'd: If there be nothing else worth notice in him, accept of his good Intention.*

SYNOPSIS

In L *there is no note about the date at the beginning of the Synopsis but a note is to be found at the beginning of Section I. In* 1 *and* 2 *at the top of the outer margin above the Synopsis, alongside the title* THE EPISTLE of St. *PAUL* TO THE *GALATIANS.*, *is printed:* Writ from *Ephesus* the Year of our Lord 57. Of *Nero* 3. (*cf. textual note for beginning of Section I*)

a	much what] L | much 1,2
c	therefore] L | therefore, Writing to the *Romans*, 1,2
h	seems] L | seems to be 1,2
h	6-10] L | 6.10 1,2
i	17.] L | 17. of the VI. *Ch*. 1,2

Section I: I.1-5

The year . . . Ephesus] L; *not in* 1,2; *but see textual note for beginning of Synopsis*

CONTENTS

b	Paul had] L | *Paul* himself had 1,2
b	truth] L | in that Truth 1,2
c	of their] L | on their 1,2

PARAPHRASE

I.1	deference on] L | deference upon 1,2

NOTES

I.1*a-b	*In* L οὐδὲ δι' ἀνθρώπου . . . 6-9 *is part of this note, and does not constitute a separate paragraph. In* 1 *and* 2 *it is a separate note, explaining* any man.
I.1*b	i e] L | *nor by Man*, i.e. 1,2
I.2*	amongst] L,1 | among 2
I.4*c	That Kingdome . . . people of god] L | The Nation of the *Jews* were the Kingdom, and People of God, whilst the Law stood. And this Kingdom of God under the Mosaical Constitution, 1,2
I.4*e	violence of] L | Violence to 1,2
I.4*f	speaks] 1,2 | speaks speaks L (*cf. manuscript note ad loc.*)

Section II. No. 1: I.6-II.21

CONTENTS

b	*Christ*] L | *Christ* v.6,7 1,2
c	servant of Christ:] L | Servant of Christ, *v*.10. 1,2
d	upon him self] L | upon himself *v*.8,9. 1,2
f	and there] L | and when he there 1,2

f	preachd to] L | Preach'd among 1,2
g	or did] L | nor did 1,2

TEXT

II.7	Peter;] 1703 | *Peter*. 1,2
II.8	Gentiles)] 1703 | *Gentiles*). 1,2

PARAPHRASE

I.6	who . . . Christ] L | (who . . . Christ) 1,2
I.6-7	Gospel which . . . else] L | Gospel; Which is not owing to any thing else 1,2
I.9	have] 1,2 | have/have L
I.9	accursed.⟨*⟩] 1,2 | accursed. L
I.17	instruction] L | instructions 1,2
I.17	into] L | unto 1,2
II.1	Then fourteen *does not begin a new paragraph in* L *but begins one in* 1 *and* 2
II.2	before them⟨*⟩] *edit.* | before them L,1,2 (2 *has a footnote sign after* which I)
II.2	preach] L | Preached 1,2 (*cf. manuscript note ad loc.*)
II.6a	here to fore] 2 | here to fore‡ L,1
II.6b	not taught] L | taught 1,2
II.10	forward to] L | forward to do 1,2
II.11	But when *begins a new paragraph in* L *but not in* 1 *and* 2; *cf. manuscript note ad loc.*
II.16	soly by faith] L | solely by Faith, 1 | solely by Faith 2
II.16	justification by faith] L | Justification by Faith, 1,2
II.17	who seek] L | seek 1,2

NOTES

I.6*a	above] L | about 1,2
I.6*b	year] L | years 1,2
I.7*a	ἕτ⟨ε⟩ρον] 1,2 | ἕτηρον L
I.7*b	V] L,1 | *Ver* 2
I.10*b	instruction] L | Instructions 1,2
I.10*c	pretence of] L,1 | pretence to 2
I.10†	*perswad* in our translation] L | translated *Perswade* 1,2
I.17*a	οὐ] L | οὐ and 1,2
I.17*a	the designe] L | Design 1,2
I.17*a	shew that] 1,2 | shew that that L
I.17*b	and apostle] L | and an Apostle 1,2

I.17*b not from] L | not with 1,2

II.2*b miracles] L | Miracle 1,2

II.2*c persons and] L | Persons, 1,2

II.2*d See Act. XXI.18-33] L*; not in* 1,2 (*cf. manuscript note on II.2* c–d*)

II.2† ⟨Phil⟩ | *edit.* | Colos L,1,2

II.2† propagateing] L | the propagating 1,2

II.2‡b concerning] L | of 1,2

II.3*d circumcision there] L | circumcision there, 1,2

II.4*, II.4†, II.4‡, II.5*, II.5† *are given in this edition in the order in which they occur in* 2. *In* L *they are arranged in the order 4‡, 4*, 5†, 4†, 5*, but are numbered differently. In* 1 *they are arranged in the same order as in* L, *except that 4† is printed there not as a separate note but as the second paragraph of 5†.*

II.4* ⟨4⟩] 2 | 5 L,1

II.4†a point that] L | point 1,2

II.4‡ ‡] *edit.* | 4* L,1 | (*d*) 2

II.5* 16 V.7] L | 19.*v*.7. 1 | 19. 2

II.4, 5b shewing] L | the shewing 1,2

II.6*, II.6†, II.6‡ *are given in this edition in the order in which they occur in* L *and* 1. *In* 2 *they are printed in the order 6*, 6‡, 6†. In* L *6* explains* But, *6†* these, *and 6‡* realy. *In* 1 *6* explains* those, *6†* realy, *and 6‡* here to fore. *In* 2 *6* explains* those, *6†* pleases, *and 6‡* men.

II.6†a here] L | there 1,2

II.6†c satisfied] L | satisfied it 1,2

II.6‡a tran⟨s⟩lation] 1,2 | tranlation L

II.6‡b ⟨9⟩] *edit.* | 3 L,1,2

II.7*a ⟨7⟩] 2*; not in* L,1

II.7*b imm⟨e⟩diate] 1,2 | immdiate L

II.7*b alter] L,2 | after 1

II.9*b he end] L | the end of 1,2

II.11*c decree] L,2 | degree 1

II.11*e were] L,1 | are 2

II.11*f from] L,2 | for 1

II.14*a else ⟨but⟩] 1,2 | else that L

II.15* 17-23] L | 17.23 1,2

II.17*a Those] L | These 1,2

II.17*a all from] 1,2 | from all from L (*cf. manuscript note ad loc.*)

II.17*b all] L | also 1,2

II.17*b selves, are,] L,1 | selves; 2

II.18* speakeing it] L | speaking 1,2

Section III: III.1-5

CONTENTS

	opend] L | open'd, 1,2

PARAPHRASE

III.1	suffering] L | Sufferings 1,2 (*cf. manuscript note ad loc.*)

NOTES

III.5*	καλ⟨έ⟩σας] *edit.* | καλήσας L,1,2

Section IV: III.6-18

TEXT

III.10	Cursed] 1 | cursed 2
III.18	*In* 1 *and* 2 *this verse of AV is at the beginning of the next section*

PARAPHRASE

III.8	Sacred] L (*reads* S:)*; not in* 1,2
III.10	their] L | the 1,2 (*cf. manuscript note ad loc.*)
III.11	for] L*; ital.* 1,2
III.14	by] L*; not in* 1,2
III.15	Brethren *begins a new paragraph in* L*and* 1 *but not in* 2
III.18	promise, to Abraham] L | promise to *Abraham*, 1,2

NOTES

III.9, 10*	See . . . note.] L*; not in* 1,2 (*see explanatory note ad loc.*)
III.12†	⟨XVIII 5⟩] *edit.* | VIII.15 L,1,2
III.14*	side is so] L | side, so 1,2
III.14†a	receiveing] L | having received 1,2
III.16†, III.16‡	*follow the order of* 2. *In* L *and* 1 *they are in reverse order.*

Section V: III.19-25

CONTENTS

	shews them] L | shews 1,2

TEXT

III.18	*See the note on the Text ad loc. in the previous section*

PARAPHRASE

III.21 blesseing] L | the blessing 1,2

NOTES

III.19† was] L; *not in* 1,2
III.20*a manifest] L | manifest that 1,2
III.20*a di⟨s⟩anulled] 1,2 | dianulled L
III.20*a both] L | by both 1,2
III.20*b giveing] L | giving of 1,2
III.20*b between the I⟨s⟩raelites] 1,2 | between the Iraelites L
III.20*f di⟨s⟩anulled] 1,2 | dianulled L
III.21† an exact] L | any exact 1,2
III.22* next verse] L | Text 1,2
III.22† 32] L | 22 1,2
III.22‡ is in] L | in 1,2

Section VI: III.26-9

PARAPHRASE

III.29 one seed] L | ones, Seed 1,2

NOTES

III.27* 27] L,2 | 25 1
III.27*a a few] L | few 1,2 (*cf. manuscript note ad loc.*)
III.29* *the promise*] L | *Promise* 1,2

Section VII: IV.1-11

TEXT

IV.5 To] 1 | to 2

PARAPHRASE

IV.2 father.] L,2 | Father? 1
IV.4 law,] L | Law; 1,2
IV.9 yea] L,2 | ye 1
IV.9 bondage⟨‡⟩] *edit.* | bondage L,1,2

NOTES

IV.3† restraints] L | restraint 1,2
IV.6*a I.11] L | 11 1,2
IV.6*a who *have*] L | *who have* 1,2

IV.6*b — as he that hath] L | as he that has 1,2
IV.7*a — the spirit] 1,2 | the the spirit L
IV.9* — 9⟨*⟩] 1,2 | 9 L
IV.9* — *or*] L; rom. 1,2
IV.9‡a — thought] L | thoughts 1,2
IV.9‡a — instate] L | instale 1 | install 2

Section VIII: IV.12-20

PARAPHRASE

IV.12 — mind] L | Mind, 1 | Mind 2
IV.16 — enemie] L | Enemies 1,2
IV.17 — might] L | may 1,2
IV.18-19 — you my] L | you My 1 | you. My 2 (*cf. manuscript note ad loc.*)

NOTES

IV.14*a — mention it] L | mention, it 1 | mention it, 2
IV.15* — it is] L | 'tis 1,2
IV.16* — *enemie*] L | *Enemies* 1,2
IV.18* — 18⟨*⟩] 1,2 | 18 L
IV.19*b — so] L | so to 1,2
IV.19*c — read it] L | read 1,2
IV.20*a — *to change*] L | to *change* 1,2

Section IX: IV.21-V.1

PARAPHRASE

IV.21 — hearing] L | having 1,2

NOTES

IV.21* — vulgat] L | Vulgar 1,2
IV.29* — the original] L | their Original 1,2
IV.30* — XXI] L,1 | 20 2

Section X: V.2-13

CONTENTS

a — 6–] L,1 | 6. and 2
f — wishing those] L | wishing these 1,2
g — seem] L | seem'd 1,2

TEXT

V.3 — do] 1; *not in* 2

PARAPHRASE

V.4	what ye] L | what you 1,2
V.5	gospel†] L | Gospel† and 1,2
V.10	mind⟨*⟩] 2 | mind L,1
V.11	am I] L,2 | am 1

NOTES

V.2*	μαρτύρομαι] 2 | μαρτυροῦμαι L,1
V.6*	repress] L | express 1,2
V.6*	13] L | 19 1,2
V.8*b	*sure*] L,2 | *sure I* 1
V.8*b	*knew*] L | *know* 1,2

Section XI: V.13-26

TEXT

V.14	self] 1 | felf 2
V.20	witchcraft] 1 | whichcraft 2

PARAPHRASE

V.13	lusts] L | Lust 1,2
V.17	propose] L,1 | purpose 2
V.22	Love,] L | Love, Joy, 1,2
V.25	estate] L | State 1,2

NOTES

V.16, 17†a	paints] L,1 | points 2
V.16, 17†a	very] L*; not in* 1,2
V.16, 17†c	terminate] L | terminate in 1,2
V.16, 17†c	that part] L | the part 1,2
V.16, 17†c	prompt] L | prompt us 1,2
V.18*, V.18†	*follow the order given in* L *and* 1. *In* 2 *they are in reverse order.*
V.18*a	those who] L | those that 1,2
V.18*b	two] L*; not in* 1,2
V.18*d	⟨2⟩ Thess] *edit.* | 1 Thess L,1,2
V.18†	*god* are] L | *God, are* 1,2
V.20*	either] L*; not in* 1,2 (*cf. manuscript note ad loc.*)
V.24*	they *through*] L | *they through* 1,2
V.24†a	observed above,] L | observed above 1 | observed, above 2
V.24†b	⟨2⟩2] *edit.* | 2 L,1,2
V.26*	much what] L | much 1,2

Section XII: VI.1-5

PARAPHRASE

VI.1	temptation] L | Temptations 1,2
VI.3	dec⟨e⟩iveth] 1,2 | deciveth L
VI.4	glorying] L | Glorifying 1,2

NOTES

VI.2†a	X⟨V⟩] *edit.* | XIV L,1,2
VI.4*a	καυχήσ⟨ω⟩νται] *edit.* | καυχήσονται L,1,2
VI.4*b	there are] L | there be 1,2

Section XIV: VI.11-18

CONTENTS

taken notice of] L*; not in* 1,2
an admonition] L | Admonitions 1,2

PARAPHRASE

VI.12	carry it] L | carry 1,2
VI.12	observance] L | observances 1,2 (*cf. manuscript note ad loc.*)
VI.18	grace] L | *favour* 1,2

NOTES

VI.12*	see . . . 26] L*; not in* 1,2
VI.12†	*In* L *this note is numbered 12†; in* 1 *13†, and in* 2 *13(k). In* L *and* 1 *it explains* Messiah *(VI.12); and in* 2 Jews *(VI.13).*
VI.16*b	A way . . . unusual] L | no very unusual way of speaking 1,2 (*cf. manuscript note ad loc.*)

L *has the subscription* 1703 Finis/John Locke*;* 1 *and* 2 *have the subscription* FINIS

1 CORINTHIANS

SYNOPSIS

c	incline] L | induce 1 (*cf. manuscript note ad loc.*)
d	any] 1 | any/any L
h	deliverd] L | had delivered 1
i	the VI] L | *Ch.* 6 1
i	proposed] L | had proposed 1
i	may] L | might 1

Section I: I.1-9

Beginning with Section I the date An: Ch: 57. Neronis 3 ***or a formal variant of it is written at the top of the left margin of each page of*** L. ***The date An. Ch.*** 57. ***Neronis*** 3. ***is printed at the top of the outside margin of each page of*** 1, ***beginning also with Section I. In the present edition the date is given in expanded form, but only once, at the beginning of Section I.***

PARAPHRASE

I.7	comeing⟨†⟩] *edit.* | comeing L,1

NOTES

I.2*b	see] L; ***not in*** 1
I.2*b	40 and they] L | 40. They 1
I.2*b	became holy 1 Pet II] L | so became holy, 1 *Pet.* 11 1
I.2†	Christian] L | Christians 1
I.7†	*This note is in* L *but not in* 1

Section II. No. 1: I.10-16

PARAPHRASE

I.12	and] L | or 1 (***cf. manuscript note ad loc.***)
I.16	for . . . Baptise] L; ***not in*** 1 ***in this section, but see textual note on I.17***

NOTES

I.10*b	use of] L | use of, 1
I.13*	βαπτισθ⟨ῆ⟩ναι] *edit.* | βαπτισθέναι L,1

Section II. No. 2: I.17-21

CONTENTS

ill⟨i⟩terate] 1 | illterate L

PARAPHRASE

I.17	But to] L | For *Christ* sent me not to baptise, but to 1 (***cf. textual note on I.16***)
I.23	expectation] L | Expectations 1
I.24	it is to those] L | but yet it is to these 1
I.25	come] L | came 1
I.27	foolish men⟨*⟩] *edit.* | foolish men L,1
I.30a	revealeing] L | revealing of 1

I.30b — unto] L | to 1
I.30b — preeminency] L | Pre-eminence 1 (*hyphen at line-ending*)
I.30b — value] L | value, 1

NOTES

I.22*a — Ἐπειδὴ is *does not begin a new paragraph in* L *but begins one in* 1
I.22*b — the 21 verse] L | *ver.* 21 1
I.22*d — though] L | and though 1
I.25, 27, 28* — *In this edition this note explains* foolishness in those *(I.25)*, foolish men *(I.27), and* men *(I.28). In* L *it explains* foolishness in those *(I.25), and* men *(I.28). In* 1 *there are no footnote signs in the text or attached to the footnote.*
I.28†b — Christian] L | Christian, 1
I.28†c — This St Paul *begins a new paragraph in* L *but not in* 1
I.28†c — stop] L | stay 1
I.28†c — (as] L | as 1
I.28†c — v.] L | (See 1
I.28†d — esteem] L | any Esteem 1
I.28†d — note] L | Note on 1
I.28†d — here he] L | here, καταργήσῃ, he 1

Section II. No. 3a: II.1-5

3⟨a⟩] *edit.* | 3 L,1

NOTES

II.1*b — said,] L | said 1
II.1*c — his founding his] 1 | his founding/his founding his L
II.1*d — upon that] L | upon 1
II.1*e — the assistance] L | by the Assistance 1
II.4*a — Apostles] L | Apostle 1
II.4*a — in miracles] L | Miracles 1
II.4*b — ⟨13⟩] *edit.* | 12 L,1
II.5* — ⟨5⟩] 1 | 4 L

Section II. No. 3b: II.6-16

3⟨b⟩] *edit.* | 3 L,1

PARAPHRASE

II.7 — obscure] L | the obscure 1
II.7 — now understand] L | understand, receive 1
II.9 — heart of man] L | Heart 1

II.15 preaches] L | preacheth 1

II.15 noe] L | not 1

II.16 it?] L | it. 1

II.16 Christ: And] 1 | Christ by his natural wisdom to instruct and rectifie the spiritual* man· But I am sure I have the spirit of Christ whereby I know his mind, his doctrine; And L (*Locke has omitted to delete material for which he has made a substitute insertion; see manuscript note ad loc.*)

NOTES

II.6*a i e] L*; not in* 1

II.6*d St] L*; not in* 1

II.6† *In* L *this note explains* the wisdome*: in* 1 the Wisdom of this World

II.6‡, II.6§ *follow the order given in* L. *They are in reverse order in* 1. *6‡ explains the two occurrences of* this world *in* L, *and the second occurrence of* this world *in* 1. *6§ explains* princes *in both* L *and* 1.

II.6§f ⟨V⟩] *edit.* | IV L,1

II.6¶a If] L*; ital.* 1

II.7†b yet by] L*; ital.* 1

II.7†b consequently the Corinthians] 1 | consequently the/the Corinthians L

II.7†b particularly concerned] L | peculiarly concerned 1

II.7†c and peculiarly] L*; not in* 1

II.7‡a doe] L | does 1 (*cf. manuscript note ad loc.*)

II.7‡b μυστ⟨ή⟩ϱιον] *edit.* | μυστέϱιον L,1

II.7‡b μυστ⟨η⟩ϱίου] 1 | μυστεϱίου L

II.7‡c ver. 6 . . . following] L | the Verse immediately preceding, and that following 1

II.7‡d ἀπ’ α⟨ἰ⟩ώνων] 1,2 | ἀπ’ ἀώνων L

II.7§a of Christian] *edit.* (*cf. next note*) | of a Christian L,1 (*cf. manuscript note ad loc.*)

II.7§a preachers and beleivers] L*; not in* 1 (*cf. manuscript note ad loc.*)

II.7§a-c Why . . . gloried in *is not placed in quotation marks in* L, *but is so placed in* 1

II.7§a-b in your . . . beleiver] L | as you do, in your distinct Teachers; the Glory that God has ordained us *Christian* Teachers and Professors to, is to be Expounders, Preachers, and Believers 1

II.7§b-c	gospel consorts . . . excelling what] L | the Disciples of *Christ*, who is the Lord of *all* Power and Glory, and herein has given us what far excels all that 1
II.7§c	ver.] L | *Vid.* ver. 1
II.7§c	That the . . . see] L | The Excellency of the Gospel-Ministration see also, 1
II.12*b	II] L | 11 1
II.12†	*this world*] L | the World 1 (*cf. manuscript note ad loc.*)
II.15*	*This note is numbered 15* in* L, *but 14, 15.(g) in* 1. *It explains* divine revelation *(II.15) in* 1, *but* But a Man . . . *(II.14) and* Animal *(II.15) in* 1
II.15*	⟨ver.⟩ 14 and 15] *edit.* | the 14 and 15 L | *ver.* 14, 15 1
II.15*	revelation.] L | Revelation. This is what appears to be meant by *natural*, or rather *animal* Man and Spiritual, as they stand opposed in these two Verses. 1
II.16*b	certain that] L | sure 1

Section II. No. 4: III.1-IV.20

CONTENTS

e	v:] L; *not in* 1
e	7.13] L | 7-13 1
f	use] L | Use and 1

PARAPHRASE

III.1b	Babes] L | Carnal(*l*), even as to Babes 1
III.2b	more advanced] L; *not in* 1 (*cf. manuscript note ad loc.*)
III.4	principles] 1 | principles† L
III.4	solely] L | wholly 1
III.4	the spirit of god.] *edit.* | the spirit of god the spirit of god. L | the Spirit of God? 1 (*cf. manuscript note ad loc.*)
III.5c	your teachers] 1 | your teachers your teachers l (*cf. manuscript note ad loc.*)
III.11	who has come†] L | (who has come 1
III.11	laid] L | laid) 1
III.15	worke] L | Works 1
III.18	incompasseing] L | in/compassing 1
III.22a	his glory] L | his Glory; 1
IV.1	As for *does not begin a new paragraph in* L, *but begins one in* 1
IV.6a	chosen to name] L | named 1 (*cf. manuscript note ad loc.*)
IV.8a	noe] L | not 1
IV.8b	you did truly] L | truly you did 1 (*cf. manuscript note ad loc.*)
IV.15	you I say] L | you, I say, 1
IV.18	Some indeed *begins a new paragraph in* L *but not in* 1

NOTES

III.1*	*In* 1, *but not in* L, *this note is followed by the following separate note which explains* spiritual *(III.1), the word explained by III.1†* *in* L. *In* 1 *note III.1† explains* Carnal.
	(*k*) Here πνευματικός *Spiritual*, is opposed to σαρκικός *Carnal*, as *ch*.2.14. it is to Ψυχικός *Natural*, or rather *animal*; so that here we have three sorts of Men, 1. *Carnal*, i.e. such as are swaid by fleshly Passions and Interests: 2. *Animal*, i.e. such as seek Wisdom, or a way to Happiness only by the Strength and Guidance of their own natural Parts, without any supernatural Light coming from the Spirit of God, *i.e.* by Reason without Revelation, by Philosophy without Scripture. 3. *Spiritual*, i,e. Such as seek their Direction to Happiness, not in the Dictates of natural Reason and Philosophy, but in the Revelations of the Spirit of God in the Holy Scriptures. (*Cf. manuscript note on III.1†*)
III.1†a	ψυ⟨χ⟩ικός] 1 | ψυκικός L
III.1†b	declareing] L*; not in* 1
III.4*c	that his] L | these his 1
III.4*c	opposer] *edit.* | opposers L,1
III.11*	v] L*; not in* 1
III.11†	*In* L *this is a separate note from III.11*, but in* 1 *it runs on from III.11* and is not a separate note*
III.11†	v] L*; not in* 1
III.12*	⟨12⟩] *edit.* | 13 L,1
III.17*b	Ch: V.6] L*; not in* 1 (*cf. manuscript note ad loc.*)
III.18*	particularise; to us] L | particularize to us, 1
IV.6†	6.9] L | 69 1
IV.16*	mislead] L | misled 1

Section II. No. 5: IV.21-VI.20

CONTENTS

a	disorder] L | Disorder which 1
f	matter that] L | matter 1 (*cf. manuscript note ad loc.*)
i	the gentils] L | Gentiles 1
j	*named*] L | *heard of* 1
l	adultery] L | and Adultery 1
o	heard named] L | heard named, 1
r	Suitable] L | Suitably 1
r	v.g] L | *v*.9. 1
u	here] L*; not in* 1

u	⟨13⟩] *edit.* | 19 L,1
u	among] L | amongst 1
w	II] L | 11 1

TEXT

VI.7	another: why] 1703 | another: whey 1
VI.9	mankind,] 1703 | mankind. 1

PARAPHRASE

V.6	know ye] L | know you 1
V.9	I wrote *begins a new paragraph in* L *but not in* 1
VI.4	among] L | amongst 1
VI.5	shame a wise*] L | Shame, who stand so much upon your Wisdom, one(*p*) wise 1 (*cf. manuscript note ad loc.*)
VI.7	ju⟨d⟩gment] 1 | jugment L
VI.8	father⟨s⟩] 1 | father L
VI.12	But* supposeing *begins a new paragraph in* L *but not in* 1
VI.17	indignity] L | in/Dignity 1

NOTES

V.1*a	The writers] L | Vid. *ch*.4.8,10. The Writers 1
V.1*b	or *Rem*] L | *or Rem* 1
V.1†	†] 1 | 1† L
V.1†a	by the Roman . . . instance] L | prohibited by the Laws of the Roman Empire, may be seen 1
V.1†b	*auctoribus, . . . scelus*] L | *auctoribus. O scelus* 1
VI.4*a	*Least* . . . Amongst] L | Ἐξουθενημένους, *Judices non Authenticos*. Among 1
VI.4*a	was *con⟨s⟩essus*] *edit.* | was *concessus* L,1 (*cf. explanatory note on VI.4*b*)
VI.4*a	determin causes] L | determine Cause 1
VI.4*a	an other *consessus*] L | another *concessus* 1
VI.4*a	*authentici*] L | *Authentick* 1
VI.4*b	it here . . . following] L | ἐξουθενημένους, those *who are least esteemed*, as our English Translation reads it, is plain from the next 1
VI.5*	*Wise man* σοφός] L | σοφός, *wise Man* 1 (*cf. manuscript note ad loc.*)
VI.5*	ordaind] L | ordained, or 1
VI.8*b	sev⟨e⟩ral] 1 | sevaral L
VI.8*b	others] L | other 1

VI.11†	*Ye are*] L | ye are 1
VI.12*c	migh⟨t⟩ pass] 1 | migh pass L
VI.12†a	seem] L | seems 1
VI.12†b	disposal] L | Disposals 1
VI.12†c	recei⟨v⟩e] 1 | receime L
VI.12†e	The context *begins a new paragraph in* L *but not in* 1
VI.12†f	brough⟨t⟩] 1 | brough L
VI.14*a	Corinthian] L | *Corinthians* 1
VI.14*d	These words *begins a new paragraph in* L *but not in* 1
VI.14*d	⟨12⟩] *edit.* | 13 L,1
VI.14*d	harlot?] L | Harlot, 1
VI.14*d	*In* 1 *the quotation marks extend to* lawfull. *In* L *they extend only to* never doe.
VI.14*e	If this *begins a new paragraph in* L *but not in* 1

Section III: VII.1-40

TEXT

VII.25	concerning] 1703 | coucerning 1

PARAPHRASE

VII.4	For the wife *begins a new paragraph in* L *but not in* 1
VII.4	refuse the wife] L | refuse his Wife 1
VII.5	ye may] L | you may 1
VII.8	To the u⟨n⟩maried] 1 | To the umaried L
VII.10	But to *begins a new paragraph in* L *but not in* 1
VII.17	one] L*; not in* 1
VII.25	Now concerning *begins a new paragraph in* L *but not in* 1
VII.28	(But if] L | But if 1
VII.31	it†)] L | it(*n*). 1

NOTES

VII.3*	injoyments.] L | Injoyments? 1
VII.12 and 13*	dismis⟨s⟩ing] 1 | dismising L
VII.20*	⟨20⟩] 1 | 18 L
VII.20*c	these] L | those 1
VII.20*d	others] L | the others 1
VII.25†	and 11] *edit.* | and. 11 L*; not in* 1
VII.31*	but] L*; ital.* 1
VII.31†	†] 1 | 31† L
VII.31†	28 ver.] L | *ver.* 28 1
VII.31†	31 ver.] L | *ver.* 31 1
VII.37*a	*Virgin* seems] L | seems 1(*cf. manuscript note ad loc.*)

VII.37*b	1 Because *begins a new paragraph in* L *but not in* 1
VII.37*c	2 The necessity *begins a new paragraph in* L *but not in* 1
VII.37*d	3 Ἐξουσίαν *begins a new paragraph in* L *but not in* 1
VII.37*d	signifie, either] L | either signifie, 1
VII.37*e	κέκρι⟨κ⟩εν] *edit.* | κεκρινεν L,1
VII.37*e	ἐν] L | ἐν τῇ 1
VII.37*g	4 Because *begins a new paragraph in* L *but not in* 1
VII.37*h	*find*] L | *finds* 1
VII.38*	*giveing*] L | giving 1

Section IV: VIII.1-13

PARAPHRASE

VIII.1	knows] L | know 1
VIII.2-6	(But if . . . father) *is in parentheses in* L *but not in* 1
VIII.2	(But if *begins a new paragraph in* L *but not in* 1
VIII.7	suffi⟨ci⟩ently] 1 | suffiently L
VIII.8	noe thing,†] L | nothing, 1
VIII.8	any thing] L | any things 1
VIII.8	our] L*; not in* 1
VIII.10	doubts] L | doubt 1

NOTES

VIII.3*	γνω⟨σ⟩θέντες] 1 | γνωθέντες L
VIII.5*b	heathen] L | Heathens 1
VIII.5*b	Lord-Agents] L | Lords Agents 1
VIII.5*c	came] L | come 1
VIII.8†, VIII.8‡	*are in reverse order in* L (*cf. manuscript note ad loc.*)
VIII.8†	*This note is in* L *but not in* 1 (*cf. manuscript note ad loc.*)
VIII.8‡	*if they . . . worse*] L | if they eat things offer'd to Idols, they were not the better; or if they eat not, were not the worse, 1

Section V: IX.1-27

CONTENTS

f	This seems *begins a new paragraph in* L *but not in* 1

TEXT

IX.12	used this power;] 1703 | used this power? 1

Section VI. No. 1: X.1-22

CONTENTS

b	and church] L*; not in* 1
c	a way] 1 | away L

TEXT

X.3 all eat] 1703 | eat all 1
X.4 all drink] 1703 | drink all 1
X.4 spiritual drink] 1703 | spiriturl drink 1

PARAPHRASE

X.20 covenant alliance] L | Covenant, Alliance 1
X.22 enter ... almighty] L | resist him when he lets loose his Fury against you? 1 (*cf. manuscript note ad loc.*)

NOTES

X.2* ceremony] 1 | cereremony L
X.10* 'Ολοθρευτο⟨ῦ⟩] *edit.* | 'Ολοθρευτός L,1
X.14* ⟨14⟩] *edit.* | 15 L,1

Section VI. No. 2: X.23-XI.1

CONTENTS

a noe virtue] L | nor Virtue 1

TEXT

X.24 wealth] 1703 | weath 1

PARAPHRASE

X.29 is my liberty ... Idolatry] L | should I use my Liberty, so that another Man should in Conscience think I offended 1 (*cf. manuscript note ad loc.*)
X.29 mans co⟨n⟩science] *edit.* | mans coscience L
X.29 Idolatry:⟨*⟩] *edit.* | Idolatry: L
X.30 for?*] L | for? 1
X.32 Jews*] L | Jews 1
X.32 gentils†] L | Gentiles 1
X.32 church‡] L | Church 1

NOTES

X.28* *For the*] L | *The* 1
X.28* Vulgat] L | Vulgar 1
X.29*, X.30*, X.32*, X.32†, X.32‡ *These notes are in* L *but not in* 1; *cf. manuscript notes ad loc.*
X.32†, X.32‡ *In* L *these notes run on after note X.32**

Section VII: XI.2-16

TEXT

XI.15 to her:] 1703 | to her. 1

NOTES

XI.3*b ob⟨s⟩erved] 1 | oberved L
XI.3*c *praying* and] L | *Praying and* 1
XI.3*d *praying* and] L | *Praying and* 1
XI.3*h women] L | Woman 1
XI.3*k ⟨XIV⟩.3] *edit.* | IV.3 L,1
XI.3*n those] L | these 1
XI.3*p II] L | 11 1
XI.3*q Mr Mede Disc. 16 *is in the margin in both* L *and* 1. *In* L *an asterisk indicates that it explains the words in this part of the note ending with* Scripture. *In this edition it has been placed in parentheses after* Scripture (*cf. manuscript note ad loc.*).
XI.3*u where] L | wherein 1
XI.3*u the women is] L | the Woman, is 1

Section VIII: XI.17-34

CONTENTS

c meal] L | Meat 1
d meal] L | Meat 1

TEXT

XI.17 you come] 1703 | ye come 1

PARAPHRASE

XI.20 come] L | came 1
XI.20 tis] L | it's 1
XI.22 sati⟨s⟩fying] 1 | satifying L
XI.32 ⟨w⟩e may] 1 | me may L

NOTES

XI.21*a suppers] L | Supper 1
XI.21*b eat] L | to eat 1
XI.21*e when] L | where 1
XI.22* and delivers] L*; not in* 1
XI.27† Ἔνοχος] 1 | Ἔννοχος L

XI.28*a discriminateing] L | direct Imitating 1
XI.28*b disorders, herein] L | Disorders herein, 1
XI.28*h the punishment] 1 | the the punishment L
XI.28†b *that let a*] 1 | *that let him a* L (*cf. manuscript note ad loc.*)
XI.29*a *Not discriminateing*] L | not *discriminating* 1

Section IX: XII.1-XIV.40

CONTENTS

b 4.5] L | 45 1
c god⟨)⟩] 1 | god L
d difference nor] L | Difference or 1
f ⟨31⟩] *edit.* | 41 L,1
g –XIII.1-13] L; *not in* 1 (*cf. manuscript note ad loc.*)

Section IX. No. 1: XII.1-3

NOTES

XII.1*a several of] L | several 1
XII.1*c vid] L | See 1
XII.3† ⟨5⟩] *edit.* | 6 L,1

Section IX. No. 2: XII.4-11

PARAPHRASE

XII.6 to] 1 | to‡ L
XII.7 and advantage] L | and Advantages 1

NOTES

XII.6†a II] L | 11 1
XII.9*c understanding] L | Understanding, 1
XII.9*c that assurance] L | the Assurance 1
XII.9*d and *the word*] L | and the *word* 1
XII.10* Sacred] L; *not in* 1
XII.10* spoke] L | spoken 1

Section IX. No. 3: XII.12-30

12-30] L | 12-31 1 (*cf. manuscript note ad loc.*)

TEXT

XII.15 body; is] 1703 | body? is 1
XII.16 body; is] 1703 | body? is 1

PARAPHRASE

XII.30 interpreters of tongues?] L | Interpreters of Tongues? But ye contest one with another, whose particular Gift is best, and most preferable(*y*); but I will shew you a more excellent way, *viz*. Mutual Good-will, Affection and Charity. 1 (*The additional material in* 1 *is a paraphrase of XII.31, a different paraphrase of which is given in* L *at the beginning of Section IX. No. 4; cf. manuscript note ad loc.*)

NOTES

XII.13*a the Gentils] L | Gentiles 1
XII.13*a them] L; *not in* 1

Section IX. No. 4: XII.31-XIII.13

XII.31-XIII.13] L | XIII.1-13. 1 (*cf. manuscript note ad loc.*)

CONTENTS

a-c St Paul haveing . . . XIII Ch:] L | St. *Paul* having told the *Corinthians*, in the last Words of the precedent Chapter, that he would shew them a more excellent way than the emulous producing of their Gifts in the Assembly, he in this Chapter tells them, that this more excellent way is Charity, which he at large explains, and shews the Excellency of. 1 (*cf. manuscript note ad loc.*)

TEXT

XII.31 *This verse is included in the previous section in* 1

PARAPHRASE

XII.31 You make . . . excelling.] L; *not in* 1 (*cf. textual note on XII.30 and manuscript note on XII.31 under Section IX. No. 3*)
XII.31 excelling.⟨†⟩] *edit.* | excelling. L
XIII.1 the sound] 1 | the the sound L

NOTES

XII.31* *This note is in this section in* L, *but in Section IX. No. 3 in* 1
XII.31*b điversity] L | Diversities 1
XII.31*c one of those of] L | one of 1
XII.31*e Besides *begins a new paragraph in* L *but not in* 1

XII.31*g-i But says . . . advanced by them.] L; *not in* 1 (*cf. manuscript notes on XII.31*g–h, h–i*)

XII.31*g ⟨κ⟩ρεῖττον] *edit.* | χρεῖττον L

XII.31*h ⟨κ⟩ρεῖττονα] *edit.* | χρεῖττονα L

XII.31*i ὠφελοῦμα⟨ι⟩] *edit.* | ὠφελοῦμαγ L

XII.31† *This note is in* L *but not in* 1. *In* L *it runs on after note XII.31*. Here it constitutes a separate paragraph. Cf. manuscript note ad loc.*

XIII.2*a *mysterys*] L | *Mystery* 1

XIII.2† †] 1 | 2* L

Section IX. No. 5: XIV.1-40

XIV⟨.1-40⟩] 1 | XIV L

PARAPHRASE

XIV.2 nobod⟨y⟩] 1 | nobod L

XIV.9 ye utter] L | utter 1

XIV.11 the force] 1 | the the force L

XIV.13 soe as] L; *not in* 1

XIV.14 tis] L | it is 1

XIV.15 also doe] L | do also 1

XIV.18 tongues] 1 | tongues* L

XIV.19 tongue] 1 | tongue* L

XIV.32 Christians] L | Christians, 1

XIV.36 What doe *begins a new paragraph in* L *but not in* 1

XIV.37 prophesie] L | Prophesies 1 (*cf. manuscript note ad loc.*)

NOTES

XIV.1*a given it] L | given it, 1

XIV.1*c besides] L | besides, 1

XIV.1*d ⟨κ⟩ρείτ⟨τ⟩ονα] *edit.* | χρειτονα L,1

XIV.2*a spir⟨i⟩tual] 1 | spirtual L

XIV.2*d wher] L | when 1

XIV.2*d gift of] L | Gifts of 1

XIV.4* unknown] L; *ital.* 1

XIV.6*a each its] L | each his 1

XIV.6*a thus] L; *not in* 1

XIV.15*c his own mind alone] L | alone his own Mind 1

XIV.20*, XIV.20† *In this edition these notes are given in the reverse order to that of* L *and* 1. *In* L *20* explains* children, *and 20†* malice. *In* 1 *20* explains* your Understandings, *and 20†* Malice (*cf. manuscript note on XIV.20**).

XIV.26*a *with*] L; *not in* 1

XIV.26*b may all] L | all may 1
XIV.27*b *although*] 1;rom. L
XIV.27‡ have an end put] L | here put an end 1
XIV.37* II] L | 11 1
XIV.38* the *any*] 1 | *the any* L

Section X: XV.1-58

TEXT

XV.41 moon] 1703 | mon 1

PARAPHRASE

XV.35 that men dead] L | to pass that dead Men 1
XV.38 hath] L | has 1
XV.48 or] L | and 1
XV.53 and from] 1 | and from/and from L
XV.54 of victory] L | of Victory(*p*) 1
XV.58 all ways] L | always 1

NOTES

XV.35*c declare that] L | declare it 1
XV.35*c other] L | others 1
XV.42*j says in] L | says 1
XV.42*l the saints] L | Saints 1
XV.42*m Takeing *begins a new paragraph in* L *but not in* 1
XV.42*m say⟨s⟩] 1 | say L
XV.42*m next] L | the next 1
XV.42*o shall all in] L | shall in 1 (*cf. manuscript note ad loc.*)
XV.42*p Paul] L | *Paul*'s 1
XV.42*p who were] L | who are 1
XV.42*p say⟨s⟩] 1 | say L
XV.42*t make⟨s⟩] 1 | make L
XV.42*v since as] L | since 1
XV.42*v all die] L | die 1
XV.42*w and *the*] L | *And the* 1
XV.44*a confor⟨m⟩able] *edit.* | conforable L | conformably 1
XV.44*b con⟨s⟩tant] 1 | contant L
XV.44*b naturaly] L | natural 1
XV.44*c meat] L | Meat and 1
XV.44*c obtain . . . dead] L; *ital.* 1
XV.44*c i e are] L | *i.e.* 1
XV.45* 45] *edit.; not in* L, 1 (*In* L *and* 1 *this note is listed as a second note*

	on XV.44. In L *and this edition it explains* power to give life *(XV.45); and in* 1 spiritual *(XV.44).)*
XV.53*a	φ⟨θ⟩αρτὸν τοῦτο *this*] *edit.* | φαρτὸν τοῦτο *this* L | φθαρτόν 1 (*cf. manuscript note ad loc.*)
XV.53*a	θνητὸν τοῦτο *This*] L | θνητόν 1
XV.53*a	νεκροί] L | νεκροί *dead* 1
XV.53*a	*dead persons*] L | *the Dead* 1
XV.53*b	makes it] L | it is 1
XV.53*c	ψυχικὸν] W | ψευχικὸν L,1
XV.53*c	both which places] L | both which 1
XV.53*c	p⟨e⟩rson] 1 | prson L
XV.53*c	any one of] L | any of 1
XV.53*f	both to] L | to both 1 (*cf. manuscript note ad loc.*)
XV.54(*p*)	*The following note, which explains* of Victory, *is in* 1, *but not in* L: 54(*p*) Νῖκος *Victory*, often signifies End and Destruction. See *Vossius* de LXX interpret, *cap*. 24.

Section XI: XVI.1-4

NOTES

XVI.2*	gains] L | Gain 1
XVI.3*a	(*1st*) δοκιμά⟨σ⟩ητε] 1 | δοκιμάζητε L

Section XII: XVI.5-12

PARAPHRASE

XVI.10	If Timothy *begins a new paragraph in* L *but not in* 1
XVI.12	As to *begins a new paragraph in* L *but not in* 1

NOTES

XVI.12†	other] L | others 1

Section XIII: XVI.13-24

CONTENTS

them] L*; not in* 1 (*cf. manuscript note ad loc.*)

TEXT

XVI.20	Greet ye] 1703 | Greet you 1

PARAPHRASE

XVI.15	You know *begins a new paragraph in* L *but not in* 1

XVI.24	Christ Jesus] L | Christ Jesus sake 1 (*cf. manuscript note ad loc.*)

NOTES

XVI.22*	Apostle?] L | Apostle, 1
XVI.22*	disorders of] L | Disorders in 1
XVI.22*	15] L | 15? 1

1 *has the subscription* FINIS *which is not in* L

2 CORINTHIANS

SYNOPSIS

At the top of the left margin of each page of L *is written the date* An. Chr. 57 Neronis. 3 *or a formal variant of it. The date An. Ch.* 57. *Neronis* 3. *is printed at the top of the outside margin of each page of* 1. *In this edition the date is given in expanded form, but only once, at the beginning of the Synopsis.*

b	II.14-VI.10. X.1-XIII] L | 2.14. and 6.10. and 10.1. and 13 1

Section I: I.1, 2

NOTES

I.1*a	1 Cor ⟨XVI⟩] *edit.* | 1 Cor XIII L,1

Section II: I.3-VII.16

II] *edit.* | II. N.I L,1

Section II. No. 1: I.3-14

CONTENTS

c	alway] L | always 1
d	Paul that was] L | *Paul* was 1
d	man had] L | Man, and had 1

PARAPHRASE

I.11	p⟨ro⟩cured] 1 | porcured L

NOTES

I.3*	is their true . . . 17] L | it agrees with St. *Paul*'s Sense, see 1 *Eph*.17. 1
I.14*	him and owned] L | him own'd 1

Section II. No. 2: I.15-II.17

CONTENTS

c	23-II] L | 23. and 2 1

TEXT

I.15	you] 1703 | yon 1
II.12	Lord,] 1703 | Lord. 1

PARAPHRASE

I.15	a second] 1 | a a second L (*cf. manuscript note ad loc.*)
I.23	be] L | is 1
II.4	an intention] L | Intention 1
II.14	gives] L | who gives 1

NOTES

I.22†e	thereby] L | there 1
II.3*b	21-] L | 21. and 1
II.5*	however] L | however, 1
II.16*, II.17*	*are in the order given in* 1. *In* L *they are in reverse order.*

Section II. No. 3: III.1-VII.16

CONTENTS

a	this)] L | this, 1
a	Corinthians:] L | Corinthians) 1

TEXT

IV.18	temporal] 1703 | temporary 1
VI.10	sorrowful] 1703 | forrowful 1
VI.11	Corinthians] 1703 | corinthians 1

PARAPHRASE

III.3	that, you] L | that you, 1
III.3	διακονηθεῖσα ⟨ὑφ'⟩ ἡμῶν] *edit.* | διακονηθεῖσα ἀφ' ἡμῶν L; *not in* 1
III.9	ministration] 1 | ministration* L
III.13	hinders] L | should hinder 1
III.18	we all] L | we, all 1
IV.3	hidden] 1 | hidden* L
IV.5	Jesus's] L | Jesus 1

IV.15a	preac⟨h⟩ing] 1 | preacing L
IV.15b	prayse] L | pray 1
IV.16	faint] L | faint not 1
V.1	heaven] L | Heavens 1
V.2	earnestly] L | earnestly, 1
V.2-3	superinduced, If soe be] L | superinduced: If so be, 1
V.5	prepares] 1 | is prepares L (*cf. manuscript note ad loc.*)
V.10	body*] L | Body 1
V.18	alone] L | alone; 1
V.19	this] L | his 1
V.19	reconciliation] 1 | reconciliation* L
V.20	b⟨e⟩seech] 1 | bseech L
VI.1	also] L | alway 1
VI.5	down,] 1 | down L
VI.6	long suffering] L | Long-sufferings 1
VI.13	affection] L | Affections 1
VII.10	(*2nd*) worket⟨h⟩] 1 | worket L
VII.14	as] L*; not in* 1

NOTES

III.4, 5*	4⟨, 5⟩] *edit.* | 4 L,1
III.4, 5*b	Πεποίθησις *begins a new paragraph in* L, *but is a continuation of the note begun in the previous paragraph. In* 1 *it begins a separate note* 5(*c*), *explaining* reckon *in III.5.*
III.4, 5*b	word] L | term 1
III.4, 5*b	λογίζεσθαι] L | λογιζεσθῶ 1
III.4, 5*c	But if] L | or if 1
III.4, 5*c	or abilitys] L*; not in* 1
III.7*a	καταργουμένη] L | Καταργουμένην 1
III.7*c	δόξ⟨α⟩] *edit.* | δοξη L,1
III.7*d	us there] L | us there, 1
III.10*b	ind⟨u⟩striously] 1 | indistriously L
III.11*	*This note is numbered 11* in* L, *and 10(i) in* 1
III.11*	and be] L | and to be 1
III.12*b	own haveing] L | having 1
III.12*c	‘Haveing therefore *does not begin a paragraph in* L, *but begins one in* 1. ‘Haveing therefore . . . my ministry’ *is in quotation marks in* L, *but not in* 1.
III.13*c	determin] L | determines 1
III.13*g	which shall . . . Lord. *is in quotation marks in* 1, *but not in* L
III.17†	†] 1 | 17† L
III.17†	*runs on after note 17* in* L *but not in* 1*; is a separate note in* L *and* 1

III.18*d 'Moses with a vayl *begins a new paragraph in* L *but not in* 1
III.18*d κατοπτριζόμενοι reflecting ... the Lord *is in quotation marks in* L, *but not in* 1
III.18*e *refle⟨c⟩ting*] 1 | *refleting* L
III.18*f therefore it] 1 | therefore it it L
III.18*l chapter] L | Chapters 1
IV.2* αἰσχύνη⟨ς⟩] 1 | αἰσχυνη L
IV.2* *by*] 1*;* rom. L
IV.2* ἀνακεκαλυμ⟨μ⟩ένῳ προσώπῳ] W | ἀνακεκαλλυμένω προσωπῳ L | ἀνακεκαλλυμμένω πρόσωπω 1
IV.2* ⟨18⟩] *edit.* | 13 L,1
IV.4† explain] L | explains 1
IV.6*a For the explication *does not begin a new paragraph in* L, *but begins one in* 1
IV.6*b those] L | these 1
IV.6*d image of Christ] L | Images of Christ 1
IV.16* 7-V] L | 7. and 5 1
IV.17* כב⟨ד⟩] *edit.* | כבר L | ככר 1
IV.17* to be *heavy* ... Paul] L | *to be heavy*, and *to be glorious* here in the Greek, St. *Paul* in the Greek 1
V.3* 15-V] L | 15. and 5 1
V.6, 8* signifie] L | signifies 1
V.9*a (w⟨h⟩ither] *edit.* | (wither L | (whether 1
V.9*a ἐνδημ⟨εῖ⟩ν or ἐκδημ⟨εῖ⟩ν] *edit.* | ἐνδημοῦν or ἐκδημοῦν L,1
V.10* *This note is in* L *but not in* 1*; cf. manuscript note ad loc.*
V.12*a other] L | others 1
V.17*a the former] L | his former 1
V.17*a shew that] L | shew 1
V.17† his] L | this 1
VII.11‡ *In* L *and* 1 *this is a separate note, but while in* L *it begins a new line, in* 1 *it runs on from the previous note*
VII.11§ *In* L *and* 1, *while this is a separate note, it runs on from the previous note*

Section III: VIII.1-IX.15

TEXT

VIII.4 saints.] 1703 | saints 1
VIII.9 your] 1703 | our 1
VIII.13 be eased] 1703 | may be eased 1

PARAPHRASE

VIII.14 came] L | come 1

VIII.21	prese⟨r⟩ved] 1 | preseved L
VIII.23	collect] L | Collection 1
IX.8	abound to] L | abound in 1
IX.11	beneficence] 1 | beneficence* L
IX.13	men)] *edit.* | men- L | Men, 1 | Men,) W

NOTES

VIII.1*	cause] L | Author 1
VIII.1*	vid. IX.15. And] L | Besides 1
VIII.1*	*given by*] L | *given in* or *by* 1
VIII.8*a	*of your love*] L.?,W | *of their Love* 1 (L *reads* 'y[r]', *which can be transcribed either* 'your' *or* 'their')
IX.8*	8⟨*⟩] 1 | 8 L
IX.9 and 10*	i e] L*; not in* 1*; cf. manuscript note ad loc.*
IX.10†	⟨10⟩†] *edit.* | †* L

Section IV: X.1-XIII.10

CONTENTS

collect] L | Collection 1

Section IV. No. 1: X.1-6

⟨PARAPHRASE⟩

The heading Paraphrase *is absent from* L *but present in* 1

X.2	manner] L | manner. 1
X.2	count] L | account 1
X.3	to the flesh] 1 | to the flesh* L

NOTES

X.6*c	therefor him] L | therefore 1

Section IV. No. 2: X.7-18

TEXT

X.15	labours] 1703 | labour 1

PARAPHRASE

X.7	adversary] L | Adversaries 1
X.9	But that] 1 | But that* L
X.12	bold*] L | bold 1
X.15	pains.‡] L | Pains: 1

NOTES

X.7*	23] L | 33 1
X.8†	*In* L *and* 1 *this is a separate note, but while in* L *it begins a new paragraph, in* 1 *it runs on from the previous note*
X.12*, X.12†	*In* L *these are two separate notes, but in* 1 *they are combined as one note, explaining the words* within themselves *and beginning* This is spoken.
X.12†a	have] L*; not in* 1
X.12†b	Apo⟨s⟩tles] *edit.* | Apotles L | Apostle's 1
X.13*	the] L*; not in* 1
X.15, 16†d	mentions . . . seting up] L | speaks of one Man, that setting up thus 1
X.15‡	*This note is in* L *but not in* 1*; cf. manuscript note ad loc.*

Section IV. No. 3: XI.1-6

TEXT

XI.1	you] 1703 | ye 1
XI.4	that] 1703 | thar 1

NOTES

XI.3*f	*Here, as in* 1, *the quotation marks end after* Judaisme. *In* L *they end after* light to this.

Section IV. No. 4: XI.7-15

NOTES

XI.7*	answers. here by] L | answers here, by 1

Section IV. No. 5: XI.16-33

TEXT

XI.26	1 *and* 1703 *read* journeying *in agreement with the 1611 edition. Modern printings of AV read* journeyings.

PARAPHRASE

XI.22	him,] L | him? 1
XI.26	from my own] L | by my own 1

NOTES

XI.17*, XI.18*, XI.19*	*Here the notes are numbered as in* L. *They are numbered* 18(*i*), 19(*k*), 20(*l*) *respectively in* 1, *where* 18(*i*) *explains* Extraction

(XI.18), 19(*k*) *explains* Fools *(XI.19), and* 20(*l*) *explains* For you bear *(XI.20).*

Section IV. No. 6: XI.1-11

CONTENTS

revelation] L | Revelations 1

NOTES

XII.1* Chapter,] L | Chapter 1
XII.7* conceale it is] L | conceal it, is 1
XII.7* came] L | come 1

Section IV. No. 8: XII.14-21

PARAPHRASE

XII.17 any one] L | any 1

NOTES

XII.19*h interposi⟨ti⟩on] 1 | interposi/siton L
XII.19*h observed] L | found 1

Section IV. No. 9: XIII.1-10

PARAPHRASE

XIII.1 This is] 1 | This is is L
XIII.5 proofs.⟨*⟩] 1 | proofs. L

NOTES

XIII.4*b causal] L | casual 1
XIII.4*b causally] L | casually 1
XIII.4*b happen] L | happens 1
XIII.5, 6, 7*b ⟨3.⟩] 1; *not in* L
XIII.5, 6, 7*b *ye*] L | *you* 1

Section V: XIII.11-14

II-1⟨4⟩] *edit* | 11–13 L,1

TEXT

XIII.14 the Lord] 1703 | our Lord 1

In L *there is a subscription* Finis 1701 *reproduced without the date in* 1

EXPLANATORY NOTES

For a discussion of notes and references, see Introduction, pp. 86-8.

THE PREFACE

p. 103[1] *To go about it . . . justify it*: these words occur in Locke's draft of the *Preface* (Appendix I, d).

p. 103[2] The difficulties mentioned in this paragraph are mentioned, but not in exactly the same words, in 'Difficulties' (Appendix IV, c-d).

p. 104[1] The point made in this sentence is also made in 'Drafts' (Appendix I, c), 'Difficulties' (Appendix IV, a), and in the last sentence of 'Difficulties' (Appendix IV, r). *Syriack* is probably intended to include Aramaic as well as Syriac.

p. 104[2] The reference to *Hiphil* is also found in 'Difficulties' (Appendix IV, a). *Hiphil* is the name given to the causative active form of the Hebrew verb, which can mean either 'to cause to be . . .' or 'to declare to be . . .'. For example the *Hiphil* of the verb 'to be righteous' can mean either 'to cause to be righteous' (i.e. 'to make righteous') or 'to declare to be righteous', a feature of the Hebrew which is important for the discussion of Paul's use of the Greek δικαιοῦν ('to justify').

p. 104[3] *warm Temper*: cf. 'Difficulties' (Appendix IV, i).

p. 104[4] *those many large Parentheses*: cf. 'From his large parentheses' ('Difficulties', Appendix IV, a).

p. 104[5] *in . . . Sense*: cf. 'in a coherent train of argumentation . . . rational coherent discourses' ('Drafts', Appendix I, h-i; cf. 'Difficulties', Appendix IV, f-i).

p. 105[1] The ambiguity of Paul's use of the first person plural is mentioned in 'Difficulties' (Appendix IV, b). See also Locke's note Eph. I.3(*d*)a-b. For the ambiguity in his usage of the first person singular see his note Rom. VII.7†.

p. 105[2] *Chapters and Verses*: cf. 'Difficulties' (Appendix IV, g), which describes the Epistles as 'chopd into verses'. See also Introduction, pp 18-19.

p. 106[1] *Tully's Epistles*: the Epistles of Marcus Tullius Cicero. Locke possessed many volumes of Cicero's works, and seems to have been well read in them. See LL, p. 21.

p. 106[2] *Selden*: John Selden (1584-1654), *Table Talk* (2nd edn., London, 1696), LL no. 2609, pp. 8-9.

p. 107[1] Cf. *Second Vindication, Works*, vi. 295: 'Thus systems, the invention of men, are turned into so many opposite gospels; and nothing is truth in each sect, but what suits with them. So that the Scripture serves but, like a nose of wax, to be turned and bent, just as may fit the contrary orthodoxies of different societies. For it is these several systems, that to each party are the just standards of truth, and the meaning of the scriptures is to be measured only by them.'

p. 108[1] *Hammond and Beza*: cf. Introduction, pp. 12-13, 25.

p. 109[1] Cf. 'Drafts' (Appendix I, n). For a discussion of the reference to *learned Divines of the Church of England* see Introduction, pp. 10-11.

p. 110[1] *frequent Perusal*: cf. 'Difficulties' (Appendix IV, j).

p. 110[2] *disjointed, loose pious Discourses*: Locke may have been thinking of the kind of criticism made by Richard Simon, *Histoire critique du Vieux Testament*, p. 39, from which he made the following entry, headed 'Epistolae', at the beginning of Romans in LL no. 2864:

> Stile. Les Hebreux ne parlent souvent qu'a demi-mot et ils ne font quelque fois qu'entamer une matiere sans l'achever: ils ne sont pas meme exacts dans l'arangement de leurs paroles. Les Epitres de St Paul fournissent des exemples de toutes ces differences de stile'.

Criticism of Paul's style goes back to the early Church, and there is evidence of its existence in the sixteenth and seventeenth centuries in the articles on Jean Adam and Peter Bembus in Pierre Bayle, *Dictionaire historique et critique* (Rotterdam, 1697), LL no. 237, i. 102, 539.

p. 110[3] Acts IX.1-19; XXII.3-16; XXVI.9-18; Gal. I.15-17. For *chosen Vessel* cf. 'Drafts' (Appendix I, g).

p. 110[4] Locke assumes that the whole doctrine of the Gospel was communicated to Paul by revelation at the time of his conversion. See his notes Gal. I.16†; I.17*.

p. 110[5] Acts XXII.3. Gamaliel was a leading rabbi in Paul's younger days.

p. 112[1] For the importance of being aware of the circumstances in which the Epistles were written, see *Reasonableness, Works*, VI. 152-3.

p. 113[1] Cf. 'Drafts' (Appendix I, a).

p. 113[2] *Notions*: in the *Essay* (II. xxii. 2; III. v. 12; pp. 288, 436) Locke gives the name 'Notions' to 'Mixed Modes'; see also Schouls, *Imposition of Method*, pp. 250-1.

p. 113[3] *Analogy of Faith*: Locke may be using *Analogy* in the sense of 'analogue', or he may be alluding to beliefs formulated by reasoning from analogy (see *Essay*, IV. xvi. 12 (p. 666)).

p. 114[1] *Contrivances of Men*: see above, p. 107[1] n.

p. 114[2] The Platonism to which he refers is exemplified by Clement of Alexandria, Origen, and, at a later date, Augustine. Its influence was to be seen in the Cambridge Platonists of the seventeenth century.

p. 114[3] The influence of Aristotle was to be traced not only in Thomas Aquinas and other medieval theologians but also in the philosophical teaching which prevailed at Oxford in the seventeenth century.

p. 114[4] *Aerial and Aetherial Vehicles*: The Cambridge Platonist, Cudworth (*True Intellectual System*, pp. 785-99), discusses the thought of the sixth-century Christian philosopher John Philoponus, who argues that while the rational soul is separable from all body, the irrational life of the soul is always united with a body. During its earthly life it has the 'gross earthy body' but afterwards it has for its 'vehicle' what is called the spirituous or aerial body. Philoponus also quotes Greek philosophers as a support for the view that there is yet a third vehicle of the soul, the celestial or ethereal body, which is of higher rank than the other two. Cudworth has no difficulty in arguing that Paul's spiritual body is the Christian equivalent of the ethereal, celestial body (1 Cor. XV.44). He claims also that the same ethereal body is alluded to in Paul's reference to the 'building from God' in 2 Cor. V.1. He also suggests that when Christ descended into hell he may have had a spirituous body (p. 805). He mentions the view that the good angels have ethereal bodies while the wicked angels have lost their ethereal but retain their aerial bodies (pp. 806-12). While he unequivocally affirms a belief in ethereal bodies, he does not commit himself to the existence of aerial ones (p. 806). But he argues that there is support for this belief in both aerial and ethereal vehicles in many early Christian writers, and that it has its origins in the writings of Greek philosophers, although its implications in pagan writers were different from those in Christian theologians.

Another Cambridge Platonist, Henry More, mentions

the aerial and ethereal vehicles, but commits himself more strongly to a belief in the latter than in the former (*Opera Omnia*, 3 vols.: London, 1675-9, VI. v. 1-2, 214).

Cudworth explains that Origen believed 'this tabernacle' (2 Cor. V.1) to be the subtle spirituous body which the soul continues to have during this earthly life at the same time as the gross earthy body. It is probably this viewpoint to which Locke is alluding in his Preface. See Introduction, pp. 53-4, and explanatory note on 2 Cor. V.1-10.

p. 114[5] For Locke's views on 1 Thess. V.23 see Appendix V. The view from which he dissociates himself is probably that which explains 'body' as the physical body, 'soul' as the will, and 'spirit' as the mind. Such an interpretation is traceable to Origen and the Neoplatonists, and is put forward by Crellius and Hammond, among others. In his notes on the verse (Appendix V), however, Locke indicates that soul and spirit refer to 'different consitutions of the same person'. He explains that the soul is that part of the blood in which there is animal life, and which is mortal. The spirit, on the other hand, is that part of the human constitution in virtue of which a person receives immortality at the resurrection of the dead. It is the pledge of immortality, although it does not of itself preserve a person from death.

p. 115[1] *Warmth*: see explanatory note on Preface, p. 104.

p. 115[2] *'Tis the same thing . . . Lord and Master*: the danger of letting anyone apart from Christ or the Holy Spirit be the interpreter of Scripture is a theme of Locke's in his *Second Vindication* (*Works*, vi. 359): 'To lead me into their true meaning, I know (as I have above declared) no infallible guide, but the same Holy Spirit, from whom these writings at first came. If the unmasker knows any other infallible interpreter of scripture I desire him to direct me to him: until then, I shall think it according to my master's rule, not to be called, nor to call any man on earth, Master.' The 'unmasker' to whom he refers is John Edwards, author of *Socinianism Unmask'd*.

p. 116[1] *Study . . . Salvation*: cf. 'Drafts' (Appendix I, k).

p. 116[2] *comparing spiritual things with spiritual things*: This phrase is taken from 1 Cor. II.13. In his paraphrase of the verse Locke explains it differently. See explanatory note on the verse.

GALATIANS

The Epistle to the Galatians was written by Paul in the midst of controversy. Teachers in Galatia were claiming that obedience to the whole of the Jewish law, including the rules about circumcision and unclean foods, was necessary for justification. A challenge had also been made to the genuineness of Paul's claim to be an apostle. To deal with these issues Paul wrote his Epistle, arguing that his apostleship had been given him directly by God, and that men and women were justified by God's grace through faith.

There has long been dispute about the date and destination of the Epistle. A variety of dates have been suggested, both before and after the Jerusalem Council recorded in Acts XV; and some scholars in recent times have tried to establish a date independent of the evidence of Acts, which they regard as untrustworthy. The identity of the churches addressed by the Epistle has also been debated. There is disagreement whether it was sent to the northern or the southern part of the province of Galatia. These issues were being discussed in Locke's and previous times (see explanatory note on Synopsis, e); they continue to be the subject of controversy.

Interpreters disagree about the precise nature of the opposition to Paul in these churches. Among seventeenth-century scholars Grotius described them as philosophers and Hammond believed them to be Gnostics. Locke merely described them as 'Judaizing seducers'. It is still a matter of controversy whether they were of Jewish or Gentile origin and whether they were members of the Church or not. It is clear enough, however, that they were trying to persuade the Galatian Christians to 'Judaize', that is, to keep the Jewish law in all its details.

The Epistle is important for its information about Paul's own life; it gives an account of his activities before and after his conversion, emphasizing his independence of the apostles in Jerusalem, and mentioning his dispute with James, Peter, and Barnabas (I.11-II.14). It contains a statement of his authority as an apostle, an authority which he believed to be derived from God and Christ (I.1-12). It includes important teaching about a variety of theological themes: grace, justification, the death of Christ, the adoption of believers, life in union with Christ, the old and new covenants, the fruit of the Spirit, and the law of love. The combination of autobiographical material with theological and ethical teaching has made the Epistle a topic of much discussion.

Locke divides the Epistle into fourteen sections (see Appendix XI). He regards Section I as an introduction, Sections II and VIII as defences of Paul's conduct, Sections III-VII as arguments against circumcision, Sections IX-XIII as exhortations, and Section XIV as a conclusion.

SYNOPSIS

a *The subject and designe*: an entry of unknown source, marked i.14, in MS Locke f. 30, fo. 63[r] reads: 'The Epistle to the Galatians is an excellent commentary on the Epistle to the Romans.' In LL no. 2864, between pp. 138 and 139, is the following entry: 'The designe of the Epistle is to dissuade them from Subjection to the law of Moses. IV.10.21. V.1.'

e *St Paul had converted*: in this paragraph and in notes Gal. I.6* and II.11* Locke states his position about the date and origin of the Epistle. He believes it to have been written in AD 57 from Ephesus during Paul's third missionary journey (Acts XIX.1-41), a viewpoint which he shares with Pearson (Appendix II). It is also dated to the same missionary journey by James Ussher, *Annales Veteris et Novi Testamenti* (3rd edn. Bremen, 1686), LL no. 3028, p. 673, Henry Hammond, *A Paraphrase and Annotations upon all the Books of the New Testament* (new edn., 4 vols.: Oxford, 1845), iv. 4, and Whitby, *Epistles*, p. 1; but Ussher gives the date as 58 and Hammond as 55. Another theory is that of Grotius, who dates the Epistle to Paul's second missionary journey, and believes it to have been written from Corinth during his first visit (Acts XVIII.1-18) rather than from Ephesus. Grotius's view, expressed in his note on Gal. I.2, is in conflict with a statement in his preface to Galatians that the Epistle was written about the same time as Romans, which he dates during the third journey. Yet another viewpoint is that of John Lightfoot, who argues that the Epistle to the Galatians was written from Rome in AD 59 during Paul's imprisonment there. This theory, which is also favoured by Walker, is based on a statement at the end of Gal. VI.18, which does not have the best manuscript support. A much earlier date for Galatians is given by Calvin and Beza (on II.1), both of whom place it before the Jerusalem Council of Acts XV. According to their theories it was written after the first missionary journey, as early as AD 48 or 49.

Like most scholars who date the Epistle after the Jerusalem Council, Locke claims that the Council is alluded to in Gal. II.1-10. In that case it took place during what Galatians describes as Paul's second and Acts as his third visit to Jerusalem after his conversion. Calvin, however, argues that the visit described in Gal. II.1-10 was identical with that mentioned in Acts XI.27-30, and was the second visit according to both these writings. Beza suggests that Gal. II.1-10 refers to another visit, not mentioned in Acts, which took place after Paul's first missionary journey but before the Jerusalem Council. While Locke claims that Gal. II.1-10 describes events which occurred at the time of the Council, he indicates in note Gal. II.2* that Paul is referring to a private meeting with Peter, James, and John, not to any public discussion.

Another controversial issue is the identity of the churches addressed in this Epistle. Scholars who date it before the Jerusalem Council have to conclude that it was written to those churches in South Galatia which Paul founded during his first missionary journey, where the inhabitants were not Galatians by race. But if the Epistle is dated after or during the second missionary journey, it is arguable that it was addressed to churches in North Galatia, where the people were Galatians by race. Locke seems to have adopted the latter explanation, since he asserts that the churches addressed were founded in AD 51, which, according to his sytem of dating, would be during the second journey.

Section I: I.1-5

PARAPHRASE

I.3 *Favour*: Locke renders χάρις as 'Favour', while AV translates it as 'grace', a translation which Locke himself uses for the word on several occasions. Both words convey the idea of God's gracious initiative. Jenkin (*Remarks*, pp. 130-1) criticizes him for not keeping to the word 'grace'.

NOTES

I.1*a For *Timothy* see explanatory note on 1 Cor. I.1. For *Titus* see explanatory note on Gal. II.1. The sending of *Judas* and *Silas* is mentioned in Acts XV.22-34. *Judas* is Judas Barsabbas, not to be confused with Judas Iscariot or with Judas (or Jude), the brother of Jesus. *Silas* was Paul's companion on his second missionary journey (Acts XV.40-XVIII.5). He was probably the same person as Silvanus, who is mentioned in 2 Cor. I.19; 1 Thess. I.1; 2 Thess. I.1; 1 Pet. V.12.

I.1*b *Matthias* was appointed an apostle to fill the vacancy caused by the death of Judas Iscariot (Acts I.15-26). The contrast between the way in which Matthias and Paul became apostles is also found in Grotius and Walker.

I.2* *the lesser Asia*: Asia Minor.

I.4* Locke argues that *evil world* or *age* refers to the Jewish nation under the Law of Moses. The usual interpretation of these words treats them as a reference to the corrupt nature of the present condition of the world. Grotius contends that they allude especially to the Jews, who expected a 'kingdom of this world'. Hammond, in his paraphrase of Gal. I.4, indicates that 'evil age' refers to both Jews and Gentiles, but in his note on Matt. XXIV.3 he explains it as a reference to the Jewish nation under the law. Such is the view of Locke in this note and also in notes 1 Cor. II.6‡ and Eph. III.11(*l*). His source for this interpretation is Richard Burthogge's *Christianity a Revealed Mystery* (see Introduction, p. 13). He exchanged correspondence about the matter with Burthogge, whose letters of 20 November 1702 and 4 May 1703 are in Locke, *Corr.* vii. 709-11, 777-80. Cf. explanatory notes on 1 Cor. II.7 and Eph. III.9. Locke's interpretation has not met with general acceptance and is criticized by Le Clerc (*Bibliothèque choisie*, xiii. 79), Jenkin (*Remarks*, pp. 132-3), and Whitby (*Add.*).

Section II: I.6-II.21

PARAPHRASE

I.16 *to reveal his son to me*: the Greek ἐν ἐμοί is understood by AV as 'in me'. Erasmus (*Para.*), Vorstius, and Grotius explain it as 'through me'. Calvin, Beza, and Whitby, like Locke, understand it as 'to me'.

I.24 *upon my account*: this is a translation of ἐν ἐμοί, which Locke renders as 'to me' in Gal. I.16. Other scholars, e.g. Calvin, Hammond, Walker, Whitby, and Le Clerc (NT) are in agreement with him regarding verse 24.

II.1 *fourteen years after*: commentators have disagreed about the time from which the fourteen years should be reckoned. Calvin and Hammond date it from Paul's conversion, and count the three years mentioned in Gal. I.18 as included in the fourteen. Locke's note Gal. II.2‡a implies that the fourteen years should be dated from the visit of Gal. I.18-20. In this respect he is in agreement with Luther, Lightfoot, and Whitby.

Barnabas: a Levite, born in Cyprus (Acts IV.36-7), who brought Paul to help him at Antioch (Acts XI.19-22). He was Paul's companion during the first missionary journey and attended the Jerusalem Council. Because of a disagreement the two men afterwards parted company (Acts XIII.1-XV.39). Except for the incident mentioned in Gal. II.11-14, Barnabas is depicted in the New Testament as a supporter of Paul in the controversy about the Jewish law. He is described as an apostle in Acts XIV.4, 14 and 1 Cor. IX.6. See also Acts IX.27.

Titus: a Gentile convert, who was Paul's emissary in his dealings with Corinth (2 Cor. II.13; VII.6, 13, 14; VIII.6, 16, 23; XII.18). The Epistle to Titus is addressed to him.

II.4 *under the gospel*: a paraphrase of 'in Christ Jesus' (AV).

II.7 *James, Peter, and John*: for *James* see explanatory note on Gal. II.7*a. *Peter* is sometimes described by Paul as 'Cephas', a transliteration of a Greek adaptation of the Aramaic Kêphā ('rock'), the name which he was actually called by Jesus. See Gal. II.9 (AV); II.9*a; 1 Cor. I.12 (AV, Para.); III.22 (AV); IX.5 (AV); XV.5 (AV). The *John* mentioned here is John, the son of Zebedee, one of the leading disciples of Jesus.

II.11 *he was to be blamed*: an entry in LL no. 309, listed under I.11, mentions Hammond's paraphrase, 'he had beene blamd', which is a literal translation of the Greek. Locke, however, in agreement with AV and most commentators of his day, explains the Greek as 'was to be blamed'.

II.16 *soly by faith*: Poole's *Synopsis* shows that some interpreters believed this verse to imply that faith was merely a supplement to works, a suggestion which is supported if ἐὰν μή is translated as 'unless' (Vulgate 'nisi') instead of 'but' (AV). Locke's paraphrase shows that he wished to avoid this suggestion. His interpretation is in agreement with Luther, Calvin, Hammond, and Whitby. The doctrine of justification is given fuller treatment in Locke's paraphrase of Rom. III.19-31.

II.19 *by the tenor of the law*: Locke does not indicate clearly the implications of his paraphrase. His cross-reference in note II.19* to Rom. III.21 suggests that he may mean 'by the tenor of the gospel law' since the passage in Romans speaks of a righteousness apart from the law of Moses. But the other cross-references, to Gal. III.24, 25 and IV.21, indicate that the law of Moses had an educative function in preparing men and women for the coming of Christ. His note Gal. II.19‡, however, does not suggest that in this part of Galatians Moses' law is being regarded as educative, but that the rule of the Gospel is understood as law.

NOTES

I.6* See explanatory note on Gal. Synopsis, e.

I.6† *from him that called you*: Vorstius and Whitby claim that this refers to God. Luther, Calvin, Crellius (*Comm., Para.*), and Grotius refer it to Christ. Locke's interpretation, which refers to Paul, is also found in Beza.

I.7* Locke's interpretation of this phrase is in agreement with Calvin, Grotius, and Le Clerc (NT). The view which he rejects, that the words 'not another' mean 'not another gospel', is supported by Erasmus (*Ann.*), Luther, Vorstius, Hammond, Walker, and Whitby.

I.10*b *his commission and instruction from him alone*: an entry for this verse in MS Locke f. 30, fo. 67[r], reads: '*men or god* i e human inventions, the devices and figments of men or the very will and commands of god?' The entry appears to be based on a book, the identity of which is not clear.

I.17*a *by immediate revelation*: an entry for I.16 from Pearson, *Annales Paulini*, p. 2 (*Opera Posthuma*), in LL no. 2864, p. 141, reads: 'Non contuli cum homine quopiam a quo Evangelii doctrinam discere potui sed abii in Arabiam ubi per revelationem Evangelium accepi' ('I did not associate with any person from whom I could learn the teaching of the Gospel, but when I received the Gospel by means of revelation, I went away into Arabia').

I.17*b Locke implies that Paul was preaching to the Gentiles during his visit to Arabia, a view which he shares with Vorstius, Crellius (*Comm., Para.*), and Grotius.

I.18* *Three years*: in dating the three years from Paul's conversion, Locke is in agreement with Calvin, Crellius (*Comm., Para.*), Grotius, Hammond, Walker, and Whitby. An entry from Pearson, p. 3, in LL no. 2864, p. 142, shares this viewpoint: '*post tres annos*. nempe a conversione sua' ('*after three years*, undoubtedly from his conversion'). Locke also mentions that Pearson gives AD 38 as the date of Paul's return to Jerusalem.

II.2*b *miracles*: Locke's (Bodleian) manuscript reads *miracles*, presumably alluding to the incidents described in Acts

XIV.3, 8-13, during Paul's first missionary journey; whereas the first and second editions read *Miracle*, which must refer to the one miracle on that journey which is described in detail (Acts XIV.8-13).

II.2*c *nempe privatim eminentioribus* ('indeed in private to those who were more distinguished') is a Latin translation of the Greek, and corresponds to AV's 'but privately to them which were of reputation'. Calvin thinks that the words refer to the apostles. Grotius claims that they refer to over zealous followers of the apostles. Locke agrees with Hammond in claiming that they refer only to Peter, James, and John. The choice of Latin words by Locke may have been influenced by Knatchbull, who uses both *privatim* and *eminentioribus* in his comments on the passage.

II.2‡ It is characteristic of Locke that he supports the evidence of revelation with an argument from reason.

II.4, 5 The idea that there is a redundancy due to a Hebrew pleonasm is found in Grotius as well as in Locke.

An entry from Claude Sarrau, *Epistolae* (Orange, 1654), p. 219, listed under I.5 in LL no. 309, mentions that the words οἷς οὐδέ are absent from the text of Gal. II.5 in Codex Claromontanus. This reading, which has support from various other authorities (Locke's entry mentions Irenaeus, III. xiii. 4), would indicate that Paul, though he was not compelled to do so, gave way to pressure and had Titus circumcised. Locke does not mention this alternative text, however, in his note on the verse.

II.6† Luther, Erasmus (*Ann.*), Beza, Grotius, and Hammond supply 'I received nothing' rather than 'I learned nothing'. They regard it as a case of anacolouthon where Paul has failed to follow up a train of thought which he has begun. If, however, the parentheses found in this verse in AV are removed, it is possible to interpret as Locke does. Calvin, Vorstius, Whitby, Walker, and Le Clerc (NT) are in agreement with Locke. The suggestion of Locke, however, that the definite article should be supplied at the beginning of the verse has no textual support and was rejected by Whitby (*Add.*).

II.7*a Locke regards James as one of the apostles most in favour with Jesus during his ministry. But this interpretation cannot be sustained if the incident described in Galatians II is the Jerusalem Council, as Locke maintains. According to Acts XII.2, James, the son of Zebedee, who was one of the leading disciples of Jesus, was beheaded long before that council. A more widespread view is that the James mentioned here was the brother of Jesus, said by Eusebius (*Historia Ecclesiastica*, II. 23) to have been the first bishop of Jerusalem. Some scholars, including Calvin (on I.19) and Whitby, *Epistles*, 'Preface to James', as well as many of the Fathers, claim that he was not strictly the brother of Jesus but James the son of Alphaeus, one of the twelve disciples and a cousin of Jesus. Grotius and Hammond, however, argue that he was not an apostle.

II.11* See explanatory note on Gal. Synopsis, e.

II.19‡b *the rule of the Gospel*: Locke interprets living to God as obedience to the rule of the Gospel. Cf. Grotius, who interprets it as 'living according to the command of Christ'.

Section III: III.1-5

PARAPHRASE

III.1 *cast a mist*: Whitby's note on the verse uses the phrase 'Mists before the Eyes'.

III.2 *miraculous gifts*: in relating the gift of the Spirit to the performance of miracles Locke is in agreement with Le Clerc (NT); Calvin, while he does not exclude miracles, understands the Spirit in this verse as primarily connected with regeneration; and Beza links it with graces and virtues.

III.5 Locke's claim that Paul is meant here as the minister of the Spirit is unusual, although, according to Erasmus (*Ann.*), it was a viewpoint mentioned by Peter Lombard and Augustine. Commentators usually explain that either God or Christ is said here to minister the Spirit.

Section IV: III.6-18

PARAPHRASE

III.6 AV and most commentators link verse 6 with verse 5. Locke is unusual in linking it with verse 7.

III.16 Whitby takes Paul literally and claims that 'the seed' refers to Christ alone. In referring it also to the body of Christ, the Church, Locke is in agreement with Beza, Vorstius, Crellius (*Comm., Para.*), Hammond, and Le Clerc (NT).

III.17 An entry in MS Locke fo. 30, f. 66r reads: '*The Covenant* sc: of grace. *The law*. i e the covenant of works'.

NOTES

III.9, 10* *Rom III.26. note*: this cross-reference to Locke's work on Romans is absent from the printed editions, presumably because his work on Galatians was printed before that on Romans.

Section V: III.19-25

PARAPHRASE

III.19b *to shew them their sins*: an entry in MS Locke f. 30, fo. 66[r] reads: '*Because of transgressions*, that it might be a glasse to shew them their sin guilt and want of righteousnesse and soe be a schoolmaster to bring them to Christ. 24', the last words being an allusion to Gal. III.24. Another entry, loc. cit., is taken from John Spencer (1630-93), Master of Corpus Christi College, Cambridge, *De Legibus Hebraeorum Ritualibus et earum Rationibus* (Cambridge, 1685), LL no. 2740, p. 28; it explains the disobedience of the Israelites in terms of their idolatry, but Locke made no special use of it in his paraphrase.

III.20 According to J. B. Lightfoot, *Saint Paul's Epistle to the Galatians* (10th edn. London, 1890), p. 146, this verse has been given between 250 and 300 different interpretations. Among those which were likely to be known to Locke was that of Erasmus (*Ann., Para.*), for whom Christ was the mediator whose function was both human and divine; because God is purely divine, there is need for Christ to mediate between God and humanity. According to Calvin, Christ was the mediator, not of one, but of two, since he mediated both the old covenant with the Jews and the new covenant with the Gentiles; the assertion that God is one is a reminder of his faithfulness to his promises.

Writers who regard Moses as the mediator include Grotius. When people are united, he argued, they do not need a mediator (a mediator is not of one); and God is self-consistent (God is one). Hammond, however, treated the whole of verse 20 as an objection to Paul, which asserted that if Moses was the mediator of the covenant between God and the Israelites, God would be obliged to obey the covenant of works. Verse 21, he claimed, was an answer to the objection, and indicated that the covenant did not annul the promise of blessing to the seed of Abraham, which, according to Paul, was concerned with justification by faith. A similar view was held by Crellius (*Comm., Para.*).

Locke adopted a different position, although he also regarded Moses as the mediator. The Gentiles as well as the Israelites, he argued, were a party to the covenant with Abraham. Since, however, the Gentiles were not present at the giving of the law, in reality only one of the parties to that earlier covenant, namely God (God is one), was truly present at Sinai. For that reason the previous covenant could not be disannulled, because both parties were not wholly present at the later covenant. Locke's interpretation was adopted in the eighteenth century by Doddridge in England and J. D. Michaelis in Germany.

Whitby's interpretation of the passage is somewhat different. He says that Moses was a mediator of only one party, the Jews. But God, who gave the promise to both parties through Abraham, is one, and is ready to justify Gentiles as well as Jews.

The publisher's Preface to the first edition of Locke's *Galatians* claims that Locke's account of this verse is an original contribution to scholarship (cf. Textual Notes, Galatians, ad init.). The claim may well be correct. Locke's interpretation is explicitly rejected by Le Clerc (*Bibliothèque choisie*, xiii. 79-82) and Jenkin (*Remarks*, pp. 133-8).

III.23 A 'JL' entry in LL no. 309, listed under IV.23, reads: 'We were kept close shut up under the law until faith should be rev⟨e⟩aled. i e til the gospel should be revealed JL.' An entry in LL no. 2862, p. 151, reads: 'πίστιν. i e Doctrinam Evangelicam' ('*Faith*, i.e. Evangelical Doctrine').

NOTES

III.19† *by the hand of Moses*: an entry in LL no. 2862, p. 151, based on J. Cappellus, *Observationes*, p. 119, reads: 'ἐν χειρὶ μεσίτου. i e Ministerio Mosis' ('*By the hand of a mediator*, i.e. by the ministry of Moses').

Section VI: III.26-9

NOTES

III.27* In LL no. 309 an entry, listed under IV.27, from Tillotson, *Sermons*, i. 251, reads '*Put on Christ*. i.e. taken upon them to be like him. said in allusion to the ancient custom of puting off their garments at baptisme which signified the puting off the body of sin. And so the puting them or perhaps new ones on again. the puting on a new life conformable to the example and precepts of Christ. vid Rom VI.2-5'. This entry is more likely to have influenced Locke's notes Rom. VI.2* and VI.3* than this present note. See explanatory notes on Romans ad loc.

MS Locke f. 30, fo. 66ʳ contains an entry from Stephen Le Moyne, *Varia Sacra* (2 vols.: Leyden, 1685), ii. 745-6, in which he describes the different types of clothing worn by different nations, classes, and sexes, and explains Christians to have put on Christ. The entry does not appear to have influenced Locke's Paraphrase for this verse.

III.29* *The Clermont Copy*: Codex Claromontanus. See Introduction, pp. 25-6. Beza accepts the same rendering here as Locke, but few scholars have favoured this reading, which is clearly a case of assimilation to the previous verse. Locke's procedure here is a good example of his approach to textual criticism: he prefers the reading 'more suitable' to the argument.

Section VII: IV.1-11

PARAPHRASE

IV.3 *the law*: in paraphrasing AV's 'the elements of the world' as 'the law', Locke is in agreement with most commentators of his time, and is consistent with his limitation of 'We' in this verse to Jewish Christians. Hammond, however, although he understands 'elements of the world' to refer to the Jewish religion in this verse, claims in a note on Col. II.8 that it can also refer to Gentile religion and philosophy. Le Clerc, in his review of the *Paraphrase* (*Bibliothèque choisie*, xiii. 82), makes a similar point about philosophy.

NOTES

IV.1* δοῦλος ('bondman' or 'slave') does not occur in verse 8, but the corresponding verb is there.

IV.9† Compare Whitby's paraphrase: 'weak, as having no power to cleanse the Soul: and beggarly, as not being able to confer upon us the Spiritual Riches of the Gospel'. Whitby's words are almost a direct translation of a comment by Grotius on this verse.

Section VIII: IV.12-30

PARAPHRASE

IV.12 Erasmus (*Ann., Para.*), Hammond, and Whitby explain 'be as I am' (AV) as an appeal to the Galatians to follow Paul's example and abandon Judaism. But Locke agrees with Luther, Calvin, Beza, Grotius, and Walker in regarding it as an appeal to establish a close and harmonious relationship with him. Locke's *Think your selves to be very me* is reminiscent of a comment by Grotius and Crellius (*Comm.*) that it is an exhortation to be as Paul's 'alter ego'.

IV.17 *to exclude me*: Locke's paraphrase differs from AV's 'to exclude you'. The reading adopted by Locke was introduced by Beza, and also adopted by Crellius (*Comm., Para.*) and Whitby.

NOTES

IV.14* Locke's reluctance to speculate about the meaning of *weakness* (which is rendered 'infirmity' in both Locke's paraphrase and AV's translation of IV.13) is understandable. Hammond explains it as a reference to persecution, Calvin and Grotius to Paul's insignificant appearance, Whitby to a bodily weakness affecting his speech, and Le Clerc (NT) to sickness.

IV.18* The Greek can be translated either 'in a good thing'; or 'to a good man'. If the former is adopted, as it is by AV and most commentators, it could mean 'in a good cause'. In preferring the latter translation Locke is close to Hammond. His paraphrase is criticized by Le Clerc (*Bibliothèque choisie*, xiii. 83) and Whitby (*Add.*).

IV.19* AV, Hammond, Walker, and Whitby link verse 19 with verse 20. Others, like Erasmus (*Ann., Para.*), take verse 19 as an exclamation on its own. In attaching it to verse 18 Locke is in agreement with Beza. The alterations made by Locke to his Bodleian manuscript give the impression that at first he agreed with Erasmus, but then changed his mind. See manuscript notes, ad loc.

Section IX: IV.21-V.1

PARAPHRASE

IV.23-9 *in the ordinary course of... miraculously*: an entry of unknown origin in MS Locke f. 30, fo. 66v reads: '*Flesh* i e son of

Abraham according to the ordinary course of nature. *Spirit*. i e by a miraculous birth, soe that he was not soe much the son of Abraham as the son and heir of the divine promise'. Le Clerc (NT) also uses the phrase 'ordinary course of nature'.

V.1 *made you free*: the Greek text, AV, and most commentators support 'made us free'. Locke's translation is in agreement with Crellius (*Comm.*, *Para.*) and Le Clerc (NT), but has not found general acceptance. Crellius (*Para.*) treats this verse as part of the previous chapter, as Locke does.

NOTES

IV.21* The Greek manuscripts which support the translation 'Read' include Codex Claromontanus. Hammond agrees with them. The best textual evidence, however, favours 'hear', which is accepted by most commentators.

Section X: V.2-13

PARAPHRASE

V.2 An entry from Mede, *Works*, i. 330, in MS Locke f. 30, fo. 70ʳ reads: '*If* etc. Because he that received circumcision did as much as affirme that Christ was not yet come'. But Locke does not make use of this comment.

V.5 *follow the truth of the gospel*: cf. an entry from LL no. 2862, p. 154: '*Faith*. i e obedience to the law of the Gospel as by *law* the Apostle means in this Ep: and Rom III legal performances in obedience to the law of Moses.'

V.8 As in Gal. I.6, the one who called them is variously identified with God (Erasmus (*Para.*), Calvin, Beza, Vorstius, Crellius (*Para.*), Grotius, Walker, Whitby, Le Clerc (NT)) or Christ (Erasmus (*Ann.*)). Locke refers it to Paul. There is a hint of such an interpretation in Hammond who explains it as a reference both to God and to 'him who brought you to the faith'.

Locke claims that πεισμονή can be translated *subjection* although in his paraphrase he renders it *perswasion*, in agreement with Erasmus (*Ann.*, *Para.*), Calvin, Beza, Grotius, Walker, and Whitby.

V.9 *one man*: the suggestion that one man was at the root of the trouble in Galatia may be compared with Locke's theory that one false apostle was the ringleader among Paul's opponents at Corinth. In the comment on Gal. V.10

Walker also suggests that Paul is referring to one person. Whitby sees 'leaven' as a reference to Paul's Jewish opponents, while Calvin claims that it alludes to doctrines, not to people.

V.10 Locke, like Hammond, claims that 'judgment' (AV) refers to ecclesiastical censure.

NOTES

V.11* This note answers a question in LL no. 2864 (between pp. 138 and 139): 'What was the persecution that the Christians who observed not the law sufferd from the Jews? IV.29. V.11. VI.12'.

Section XI: V.13-26

PARAPHRASE

V.16 *the light that is in your minds*: this is Locke's paraphrase for 'spirit'. Compare Le Clerc (NT), 'light of the spirit'. Some commentators (e.g. Luther, Calvin, and Grotius) regard 'spirit' here as the Holy Spirit. Vorstius explains it as a reference to the teaching of Christ, and Hammond as 'gospel rule'. Locke's position is outlined in note Gal. V.16, 17†c. The spirit, he explains, is 'that part of a man which is endowed with light from god to know and see what is righteous, just, and good'. This is the 'light of nature' which he mentions in his introduction to Rom. I.16-II.29 and in his paraphrase of Rom. II.14. His note Rom. VII.18* explains that human beings consist of two parts: flesh, which is the natural inclination urging the satisfaction of sinful desires; and mind, which means 'the judgment and purpose of the mind, guided by the law of right reason'. In Gal. V.16, 17†e he explains that the spirit (or right reason) has not of itself the strength to do the right but needs renewal 'by the assistance of the Spirit of God'. His position is in basic agreement with that of the *Essay*, IV. xviii. 8 (p. 694), where the light of reason is said to be given by God, and where Locke claims that moral truths can be discovered by reason (III. xi. 16; IV. iii. 18, pp. 516, 549). The *Essay* does not, however, deal with human inability to will what is good with the aid of reason alone. In the *Reasonableness* (*Works*, vi. 151) Locke says that if we do what we can, Jesus 'will give us his Spirit to help us to do what, and how we should'. His note here on Gal.

V.16, 17 goes further than the *Reasonableness*, and argues that the Holy Spirit's function is to renew the mind and the inward person.

V.16 *doe not give your selves up*: Beza, Hammond, and Locke translate the Greek here as an imperative. But the Greek is most naturally translated 'you shall not give yourselves up', which is the position adopted by AV and by Luther, Calvin, Crellius (*Comm.*), Walker, and Whitby.

V.19 An entry from Allix in LL no. 309, listed under IV.19, explains the works of the flesh as those of carnal Jews, and the fruit of the Spirit as the life of spiritual Christians who rejoice in the gifts of the Spirit.

V.22 Locke's omission of 'Joy' from his paraphrase may be an oversight. See textual note ad loc.

NOTES

V.17* Hammond and Walker also make the point that in V.17 the Greek is at variance with AV.

V.20* Various other writers, including Erasmus (*Ann.*, *Para.*), mention that the word φαρμακεία can refer to poisoning.

V.24† Locke sees the crucifixion as an illustration of what happens to anyone in whom the evil principle is subdued. In this respect his account resembles that of Grotius. He mentions nothing of the explanation, found in Hammond, that links it with the renunciation of the desires of the flesh in baptism.

Section XII: VI.1-5

PARAPHRASE

VI.1 *eminent in the church*: compare Hammond, who explains 'spiritual' (AV) as a reference to 'the governors in the churches', and Whitby, who relates it to the spiritual gifts which equipped people for service in the Church.

NOTES

VI.4*a Locke correctly observes that the Greek can be translated 'glorying' as well as 'rejoicing' (AV).

VI.4*a *having brought him to circumcision*: an entry in LL no. 2862, p. 154, reads: '*and not in an other* viz whom he hath got to be circumcised. ver. 12', the cross-reference being to Gal. VI.12.

Section XIII: VI.6-10

PARAPHRASE

VI.8 An entry in LL no. 2862, p. 154, reads: '*he that soweth to his flesh*. i e he that relys on the circumcision of his flesh. *corruption*. i e eternal death'. In MS Locke f. 30, fo. 70ᵛ, another entry reads: 'φθοράν *corruption*. i e eternal death and losse of being as is evident by the opposition here to φθοράν in ζωὴν αἰώνιον and ἀφθαρσίαν which we translate immortality Rom. ii.7'. This entry is followed by the letter 'K', which presumably alludes to a pamphlet from which it has been taken (see LL, pp. 51-2).

Section XIV: VI.11-18

PARAPHRASE

VI.11 Like Calvin, Beza, and Grotius, Locke treats πηλίκοις as an adjective of number. The Greek would then be literally translated 'with how many letters', although both AV and Locke translate 'letter', referring to the Epistle as a whole. According to this interpretation Paul was alluding to the length of the Epistle. An alternative translation, 'with what large letters', indicates that the Epistle, or at least part of it, was in Paul's own large handwriting, a view advocated by Erasmus (*Ann.*) and Hammond.

VI.14 An entry in LL no. 2862, p. 155, reads: '*Save in the crosse of Christ* opposed to glorying in circumcision and the law'.

VI.15 *the new creation*: cf. an entry in LL no. 309, listed under Eph. II.15, which reads: 'r: *but the new creation*. JL. v. 2 Cor V.17'.

VI.16 The meaning of Israel in this verse has been much discussed. Some scholars, including Grotius, explain that it means Jewish Christians. But most of them, including Erasmus (*Ann.*), Calvin, Vorstius, Crellius (*Comm., Para.*), and Walker, take the same viewpoint as Locke and refer it to all Christians. In LL no. 2862, p. 155, an entry which gives an interpretation like Locke's reads: '*The Israel of god*. i e Christians in contradistinction to Israel of circumcision.'

VI.17 *markes of the stripes*: cf. Whitby, 'wounds and stripes'.

VI.18 Locke's paraphrase omits the traditional subscription (see AV), which indicates that the Epistle was written from Rome. This subscription does not have the best manuscript attestation. See also explanatory note on Gal.,

Synopsis, e. A subscription is found in the AV copy-text of Galatians but not of 1 and 2 Corinthians, Romans, and Ephesians.

NOTES

VI.12* The cross-reference to Locke's note Rom. II.26* is not reproduced in the printed editions, since the paraphrase and notes on Galatians was published before that on Romans; see textual note ad loc.

1 CORINTHIANS

Situated on the isthmus which divided the Peloponnese from the rest of Greece, Corinth was a busy commercial centre and the capital of the Roman province of Achaia. It was the meeting place of many religions and philosophies, and was also famed for its permissive morality. The founding of the church there by Paul is recorded in Acts XVIII.1-18. The first Epistle seems to have been sent from Ephesus (1 Cor. XVI.8); and, if the Acts of the Apostles is regarded as trustworthy, it must have been written during the visit to that city described in Acts XIX.1-41. Various dates have been suggested for its composition, among which are AD 51 (L. Cappellus; see Appendix II) and 59 (Ussher, *Annales*, p. 673). Locke, following Pearson, dates it to 57 (Synopsis, e; Appendix II).

Some modern scholars regard the Epistle as a conflation of two or more different writings, but others believe that it was written by Paul in its present form. Its unity was not disputed in Locke's day. If it is regarded as one letter, it was written to deal with trouble in the church at Corinth. He had already had occasion to write to it, but his instructions had been misunderstood (1 Cor. V.9). Information had reached him about the state of affairs there, and various points had been raised in a letter which he had received (1 Cor. I.11; VII.1). The members of the church were divided among themselves, some claiming to be supporters of Paul, some of Apollos, and others of Peter (1 Cor. I.12; see explanatory note ad loc.). There was immorality in the church (1 Cor. V.1-2). Questions were being raised about marriage and divorce (1 Cor. VII.1-40), the eating of meat sacrificed to idols, participation in meals in pagan temples (1 Cor. VIII.1-13; X.14-XI.1), and a variety of issues connected with Christian worship (1 Cor. XI.2-XIV.40). Another problem was the denial by some Church members of a belief in the resurrection of the dead (1 Cor. XV.1-58). In addition to these matters, Paul was facing intense personal opposition, and felt the need to defend his position as an apostle (1 Cor. IX.1-27).

The source of the trouble has long been a matter of dispute. Hammond regarded the unrest as primarily the work of Gnostics and Judaizers. Whitby ascribed it to philosophers and Judaizers. According to Locke, it was instigated by a Jewish false apostle, who was probably a Judaizer, and had gathered a faction around himself (1 Cor. Synopsis, e-f; I.10-VI.20, Contents, a-c; IV.21-VI.20, Contents, a-i; IX.1-27, Contents, a-e; XI.17-34, Contents, a-e; etc.).

As Paul dealt with the church's problems, he unfolded his views on the various practical issues which had arisen, but also developed his teaching about the Church, the Lord's Supper, the resurrection, and other theological matters. Moreover, the Epistle gives a vivid picture of life in an early Christian community.

Locke divides the Epistle into thirteen sections (see Appendix XI). Three entries in LL no. 2864, between pp. 54 and 55, provide evidence of his work on the Epistle. The outlines in these entries do not completely agree with that which he follows in the *Paraphrase*; but they appear to have provided Locke with a basis for his treatment of the Epistle.

The first entry gives the following summary of the Epistle's contents:

	He writes to them as to converted Gentils XII.2
I.1-9	Thanks god for their state in Christianity.
10-IV	Reproves their being of parties
V	What to doe with the Fornicator and other irregular brethren
VI.1-13	Reproves their law sutes and injustice
VI.13-VII.	Against fornication, and occasionaly of mariage and other ties
VIII	Meat offered to Idols
IX	His right to maintenance without useing it
X.1-22	Against Idolatry. The sacraments priviledg Christians in sining more than Jews.
X.23-33	Against giveing Scandal by eating things offered to Idols
XI.1-17	Women to be coverd in their Assemblys 17 Lords supper how to be eaten 34
XII.-XIV.	The different excellency of Spiritual gifts. Prophesieing to be preferred to the rest, but charity to them all
XV	The dead shall rise and how
XVI	Exhortations and Salutations

The second entry outlines the argument of the Epistle, and reads as follows:

1 Ep: ad Cor

After a preface wherein he speaks favourably of those whom he is goeing to reprove

1 The businesse of this Epist is 1st to reprove their contentions I.10-IV

Their divisions seem not to have been about opinions but about teachers which they were conceited of and distinguished themselves by. *I am of Paul. I of Apollos and I of Cephas*. Not that these were in truth those under whose names they rankd themselves into factions for St Paul says *These things I have in a figure transferd to my self and to Apollos for your sakes* IV.6. i e because I would not personaly tax those heads of factions amongst you. For his reproof seems to aime at some amongst them, who seting up them selves for wise† got followers that cried them up as more learned and better preachers than St Paul himself whom they found fault with or at least lessened.* There appears to be something personal to St Paul in the case as may be seen al along where he gives an account of his way of preaching II.2-5 that he laid the foundation of their faith whatever others may build on it. III.10 and expresly where he says, *With me it is a very small thing that I am judged of you* IV.3. The designe therefor of the IV first Chapters is to take away the pride of these Corinthian teachers and to stop the glorying of their followers by shewing that the doctrine of the Gospel is {a} a plain and simple, and to the wisdom of this world a mean contemptible and foolish thing. And that which makes a man a preacher of it is not parts or learning, or wisdom of the world but the Grace and Gift and Spirit of god. And therefor if one be a preacher and an other not, or one a better preacher than an other he has thereby noething to glory in. This is the drift of his discourse all along particularly. IV.7

2 The next thing is his reproof about the Incestuous man V

He orders them to deliver him to Sathan by his spirit 4 i e of workeing miracles whereby he seems to shew some difference between himself and those Teachers they gloryed in. But their *glorying could not be good*. 6 whilst they reteind such an offender amongst them that might corrupt their morals

3 In the next place he rebukes their goeing to law one with an other and that before heathen judges VI.1-7 and there upon he takes occasion to reprove other faults in them and particularly Fornication VI.8-20· The connection of ver. 12 with what goes before seems not very obvious. ver. 12-13 *and them* seem to come in more naturally at the end of VIII but that there are noe MSS that support any such transposition

4 In answer to their demands he tells them it is best to be unmaried but that those who have not the gift of continence should mary as a remedy against fornication, and then he gives them directions about conjugal dutys; and in case the husband or wife remained unbeleiver, the converted was not to forsake the unbeleiver if he were willing to continue: And upon this occasion he lays it down as a rule that conversion to Christianity changes noething in any ones civil state; but leaves every one maried or unmaried, bond or free just as it found him. After this incidental discourse concerning the unchanged estate of servants as well as maried upon their conversion to Christianity, he reassumes his answer to their question about mariage and informes them that in the present distresse of the church celibate was the better estate; that mariage has always most care, and celibate most leisure to minde religion, but that every one had their liberty herein· only that all that had wives or other enjoyments should use them as if they had them not VII

5 In his entrance upon his answer concerning things offerd to Idols he

reproovs those who followed or presumed on their knowledg to the prejudice of their charity, and then tells them that he who knows that there is but one god and that Idols are noe thing may eat things offerd to Idols but he must take care that he doth not thereby scandalize his weak brother who haveing not soe much knowledg in the case thinks an Idol to be some thing and yet incouraged by his example eats things offered to Idols and thereby sins VIII

6 He answers those who questioned whether he ought to be mainteind by those to whom he preachd, and proves by the example of other Apostles; by the law; by equity that he who spent his time in preaching the Gospel he and his family ought to be mainteined by those he preachd to: but however with them he had and would decline it. for the gospels sake. only he seems to take notice of their particular unkindnesse to him which agrees with what he had said in the begining of the Epist IX

7 He dehorts them from Idolatry shewing that their being baptised and partakeing of the Lords supper excuses not but aggravates their Idolatry as well as other sins, and will draw on them the judgments of god. This he proves by the example of the Israelites who were punished for their Idolatry and other sins though they were baptised into the law of Moses and eat Spiritual meat X.1-22

8 He again gives them cautions about eating things offerd to Idols, which though lawfull yet scandal was carefully to be avoided X.22-33

9 Directions concerning their assemblys XI.1-16
concerning the Lords supper XI.17-34

10 Spiritual gifts are various but all for the benefit of the Church, but Charity exceeds them all. Those of them are to be preferd which are most for edification XII-XIV

11 The sum of the Gospel Christs death, burial and resurrection from whence he proves the resurrection of the dead XV

12 Directions concerning their collection for the church at Jerusalem XVI.1-4

13 He tells them when he will come to them XVI.5-9

14 He bespeaks their civility to Timothy XVI.10.11

15 Exhortations and Salutations XVI.13-24

† vid 2 Ep: X.12

* The great occasion and cheif businesse of both St Pauls Epistles to the Corinthians seems to be the Vindication of himself against some enemies or rivals he had amongst them· vid II Ep. V.12.13. X.2.12 XI.12.13. XIII.3

A third entry in LL no. 2864 deals with the faults of the church at Corinth which are mentioned by Paul:

The faults that the Apostle in this Epistle seems to take notice of or glance at among the Corinthians seem to be

1 Corinthians

1 A great opinion of them selves for
   Knowledg I.5. VIII.1
   Wisdome I.17.19.22.24-27.29.30. II.1.4-7.13. III.18 IV.10
   Gifts I.7. IV.8.10. I.29. IV.7. V.2.6.
   Eloquence I.5.17. II.1.4.
2 Divisions I.10
3 Assumeing to themselves the glory of an others labour III.10
4 Their cariage to St Paul
   Censureing him IV.3. IX.3
   Questioning his Apostleship IX.1
   Pretending to looke into and judg him IX.1. II.15.
   Puffed up as if he would not keep his word and dare to come to them IV.18.
5 Incest V.1
6 Goeing to law before the heathen VI.1
7 Fornication VI.13.
8 Thinking their sins excused by their partakeing in the Sacraments X.6.
9 Confidence in their own strength X.12
10 Eating what they knew offerd to Idols. X.25.27.28 and that without regard to their weak brethren X.28-33
11 Suffering their women to assist in the assembly uncovered XI.1-16
12 Disorders in eating the Eucharist XI.17.34

In LL no. 2864, also at the beginning of the Epistle, between pp. 54 and 55, the following loose-leaf summary of chapters V-X has been deleted:

V.1-13 Directions of discipline concerning the incestuous person. Their miscariages there in was their not punishing him as they ought

Pride a fault of the Corinthians all through the epistle. I.29.31. II.18.21. IV.6.7-10.18.19 V.2.6. VIII.1

VI.1-8 He reproves their goeing to law before the Heathen

VI.9-11 Upon occasion of this their injustice he joyns with it several other sins whereof they probably were guilty which would exclude them from the Kingdom of heaven and better possession than any thing of this world which they went to law about

VI.12-20 Amongst these he particularly dehorts them from fornication which tis probable from his way of argueing was allowd by some of their teachers reteining still too much of the pagan doctrine amongst whom it was looked on as lawfull. v. Act XV.20

12 1st he argues that though a promiscuous use of meats were lawfull meat being made for the belly and belly for meat yet there might be many reasons that might obleige a man to abstein. But promiscuousnes⟨s⟩ could not be ṣọç the body was not made for any woman promiscuously. but belongd to Christ who had purchased it

What follows is in answer to some questions they had proposed to him

VII.1-16 About marrying he rules for the married

VII.17-24. Haveing occasion to let the Corinthians see that Christianity changed not the state of Matrimony they were in before but they were subjected to the civil law as before he in the 17 verse makes the rule general viz that Christianity changed noe thing in a mans civil state as particularly a slave converted was a slave still.

VII.25-40 He answers concerning Celibate

VIII.1-13 He answers concerning things offerd to Idols

IX.1-27 He answers those who question him about his preaching gratis from which they seem to have contemned him as not being an Apostle because he claimed not what was due to that Character or else because he knew not what maintenance was due to an Apostle· to both which he answers.

X.1-13 The being in the Church and partakeing in the Sacraments excuseth not from sin nor from the punishment of it.

X.14-22 Particularly he makes use of their partakeing in the Lords Supper as an argument to disswade them from communicateing with the heathen in their worship where he shews how far it is unlawfull

X.23-33 He diswades them as before VIII from it because though to some degree it might in it self be lawfull yet Scandal makes it unlawfull.

Section I: I.1.-9

INTRODUCTION

In this Epistle, as in 2 Corinthians, Locke gives the title 'Introduction' to the paraphrase of the opening section.

I.1 *Sosthenes* is mentioned here along with Paul, because he was his companion in Ephesus. It is unlikely that he was responsible for any of the contents of the Epistle. Note I.1† refers to Acts XVIII.17, which mentions a Sosthenes who was ruler of the synagogue in Corinth. It is not clear, however, that this was the person mentioned in 1 Corinthians.

I.2 *called by the name*: in his paraphrase and note on this verse Locke is influenced by Hammond in rendering τοῖς ἐπικαλουμένοις as passive, 'who are called by', instead of middle, 'who call upon'. This latter interpretation is accepted by AV and most commentators, although Walker mentions the passive as an alternative. Whitby explicitly rejects Hammond's treatment of the word. An entry in LL no. 2864, p. 56, records Lightfoot's view that the word refers to those who are 'professione sanctis' ('saints by profession of faith'), a view which assumes that the word is in the middle voice.

I.5 *all extraordinary gifts*: LL no. 2864, p. 56, mentions Lightfoot's comment 'donis linguarum et prophetandi' ('with gifts of tongues and prophesying'), and adds a 'JL' entry: 'That knowledg here signifies some supernatural gift and not a true and ful sense of the Gospel is evident from ver. 7 and III.1-3 JL'.

I.6 *miraculous gifts*: LL no. 2864, p. 56, repeats the reference to Lightfoot's comment about tongues and prophesying (see explanatory note on 1 Cor. I.5), and adds the following: 'By supernatural gifts. This he cals δοκιμήν a proof of Christ speakeing in his 2 Cor. XIII.3'.

NOTES

I.7† The cross-references in this note are found also in an entry in LL no. 309: 'vid-Rom XIII.11.12. 1 Cor VII.29.31'. In fact, while Locke's note Rom. XIII.11, 12* refers to the expectation of Christ's imminent return, his note 1 Cor. VII.29* speaks only of Nero's persecution. The note 2 Cor. V.3*, as well as the note Rom. XIII.11, 12*, indicates that Paul expected Christ to return in the near future. In his notes on 1 Cor. XV.52 and 1 Thess. IV.15 Grotius asserts that Paul entertained the possibility that this event was imminent. Such an interpretation of Paul is rejected by Walker (on 1 Thess. IV.15). Whitby gives an extended criticism of the viewpoint in his *Additional Annotations* (Appendix to 2 Thessalonians), where he replies to William Whiston, *An Essay on the Revelation of Saint John* (Cambridge, 1706).

Section II. No. 1: I.10-16

PARAPHRASE

I.10 *affection*: in rendering γνώμη as *affection* Locke agrees with Grotius and Hammond. The usual interpretation is that given by AV, 'judgment', in the sense of 'opinion'.

I.11 *Cloe*: such also is the spelling in the first edition (1611) of AV. The correct transliteration of the Greek is 'Chloe'. Nothing is known of her apart from the reference in this verse.

I.12 *Apollos*: an Alexandrian Jew, who had been converted to Christianity, and had ministered in Ephesus and Corinth (Acts XVIII.24-XIX.1).

Cephas: i.e. Peter; see explanatory note on Gal. II.7. The mention of him in 1 Cor. I.12 has led to the suggestion that he also ministered in Corinth.

I.13 *only head and master*: LL no. 2864, p. 57, has an entry for 1 Cor. I.12 from Lightfoot, which reads: 'Χριστοῦ Messiae unici ducis, sub quo unumquemque conscribendum esse et non {s}⟨c⟩um aliquo deputato olim edocti sumus' ('*Of Christ*: of the Messiah, the one and only leader, under whom, we have previously been taught, everyone is to be enrolled, and not under someone appointed as his deputy').

NOTES

I.10* *Of whom the whole family*: cf. Eph. III.15 (AV).

I.13* *the French*: it is not clear to which translation Locke is referring. His interleaved Testament, LL no. 2864, translates 'au nom', which does not support his point.

Section II. No. 2: I.17-31

PARAPHRASE

I.19 A quotation from Isa. XXIX.14.

I.20 In LL no. 2864, p. 57, there are two entries for this verse. The first is from Lightfoot: 'σοφός qui docet alios· γραμματεύς literatus ut d{e}⟨i⟩ stinctus a plebe· συζητητής qui profundius concionatur et legem interpretatur' ('*wise man*: one who teaches others; *scribe*: a learned man, as distinguished from the common people; *disputer*: one who speaks and interprets the law more profoundly'). The second entry is from Le Clerc's *Bibliothèque universelle*, xiii. 437: 'Amongst the Rabins were different titles and different ways of teaching which the Apostle has here comprehended under. *Wise* i e those who had a power of binding and looseing i e resolveing of cases of Conscience; and of teaching· *Scribes* i e who taught the traditions on the law. *Questioners* i e who taught the mystical and allegorical sense'. Both these entries explain these terms in relation only to the Jewish world. While Locke, however, explains the word 'scribe' solely with reference to Judaism, he relates the other terms to the world of Greek culture, in agreement with Grotius.

I.21 *by their natural parts . . . wisdome* explains 'by wisdom' (AV); *wise contrivance . . . creation* explains 'the wisdom of god' (AV). Cf. an entry in LL no. 2862, p. 135, listed under II.21, from Crellius, *Liber de Deo*, i. 222: 'For since in the wisdom of god [i e by the works of god in which his wisdome manifestly appears] the world per sapientiam [sc: suam] deum non cognovit placuit deo per praedicationem quae hominibus animalibus et nil nisi terrenum spirantibus ut ut secundum carnem sapientibus stulta videatur salvos facere credentes'. The Latin part of the entry may be translated: 'through (sc: its own) wisdom did not know God, it pleased God to save believers through preaching, which seems foolish to animal human beings who breathe only what is earthly, howsoever wise they may be according to the flesh'.

Locke's interpretation is also consistent with an entry in LL no. 2864, p. 58, where ὁ κόσμος ('the world', AV) is interpreted as 'mankind', and ἐν τῇ σοφίᾳ τοῦ θεοῦ ('in the wisdom of God', AV) as 'by considerin⟨g⟩ the works of the Creation wherin the wonderful wisdom of god appears'.

Another entry in LL no. 2864, p. 58, taken from Cudworth, *True Intellectual System*, p. 477, is consistent with Locke's account of the verse. It reads: 'The generality of the world before Christianity by their natural light and contemplation of the works of god did not attain to such a practical knowledg of god as might both free them from idolatry, and effectualy bring them to a holy life.'

A different interpretation is found in an entry in LL no. 2864, p. 58, from Lightfoot, explaining 'the wisdom of God' as 'human wisdom about God'. It reads: 'σοφίᾳ τοῦ θεοῦ Sapientia circa deum: i e Mundus in Theologia sua non potuit per sapientiam suam scire deum' ('*The wisdom of God*. Wisdom about God: i.e. the world in its theology was unable through its wisdom to know God').

I.22 While AV treats I.22 as a main clause, and translates it 'For the Jews . . .', Locke translates it 'Since both the Jews . . .', and treats verses 22 and 23 as subordinate to the main clause in verse 24. He explains his position in note I.22*.

NOTES

I.22*b *did not attain to a right and saveing knowledg*: an entry for I.21, ascribed to Lightfoot in LL no. 2864, p. 58, reads: '*Knew not*, i e Saveingly'. This does not, however, clearly correspond to any note in Lightfoot.

I.22*d *wisdome*: cf. an entry for this verse from Lightfoot (on II.6) in LL no. 2864, p. 58: 'σοφίαν ethnicam vel philosophorum' ('*wisdom*, of the Gentiles or of the philosophers').

I.22*d *both Jew and Gentil*: in affirming that believers find Christ himself to be the power and wisdom of God, Locke differs from an entry under II.24 in LL no. 2862, p. 135, from Crellius, *Liber de Deo*, i. 193: 'But those who are called both Jews and Gentils perceive in the things donne by Christ the power and wisdome of god'.

I.25, 27, 28* In agreement with Calvin and Crellius (*Comm.*) Locke regards 'foolish things', 'weak things', and 'base things' (AV) as references to people rather than things. Grotius and Whitby claim that they allude to methods of instructing people as well as to the people themselves.

I.28† In explaining 'things that are not' as Gentiles, Locke is in agreement with Whitby. Such an interpretation understands Paul to be speaking of the calling of the Gentiles to be God's people, not, as Calvin understands it, of the calling of the elect. Locke's position is also in agreement with an entry from Allix in LL no. 309, where it is listed under I.26:

> 'Hoc non ad particularium electionem detorquendum. Nonne singuli quos alloquebatur Paulus ad electionem pertinebant· Eodem modo Paulus loquitur hic ad Corinthios quo olim Moses ad Judaeos ut illis humilitatis inculcaret studium' ('This is not to be distorted into a reference to the election of individuals. Did not the individuals whom Paul was addressing belong to the election? Paul speaks here to the Corinthians in the same way as Moses did in the past to the Jews, to implant a zeal for humility in them').

Section II. No. 3a: II.1-5

NOTES

II.1* Locke's paraphrase of this verse assumes the reading μαρτύριον ('testimony', AV) in agreement with the majority of manuscripts. But this note by Locke follows Codex Alexandrinus in reading μυστήριον ('mystery'), a reading which had been explicitly rejected by Whitby in his first edition. The position adopted in the note is characteristic of Locke's preference for the text which he believed to be more consistent with Paul's argument. See Introduction, p. 28.

II.4*a *miraculous gifts*: in LL no. 309 an entry, probably from Allix, explains parts of II.4 and 5: '*Demonstratione spiritus. et virtute dei*. i e Donis miraculosis. v. 1 Joh: V.8. Apo. XIX.10' ('*In demonstration of the Spirit, and by the power of God*, i.e. by miraculous gifts, vid. 1 John V.8; Rev. XIX.10'). This entry probably influenced Locke in his note II.4*a and also in his choice of the words 'miraculous operations' in his paraphrase.

Section II. No. 3b: II.6–16

PARAPHRASE

II.6 *are throughly instructed* . . . *true principles*: cf. Whitby: 'fully instructed in the Principles of the Christian Faith'.

II.7 *before the Jewish constitution*: AV, Walker, and Whitby render πρὸ τῶν αἰώνων as 'before the world', but a literal translation is 'before the ages'. Grotius renders 'many ages ago' and Hammond 'from the beginning'. Locke's interpretation is indebted, as he explains in note II.7‡c, to Richard Burthogge. In LL no. 309 an entry reads: 'πρὸ τῶν αἰώνων r: before the ages i e before the Jewish constitution. The Apostle is speaking of the Jews ver. 6. and 8 immediately before and after this and therefore here too. vid Isa: XXVI.4. Act. XV.18. 1 Cor X:11'. Le Clerc, who understands it to mean 'a long time ago' (NT), rejects Locke's interpretation (*Bibliothèque choisie*, xiii.89-90).

II.9 This verse is quoted by Locke, *Essay*, IV. xviii. 3 (p. 690), with reference to revelations that cannot be communicated to others. In his paraphrase of 1 Cor. II.10 a similar interpretation is given, namely, that these truths cannot be discerned by the natural faculties and powers of human beings. An entry from Lightfoot in LL no. 2864, p. 60, understands the verse to speak of the difference in clarity between the revelation given through the Gospel and that given through the prophets: '῞Α ὀφθαλμός etc: i e clariorem longe esse revelationem sub evangelio quam assecuti sunt prophetae' ('*What eye* etc., i.e. that the revelation under the Gospel is far clearer than that to which the prophets attained').

II.10 *natural faculties and powers*: the phrase is similar to 'natural parts and faculties' in note 1 Cor. II.6†. In *Essay*, II. ix-xi (pp. 143-63), the faculties of the mind are said to be perception, retention, discerning, comparing, composition, and abstraction. Also in *Essay*, II. xxi. 20 (pp. 243-4), Locke writes: 'For *Faculty*, *Ability*, and *Power*, I think, are but different names of the same things'. In the same paragraph he mentions two faculties of the mind, 'the *intellectual Faculty*, or the Understanding' and 'the *elective Faculty*, or the Will'.

II.13 *which the holy ghost teacheth*: LL no. 2864, p. 60, contains the following 'JL' entry: 'ἐν διδακτοῖς πνεύματος. i e words taught by the spirit. i e the words of revelation in the Sacred Scripture. πνευματικά. i.e. things or revelations relateing to the Gospel JL'.

II.13 *compareing one part of revelation with an other*: apparently Locke understands Paul to be alluding here to the comparison of one part of the scriptures with another. Grotius, Hammond, Walker, and Whitby are more specific, referring it to a comparison of the Old Testament with the Christian revelation. Whitby opposes the interpretation of Le Clerc (*Supp.*, NT), who explains it as a reference to 'speaking spiritual things to spiritual men'. At the end of his Preface Locke alludes to this part of 1 Cor. II.13.

II.14 *natural faculties*: a 'JL' entry in LL no. 2864, p. 60, reads: 'The animal powrs. i e faculties of the soul unassisted by the spirit or revelation cannot discover the things of revelation because they are discoverd or discerned only by the help of revelation. JL'. Another 'JL' entry in LL no. 2864, p. 60, reads: 'πνευματικός he that builds his Christianity upon revelation cannot be tried or judg⟨d⟩ of by one who builds only upon his natural faculties and the knowledge that is got barely by them. Such an one he cals ψυχικός ver. 14 JL'. (AV translates πνευματικός as 'spiritual' and ψυχικός as 'natural'.) Yet another 'JL' entry in LL no. 2864, p. 60, reads: 'ψυχικός. i e who is lead by the animal appetite ruleing in him. JL'. In LL no. 309 an entry from Stillingfleet, *Answer to Cressy* (London, 1675), p. 33, explains 'natural man' or 'animal man' as 'The man that supposes such a natural sufficiency in the humane soul in order to its own perfection and happinesse, (as the philosophers did) that there was noe necessity either of divine revelation to discover any new doctrin or of divine grace to conduct us to our happinesse.' These accounts are similar to those of Grotius and Whitby, who explain 'natural' as a reference to somebody who is led only by the light and principles of human reason. Calvin's account is not far removed. He explains it as meaning somebody who relies only on the faculties of nature. Le Clerc, however (*Supp.*,

NT), claims that the word refers to a person who is not concerned with spiritual things but resembles the animals. Whitby explicitly attacks Le Clerc's interpretation. The terminology examined in Locke's note is also discussed by him in his note 1 Cor. II.15*, where he takes a position consistent with the above-mentioned entries and at variance with Le Clerc.

II.16 *instruct him*: in understanding 'him' as a reference to 'the spiritual man' Locke is in agreement with Vorstius, Hammond, and Whitby. Many scholars, however, including Grotius and Walker, refer it to 'the Lord'. Grotius defends his position by pointing out that he is true to the meaning of Isa. XL.14-15, from which the words have been taken.

II.16 *the mind of Christ*: according to Locke, 'having the mind of Christ' is taking one's message from divine revelation. Grotius gives a similar interpretation.

NOTES

II.6‡ An entry from Lightfoot in LL no. 2864, p. 59, reads: 'Adventus Christi erat αἰὼν ὁ μέλλων. Tempus antecedens αἰὼν οὗτος' ('The coming of Christ was *the age to come*. The preceding time was *this age*').

II.6§ In explaining the *princes of this world* as Jewish leaders, Locke is in accord with Vorstius, Hammond, Walker (on II.8), and Whitby. Other interpretations include that of Calvin, who thinks that Paul is referring to people of intellect or stature, and that of Goodwin (see above, p. 5), to which Locke later assented.

II.6¶a *wisdome and learning . . . doctrine of the gospel*: an entry in LL no. 2864, p. 59, from Lightfoot, reads: 'σοφίαν τοῦ αἰῶνος τούτου sapientiam quam assequi quis potuit ante revelatum evangelium' ('*wisdom of this age*, the wisdom which anyone could obtain before the gospel was revealed').

II.12* Locke's claim that *we* refers to Paul alone rather than to Paul and others contrasts with an entry from Allix in LL no. 309, which reads: '*We* i e Apostoli et viri Apostolici' ('*We*, i.e. apostles and apostolic men').

II.15* *noe higher principles to build on*: cf. the second 'JL' entry in the explanatory note on II.14: 'he that builds his Christianity upon . . .'.

Section II. No. 4: III.1-IV.20

PARAPHRASE

III.11 *which is Jesus the Messiah*: according to Locke, the foundation is the doctrine of Jesus's Messiahship, as he explicitly states in Contents, c, of this section. The same interpretation is given by Grotius, Crellius, and Le Clerc (NT). It is consistent with Locke's position in the *Reasonableness*.

III.12-14 *wood, hey . . . pretious stones*: in explaining the material built on the foundation as doctrines, Locke is in accord with most of the interpreters with whom he was acquainted. The viewpoint is found in a 'JL' entry for III.13 in LL no. 2862, p. 136: '*Every mans work*. i e Every preachers doctrine. JL. v. V 9-10.' Locke does not, however, reproduce the claim made by Lightfoot that the false doctrines were Jewish. This claim is recorded in entries in LL no. 2864, p. 62, and listed under III.12. According to one of them, gold, etc., stands for 'doctrinam pretiosam puram solidam' ('precious, pure, and sound doctrine'), while wood, hay, etc., stands for 'vilem, nullius pretii nec soliditatis. i e doctrinas Judaismi' ('cheap, of no value or soundness, i.e. doctrines of Judaism'). Another of the entries reinforces the point: 'Doctrinas Judaismi sparserunt non nulli in ecclesia Cor:' ('Some spread abroad the doctrines of Judaism in the Church at Corinth').

III.12-13 *last day*: Locke's interpretation, which relates Paul's thought here to the Last Judgement, is vastly different from that of Lightfoot, who claims that Paul is referring to the judgement of the Jews when Jerusalem was destroyed in AD 70. An entry listed under III.13 in LL no. 2864, p. 62, is taken from Lightfoot, and asserts that Paul is speaking of 'dies domini brevi venturus atque ignis divinae indignationis effundendus in gentem Judaicam . . . qui et superstructionis istius ineptiam revelabit ipsamque destruet' ('the day of the Lord which is soon to come, and the fire of divine indignation which is to be poured out on the Jewish nation . . . which will also reveal the folly of that superstructure and destroy it').

III.14 *stand the triall*: an entry for this verse from Lightfoot (on III.13) in LL no. 2864, p. 62 reads: 'ἔργον μενεῖ si cuiusquam doctrina istius ignis examen ferat' ('*the work will remain*: if anyone's teaching endures the trial of that fire').

III.15 *all his pains in building is lost*: an entry for this verse from

Lightfoot (on III.13) in LL no. 2864, p. 62, reads: 'κατακαήσεται examen non ferat' ('*It will be burned up*, it will not endure the trial'). Another entry for this verse from Lightfoot (on III.13) in LL no. 2864, p. 62, reads: 'ζημιωθήσεται sc: ole{o}⟨um⟩ et opera⟨m⟩ perditis' ('He will be penalized, sc. you lose your time and trouble').

III.15 *should escape*: cf. two entries listed under IV.15 in LL no. 309. One of them is from Thomas Burnet (1635-1715), Master of Charterhouse, *The Theory of the Earth*, i (London, 1684), LL no. 534, pp. 55, 73: '*Yet soe as by fire·* A proverbial speech to expresse the risque they run, to be such, as of one that escapes out of the fire Vid Zach. 3.2 Jude. 23.' The other entry, from Tillotson, *Sermons*, ii. 57, explains that the Greek means 'as out of the fire', and comments: 'To be saved out of the fire, signifies a narrow escape out of a great danger'.

III.17 *corrupt doctrine*: cf. an entry in LL no. 2862, p. 136: '*The temple of god* i e ye are the church of god in which the spirit of god dwelleth· *if any one defile*. i.e introduce false or erroneous doctrines.'

III.22a *for your sake and use*: cf. Le Clerc (*Supp.*), 'made for your use'.

IV.6a *I have chosen to name*: for the view that Paul is not really speaking of himself and Apollos, cf. an entry from Lightfoot in LL no. 2864, p. 64: 'μετεσχημάτισα sc: loquens de praedicatione plana, rudi et a sapientia humana quam remota ad me ipsum inquit transtuli, de eleganti exculta et profundiori ad Apollo' ('*I have transferred*, sc: When he speaks of preaching which is simple, uncultivated, and far removed from human wisdom, he says, "I have transferred it to myself". When he speaks of that which is elegant, refined, and more profound, he says, "I have transferred it to Apollos"').

IV.7 *what knowledg of the Gospel*: a 'JL' entry in LL no. 309 reads: '*What has‹t› thou?* i e of the knowledg of the gospel. JL'.

NOTES

III.1† This note understands σαρκικός ('carnal') to mean the same here as ψυχικός ('natural') or ('animal'). A note deleted from L but retained in 1 makes a distinction between the two words. See textual note on III.1*.

The note retained in L is consistent, though by no

means verbally identical, with some 'JL' entries on II.15-III.1 in LL no. 2864, p. 61:

'πνευματικός i e enlightend by the Spirit of god in the knowledg and mystery of the gospel, opposed to ψυχικός. i e the mere animal man proceeding only upon natural i e unreveled principles. ἀνακρίνει i.e. explores and can discerne what is from the spirit of god and what not. But such an one is above the discovery and judgment of others. i e I who {who} have the spirit and mind of Christ. 10 and 16 cannot be examined and tried by those carnal men who pretend to tell you that I act out of crafty and carnal designes JL· πνευματικός is a man enlightend by revelation. ψύχικός, one that has only the light of his natural parts JL

What man by strength of his bare natural parts can come to the knowledg of the gospel and its wonderfull contrivance. Soe St Paul understands this place of Isai Rom XI.34. But the designe of the gospel is reveald to me. which I could not at large deliver to you as to πνευματικοῖς. i e such as depended only on revelation for the knowledg of the gospel; but as to σαρκικοῖς such as depended on their natural faculties. σαρκικοί here signifies the same with ψυχικοί II.14 JL'

III.3* The thought of this note and note III.1†d is consistent with that of an entry for III.3-4 in LL no. 2864, p. 61: 'κατ' ἄνθρωπον. doe ye not depend upon your natural abilities when you distinguish your selves and your tenets or knowledg in Christianity by your teachers· περιπατεῖτε Doe ye not governe your selves by barely humane and unreveled principles. v. IX.8'.

Section II: No. 5: IV.21-VI.20

PARAPHRASE

V.4 *and my spirit*: cf. an entry in LL no. 309 from an anonymous book entitled *Grallae* (Franeker, 1646, LL no. 1306), p. 166: '*Vobis et spiritu meo*. i e potestate clavium quae solis Apostolis concredita sine qua Corinthiorum ecclesia quemvis Satanae tradere non poterat vid Math. 16.19' ('*to you and my spirit*, i.e. by the power of the keys entrusted to the apostles alone, without which the church of the Corinthians was unable to deliver anyone to Satan. See Matt. XVI.19'). And in LL no. 2864, p. 66, an entry from Lightfoot indicates that the mention of the Spirit in 1 Cor. V.4

implies that a miraculous power has been given to Paul. But Locke interprets 'spirit' here as a reference to Paul's vote exercised at Corinth in his absence. An entry under IV.4 in LL no. 2862, p. 136, from an unnamed source, reads: 'When you are gatherd togeather, where my minde my vote shall be with you.'

V.5 *deliver the offender up to Sathan*: Hammond explains this as a reference to being delivered up to demon possession. And such an explanation may have been in Locke's mind. An entry from *Grallae*, p. 167, in LL no. 309 reads: '*Tradere Satanae* i e Corpus Cruciandum tradere' ('*To hand over to Satan*, i.e. to hand over the body to be tormented'). Cf. also an entry from Lightfoot in LL no. 2864, pp. 66-7: 'Παραδοῦναι τῷ Σατανᾷ. sc reali et miraculosa traditione in manus Satanae ut ab eo morbis torturis terroribus cruciaretur' ('*To hand over to Satan*, sc. by a real and miraculous deliverance into the hands of Satan to be tormented by him with diseases, tortures, and terrors').

V.9 *I wrote to you before*: Locke appears to understand this to refer to a previous letter; this was the view also of Calvin, Crellius, and Le Clerc (*Supp.*, NT). An entry, without named source, in LL no. 2864, p. 67, which is in fact taken from Lightfoot, supports this view, but goes on to suggest that it was sent with Timothy and suppressed by Paul after he had decided to send 1 Corinthians in its place. Whitby, however, regards it as an allusion to a previous draft of 1 Corinthians, and Vorstius and Hammond explain it as a reference to an earlier part of 1 Cor. V.

V.10 *unconverted heathens*: an entry, without named source, in LL no. 2864, p. 67, which is taken from Lightfoot, placed by Locke under V.10 but by Lightfoot under V.9, says that the 'fornicators of this world' are heathens ('Ethnici'), and that Paul is telling his readers to keep away from erring Christians rather than heathens: 'quod non intellexi tam de scortatoribus ethnicis quam de iis qui vocantur fratres aut Christiani' ('which I have understood not so much of heathen fornicators as of those who are called brothers or Christians').

VI.3 *evil spirits*: Locke agrees with most commentators of his day in explaining that the angels mentioned by Paul are evil spirits, although Walker suggests that it refers to both good and bad angels. It is not perfectly clear, however, how Locke understands Paul's remarks about judging the world and judging angels. In verse 2 the paraphrase appears to refer to a future judgement of the world. But in verse 3 it appears to speak of a present judgement of angels, even though the Greek and AV use the future tense of the verb. Locke certainly does not adopt the interpretation of Lightfoot, alluded to in two entries in LL no. 2864, p. 68, according to which the judgement of the world was the rule to be exercised by Christian magistrates when the Roman Empire became Christian. Lightfoot claims that the judgement of the angels is to be carried out, not by Christians as a whole, but by the ministers of the Gospel, who by successful evangelism will deprive the evil angels of their power and influence.

VI.4 *let the partys* etc.: although Locke's paraphrase agrees with AV in rendering the Greek as an imperative, a 'JL' entry in LL no. 2864, p. 68, argues that it should be understood as a question:

> *Doe you make those judges of it who are in the church of noe esteem of noe authoritie?* i e. Unbeleivers. That this is an interogation appears by the whole scheme of the Apostles discourse here which both before and after is interrogatory. As also by the words immediately following. *I speake to your Shame*. For the preceding words being imperative could not be spoken to their shame, as they were being interrogative. As farther appears by the next words. Have you not soe much as one wise man amongst you fit to be a judg? And therefor he could not think the most contemptible amongst ⟨you⟩ fit to be {a} judges of their differences, since he requires a wise man for it and asks whether they have not one wise enough {to} for that office, if the meanest would serve there was noe room for such a question. JL.

Whitby also explains the Greek as a question.

VI.5 *Is there not among you*: an entry in LL no. 2864, p. 68, apparently representing Locke's view, reads: 'Is there not soe much as one wise man amongst you who'. In LL no. 2864, p. 68, is also a 'JL' entry, listed under VI.4, which reads: 'You that have such wise and able teachers whom you distinguish your selves by, and whom you glory in have you not one man amongst you wise enough to determin your differences? JL'.

VI.11 *washed . . . sanctified . . . have made some advances*: Locke connects 'washed' with baptism and cleansing, a connection which is made in an unidentified entry in LL no. 309 listed under V.11, possibly derived from Allix: '*Washed*. i e. Per lavacrum sanctificatio contigit Gentibus, quae apud Judaeos pro ἀκαθάρτοις habebantur. Hic locus lucem foeneratur Rom. VI.19.20' ('*Washed*, i.e. Through washing sanctification came to the Gentiles, who were regarded by the Jews as *unclean*. This place gives light to Rom. VI.19, 20'). Most commentators in Locke's day linked washing here with baptism, but Calvin had not made the connection.

Especially noteworthy is Locke's rendering here of ἐδικαιώθητε ('are justified', AV) as *have made some advances in the reformation of your lives*. Calvin, Hammond, Whitby, and Le Clerc (*Supp.*, NT) see it as a reference to the beginning of the Christian life. But Locke sees it as an allusion to progress in that life, in agreement with Grotius, who explains it as meaning, 'You have daily made steps forward in righteousness.'

An entry in LL no. 309, listed under V.11, indicates that the Greek should be translated 'have been justified' (AV has 'are justified'), and refers to Rom. V.9.

VI.13b *our Lord Christ has taken a body*: this statement in the paraphrase seems to imply the pre-existence of Christ.

VI.20 *the pretious bloud of Christ*: these words, which have no equivalent here in Greek, are also found in Whitby. But this need not be evidence of Locke's dependence here on Whitby, because most commentators see a reference in this verse to Christ's death, e.g. Crellius, 'by the precious blood of his Son'.

NOTES

V.1* As Locke says, זנות (*zenuth*) does not refer to fornication merely in the narrow sense of sexual relations between an unmarried man and an unmarried woman. While it is always translated 'whoredom' in AV, it usually refers to the faithlessness of the Israelites in forsaking God for the false gods of other nations (e.g. Jer. III.2, 9), but it sometimes refers to literal harlotry (e.g. Gen. XXXVIII.24; Deut. XXII.21; Josh. VI.17). It is an exaggeration to claim, as Locke does, that *zenuth* can refer to 'any flagitious scandalous crime'.

V.1† Locke's source for this note is to be found in an entry in

LL no. 309, mistakenly assigned to 1 Cor. IV.1, and taken from Jeremy Taylor (1613-67), Bishop of Down and Connor, *Ductor Dubitantium* (London, 1660), ii, ch. 1, sec. 23:

> Silenius gave Antiochus his Sonne his owne wife and made it a law for the future. Cicero mentions an other instance. Nubit genero Socrus, auspicibus nullis, nullis authoribus, funestis ominibus, o mulieris scelus, incredibile, et praeter hanc unam in omni vita inauditum. (Ora: pro Clu) something like St Paul's ἥτις οὐδὲ ὀνομάζεται.

The Greek means 'which is not even named'. The Latin is almost the same as that which Locke includes in his note V.1†, where it may be translated: 'The mother-in-law marries her son-in-law with no auspices, no witnesses, and with deadly forebodings about everything. O the unbelievable wickedness of the woman, a wickedness apart from her alone unheard of in all history!' The reference is to *Pro Cluentio* 14-15 (or, on the older system, v. 14-vi. 15, not iv).

V.6‡ The Latin, from Juvenal, ii. 79-80, may be translated: 'The whole herd dies in the field because of the mange and scurf of one pig.'

VI.1* An entry without named source, but in fact from Lightfoot (on VI.2), in LL no. 2864, p. 68 explains ἐπὶ τῶν ἀδίκων ('before the unjust' or 'before the unrighteous') as a reference to 'tribunalia Ethnica' ('heathen courts'), and renders ἁγίων ('saints') as 'Christiani'.

VI.4*b *de Dieu*: Ludovicus (Louis) de Dieu (1590-1642), *Animadversiones* (Leyden, 1646), pp. 203-4. The contents of Locke's note also closely resemble some of Lightfoot's comments on this passage. The remarks of Lightfoot are not extensively recorded in the interleaved Testament, LL no. 2864, but it mentions his explanation of βιωτικὸν κριτήριον as 'consessus non authorizatus' ('unauthorized session').

VI.8*b *chopd in peices*: cf. Preface, p. 105.

VI.11† The verb δικαιοῦν ('justify') is not found in Rev. XXII.11, but the noun δικαιοσύνη ('righteousness') and the adjective δίκαιος ('righteous') occur there.

VI.12* and 12† In these notes Locke argues that Paul is answering arguments put forward on behalf of the Fornicator in defence of immoral behaviour. Three entries from Lightfoot for VI.12, 13 in LL no. 2864, p. 69, name the

Nicolaitans as the source of these arguments; and Lightfoot believed the Nicolaitans to have been Gnostic. Locke himself gives no sign of regarding Paul's opponents as Gnostics, but believes them to be Jews and Judaizers who tolerate the Fornicator's behaviour.

VI.14* This note has made use of a 'JL' entry in LL no. 309, listed under V.14, parts of which it transcribes verbatim:

> Διὰ τῆς δυνάμεως αὐτοῦ. I think should be translated *into his power* Διά signifying here *into* as it does Rom. VI.4. and 2 Peter I 3. And so this verse has a very clear and pertinent signification here, where St Paul is makeing out to the Corinthians that they have a power to judg he tels them ver. 2 That they shal judg the world. and that they shall judg angels much more things of this life ver. 3: And for this their not judging he blames them and tells them 'tis a lessening to them not to exercise this power ver. 7. And for it he gives a reason in this verse because Christ is raisd into the power of god and so should they be. Twould yet be Stronger for this sense if ἐξεγερεῖ were at first writ ἐξήγειρε as the two καί's in this ver. would incline one to think. As it is this ver. seems to stand alone here and out of its place unless it be taken in this sense, for what connection has the mention of the resurrection or of the power of god with what the apostle was saying here? JL.

A similar allusion to 2 Pet. I.3 is found in note Rom. VI.4*.

Section III: VII.1-40

PARAPHRASE

VII.31 *the Scene of things is always changeing*: although Locke believed that Paul expected Christ to return in the near future, he treated this passage, as did Crellius, as an allusion to the changing nature of life in this world. Grotius and Hammond saw it as a prediction of Nero's persecution and the Jewish War which culminated in the destruction of Jerusalem. Le Clerc (NT) believed that Paul spoke of a change in the Romans' attitude to Christians when they began to persecute them. Whitby claimed that Paul might be referring either to the dissolution of this world or to our passing out of it.

VII.39 *as a Christian fearing god*: Locke's paraphrase of μόνον ἐν κυρίῳ ('only in the Lord', AV) is in general agreement with Calvin, Beza, Vorstius, and Hammond, and contrasts with the rendering 'only to a Christian' favoured by Grotius, Walker, Whitby, and Le Clerc (NT).

NOTES

VII.14*a-b The distinction made in this note between *proles genita extra sanctitatem* ('children born outside holiness') and *Genita intra sanctitatem* ('Born within holiness') is taken from Lightfoot's note on this verse, although there is no entry for it in the interleaved Bible and Testaments or the New Testament notebook.

VII.14*b *all that are of the Christian church . . . all that were out of it*: the same distinction is found in an entry in LL no. 2864, p. 72, based on Lightfoot, explaining ἀκάθαρτα ('unclean') as 'extra Christianismum' ('outside Christianity') and ἅγια ('holy') as 'Christiani'. An entry in LL no. 309 from Hammond, *Practical Catechisme* (vi. 3), goes into more detail. ἀκάθαρτα is explained as 'not capable of the privilidges of visible members of the church'; and ἅγια as 'thought fit to be admitted into baptisme without scruple'.

VII.25* Most interpreters known to Locke understand *Virgins* here to refer to women only. The view, advocated by Locke, that it refers to single persons of both sexes is also found in a note on VII.26 in Lightfoot which is not recorded in the interleaved Bible and Testaments or the New Testament notebook.

VII.29* Calvin, Vorstius, and Crellius think that in this verse Paul was merely referring to the brevity of human life when he spoke of the time being short. Grotius and Hammond understand it as a reference to the troubles of the times. Locke's suggestion that it is a *prophetical foresight* of the persecution under Nero is in agreement with Walker (on VII.26), Le Clerc (NT) and an entry, listed under VII.26, in LL no. 2864, p. 73, taken from Lightfoot: 'asperrima tempora futura ante excidium Hierosolymae a Christo praedicta.' ('very rough times which would precede the destruction of Jerusalem and were foretold by Christ.') Another entry in LL no. 2864, p. 73, based on Lightfoot's note, and listed under VII.29, reads: 'calamitates praedictae brevi venturae' ('the predicted calamities soon to come'). Nero's persecution of the Christians in Rome took place in AD 64, and the Romans destroyed Jerusalem in

AD 70. Locke's note 1 Cor. I.7*, however, implies that this passage refers to the return of Christ. An entry for VII.29 in LL no. 309 makes a cross-reference to 1 Cor. I.7, but there is no trace of this interpretation in his comments on chapter VII in the *Paraphrase*.

VII.31* *abuseing* is the meaning favoured by the Vulgate, AV, Crellius, and Grotius. Locke agrees with Erasmus (*Ann.*) and Beza in translating it *intently useing*.

VII.37*a Locke's claim that *Virgin* here refers to the *virgin state* is sharply criticized by Le Clerc (*Bibliothèque choisie*, xiii. 89-91) and Jenkin (*Remarks*, pp. 139-40). Locke describes the interpretation as his own *conjecture* but Whitby gives the same interpretation. Explanations of the meaning of VII.36-7 are diverse. It is generally agreed that 'let them marry' (AV) in VII.36 refers to the marriage of a virgin with a suitor. But 'any man' (AV) in VII.36 refers to a virgin's father, according to Calvin, Grotius, Crellius, and Walker; to the suitor, according to Hammond. In the view of Calvin, Grotius, Crellius, and Walker, VII.37 refers to a father's attitude to his virgin daughter, while Hammond interprets it as a reference to a suitor's attitude to the woman he wishes to marry. In his paraphrase Locke implies that VII.36 speaks of a suitor's attitude to the virgin with whom he contemplates marriage, but that VII.37 speaks of a man's attitude to his own virginity. In his note VII.37*, however, he takes the position, maintained also by Whitby, that both these verses deal with a man's attitude to the question of his own virginity. It was only later that some scholars began to adopt the view that Paul was talking here of the relationship between unmarried Christians of opposite sexes who shared the same residence without having sexual relations.

VII.38* Locke prefers the reading γαμίζων ('marrying') to ἐκγαμίζων ('giving in marriage') because it is consistent with his interpretation of παρθένος ('virgin') as 'virginity' in VII.37. The reading which he has chosen is also supported by the most reliable manuscripts, and among those of them known to him were Codex Vaticanus, Codex Alexandrinus, and Codex Claromontanus.

Section IV: VIII.1-13

PARAPHRASE

VIII.2 In LL no. 309 is a lengthy entry from René Descartes (1596-1650), *Opera Philosophica* (3rd edn. Amsterdam,

1658), LL no. 601a (*Responsiones*, vi. 5), which opens with the following statement about this verse:

> Debet locus intelligi tantum de scientia, quae non est cum charitate conjuncta. i.e. de scientia Atheorum quia quisquis deum ut par est novit, non potest ipsum non d{e}⟨i⟩ligere, nec charitatem non habere. ('This passage ought to be understood only of the knowledge which is not joined with love, i.e. of the knowledge possessed by Atheists, because whoever rightly knows God, cannot avoid loving him or having love.')

The words of Descartes may have influenced Locke in his reference to *a science for speculation and dispute*.

VIII.3 *made . . . from god*: Locke, in agreement with Beza, gives an unusual rendering of the Greek, which is generally translated 'known of him' (AV) or 'known by him'.

VIII.6 *to whom . . . service*: this paraphrase of ἡμεῖς εἰς αὐτόν ('we in him' AV, or literally 'we into him') is like Grotius's 'that he might be honoured by us' and Hammond's 'to whom all men's prayers may be addressed'. Very different is Calvin's 'we are preserved by him'.

VIII.7 *conscious to themselves*: in LL no. 2864, p. 76, a 'JL' entry comments: 'with consciousnesse to them selves that they think the Idol to be something JL'.

VIII.8 In LL no. 2864, p. 76, a 'JL' entry reads: 'For neither if anyone has soe much knowledge that he eats without scrupule does he excell i e. he is not thereby recommended to god. Nor if any one scrupuls to eat is he thereby inferior or lesse recommended to god JL'.

NOTES

VIII.5* This note has many similarities, some of them verbal, to an entry for VIII.5-6 from Mede, *Works*, i. 318, in LL no. 2864, p. 75:

> εἴτε ἐν οὐρανῷ. The heathen had 1° Soveraign and supreme gods, whom they supposed eternal remaining always in the heavens, yea to dwell in the heavenly lights. These in scripture are called *the host of heaven*· Εἴτε ἐπὶ τῆς γῆς· 2° Under gods. which the Greeks called Daemons. The Scripture cals Baalim. i e Lords who were mediators or agents between the suprem gods and men. θεοί. i e Celestial Soveraign gods. Κύριοι. i e Baalim or presidents of earthly things·

But to us Christians *there is but one* soveraign *god the father* etc to whom as suprem we are to direct all our services. καὶ εἷς κύριος etc i e Mediator or agent instead of their many Baalim. δι' οὗ τὰ πάντα. i e which come from the father to us, and through whom alone we find accesse unto him.

Another comment is added, taken also from Mede: 'These Baalim were the canonized soules of men worshiped for gods', to which are added cross-references to Num. XXV.2, 3 and Ps. CVI.28. A 'JL' entry in LL no. 309, listed under IX.5, asks whether polytheism might have its origin in 'the tradition of the Persees . . . That god to prevent the Mischeif of Malignant Lucifer deposed and his confederates set certain Supervisors over his Creatures to preserve them in the State wherein they were at first created.' The note, which is dependent on Henry Lord, *A Display of Two Forraigne Sects in the East Indies* (London, 1630), pt. ii, p. 8, goes on to give the names and functions of these supervisors. It has exercised no direct influence on the *Paraphrase*.

VIII.5*b *Baalim*: the plural of the Hebrew 'Baal', which means 'Lord' or 'Master', and is often used in the Old Testament to describe a Canaanite fertility god. In its plural form it probably refers to various local manifestations of the god (Judges II.11; III.7; VIII.33; X.6, 10).

VIII.5*c *Lord-Agent Jesus Christ*: Winch Holdsworth, *Defence of the Doctrine of the Resurrection of the same Body*, accused Locke of Socinianism for describing Jesus in this present note as Lord-Agent. In reply Catharine Cockburn, *A Vindication of Mr. Locke's Christian Principles*, argued that to call him Lord-Agent does not preclude his being Lord in the sense of being God (Cockburn, *Works*, i. 196). It should also be noted that Mede, in the entry quoted in the explanatory note on VIII.5* above, describes Jesus as a mediator or agent; and this description is likely to have influenced Locke's choice of terminology in this note.

Section V: IX.1-27

PARAPHRASE

IX.1 *to see Jesus Christ*: an entry in LL no. 2864, p. 77, makes a cross-reference to Acts IX and XXII.21, both of which are accounts of Paul's conversion.

IX.3 *to those . . . upon me*: a 'JL' entry in LL no. 2864, p. 77, explains τοῖς ἐμὲ ἀνακρίνουσι as 'exp{r}⟨l⟩oratoribus meis. i e who pronounce of me as if they had discoverd I know not what in me. v 11.14.15 JL'. The Latin may be translated 'to my examiners'.

IX.8-9 The reference to arguments from both reason and revelation is also found in Contents, c of this section. An entry in LL no. 2864, p. 77, explains κατὰ ἄνθρωπον ('according to man' or 'as man', AV) with the comment: 'upon meerly humane and unreveled grounds, noe the reveled law of god makes it good v: III.3'. The point about reason and revelation is made here by Grotius, Hammond, Crellius, and Whitby.

NOTES

IX.1* This note is probably derived from Lightfoot, from whom there is an unnamed entry in LL no. 2864, p. 77: 'Ἐλεύθερος. sc: a jure Judaeorum quo non permissum ut ab Ethnicis recipiatur alimonium' ('*Free*, sc. from the law of the Jews by which alms are not allowed to be accepted from Gentiles').

IX.5* In this context Locke understands γυναῖκα as 'woman' rather than 'wife'. His explanation is consistent with that of Hammond, who suggests in his paraphrase of this verse and in his note on Rom. XVI.1 that Phoebe may have been a woman who accompanied the apostles on their travels. See explanatory note on Rom. XVI.1*. The word is explained as 'wife' in this context by many interpreters, including Calvin, AV, Grotius, Whitby, and Le Clerc (NT).

IX.12* Although Locke's note suggests that οὐσίας ('resources') should be adopted as the reading instead of ἐξουσίας ('authority'), his paraphrase is based on the retention of ἐξουσίας. The origin of the reference to Vossius (see explanatory note on 1 Cor. XV.54) has not been traced. Locke may have intended to refer to Vorstius, who mentions the reading οὐσίας, but rejects it. Other commentators accept ἐξουσίας without question.

Section VI. No. 1:X.1-22

PARAPHRASE

X.2 *into the Mosaical . . . government*: in LL no. 2864, p. 80, an entry based on Vorstius reads: 'εἰς τὸν Μωϋσῆν. i e into the doctrin of Moses as the messenger of god: as the cloud and the passage through the red sea were designed for a confirmation of the ministry of Moses.' LL no. 2862, p. 139, contains an entry from Hammond: 'εἰς τὸν Μωϋσῆν ἐβαπτίσαντο significat obligationem e{r}orum ut deo parerent sub ductu Mosis' ('*They were baptized into Moses* indicates their obligation to obey God under the leadership of Moses'). An entry in LL no. 309 translates εἰς τὸν Μωϋσῆν as 'into Moses'.

X.3 *a typical . . . signification*: in LL no. 2864, p. 80, an entry from Mede, 'Discourse xliii', *Works*, i. 327, explains πνευματικόν ('spiritual') as 'by being signs of Christ and the Spiritual blesseings through him'.

X.4 *typified Christ*: Locke's interpretation of the rock as a type of Christ rather than the pre-existent Christ himself does not mean that he was a Socinian. Although such an interpretation is found in the Socinian, Crellius, and in the Racovian Catechism, iv. 1 (p. 111), it occurs also in Calvin, Vorstius, Grotius, Hammond, Walker, and Whitby. An exception is Le Clerc (NT), who refuses to admit here that the rock typified or signified Christ, but argues merely that what could be said in a carnal sense of the rock could be said in a spiritual sense of Christ, an interpretation which is attacked by Whitby.

X.13 *persecution*: Grotius also explains temptation as taking the form of persecution.

X.16 *partake of the benefits . . . symbolically drink*: Locke's interpretation is close to that given in an entry in LL no. 2864, p. 82, from Cudworth, *A Discourse Concerning the True Notion of the Lords Supper*, p. 26: 'The eating and drinking in the Lords supper is a real communication in his death and sacrifice.' The following entry from the same page of Cudworth's work is found in LL no. 309, under X.16-18:

> *communion of the bloud and of the body*. i e The eating and drinking the body and bloud of Christ, offerd up to god upon the cross for us, in the Lords supper is a real communication in his death and sacrifice. As amongst the Jews those who eat of the Sacrifice were *partakers of the altar* i e of the sacrifice offerd upon the Altar: so to eat of things offerd up to Idols i e divils is to be made partaker of the Idol Sacrifice

X.18 *share . . . for them*: an entry from Cudworth, *Discourse* (no page number given), in LL no. 2864, p. 82, says that they 'were looked on as partakers of the Sacrifice as if it had been offerd for them'.

X.19 *any thing really different*: an entry from Cudworth, *Discourse*, in LL no. 2864, p. 82, reads: 'not physicaly different from other meats'.

NOTES

X.10* The note bears similarities to an entry from Lightfoot in LL no. 2864, p. 81: ''Ολοθρευτοῦ. Angelo mortis. i.e. communi morte. sine aliqua violenta et evidenti plaga' ('*by a destroyer*: by an angel of death, i.e. by a common death without any violent and obvious affliction').

X.11† Locke indicates his preference for the translation 'the ends of the ages' to AV's 'the ends of the world'. His position, for which he is indebted to Burthogge, is outlined in his note 1 Cor. II.7†, where he claims that the ages refer to the different dispensations in history, one of which was the Jewish dispensation. The entries for 1 Cor. X.11 in LL nos. 2864 and 309 show that he was also influenced by Lightfoot. In LL no. 2864, p. 81, an entry from Lightfoot, which does not name him, reads: 'Αἰών scripturae est vulgatissime saeculum Judaicum' ('*Age* in Scripture is most commonly the Jewish age'). Another unattributed entry from Lightfoot in LL no. 2864, p. 81, explains αἰώνων as 'Oeconomiae Mosaicae' ('of the Mosaic dispensation'). A 'JL' entry in LL no. 309 reads: 'τὰ τέλη τῶν αἰώνων: r the ends of the ages. i e the end of the Jewish constitution. v Isa. XXVI.4. 1 Cor II.7. Eph. III.9 11. JL'.

X.16* An entry from Lightfoot in LL no. 2864, p. 81, reads:

> Τὸ ποτήριον τῆς εὐλογίας. Sic vocabatur poculum in paschate super quod actae sunt gratiae post cibum et in quo salvator instituit poculum Eucharisticum. Mat. 26.27. ('*The cup of blessing*. This was the name for the cup at the Passover, over which thanks were given after food, and in which the Saviour instituted the eucharistic cup. Matt. XXVI.27.')

X.21* *federal right*: 'federal rite', i.e. one which is connected with a covenant (Latin *foedus*). Cf. an entry from Cudworth, *Discourse*, p. 35 in LL no. 309, listed under X.20, which includes the statement: 'And therefor the Apostle would not have federal communion with Devils by eating of the sacrifice offerd to them'.

Section VI. No. 2: X.23-XI.1

PARAPHRASE

XI.1 *Immitate*: Locke understands μιμηταί as 'imitators' rather than 'followers' (AV).

NOTES

X.28* The omission of these words from this verse is supported by Calvin, Grotius, and Hammond but not by Whitby. The 'other Greek copys' which Locke claims as support for the omission of the words include Codex Vaticanus and Codex Claromontanus. The French translation to which he alludes may be the one printed in the interleaved Testament LL no. 2864. Le Clerc (NT) does not omit the words from his French translation, although he notes that a copyist may have inserted them in the text. The words, which already occur in 1 Cor. X.26, are taken from Ps. XXIV.1.

XI.1* In linking this verse with the previous chapter Locke is in agreement with Vorstius and also with Calvin, who notes, 'From this it can be seen how unsuitable are the chapter divisions'.

Section VII: XI.2-16

PARAPHRASE

XI.4-5 *Christ his head . . . the man who is her head*. Vorstius, Grotius, and Hammond refer 'dishonoureth his head' (XI.4, AV) to a man's literal head, and 'dishonoureth her head' (XI.5, AV) to a woman's literal head. Locke, like Calvin, Lightfoot, and Whitby, explains 'his head' as 'Christ' and 'her head' as 'the woman's husband'. The point is also made in an entry from Lightfoot (on XI.5), listed under XI.4-5 in LL no. 2864, p. 84:

> Vir orans velatus ut pudefactus de facie sua coram deo dedecorat caput suum Christum qui faciem gestarit similem masculam et virilem, praecipueque munus Christi dedecorat, per quem accessionem ad deum habemus cum fiducia. Et foemina orans aut psallens non velata ac si faciei suae eam non puderet, caput suum virum dedecorat dum ea tam formosa prae eo videri vult, cum quidem sit tantum gloria viri. Vir autem sit gloria dei ('A man praying veiled, as one ashamed of his

face in God's presence, dishonours his own head, which is Christ, who wore a similar masculine and manly countenance. And he especially dishonours the office of Christ, through whom we have access to God with confidence. And a woman who prays or sings unveiled, as if she were not ashamed of her face, dishonours her head, which is her husband, as long as she wishes to appear more handsome than he, although indeed she is only the glory of her husband; but the husband is the glory of God').

XI.5 *garb and dress of the other sex*: an entry from Mede, *Works*, i. 80, in LL no. 2864, p. 84, reads: '*dishonoureth*. i e by being in the guise and dresse of the other sex.'

NOTES

XI.3*d-e In this note Locke rejects the suggestion that *praying* and *prophesieing* refer to women's participation in worship merely as members of the congregation, an interpretation put forward by Hammond, and also by L. Cappellus (on XI.4), from whom there is an entry listed under XI.5, in LL no. 2864, p. 84: '*Orans aut prophetans*. i e quae interest precibus vel concionibus publicis' ('*Praying or prophesying*. i.e. who is present at public prayers or assemblies'). Such also is the interpretation given by Mede, *Works*, i. 76-7, from whom there is the following entry for XI.4-5 in LL no. 2864, p. 84: 'The prophets of old did 1° Foretell things to come. 2° Notifie the will of god unto the people. 3° Utter themselves in musical wise, in a poetical strain and composure. Hence to prophesie in Sacred Scripture signifies any of these three, and here to prais god in verse or musical composure'. With this kind of interpretation there is no conflict between the mention here of women praying and prophesying, and the command in 1 Cor. XIV.34-5 that women should keep silence in church.

Locke maintained, in agreement with Grotius, that Paul was referring to women who individually prophesied under the special impulse of the Spirit. These ecstatic utterances were to be treated as exceptions to the general rule that women should be silent in church, as Locke affirms in note XIV.34, 35*. This was an unusual interpretation in Locke's day. Even those scholars who rejected the account given by Hammond, L. Cappellus, and Mede claimed that Paul admitted no exceptions to the rule given in XIV.34-5. Calvin and Whitby, for example, argue that in XI.4-5 Paul's purpose was to forbid women to be unveiled, not to permit them to pray or prophesy; and that in XIV.34-5 Paul dealt with the further problem of women speaking in church. Le Clerc (*Supp.*, NT) claimed that in 1 Cor. XI Paul was dealing with praying and prophesying at home, not in the church assembly. Locke's interpretation, restrained and cautious as it appears to be, posed a threat to the accepted practice of restricting leadership in public worship to the male sex. There was discussion of Locke's interpretation of this passage by the Quakers Benjamin Coole and Josiah Martin. See Introduction, pp. 68-9.

XI.3*q-r *Mr Mede*: the information from Mede, *Works*, i. 80, is given in an entry from Mede in LL no. 2864, p. 84, listed under XI.5: 'It was counted immodest and unseemly for women to appear barefaced in publick. The women therefor seem here to have fallen into a phantastical imitation of the She-priests and Prophitesses of the Gentils as their Pythiae, Bacchae and Maenades etc who in their Sacrifices and uttering their oracles had their faces discoverd.'

Pythiae were priestesses of Apollo at Delphi. It was their function to deliver the answers of the god to people who consulted the oracle. When a priestess delivered the oracle she would behave in a convulsive, ecstatic manner.

Bacchae were priestesses of Bacchus or Dionysus. They dressed in animal skins and were renowned for their wild and violent behaviour during their orgies. They were also called Maenads.

XI.3*s *Joel*: a reference to Joel II.28.

XI.10* Of the many interpretations given of this reference to angels, Locke mentions two in entries in LL no. 2864, p. 84. The first is Lightfoot's view that the angels are 'nuntiis desponsationum' ('messengers of espousals'), deputed by a man to espouse his wife for him. The second is from Mede, *Works*, i. 80: 'because the angels who were present at their devotions loved a comely accomodation agreeable to nature and custome'.

Section VIII: XI.17-34

CONTENTS

a-e Locke's explanation of the causes of trouble at the Lord's Supper in Corinth resembles in some but not all respects that given by Lightfoot, from which there are several excerpts in LL no. 2864, pp. 85-6. Both Locke and Lightfoot agree that some members of the church followed the Jewish Passover custom of eating a proper meal. Both agree that these Judaizers subordinated the Christian Eucharist to the common meal, and that they failed to give adequate recognition to the special significance of the Lord's Supper (see also Locke's notes XI.21*e; 27*; 28†a-b). But the two writers differ from each other in several matters. The reference to those who are hungry (XI.21) is explained by Lightfoot as an allusion to the Gentiles who fast before taking part in the Lord's Supper. According to Locke, it refers to those whose penury prevents them from bringing adequate provisions to participate in the feasting (Contents, d; note XI.21*c). Locke claims that the source of the trouble is the head of the Judaizing faction (Contents, b), whereas Lightfoot mentions no such person. Lightfoot sees the trouble entirely in terms of the tendency to treat the Lord's Supper as an appendage to the Passover meal. Locke lays great emphasis on the confusion with Passover customs as the source of the trouble. So in note XI.29*b he claims that they did not sufficiently distinguish the Christian observance from 'common eating for bodily refreshment' not from the 'Jewish Paschal supper'. He gives no evidence of accepting Lightfoot's theory about the Supper being an appendage to the Passover meal.

Lightfoot's position is partly stated in an entry for XI.21, listed under XI.17 in LL no. 2864, p. 85:

> Ut intelligantur quae hic et in sequentibus dicit Apostolus sciendum epidemicum fuisse inter Judaeos ad evangelium conversos, ut Christianismum ample{ct}⟨x⟩arentur at Judaismum non abdicarent. Adeoque pars ecclesiae Corinthiacae Judaizans existima{sse}⟨bat⟩ Eucharistiam ap⟨p⟩endicem solum fuisse paschatis. olim ab incunabulis edocti Messiam cum advenerit nihil rituum Mosaicorum exterminaturum ast omnes in splendidiorem formam evecturum· hosce Judaizantes Christianos Castigat hic Apostolus ('In order that the Apostle's words in this and the following verses might be understood, it should be known that Jewish converts to the Gospel had a widespread tendency to embrace Christianity without renouncing Judaism. And so the

Judaizing part of the Corinthian church thought that the Eucharist was only an appendage to the Passover, having in the past been taught from their cradles that when the Messiah came he would destroy none of the Mosaical rites but would advance them all to a more splendid form. It is these Judaizing Christians whom the Apostle reproves here')

Another entry from Lightfoot, listed under XI.21 in LL no. 2864, p. 85, reads: '"Ἴδιον δεῖπνον i e procoenium paschativum. ὃς μέν i e pars Gentilitia, πεινᾷ i e non coenata ad sacramentum accedit, ὃς δὲ μεθύει. i e pars Judaica in procoeniis paschatizans laute convivatur.' ('*his own supper*, i.e. a Passover Ante-supper. *one*, i.e. the Gentile part. *is hungry*, i.e. comes to the sacrament without having eaten. *another is drunken*, i.e. the Jewish part feasted sumptuously, celebrating the Passover in their Ante-suppers.')

Other entries from Lightfoot in LL no. 2864, p. 86, emphasize that the Christian rite is not a commemoration of the Jewish Passover but of Christ's death.

A different account of the origin of these troubles at Corinth is to be found in Hammond, Walker, and Whitby (on XI.22), who claim that the Lord's Supper is being combined here with the early Christian Love-Feast, which was being abused by some of the members of the Corinthian church.

NOTES

XI.27*a *Unworthily*: Locke argues that 'unworthily' refers to a failure to celebrate the Lord's Supper in accordance with Christ's institution of it. It was a reference to the 'manner' of their participating in it, to their failure to distinguish adequately between it and other meals; he explains that it does not refer to 'unbeleif or any of those sins which are usualy made the matter of examination' (XI.28*g). A similar interpretation is given by Lightfoot in a note on XI.29, although it is not recorded in the interleaved Bible and Testaments or New Testament notebook. A different account is given by Calvin, Hammond, and Walker, who argue that Paul is referring to moral unworthiness. Locke's interpretation is criticized by Le Clerc, *Bibliothèque choisie*, xiii. 94-6, and Jenkin, *Remarks*, pp. 140-5.

XI.28*g *unbeleif*: Locke rejects the idea that the unworthiness refers to *unbeleif*. An entry in LL no. 2864, p. 86, from Lightfoot reads: 'Δοκιμαζέτω. i e approbatum se fide et doctrina Christiana exhibeat' ('*let him examine*, i.e. let him show himself approved by Christian faith and doctrine'). Lightfoot here goes beyond Locke's position that the unworthiness consists in a failure to celebrate the sacrament in the correct manner.

XI.29*b *as became a religious and Christian observance*: cf. an entry in LL no. 2864, p. 86, from Mede, *Works*, i. 10: 'Not differenceing. i e not sanctifying or useing it as became soe holy a thing.'

XI.29† Locke agrees with Lightfoot in rendering κρίμα as 'punishment' in preference to AV's 'damnation'. An entry from Lightfoot in LL no. 2864, p. 86, reads: 'κρίμα. i e morbos et mortem, ut ver. 30' ('*judgement*, i.e. diseases and death, as in ver. 30'). A similar interpretation is given by Whitby. An entry in LL no. 2862, p. 141, reads: '*Judgment*. i e temporal chastisement. ver. 30.32.'

XI.31* In translating διακρίνειν as 'discriminate', and applying it to the discriminating use of the Lord's Supper, Locke differs from AV's 'judge'.

Section IX. No. 1: XII.1-3

PARAPHRASE

XII.1 *men assisted and acted by the spirit*: AV, like most commentators of that time, understands πνευματικῶν as neuter ('spiritual gifts'). Locke, in agreement with Grotius and Hammond, treats it as masculine ('spiritual men'). Whitby mentions both alternatives.

XII.3a *the Messiah the Lord*: the Greek text does not mention 'Messiah', but only 'Lord'. Locke, however, regards the confession of Jesus as Lord as an equivalent of the confession of his Messiahship. Le Clerc (NT) gives a similar interpretation. Locke treats the two confessions as equivalent in his paraphrase of Rom. X.9. The confession that Jesus is Messiah is understood by him to be the fundamental article of faith (*Reasonableness, Works*, vi. 12-13; *Second Vindication, Works*, vi. 231).

NOTES

XII.3* Cf. an entry from Lightfoot in LL no. 2864, p. 87:

> Quicquid Magi aliqui Judaei jactant de spiritu sancto certi estote eos non habere spiritum dei, quod Jesum

dicunt Anathema. Cumque gentiles fatentur Jesum esse dominum, hoc non faciunt nisi per spiritum sanctum, quamvis negant Judaei dari spiritum Sanctum gentilibus. ('Whatever some Jewish magicians boast about the Holy Spirit, be assured that they do not have the Spirit of God, because they call Jesus "Anathema". And when Gentiles confess that Jesus is Lord, they do it only through the Holy Spirit, although the Jews deny that the Holy Spirit is given to the Gentiles.')

Another entry, very similar in content, based on the same passage in Lightfoot, is also included in LL no. 2864, p. 87.

Section IX. No. 2: XII.4-11

PARAPHRASE

XII.7 *not . . . church*: cf. Grotius, 'not for their sakes but for the sake of the Church', and Hammond, 'for some benefit and advantage of the Church'.

XII.9 *steadfast confidence*: an entry for this verse from Lightfoot (on XII.8) in LL no. 2864, p. 88, explains πίστις ('faith', AV) here as 'Fiducia et audacia' ('confidence and boldness').

XII.10 *the discerning . . . operation*: these words may have been influenced by an entry for this verse from Lightfoot (on XII.8) in LL no. 2864, p. 88: 'Διακρίσεις πνευμάτων. i e Dijudicatio inter spiritus diabolicos eorumque operationes, et inter operationes spiritus sancti' ('*Distinguishings of spirits*, i.e. distinguishing between diabolical spirits and their operations, and the operations of the Holy Spirit').

NOTES

XII.8* and 8† *wisdome . . . knowledg*: similar explanations of these words are given by Whitby. While Hammond gives a similar account of 'knowledge', his explanation of 'wisdom' as the ability to speak parables and veil wise conceptions is different from Locke's.

XII.9* In connecting 'wisdome' with the apostles, 'knowledg' with the prophets, and 'faith' with teachers, Locke is following Lightfoot (on XII.8), from whom an entry is contained in LL no. 2864, p. 88, listed by Locke under 1 Cor. XII.8-9. According to this entry, the word of wisdom is said to be attributed 'Apostolis ver. 29 qui totum mysterium profundissimae sapientiae dei de Christo et salute human{e}⟨a⟩ patefecerunt' ('to the apostles, ver. 29, who unfolded the whole mystery of God's profoundest wisdom about Christ and human salvation'); the word of knowledge is described as 'cognitio futurorum' ('knowledge of future things'), attributed to prophets; and faith is said to be 'Fiducia et audacia' ('confidence and boldness'), attributed to teachers. An entry from Allix in LL no. 309, mistakenly listed by Locke under 1 Cor. XI.9, describes faith as 'miraculosa'. But in the *Paraphrase* Locke does not speak of the miraculous function of faith in this context.

XII.10* This threefold division of prophecy resembles that given by Mede. See explanatory note on 1 Cor. XI.3*d-e. In 1 Cor. XI, however, Mede understands prophesying as participating in worship, under the leadership of others, while Locke understands it of immediate inspiration. In chapters XII-XIV both Locke and Mede understand prophecy in the latter sense. An entry for 1 Cor. XIV.4 from Mede, i. 77, in LL no. 2864, p. 92, reads: '*prophesieth*. i e by the gift of interpreting Sacred Scripture, or by instruction . . . by the instinct of the Spirit interpret and apply Sacred Scripture'.

Section IX. No. 3: XII.12-30

PARAPHRASE

XII.13 *the Lords supper*: the Greek text makes no explicit reference to the Lord's Supper here, but Hammond and Walker, like Locke, introduce it into their paraphrases.

NOTES

XII.28* Locke follows here a note on 1 Cor. XII.8 by Lightfoot, from whom an entry in LL no. 2864, p. 90, reads:

> 'Αντιλήψεις. i e Illi qui comitati sunt Apostolos atque baptizarunt ab iis conversos atque huc illuc sunt ab iis missi. Ut Marcus. Timotheus Titus etc: ('*Helps*, i.e. those such as Mark, Timothy, Titus, etc., who accompanied the apostles and baptized their converts and were sent by them to various places').

The more generally accepted explanation, that 'helps' are deacons, is given by Calvin, Vorstius, and Walker. A similar explanation is that of Whitby, who regards the word as an allusion to those who look after the poor.

XII.28† Here Locke is following the same note by Lightfoot which is mentioned in the preceding explanatory note, and from which there is an entry in LL no. 2864, p. 90, where κυβερνήσεις ('governments', AV) are described as 'Solertia distinguendi spiritus' ('Skill in distinguishing spirits'). Another entry in LL no. 2864, p. 90, based on the same note in Lightfoot, gives the same explanation. The generally accepted explanation was that it referred to 'Rulers of the Church' (Whitby) or, more specifically, to bishops or presbyters (Calvin, Vorstius, and Walker).

Section IX. No. 4: XII.31-XIII.13

PARAPHRASE

XII.31 While AV and most commentators understand ζηλοῦτε as imperative ('covet earnestly'), Locke treats it as indicative, a treatment which is grammatically acceptable. At first Locke included this verse under the previous section (IX, No. 3), in accordance with the chapter-divisions; subsequently, however, he moved it to this section and made considerable changes in the wording, which were not carried over into the first edition. See textual and manuscript notes on this verse. His disregard of chapter-divisions is in harmony with the principles stated in his Preface, p. 105. See also his note 1 Cor. XI.1*.

XIII.2 *power of miracles*: the link between faith and the power to perform miracles is asserted in an entry in LL no. 2864, p. 90, from Calvin, *Institutes*, III. ii. 9, which indicates that πίστις ('faith') is the same as δυνάμεις ('powers'), which Locke explains in this entry as 'power of miracles'. See also the entry from Allix in LL no. 309 mentioned in the explanatory note on XII.9*.

XIII.10-13 Themes contained in the paraphrase of these verses include the contrast between intuitive knowledge and the knowledge obtained by deductions and reasoning, the expectation of a future state of perfect knowledge, and the affirmation that this perfect knowledge is already possessed by angels. These themes are also found in *Essay*, IV. lxvii. 14 (p. 683):

> And this, therefore, as has been said, I call *Intuitive Knowledge*; which is certain, beyond all Doubt, and needs no Probation, nor can have any; this being the highest of all Humane Certainty. In this consists the Evidence of all those *Maxims*, which no Body has any Doubt about, but every Man (does not, as is said, only assent to, but) knows to be true, as soon as ever they are

proposed to his Understanding. In the Discovery of, and Assent to these Truths, there is no Use of the discursive Faculty, *no need of Reasoning*, but they are known by a superior, and higher Degree of Evidence. And such, if I may guess at Things unknown, I am apt to think, that Angels have now, and the Spirits of just Men made perfect, shall have, in a future State, of Thousands of Things, which now, either wholly escape our Apprehensions, or which, our short-sighted Reason having got some faint Glimpse of, we, in the Dark, grope after.

NOTES

XII.31† *Beza*: the reference is to his Latin translation of the New Testament, where the cited Latin phrase means 'a way to excellency'.

XIII.1* *conception of the Jews*: an entry from Lightfoot in LL no. 2864, p. 90, reads: 'Γλώσσαις τῶν ἀγγέλων. Loquitur apostolus pro conceptu gentis Judaicae' ('*with tongues of angels*: the apostle is speaking according to the conception of the Jewish nation'). Locke, however, does not explain what is the conception of the Jews. But Lightfoot and Whitby mention the tradition that Rabbi Jochanan ben Zachai understood the language of angels.

XIII.1† Locke's account of *cymbal* agrees with an entry from Lightfoot in LL no. 2864, p. 90: 'erat cum contunderentur duo globuli ex aere absque ullo musicae vel modo vel tono' ('It was when two balls of brass were struck together without any measure or tone of music'). In treating these sounds as unmusical Locke is in agreement with Le Clerc (NT). His account is at variance with that of Hammond, who claims that Paul was thinking of the musical capacity of the cymbal.

XIII.2*b *truths . . . old testament*: an entry from Lightfoot (on XIII.1) in LL no. 2864, p. 90, explains that 'to know all mysteries' means 'secundum Judaeos Scripturam, traditiones, illustrationes parabolas etc scire' ('according to the Jews, to know the Scripture, the traditions, illustrations, parables, etc.').

XIII.2† *what is next to impossible*: an entry from Lightfoot (on XIII.1) in LL no. 2864, p. 90, reads: 'ὄρη μεθιστάνειν significat apud Judaeos impossibilia fere praestare' ('*To remove mountains* signifies among the Jews to do what is well-nigh impossible').

Section IX. No. 5: XIV.1-40

PARAPHRASE

XIV.12 *spiritual gifts*: Locke agrees with AV and most commentators in understanding πνευμάτων as a reference to 'spiritual gifts'. The literal translation 'spirits' is supported in an entry in LL no. 2862, p. 142, in John Biddle, *The Faith of One God*, p. 24, which reads: '*Zealous of Spirits*. i e ministring spirits who inspired the several Linguists and prophets.'

XIV.15 *What... case?* Cf. an entry from Lightfoot in LL no. 2864, p. 93, which reads: 'Quid ergo agendum est?' ('What then is to be done?')

XIV.15 *that... others*: this paraphrase is similar to Whitby's 'that I may be understood by others' and to an entry from Lightfoot in LL no. 2864, p. 93: 'ut intellegar ab aliis' ('that I may be understood by others'). Le Clerc (*Bibliothèque choisie*, xiii. 97-8) complains that Locke gives him no credit for this interpretation, which is found in both his *Supplement* and his *Nouveau Testament*. The entry in LL no. 2864, however, shows that Locke was indebted to Lightfoot rather than Le Clerc.

XIV.16 *who... unlearned*: an entry from Lightfoot in LL no. 2864, p. 93, reads: 'sustinens conditionem privati quoad actionem praesentem' ('being in the state of an unlearned person in respect of the immediate activity').

XIV.32 Paul's statement that the spirits of the prophets are subject to the prophets is understood by Locke to refer to the Christian prophets' self-control, which he contrasts with the failure of the heathen prophets to master the spirits which possess them. The same point is made by Grotius, Hammond, and Whitby. A similar interpretation is given in an entry from Biddle, *The Faith of One God*, p. 24, in LL no. 2862, p. 142: '*The Spirits of the prophets*. i e the spirits that inspired them. *are subject to the prophets*, because they could either utter their inspirations or suspend the use of them by permitting others to speak: insomuch as those spirits did not hurry the prophets so violently, as evil spirits are reported to drive false prophets amongst the Heathen.' A different interpretation, in Calvin, Vorstius, and Walker, is that the spirits of the prophets are judged by other prophets.

NOTES

XIV.4* This explanation of 'an unknown tongue' as the Hebrew language is derived, as Locke says, from Lightfoot's comments on this chapter. In LL no. 2864, p. 92, an entry, listed under XIV.2, from Lightfoot (on XIV.2) describes the tongue as 'Hebraica'. Perhaps Locke has in mind another comment by Lightfoot (on XIV.2), from which there is an entry under XIV.2 in LL no. 2864, p. 92:

> Etiamsi lingua Hebraea jam olim ex usu vernaculo dissueverat. In synagogis tamen lecta est scriptura, preces (excepta una et altera) et conciones habitae Hebraice. Quem morem Synagog{i}⟨ae⟩ Corinthii hi Judaizantes imitati videntur. ('Although the Hebrew tongue had long ago fallen out of vernacular use, in the synagogues the Scripture was read, prayers (with one or two exceptions) were offered, and discourses were spoken in Hebrew. It was this custom of the synagogue that these Judaizing Corinthians appear to have copied.')

The interpretation given by Lightfoot and Locke is an unusual one. In their day the prevailing view was that Paul was speaking of fluency in a foreign language. The view that he was referring to ecstatic speech, not necessarily connected with any particular language, is widely accepted by modern interpreters, but was not being advocated in Locke's day.

XIV.6* Locke's comments do not entirely agree with those of Hammond, for whom revelation is 'expounding sacred figures', knowledge is the communication of great mysteries, and prophecy is the interpretation of 'difficulties of scripture'.

XIV.6*b LL no. 2864, p. 92, has an entry under XIV.3, from Lightfoot (on XIV.2), in which prophesying is explained as 'vel psallens, ut 1 Sam. 10.5. et 1 Sam 19 24 25. vel concionans. vel futura praedicens' ('either singing psalms, as 1 Sam. X.5 and 1 Sam. XIX.24, 25, or preaching, or foretelling the future'). It is the first of these alternatives which Locke adopts in his note on this verse.

XIV.21* An entry in LL no. 2864, p. 94, explains 'in the law' as 'In Scriptura'.

XIV.27‡ The influence can be seen here of an entry for this verse from Lightfoot (on XIV.2) in LL no. 2864, p. 95:

> Ἀνὰ μέρος. Verisimile est eos Judaizasse ad morem Synagog{i}⟨ae⟩, ubi haec erat regula. In lege unus legit et

unus interpretatur. In prophetis unus legit et duo interpretantur. In libro Esterhae decem legere possunt et decem interpretari ('*In turn*. It is probable that they had Judaized according to the custom of the synagogue, where this was the rule: In the law one reads and one interprets; in the prophets one reads and two interpret; in the Book of Esther ten may read and ten interpret')

This rule is taken from the Talmudic Tractate *Megillah*, 21.2.

XIV.34, 35* Locke has made use here of an entry in LL no. 2864, p. 96, from Lightfoot's note on 1 Cor. XIV.35, which is based on the Talmudic Tractate *Megillah*, 23.1:

> Non permissum faeminae legere in lege propter honorem Synagogae· Usitatum etiam erat ut hic aut ille assidens docentem in synagoga interrogaret de hoc aut illo articulo, At et hoc etiam faeminis prohibet apostolus ('For the honour of the synagogue a woman was not allowed to read from the law. It was also the practice for one person or another to sit by the teacher in the synagogue and ask him about particular points. But this also the apostle forbids women to do')

Section X: XV.1-58

PARAPHRASE

XV.8 *borne before my time*: two entries from Lightfoot are included in LL no. 2864, p. 97; one in Latin: 'Massa informis difformisve abortivo partu edit{o}⟨a⟩' ('A misshapen or deformed lump, brought forth by an abortive birth'); and the other in English: 'As to a thing born out of due forme'.

XV.17 *still liable to the punishment*: in LL no. 2862, p. 143, an entry reads: '*Your faith is vain*. i e you in vain hope for eternal life by faith in Christ· *You are yet in your sins*. i e you are still under the curse of the wages of sin which is death. The next verse makes good this sense'.

XV.18 *are perished and lost*: in LL no. 2862, p. 143, an entry reads: 'i e those who died in the faith of Christ are dead or lost forever. soe that to *be in ones sins*. is to be in that state of eternal death when death once comes.'

XV.30-1 Cf. an entry from Lightfoot (on XV.31) in LL no. 2864, p. 99, on XV.31:

> In dies morior, spernor, proculcor, periclitor· in hui⟨us⟩ rei testimonium appello ipsissimam vestram contra me gloriationem, quam quidem ego pro gloriatione mea in

Christo habeo ('Daily I die, I am despised, I am trodden on, I am placed in danger. As evidence of this I appeal to your very boasting against me, which indeed I reckon as something for me to boast about')

XV.33 *minds*: this is Locke's rendering of ἤθη ('manners', AV), which is translated 'dispositions' by Hammond.

XV.34 *Atheistical people*: such an interpretation is in agreement with a note by Le Clerc (NT).

XV.35-50 Locke's treatment of these verses is consistent with his contention in his correspondence with Stillingfleet that the righteous are raised from the dead with bodies different from those in which they lived their mortal lives. In note XV.35*b he speaks of 'attaining other bodys'; in XV.38, Para. of 'a quite different body'; and in note XV.39* of 'bodys of very different constitutions and qualitys from those they had before'. This train of thought is in harmony with an allusion to 1 Cor. XV.37 in his *Second Reply* to Stillingfleet: 'if the body that is put in the earth in sowing, is not that body which shall be, then the body that is put in the grave, is not that, i.e. the same body that shall be' (*Works*, iii. 316).

XV.50 *we shall not . . . now*: again Locke takes the position maintained in his controversy with Stillingfleet (see preceding explanatory note).

XV.54 *Death is swallowed up . . . complete victory*: cf. an entry in LL no. 2864, p. 102, from Simon Patrick (1626-1707), Bishop of Ely, *Jesus and the Resurrection Justified by Witnesses in Heaven and in Earth* (London, 1677), LL no. 2235, p. 130, which explains 'Absorpta' ('Swallowed up') as 'so perfectly conquered that it shall never recover the least power any more'. εἰς νῖκος ('in victory', AV, or 'into victory') is paraphrased *of victory* by Locke, who explains it as *by a complete victory*. An entry in LL no. 2862, p. 144, from Le Moyne, *Varia Sacra*, ii. 305, reads: 'εἰς νῖκος. i e in aeternum. adeo ut per Christum prostrata jaceat nec possit in posterum vires suas recuperare' ('*into victory*, i.e. eternally, so that it lies prostrate through Christ, and cannot afterwards recover its strength').

A note in 1, but not in L (see textual note ad loc.), is based on an entry in LL no. 309 from Isaac Vossius (Voss) (1618-89), a Dutch scholar who emigrated to England and became a Canon of Windsor; the entry from *Appendix ad Librum de LXX Interpretibus* (The Hague, 1663), LL no.

3114, p. 82, reads: 'κατεπόθη ὁ θάνατος εἰς νῖκος. νῖκος saepe significat finem et interitum' ('*Death is swallowed up into victory. Victory* often signifies end and destruction').

XV.54 *shall be noe death any more*: a 'JL' entry in LL no. 2864, p. 102, reads: 'Suitably hereunto St John says Rev XX.14 Death and hell were cast into the Lake of fire. i e to be consumed that there might be noe more death. Death and Hell are made persons. v. XXI.4. JL'.

NOTES

XV.12* Locke claims that the denial of the resurrection stemmed from the Judaizing false apostle, who was tainted with Sadduceeism. Le Clerc (NT) agrees that the trouble arose from the Sadduceeism of Judaizing Christians. Hammond, in his Preface to 1 Corinthians, argues that Paul's opponents were both Gnostics and Judaizers. Grotius and Whitby contend that the denial of the resurrection was the result of the influence of Greek philosophers.

XV.29† *exposed them selves to the danger of death*: Grotius, Crellius, and Walker interpret this passage as an allusion to those who undergo baptism by proxy on behalf of people already dead. Hammond thinks that Paul is referring to baptism as itself a kind of resurrection from the dead. Locke, however, appears to be influenced by Lightfoot, who thinks that Paul is speaking here of martyrs, and that he regards martyrdom as a kind of baptism. An entry from Lightfoot in LL no. 2864, p. 99, points out that in Matt. XX.22, 23 'Baptismus pro martyrio sumitur' ('Baptism is taken for martyrdom'), and that ὑπὲρ τῶν νεκρῶν ('for the dead', AV) means 'sub notione mortuorum' ('under the notion of the dead').

XV.42*b-w The section of this note, '*and soe never comes . . . plain from the context*', is taken almost verbatim from Locke's unpublished paper, 'Resurrectio et quae sequuntur', which is transcribed in Appendix VI, c-q. Le Clerc (*Bibliothèque choisie*, xiii. 98) says that although Hammond mentions in passing that this verse refers only to the resurrection of the just, Locke is breaking fresh ground in emphasizing the point. In fact, however, Walker and Whitby (on XV.44) also make the point.

XV.42*j *51 ver*: the reference actually includes material from both verses 51 and 52.

XV.43* Locke agrees with Calvin and Vorstius in regarding 'sowing' as a reference to this present life. Beza and Grotius believe it to refer to death.

XV.44*c *without the help of meat drink or air*: an entry in LL no. 2864 from Episcopius, *Institutiones*, IV. iv. 1 (p. 352), in *Opera*, vol. i, explains πνευματικόν ('spiritual') as 'quod cibo aere somno non opus habet ad sui sustentationem et anima⟨e⟩ conservationem' ('which has no need of food, air, and sleep for its sustenance and the preservation of its life').

XV.45* The cross-reference to Phil. III.21 is also found in an entry in LL no. 2862, p. 143, from Volkelius, *De Vera Religione*, iii. 40.

XV.53* This note has been transcribed almost verbatim from a 'JL' entry in LL no. 309, which reads:

> τὸ φθαρτὸν καὶ τὸ θνητόν. have not here σῶμα for their substantive as some suppose but are put in the neuter gender absolutely and stand to represent νεκροί *the Dead* as appears by the immediately preceeding verse and vers 42 οὕτω καὶ ἀνάστασις τῶν νεκρῶν σπείρεται ἐν φθορᾷ. i e Mortal corruptible men are sown being corruptible and weak. Nor can it be thought strange or straind that I interpret φθαρτόν and θνητόν as adjectives of the newter gender to signifie persons when in this very discours the Apostle uses two adjectives in the newter gender to signifie the persons of Adam and Christ. v: 46. 'Αλλ' οὐ πρῶτον τὸ πνευματικὸν ἀλλὰ τὸ ψυχικὸν ἔπειτα τὸ πνευματικόν. The like way of speaking we have Mat. I.20 and Luk I.35 in both which the person of our savior is expressed by adjectives of the neuter gender. To either of which places I doe not think any one will adde the substantive σῶμα to make out the sense. That then which is meant here being this. viz That this mortal man shall put on immortality; and this corruptible man incorruptibility. Any one will easily finde another nominative case to σπείρεται and not σῶμα when he considers the sense of the place wherein the Apostles purpose is to speak of νεκροί mortal men being dead and raised again and made immortal. Those with whom grammatical construction and the *nominative case* weighs soe much may be pleased to read the passage of Virgil·
>
> Linquebant dulces animas, aut aegra trahebant
> Corpora· Aeniad Lib. 3. ver. 140

where by findeing the nominative case to the two verbs in it he may come to discover that Personality as contradistinguished both to body and soule may be the Nominative case to verbes JL.

The quotation from Virgil may be translated: 'They were giving up the sweet breath of life or were dragging along their diseased bodies.' But Locke is making a contrast between soul and body; and it would be more in accord with his purposes to translate 'dulces animas' as 'their sweet souls' than as 'the sweet breath of life'.

This entry in LL no. 309 is itself derived from a note written by Locke on a loose leaf found between pages 106 and 107 of his copy of Whitby's *A Paraphrase and Commentary on all the Epistles of the New Testament*, but now included in Locke's papers as MS Locke c. 39, fo. 25. The note is headed 'Whitby on the Epistles. p. 106 1 Cor XV.53'. It reads:

τὸ φθαρτὸν τοῦτο καὶ τὸ θνητὸν τοῦτο ver. 54 has not σῶμα for its substantive as the Dr. here supposes but is put in the neuter gender absolutely. and stands to represent the dead as appears ver. 42 οὕτω καὶ ἀνάστασις τών νεκρῶν σπείρεται ἐν φθορᾷ i e τὸ φθαρτὸν τοῦτο σπείρεται i e mortal corruptible men are sown being corruptible and weake nor let it be thought Strange that I interpret φθαρτόν and θνητόν two adjectives of the neuter gender to signifie persons, where in this very Chapter the Apostle uses two adjectives in the newter gender to signifie the persons of Adam and Christ. ver. 46 Ἀλλ οὐ πρῶτον τὸ πνευματικὸν ἀλλὰ τὸ ψυχικὸν ἔπειτα τὸ πνευματικόν. To which might be added Math. I.20. and Luk. I.35 in which the person of our saviour is spoken of in the newter gender to either of which places here mentiond I hope the Dr will not adde the substantive σῶμα to make out the sense. Soe that here is meant this mortal man shall put on immortality and this corruptible man incorruptibility The doctor will easily finde another nominative case to σπείρεται when he a little better considers the sense of the place wherein the Apostles purpose is to speak of νεκροί mortal men being dead and raised agen and made immortal. The better to lead him into it since Grammatical construction and *the nominative case* soe much weighs with him I will quote him a verse out of Virgil where by findeing the nominative case to the two verbs in it he may come to discover that personality as contradistinguishd both to body and soule may be the nominative case to verbes. The verse is

Linquebant dulces animas, aut aegra trahebant
Corpora—— Aeniad Lib. 3. ver. 140

In both the entry in LL no. 309 and note 1 Cor. XV.53* Locke has removed any specific mention of Whitby, although he is obviously replying to arguments put forward by Whitby in his comments on 1 Cor. XV.53. In his first edition Whitby claimed that in this verse φθαρτόν and θνητόν referred to the corruptible and mortal body. In fact Whitby was maintaining the same interpretation of the verse as had been given by Stillingfleet (*Answer to Mr Lockes Second Letter* (London, 1698), LL no. 2790, p. 43). And he appears to have been reacting to Locke's rejoinder to Stillingfleet in his *Second Reply* (*Works*, iii. 326). In that *Second Reply* Locke did not specifically discuss the interpretation of verse 53, but made the general point: 'He who reads with attention this discourse of St. Paul, where he discourses of the resurrection will see that he plainly distinguishes between the dead that shall be raised, and the bodies of the dead.' It is probably to this comment that Whitby alluded in his first edition of his work on the Epistles, although he may also have been thinking of Crellius, who argued that the words φθαρτόν and θνητόν need not refer to the body in verse 53. Locke's rejoinder to Whitby in his note 1 Cor. XV.53* provoked a further comment from Whitby in his *Additional Annotations*, where he rejected Locke's account of verse 46 as a reference to Adam and Christ.

Le Clerc (*Bibliothèque choisie*, xiii. 98-9), in his discussion of Locke's treatment of verse 53, claims that it would have been preferable not to deny outright that Paul spoke of the resurrection of the body, since such a belief is stated in verse 44.

Crellius, to whom Le Clerc alludes, claimed that it was not certain that Paul was referring to the mortal and immortal body in verse 53. But he also argued that if Paul was speaking of the body here, it was only of the bodies of those who survived until the coming of Christ. Such people, he claimed, would put on their immortal bodies, and their mortal bodies would be absorbed and reduced to nothing. Locke did not adopt this second suggestion by Crellius, but was in agreement with his first assertion, that this verse need not be speaking of the body.

Locke's position is criticized by Jenkin (*Remarks*, pp. 148-51).

This whole note, XV.53*, is an addition by Locke to what he first wrote in the Bodleian manuscript (see manuscript note ad loc.). The manuscript of his work on the Corinthian Epistles is dated 1700. Whitby's work on the Epistles was published in the same year, but apparently Locke had completed the manuscript before he decided to allude to Whitby's comments. He was aware of Whitby's position early in the previous year. On 11 January 1699 Whitby sent Locke a copy of part of his Preface to 1 Corinthians (MS Locke e. 11; the accompanying letter is in *Corr.* vi. 545), in which he criticized Locke's views on the resurrection of the body. Although the loose leaf found in Locke's copy of Whitby's book is dated 19 September 1699 on the back, it refers to the published copy of the book. Both it and the addition to Locke's manuscript must have been written after Whitby's work was published.

Section XI: XVI.1-4

PARAPHRASE

XVI.3 Since there was no punctuation in some of the early manuscripts, the translation of this verse is uncertain. Beza and AV link 'by letters' with 'approve'. Locke, along with Grotius, Whitby, and Le Clerc (NT), links the words with 'send'.

Section XIII: XVI.13-24

PARAPHRASE

XVI.22 *The Lord cometh*: AV reads 'Maranatha', a transliteration of the Greek, which itself transliterates the Aramaic for 'Our Lord, come' rather than *cometh*. Locke does not go as far as Walker, Whitby, and Le Clerc (*Supp.*, NT), who, in addition to recognizing its Aramaic background, explain it as a formula for excommunication. Nor does he adopt the interpretation in two entries from Lighfoot in LL no. 2864, p. 105. According to one of them 'Maranatha' means that Christ will come to punish the Jewish nation. According to the other, which is from Lightfoot but does not name him,

Paul uses the word to threaten imminent destruction to the Jews. While Locke connects the word with the infliction of punishment, he explains it as a punishment meted out to anyone who is an enemy of Christ and the Gospel.

2 CORINTHIANS

In Locke's day it was believed that the Second Epistle to the Corinthians was written a year or two after the First Epistle, and was sent to condemn Paul's opponents at Corinth and also to express his gratitude for a change of heart among many members of the church. Such is also the opinion of some modern scholars; but others believe it to be a conflation of material from more than one Epistle. Whichever theory is adopted, the contents of the Epistle supply evidence of continuing controversy in the Corinthian church.

Conjectures made by seventeenth-century scholars about the date of the Epistle varied from 51 (L. Cappellus; see Appendix II) to 60 (Ussher, p. 673). Locke, who as usual follows Pearson (Appendix II), dates it to 57 during Paul's journey through Macedonia after his departure from Ephesus (Acts XX.1-2; see 2 Cor. I.15-II.17, Contents, a-f).

It is usually supposed that the troubles mentioned in the Second Epistle to the Corinthians arose from the same source as those mentioned in the First. Locke reaches that conclusion, and argues that the chief instigator of the disturbances was a Jewish false apostle (2 Cor. Synopsis, d; I.15-II.17, Contents, e; III.1†; V.17*a-c; X.7-18, Contents; XI.1-6, Contents; XI.16-33, Contents; etc. See also the first explanatory note on 1 Cor.).

The Epistle reveals a great deal about Paul's personal life. It shows him in conflict with his opponents and gives a sustained defence of the genuineness of his apostleship. Within its pages are autobiographical passages which describe his sufferings and mention his achievements and the revelations which he received (2 Cor. IV.8-12; VI.3-10; XI.21-XII.12). It also contains important statements about the contrast between the old and the new covenants (2 Cor. III.1-18), the future life (2 Cor. V.1-10), and Christ's work of reconciliation (2 Cor. V.14-21).

Locke divides the Epistle into five sections (see Appendix XI). It is possible that he used two loose-leaf entries in LL no. 2864, between pp. 105 and 106, in preparing his paraphrase and notes on the Epistle. But the outline given in these entries is by no means in complete agreement with that given in the *Paraphrase*.

The first of the entries in LL no. 2864 is as follows:

2 Ep: ad Cor

I-VII In the 7 first chapters his designe seem⟨s⟩ to be to excus⟨e⟩ his former sharp Epistle, which if it had greived them he had been a greater sufferer for the gospel whereof he was a minister and which he preachd to every one

sincerly and that his not comeing to them as he promised and intended was not out of displeasure. That this trouble had been to their advantage but yet that he was rejoyced in their being consoled again
VIII. IX Exhorteth to a liberal contribution, which was for the releif of the bretheren in Judaea
X-XIII Justifieth him self and his Apostleship against some calumnies which he also seems to have an eye to in the 7 first Chapters.

This whole Ep:, except the VIII and IX Ch: (wherein he ex⟨h⟩orts them to a liberal contribution) and a few verses in the close, seems to be expostulatory with them about his former epistle, their cariage there upon and some discourses and calumnies amongst them against him. wherein he vindicates his authority, his sincerity in preaching the true doctrine of the Gospel without any worldly designe, and his love and concerne for them in particular

I.1-14 He mentions his sufferings {from} to comfort them
I.15-II.11 Twas not out of lightnesse that he came not as he purposed but to spare them.
II.12.13 And because he found not Titus at Troas he hasted to Macedonia without comeing to them.
II.14-V.19 Which journey god had blessed with successe and thereupon declares the sincerity constancy unbiassednesse freedom of his preaching, dangers and sufferings in it for a vindication of him self from some imputations laid on him by teachers of an other make
V.19-VI.10 Assert⟨s⟩ his commission from god: beseeches their teachers to behave themselves as they ought. The pattern whereof nameing himself he seems to draw from what he had done and sufferd
VI.11-VII.3 He proceeds in Exhortations which seem to be more general to the whole body of Christians
VII.4-16 He lets them know how much he was comforted in Macedonia amid his sufferings by the news Titus brought him of their cariage upon the receit of his former Epistle, the inten⟨t⟩ whereof he here explains
VIII.IX.15 He exhorts them to a liberal contribution to the Church at Jerusalem by the Example of the Churches of Macedonia
X-XIII.10 He justifies himself against those who thought of him as if he walked in the flesh
XIII.11-end General exhortations

A further loose-leaf entry at the same place in LL no. 2864 reads:

2 Ep: Cor:

This whole Epistle, excepting the VIII and IX Ch: and a few verses in the close, seems to be writ by St Paul to vindicate himself in the minds of the Co⟨n⟩verted Corinthians from the slanders and disparagements which some enemies he had in that church took all occasions* to lessen him with. as

1° That his preaching was managed with worldly interest and designe craftily espetialy his cariage towards the Corinthians I.12.13. X.2· To which he answers I.1-14. IV.1-VII.16. XII.16-19

2° That he broke his word in not comeing to them. I.18. To which he answers I.15.-II.17. XII.20-XIII.10

3° That he commended himself. To which he answers. III.1-18. X.1

4° That his letters were powerfull but he himself when present weak and his speech contemptible. X.10· To which he answers. X.1-XIII.10

5° They question his mission XIII.3. To which he answers XIII 3-10

The VIII and IX are imploid to exhort them to a liberal contribution to the Church at Jerusalem.

* XI.12

SYNOPSIS

c The references to XI.11 and XII.15 are perplexing because these verses do not illustrate Paul's sharpness towards his opponents. Perhaps Locke meant X.11 or XI.12 instead of XI.11, and XII.16 instead of XII.15.

Section I: I.1-2

INTRODUCTION

Introduction: in this Epistle, as in 1 Corinthians, the paraphrase of the opening section is entitled *Introduction*.

PARAPHRASE

I.1 *Timothy*: a companion of Paul (Rom. XVI.21; Acts XVI.1-3; XVII.14-15; XVIII.5; XIX.22; XX.4), and associated with him in the opening words of Philippians, Colossians, 1 and 2 Thessalonians, and Philemon, as well as 2 Corinthians. On several occasions he was Paul's messenger (1 Cor. IV.17; XVI.10; Phil. II.19; 1 Thess. III.2). His mother was a Jewish Christian and his father a Gentile (Acts XVI.1).

NOTES

I.1*c *in the opinion of some very learned men*: whether or not Locke had any other scholars in mind, he was certainly thinking here of Pearson, who claimed that 1 Timothy was written in 65. By this reckoning 1 Timothy was dated at least fifteen years after Timothy had first become Paul's companion and eight years after his visit to Corinth, mentioned in 1 Cor. IV.17 and XVI.10-11, which took place, according to Locke, between the writing of 1 and 2 Corinthians. Locke uses Pearson's dating of 1 Timothy and the comment in 1 Tim. IV.12 to stress the youthfulness of Timothy at the time of the composition of 2 Corinthians. In his notes on chronology, however (see Appendix II), he rejects Pearson's dating because the reference to Timothy's youth in 1 Tim. IV.12 would not be appropriate as late as AD 65.

Section II. No. 1: I.3-14

PARAPHRASE

I.3 Hammond, Walker, and Whitby agree with AV in translating 'Blessed be God, even the Father of our Lord Jesus Christ'. But Locke renders it 'Blessed be the God and Father of our Lord Jesus Christ'. Le Clerc gives a similar translation in French (NT). Cf. an entry in LL no. 309: 'r: *the god* and *father*. v. 1 Pet. I.3. Rom. XV.6.'

I.5 Like Calvin, Beza, Hammond, and Le Clerc (NT), Locke regards this verse as a reference to sufferings endured on behalf of Christ. He does not regard it, as does Walker, as an allusion to sufferings like those of Christ. Nor does he adopt the position of Beza, who regards it as a reference to the sufferings endured by Christ himself in his followers.

I.6 In Locke's day most commentators believed this verse to allude to eternal salvation. Locke, in contrast, interprets salvation in this context as relief from sorrow in the present life. Hammond also mentions relief, but, unlike Locke, includes the idea of an eternal reward.

I.6 *which is effected*: like Calvin and Grotius, Locke treats ἐνεργουμένης as a passive participle. AV, however, and Erasmus (*Para.*) regard it as a middle participle with an active sense, 'which is effectual'.

I.14 Locke prefers *glory* to AV's 'rejoicing'.

Section II. No. 2: I.15-II.17

PARAPHRASE

I.15 *a second gratification*: Calvin and Whitby explain δευτέραν χάριν ('a second benefit', AV) as a second gift from God, a confirmation in the faith in addition to the first gift of grace received at conversion. According to Locke this second grace or benefit was the gratification and satisfaction which the Corinthians would receive from Paul's visit to them. See also Locke's note I.15*.

II.5 *in some degree . . . load on him*: Locke's paraphrase is markedly different from AV's 'that I may not overcharge you all'. There are two ways of punctuating the passage. If a comma is placed after ἐπιβαρῶ ('lay load'), the word 'him' may be supplied in translation, and an interpretation like Locke's may be adopted. Such an interpretation is found also in Calvin, Beza, and Hammond; whereas if no comma is placed after ἐπιβαρῶ, AV's rendering has to be adopted, as it is by Walker and Whitby.

II.14 *makes me triumph*: in giving this paraphrase, Locke takes a position like that of Calvin, AV, Hammond, and Le Clerc (NT). An alternative translation, 'triumphs over us', is supported by Beza and Walker.

II.17 *Hucksters*: this same word is used by Whitby in his note on this verse.

NOTES

I.21* and I.22* Locke may have been influenced in these notes by Grotius, who refers the anointing to the internal gift of the Spirit, and the sealing to external, miraculous gifts.

I.22†a This note may have been influenced by an entry for I.21 in LL no. 309, which explains *earnest* as 'pledge' and makes a cross-reference to Eph. I.13: '*Earnest of his Spirit*. caled the *spirit of promise* Eph. I.13. i e Donorum miraculosorum complementum est pignus complementi aliarum promissionum. v. Eph. I.13.14'. (The Latin may be translated: 'That which completes the miraculous gifts is a pledge of the completion of the other promises'.) The entry is probably based on Allix.

II.1* This verse seems to imply that Paul had already made a sorrowful visit to Corinth before he wrote 2 Corinthians. But the Acts of the Apostles mentions no such visit. One solution to the problem, supported by Calvin, Beza, and Hammond, is that the first sorrowful visit was not a literal visit, but the sending of 1 Corinthians with its instructions for the punishment of the man who was living with his father's wife. In that case, Paul was not writing about the prospect of a second sorrowful visit but about a second visit which would prove to be sorrowful. The difficulty with this explanation is that it does violence to the Greek.

But it is this explanation which Locke prefers, as does Grotius. In more recent times scholars have suggested that Paul made a sorrowful visit to Corinth which has not been recorded in the Acts of the Apostles.

II.3*a *I writ to you*: Locke agrees with most of the commentaries then available in treating this verse as a reference to 1 Corinthians. Grotius, however, regards ἔγραψα as an epistolary aorist, meaning 'I write', and referring to 2 Corinthians itself. It was not until later that scholars suggested that Paul was referring to yet another letter, part of which might have been incorporated by a redactor into 2 Corinthians.

Section II: No. 3: III.1-VII.16

PARAPHRASE

III.3 *amanuensis*: Grotius uses the same word in his comment on this verse.

III.12 A 'JL' entry in LL no. 2864, p. 112, reads: 'παρρησίᾳ. i e I preach plainly and literaly the Gospel which was figuratively and typicaly deliverd in the law but soe obscurly that the Jews doe not yet see and understand it. v: παρρησία. Joh: XI.14 and XVI.29 JL'. The Greek word may be translated 'boldness' or 'openness of speech'. This entry appears to have been used for the paraphrase of III.14 as well as III.12.

III.18 Locke interprets 'we' in this verse as 'ministers' of the Gospel. Grotius, Hammond, and Whitby understand it of believers in general.

III.18 *as mirors reflecting the glory of the Lord*: Locke's paraphrase *reflecting* is in agreement with Erasmus (*Ann.*, *Para.*) and contrasts with AV's 'beholding', which is the interpretation also found in Calvin, Grotius, Hammond, Walker, Whitby, and Le Clerc (NT).

III.18 *the Lord who is the Spirit*: Locke's paraphrase is in agreement with Beza. An alternative translation is 'the Spirit of the Lord' (Calvin, AV, Grotius, Hammond, Walker, and Le Clerc (NT)).

IV.10-12 An entry in LL no. 2864, p. 115, reads: 'i e That our sufferings might be a proof of Christs resurrection, and that life of his worke upon you, it being the great proof of the truth of the Gospel'.

IV.13 *David*: Locke quotes here from Ps. CXVI.10, which he believes to have been written by David.

V.1-10 There are several important questions of interpretation in this passage. One of the problems is the meaning of 'earthly house of this tabernacle' (V.1). Whereas Cudworth, without expressing agreement, mentions Origen's claim that the 'earthly house' referred to the physical body, while the 'tabernacle' meant the subtle aerial body which adhered to the soul (*True Intellectual System*, pp. 818-19), Locke agrees with most interpreters of his day in understanding the tabernacle and the earthly house both to mean the physical body.

Another issue is the meaning of 'a building of God, an house not made with hands' (V.1, AV). Locke, like most interpreters, understands this to mean the body which believers will receive at the resurrection, although he does not wish to describe it as an 'ethereal body', a phrase used by Cudworth (*True Intellectual System*, p. 817). His position differs from that of Calvin, who claims that the 'building from God' has its beginning in the state of immortality entered into at death, and will reach its consummation at the resurrection.

A further problem is the meaning of the word 'naked' in V.3. In his paraphrase Locke explains it in terms of putting off this body, which would imply a state in which a person was without a body, between the moment of physical death and the day of resurrection. Other explanations are that 'naked' refers to the sinful condition of human beings (Walker), or to the state of the damned at the day of resurrection who will not have glorious, celestial bodies (Calvin, Whitby).

Locke indicates in note V.4* that he has difficulty in understanding the meaning of 'clothed' in V.2-4. His paraphrase implies that it refers to the reception of a celestial body at the resurrection. Yet his note sees a difficulty in this interpretation because it might suggest that even the wicked receive this celestial body, the 'house which is from heaven'. This was not an insuperable difficulty for him. In his comments on 1 Cor. XV.42 in his manuscript, 'Resurrectio et quae sequuntur' (Appendix V, n-r), he asserts that the resurrection of the just will precede the resurrection of the wicked, which will be a completely separate event. It would be quite consistent, therefore, for him to contend that 'clothed' describes the condition of the righteous at their resurrection and has nothing to do with the fate of the wicked.

Yet another problem arises from Paul's assertion in V.8 that 'we' are willing 'to be absent from the body, and to be present with the Lord'. One interpretation sees here a reference to an intermediate state of conscious existence between physical death and the resurrection. This was a widely accepted account of the verse and was supported by Calvin, Walker, and Whitby. Some theologians, however, believed that the soul died or fell asleep at the moment of physical death, and was not awakened or brought to life again until the day of resurrection. Such views were held by the Socinians and by Milton, Hobbes, and others. Locke himself was supposed by some of his critics to be a mortalist (see Introduction, p. 54). But his position is not clear in his comments on 2 Cor. V.1-10. In his note V.9* he says that neither the word translated 'be present' nor that translated 'be absent' can signify 'his being with Christ in heaven'. This comment gives the impression that he does not understand the passage to refer to an intermediate state.

A 'JL' entry for 2 Cor. V.4 in LL no. 309 rejects the view that Paul is speaking of immaterial souls in this passage. Locke argues that persons are spoken of as distinct from soul and body, and that when Paul refers in these verses to 'we', he is speaking of persons, not of souls or bodies. Locke does not actually deny an intermediate state in this entry, but the general attitude which he displays would suggest that he rejects the belief. An entry for 2 Cor. V.1-4 in LL no. 309 speaks slightingly of the doctrine of aerial and ethereal vehicles, which was sometimes associated with a belief in an intermediate state. He also writes disparagingly of that doctrine in the Preface, p. 114. But rejection of the doctrine need not imply rejection of a belief in an intermediate state.

The only indication that Locke may have believed in an intermediate state is in his note 2 Cor. V.9†c, where he writes of 'death which brings me home to Christ', and in his paraphrase of 2 Cor. V.8, where he mentions 'quiting this habitation to get home to the Lord'. It is possible, however, that he understood the passage in the same way as Crellius, who believed that the salvation of 'those who die in the Lord' was 'in port' while that of 'those who live in the Lord' was still 'on the stormy sea'. This explanation was understood by Crellius to be consistent with the rejection of any belief in an intermediate state. For a discussion of Locke's views on these matters see also Introduction, pp. 51-6.

Entries in LL no. 309 provide evidence of Locke's thoughts on this part of the Epistle, and show which writings he was consulting. An entry for 2 Cor. V.4 from Cudworth, *True Intellectual System*, p. 795, reads: '*Unclothed*. i e Stripd quite naked of all body'. A 'JL' entry for the same verse, to which reference has already been made, reads:

> *We·* By the prejudice of the received philosophie of immaterial soules, *we* is generaly interpreted to be the immaterial soules whereas the scripture noe where authorizes any such interpretation, but the plain genuine scripture sense is *we*. i e the same persons shall be in or have different and more spiritual bodys and that this is a way of speaking not peculiar to scripture. but common to other languages and authors of good sense wherein the person is considerd abstractly and spoke of in contradistinction both to soule and body. I shall content my self here with one but that a very convinceing instance taken from Virgil Aeniad lib. 3. ver. 140
>
> Linquebant dulces animas {animas}, aut aegra trahebant
>
> Corpora
>
> where it is plain that *illi* the nominative case to trahebant i e the persons are considerd and spoken of as distinct from soule and body and soe *Nos* or *we* in this passage of St Paul. And I doe not remember any place in Sacred Scripture where the person is put for the soule. but for the personality in whatsoever sub⟨s⟩tance it is continued JL

The quotation from Virgil in the above entry is found also in Locke's note 1 Cor. XV.53*, in an entry from LL no. 309 for 1 Cor. XV.53, and in a note about Whitby's views of the same verse (see explanatory note on 1 Cor. XV.53*). For Locke's views on the relationship of 'person' to 'soul' and 'body', see also Appendix V.

An entry for 2 Cor. V.1-4 from LL no. 309, which makes reference to Tillotson, *Sermons*, iii. 216, and to Cudworth, *True Intellectual System*, p. 818, reads:

> Knowing that when this earthly body of ours which is but a tent that must soon be taken down shall be dissolved we shal have habitations not like those of mens makeing i e mouldering and comeing to decay but heavenly and eternal bodys. For while we are in this body we groan by reason of the pressures and afflictions of it; which yet we could wish not to put off by death; but to be of the number of those who at Christs comeing shall without dyeing be clothed upon with those spiritual glorious and heavenly bodys which men shall have at the resurrection. v 1 Cor XV.51. If soe be at Christs comeing to judgment [which they thought not far off] *clothed*. i e in the body alive and *not naked* i e not devested of the body or not dead. For we that are in these bodys doe groan with the afflictions and pressures of this life· not that we desire by death to be devested of these bodys but we had rather be found alive and changed and without putting off these bodys have immortality as it were superinduced. v: ... Tillotson Serm: on 2 Cor. V.6.... This seems to me the true meaning of the Apostle both for the reasons given by Dr Tillotson and because it does not appear very probable that the Apostle should discourse to the Corinthians upon a supposition of a philosophical speculation about aerial and aetherial vehicles. v: Cudworth

LL no. 309 contains the following entry for 2 Cor. V.2 from Cudworth, *True Intellectual System*, p. 795: '*Clothed upon with our house which is from heaven*. i e with ethereal bodys.' There is also in LL no. 309 a cross-reference, relating 'we groan' (V.2) to Rom. VIII.23, and a reference to Tillotson, *Sermons*, iii. 218, explaining verse 3 as '*If so be we shall be found clothed and not naked*'.

V.10 This verse is used in combination with 1 Cor. XIV.25 in an allusion to Paul in *Essay*, II. xxvii. 26 (p. 347), where Locke argues that personal identity consists in the consciousness of having committed one's past actions:

> And therefore conformable to this, the Apostle tells us that at the Great Day, when every one shall *receive according to his doings, the secrets of all Hearts shall be laid open*. The Sentence shall be justified by the consciousness all Persons shall have, that they *themselves* in what Bodies soever they appear, or what Substances

soever that consciousness adheres to, are the *same*, that committed those Actions, and deserve that Punishment for them.

V.16 *that Christ himself . . . my blood and nation*: Walker and Le Clerc (*Supp.*, NT) claim that 'knowing Christ according to the flesh' in this verse refers to a personal acquaintance which Paul had with Jesus during his earthly life. According to Grotius and Hammond, however, Paul is saying that he formerly expected Christ to be a 'temporal king'. Yet another explanation is given by Locke, who says that Paul has ceased to glory in the fact that Jesus belonged to the Jewish nation. For Locke this passage is part of Paul's polemic against his Judaizing opponents.

V.17 κτίσις can refer to either a creature or an act of creation. Calvin, AV, and Le Clerc (NT) prefer the former, and Locke the latter, while Grotius comments that both meanings are valid here. Locke's paraphrase shows dependence on a 'JL' entry in LL no. 309: 'r: *Soe that if any one be in Christ it is a new Creation*. i e he is in an estate as if he were created a new for in this new estate all former Mundane relations considerations and interests are ceased and at an end JL. v. Gal VI.15'.

Locke also suggests in note V.17† that 'old things' refers to 'the Jewish œconomie', an interpretation which would certainly be in harmony with Paul's experience. Most commentators explain it in a more general sense as an allusion to a former mode of life, whether Jewish or Gentile.

V.19 AV's translation 'God was in Christ . . .' gives support to the doctrine of the incarnation, in agreement with Erasmus (*Ann.*), Calvin, Beza, and many others. Locke's paraphrase, which presupposes the translation 'In [or 'by'] Christ God was . . .', is in agreement with Hammond and Le Clerc (NT).

V.21 In his paraphrase of this verse Locke comes very close to asserting that Christ paid the penalty for the sins of men and women by acting as their substitute. His treatment of the verse provides strong evidence that he regarded the death of Christ as uniquely redemptive. His position is similar to that of Le Clerc (NT), who indicates that God treated Christ as a sinner. Cf. an entry in LL no. 309: '*Sin*. i e An offering for Sin. v. Gen. IV.7'. Another entry in LL no. 309 is identical (apart from formal features).

made righteous: cf. an entry in LL no. 2862, p. 147, from Crellius, *Liber de Deo*, i. 301: 'justi. vel justificati' ('righteous or made righteous').

VII.8 It was the usual view in Locke's day that in this verse Paul was referring to 1 Corinthians. But Locke makes no comment on the matter.

VII.11b *what fear to offend me*: like Whitby, Locke explains 'fear' (AV) as fear of Paul. Calvin explains it as fear of God.

VII.11b *revenge against your selves*: Locke agrees with Hammond in explaining 'revenge' in this way. Grotius understands it as revenge against false teachers, and Calvin, Le Clerc (NT), and Whitby as revenge against the fornicator.

VII.11b *to be set right*: Locke's paraphrase implies a reference to a moral change in the Corinthians. On the other hand, Calvin, Grotius, Walker, and Le Clerc (NT) understand it to mean that the Corinthians were shown to be free from blame.

VII.11b *by this cariage of yours*: Locke differs here from AV, which translates ἐν τῷ πράγματι as 'in this matter'. His rendering of the Greek is unusual, and is explained by him in his note on this verse. Modern texts prefer τῷ πράγματι, but many editions in Locke's day, e.g. Erasmus, Beza, Walton, had ἐν τῷ πράγματι.

NOTES

III.17* *mystical and spiritual meaning*: Cf. an entry in LL no. 2864, p. 113: 'Dominus [Lord] etc. i.e Christ is that spiritual or mystical sense conteined in the letter of the law. ver. 6. and Rom II.6.'

IV.1*a Editions in Locke's day read ἐκκακοῦμεν. Modern editions prefer ἐγκακοῦμεν. Whichever word is selected, the translation is the same.

IV.6*d *knowledg of god in the gospel*: a similar interpretation of 'glory' is given in an entry in LL no. 2862, p. 146: '*glory of god*. i e the glorious gospel. v. III 7-11'.

IV.17* Cf. an entry in LL no. 309, listed under V.17: 'כבד signifies, grave esse et honorari, here they are both joynd'. The Latin may be translated: 'to be heavy and to be honoured'.

V.3* Locke's statement here about Paul's expectation of Christ's imminent return is criticized by Jenkin (*Remarks*, pp. 151-3). See also explanatory note on 1 Cor. I.7†, and Introduction, p. 29. His note on Rom. XIII.11, 12, verses to which he makes cross-reference in this present note, also speaks of Paul's belief in the imminence of Christ's return. His cross-references here also include 1 Cor. VII.29, 31 and X.11, but he gives a different interpretation of them in his paraphrase and notes.

VI.15* *Belial* is usually understood as a name for the devil. Locke explains it in this context as a reference to pagan gods.

Section III: VIII.1-IX.15

PARAPHRASE

VIII.1,4,6,7,9,19 In 2 Cor. VIII.1, 6, 7, 9, 19 AV translates χάρις as 'grace', and in 2 Cor. VIII.4 as 'gift', whereas Locke paraphrases it as *gift by which the grace of god is given* (VIII.1), *contribution* (VIII.4), *charitable contribution* (VIII.6), *act of charitable liberality* (VIII.7), *munificence* (VIII.9), and *liberal contribution* (VIII.19). Locke's interpretation is consistent with three 'JL' entries in LL no. 309. The first of them makes the following comment on 2 Cor. VIII.1 (listed as VI.1): 'r: *we make known to you the gift of god in the churches of Macedonia*: vid. ver. 6.7.19 IX 15. *Gift of god.* i e Charitable contribution to which god moved their hearts JL v: 1 Cor XVI.3'. The second entry, for 2 Cor. VIII.6, 7, 19 (listed as X.6, 7, 19), is: 'r: *gift*. vid. ver. 1. and IX.15. 1 Cor XVI.3 JL'. The third, for 2 Cor. VIII.9 (listed as X.9), is: 'r *gift* or *munificence*. as in the fore mentioned verses JL'. Locke's greater readiness than AV to explain χάρις as 'gift' is shared by both Le Clerc (NT) and Whitby.

NOTES

VIII.18* *Brother*: Locke's view that the 'brother' mentioned in VIII.18 was Luke is shared by Grotius, Hammond, Walker, and Whitby. Other suggestions were made: Calvin thought that it was Barnabas, and Lightfoot (*Works*, i. 310-11) conjectured that it was Mark.

IX.9 and 10* *Liberality*: in explaining δικαιοσύνη as liberality rather than 'righteousness', Locke differs from AV, but agrees with Hammond and Whitby. The cross-reference made by Locke to Matt. VI.1 is found also in Le Clerc (NT).

Section IV. No. 1: X.1-6

PARAPHRASE

X.5 *reasonings*: this explanation of ὕψωμα is found also in

Hammond. Cf. Le Clerc's 'raisonnements' (NT). Walker and Whitby introduce the word, but retain AV's 'imaginations' as well.

Section IV. No. 2: X.7-18

PARAPHRASE

X.12 Cf. a 'JL' entry in LL no. 309, listed under XI.12: 'r: *measureing them selves within them selves and compareing them selves to them selves* JL'.

NOTES

X.15‡ The cross-reference to Rom. XV.20 is found also in an entry in LL no. 309, listed under XI.15.

Section IV. No. 3: XI.1-6

PARAPHRASE

XI.3 *singleness which is due to Christ*: in translating εἰς Χριστόν as 'to Christ', Locke agrees with Grotius and Le Clerc (NT). The translation 'in Christ' is preferred by Calvin, Beza, AV, and Hammond.

XI.4 *this intruder*: this verse gives more support than most to Locke's theory that there was one false apostle who led the opposition to Paul in Corinth. Le Clerc (NT) also sees in this verse a reference to a Jewish Christian leader opposed to Paul. The more generally accepted interpretation of the verse regards 'he that cometh' (AV) as indefinite, and not limited to one particular person.

Section IV. No. 4: XI.7-15

PARAPHRASE

XI.12 *But what I doe and shall doe*: both the paraphrase and the note on this verse show the influence of a 'JL' entry in LL no. 309:

> r: *But what I doe and shall doe*. So in the Greek and soe in the sense. For it is a continuation of the matter of the immediately preceding verse and is to convince the Corinthians that he refused not to receive maintenance from them out of any unkindness to them but for an other reason mentioned in the following words JL

Locke's paraphrase differs from AV's 'But what I do, that will I do.'

Section IV. No. 5: XI.16-33

PARAPHRASE

XI.18 *their circumcision or extraction*: while Locke and Whitby explain 'flesh' (AV) as a reference to the Jewish heritage, Calvin, Grotius, and Hammond explain it in a more general sense as a reference to externals.

XI.20 *If he take . . . a salary from you*: an entry in LL no. 309 explains *take* as taking 'a bribe or fee'.

XI.22 *Is he an Hebrew*: in his attempt to trace the opposition back to one false apostle, Locke does violence to this passage by turning the plurals into singulars. The Greek should be translated as in AV, 'Are they Hebrews', etc.

XI.22 *by language an Hebrew*: Locke's claim that Hebrew in this verse refers to a speaker of the Hebrew language is similar to Whitby's. The usual view, found in Calvin and Grotius, is that it refers to someone who is Hebrew by descent.

XI.23 *In stripes I am exceedingly beyond him*: the Greek, translated literally by AV as 'in stripes above measure', does not indicate that Paul is comparing himself with particular individuals. Hammond, however, thinks that he is comparing himself with the twelve apostles. Locke supposes that there is a comparison with the false apostle.

XI.26 *in the country*: AV translates ἐν ἐρημίᾳ as 'in the wilderness'. Locke's paraphrase shows the influence of Lightfoot's comments on Matt. III.1 to which allusion is made in an entry for 2 Cor. XI.26 in LL no. 2864, p. 134, which explains the Greek as 'ruri' ('in the country'). In his comment Lightfoot contrasts 'in the country' with 'in the city'.

NOTES

XI.20*a *bondage*: Walker and Whitby regard this as a reference to bondage to Jewish rites and ceremonies. Locke's position is similar to that of Calvin, who speaks of bondage to false apostles, although Locke characteristically mentions only one such apostle.

Section IV. No. 6: XII.1-11

PARAPHRASE

XII.1 The textual evidence for the first part of this verse is varied. AV's 'It is not expedient for me doubtless to glory' is based on the reading which begins καυχᾶσθαι δὴ οὐ συμφέρει μοι. Locke adopts the reading which begins εἰ καυχᾶσθαι δεῖ . . . 'If I must glory', or, as he expresses it, 'If I must be forced to glory'. This reading, as Locke points out, is supported by the Vulgate (see his note XII.1*). Some of the Syriac versions give partial support, in that they read 'I must glory', although they omit the word 'if'. It is probably to these that he alludes when he mentions the Syriac in note XII.1*. Characteristically Locke selects the reading which, he thinks, suits 'better with the context' than other readings, and 'renders the sense clearer'.

XII.2 *by the power of Christ*: Locke regards *in Christ* (AV) as adverbial, as also does Hammond. Another explanation treats it as adjectival. For example, Calvin explains 'a man in Christ' as one who 'looks exclusively to Christ', while Vorstius, Grotius, and Le Clerc (*Supp.*, NT) interpret it as meaning 'a Christian'.

XII.4 *what is not in the power of man to utter*: Locke differs from AV, which translates 'which it is not lawful for a man to utter'. Most commentators of Locke's time agreed with AV in understanding οὐκ ἐξόν to mean 'it is not allowed'. Locke preferred the meaning 'it is not possible', while Whitby brought out both meanings.

Locke's interpretation of this verse is consistent with his allusion to it in *Essay*, IV. xviii. 3 (pp. 689-90), where he argues that '*no Man inspired by* GOD, *can by any Revelation communicate to others any new simple Ideas* which they had not before from Sensation or Reflexion'. Locke's discussion in the *Essay* includes the following comments:

> For Words seen or heard, re-call to our Thoughts those *Ideas* only, which to us they have been wont to be Signs of: But cannot introduce any perfectly new, and formerly unknown simple *Ideas*. The same holds in all other Signs, which cannot signify to us Things, of which we have before never had any *Idea* at all.
>
> Thus whatever Things were discovered to St. *Paul*, when he was rapp'd up into the Third Heaven; whatever new *Ideas* his Mind there received, all the description he can make to others of that Place, is only this, That there are such Things, *as Eye hath not seen, nor Ear heard, nor hath it entred the Heart of Man to conceive*.

While the latter part of this allusion to Paul refers to 1 Cor. II.9, the former part refers to 2 Cor. XII.1-5. In this passage in the *Essay*, as in the paraphrase of 2 Cor. XII.4, Locke emphasizes the impossibility, not the unlawfulness, of Paul's uttering what he heard in his vision.

NOTES

XII.1* *vulgare translation*: the Vulgate.

XII.7* *Thorn in the flesh*: among the explanations of this phrase which are likely to have been known to Locke are 'a sharp pain' (Grotius), beatings and imprisonment (Hammond), 'some publicly observed infirmity of body, presence, speech' (Walker), 'a stammering in speech' (Whitby). Locke's refusal to take part in the guessing-game is understandable.

Section IV. No. 8: XII.14-21

NOTES

XII.19* See explanatory note on XIII.1.

Section IV. No. 9: XIII.1-10

PARAPHRASE

XIII.1 *This is now the third time I am comeing to you*: in an entry in LL no. 2864, p. 137, Locke claims that Paul is speaking not of a third visit to Corinth but of a third intention to visit the city. He explains that the proposed visit would be the second made by Paul, the first having been made in AD 52. It is this second visit that he had previously intended to make on two occasions, and that now for the third time he has resolved upon. In his note 2 Cor. XIII.19* he explains that Paul's first unfulfilled intention to make the visit is mentioned in 2 Cor. I.23, where he indicates that he refrained from coming because he wanted to spare the Corinthians. Probably Locke believed that the second unfulfilled intention of Paul to make the visit coincided with his decision to send Titus to Corinth as his representative (2 Cor. XII.18-19). His note XII.19* indicates that on that occasion Paul forbore *comeing merely out of respect and goodwill to them*.

This kind of explanation was popular in Locke's day, and is found, for example, in Vorstius (on XII.14), Grotius (on XII.14), Le Clerc (*Supp.*, NT, on XIII.1), and Whitby (on XII.14). According to Erasmus (*Para.*) and Calvin, however, this would be his third actual visit to the city, an interpretation which would imply that he had already made a second visit in addition to that of Acts XVII.1 ff. Locke's opinion about the matter is contained in an entry for XIII.1-2 in LL no. 2864, p. 137:

Tertio. The 1st real comeing of St Paul to Corinth was from Athens Act. XVIII.1 Anno aerae vulg: *52*. The 2d when he came out of Macedonia to Greece Act. XX.2. anno *57* and then he writ his Epistle to the Romans from Corinth. but this Epist to the Corinthians was writ to them out of Macedonia before his actual comeing to Corinth this 2d time. therefor this Τϱίτον τοῦτο ἔϱχομαι according to the Hebrew way of speaking must be understood *I prepare* or *resolve to come this 3d time* haveing been twice disappointed. But you may be sure I will now come upon this my 3d resolution which will as certainly stand, as what is confirmed by 2 or 3 witnesses stands

I forewarnd you before and forewarn you as just comeing to you this second time. and being absent write it to you that if I come I will by the extraordinary power I have make some of you examples.

XIII.2 *these two letters are my witnesses . . . rule*: Calvin claimed that in speaking of witnesses Paul was referring only to himself in so far as he paid his different visits to Corinth. Lightfoot, however, argued that Paul was alluding to Stephanas, Fortunatus, and Achaicus, who are mentioned in 1 Cor. XVI.17, and who, according to Lightfoot, were the messengers who took 1 Corinthians to Corinth. It is Lightfoot's explanation which Locke rejects in note 2 Cor. XIII.2*e-h. Locke's theory, that the witnesses were Paul's two Epistles to the Corinthians, had already been propounded by Hammond.

Locke's paraphrase also indicates that the requirement for witnesses is 'according to our Saviours rule'. In his note 2 Cor. XIII.2* he claims that Paul quotes the requirement about witnesses from Jesus's teaching in Matt. XVIII.16, not from the Jewish Law (Deut. XIX.15), although it is found in both these places. Calvin and Whitby, on the other hand, argue that the Jewish Law is Paul's authority here. Locke's explanation is consistent with his repeated emphasis on the rule of Christ as an adequate guide for conduct. See Introduction, p. 47.

XIII.3 *Since you demand a proof of my mission*: the paraphrase here is probably influenced by an entry in LL no. 2864, p. 138: 'δοκιμὴν a proof. i e by some supernatural miraculous act, this he cals the testimony of Christ. 1.Cor I.6. Since you require a proof of my mission and authority for what I speake as from Christ. Though you methinks.need not put it to this trial. I haveing given sufficient proofs of it amongst you already. v. XII.12'.

XIII.4 Both the paraphrase and the note on this verse show the influence of an entry in LL no. 2864, p. 138: 'For though it seemd weaknesse and want of power in Christ to die by crucifiction yet he lives and has all power from god. Soe though I appear weak and of noe power by my suffering for Christ. v. XII.10. yet I shall have life and strength enough from god and Christ to make you feel the power I have.'

XIII.5 The punctuation of the second half of this verse is uncertain. AV puts a question-mark after 'reprobates', while Locke, and also Hammond, put it at the end of the verse.

Another issue in this verse is the translation of ἀδόκιμοι, which AV, Hammond, Walker, and Whitby render 'reprobates'. Locke renders it *destitute of proofs*, and explains his position in note 2 Cor. XIII.5, 6, 7*. An entry in LL no. 309 mentions Hammond's translation, 'reprobates' (*Practical Catechisme*, v. 3), and a 'JL' entry in LL no. 2864, p. 138, paraphrases the verse as follows, in a way consistent with that which is used in the *Paraphrase*: 'Trie your selves whether you have faith or noe, make proof in your selves: or you, who pretend to know me soe well, doe you not know your selves, and that if you are not ἀδόκιμοι (i e if you can give proofs by the extraordinary gifts of the holy-ghost) Christ is in you?'

See also Locke's note Rom. I.28†.

XIII.6-9 There is a general, but not a detailed verbatim, correspondence between the paraphrase of these verses and the following 'JL' entry in LL no. 2864, p. 138:

> 6 And I trust you shall find I am not without such proofs that Christ is in me
>
> 7 But I wish to god that you may doe noe evil, and not that by your persisting in your faults I may when I come shew by miraculous punishments that I have proofs of my mission; but that you may live as becomes true Christians and I there by be as one who can give noe such proofs.

8 For I can doe noe thing against those who are in truth Christians but for the promoteing of the truth of the Gospel by supernatural punishments on those who professeing Christianity are not obedient to it.

9 For I am glad when I am weak. i e have noe occasion and consequently noe power to inflict any supernatural punishment; but that ye are strong and vigorous in the Christian life. And I wish that ye may moreover be perfectly set right by a return to unity, integrity and the restoration of the offender delivered to Sathan

10 I write these things before I come, that when I come I may not be forced to use severity in the exercise of that extraordinary power which Christ hath given for edification and not for destruction

This meaning of this Chapter will be evident to any one who will consider the words δοκιμὴν ἀδόκιμοι δόκιμοι as they stand ver. 3.5.6.7 JL